TALENTED CHILDREN AND ADULTS
Their Development and Education

Second Edition

Jane Piirto
Ashland University

Merrill,
an imprint of Prentice Hall

Upper Saddle River, New Jersey   Columbus, Ohio

Library of Congress Cataloging-in-Publication Data

Piirto, Jane
   Talented children and adults : Their development and education /
Jane Piirto. — 2nd ed.
      p. cm.
   Includes bibliographical references (p.   ) and index.
   ISBN 0-13-096146-9
   1. Gifted children—Education—United States.   2. Gifted children—
United States—Identification.   3. Talented students—United
States.   4. Gifted persons—United States.   I. Title.
LC3993.9.P55 1999
371.95' 0973—DC21   98-21644
                                                                                        CIP

Cover art: © Nicholas Hill
Editor: Ann C. Davis
Production Editor: Julie Peters
Editorial/Production Supervision: Custom Editorial Productions, Inc.
Cover Designer: Rod Harris
Design Coordinator: Diane C. Lorenzo
Production Manager: Laura Messerly
Director of Marketing: Kevin Flanagan
Marketing Manager: Suzanne Stanton
Advertising/Marketing Coordinator: Krista Groshong

This book was set in Optima by Custom Editorial Productions, Inc., and was printed and bound by
R.R. Donnelly and Sons Company. The cover was printed by Phoenix Color Corp.

Photo credits: Andy Brunk/Merrill, p. 90; Paul Conklin, p. 186; Scott Cunningham/Merrill, pp. 262, 416, 485; "Life Choices," p. 332;
Anthony Magnacca/Merrill, pp. 224, 358; NASA, p. 519; Steven Navarre, pp. 46, 66, 268, 304; Jane Piirto, pp. 2, 124, 136, 203,
431, 530; Barbara Schwartz/Merrill, pp. 20, 159, 284, 394, 522; Silver Brudett Ginn, p. 143; UPI/Corbis-Bettmann, p. 561;
Anne Vega/Merrill, pp. 131, 216; Ulkrike Welsh, p. 462; David Zalubowski, p. 316.

Printed in the United States of America

10 9 8 7 6 5 4 3 2 1

ISBN: 0-13-096146-9

Prentice-Hall International (UK) Limited, *London*
Prentice-Hall of Australia Pty. Limited, *Sydney*
Prentice-Hall of Canada, Inc., *Toronto*
Prentice-Hall Hispanoamericana, S. A., *Mexico*
Prentice-Hall of India Private Limited, *New Delhi*
Prentice-Hall of Japan, Inc., *Tokyo*
Simon & Schuster Asia Pte. Ltd., *Singapore*
Editora Prentice-Hall do Brasil, Ltda., *Rio de Janeiro*

This book is dedicated to all my students

PREFACE

The journey of this book began in 1990 when a sales representative for Merrill Publishing stopped into my office. Knowing that I am a writer, he asked me whether I would be interested in writing a textbook. I wasn't, as I had another novel and some poems on my mind. Then he asked me whether I had any ideas for books needed in the field of education. I did. He wrote my ideas down, and I received a call of interest from acquisitions editor Ann Davis. After I wrote three sample chapters and they were sent to reviewers, I was offered a contract.

The process of writing the text was long and grueling. I had cardboard boxes full of files of articles for every topic in each chapter. I wrote every day for a year. I submitted the manuscript. Ann sent it to reviewers, who told me what they thought about it. I made revisions and it was accepted. Editors began calling me about photographs and art. My mail held permission forms and advertising copy. My voice mail box (this was before I had e-mail) contained messages from one and all. The publishing company merged and re-merged, and changed its name. Somehow the book got done, on schedule, and on time. I remember the day I stopped into their office in Columbus. They brought out a copy of the book, newly printed. It was beautiful! The cover art by artist Nicholas Hill was just right. The book was fat and fine. It was late 1993 and it had a 1994 copyright.

This company, one of the largest college textbook companies in the world, sent the book to various periodicals and I waited for the reviews. The year ended. No reviews. The next year ended. No reviews. Then, near the end of 1996, there was one review, by Joan Smutny, in *Roeper Review*. Thank you, Joan. Other reviews followed, including the one in *Gifted Child Quarterly* by Bonnie Cramond and Karen Higginbotham. Thank you, Bonnie and Karen. The one in the *Journal for the Education of the Gifted* by Cheryl Adams arrived at the end of 1997. Thank you, Cheryl. The other day I received a review from Poland. In Polish. Thank you, Wieslawa. I hope you said good things. Every time I go to speak at a conference, someone comes over and asks me to sign their book. I am grateful. The other day, I talked with Australian professors who use the book with their undergraduates. People tell me they like all the charts and tables. They tell me the book is readable—and to make it read well was my goal.

Simultaneously, my editor was already talking of the future, urging me to finish a plan for the second edition, sending me a contract to sign after she sent my plan to reviewers, who told me what they thought.

"Second edition?" I said. "The first edition seems barely born."

But that is the way it is with textbook publishing. Now, as I write this, it is late spring 1998, and we are at the end of a year-long process involving as many people with the first edition. I thank Merrill/Prentice Hall for having enough faith in this book targeted for a very small audience to put it into production for a second edition. I would especially like to thank my editor, Ann Davis, her assistant Pat Grogg, production editor Julie Peters, and photography editor Nancy Ritz. James Reidel and Julie Hotchkiss have copyedited with patience and grace. Their attention to detail has been most professional and while tracking down those last few references, enough to make any author testy, I was also grateful for their raptor eyes.

Now that I have indeed written a textbook (but not that third novel), I recommend it for those who want to keep abreast of thought in their field. When you have to write, you have to read. Strangely enough, I am proud that I was able to keep all these references and sections straight. To write such a big book as a single author is daunting. To finish it is almost a personal triumph. The process has been both gratifying and educational, and when I count up my life's accomplishments, I think I will mention this book.

AN OVERVIEW OF THE BOOK

Chapter 1 tries to put into focus the various theories of intelligence and intelligences that have guided the field since its inception. It's a difficult chapter, but a necessary introduction to issues that continue to engage us. This edition includes the new information on serving and identifying the underserved populations that has come out of the Javits grants from the federal government. It includes the results of studies from the National Research Center for the Gifted and Talented at the University of Connecticut, the University of Virginia, the University of Georgia, and Yale University. I have tried to get a handle on the move toward inclusion and the quandary about middle school education. Many controversies accompany the need to educate learners who have outstanding academic abilities and talents, and I hope the process is clarified somewhat through this book. The developmental approach taken here considers talents by domain, which are a reflection of my thought in formulating the Pyramid of Talent Development.

As a former English teacher, curriculum continues to interest me as the most important part of the puzzle of educating the talented, and I have expanded the two chapters that deal with curriculum, Chapters 9 and 10. The results of the Third International Mathematics and Science Study (TIMSS) are included, with a comparison of how the brightest U.S. students do in comparison with other countries. Recently I have been studying the thinkers in postmodern curriculum theory, and I have included a nod to their provocative thinking. Critical pedagogy informed by equity questions about class, race, and gender may give our field the direction it needs.

As a former guidance counselor, I have definite ideas about this area, and they are included. The chapter on counseling and guidance, Chapter 11, has been reorganized and expanded. Readers find the Individual Educational Plan included there to be user friendly. I invite you to try it with a student. Chapter 12, on populations that are underserved and underidentified, has also been streamlined, and much information gleaned from the Javits grants in the past few years has been included.

As a former school administrator, I appreciate the need for recommendations and clarity in setting up and evaluating programs. In Chapters 2 and 3, the caveats and recommendations for setting up traditional programs have been condensed into a chart that can be used as a checklist. I have tried to be helpful as well as clear, and have listed, in Appendix A, the merits of various standardized tests and instruments used in identification. In Appendix B, I have again included the helpful questionnaire used in the Cox, Daniels, and Boston study of 1985.

With all the writing, speaking, and thinking I do on creativity, you would think I would have increased the amount of discussion on creativity. Instead, I have streamlined the research review into charts, and condensed the two creativity chapters into one, Chapter 4, with an emphasis on authentic assessment and portfolios and on creative products as means of identification. There are many new case examples in this edition. Much has been left out as well, as my editor did not want the book to be longer than the first edition.

I'm glad I had a chance to survey the literature again. As a professor who directs a licensure program for teachers who will teach the gifted and talented, I appreciate the back and forth of research, teaching, and scholarship. I hope this book is a good introduction to the field of the education of the gifted and talented for those of you who are reading this book as an assignment in your courses. I hope it is readable and engages you, and that the challenge of educating these youngsters begins to obsess you as it has me for the past 20 years.

ACKNOWLEDGMENTS

Thanks to reviewers of this edition: Art Attwell, University of Arkansas at Monticello; June Kreutzkampf, University of Minnesota at Duluth; Bruce M. Mitchell, Eastern Washington University; and Jay A. Monson, Utah State University.

Thanks to my students in Ohio and Georgia for the past few years. While you may never see your names here, because you are out of school now, and in the field teaching gifted and talented students, I am ever grateful for the opportunity to be your professor for awhile: Joel Abbott, Sandra Akin, Jennifer Allen, Anne Allendorf, Michelle Barbosa, Jeanette Beabout, Lori Beach, Jillian Bichsel, Barb Bodart, Luetta Booth, Linda Bracken, April Brooks, Kathryn Brown, Sheryl Buckley, Jenny Burke, Shawn Carter, Ellen Casey, Peggy Cawley, Tamra Clausen, Cynthia Collins, Rebecca Coppock, Diana Crabtree, Susan Crews, Sheryl Cubbins, Linda Cullison, Stephanie Cutlip, Joanne Damico, Khrista Darden, Marjorie Davis, Donna DeTray, Joy Dials, Martha Edwards, Jackie Eitel, Bonnie Elias, Cheryl Ellis-Solomon, Sheila Fagan, Susan Filler, Lori Flint, Tonjua Freeman, Carol Froelich, Beth Gantz, Don Garvick, Joyce Garvick, Alice Gay, Sandra Gibson, Daphne Golden, Susan Graham, Jennifer

Greer, Lee Ann Hall, Theresa Hancock, Mary Jo Harris, Jean Herendeen, Karen Higginbotham, Jan Hogle, Amanda Hogue, Larry Hohman, Cameron Hoxie, Kelly Holloway, Debbie Howell, Ruth Huber, Karnel Hudson, Elizabeth Hughes, Leslie Hunnicutt, Marjorie Hursey, Stacy Hutton, Theresa Jansen, Christine Keaton, Nancie Kennedy, Sara Kennedy, Karen Kessler, Joy King, Karen King, Lisa Koch, Connie Kramer, Vicki Krugman, Emily Krysanick, Jodi La Coppola, Victoria Lamb, Dawn Landoll, Janee Larson, Ann Lewis, Charlotte Lewis, Yu-shu Lin, Cindy Linzell, Andrew Llewelyn, La Tease Long, Lynn Lundholm, Kathleen Machan, Helen Mack, Patty Maczka, Teri Manion, Francie Marshall, Jill Mazzocca, Cherie Allen McAdams, Vanessa McEndree, Beverly McFarland, Teneh McMahan, Ann McNeil, Michelle Merton, Gwen Miller, JoSue Miller, Cynthia Minick, Linda Mitchell, Scott Mitchell, Carol Minocchi, Sylvia Rodriguez-Mylinski, Kendra Murray, Evelyn Newman, Mary Nickle, Diane Oplinger, Alexi Otis, Valerie Miller, Suzanne Palmer, Katy Peppers, Susan Pinion, Kathy Preston, Lynn Ramsay, Dana Randall, Mimi Reinhoudt, Ellen Reiss, F. Christopher Reynolds, Mary Rogers, Robbin Rogers, Barbara Rosalez, Amy Rose, Karen Ross, Karen Rowley, Robin Ryan, Angela Salmons, Martha Sherpely, Nancy Schottke, Betsy Schuman, Christine Self, Jane Sellers, Constance Shicks, Kelly Sherrill, Zayda Sierra, Sandra Siers, Marianne Smietana-Harner, Mark Solars, Margaret Sottosanti, Kathryn Sowash, Jennifer Stroup, Thom St. Clair, Mark Steffan, Tammy Stevens, Phyllis Swartz, Carol Swiatek, Janel Swonger, Gina Tabacca, Ria Terranova-Webb, Susan Tolbert, Dawn Upchurch, Jane Vandré, Mimi Verdone, Linda Wade, Karen Waldeck, Mary Wentz, Gail Wetteraurer, Therese Wilson, Ann Winer, Brenda Wheat, Sherry Wilkerson, Sandra Willmore, Michelle Woodard, Kim Wuenker, and Li Zuo.

Thanks to colleagues and friends: Sue Amidon, Jill Burrus, Geri Cassone, Bonnie Cramond, Roberta Daniels, James Delisle, Pat Edwards, Kathy Flanagan, David Henry Feldman, John Feldhusen, Ellen Fiedler, Darlene Freeman, Donna Ford-Harris, Greg Gerrick, Jeannie Goertz, Alan Guma, Merri Jamieson, Patricia Johnson-Kwartler, Sanda Kay, Dorothy Kennedy, Tom King, David Kowalka, Susan Larson, Sharon Lind, Paula Olszewski-Kubilius, Patricia Lambert, Amy Liebov, Betty Maxwell, John Memmott, Anthony Miserandino, Diane Montgomery, Katherine Payant, Michael Piechowski, Diane Pool, Michael Pyryt, F. Christopher Reynolds, Karen Rogers, Rose Rudnitski, Beverly Shaklee, Linda Silverman, Patrick Slattery, Rebecca Spehler, Kay Spore, Tom Southern, Rena Subotnik, Ray Swassing, Gene Telego, Kari Uusikylä, Joyce VanTassel-Baska, James Webb, Betty Whitted and Paula and Rachel Wilkes. Your suggestions and support have been appreciated. Thanks especially to the library staff at Ashland University, Bill Weiss and Sue Ellen Ronk.

And thanks to my creative mother, Pearl Piirto, my sisters Ruth and Rebecca and their families, and my children Steven, Denise, Ralph, and Danielle—outstandingly talented, one and all.

Jane Piirto, Ph.D.
Trustees' Professor
Ashland University
jpiirto@ashland.edu

CONTENTS

CHAPTER
3

IDENTIFICATION OF THE ACADEMICALLY TALENTED:
HIGH-IQ TALENT AND SPECIFIC ACADEMIC TALENT   **90**

CHAPTER
4

IDENTIFICATION OF CREATIVITY

136

CHAPTER
8

TALENTED ADULTS

316

CHAPTER
11

SOCIAL-EMOTIONAL GUIDANCE AND COUNSELING
NEEDS OF THE TALENTED   462

OVERVIEW OF THE FIELD OF TALENT DEVELOPMENT EDUCATION

1 WHO ARE THE TALENTED? GIFTEDNESS, TALENT, AND INTELLIGENCE

FOCUSING QUESTIONS

1. Should the word "gifted" be used to describe children?
2. What is your definition of *intelligence*? How does it relate to the common-sense definitions and the information-processing definitions?
3. What is your definition of *giftedness*?
4. What is your definition of *talent*? Is talent the same or different from giftedness?
5. Historically, genius has been equated with intelligence, giftedness, and talent. What are the common threads in the definitions?
6. Why do discussions of the heritability of IQ provoke passionate reactions.
7. Are you more of a hereditarian or more of an environmentarian? Why?
8. What aspects of the various ways of looking at talent are common to all the theories?
9. Discuss the new paradigm for the education of the talented (or "gifted") as shown or not shown in a nearby school district.

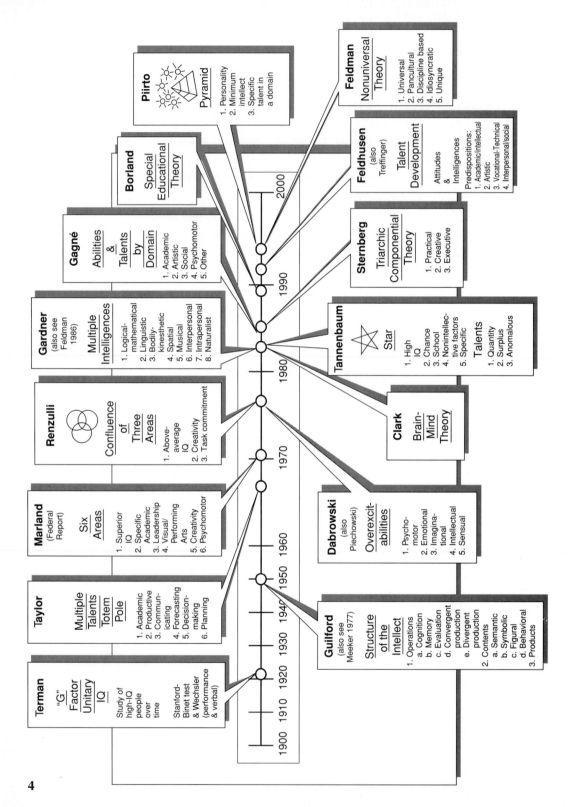

Figure 1.1 Time Line of Various Theories and Theorists That Have Had an Impact on the Field of Gifted and Talented Education

4

Alice Kellogg, a teacher of the gifted and talented, was talking to a colleague, Mrs. Kenyon, about Mike, one of the students in her eighth grade English class who had been identified as gifted. Mrs. Kenyon said to Alice, "But he's not gifted."

Alice said, "Well, he has an IQ on a Stanford-Binet individual intelligence test of 140. That's in the 99th percentile."

Mrs. Kenyon insisted, "But he's not gifted."

Alice continued, "But he has all A's in all his subjects."

"But he's not truly gifted," Mrs. Kenyon said.

"But he scores in the 97th percentile, the ninth stanine, on the Iowa Test of Basic Skills that we give, the standardized achievement test."

"But he's not gifted, as I think of gifted," Mrs. Kenyon said. She was getting perturbed.

"But you have chosen him as your student aid, because he is so organized, and gets everything done on time, and is responsible, and can be trusted."

"I know, but to me, he's not gifted."

Alice thought, and then said, "Well, he's not a very exciting personality, I guess. Is that what you mean?"

Mrs. Kenyon seemed relieved. "Yes, I guess so. He's just so goody-goody. That's not gifted to me. He just works hard. He's an overachiever, not a gifted student."

By all the standards of the State Board of Education in that state, Mike was gifted, but to his favorite teacher, he wasn't. This story illustrates the wide confusion about the concepts of giftedness, talent, and intelligence. This confusion is not new.

DEFINITIONS OF INTELLIGENCE, GIFTEDNESS, TALENT, AND GENIUS

Much confusion surrounds the terms *intelligence, giftedness, talent,* and *genius,* as people have used them and as they have been applied in the educational world. Makers of tests have often defined intelligence as having strengths in certain verbal or mathematical areas. People often use the word *gifted* to describe all children, as in the commonly heard statement, "But aren't all children gifted?" Some people think genius runs in families; others think that talent is acquired by experience or that talent is God-given.

School Definitions of Giftedness

In the United States, attempts have been made to get away from the use of a single, unitary IQ score in the definition of giftedness and talent. The federal government, through the U.S. Office of Education, has made three major initiatives in this direction: the 1971 Marland Report, the 1988 Javits Act, and the 1993 *National Excellence* report.

The Marland Report

In 1971, the report *Education of the Gifted and Talented* was issued by then-commissioner of the U.S. Office of Education Sidney Marland to Congress. The report listed six kinds of giftedness: (1) intellectual; (2) specific academic; (3) creative; (4) visual and performing arts; (5) leadership; and (6) psychomotor. It is evident that the Marland definition was influenced by the work of such thinkers and writers as De-Haan, Havighurst, Hollingworth, French, Ward, Witty, Passow, Ehrlich, and Kough.

Public Law 91-230

Gifted and talented children are those identified by professionally qualified persons who by virtue of outstanding abilities are capable of high performance. These are children who require differentiated educational programs and/or services beyond those normally provided by the regular school program in order to realize their contribution to self and society.

Children capable of high performance include those with demonstrated achievement and/or potential ability in any of the following areas, singly or in combination:

1. general intellectual ability
2. specific academic aptitude
3. creative or productive thinking
4. leadership ability
5. visual and performing arts ability
6. psychomotor ability

It can be assumed that utilization of these criteria for identification of the gifted and talented will encompass a minimum of 3 to 5 percent of the school population. (Marland, *Education of the Gifted and Talented*, 1971, p. 5)

The Marland Report said that most experts, by 1971, thought that the "gifted" were 5 percent or less of the population, and the "talented" were 11 to 15 percent of the population, though "these terms are, of course, not mutually exclusive" (p. 23). The Report went on to say that there was "apathy or hostility" in many school districts, and that more than half of schools reported that they had "*no* gifted students in their schools!" (p. 38). Fincher (1976) said that the report was greeted with great apathy throughout the nation:

The nation's approach to the gifted, limited as it is, is dogged by virtually every administrative and bureaucratic ill that can afflict government enterprise: lack of funds, lack of leadership, lack of trained personnel, lack of public understanding, lack of priority, lack of legislation, appallingly poor diagnosis of the very population it is supposed to serve, too much isolation, too little organization, and a stubborn history of nonintervention and state autonomy in how federal funds should be used. (p. 281)

By the mid-1980s, most gifted and talented education programs in schools in the United States had appropriated these types of giftedness in their definitions of the term. However, in practicality, these gifted education programs also mainly served and identified those who had high scores on either intelligence or achievement tests.

Pedagogical or school-related definitions in the U.S. and Canada are variations of the 1971 Marland Report. Marland said that the country had an obligation to pay attention to the educational needs of these children out of a duty to conserve: "Conservation of the gifted and talented requires that society tolerate the right of the individual with exceptional abilities and talents, even though unconventional, to attain his goals" (p. 22).

1988: The Javits Gifted and Talented Act

In 1988, the Congress of the United States passed the Jacob K. Javits Gifted and Talented Students Education Act of 1988, under the Elementary and Secondary Education Act, Title IV. This act noted that gifted and talented students were a "natural resource vital to the future of the Nation and its security and well-being" and as such their potential must be discovered early or else their contribution to the "national interest" was "likely to be lost." "At greatest risk" were children from "economically disadvantaged families and areas," and children of "limited English proficiency." Declaring that the Federal government had a "limited but essential role" in the education of these youth, the Javits Act set up a national agenda for research, demonstration, the training of personnel, and the supplementing of state and local funds. Gifted and talented students were defined thus:

Children and youth who give evidence of high performance capability in areas such as intellectual, creative, artistic, or leadership capacity, or in specific academic fields, and who require services or activities not ordinarily provided by the school in order to fully develop such capabilities.

National Excellence: A New School Definition of Giftedness

In 1991, an advisory panel to the Javits Act administrators in the U.S. Office of Educational Research and Improvement proposed a revised definition of gifted and talented children that was motivated by new cognitive research and by concerns for the inequity in participation in programs for the intellectually gifted. The full title of the report, which came out in 1993, is *National Excellence: A Case for Developing America's Talent*, and it was authored by Patricia O'Connell-Ross of the U.S. Office of Educational Research and Improvement. The definition proposed that giftedness—or talent—occurs in all groups across all cultures and is not necessarily seen in test scores, but in a person's "high performance capability" in the intellectual, in the creative, and in the artistic realms. The importance of environmental influence is apparent in this definition, as the concept of giftedness has been revised. Giftedness is said to connote "a mature power rather than a developing ability." Talent is to be found by "observing students at work in rich and varied educational settings." The best way to find talented children is by "providing opportunities and observing performance" (pp. 54, 55). The report noted a "quiet crisis" was apparent in the land. This crisis was the state of affairs in the education of our outstandingly talented children. The word *gifted* was eliminated, and the terms *outstanding talent* and *exceptional talent* were embraced. The new definition was as follows:

A Definition of Children with Exceptional Talent

Neuro-science and cognitive psychology have given us new insights into what it means for children and youth to be exceptionally talented and require us to develop a new definition of this population. The term "gifted" connotes a mature power rather than a developing ability and, therefore, is antithetic to recent research findings about children. The following definition, based on the definition used in the federal Javits Gifted and Talented Education Act, reflects the knowledge and thinking of today.

Children and youth with outstanding talent perform or show the potential for performing at remarkably high levels of accomplishment when compared with others of their age, experience, or environment.

These children and youth exhibit high performance capability in intellectual, creative, and/or artistic areas, possess an unusual leadership capacity, or excel in specific academic fields. They require services or activities not ordinarily provided by the schools.

Outstanding talents are present in children and youth from all cultural groups, across all economic strata, and in all areas of human endeavor.

To put this definition into practice, schools must develop a system to identify gifted and talented students that accomplishes the following:

1. *Seeks variety.* It must look throughout a range of disciplines for students with diverse talents.
2. *Uses many assessment measures.* It must use a variety of appraisals so that schools can find students in different talent areas and at different ages.
3. *Is free of bias.* It must provide students of all backgrounds with equal access to appropriate opportunities.
4. *Is fluid.* It must use assessment procedures that can accommodate students who develop at different rates and whose interests may change as they mature.
5. *Identifies potential.* It must discover talents that are not readily apparent in students as well as those that are obvious.
6. *Assesses motivation.* It must take into account the drive and passion that play a key role in accomplishment. (*National Excellence*, 1993, pp. 54-57)

HISTORY OF INTELLIGENCE TESTING

While the *National Excellence* report of 1993 spoke of differences in *achievement* tests across nations, the field of gifted education was first defined by the *intelligence* test. Those who were *gifted* scored in the upper ranges, the upper three percent, on such a test.

Sir Francis Galton (1822–1911), a British scientist and Charles Darwin's cousin, is considered the founder of the normal (bell-shaped) curve (see Figure 3.3). He became interested in heredity and the measurement of humans; he collected statistics on height, dimensions, strength, and other characteristics of large numbers of people. Galton also demonstrated fundamental techniques in statistical measurement. Among his works are *Hereditary Genius* (1869), *Inquiries into Human Faculty* (1883), *Natural Inheritance* (1889), and *Finger Prints* (1892). Galton theorized that psychological traits are based on physiological traits, and, therefore, that the normal distribution on a bell-shaped curve must also be true of human intelligence.

Galton set out to prove his theory, using the *Who's Who* of Britain. He reasoned that "eminence" showed "intelligence." Galton compared these eminent people with the mythical "average" man, thus extrapolating a normal distribution. Of course, the average man is a statistical phenomenon, a "mythic figure" created by statistics. Galton also explained why even in eminent families, children often had different levels of intelligence. He invented the terms *regression toward the mean* and *correlation*, statistical explanations for the phenomenon. Below-average parents often had slightly closer to average children, and above-average parents often had slightly closer to average children.

After Galton's appropriation of the idea of the statistical "average," against which all intelligence must be compared, Alfred Binet, in France, came into the picture. Binet was the director of the psychology lab at the Sorbonne. Jean Piaget was one of his assistants at the time. With universal education being a by-product of the Industrial Revolution, Binet was asked to try to find a way to identify students who would have trouble in school.

The idea of establishing age norms and comparing them to mental norms was born. By 1905, Binet and his colleague Theophilus Simon had tested many children and had some rough estimates about what could be expected of children from the ages of 3 to 11. But a German psychologist, William Stern, made a better suggestion. He theorized that a mathematical formula, dividing the child's *mental age* by the child's chronological age and multiplying that by a standard of 100, would yield a quotient of intelligence. The IQ was born, never to die, only to be modified and reified and referenced and used to categorize, to label, and to define. What is most surprising is the rapidity with which this numerically-based concept of intelligence was accepted throughout the infant profession of psychology, and the lack of validation the concept underwent before large numbers of people were subjected to testing and then to the decisions based on that testing.

The *g* Factor

The popularization of the notion of an intelligence quotient took the psychological world by storm, and more and more tests and items on tests were developed. In Great Britain, two psychologists, Charles Spearman and Cyril Burt, led a team that the Association for the Advancement of Science had charged to develop tests that would assess the mental abilities of British schoolchildren. No one had as yet defined what intelligence was, although all the psychologists were intent on measuring it. Spearman theorized that intelligence was a sort of faculty, a general capacity, present in all special abilities. This came to be called Spearman's "*g*," or "general intelligence."

Use of the IQ to Sort and Discriminate

By the 1920s, the fledgling psychometric field was also active in the United States, which was experiencing great floods of immigrants. Some immigrants were given intelligence tests at Ellis Island, and were deported based on the results. Racism and classism were defended by the intelligence testing profession. In 1916, Henry Goddard, director of research at the Vineland, New Jersey, School for the Feeble-Minded, himself tested European immigrants at Ellis Island, and found that "83 percent of the Jews, 80 percent of the Hungarians, 79 percent of the Italians, and 87 percent of the Russians were not just backward, but feeble-minded" (Fincher, 1976, p. 176). During World War I, the Army Alpha tests were given to draftees, and the results came out along race and class lines, with those draftees who had come from Britain scoring highest, and those from the Slavic and Mediterranean countries scoring lowest.

Carl Brigham, a psychologist from Princeton University, saw these results as heralding the superiority of Nordic and German stock. Brigham then became the secretary of the College Entrance Examination Board, and he developed the Scholastic Aptitude Test. It took him several years to recognize the variable of adopted language, but by then Congress had passed the 1924 immigration law that restricted the numbers of immigrants from certain countries. Few people in the field of gifted education mention the field's close ties to theories of eugenics. These theories later were instrumental in the philosophizing that formed the German Third Reich.

Lewis Terman, a psychologist at Stanford University, began a study called *Genetic Studies of Genius* in 1922. Terman, who had developed the Army Alpha test, and whose longitudinal study of high-IQ individuals is among the most referred to in the study of giftedness, got into the debates about genetically inferior races, saying about two Mexican-Indian children that these children should be "segregated into special classes" because they would be good workers, but they couldn't think abstractly. He said the "unusually prolific breeding" of their race posed a threat to society. These so-called scientific findings are among the reasons that IQ testing has been looked at with fear.

However, the psychologists began to try to improve the tests through better sampling and selection of test items. By the early 1930s, the concept of the Intelligence Quotient was believed in the United States, and widespread testing yielding IQs was entrenched in the schools. The next 60 years saw only deeper entrenchment, especially in the fields of special education and what came to be called *gifted education*. Fincher (1976) noted that the controversies over the IQ test exemplify a historical split in the social history of the United States, "with its roots plunged deep in our turbulent political past: the war between Jacksonian democracy, with its emphasis on the greatest good for the greatest number, and Jeffersonian democracy, with its concern for the unique needs of the individual" (p. 278).

Then in 1994, a book called *The Bell Curve* (Herrnstein & Murray) was published. This book made the front pages of the newspapers much as the *National Excellence* report had the year before. The researchers purported to "prove" that minorities had lower IQs than whites and this accounted for their presence in the lower social classes. In the 1960s, Herrnstein, a professor at Harvard, along with Arthur Jensen, a professor at UC-Berkeley, had already achieved notoriety for such a theory. This time educators were incensed and such books as *Measured Lies:* The Bell Curve Examined (edited by Kincheloe, Steinberg & Gresson, 1996) took the Herrnstein and Murray theory apart chapter by chapter. Kincheloe and Steinberg (1996b) wrote, "Not only is *The Bell Curve* marked by unreliable sources, the dismissal of problematic data, logical non-sequiturs and misguided purposes, it emerges from a crumbling paradigm often deemed inadequate for the study of human intelligence" (p. 28).

The shock wave of this best-selling book is still being felt in education circles, and it will probably finally herald the death of the IQ test in schools.

DEFINITIONS OF INTELLIGENCE

People on the street, when asked what intelligence was, agreed that there are three facets to intelligence (Neisser, 1979): (1) the ability to solve practical problems; that is, seeing all sides of the problem, being able to reason logically and with open-mindedness; (2) having verbal strength (being able to hold a good conversation, reading well, reading often); and (3) having social knowledge (understanding social cues; admitting when one is mistaken; having a general interest in the world).

Adults think that as children grow older, their intelligence is shown by how well they can solve problems and reason, while when children are young, their intelligence shows in their quickness of perception and their motor ability. After age 2, the ability to be verbal is a determining aspect of intelligence, and this continues right through adulthood.

More on *"g"*

What *"g"* is could be called the "sparkle in the eye" theory of intelligence, that "something" that some people think gifted people have. Like casting directors who just know what qualities the character in a movie or play should display, or like people who go to an art museum and look at the paintings, saying, "I know what good art is when I see it," the *"g"* factor believers cannot define it but they know it when they see it. One school principal once asserted that she could identify gifted children who are gifted just by watching them and talking to them. She said that those children who are gifted have "that certain something" that is the same in all of them, no matter what their talents are. Spearman called this *general intelligence,* and he theorized that mathematicians have four times as much general intelligence as musicians, and 36 times as much general intelligence as those who could draw well. (Both Spearman and Burt were mathematicians. IQ tests seem to work best in finding potential mathematicians and scientists.)

What was this *"g"*? It was a nebulous higher faculty for reasoning that was innate, or inborn. Burt developed a hierarchy of the general, the group, and the specific, which combined to make up a theory of what intelligence was. General intelligence involved judgment, reasoning, and how to apply concepts. The specific were sensory and motor skills, and the group were abilities such as perception of patterns and memory.

L.L. Thurstone, a psychologist from the Carnegie Institute of Technology, used factor analysis to separate *"g"* intelligence from *"S"* intelligence, or specific intelligences. These were called *primary mental abilities,* or PMAs. To this day, attempts to disprove the existence of *"g"* are being made, but for the most part they have failed. The mystical *"g"* has not yielded to psychometric factoring.

Researchers have continued to stubbornly try to find *"g,"* that certain something that is genetic, a "gift." Another theorizer, Eysenck (1985), said there are three intelligences: Intelligence A, which is "the biological substratum of all cognitive behaviour, giving rise to individual differences of a largely or entirely genetic nature"; Intelligence B, which is "the application of this ability in everyday life," which is influenced by environment, culture, and personality; and Intelligence C, which is "the IQ measurement of intelligence," the attempt to come close to A and to predict B (p. 118).

Fluid and Crystallized Intelligence

The theory race was on. Many psychologists proposed theories of intelligence. *"G"* factor intelligence came to be called *fluid* intelligence, similar to Eysenck's "Intelligence A," Burt's "general," or Thurstone's "general." To R.B. Cattell, fluid intelligence was the ability to perceive relationships and to integrate them mentally, apart from sensory knowledge. *Crystallized* intelligence was what we learned from our senses, from experience. Fluid intelligence was thought to be innate, but Lohman (1992) disagreed. Performance intelligence tests supposedly measure fluid ability, while achievement tests supposedly measure crystallized ability. Lohman said that fluid and crystallized abilities are on a continuum of transfer, and that both are developed as a result of education.

Fluid abilities are those that help an individual solve unfamiliar problems in a domain, and these fluid abilities can be improved with education in the organization of a discipline and with more emphasis on transfer. Cattell's theory of fluid and crystallized intelligence (called *Gf* and *Gc* for General fluid and General crystallized intelligence, respectively) was adopted in the development of the newest version of the Stanford-Binet intelligence test, the Stanford-Binet IV (N.M. Robinson, 1992). Thus even the revisers of the original intelligence test left behind the "*g*"-factor theory.

The Lumpers and the Splitters

Various theoreticians defining what intelligence is have come to be classified into the categories of *lumpers* and *splitters* (Mayr, 1982; Weinberg, 1989). The lumpers were those who thought that intelligence was a unitary trait with different specific abilities showing that intelligence. In 1967, J.P. Guilford published his work, *The Nature of Human Intelligence*. The ultimate splitter, Guilford posited that there were over 120 different kinds of intelligences, spread across four contents: the Figural, the Symbolic, the Semantic, and the Behavioral. These he called "the Structure of Intellect."

Guilford's idea of separate kinds of intelligence, or talent, has been quite influential in the thinking of psychologists about intelligence. The most famous current splitter is Howard Gardner, whose multiple intelligence (MI) theory in *Frames of Mind* (1983; see also 1996) posited eight kinds of intelligence: linguistic, musical, logical-mathematical, spatial, bodily-kinesthetic, interpersonal, intrapersonal, and naturalist.

Vernon (1971) took a position in the middle, between the lumpers and the splitters, saying that intelligence is hierarchical from the general to the more specific. Horn (1986) also proposed a hierarchical structure of intelligence. Educators should be familiar with these thinkers.

HEREDITY OR ENVIRONMENT

In addition to making theories about general and specific, structures and frames of intelligence, the psychologists and educators debate whether intelligence is nurtured or inherited. The great nature/nurture debate still rages: What part of a person's abilities are inherited, and what part are produced by environment?

Darwin and Galton and the Statistical Average

Perhaps the major figure in the nature/nurture debate was and still is Charles Darwin, who, with his extraordinary voyage to the Galapagos, and the resulting *On the Origin of Species* (1859), proposed that all creatures have evolved, that the fittest survive, and, therefore, heredity is more powerful than environment, although environment acts slowly to change the creature from one thing to another. The aforementioned Francis Galton, the father of modern testing, studied families of prominence, and "proved" in his famous book *Hereditary Genius* (1869) that genius is hereditary. Galton's work preceded that of the French psychologist Alfred Binet by 30 years.

Karl Marx's *Das Kapital* came out the same year as *Hereditary Genius*, and both books have had a great influence on the world's thought. Marx's point of view was that all people are overwhelmingly formed by the environment, and Galton's followers tried to show that people are overwhelmingly formed by their inherited genes. Galton was an advocate of eugenics, the interbreeding of highly intelligent people in order to improve the human species, while Marx was an advocate of social action against the prevailing system in order to provide change. To Marx, the common man was the revolutionary tool by which society would become more fair and equitable, and to Galton, the common man was an object for genetic experimentation, a statistical phenomenon, whose intelligence could be raised by a process of hereditary blending.

The debate was formed, and still continues today. Geneticists and other scientists who study heredity and environment have themselves been studied. One study (Pastore, 1949) found that scientists who believed that intelligence was inherited were conservatives and those who believed that intelligence was formed by environment were liberals. Another study (Sherwood & Nataupsky, 1968) found that scientists who believed that intelligence was inherited came from families whose grandfathers had been born in the United States, and scientists who believed that intelligence was formed by environment were children of immigrants and came from lower socioeconomic status backgrounds. This is to illustrate that a person's beliefs (even those of a supposedly neutral scientist) influence the hypotheses one forms and the theories one makes. Stephen Jay Gould, in *The Mismeasure of Man* (1981) pointed out that the whole testing movement that presupposed intelligence was inherited was fraught with bias and even fraudulence.

What Twin and Adoptive Studies Have Shown About Heritability of Intelligence

The study of identical twins is intriguing from the nature/nurture point of view. If identical twins formed from the same egg, more alike than any other two human beings, could be shown to have differences if they were raised apart, the environmental viewpoint—that environment, or experience, shapes intelligence and behavior—would prevail. If twins raised apart had few differences, the hereditarian viewpoint—that genetics is the overwhelming factor in determining how a person turns out—would prevail. If people who were adopted at a young age showed more similarity to their adoptive parents than to their biological parents, environmental influences would be shown to be dominant. If people who were adopted showed more similarity to their biological parents, the dominance of genes would be shown.

Over the years, much has been made of the similarities found between identical twins who have been raised apart. Galton included twins in his studies. He influenced Cyril Burt who purported to find significant results showing that intelligence is overwhelmingly inherited. Burt's data were later discredited; in fact, he was found not to have even studied twins he said he studied. Kamin (1981) and Lewontin, Rose, and Kamin (1984) pointed out that environmental factors were still predominant even in studies of twins raised apart, for many of these twins had been raised by branches of the same extended families, or in close geographical proximity.

The more recent Minnesota Study of Twins Reared Apart Project at the University of Minnesota (Bouchard, Lykken, McGue, Segal & Tellegen, 1990) has revealed great similarities between twins raised apart; however, the greatest similarities are between identical twins raised together. Researchers found that approximately 70 percent of the difference in IQ was attributable to genetics: "On multiple measures of personality and temperament, occupational and leisure-time interests, and social attitudes, identical twins (monozygotic) reared apart are almost the same as identical twins reared together" (p. 223). Even in an area that would seem to be strictly environmental, the choice of occupations, they found that 40 to 50 percent of the variation in vocational interests is genetic (Moloney, Bouchard & Segal, 1991). Bouchard said on a *Nova* program about the twin studies (1987) that he had begun them with a strong bias toward the overwhelming influence of environment, as a good educator/psychologist would, but he had become more and more convinced of the preeminence of hereditary factors.

While these findings are frightening to some people, the researchers pointed out that how the person reacts to the environment can also be genetically influenced. Responding to criticisms, the Minnesota researchers in 1991 said that it is "highly unlikely" that unforeseen similarities in the environments of twins raised together and twins raised apart could cause the similarities in personality, temperament, occupations, and social interests.

Other studies about the heritability of intelligence have taken place using adopted children, their adoptive parents, and their birth parents (Munsinger, 1975). Adopted children were found to resemble their natural parents more closely than their adoptive parents in intelligence. The results of these studies are also in question, for Kamin (1981) pointed out that the researchers did not correct for the influence of socioeconomic status. Eysenck (1985) disagreed. He said that the similarities between the adoptive children's IQs and their natural parents' IQs "increase during the time he is being brought up by others, and that the difference between the child's IQ and his adoptive parents goes down!" (p. 124).

In 1997 Plomin summarized the genetic studies about the relationship between general cognitive ability, heredity, and environment: "Genetic contributions to individual differences in IQ test scores are significant and substantial," he said. Correlations between twins raised apart are greater than for nonrelated siblings raised together. "About half of the IQ differences among individuals in the population can be accounted for by genetic differences among them" (p. 70). Verbal abilities and spatial abilities are more heritable than memory and speed of information processing. As people get older, they show more similarity to their genetic relatives. An interesting finding was that ability (or IQ) test scores and achievement test scores, though they are often similar, reveal differences. "The overlap between intelligence and scholastic achievement is due entirely to genetic factors, whereas the differences between them are environmental in origin" (p. 73). In other words, underachievement (a disparity between achievement test scores and ability test scores) seems to be environmental.

The controversy surrounding these studies continues, and the educational practitioner is, after all, not a genetic psychologist nor a psychometrist. If IQ is all inherited, why teach? If IQ tests that purport to measure intelligence are biased toward socioeconomically or environmentally advantaged children, why are they still used? Why is intelligence confounded by income? The controversy has not died down. The 1995 meeting of the American Educational Research Association in San Francisco that featured a panel on Herrnstein and Murray's 1994 book *The Bell Curve* with psychologist Arthur Jensen found staid educational researchers booing him, walking out, and turning back to shout as they did so.

DEFINITIONS OF GIFTEDNESS AND TALENT

From Plato to Gardner, from the patriarch Moses to the matriarch Grandma Moses, human society has struggled to define and deal with those individuals who stand out by virtue of their abilities. The recognition that people differ in their aptness for study was seen at the very roots of Western culture, in Greece. Plato, in his ideal society led by the philosopher-king, said that people should serve society with their strongest abilities, and he recognized that different people had different abilities.

Etymology of the Word *Gifted*

The word *gift* originates in Old Teutonic and it originally meant "payment for a wife." Another root of the word is in Old French, where it meant "poison." According to the *Oxford English Dictionary* (3rd edition, 1981), in the English language, the first mention of the word *gifted*, meaning "endowed with gifts," or "talented," appeared in 1644 when it was used in the sense of a person having a special talent for public speaking. The term has generally referred to people who have abilities that are different and higher than normal.

Historical Views

In the "Allegory of the Cave" in Plato's *Republic*, Socrates said that the ideal leader must be both a soldier and a philosopher, and must be good in "the contemplation of numbers," or mathematics, for "natural reckoners are by nature quick in virtually all their studies." He recognized that some people take better to their studies than others, and said that these people have "gifts of nature" such as "a certain keenness for study." They learn easily and are relatively rare to find, "for souls are much more likely to flinch and faint in severe studies than in gymnastics," and thus the state must "demand a good memory and doggedness and industry." They must be both physical and philosophical, equally good at the work of the body and of the mind, and he even advocated equal opportunity for women, saying "for you must not suppose that my words apply to the men more than to all women who arise among them endowed with the requisite qualities."

Today's thinkers about intelligence, giftedness, and talent also say that those who have a quickness for study have "a good memory," have "doggedness," and have "industry." They are said to learn more rapidly. Plato was perhaps the first, but not the last, to recognize that some people differ in their school abilities, and that those people should have a different education.

That Descartes was a talented philosopher and mathematician (logical-mathematical or symbolic intelligence), that Tiger Woods is a talented golfer (bodily-kinesthetic or behavioral intelligence), that Anne Frank was a talented writer (linguistic or semantic intelligence), that Moses was a prophet (intrapersonal or social intelligence), that Grandma Moses was an artist (spatial or figural intelligence) whose talent was not recognized until she had aged, that Margaret Thatcher was a talented politician (interpersonal or social intelligence), that Audubon was a talented collector and cataloguer of birds (naturalist intelligence), that John Lennon had a talent for writing incomparable popular songs (musical or symbolic intelligence) illustrate that talent, or the manifestation of talent, takes many forms. Yet the persistent belief that intelligent people have a certain score on a general intelligence or IQ test continues.

Issues of Labeling

In the United States we label children as *gifted*, implying that they have special talents and high intelligence. Throughout history, this has meant that the child has been bestowed with some talent. In fact, the terms *gifted* and *talented* are often used interchangeably, although some state departments of education define *gifted* as having a high IQ, and *talented* as being in the visual or performing arts. This text prefers the term *talented*, although the author finds it difficult not to use the word *gifted* in her speech, as the word is widely used within the field (while looked at suspiciously by educators and people from outside the field). Few adults would state they themselves are *gifted*, though they have no hesitation about labeling small children so. Armenta (1997) found that bright adults confirmed that "the gifted label is hard to bear … gifted children know their own label but when they look around, they can hardly find a single gifted adult who volunteers to become a role model" [in assuming the label of *gifted*]. In 1997 Feldman said, "No mere semantic preference, the definition of the term *gifted* is perhaps the most important task faced by the field as it moves toward the next century" (p. 11).

In 1993 the word *gifted* was removed from federal authorizing legislation, and the word *talented* was retained. At present, the term *talent development* is seen with more and more frequency, and name changes are in the air. For example, the Iowa Center for the Gifted changed its name to the Iowa Center for Giftedness and Talent Development.

In 1994 Margolin criticized the field's use of the term *gifted*. He noted that in the premier journals of the field, the *Gifted Child Quarterly, The Journal for the Education of the Gifted,* and the *Roeper Review*, the terms are used as if there is an implicit definition, but upon close reading, one can see that the authors of the articles rarely define what they mean by using the word gifted. Sometimes it means high IQ. Sometimes it means high academic achievement. Sometimes it means high mathematical achievement. Sometimes it means having scored high on a creativity test or having obtained high grades.

Etymology of the Word *Talented*

In contrast to *gifted*, the word *talent* originated in Latin, and it was the term for a sum of money. As the term evolved, it came to mean an inclination, a leaning, a desire, a wish. Its first use in the contemporary sense of having a natural ability or a mental endowment evolved from the Gospel of Matthew, in his story of Jesus's "Parable of the Talents." According to the *Oxford English Dictionary*, by 1600 the word was used as we use it today. To be talented is to possess the skills to do something well.

Most educational programs say that they are programs for the "gifted and talented," where the term *gifted* implies having a high IQ, and the term *talented* means being able to do something well, such as paint, sing, dance, or act. Having a high IQ is not necessary for having talent, though the *Oxford English Dictionary* lists *gifted* as being synonymous with *talented*: Talented means "possessing talent, gifted, clever, accomplished." The inclusion of both terms in almost all descriptions of programs implies that program definers feel uneasy about the difference between the two. Some state department of education definitions differentiate gifted from talented in this way, but most states do not differentiate, using the terms synonymously, even putting a slash between them, as in G/T (gifted/talented).

In 1992 and 1994 (in the first edition of this book) I argued for the consideration and identification of talents by domains, and organized the book developmentally, discussing talent according to domain. In 1996, Winner also said that talents exist in domains, and she said that differentiating between *gifted* as having high IQ or being good in "schoolhouse" subjects, and *talented* as being good in music, art, or athletics, is a useless differentiation. She said, "Children gifted in academic and aesthetic domains should be labeled either all talented or all gifted" (p. 102).

The confusion about these terms illustrates the evolutionary character of language. The reader should be aware of the confusion, which continues today just as it has for centuries. The confusion deepens when one takes into account whether intelligence, giftedness, talent, or genius—pick your term—are inherited or acquired by experience.

THEORIES OF GIFTEDNESS THAT HAVE INFLUENCED THE FIELD

The call for a comprehensive theory of giftedness—or talent—has continued. Cohen (1988) summarized the current theories of giftedness, and said that a theory should take into account (1) the nature of the gifted child; and (2) the education and identification of the gifted child. In addition, a theory should have a clear framework and should meet certain criteria such as consistency, logic, simplicity, and wholeness.

The field has been influenced by the single, unitary IQ theory since Terman (1877–1956). As mentioned above, Terman devised the term *intelligence quotient* (IQ), which became an index of measurement of the intelligence level of both children and adults, with a normal standard of 100. He also developed the so-called Stanford-Binet intelligence tests to measure the IQ. Among his many works are *The Measurement of Intelligence* (1916), *The Intelligence of School Children* (1919), *The Stanford Achievement Test* (1923), and *Genetic Studies of Genius* (1925–1959), a five-volume study of 1500 gifted children from adulthood through midlife.

Creativity research was called for by Guilford in 1950. Several conferences were held at the University of Utah. These were coordinated by Calvin Taylor, who formulated a Multiple Talents theory based on creativity research. This model was validated by the National Dissemination Network and is still used widely in the field of talent development education. Called Multiple Talent Totem Poles, the theory features (1) academic; (2) creative; (3) planning; (4) communicating; (5) forecasting; and (6) decision making. Taylor and Ellison (1975) said, "teachers are talent developers, having all children use knowledge to activate and develop a multiplicity of their talents" (p. 201).

Guilford's model of the Structure of the Intellect had its application to the field of the education of the talented. Mary Meeker took 26 of Guilford's 120 subtests and made a test called the SOI Learning Abilities Test (SOI-LA). She further made a Gifted Screening Form, where a gifted person is someone who scores in the "gifted" range on 10 or so subtests (mostly semantic and symbolic). Meeker was on the board of the National Association for Gifted Children for many years.

A New Paradigm

Feldman (1991, 1992) postulated a new paradigm for giftedness. He was on the committee that advised the U.S. Office of Educational Research and Investigation for the *National Excellence* report. He said that the times were changing. The *old* paradigm for giftedness said that giftedness was contained in one score, the IQ score. The *new* paradigm suggests that there are many types of giftedness. The *old* paradigm was trait based; the emerging paradigm is *qualities* based. The *old* one was often considered elitist; the *new* is based on a consideration of individual excellence. The *old* moved from the inside to the outside (that is, giftedness is somehow in there and it comes out without special intervention); in the *new,* emerging paradigm the framework is contextual: giftedness is defined by the context in which the gifted person finds himself. The *old* was test driven; the *new* is achievement driven; that is, giftedness is a developmental process. The *old* was authoritarian: that is, authorities determined that "you are gifted" and "you are not gifted"; the *new,* emerging paradigm is collaborative; that is giftedness is determined by consultation. The *old* was school oriented; the *new* is field and domain oriented; that is, a person is gifted in something—in a domain. The old was ethnocentric; the new is diverse. Feldman went on to say that no theory of giftedness is "right"; the question is which theory has the most transformational impact (see Figure 1.2).

Developmental theories such as those of Piaget, Feldman, and Vygotsky have been proposed. Cognitive theories such as Gardner's multiple intelligences theory (MI) and Sternberg's triarchic theory as discussed previously have been gaining currency. Other theories are the Dabrowski overexcitability theory, the Feldhusen TIDE model, the Gagné differentiation between giftedness as aptitude and talent as achievement, psychosocial theories such as the Renzulli theory and the Tannenbaum theory, and my own Pyramid of Talent Development (Figure 1.6 on p. 30).

Developmental Theories of Intelligence

Besides the psychometricians, the test-makers discussed above, another type of intelligence theorist has been the developmental theorist. Piaget (1947/1960) was among them. Intelligence is "the state of equilibrium towards which tend all the successive adaptations of a sensorimotor and cognitive nature, as well as all assimilatory and accommodatory interactions between the organism and the environment" (p. 11). The Piagetians focused on qualitative changes in development of perception, understanding, and environmental functioning. The hierarchies of development—sensorimotor, preoperational, concrete operational, and formal operational—were viewed as ways of thinking and not as what the person knew. The person reaches a state of equilibrium through the processes of assimilation and accommodation. The intelligent person does so "through a reflection of thought on itself" (p. 15). To Piaget, the highest

Figure 1.2 Emerging
Paradigm of Giftedness
From "Has there been a paradigm
shift in gifted education?" by D.
Feldman, 1992, in N. Colangelo, S.
G. Assouline, and D. L. Ambroson
(Eds.), *Talent Development: Pro-
ceedings from the 1991 Henry and
Jocelyn Wallace National Research
Symposium on Talent Development*
(pp. 89–94). Unionville, NY: Trillium
Press. Copyright 1992 by Trillium
Press. Reprinted by permission of D.
Feldman.

Old	New
Giftedness is High IQ	Many Types of Giftedness
Trait Based	Qualities Based
Subgroup Elitism	Individual Excellence
Innate, "In There"	Based on Context
Test Driven	Achievement Driven, "What You Do" Is Gifted
Authoritarian, "You Are or Are Not Gifted"	Collaborative, Determined by Consultation
School Oriented	Field and Domain Oriented
Ethnocentric	Diverse

form of intellectual operation was that found in logic and in mathematics. Logic is able to translate "the vagueness of verbal language" to algorithms and finally to axioms similar to those in geometry. Piaget equated intelligence with mathematical intelligence, overlooking the intelligences requisite in other domains, such as visual arts or writing.

Piaget said that intelligent behavior was manifested progressively as a child moved from one developmental state to another, from the sensorimotor through the preoperational, from the concrete to the formal. It was previously thought that all adults reached formal operations sooner or later, but some studies have shown that some adults never reach formal operations, and that is perhaps why our newspapers are written on a 12-year-old reading level (Flavell, 1977; Martorano, 1977; Niemark, 1975). To Piagetians, giftedness would be the rapid passing from one stage to another, that is, though the normal eight-year-old child would be in concrete operations, the gifted eight-year-old child would possibly be into formal operations.

Recently, developmentalists have posited that perhaps giftedness is manifested in adulthood by the gifted adult reaching a *post*formal stage of development, a stage where problem *finding* is the giftedness, whereas in the formal developmental stage, problem solving is the determinant. Indeed, Getzels and Csikszentmihalyi (1976) indeed found that those visual artists who were the most distinguished were those who found the most challenging and interesting artistic problems on which to work.

Another developmental approach has been to look at prodigy as Feldman (with Goldsmith, 1986) has done, in the belief that looking at rapid development will provide knowledge about all development. Feldman said, "Although the prodigy's gifts are awesome and extremely uncommon, I believe that the processes by which they grow and flower are nonetheless similar to the ones by which all intellectual development proceeds" (p. x).

In 1994 (Feldman; see also Feldman, Csikszentmihalyi & Gardner, 1994) Feldman proposed a theory of talent development called *nonuniversal theory* (see Figure 1.1 on p. 4). While not a theory of giftedness, nonuniversal theory concerns the development of the intellect that explains "transitions and transformations in understanding and

Students learn classification with manipulatives.

extending bodies of knowledge, acquisition of expertise and creative advances in knowledge" (Feldman, 1997, p. 22). Proposing a continuum of developmental domains ranging across (1) *universal*; (2) *pancultural*; (3) *discipline based*; (4) *idiosyncratic*; and (5) *unique*, Feldman asked four questions relevant to the field of the education of the gifted and talented:

1. What kinds of special talents, general and specific, in what combinations seem to be necessary for mastery in various developmental domains?
2. What kinds of conditions (external and internal) seem to be necessary for extraordinary mastery to occur?
3. What are the special circumstances, including more specific as well as more general talents, in addition to those required for initial mastery, that seem to be involved when domains are mastered and transformed?

4. How do we characterize those extremely rare events when a well-established developmental domain is transformed so fundamentally that its principles and psychological organization are irreversible altered, i.e. when contributions of *genius* have occurred?

A third developmental approach to understanding intelligence was proposed by Vygotsky (1962). L.S. Vygotsky, a Russian psychologist working during the 1920s, in the Marxist intellectual fervor after the Russian Revolution, proposed that a child's intelligence cannot develop apart from social structures. Vygotsky's views were suppressed in the former Soviet Union when behaviorism was viewed as being more politically correct; that is, a person could be conditioned to learn; learning was environmental and not a genetically induced capacity (Wertsch, 1988).

Cognitive Theories of Intelligence

Another view of what intelligence is has been called the *cognitive* view. The cognitive sciences are philosophy, psychology, linguistics, artificial intelligence, anthropology, and neuroscience. Of these, psychology and artificial intelligence have formulated views of giftedness. Cognitive science has widened the consideration of what intelligence is, from the narrow psychometric view that intelligence is what intelligence tests measure to the broad view of what happens in the human mind when intelligent thinking takes place. Artificial intelligence is related to the "information-processing" theory of giftedness.

Information Processing as Intelligence

One of the information-processing theorists is Robert Sternberg of Yale University (1985). Sternberg proposed a triarchic theory with three subprocesses (see Figure 1.1 on p. 4). These are as follows: (1) individuals with intelligence are able to monitor their internal thinking processes; that is, they can show metacognitive ability in an executive manner; (2) individuals who show intelligence can produce novel products, which are often made after a person learns something to the point where it is automatic, and this is the creative subprocess; and (3) intelligent individuals also have the ability that is often called "common sense." For example, they can change their behavior after experiencing difficulties. They possess tacit knowledge, or practical knowledge of how to get along in the world and are able to adapt, select, and shape their environments. The person who possesses all three of these subprocesses to the highest degree is the most intelligent. Essentially Sternberg is describing what makes up general intelligence as most of his studies have used a baseline of IQ for comparisons and analysis.

Sternberg's theory has great popularity with academicians at the time of this writing. Sternberg is in the process of developing and validating the Sternberg Multidimensional Abilities Test, which is to measure these abilities. To simplify Sternberg's idea, intelligent behavior is made up of three components: (1) practical; (2) creative; and (3) executive ability.

Sternberg conducted four projects funded by the Javits grants to the National Research Center/Gifted and Talented. Project I, a construct validation and educational application of Sternberg's triarchic theory of human intelligence, revealed that students who are instructed and whose achievement is evaluated in a way that matches (at least partially) their profile of abilities will perform better in school than children who are mismatched. Project II, which examined the construct validity of Sternberg's theory of mental self-government, found that teachers tend to (1) evaluate more positively students who match their own profile of style; and (2) overestimate the extent to which students match their own style of thinking. Project III, construct validation of Sternberg and Lubart's investment theory of creativity (1991), found that creative individuals are people who "buy low and sell high" in the world of ideas. Project IV, an investigation of Sternberg's pentagonal implicit theory of giftedness, found that society labels people as gifted to the extent that the people meet five criteria—excellence, rarity, productivity, demonstrability, and value.

Sternberg is among many researchers who have disputed that intelligence is merely having scored high on an IQ test. In 1997 he proposed that his theory be called "successful intelligence." He said, "Ultimately, successful intelligence is about figuring out what you do well, figuring out what you do poorly; and then finding out a way of capitalizing on strengths and compensating for or remediating weaknesses" (p. 2).

Recent research has begun to unravel what happens in the mind while people think. These studies are beginning to yield hard information about how people process information. Thus, they are called information-processing studies. Among these are studies of *rapidity of mental processing* (Eysenck, 1985; Vernon, 1987), of *metacognition* (Borkowski & Peck, 1986; Chan, 1996; Dover & Shore, 1991; Flavell, 1979 ; Geary & Brown, 1991; Hannah & Shore, 1995; Schwanenflugel, Stevens & Carr, 1997), of *metamemory* (Borkowski & Peck, 1986; Carr & Borkowski, 1987; Kurtz & Weinert, 1989), of *insight* (Davidson, 1986, 1992; Sternberg & Davidson, 1985, 1995), and the like.

The knowledge these studies produce is rudimentary. Though "metacognition" is a hot word in education nowadays, the practical applications for educators of the talented seem to be the same as for all educators. If students are directly taught strategies for planning, selecting, monitoring, and evaluating their work, they are more likely to use these strategies to good effect. Researchers don't know yet whether the differences between high IQ students and average IQ students are only present in middle childhood, and the average intelligence students eventually catch up in high school, whether high IQ children learn more quickly when general guidelines for planning and monitoring are taught, or even whether the superiority of metacognition in some high IQ students continues over the life span.

The insight research has also shown that high-IQ students are able to apply insight when they solve tricky problems. High-IQ students performed better spontaneously in three areas of insight: (1) selective encoding; (2) selective combination; and (3) selective comparison. This happened for both seventh graders and college students. Like metacognitive theory, insight theory as presently constituted is vague.

The memories of high-IQ students process more efficiently and information is retrieved more efficiently, both in long-term and short-term memory. High-IQ students can also better remember remembering (Carr & Borkowski, 1987). Researchers have found that there are "qualitative differences" in the sort recall and the metamemory of high-IQ and average-IQ children.

All of these avenues of research are fascinating. However, what these emerging studies illustrate is that evolving definitions of intelligence are still theoretically tied to measures of IQ, and to the entrenched idea that high IQ means giftedness. It seems that the studies are yielding breakdowns as to what having a high IQ means, but they are not throwing out the IQ as a means of defining intelligence, or the definition of giftedness as having a high IQ. As Michael Pyryt (1996) said, IQ is "easy to bash, hard to replace" (p. 255).

Expertise Theory

Another avenue of research on intelligence that is applicable for educators of the talented is the expertise research. This is domain- or discipline-based and includes research on transfer; that is, how do children master the subject matter? (It is content specific and context bound) (Corner & Hagman, 1987). Research on expert–novice comparisons have shown that experts, unsurprisingly, have a large knowledge base of patterns in how the domain works. They can rapidly recognize situations where the patterns apply, and they can therefore reason forward, manipulating the patterns in order to reach solutions. Again, this is logical, and not earthshaking.

Multiple Intelligence Theory: Gardner's Eight Intelligences

Another cognitive theory of intelligence is Multiple Intelligence (MI) theory (see Figure 1.1 on p. 4). Project Spectrum, a joint effort of Gardner's colleagues Mara Krechevsky of Harvard's Project Zero and David Feldman of Tufts University, engaged in studying seven of the intelligences in preschool children and developing assessments for these intelligences. (See Chapter 5 for a detailed description of these assessments.) Founded in 1984, Project Spectrum researchers set out to determine whether or not children as young as four years old had "distinctive profiles of intelligences." They found that indeed this was so; "even students as young as four years old present quite distinctive sets and configurations of intelligences" (Gardner, 1991, p. 206). Gardner claims that each of these types of intelligence is discrete, and is formed by its own peculiar kinds of learning, as well as its own kind of memory and perception. He proposed eight criteria for the existence of an intelligence.

Gardner's Criteria for an Intelligence

1. Potential isolation by brain damage
2. Existence of idiots savants, prodigies, and other exceptional individuals
3. An identifiable core operation or set of operations
4. A distinctive developmental history, along with a definable set of "end-state" performances
5. An evolutionary history and evolutionary plausibility
6. Support from experimental psychological tasks
7. Support from psychometric findings
8. Susceptibility to encoding in a symbol system

However, the researchers also have found that certain intelligences combine to form certain types of what could be called talent. For example, physicists would combine logical-mathematical intelligence and spatial intelligence.

Mainstream educators have demonstrated a substantial interest in Gardner's work. Articles about his theory have appeared in every mainstream educational journal, from *Phi Delta Kappan* to the *Instructor*, to the *Middle School Journal*. Workshops conducted by educational consultants are available throughout the country. Gardner's theory is transforming the educational landscape at the millennium. Educators have always known intuitively that children are intelligent in many ways, and not just in the mathematical and verbal ways that are usually tested. The eight intelligences are assessed by looking directly at the intelligence as it is manifested, and not by abstract paper and pencil testing. Like IQ theory, the theory of intelligence that has the most sticking power is the theory that is adopted by the schools.

The field of the education of the gifted and talented embraced Gardner's theory as soon as he proposed it, in the middle 1980s. Several Javits projects have explored MI identification and programming.

Psychosocial Theories of Giftedness

Overexcitability Theory

Among several other theories gaining currency is the Dabrowski theory. Though proposed in the 1960s, it is only recently that the theory has been cited in the field of the education of the gifted and talented (see Figure 1.1 on p. 4) . The Dabrowski theory is a theory of emotional development that is particularly suitable for an understanding of giftedness. Dabrowski posited that people develop through a series of stages brought on by positive maladjustment. The theory, called Theory of Positive Disintegration (TPD), emphasizes the role of suffering and inner conflict in advancing development. Two essay response instruments, the Definition Response Instrument (DRI) and the Overexcitability Questionnaire (OEQ), are utilized. An objective test is in the developmental stages. Both go far beyond the IQ test, emphasizing the presence or absence of overexcitabilities.

Dabrowski was interested in describing human personality as it actually expresses itself. He observed a "multileveledness" in human behavioral phenomena, from egocentric to altruistic, from nonreflective to intensely self-aware, from developmental (not capable of psychological growth) to highly developed. The theory emphasizes affective and emotional development, not just cognitive development, and it explains developmental transformation in a sequence of five levels. These levels are useful in considering adult moral and emotional giftedness.

In addition, Dabrowski proposed five types of "overexcitabilities" predictive of developmental potential: (1) psychomotor; (2) sensual; (3) intellectual; (4) imaginational; and (5) emotional. Michael Piechowski (1979) has become the leading researcher in the field of the education of the talented and gifted into the Dabrowski theory since Dabrowski's death. These overexcitabilities are useful in considering the differences that some children have from other children. Again, much of the Dabrowski theorizing compares children with high IQs with others, and thus, like most of the theories in the field, it is an explication of what it means to have a high IQ. The theory of overexcitabilities is discussed in Chapter 11.

Renzulli Theory

Another theory of giftedness that has gained wide currency is the Renzulli theory (see Figure 1.3). Cox, Daniel, and Boston (1985) said that Renzulli's theory captures the Whitehead dictum that education should have a rhythm of "romance, precision, and generalization" (p. 142). Henry Levin, founder of the accelerated schools movement, has embraced Renzulli's theory and his corresponding model of schoolwide enrichment. Renzulli's theory shows a Venn diagram, which posits that a gifted person has equal amounts of above-average intelligence, creativity, and task commitment (Figure 1.3). How one measures above-average intelligence and creativity is left to the school system, but instruments such as behavior checklists and creativity tests are advocated. A gifted person exhibits gifted behaviors:

> Gifted behavior reflects an interaction among three basic clusters of human traits—these clusters being above-average general and/or specific abilities, high levels of task commitment, and high levels of creativity. Individuals capable of developing gifted behavior are those possessing or capable of developing this composite set of traits and applying them to any potentially valuable area of human performance. (Renzulli & Reis, 1989)

Tannenbaum's Theory

Tannenbaum (1983, 1997) called giftedness a psychosocial phenomenon (see Figure 1.4). His definition encompassed five factors: (1) a "sliding scale" of general intelligence; (2) special ability; (3) nonintellective factors; (4) environmental factors; and (5) chance factors. Each of these has its static and its dynamic dimension. There are two types of gifted people, the performers and the producers. The producers produce thoughts and tangibles and the performers perform staged artistry and human services. He said that when we look for giftedness in children, we know certain things about the nature of giftedness:

> First, we may regard it as extraordinary promise for productivity or performance in areas of work that are publicly prized; it is not a facility for consuming knowledge in abundance or at a rapid pace. Second, we may consider its parameters as encompassing surplus, scarcity, and quota talents, and perhaps some anomalous talents as well. Third, we may assume its existence in children to be a moderately reliable herald of their distinction as adults. Finally, there is enough empirical evidence to help us locate at least part of the "terrain" in a person's psyche and surroundings where factors associated with extraordinary potential and its realization are most likely to exist. (1983, p. 89)

Tannenbaum said that the identification of giftedness is risky business because there is no guarantee that precocity will be realized in adult performance. He continued:

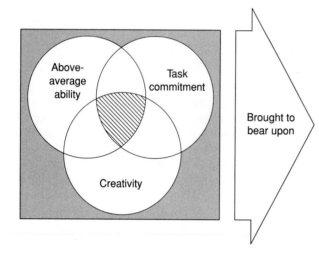

General Performance Areas

Mathematics • Visual Arts • Physical Sciences • Philosophy • Social Sciences • Law • Religion • Language Arts • Music • Life Sciences • Movement Arts

Specific Performance Areas

Cartooning • Astronomy • Public Opinion Polling • Jewelry Design • Map Making • Choreography • Biography • Film Making • Statistics • Local History • Electronics • Musical Composition • Landscape Architecture • Chemistry • Demography • Microphotography • City Planning • Pollution Control • Poetry • Fashion Design • Weaving • Play Writing • Advertising • Costume Design • Meteorology • Puppetry • Marketing • Game Design • Journalism • Electronic Music • Child Care • Consumer Protection • Cooking • Ornithology • Furniture Design • Navigation • Genealogy • Sculpture • Wildlife Management • Set Design • Agricultural Research • Animal Learning • Film Criticism • etc.

Figure 1.3   Renzulli's Graphic Definition of Giftedness
From "What Makes Giftedness? Reexamining a Definition" by J.S. Renzulli, 1978, *Phi Delta Kappan, 60*, p. 184. Copyright 1978 by J.S. Renzulli. Reprinted with permission of the author.

> Keeping in mind that developed talent exists only in adults, a proposed definition of giftedness in children is that it denotes their potential for becoming critically acclaimed performers or exemplary producers of ideas in spheres of activity that enhance the moral, physical, emotional, social, intellectual, or aesthetic life of humanity. (1986, p. 33; 1997, p. 27)

All of these definitions are theory based; that is, they spring from a philosophical position about the nature of the talented.

Comprehensive Theories

Feldhusen's TIDE Model

Feldhusen sees talents as being genetically induced, with those who will demonstrate talent showing that talent in precocious behavior. Motivation, style, and ability are environmentally influenced. Insight, knowledge, and skills in thinking creatively are essential in the realization of specific talents. Feldhusen said there are four domains of talent with specific subcategories (see Figure 1.1 on p. 4) : (1) academic/intellectual; (2) artistic; (3) vocational-technical; and (4) interpersonal/social, and that children differ in their talents and in their levels of talents, that the heritability element is simply potential and not manifestation of talent, and that talent development is the business of the schools (Feld-husen, 1992b, 1995). Like Gardner, Feldhusen is among the theorists who do more than describe what it means to have a high IQ. His theory is broad and inclusive.

Gagné's Model of Giftedness and Talent

The Canadian psychologist Françoys Gagné (1985, 1990, 1992, 1993, 1995, 1996) presented a theoretical model of talent (see Figure 1.1 p. 4). Calling talent "the developmental product of an interaction between aptitudes and intrapersonal

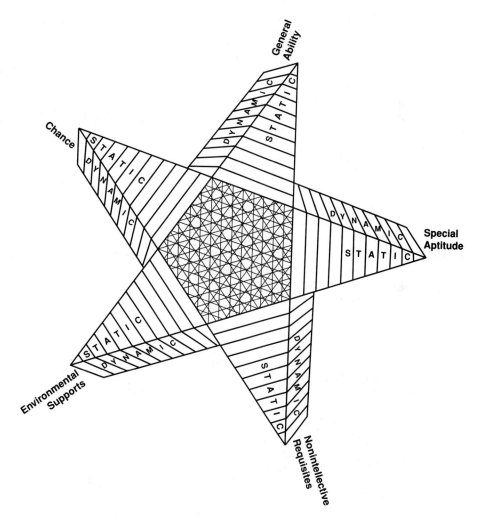

Figure 1.4 Tannenbaum's Five Factors of Giftedness

Reprinted with the permission of Macmillan Publishing Company from *Gifted Children: Psychological and Educational Perspectives* by Abraham J. Tannenbaum. Copyright 1983 by Abraham J. Tannenbaum.

and environmental catalysts" (1990, p. 66) he has delineated five general fields of talents. People can have talents in academic, technical, artistic, interpersonal, and athletic fields. On the other hand, he said that giftedness is the *aptitude* for achievement in these fields. The domains of giftedness are intellectual, creative, socioaffective, and psychomotor, as shown in Figure 1.5. In 1995, Gagné said that democratization of the field of the education of the gifted can be achieved by the three following means:

1. Reexamine the thresholds of IQ by which academic talent is defined and move the threshold from two standard deviations above the mean (about 130 IQ) to one standard deviation above the mean (about 115 IQ). Create quantitative subcategories above 115 IQ.
2. Create qualitative subcategories that recognize other talents, for example, socioaffective talents such as moral precocity and the ability to negotiate, or creative talents such as the ability to improvise in any of the arts, or technological and mechanical talents such as the ability to fix machines.
3. Recognize there are fields where talent is needed other than the usual professional fields such as medicine, law, and academics. Such fields would include cooking, gardening, popular music, teaching, sales, social work, electrical work, etc. That is, the concept of talent should embrace more domains and aptitudes. A talented cook is a chef, for example, just as a talented academic is a professor.

Whether the aptitude will be realized depends on environmental, interpersonal, and motivational catalysts. Gagné said that while all people may achieve competence in a domain, all people do not have talent: "The concept of talent singles out a small percentage among competent persons as exemplary performers in their field. Talent is synonymous with expertise, excellence, outstanding performance: talent is to a minority what competence is to a majority" (1996, p. 7). Gagné's model has had significant influence on the latest thinking in the field of talent development.

The Author's Position

My own theoretical position is that the "gifted," for the purposes of the schools, are those individuals who by way of learning characteristics such as superior memory, observational powers, curiosity, creativity, and the ability to learn school-related subject matters rapidly and accurately with a minimum of drill and repetition, have a right to an education that is differentiated according to these characteristics. All children have a right to be educated according to their needs. These children become apparent early and should be served throughout their educational lives, from preschool through college.

They may or may not become producers of knowledge or makers of novelty, but their education should be such that it would give them background to become adults who do produce knowledge or make new artistic and social products. These children can be found in all socioeconomic and ethnic groups by those who look hard enough. Standardized testing is a good way to find them but not the only way, especially for disadvantaged groups where observation, portfolio assessment, and other methods should be utilized. These children have no greater obligation than any other children to be future leaders or world-class geniuses. They should just be

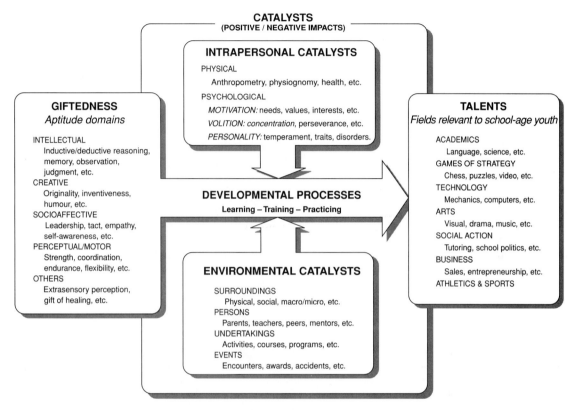

Figure 1.5   Gagné's Differentiated Model of Giftedness and Talent
Used with permission of Françoys Gagné, 1998.

given a chance to be themselves, children who might like to classify their collections of baseball cards by the middle initials of the players, or who might like to spend endless afternoon hours in dreamy reading of novels, and to have an education that appreciates and serves these behaviors.

This education should be focused on developing children's proclivities in certain domains of achievement. The child who is a dreamy reader of many novels will perhaps become a novelist or poet; the baseball card collector and reader of nonfiction may perhaps become a scientist, but these choices will come in adulthood.

The point to be emphasized is this: Many schools already have in place the mechanisms, the curriculum sequences, and the advanced level courses needed. The specialist in talent development education is part of a whole, a school *system*, and needs to view each child individually and to facilitate the placement of the child into the stream where the teachers know how to develop talent in that field. By viewing each student individually, rather than as a generic "gifted" child, one can plan the optimal educational and developmental experience. The student is one person. The diagram in Figure 1.6 illustrates this position, and it is explained in more detail in the following section.

Figure 1.6   The Piirto Pyramid of Talent Development

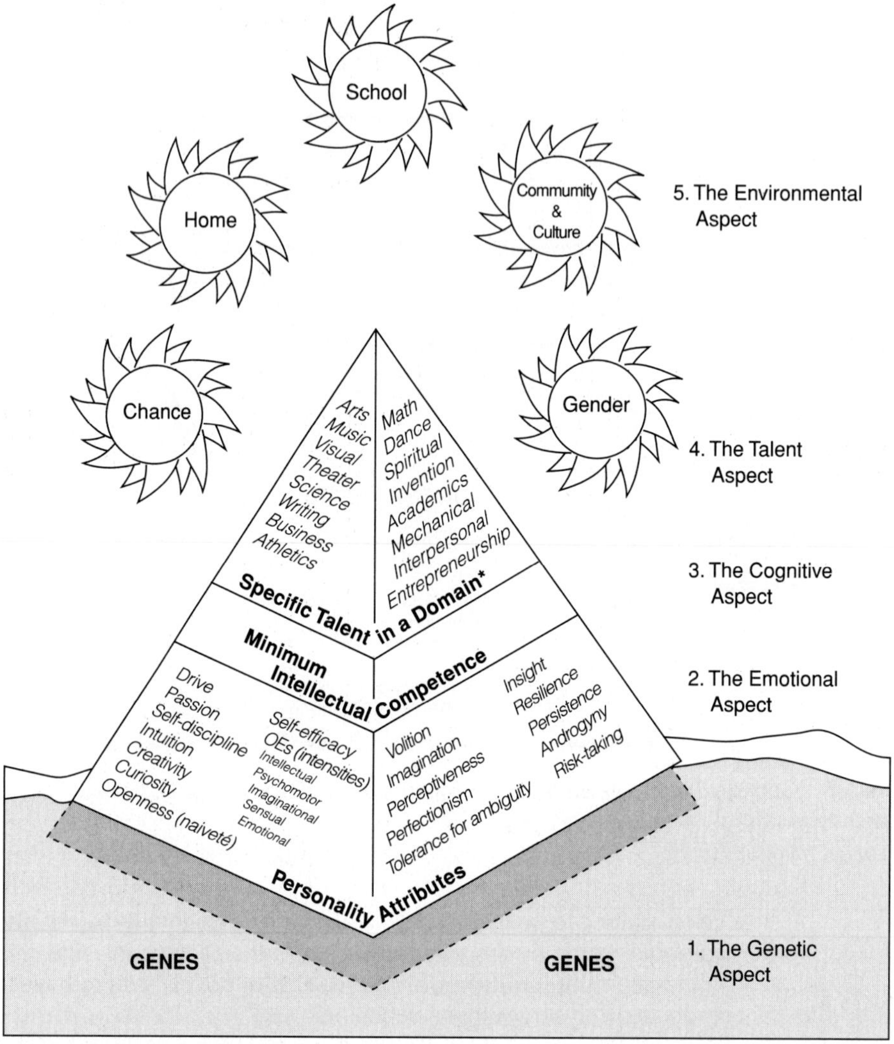

* Talent becomes a "calling."

THE PIIRTO PYRAMID OF TALENT DEVELOPMENT

1. The Genetic Aspect

We begin with our genetic heritage. We have certain predispositions, and studies of twins reared apart at the University of Minnesota and elsewhere have indicated that as we become adults, our genetic heritage becomes more dominant (Plomin, 1997). Our early childhood environment has more importance while we are children than when we are adults, according to this theory.

2. The Emotional Aspect: Personality Attributes

In the early 1990s, while researching for the first edition of this synoptic textbook, I reflected on what I had learned. I realized that all the studies I had surveyed emphasized that successful creators in all domains had certain *personality attributes* in common. For example, the studies done at the Institute for Personality Assessment and Research (IPAR) at the University of California, Berkeley, had assessed the personality attributes of many world-class creators (e.g., Barron, 1968, 1995; MacKinnon, 1975); I thus made those common personality attributes the squat base of the model. Frank Barron called the Pyramid "excellent—a compact, elegant, graphic synthesis" (F.X. Barron, personal communication, October 30, 1996). These are the *affective* or *emotional* aspects of what a person needs to succeed, and while some of these are traits or temperaments (that is, by and large inherited), others can be developed in people.

Such aspects of personality are just now beginning to be studied and the necessity for their presence or development to be emphasized. For example, resilience, or the ability to bounce back after adversity, trauma, or rejection, is an aspect of personality that has recently begun to engage such psychoanalysts as Alice Miller (in her 1990 book, *The Untouched Key*) and such psychiatrists as Lenore Terr (in her 1990 book, *Too Scared to Cry*). Why do some children overcome trauma and lead creative and productive lives, but others do not? What is the influence of the home and of parents on the manifestation of talent potential?

The field of personality psychology within the domain of psychology has recently reconfigured personality attributes to what are called the "Big Five" (Wiggins, 1996). These describe individual differences in terms of (1) extraversion; (2) agreeableness; (3) conscientiousness; (4) emotional stability; and (5) openness to experience. The model provides a common language for the field of personality psychology while, at the same time, it supports widely divergent approaches. While personality psychologists are debating the efficacy of this model, I have surveyed the literature on genius, eminence, giftedness, and such, listing the personality attributes that seem to be most salient in the development of talent.

Among the personality attributes are *androgyny* (Barron, 1968; Csikszentmihalyi, Rathunde, & Whalen, 1993; Piirto & Fraas, 1995); *creativity* (Piirto, 1992a, 1998; Renzulli, 1978; Tannenbaum, 1983); *imagination* (Piirto, 1992); *insight* (Davidson, 1992; Sternberg & Davidson, 1985); *intuition* (Myers & McCaulley, 1985); *openness,* or *a sense of naiveté* (Ghiselin, 1952); the presence of *overexcitabilities,* called OEs (Piechowski, 1979; Silverman, 1993); *passion for work in a domain* (Benbow, 1992; Bloom, 1985; Hillman, 1996; Piirto, 1992a, 1998); *perceptiveness* (Myers & McCaulley, 1985); *perfectionism* (Silverman, 1993); *persistence* (Renzulli, 1978); *resilience* (Block & Kremen, 1996; Ford, 1994; Jenkins-Friedman, 1992; Noble, 1996); *risk taking* (MacKinnon, 1978; Torrance, 1987a); *self-discipline* (Renzulli, 1978); *self-efficacy* (Sternberg & Lubart, 1992, Zimmerman, Bandura & Martinez-Pons, 1992); *tolerance for ambiguity* (Barron, 1968, 1995); and *volition* or *will* (Corno & Kanfer, 1993).

This list is by no means discrete or complete, and one may argue whether insight is a cognitive trait or a personality attribute, or whether creativity is a way of life or an aspect of personality, but personality theory is quite vague and the English language lists many synonyms that bespeak shades of connotation among terms. What one calls "motivation" another calls "task commitment" or "persistence," which may be what is between motivation and task commitment. This list indicates some of the good work that has been done on the personalities of effective people and indicates that this work has converged to show that effective adults have achieved effectiveness by force of personality. Talented adults who achieve success possess many of these attributes.

For example, Csikszentmihalyi, Rathunde, and Whalen (1993) said such personality attributes make up the autotelic personality, where "flow," or the ability to tap into optimal experiences, is accessible. Likewise, Winner (1996), in her synthesis of research, listed among the nine myths about giftedness that IQ level as a determiner of who should receive special programming should be set to rest as being inefficient, and that personality factors should be looked at. These aspects of personality are present in some way in highly effective people. One could call these the foundation, and one could go further and say that these may be innate but they can also be developed and directly taught, as Wilkes, in the case example at the end of this chapter (on p. 40), has found.

3. The Cognitive Aspect

The *cognitive* dimension, or IQ, has been overemphasized. If there were no IQ tests, we would still be able to find and serve talented children; that is, the IQ test is often an abstract, "out there," screen that obfuscates, confuses us. However, perhaps the g-factor, since it won't die, has some merit in terms of functioning in the normal world; special educators assert that a "normal" IQ is about 100, and they serve "below normal" students with the intent of helping them to function in the world of work and of community living. Thus I designated the IQ as a minimum criterion, mortar and paste, necessary for functioning in the world, especially useful if it is average or above average. However, having a high IQ or a very high IQ is not necessary for the realization of most talents (e.g. Baird, 1985). Rather, college graduation seems to be necessary (except for professional basketball players, actors, and entertainers), and most college graduates have above-average IQs but not stratospheric IQs (Simonton, 1994).

There is a minimum IQ threshold that is different for different manifestations of talent. Simonton (1986) thought it was about 120. He said, "Beyond an IQ of around 120, further gains in IQ do not increase the likelihood of creative achievement. An IQ of 120 is not a very selective cutoff point; it marks the average intelligence of college graduates (Cronbach, 1960); and about 10 percent of the general population has an IQ of 120 or higher" (p. 45). Freeman (1986) thought that after two standard deviations above the mean, IQ is not terribly predictive of innate ability but of home environment; above 130, IQ should be regarded "as reflecting achievement as much as native intelligence" (p. 10).

Generally speaking, as Renzulli pointed out, above-average scores on an intelligence test seem to be enough for the manifestation of talent, because social effects and talent also enter into the determination. A high IQ does not hurt, and is necessary, especially in science talent, as Simonton (1986) pointed out. However, depending on the test given, IQs will vary. People who score high on IQ tests seem to have such cognitive characteristics as good memories and the ability to solve unfamiliar problems. People who score very high on IQ tests are also constitutionally different, "asynchronous," as Morelock (1992), Tolan (1992a, 1992b), and Silverman and Kearny (1992) pointed out. These are a special type of gifted people, those with the high IQs, but they are not the only gifted people.

4. The Talent Aspect

Then I reflected on what was absolutely necessary, and that was the *talent* itself—inborn, innate, mysterious. That became the tip of the pyramid reaching toward the suns. When a child can draw so well he is designated the class artist, when a boy can throw a ball 85 miles an hour, when a student is accused of cheating on her short story assignment because it sounds so adult, talent is present. Most talents are recognized through certain *predictive behaviors*. For example linguistically talented students often do extensive and passionate reading of fiction; or mathematically talented students may prefer to do the statistics for the basketball games rather than be the cheerleaders at those games (Piirto, 1995a, 1995b). These talents are demonstrated within domains that are socially recognized and valued within the society. These are at the tip of the pyramid.

There must be specific talent in a specific domain such as visual arts, music, literature, acting, dance, athletics, invention, mathematics, science, and the like. This talent is manifested in physical as well as mental ways. For example, creative writers scored very high on verbal concepts as measured on the Terman Concept Mastery Test, indicating their ability to synthesize and to understand verbally (Barron, 1968). Inventors scored quite low on the same test, because their abilities are often spatial and not verbal (MacKinnon, 1978). No one questions that both writers and inventors are talented. No one asks dancers what their IQs are, for their abilities, like those of athletes, are in their bodies.

Although Gardner (1983) called his "frames of mind" intelligences rather than talents, the multiple intelligences are combined and recombined to concrete applications *within talent domains*, and so I prefer to call the talents what they are: socially recognized within talent domains—for example, academic (literature, mathematics, science, social studies, philosophy), arts (visual, performing), athletic, spiritual, or entrepreneurial.

Talent Multipotentiality: Feeling the Call, or the "Thorn"

However, although absolutely necessary, the presence of talent is not sufficient. Many people have more than one talent, and wonder what to do with them. What is the impetus, what is the reason, for one talent taking over and capturing the passion and commitment of the person who has the talent? A useful explanation comes from Socrates, who described the inspiration of the Muse (Plato, *Ion*; see Piirto 1992a/1998). Carl Jung (1965) described the passion that engrosses; Csikszentmihalyi (1991) described the process of flow, and depth psychologist James Hillman (1996), described the presence of the *daimon* in creative lives. All these give clue to what talent a person will choose to develop.

Hillman (1996) described the talents in a way similar to Plato and Jung: "The talent is only a piece of the image; many are born with musical, mathematical, and mechanical talent, but only when the talent serves the fuller image and is carried by its character do we recognize exceptionality" (p. 251). Hillman's idea is similar to the notion of a "vocation" or "call." I would call it inspiration or passion for the domain. Philosophers would call it "soul." Thus I have put an asterisk, or "thorn" on the pyramid to exemplify that talent is not enough for the realization of a life of commitment. Without going into the classical topics of Desire, Emotion, Art, Poetry, Beauty, Wisdom, or Soul (Adler, 1952), suffice it to say that the entire picture of talent development ensues when a person is pierced or bothered by a thorn, the *daimon*, that leads to commitment.

Feldman was close when he described the *crystallizing experience* (Feldman, 1982), but the thorn is more than crystallizing; it is fortifying. As mentioned above, one of the definitions of *gift* comes from Old French for "poison" and this is what the talent that bothers may become to a person if the person doesn't pay attention to it. As well as a joy it is a burden. As well as a pleasure it is a pain. However, the person who possesses the talent also must possess the will and fortitude to pursue the talent down whatever labyrinth it may lead.

5. The Environmental Aspect

These first four levels of the Piirto Pyramid could theoretically be called the individual person. From the ground of genes, the base of personality, the cement of cognitive ability, and the presence of talent comes the person. In addition, everyone is influenced by five "suns." These suns may be likened to certain factors in the environment. Many teachers feel that they are merely putting their finger into the dike because the students have so many outside-of-school influences that bear upon their school performance, and even upon whether or not the students can be taught.

The Environmental "Suns"

The three major suns, the Suns of "Home," "Community and Culture," and "School," refer to a child's being (1) in a positive and nurturing *home* environment, and (2) in a *community and culture* that conveys values compatible with the educational institution, and that provides support for the home and the school. The (3) *school* is a key factor, especially for those children whose other "suns" may have clouds in front of them.

Other, smaller suns are the Suns of "Gender" and "Chance," and refer to (4) the influence of *gender*, and (5) what *chance* can provide. The presence or absence of all or several of these make the difference between whether a talent is developed or whether it atrophies.

Unfortunately, it could be said that when a student emerges into adulthood with his or her talent nurtured and developed it is a miracle, because there are so many influences that encroach on talent development. We all know or remember people with outstanding talent who did not or were not able to use or develop that talent because of circumstances such as represented by these "suns." For example, a student whose home life contains trauma such as divorce or poverty may be so involved in that trauma that the talent cannot be emphasized. The school's role becomes recognizing the talent and encouraging lessons, mentors, or special experiences that the parents would otherwise have provided had their situation been better. The "suns" that shine on the pyramid may be hidden by clouds, and in that case, the *school* plays a key role in the child's environment.

As another example, in a racist society, the genes that produce one's race are acted upon environmentally; a person of a certain race may be treated differently in different environments. The *school* and the *community and culture* are important in developing or enhancing this genetic inheritance. Retired general Colin Powell has said that he entered the army because he saw the military as the only place in a racist society where he would be treated fairly, where his genetic African-American inheritance would not be discriminated against, where he could develop his talents fully.

This sketch of a pyramid was developed with a view that students, teachers, and parents should find it understandable and usable, and yet that it be research-based and powerful, simple and elegant. Perhaps the situation that leads students to often not make use of their talents can be helped when they are directly taught about the factors that lead to optimum development conditions; when we do not do things *to* children ("surprise, surprise; you're gifted and talented because we got the results of that IQ test! Now sit back and we'll put you into a program"), but instead we work *with* students as they are empowered to work with themselves.

In fact, it would seem that if all five of the "suns" shine evenly and brightly, creativity may not develop, for *creativity* (which I call an attribute of personality in this model) requires risk taking, openness, and persistence or fortitude, and these may not be developed without some little adversity (Miller, 1990; Piirto, 1992a/1998). One's resilience is crucial; one's ability to create an image or metaphor out of pain is also. The Dabrowski theory of emotional development lends light to the influence of challenge and pain upon growth. One grows through pain, not in avoiding pain. Dabrowski called it "positive disintegration" (Dabrowski, 1964). One disintegrates and reintegrates at a higher level, according to the theory.

The mere accident of birth provides for the child's development and for the realization of that child's potential. This is a sobering fact, and it should provide the impetus for the schools to find, and help, those children whose "luck" may not have permitted them to be born into an environment that will nurture their great potential. In all cases, the school is merely an environmental factor in the development of talent, but the school can be either a powerful shaper or a deterrent to that development.

A GIFTEDNESS CONSTRUCT

Researchers (Baird, 1985; Hoge, 1988) have pointed out that although studies are available, no studies have included the children with lower cognitive ability, to see whether they would have done just as well in life as children with higher cognitive ability if other factors had been equal, especially if they went to college, or if their "suns" of environment were present in relatively equal magnitude.

Controversies over the Giftedness Construct

Critics have attacked the Marland definition of giftedness as having aspects that are too difficult to identify or to measure. One critic called for a renewed definition of what he calls the "construct of giftedness" (Hoge, 1988). Hoge argues that educators have misused the tests used to identify giftedness, and that instead the tests have become the definitions of giftedness. The typical scenario for the identification of giftedness goes like this: The local school board develops a definition that usually goes along with the

Marland definition; this is generally close to the one developed by the state or county. This definition generally states that the gifted have high levels of intellectual potential, or high aptitudes in something such as mathematics or reading, have high motivation levels, and have creativity. All of these are vague and globally defined.

In 1995 Sternberg and Zhang examined implicit, or underlying, intuitional ideas of giftedness and said that in order to be called gifted, a person must meet five criteria: (1) *excellence*—the person must be superior with relation to contemporaries in at least one field; (2) *rarity*—the ability in which the person is excellent must be rated as being relatively rare; (3) *productivity*—the person must produce; that is, a test score isn't enough; (4) *demonstrability*—the productivity and the ability must be able to be tested by a valid test; (5) *value*—something meaningful to the society must be given by the gifted person.

In 1994 Margolin and Sapon-Shevin, in two books critical of the idea that giftedness exists, wondered whether there even is a giftedness construct. Along with many others in the field of gifted education, they also believe that giftedness is not absolute, the results of a test score, but that giftedness is a socially constructed phenomenon. Margolin and Sapon-Shevin, critics from outside the field, believe that gifted education benefits the privileged classes. (Sapon-Shevin also argued for full inclusion, that is, for full heterogeneous grouping in classrooms, with no special services or programs for any children. Not to do so, to treat some children differently, to make the curriculum different, is to go against the idea of community, she thought.)

In 1996 Borland took up the cry and asked the field to criticize itself in these areas:

1. Is there such a thing as a gifted child?
2. Is gifted education racist, sexist, and classist?
3. Is there a need for ability grouping?
4. Does gifted education interfere with community?
5. Is the field irrelevant?

Borland said that removing gifted education programs from schools would exacerbate the problem of inequity, for who would be most impacted by such removal? Affluent parents would find their children special schools and special programs, but parents who are in poverty would not be able to afford to do so.

A Proposed Giftedness Construct

People have indicated that the exact words don't matter, but as a poet and a studier of words (Piirto, 1995a, 1995b), the author would like to indicate here that it is evident by now that what has been called the giftedness construct can be made more functional and helpful when the field decides on accurate terminology. All kinds of talent make up the giftedness construct. When calling a person "gifted," we should be accurate in our language. If we mean *high IQ*; that is, if we identify a child's talent potential by means of an IQ test, we should say *high IQ*. If we identify a child's talent potential by means of an academic achievement test, we should say *academic talent*. Academic talent may or may not be synonymous with high-IQ talent, especially if the child with a high IQ does not get good grades or high scores on a standardized achievement or ability test such as the SAT or the ACT.

If we say a child is *creative*, do we mean the child scored high on a divergent production test or ranked high on a creativity characteristics checklist? Then we should say the child has cognitive divergent production characteristics. We should not confuse creativity with either of these two identification tools. Whether creativity is a construct or an aspect of personality is not yet clear (Piirto, 1992a/1998). If we identify a child's talent potential by means of expert opinion and concrete products within a domain such as music, visual arts, theater, dance, or athletics, we should call that talent *musical talent, visual arts talent, theatrical talent, dance talent, mechanical talent, athletic talent* and the like. If a child can relate with skill and grace to others, enhancing their lives with his/her presence, we should call that talent *relationship talent*. If we notice that a child has talents in several areas, we should say the child has *multiple talents*. Accuracy in naming the talent will clarify our thinking about giftedness and talent.

All these talents could be shown to be within a giftedness construct. This would be a comprehensive and inclusive model, with high IQ being helpful especially in realizing science talent, mathematics talent, and verbal talent, as well as other academic talents that are generally the province of people in the professions. Having a high IQ is good (though the higher the IQ, the more adjustment difficulties people seem to have), and can inform and help in developing all talents. Then there could be creating talent, performing talent, mechanical talent, spiritual talent, relationship talent, and other talents that do not *require* a high IQ, though having high general ability is always a plus.

For example, the performing talent of athletics requires the ability to move the body in space, and the mechanical talent of being able to sew or suture requires small or fine motor ability, another manifestation of what Gardner (1983) called bodily-kinesthetic intelligence and Guilford (1967) called behavioral intelligence. The creating talent of musical composition requires the auditory ability to hear acutely in one's head, various combinations of musical notes and rhythms or musical intelligence (Gardner, 1983), while the creating talent of easel painting requires the ability to see or visualize colors, forms, shapes (figural or spatial intelligence) and to place these in harmony on a given space (bodily-kinesthetic intelligence).

This postulated giftedness construct should include all forms of talent. Schools and colleges should focus on academic talent. Conservatories, camps, and special programs and coaches can focus on the other talents. Creative talent is present in all the other talents.

Once we are exact about our terminology, we can better serve the student's needs, for exact terminology leads to clear thinking. The somewhat justified, pervasive, and ringing charges by critics of the field that we are elitist and have fuzzy definitions should be met with a philosophy of talent development where individual talent needs and rights can be realized. Frasier et al. (1995) proposed that there are several core attributes common to talented and gifted people of all races, ethnicities, and cultures. These are detailed in Table 1.1. They are similar to the personality attributes on the base of the Pyramid of Talent Development.

This inclusive attitude can serve as a spur to talent development in general in the context of an expanded giftedness construct. I have taken the liberty of sketching one in circular (not linear) form to indicate that the giftedness construct is not lines and angles, but a sphere, a circle, which enfolds all kinds of talent (Figure 1.7).

Table 1.1   Ten Core Attributes of Giftedness

Core Attributes	General Description
Motivation: Exhibits evidence of desire to learn	Forces that initiate, direct, and sustain individual or group behavior in order to satisfy a need or attained goal
Communication skills: Highly expressive and effective use of words, numbers, symbols, etc.	Transmission and reception of signals or meanings through a system of symbols (codes, gestures, language, numbers)
Interest: Intense (sometimes unusual) interests	Activities, avocations, objects, etc., that have special worth or significance and are given special attention
Problem-solving ability: Effective (often inventive) strategies for recognizing and solving problems	Process of determining a correct sequence of alternatives leading to a desired goal or to successful completion or performance of a task
Imagination/Creativity: Produces many ideas, highly original	Process of forming mental images of objects, qualities, situations, or relationships that are not immediately apparent to the senses; solves problems by pursuing nontraditional patterns of thinking
Memory: Large storehouse of information on school or nonschool topics	Exceptional ability to retain and retrieve information
Inquiry: Questions, experiments, explores	Method or process of seeking knowledge, understanding, or information
Insight: Quickly grasps new concepts and makes connections; senses deeper meanings	Sudden discovery of the correct solution following incorrect attempts based primarily on trial and error
Reasoning: Finds logical approaches to figuring out solutions	Highly conscious, directed, controlled, active, intentional, forward-looking, goal-oriented thought
Humor: Conveys and picks up on humor well	Ability to synthesize key ideas or problems in complex situations in a humorous way; Exceptional sense of timing in words and gestures

Based on information from Frasier et al. (1995). *Core Attributes of Giftedness*. National Research Center on the Gifted and Talented. Storrs, CT: University of Connecticut.

Figure 1.7   A Proposed Giftedness Construct

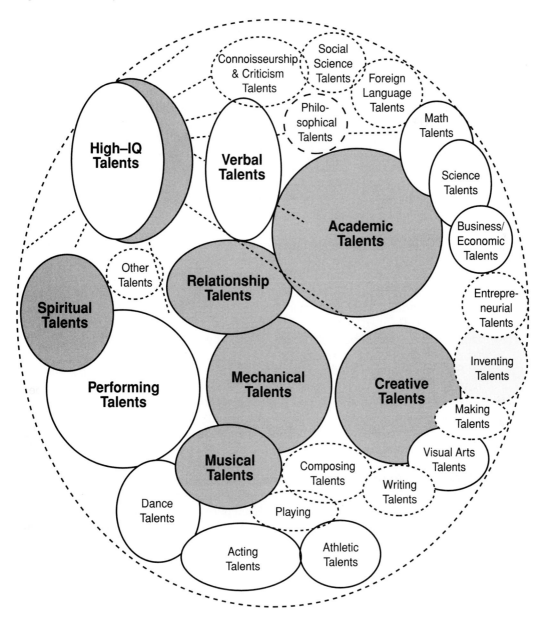

Case Example: Using the Pyramid of Talent Development in the Inclusionary Classroom

by Paula Wilkes, Ph.D., Teacher and Educational Consultant, Eugene, Oregon, Public Schools
(Used with permission of author)

During the past 20 years, I have been trying new strategies that have helped increase the effort and quality of work by my students. I have taught them to use mind-mapping, the Structure of Intellect, multiple intelligences, portfolios, emotional intelligences, self-assessment rubrics, and project-based learning. I do a lot of consulting and speaking to other teachers, and I have also used these strategies with them. However, the real breakthrough came to me in January 1995, when a colleague who knew I was interested in Howard Gardner's MI theory and the misuse of IQ as a measure of intelligence told me of Jane Piirto's "Pyramid of Talent Development" and gave me an article that had been published in Europe (Piirto, 1995a).

After reading Piirto's explanation of the Pyramid, which had first been written as part of the first edition of this textbook, *Talented Children and Adults: Their Development and Education* (1994a), I knew with a little modification and work I could make it a model for my classroom, a full-inclusion classroom of 34 fourth and fifth graders. That classroom was comprised of five students with special education IEPs (two with behavior plans) and 12 identified talented and gifted students, so it would be a challenge to find any model that would have meaning for such a diverse group of students.

The only change I made to the model so that nine- and ten-year-old students could understand it, was to relate the top third to the seven multiple intelligences, which they already knew. Thus I linked talent in writing to linguistic intelligence; talent in mathematics and science to logical-mathematical and spatial intelligence; athletic talent to bodily-kinesthetic intelligence; acting talent to bodily-kinesthetic, linguistic, and the personal intelligences, and so forth.

Piirto has linked these in her book *Understanding Those Who Create* (1992a/1998) as well as in the 1994 textbook, and I felt using multiple intelligences clarified the top of the pyramid for the students, who were used to working with them. At the bottom of the pyramid I deleted personality attributes that the students might not understand, such as "androgyny," which Piirto said means flexibility and lack of rigidity in sex role stereotyping. I chose key words that the students could relate to such as "self-discipline," "drive," "persistence," "passion," "resilience," "leadership," and "imagination." Each student was given a copy of the Pyramid and the "suns" were colored as I gave concrete examples, and then that copy was put in the "self-smart" section of their portfolios.

One school year, I taught 28 fifth graders, 12 of whom I had the previous year, and who were familiar with the Pyramid. I decided to start off the first day with an overview of the Pyramid of Talent Development. It was wonderful to have students who were able to give "kid examples" of the meaning the Pyramid held for them. Two students built a 3D poster of the Pyramid and it became a year-long bulletin board. When students or I would find articles in magazines or the newspapers that typified an aspect of the Pyramid, we would discuss it and add it to our growing collection.

For example, we found articles about the motivational speaker Les Brown who, because of his personality attributes and the shining sun of his adoptive mother, was able to overcome great hardship (Terry, 1996). We talked about a local high school senior who was among 40 students nationwide in the Westinghouse Science Talent Search. In an article in our local paper, this high school student said that she didn't consider herself that much brighter than anyone else. She said, "I work hard. I love to do it. That's what makes the most difference. Perhaps it's not a matter of innate ability as much as knowing what you love to do" (Bishop, 1995). We talked about her personality attributes and the fact that the "suns" of home and school had been shining on her by providing her with challenging learning experiences.

We also read articles about a teenager trying to escape three generations of poverty by being the first member of her family to attend college. We read about and later met a 15-year-old tuba player whose innate talent and self-discipline had won him a prestigious scholarship to a music academy. We also talked about a dyslexic college student whose hard work earned him an international mathematics award. It seemed as though nearly every week we were able to find examples about how the personality attributes of individuals and/or the suns that were shining on them had made a significant difference in helping them realize their talents. We used the media to illustrate the Pyramid. Table 1.2 is a list of possible books and articles suitable for use on personality attributes with the Piirto Pyramid.

The Pyramid made its way into "Back to School Curriculum Nights," parent conferences, and newsletters to families. It became an important framework for the way I taught and the way students worked. At the end of major projects, the students were asked to assess their effort, their persistence, and/or the quality of their work. By the end of the year, most of the students had realized that they were in control of the amount they learned and the projects that demonstrated that learning. For students who did not have the "sun" of home shining down on them, I made an effort to get them to reach out to others when they needed assistance rather than using that "cloud" as an excuse.

Not only were students aware of the progress they had made, but so were many of the parents. "Carolyn" was a student who had felt that she wasn't "smart," and her mother had spoken with the school psychologist several times the previous year about her negative self-image. Carolyn was really taken with the idea of the Pyramid and discussed examples with me. During fall term, she and her classmates were asked to read an historical novel and then illustrate and summarize six of the sixteen chapters. Carolyn made an outstanding illustration and summary for all sixteen chapters! She realized that she was in charge of the base of the Pyramid, and there was no stopping her. In May, she entered her portfolio in a county-wide competition and earned a medal.

"Maggie" was the only student I've ever had who had gifted abilities in all seven intelligences. She took the SAT in the Johns Hopkins Center for Talented Youth Talent Search program and scored "high honors" in both the verbal and mathematical categories. At a district track meet, she won the 100-yard dash, and was an outstanding soccer and basketball player. Her musical skills included not only singing and playing the piano and recorder, but she was also able to put a poem to music. Perhaps her greatest talents were in the "personal

Table 1.2   Books and Articles That Illustrate the Pyramid of Talent Development

Name	Personality Attributes	"Suns"	Reference
Ron Howard The son ("Opie") of actors who became a director	Passion, Self-Discipline, Drive	Home and Genes	Rader, D. (1996, October 10). A nice guy and a winner. *Parade Magazine.*
Matilda Librarian	Passion, Resilience, Persistence, Drive	"Clouded" Sun of Home and Shining Sun of Community	Tri Star/Jersey Films. (1996). *Matilda* [Film, rated PG]. Use first ten minutes of this fictional tale to demonstrate the Personality Attributes over-coming the neglectful home environment.
Gary Paulsen Author of children's books	Imagination, Passion, Resilience, Androgyny	Home (Grandmother) and Community (Older workmen)	The Trumpet Club, Inc. (1993). *Trumpet Video visits Gary Paulsen* [film]. Mother had "problems" so Paulsen spent time with Grandmother who showed him the "feminine side." He says he was "raised by bears," the older men who drove big machines and took him under their wings.
Angelina and Sarah Grimke Early pioneers in social reform—abolition and women's rights.	Passion, Drive, Resilience, Persistence		Teacher Created Materials, Inc. *Focus on Women.* (1995).
Mildred Taylor Successful novelist for children, winner of the Newbery Award, 1976	Imagination, Self-Esteem		Teacher Created Materials, Inc. *Focus on Women.* (1995).
Tiger Woods Champion golfer	Passion, Drive, Self-Discipline, Compulsiveness	Home, Foundation of Genes	Woods, E. (1997). *Training a Tiger.* New York: Harper Collins. A plan for raising a winner in both golf and life.
A CD of songs from, and a story about, "women in a World War II prison camp who freed their spirits through song." This article is written by one of the women who lived through it.	Imagination, Resilience, Persistence		*Paradise Road—Song of Survival.* [Soundtrack]. From the book by Helen Colijn (1997). Reader's Digest.

Table 1.2 *Continued*

Name	Personality Attributes	"Suns"	Reference
R. Buckminster Fuller An inventor who held over 2,000 patents. For two years, he slept only only two hours per night.	Imagination, Drive, Resilience, Compulsiveness		Teacher Created Materials, Inc. *Focus on Inventors.* (1994).
Levi Strauss An immigrant who designed the first jeans.	Resilience, Imagination		Teacher Created Materials, Inc. *Focus on Inventors.* (1994).
Louis Braille Left blind by an accident, it "did not put a damper on Louis's willingness to learn."	Resilience, Imagination		Teacher Created Materials, Inc. *Focus on Inventors.* (1994).
Shania Twain Grew up poor, parents died, and she was left to raise siblings. She had an unwavering belief in her talents and a passion for music.	Resilience, Passion, Self-Esteem	Home	Buchalter, G. (1996, July 21). Now I know I can't fix everything. *Parade Magazine.*
Sonya Carson "Sonya Carson had no wealth and little education, but the wisdom she gave her sons helped them to succeed mightily."	Resilience, Self-Discipline, Drive, Self-Esteem	Home	Ryan, M. (1997, May 11). If you can't teach me, don't criticize me. *Parade Magazine.*
Charles Johnson "But the love of violins did more than stick with Charles. It got inside like part of his chemistry."	Passion, Drive, Compulsiveness	Home, Foundation of Genes	Associated Press. (1996, May 5). Musical family follows the fiddle for 5 generations. Eugene, Oregon *Register Guard.*
Les Brown "The thought of failing doesn't matter to me … Most people allow their fears to prevent them from succeeding … Born in an abandoned building and given up for adoption by his mother." He learned to be unstoppable from watching his adoptive mother.	Imagination, Self-Discipline, Passion, Resilience, Drive, Self-Esteem	Home	Terry, W. (1996, January 7). How he found himself—again and again. *Parade Magazine.*

intelligences." She was quite reflective about her work and her relationships, and she was chosen as a peer conflict manager. This was a student whose personality attributes headed her for success while keeping her relatively free of stress. She displayed great emotional intelligence (Goleman, 1995). I came to realize that directly teaching about personality attributes and encouraging students to develop these attributes was what Goleman had been talking about in his recent book, which fit right in with the Pyramid and the multiple intelligences focus I had been using.

"Simon" was a boy who had experienced the loss of two significant male relationships due to divorce, and he appeared to lack self-esteem in most areas of his academic life. During his fifth grade year, his first project was of very poor quality, so I asked him to redo the assignment. Rather than doing it on his own, he was rescued by his mother, who did most of the work. When he presented it to his peers they asked who had done the drawing and he said his mom had. There wasn't a real sense of ownership. I sat down with Simon and talked with him about how it would be his personality attributes that would determine whether he would realize his talents. At the end of last school year, after a year and a half of focusing on what the Pyramid was showing, Simon submitted a wonderful portfolio of learning. He told his classmates in a final class meeting in May that he had learned how important it was to work hard and produce quality work, and that he was proud of himself for the effort he was now putting into his learning.

Is every one of my students realizing their talents? Definitely not! But the Pyramid gave us a good place to focus our attention. At the end of the year I gave my students a blank pyramid and asked them to color the suns that were shining on them, identify the talents they possessed, and list personality attributes they were "currently using" in one column, and in another column, list the personality attributes they were "still learning about." Although all the students had made progress toward becoming independent learners, the three students I continued to worry about had listed "drive" and "self-discipline" as areas still needing to be developed. Perhaps their middle school teachers would see the applications of the Pyramid of Talent Development.

In *Emotional Intelligence* (1995), Goleman cites several psychologists who suggest that being able to get into "flow" while doing work is the difference between students who do well in school and those who do not. It is not a matter of IQ or other measures of "intelligence," but of being challenged by and getting satisfaction from the work we do. I believe that understanding the Pyramid of Talent Development gave my students the impetus to work harder, and the result of that effort was a sense of accomplishment and a willingness to continue to strive to be the best that they can be. The Pyramid of Talent Development, with its strong visual presentation, and ideas that can be understood by parents and students alike, is a powerful tool that should be shared with students.

➤ ➤ ➤ ➤ ➤ ➤ ➤ ➤ ➤ ➤ ➤ ➤ ➤ ➤ ➤ ➤ ➤

SUMMARY

1. Historically, the terms *genius, intelligence, giftedness,* and *talent* have different origins, but they have come to be used somewhat interchangeably.
2. Several definitions of giftedness are in use at present.
3. The definitions of intelligence have also varied, although intuitive definitions have remained remarkably the same.
4. The concept of talent development has been discussed in the past few years but a theory-based definition is needed.
5. Intelligence is often equated with a score on an IQ test, although recent definitions have questioned the use of IQ tests.
6. Studies of twins raised apart have raised startling questions about the heritability of intelligence.
7. The definition and realization of talent potential depends on the milieu, on the family and home environment, on the commitment of the school, on chance, and on the personality attributes and specific talents of the individual talented person.
8. A giftedness construct was proposed.
9. The case example shows how one teacher has used the Pyramid of Talent Development in her classes.

CHAPTER

2 GETTING STARTED: DEVELOPING A PROGRAM FOR THE TALENTED

The Need for Awareness
History of U.S. Education of the
    Talented
Typical Historical Arrangements
    for Talented Children
Zeitgeist and the Education of
    Talented Children
State of the States
The Law and Academically
    Talented Children
Setting up a Program
Outcome-based Education for the
    High-Ability Student
Educational Program Options
Teachers of the Talented
Program Evaluation
Case Example: Four Years as a
    Consulting Teacher for the
    Gifted and Talented
Summary

FOCUSING QUESTIONS

1. Discuss the historical ebbs and flows of the education of the talented and try to predict for the future from a knowledge of the past.

2. How does the temperature of the times, or *Zeitgeist*, affect the education of the talented?

3. Describe the responsibility of the states to the education of the talented.

4. Why should administrators and teachers be aware of the law and its relationship to the education of the talented?

5. Discuss the planning committee and its responsibilities.

6. Why should there be a written philosophy for a program for the talented?

7. List and discuss several outcomes suitable for outstandingly talented students.

8. Compare and contrast XYZ grouping, within-class grouping, cluster grouping, and cross-grade grouping.

9. What are the advantages and disadvantages of each type of grouping mentioned in question 8?

10. Why are acceleration and enrichment necessary for the education of the talented?

11. Discuss cooperative learning as a technique for use with talented students.

12. What are the advantages and disadvantages of pullout programs? Take a stand. Do you advocate this type of program?

13. What are the advantages and disadvantages of self-contained programs? Take a stand. Do you advocate this type of program?

14. What are the advantages and disadvantages of educating talented students in the regular classroom? Take a stand. Do you advocate this type of program?

15. What should a teacher think about before specializing in the education of the talented? Why?

16. What are the features of a successful consulting (facilitation, intervention-specialist) teacher program?

47

Figure 2.1   Overview of Chapter 2

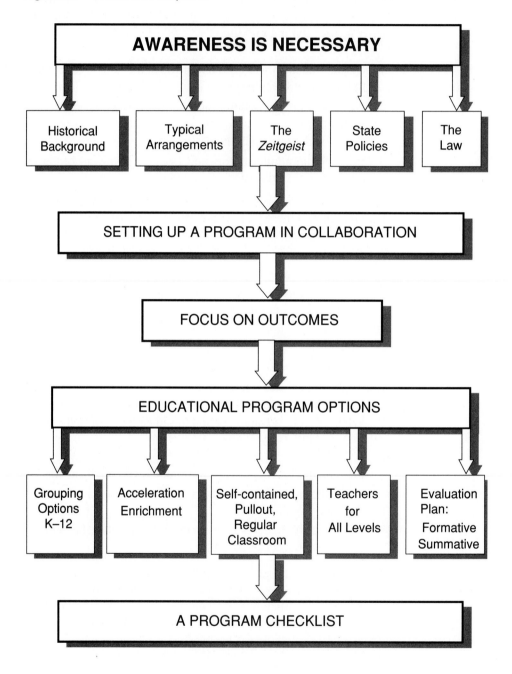

Consider the following scenario: The state has just mandated that all talented students be identified, although it has not mandated that they be served. Jane Rushton, the superintendent, herself a former talented child, with a background as a high-school chemistry teacher, receives the notice from the State Department of Education. Parents in the district have occasionally buttonholed her when they've seen her in the grocery store or at church, and have asked her when the district is going to start a program for talent development. Dr. Rushton has answered them all with the same reply: "When we pass the millage."

It is May 15, and the townspeople have voted to pass the millage, meeting the district's expenses for the next three years. Dr. Rushton means to keep her promise. The district is in the middle of the state's per-pupil expenditures, about $5,000 per child, and the size of the town, about 25,000 people, permits six elementary schools, one middle school, and one comprehensive high school. There is also a regional vocational high school where students from two counties attend. The regional office of education has a consultant for programs for talent development. Dr. Rushton calls him and makes an appointment. "It's time to get serious about our talented children," she says. "What do you suggest we do?"

THE NEED FOR AWARENESS

The first role of the administrator in the education of the talented is to become aware (Booth, 1985). The administrator should be aware of the characteristics of talented students, aware of the community's values and goals for its talented youth, and aware of whether or not the community will support programming for talented students. The administrator also should be aware of whether the local curriculum is adequately serving the needs of talented students at the present time, and should be aware of what local resources are available to meet the needs of these students. The administrator also needs to become aware of the history of the education of the talented, and of the state's structure for educating talented students.

HISTORY OF U.S. EDUCATION OF THE TALENTED

The definitions have varied, yet children who will be called *gifted* and *talented* have been and continue to be born and to enter school, and the schools have been and will continue to be challenged to provide suitable educations for these children. No matter how much the school reformers wish that all children could be taught in large classes by one teacher who teaches to the middle, the fact is that those teachers have always and will continue to encounter children whose abilities call for different treatment. As far back as 1940, Herbert A. Carroll said:

> The principal objection to enrichment for gifted children in the heterogeneous classroom is that in most cases it fails to work. Teachers are human beings with all the failings of human beings. Consequently most of them prefer teaching procedures which require the least

amount of time. They find it much easier to treat the class as a unit than as a loosely organized group of subgroups and individuals. (p. 246–247)

The comment still applies. In 1996, after completing a four-year study of how elementary teachers plan for individual students, researchers said:

Teachers generally focused their planning on the class as a whole. When they did think
about individuals, their focus was mainly on the students' social and emotional needs, or
on global and unconditional traits. The implication was that such traits and social/emo-
tional issues were beyond the boundaries of the teachers' influence. (Morocco, Riley,
Gordon & Howard, 1996, p. 164)

Teachers still prefer to treat the class as a unit and to teach the same to all students
(Archambault, Westberg, Brown, Hallmark, Emmons & Zhang, 1993; Lawton, 1992).
The education of children who have been called gifted and talented has been characterized by peaks and valleys according to the prevailing attitudes of the society towards
these children. Tannenbaum (1983) in Table 2.1 summarizes these peaks and valleys.
This ragged time line traces the ebb and flow of interest in the education of talented
students. The late 1970s to the mid-1990s saw a "flow," with more and more local and
state districts instituting programs for the talented, with the identification procedures
becoming more and more standardized across the nation. Recently, an "ebb" has occurred, with several states enfolding gifted education into general education, saying
that the pedagogy for the gifted is good for all children. That is certainly true.

TYPICAL HISTORICAL ARRANGEMENTS
FOR TALENTED CHILDREN

Throughout the short history of public education in the United States, talented children
have been taught in several logical ways. These are *acceleration, grouping*, and *special
schools*.

Acceleration

Arrangements for the education of the talented have varied over the past century in the
United States. The first arrangements were to allow faster students to move through the
curriculum at a faster speed. This is called acceleration, and though it has been found to
be a very efficient means of educating precocious students, acceleration has met with
emotional reactions from educators. This emotional reaction is because of the dual roles
that formalized public education must assume. The first role is to socialize students to
be citizens and good workers. The second role is to educate students and make them literate. The two roles often conflict, and educators who object to acceleration often cite
the fact that the student who is permitted to be accelerated may suffer peer rejection.
This is more often cited with boys than girls, because an accelerated boy's small size in
junior high school may prevent him from playing sports.

Images of talented boys in the popular culture reflect the society's attitudes. The
popular movie *Lucas* showed acceleration as a negative peer influence on the main

Table 2.1   Peaks and Valleys in the Education of Talented Children

Date(s)	Place	Event
1868	The St. Louis Plan	Flexible promotion in the St. Louis schools
1886	Elizabeth, New Jersey	Three-track system in grades 1 through 8
Late 1800s	Santa Barbara, California Concentric Plan	Similar to track system
Late 1800s	New York and Chicago, Constant Group System	
1891	Cambridge, Massachusetts Double Track Plan	Classes could cover six years of work in four years
1900	New York City	Rapid advancement classes; beginning of special progress classes; junior high could complete three years of work in two years
1901	Worcester, Massachusetts	First special school for academically able, grades 7 through 9
1902	Baltimore, Maryland	Special school for academically able
Early 1900s	Summer vacation schools	Higher level material studied so children could move in grades
Early 1900s	Special high schools in urban areas	
1918	Louisville, Kentucky	School for high-IQ children; first school selecting by mental tests; followed by schools in New York City; Urbana, Illinois; Columbus, Ohio; Berkeley, California
1918	Cardinal Principles of Secondary Education	These principles established that high schools should create separate courses of study for college preparatory and vocational interests.
1921	Terman Study of children with high IQs	*Genetic Studies of Genius,* Stanford University, California
1922	New York City, Experimental classes for gifted children at P.S. 165	Hollingworth studies
1922	Speyer School	Laboratory school at Teachers College ultimately continued with special classes
1920s	Progressive Education Movement	Prior to this, schools had advanced learners rapidly (acceleration) but now bright students were to be taught in depth (enrichment). Developmental concerns were voiced, and children were kept with their age-mates but intellectual peers. Ability grouping

(continued on next page)

Table 2.1 *Continued*

Date(s)	Place	Event
1930s and		Decline in ability grouping; enrichment of gifted children in regular 1940s classrooms
1950s	*The Gifted Child*	Publication of *The Gifted Child* (Witty, 1951) by the American Association for Gifted Children
1950	Educational Policies Commission	Called neglect of mentally superior students a "social waste"
1954	School desegregation	Supreme Court decision; focus on equity
1957	*Sputnik*	Revives interest in the education of gifted students; focus on excellence
1958	National Defense Education Act	Encourages students in mathematics, science, and foreign language
1960	Implicit meritocracy	Created by Kennedy's call for the brightest to serve the public
1963 ff.	Civil Rights Movement/ Vietnam War	Gifted college students lose faith in the purposes of the government and the life of the mind; devaluation of science
1971	Marland Report	Notes deteriorating emphasis on the education of the gifted and talented
1975	Public Law 94-142	Education of the handicapped: Special students are to have individual education plans (IEPs). Prescriptive/ diagnostic approach to education; focus on equity
1976	New U.S. office	Creation of the Office of Gifted and Talented in the U.S. Department of Education
1977	Title IV-C Grants	Inclusion of the gifted in Title IV-C grants
1982	New U.S. office closed	Demise of the Office of Gifted and Talented in the U.S. Department of Education
1988	Javits Act	Enactment of the Javits Gifted and Talented Students Education Act
1989	U.S. office revived	Javits Gifted and Talented Director in the U.S. Department of Education, Office of Educational Research and Improvement; national research centers established
1992	States create offices	By this time there are gifted/talented education offices in 49 state departments of education.
1993	Talent development	*National Excellence* report from U.S. Department of Education, O.E.R.I., emphasizes talent development and world-class standards

Based on historial information in *Gifted Children: Psycological and Educational Perspectives* by A. Tannenbaum, 1983. New York: Macmillan. Copyright© 1983 by Macmillan.

character. The main character of the television show "Doogie Howser" had peers of his chronological age and of his mental age. The boy in the movie *Little Man Tate* experienced rejection from his age peers and then peer acceptance from his mental peers when he was finally able to enter a special school. (No films with a bright girl with the same problems have been made, though Harriet, in *Harriet the Spy,* exhibited behaviors common to bright students.) Another was *Good Will Hunting.*

The influence of the Gesell Institute studies of child developmental stages and ages in the 1940s and 1950s convinced educators that students benefit most from being with their chronological-age mates, and precipitated a fear that students who would be accelerated would experience developmental and personal difficulties. The continuance of DA (developmentally appropriate) rhetoric in today's education also mitigates against acceleration. Although most of the evidence is to the contrary, as we shall see, educators continue to fear acceleration.

Grouping

Another common means used historically to educate faster children was once called *tracking.* Now called grouping, there are several ways of doing it. Research (Kulik, 1992a, 1992b; Kulik & Kulik, 1984a, 1984b; Kulik & Kulik, 1991) has shown that the achievement of medium-ability and slow-ability students is either not affected by ability grouping or is negatively affected by ability grouping, but that the achievement of high-ability students is positively affected by ability grouping that includes curriculum modification according to the learning characteristics of high-ability students. Those who decry that a special education for academically talented students is elitist often cite ability grouping as being discriminatory. With the surge of interest in cooperative learning in the early 1990s (Johnson & Johnson, 1987; Slavin, 1987, 1991), heterogeneous grouping has been called for as fitting the democratic ideals of the society (Oakes, 1985; Sapon-Shevin, 1994). Some researchers (Mills & Durden, 1992; Robinson, 1990; Rogers, Cussler & Anderson, 1991; Roy, 1991) have cautioned that educators of the talented should get on the cooperative education bandwagon cautiously, for in cooperative education grouping, the gifted child often serves as the "teacher" and as the "group leader," both roles which may not be the most suitable for the development of social relationships for talented children. The subject of grouping will be discussed further later in this chapter.

Special Schools

A third historical means of educating talented students has been the establishment of special schools for the talented. Special schools for high school students began in the early twentieth century, with the establishment of Stuyvesant High School in New York City. The Hunter College High School for Gifted Girls came even earlier. The Hunter College Elementary School for gifted students opened in 1941. Children were chosen for these schools by competitive examination or by individual IQ. These arrangements for academically talented children became popular in the 1980s as mandates for desegregation caused urban school systems to change the concept of the neighborhood school to the concept of the magnet school. Even on the elementary school level in many urban areas, special magnet schools emphasize various themes: for example, Columbus, Ohio, has a French language school; most cities have a special high school for the visual and performing arts and special schools for mathematics and science. Recently a trend has been noticed for a return to neighborhood schools. While the establishment of these schools may meet federal desegregation guidelines, their worth as schools for talented students is not known.

ZEITGEIST AND THE EDUCATION OF THE TALENTED

For the academically talented, public relations has always been a difficulty. It is somehow un-American to be intellectual, to be talented in academic areas. Howley, Howley, and Pendarvis (1995) traced the roots of anti-intellectualism in American schools in *Out of Our Minds: Anti-intellectualism and Talent Development in American Schooling.* They noted that cultivating the intellect through reason is dangerous to a society, because most education exists to serve the dominant interests. "The cultivation of reason, especially through literacy, is intellect. Only intellect possesses the authority to examine, critique, and judge the conditions of existence in an articulate fashion" (p. 42). When reason and intellect are educated, a discourse results. "Such discourse elaborates discussions that the commitments of vested interests would sooner suppress" (p. 42).

Special educational opportunities for academically talented children have had to be a response to what was in the air. In the 1950s, the academically talented child was seen as the potential savior of the society, as the Cold War and Sputnik defined being competitive with the Soviet Union as necessary to the survival of the United States. These students, who graduated from high school in the late 1950s and early 1960s, took their scholarships and grants and began to study science, mathematics, and foreign languages in many of the universities of the country.

They had just graduated from college when the next generation, the antiwar protestors and the civil rights activists, began to deny that being intellectually able was important or necessary. It is ironic that many of the leaders of these movements were themselves academically talented, attending many of the elite colleges of the nation (such as Berkeley, Columbia, the University of Michigan) when they began promoting egalitarian rhetoric such as "All thoughts are just as good as all other thoughts," and "Everyone is as intelligent as everyone else." They began to strive for a higher consciousness, a consciousness that Reich (1971) defined as Consciousness III. Perhaps they felt guilty for having academic talent.

States of altered consciousness were often evoked by hallucinatory drugs, and new ways of being were manifested in communal living and the sexual freedom made possible by the invention of the birth control pill. Sexual equality came along with that sexual freedom, and experimental ways of living began to evolve: open marriages, communes, and retreats such as Esalen, and movements such as "est," where people went to "get it." Along with this freedom and equality of thought came a sense of responsibility to the environment, and the Environmental Protection Agency was created, along with such volunteer organizations as Greenpeace and the Sierra Club. Talented individuals were participants and leaders in these social changes.

After the passage of the Voting Rights Act and Public Law 94-142, the act which authorized increased funding for handicapped students, the next generation of academically talented students settled down to make money and to become consumers. The purpose of their education was not to save the world, but to get the highest paid job in commerce that they could. While talented students ten years earlier had gone into the Peace Corps, or had gone to be schoolteachers in Harlem, the next generation went to the Wall Streets of the large cities. They bought boats and condos and fast cars, and they decided that their purpose in the world was to get a nice sublet during the summer in The Hamptons, or a *pied-à-terre* in Cancun.

The words *networking* and *connections* came to be bywords of the ways they saw to make it. Not only consumption, but conspicuous consumption became the goal of many of the talented youth of the 1970s. The way to become a "Master of the Universe," as Wolfe put it in *Bonfire of the Vanities*, was to use one's intelligence in finance and business. Therefore, the numbers of students choosing the sciences, mathematics, and the humanities dropped lower than the number of students choosing business and an MBA. The life of the mind as exemplified by doing research in academe or by teaching in a public school was not appealing to these talented students. The number of lawyers soared. This period lasted from the end of the Vietnam War into the 1990s. Calling themselves Generation X, they seem to be most interested in buying the house, having the baby, settling down with the mortgage and the job and the pension.

Crass consumerism seems to be losing popularity at the end of the millennium, as some youth seem to want to simplify their lives according to a public television show called *Affluenza* (1997). Popular newsmagazines propose that the brightest are leaving the fast track. At this writing, it is too soon to tell whether talented youth have turned from self-promotion to selflessness. Many students still graduate from college, get the job, get married, buy the house, acquire the mortgage, have the baby, and settle in to frazzled, conventional lives. There seems to be no mass movement towards altruism or intellectualism.

STATE OF THE STATES

In a comprehensive policy analysis in 1992, Coleman and Gallagher surveyed all 50 states as to their policies about the identification of and programming for talented students. The study found that most of the states had policies that addressed the identification of talented students, and that 40 states paid attention to cultural diversity among talented students. However, most states did not mandate programming for any talented students, let alone underserved talented students. The state policies were permissive, but state funding was lacking. The types of outstanding talent emphasized were usually high IQ and specific academic talent.

By 1995, all 50 states addressed the education of gifted and talented children (Passow & Rudnitski, 1995). Twenty-three of the 49 directors of gifted and talented education in state departments were housed in special education settings, where due process and other policies related to Public Law 94-142 are followed. Twenty-seven states had policies on due process for gifted and talented students.

THE LAW AND ACADEMICALLY TALENTED STUDENTS

Karnes and Marquardt (1991a, 1991b) summarized the types of suits brought on behalf of academically talented children. Early admission cases, admission to programs, race and admission to programs, desegregation issues with relation to talented children, magnet school issues, modification of curriculum and course work, placement and certification of teachers in the education of the academically talented, and the lack of school programming for academically talented students have all drawn suits.

The *Centennial* case in Pennsylvania is an example. Karnes and Marquardt called it "the seminal case in gifted education" (1991b, p. 62). A child was placed in a pullout program instead of receiving suitable course placement for his mathematics and reading academic talent. The court ruled that pullout placement was not adequate placement, and that the child's Individual Educational Plan (IEP) indicated that he needed more rigorous course selection and placement. (An Individual Education Plan is a written statement by the school that specifies the long-term and short-term goals for an instructional program including where the program will take place and who will deliver the program, as well as how the student's progress will be evaluated.) The school district was enjoined to provide the student appropriate training in mathematics and reading, according to their present resources: "the school district was required to do more than just place a student in a class with other gifted students 150 minutes a week because Pennsylvania law focused on providing appropriate education for individuals" (1991b, p. 61). Parents have also sued schools for other aspects of appropriate placement, for example, early entrance and early graduation.

SETTING UP A PROGRAM

The Planning Committee

While service to talented students is not mandated in most states, a district would do well to plan ahead and to set some goals for the education of the talented. To meet these goals, the district should choose a planning committee. The makeup of this planning committee should include interested teachers, administrators, parents, community members, and talented students. The size of the committee should be workable; twelve is too many and four is too few. Many districts choose to have a teacher from each level (primary, intermediate, secondary), one or two interested parents, a principal or central office person such as the school psychologist or a curriculum specialist, and a school board member. A talented student from the middle school or high school should also be invited to join.

The first task of this planning committee is to do a self-analysis. What are their beliefs about talent development education? What visions do they have for the future? Each person writes down statements of belief about talented students. A general discussion is held and about 10 to 15 beliefs are generated from the group. Then another list is generated, this time of belief statements about programming for gifted and talented students. Such belief statements locate the education for talented students within the context of education for all students. Should it be different? Should it be the same? From the belief statements comes a vision statement, and from the vision statement comes a list of goals and desired results (Hanninen, 1994).

The committee then narrows the discussion to the five most important critical issues that have come from the belief statements. Five strategies were recommended by Hanninen (1994):

1. Analyze the language. That is, interpret what is really being said in school documents and in vision statements. Can any of it apply to the education of the gifted and talented? Of course it can.

2. List key decision makers, stakeholders, and risk takers. Who are the "influencers" in the school community?

3. Infuse the words *gifted/talented* into several school policies, especially in curriculum documents, statements about special populations, staff development documents, and documents about parental involvement. In addition, there should be a separate policy statement about the program for the education of the talented.

4. Visualize the desired direction. A framework with a continuum of services from preschool through grade 12 should be designed. How the services for talented children relate to services for all children should be defined. Accountability strands should indicate who is responsible for what.

5. Enact equitable access to resources. Students, teachers, and families should have the same opportunity for all resources. Academically talented students are no different from athletically talented students in this regard. Buses, uniforms, and special teachers should not be provided for one population and not for another. The policy statements should reflect such equity.

In all, the educators and advocates for the talented should work within the larger framework of the school, and not separate themselves. After the belief statements and vision statements have been penned, the planning committee needs to see what the district is already doing for talented students. A needs assessment or a survey should be administered and compiled. Often these surveys are variations on that given by the Richardson Foundation in its Pyramid Project, a study of gifted education in 1,158 school districts in the early 1980s (Cox, Daniel & Boston, 1985). This data-gathering questionnaire is presented in Appendix B.

The data collected will provide a starting place for the district. Usually the planning committee finds that some of the needs of talented students are being met, and that as students get older, their academic needs are met through various course selection options. To design a full, continued program for talented students is the challenge the committee will have to deal with. A continuum of services for talented children, ranging from kindergarten to grade 12, is a rarity in most districts. However, pre-K to 12 service to talented students should be the goal for the planning committee.

Besides the ideas that may be included in the survey, the planning committee should consider the latest innovations in education. Talent development education programs often have had a great influence on regular education. What used to be differentiation for talented students is now part of the curriculum for all. This is wonderful. Now educators of the talented must differentiate in *levels of challenge* for the academically able and cannot call "creativity" or "critical thinking" differentiation enough.

The Necessity for Collaboration Between General Education and Talent Development Education

The program is nested within a school *system*. Ideally, the students interact with each other no matter what their race, creed, or social class. However, the educators sometimes do not interact with each other. The teacher stays in her classroom and sends the children to the talent development specialist at the appointed hour. Some teachers and administrators even doubt whether there is such a species as a gifted child. The talent development education specialist often feels alone, as lonely as the Maytag repairman, sitting there in her room, unconnected to the flow and liveliness of the school around her.

A study by a task force of the National Association for Gifted Children (Tomlinson, Coleman, Allan, Udall, and Landrum, 1996) indicated that both the educators of the gifted and talented and general educators feel communication is enhanced through collaboration. Suggestions were made in six areas: (1) perceptions about gifted education; (2) about instructional practice and programming; (3) about preservice, inservice, and graduate preparation; (4) about policy and political action; (5) about school reform issues; and (6) about research and dissemination. The recommendations the task force made are explained in more detail in Figure 2.2.

A Program and Not a Provision

Tannenbaum (1983) and Borland (1989) cautioned that the education of the talented should be programmatic and not provisional (that is, education of the talented in any school district should be a right—not a privilege for talented youngsters). Tannenbaum said that the program should be "prescribed, sequential, and a permanent part of the curriculum rather than an occasional frill" (p. 431).

The budget for the education of talented students should be a budget for a *program*, and should be part of the whole budget so that it is not capriciously reduced during budget cutting times. If the board looks at budgeting for the talented as a priority similar to budgeting for handicapped, learning disabled, and other special education children, or for children who attend the local vocational school, or for the school athletes, the program is unlikely to be cut. Essentially, program planning for the talented is the same as any program planning for any other school program. The program goals should be determined through needs assessment and consensus should be reached about the objectives. Objectives flow out of goals. A chart could be used, in which the goals are broken down and made doable. In many districts, each individual student has an *individual educational plan* (IEP). Whether or not a district chooses to use the IEP procedure, the plan should evolve from the philosophy and from the goals and objectives.

Since talent is varied and arises at various ages (for example, academic talent in reading and in mathematics is apparent early; mechanical talent is often not apparent until motor skills are developed), the planning must take into account what kinds of

Figure 2.2 Selected Recommendations About Collaboration

1. **Suggestions for Improved Perception About Gifted Education**
   a. Use broadened conceptions of intelligence. Focus on gifted education as a resource for talent development in a broad range of students.
   b. Develop videotapes of effective examples of gifted education and use them widely.
   c. Provide in-depth training for educators of the gifted on the larger perspectives of assessment (standards, rubrics, portfolios).
   d. In interactions with general education, be patient.
   e. Become active in organizations of general education.

2. **Suggestions Regarding Instructional Practice and Programming**
   a. Focus on assessing student needs and not on identification and grouping.
   b. Provide leadership in performance-based assessment.
   c. Focus on the regular classroom more than on special programs/classes.
   d. Focus on flexible use of time with gifted learners in the classroom.
   e. Take the lead in establishing differential rubrics and performance outcomes for use with gifted students in the regular classroom.
   f. Emphasize coplanning and coteaching.
   g. Create and share differentiated instructional and grouping models.

3. **Suggestions Regarding Preservice, Inservice, and Graduate Preparation**
   a. Encourage university level educators to collaborate with special educators.
   b. Prepare educators of the gifted to model a variety of instructional strategies in the regular classroom.
   c. Actively recruit and support minority teachers of the gifted.

4. **Suggestions for Policy and Political Action**
   a. Plan conferences in concert with other organizations in general education and encourage sharing.
   b. Nurture support from teacher unions.
   c. Hold special workshops on political action and policy development.
   d. Establish working relationships with businesses and industries which have an interest in high-end excellence.

5. **Suggestions Regarding School Reform Issues**
   a. Advocate and work for educational environments in which all students have an opportunity to explore meaningful content, think critically and creatively, and become engaged in worthwhile production.
   b. Teach educators of the gifted to respond to diversity.
   c. Encourage development of multicultural curricula.
   d. Adapt school schedules for collaborative planning.
   e. Join other educators in working for reduced class size, longer blocks of instructional time, improved teacher salaries, and other initiatives likely to improve quality of instruction in schools.

6. **Suggestions Regarding Research and Dissemination**
   a. Work to strengthen research base for practices advocated for gifted learners.
   b. Conduct longitudinal studies on modifying teachers' attitudes about giftedness.
   c. Invite collaborative participation in journals.

Based on suggestions by Tomlinson et al. (1996). NAGC Task Force Report.

talent are to be served. The point is that philosophically speaking, the planning committee, in deciding to serve and develop talents in children, will need to decide *which* talents and *how* to develop them, before proceeding with a wholesale identification procedure.

OUTCOME-BASED EDUCATION FOR THE HIGH-ABILITY STUDENT

Nationwide trends in the school reform movement have stressed outcomes. Many states have engaged in dialogue and decision making about *outcome-based education* (OBE). Because many of the outcomes were in the *affective* (i.e., "Students will get along with others individually and in groups"), rather than the *academic* (i.e., "Students will be able to read the daily newspaper") areas, members of the religious right and parents took issue with outcome-based education. The term "outcome" may be dangerous to use, but the idea that students should be academically different when they graduate than when they enter, that they should be literate in mathematics, science, social science, and reading, should be considered.

When one looks at what the effect of a specialized education should be, perhaps one effect could be that students who have experienced a differentiated education according to their academic ability should be admitted to any college they choose, without regard to income. College admission seems to be the implicit purpose of most programs for the academically talented. Many districts have developed rubrics (written directions on how to assess student work) for each course and program. These rubrics are then compared to the state and national assessment standards to see whether the school's achievement goals interface with what the rest of the state or country seems to be requiring.

VanTassel-Baska (1994) cautioned that the learner outcomes developed in most states may be too low level, academically, for able learners. The learner outcomes should be differentiated for the academically talented. She gave an example of ninth grade English curriculum outcomes for all learners juxtaposed with outcomes that were developed specifically for academically talented students at that same grade level:

Generic	*Academically Talented*
1. Comprehends a variety of materials	1. Evaluates diverse materials according to a set of criteria or standards
2. Is familiar with the structural elements of literature.	2. Creates a literary work in a self-selected form, using appropriate structural elements
3. Develops an understanding of the chronology of American literature	3. Analyzes and interprets key social, cultural, and economic ideas as expressed in the literature, art, and music of America at 40-year intervals

The outcomes (standards, benchmarks) for the academically talented students should logically be more intellectually challenging; they should be harder. Academically talented students often are able to comprehend high-level reading material, and they can synthesize what they have read to look for themes and trends. Van-Tassel-Baska (1997) cautioned educators of the talented to use the standards set by the national curriculum groups (e.g., National Teachers of Mathematics; National Association of Teachers of English), rather than those at the state or local level, because the standards tend to get watered down at farther removes from their origin.

Four suggestions for setting standards for the gifted and talented have been made (Baker & Schacter, 1996): (1) The standards (or benchmarks or outcomes) toward which a program should aim may also be based on what expert adults in the domain do; (2) The standards could be set by teachers who have high-level content knowledge about the domain; (3) The standards could be "developmentally appropriate"; that is, they could be based on what gifted and talented learners in similar learning environments have achieved in this domain; and (4) The standards could be based on what students one or two grades above those being assessed can do. The first two suggestions already have accumulated data, but the last two have not. The notion that students should aim for what experts in the domain do is gaining credence.

Wiggins (1996) stated that standards should be set for a full range of performances, with "examplars" or models available for students to see. How will students know what they should achieve if they never see examples of the best? Such examples should be from the real world. These examples will not limit creativity but will anchor the products in a real-world domain.

EDUCATIONAL PROGRAM OPTIONS

In recent years, a debate has been raging among educators. Some educators, such as Jeannie Oakes and Robert Slavin, have insisted that talented students should not be taught in separate groups or classes, but that everyone should be taught in heterogeneous groups. Other educators, including those of the talented, have said that whole group, heterogeneous group instruction, means that the talented students will not be able to reach their potential. What has research about grouping practices shown? The planning committee for the program for talented students must make certain decisions about program options, and how, or even whether, to group students is among these decisions.

Ability Grouping

Ability grouping has been used in schools for more than a hundred years. As soon as the numbers of students in any classroom or school got to be so many that the differences in their abilities to learn stood out, teachers automatically put the students into groups for subject matter learning. These groups were often informal, consisting of two or more students who could keep pace with each other. When students started to be grouped according to chronological age, when developmental experts cautioned that students should remain in classes only with their age-mates, ability grouping began to be the norm rather than the exception.

The social upheavals of the 1960s and 1970s increased the calls for "equity," and equity was defined in the 1990s as heterogeneous grouping, so that no students would move faster than any other students, even though the students' abilities indicated that they could do so. Several types of ability grouping are available as discussed in the following sections.

XYZ Grouping

XYZ grouping is done according to high-, middle-, and low-ability based on test scores or other performance indicators. Detroit had such a plan as early as 1919. Students had the same curricula and the same textbooks; the only differences were in pace of instruction and depth of enrichment. The top 20 percent in achievement were in the "X" classes, the next 60 percent were in the "Y" classes, and the lowest 20 percent were in "Z" classes.

A meta-analysis (a study of all the studies) by Kulik and Kulik (1992a, 1992b) of 51 studies of the effectiveness of XYZ grouping showed that high-aptitude learners gained about one-tenth of a year with such grouping and curricula (Kulik, 1992a). Similar studies by Slavin (1987, 1991) showed no difference in the achievement gains among students in XYZ groups. Likewise, self-esteem of students in XYZ groups was studied by Kulik and Kulik (1984a, 1984b, 1987, 1990, 1991; Kulik, 1992a), and their studies showed that students in the lower group, the "Z" groups, had slightly higher self-esteem in such a configuration, but that students in the higher group, the "X" students, had slightly lower self-esteem.

In commenting on why the achievement and self-esteem effects were so small in XYZ groups, James Kulik (1992b) said that "curricular uniformity" was probably the main reason, for they were placements of "differential placement but not differential treatment." He said, "For example, children in the high group in a Grade 5 program may be ready for work at the sixth grade level; children in the middle group are ready for work at the fifth grade level; and children in the low group may need remedial help" but all had the same curricula (p. 4).

Another name for XYZ grouping is *tracking*. Critics such as Jeannie Oakes have called for an elimination of all grouping—not only XYZ grouping—after studying the results of XYZ grouping on achievement. A call to "detrack America" has been raised by many educators. Kulik (1992b) said that "Meta-analytic evidence suggests that this proposed reform could greatly damage American education. Teachers, counselors, administrators, and parents should be aware that student achievement would suffer with the total elimination of all school programs that group students by aptitude" (p. 6). He said that achievement results from schools replacing all XYZ classes with heterogeneous classes would show that students of higher aptitude would "fall slightly," while the level of achievement of the rest of the students would stay about the same. He cautioned, "If schools eliminated grouping programs in which all groups follow curricula adjusted to their ability, the damage would be greater, and it would be felt more broadly" (p. 6).

It seems that Kulik's advice is being followed, and many districts are deciding to continue with honors classes, especially in academic subjects such as science, mathematics, social studies, and language arts, with all other students not in the honors classes grouped together for instruction. Qualification for honors classes is being broadened in many districts to include more criteria than aptitude or achievement test scores from tests given at very young ages. Such criteria often include self-nomination by students, and meeting certain knowledge requirements on criterion-referenced assessments geared for honors classes.

Within-Class Grouping

A second type of ability grouping is *within-class grouping*, in which students within the same class are grouped for instruction according to their achievement. Common types of within-class grouping are (1) mastery learning and (2) individualized instruction. In the most common form of within-class grouping, (3) regrouping by subject, students are generally grouped into three or more levels, and they study material from different textbooks at different levels. Meta-analytic studies from the University of Michigan (Kulik, 1992a, 1992b; Kulik & Kulik, 1984a, 1984b, 1987, 1990, 1992a, 1992b) and from Johns Hopkins University (Slavin, 1987, 1991) found that this type of ability grouping had positive results, with gains for low-, middle-, and high-ability students averaging 1.2 years in a school year. A review of research by Balzer (1991) indicated that students should probably be grouped by ability for reading and mathematics, and that if students are grouped, the content would be differentiated.

Cluster Grouping

A type of within-class grouping is *cluster grouping.* This is where several talented students are placed with a teacher who will treat them as talented and differentiate their instruction accordingly. Winebrenner and Devlin (1991) said that four to six talented students should make up a cluster; the teacher will be able to differentiate for their instruction and the workload will not be horrendous. This way, the students can be talented all the time, and not just in their resource room or pullout class. Cluster grouping may be used at all grade levels and in all subject areas. Gifted students may be clustered in one section of any heterogeneous class, especially when there are not enough students to form an advanced section for a particular subject.

Cluster grouping is also a welcome option in rural settings, or wherever small numbers of gifted students make appropriate accommodations difficult. The advantage of this type of grouping is that it fits, philosophically, with the special educational practice of *inclusion*, and it still provides the students with a peer group. Teachers have found that cluster grouping helps the achievement of the other students as well. The positive effects of the cluster grouping practice may be shared with all students over several years by rotating the cluster teacher assignment among teachers who have had gifted education training and by rotating the other students so all students eventually have a chance to be in the same class with a cluster group. Individual or small group educational plans (Differentiated Educational Plans) should be kept as records.

Schuler (1997) reported on national study of cluster grouping that found it is a viable option for the education of the talented. First, a district should adopt a formal policy on cluster grouping *before* selecting students. Selecting cluster teachers is extremely important. A cluster teacher should "understand the unique attributes and needs of talented students; be intellectually alive; be creatively productive; be flexible and willing to find appropriate outlets for student products; be attuned to the process of teaching, not just the content; be a role model for students; and be able to foster positive feelings among students and faculty toward the gifted and talented program" (Schuler, 1997, p. 2).

Cluster teachers can use these strategies: curriculum compacting, speeding up the coverage of the content, going beyond the content, projects and readings based on interest, and working with other talented students in other grades. Support and special services are essential components for cluster grouping to be effective. The cluster teacher should work with a consultant who is a specialist in talent development education. The counselor should also be part of the team. The results of the Cluster Grouping Survey showed that academically talented students do benefit from cluster grouping.

Cross-Grade Grouping

Cross-grade grouping is another type of ability grouping. This was first tried in the Joplin Plan in Missouri in the 1950s. In this model, students in the fourth, fifth, and sixth grades were broken into nine groups reading from the second grade to the ninth grade level. Students went to reading class at the same hour, but to the level of instruction at which they were achieving. Other types of cross-grade grouping are (1) ability-grouped class assignment; (2) ability grouping for selected subjects; (3) nongraded plans; and (4) special classes (Mills & Durden, 1992). Meta-analysis showed that cross-grade grouping is an effective means of delivering instruction, and achievement gains similar to those of within-grade grouping were found. The key element, it seems, is that students study different curricula for different ability levels.

Acceleration/Enrichment

The subject matter for grouping is either accelerated or enriched classes. While these have generally been separated as options for talented students, researchers such as Stanley (1989), Kitano and Kirby (1986), and Davis and Rimm (1989), as well as Southern and Jones (1991), pointed out that they are, at base, alike. Enrichment is supposed to broaden the curriculum and include material that is not in the regular course of study. Acceleration also contains advanced material that is not in the regular course of study.

Treating some students according to their special needs is a common practice; we have special remedial mathematics and reading classes and special classes for learning-disabled learners. Now, in inclusive classrooms, some people say that the whole class functions at the lowest level, as teachers must slow down. Accelerated classes are those that move rapidly through the subject matter; enriched classes are those that cover more subjects in greater depth. In meta-analysis of 23 studies of acceleration, Kulik (1992a, 1992b) found that students whose classes were accelerated (this is not individual acceleration of one student, but of classes of students) generally outperformed those who were not accelerated but who were of the same ability levels. Average gains in grade-level competencies were one year for the accelerates compared with the nonaccelerates.

Enrichment, or adding more to the traditional curriculum (for example, foreign language, anthropology, law, special art and music classes), is another way that grouped students of high ability have been taught. Of 25 studies that were analyzed (Kulik, 1992a, 1992b), 22 studies showed that high-ability students who had enriched curricula achieved more than high-ability students who did not have enriched curricula. The gains averaged about five months; that is, students with enriched classes gained about 1.5 years while the other students gained about a year. An adjusted curriculum in both the cases of acceleration and of enrichment was thought to be the reason for these gains.

The National Research Center on the Gifted and Talented has published several guidelines based on the meta-analytic studies (Kulik, 1992b):

Guidelines from Meta-Analytic Studies of Ability Grouping

Guideline 1: Although some school programs that group children by ability have only small effects, other grouping programs help children a great deal. Schools should therefore resist calls for the wholesale elimination of ability grouping.

Guideline 2: Highly talented youngsters profit greatly from work in accelerated classes. Schools should therefore try to maintain programs of accelerated work.

Guideline 3: Highly talented youngsters also profit greatly from an enriched curriculum designed to broaden and deepen their learning. Schools should therefore try to maintain programs of enrichment.

Guideline 4: Bright, average, and slow youngsters profit from grouping programs that adjust the curriculum to the aptitude levels of the groups. Schools should try to use ability grouping in this way.

Guideline 5: Benefits are slight from programs that group children by ability but prescribe common curricular experiences for all ability groups. Schools should not expect student achievement to change dramatically with either establishment or elimination of such programs.

Another form of enrichment is *process training*; that is, skills training, higher level thinking, Bloom's taxonomy, creative thinking, study strategies, and the like. Rather than difference in type of subject matter, as enrichment in the form of a class in foreign language or a class in economics is (and why should the academically talented be the ones who should get such differentiation in subject matter; shouldn't all students get it?), process training is often chosen as the curriculum so that the teachers of the talented won't step on the toes of the teachers in the regular classroom. "You can't read *Romeo and Juliet* in the seventh grade enrichment class; students read *Romeo and Juliet* in the ninth grade English class!" is the complaint, as if *Romeo and Juliet* is the only play Shakespeare ever wrote, or that one visit to the play will probe all of its richnesses.

Among critics of process enrichment are Howley, Howley, and Pendarvis (1995), who said: "gifted programs typically 'teach' cognitive and affective processes disconnected from real intellectual substance. The applicability of these processes to academic problems or to problems in the 'real world' is questionable" (p. 94). While such process education as advocated by Bruner and Bloom was well-intentioned, as a means for provoking inductive thinking and the making of high-level products in science, mathematics, humanities, and social science, the applications in talent-development education classrooms have been uneven. "Inquiry training, brainstorming, synectics and many other game-like methods predominate. To the extent that the process-oriented approach has been routinized and trivialized, it ignores the ends for which it was originally intended" (Howley, Howley & Pendarvis, 1995, p. 97). Process training is not acceptable academic content to these critics.

Cooperative Learning as a Technique for Teaching the Talented

Since the mid-1980s, when Johnson, Johnson, and Holubec (1986) published their work on cooperative learning, cooperative learning has been touted as being a good way to improve achievement. This teaching technique has also been praised for its effects on socializing students to work with others in groups.

Robinson (1990) made several recommendations about the use of cooperative learning, suggesting that cooperative learning should not be the only teaching technique used, and that talented students should not always be in heterogeneous groups. Mills and Durden (1992) affirmed that "ability grouping and cooperative learning can be used effectively in combination or alone" (p. 15) and so the school should not be put into a position where one option is chosen over another. In a study of the use of cooperative learning as a teaching tool in advanced high school English classes, Rogers showed that cooperative learning techniques were popular among the advanced students and that cooperative learning techniques did, as they were supposed to do, promote social interaction and cooperation (Rogers, 1991). Thus it

Academic competitions across districts are quite common.

is apparent that the teaching technique of cooperative learning can be used with talented students, but it is better used in homogeneous groups of talented students, so that the talented students are not exploited.

Flexible Grouping

Grouping is not going to go away, but it should always be flexible. That is, students should be able to move in and out of groups, depending on task and subject, and even on whim. The days of a child being put into the redbird reading group in first grade and remaining with the same students until high school graduation are over. Ability grouping, correctly used, produces academic gains for academically talented students when high-challenge materials are also used. When the teacher has been trained in differentiation techniques or when the teacher knows the high-level material well, the gains are even greater. If students are grouped across grades for high-level instruction, there seem to be no lasting social or emotional effects. Rogers (1991) said a "Robin Hood Effect" is present when group-paced mastery learning classes do not take into account the needs of high-ability students for challenging material.

Shore, Cornell, Robinson, and Ward (1991) said that part-time grouping seems as effective as full-time grouping. They suggested that identifying who should be grouped should "err, if one must, on the side of providing differentiated service for too many rather than too few students" (pp. 86–87). Languages and mathematics seem most amenable for ability grouping. And if there is to be grouping, the curriculum should be adapted as well. While this may seem obvious, some teachers seem to think that just putting children into groups is enough, and they don't provide different kinds of challenging materials. Shore et al. (1991) also recommended that both the risks and the benefits of grouping be carefully weighed and that joint activities be planned among students of varying academic abilities. If the educators of the academically talented are persuaded to abandon ability grouping, they should make sure that their students have their learning needs (that is, increased pace and greater depth) fully accommodated in the alternative setting.

Teaching, Waiting, and Helping

A colleague who had won big on the "Jeopardy" television show visited my class. Though his primary teaching responsibility as a teacher of music composition is with undergraduates and not the graduate students in my class, he prefaced his talk this way: "I'm not nervous teaching adults. I have been teaching since I was six years old." At the age of three he was counting backwards by threes; by the age of 12 he had taught himself calculus as his school system didn't know what to do with him and put him in the back of the room reading mathematics textbooks. For socialization, he was asked to tutor and to teach his peers.

A fourth grade girl came home from school. "What did you do in school today?" asked her father, who was the at-home parent, working from home as a freelance writer. "I waited," said the girl. "The teacher says 'Wait,' every time I ask her a question. Lots of the kids are slower than I. I finished the book the first week, reading ahead. Now I just wait."

"What do you do while you're waiting?" her father asked.

"I memorize all my classmates' middle names, and alphabetize them. I try to write everything backwards. I made up a new language that's like Pig Latin, but not really. I read a book behind the book we're reading. I draw on a tablet in my desk. I do the problems twice."

I asked two of my colleagues, both senior administrators in our department, how their curriculum had been differentiated when they were in high school. "I was the class monitor," said our department chair. "I took the attendance, took notes to other teachers and to the principal, clapped the erasers, graded papers, and gave the announcements over the intercom. As I had all As, the teachers and the principal said that they would give me these privileges. I am still the monitor, I guess."

"I was the substitute teacher," said the head of one of our program teams. "I taught physics, mainly, to my classmates. Once I taught for two whole weeks. I guess it's no surprise I turned out to be a physics teacher before I moved into administration and became a superintendent."

These are true stories. Academically talented students seem to have had universal experiences as teachers, helpers, and those who wait. The strategies they have used for relieving boredom in the classroom would make an interesting article. You may say, "So what?" But in an era where we say that all children should be challenged academically, one may ask whether this is appropriate differentiation, developmentally appropriate, that is, for those whose minds seem to be able to handle more appropriate tasks than taking attendance, clapping erasers, teaching basic skills to slower peers, or even teaching physics at the age of 16, without the requisite teacher's license required in our schools for science teachers. Some parents have begun to say to the schools, "My understanding is that teachers need to be certified. My child is not a certified teacher."

Pullout or Self-Contained?

The most commonly practiced way of educating talented children is to have a pullout program. Students who are identified as talented leave their regular classroom and go to a special teacher in a special room for a certain number of hours per week. Advantages of such an arrangement are shown in Figure 2.3 on p. 73.

Cox, Daniel, and Boston (1985) called pullout programs "patchwork" and "fragmented," and said, "we think it is a model whose time has come—and gone" (p. 44). They also noted that a district can falsely rest on its laurels by saying that it has a pullout program and that the needs of the academically talented are therefore being met. VanTassel-Baska (1987) said that since the pullout program is formulated to diverge from the regular school curriculum, it is doomed to be considered frivolous since most pullout programs do not give grades, do not have instruction in traditional subject matters, focus on the affective rather than the academic, and do not have written curricula.

Kitano and Kirby (1986) commented that teachers in pullout programs must plan a program that is carefully coordinated with that of the regular classroom teacher to "prevent unnecessary duplication of effort and to determine what will be required of the gifted student" (p. 118). Davis and Rimm (1989) commented that regular classroom teachers often oppose pullout programs: "friction often develops when teachers are saddled with the dilemma of permitting students to miss important content or else forcing them to make up missed work—thus punishing them for their G/T participation" (p. 131). Clark (1992) said that special pullout classes have "little time for meeting all of the gifted needs, teachers may resent interruption of their program, and other students in the regular classroom may envy and isolate the gifted child because of the special class" (p. 176). However, the pullout program remains one of the most popular options for the education of talented students.

How successful are pullout programs? The PACE (Program for Academic and Creative Enrichment) program, an elementary school model in Indiana, was studied to assess its long-term effects (Moon & Feldhusen, 1991). Moon and Feldhusen did a multiple-case study using a questionnaire and then interviews of 10 families whose children had participated for at least three years. This pullout program was for two hours a week. The families and the students felt that the PACE program had provided many benefits and few hindrances to the talented students. Students felt they learned to think and to problem-solve, and, in particular, they felt that the personal and emotional benefits were great. The students felt that being in the pullout program gave them more self-confidence, self-esteem, and "the courage to be different" (p. 2).

Vaughn, Feldhusen, and Asher (1991) conducted a meta-analysis of nine studies of pullout programs. They found that pullout programs have some positive effect on students' achievement and on their scores on critical thinking tests. They also found little or no effect on self-concept as measured by the Piers-Harris Children's Self-Concept Scale.

In an ethnographic study for the U.S. Office of Research and Evaluation, I observed three academically talented children during their fourth and fifth grade years, both in their regular classroom and in their pullout classroom (Resource Module 2.1). I found that, while in the regular classroom and at their other special classes such as physical education, music, and art, the academically talented students were "good kids," obedient, law-abiding, friendly, raising their hands, and getting good grades. However, they truly came alive in their pullout gifted and talented classroom, where, with eight other children, they argued, debated, did independent studies, and had a good time with such programs as Philosophy for Children and Junior Great Books. The qualitative difference was great, and someone who had not observed the children in both settings would not notice how they changed, for they went along and were good students in their regular classroom, but in their pullout classroom they bloomed. Resource Module 2.1 gives an example of the kind of dialogue possible in a pullout program that would perhaps not be possible in an inclusive classroom as most children would probably not be interested.

Resource Module 2.1 Dialogue from a Pullout Program for Academically Talented Fourth Graders

This is a Philosophy for Children lesson. *Pixie* is the Philosophy for Children novel used for grades three and four, and it emphasizes relationships and looking for meaning. Philosophy for Children is a nationwide program for all children, but perhaps the level of dialogue is more advanced among academically talented students.

The students had been discussing the difference between thinking and feeling, and Dr. Hill had put their responses on the bulletin board. Among the answers were these: "Thinking is a form of having complex thoughts in the mind about someone or something." "Feeling is connected to hunches. It is a thing you're not sure of, something you wouldn't bet your life on, but your gut instinct tells you it is true." "Knowing is what is already in your mind." "Thinking is the step that has to come before feeling or knowing."

The class had a long discussion on the first sentence of a novel, arguing about it. For the next class, Dr. Hill said, "We could have challenged every sentence, but basically we need to discuss how we know something is true. You can tell something is true for two basic reasons." She pointed to the board. On the board was written:

On Truth

Reasons:

1. Definition

2. Evidence

She instructed them to write whether the sentence she read was true or false by reasons of definition or of evidence. She read sentences such as "Firemen are usually brave." "Every circle is round." "Fire always burns paper." "There's always a tomorrow." As they discussed the sentence about circles being round, Patrick began drawing circles. He leaped up and went to his bookbag, got his compass and protractor and began using them. He muttered, "What's a perfect circle?" The other students were jumping up and going to the board to draw circles. There was much lively discussion, and the students were interrupting, even shouting in their enthusiasm. Stacy said, "On a car radio, my dad said that the knobs have to be perfect circles because otherwise people can't use them." Dr. Hill interrupted. "I'm going to read a definition. I don't usually do this in philosophy, but since we're talking about definition—" She read the definition of a circle. The students discussed what "equidistant" means. They finally concluded that there is a *perfect* circle, but that that is the *ideal*, which can never be reached, and that there is the *idea* of a circle, which is what all other circles are.

The disadvantage cited by researchers, that pullout programs are a "part-time solution to a full-time problem" is magnified when one considers that most pullout programs are for students in grades four through six. The most crucial need for programming is for young students, whose precociousness is often squelched when they enter school. Academically talented students are academically talented all the time, every day, and some schools have pullout programs for as little time as 30 minutes or one hour per week. This places a responsibility on the regular classroom teacher, a responsibility to program for, to modify curricula for, and to adequately teach talented students. Do regular classroom teachers do this? Some do and some don't.

Regular Classroom Modifications

A 1992 report by the National Research Center on the Gifted and Talented (Gubbins, 1992) consolidated three studies. One study surveyed 3,600 third and fourth grade teachers, asking them what modifications they made of their curricula in the regular classroom to serve the needs of the gifted and talented students they had. The teachers made few, if any, changes. This held true for rural, suburban, urban, public, private, small, large, mostly white, or mostly minority classrooms. Those teachers who did provide some special modification for academically talented students did so by such passive changes as giving more advanced readings, more independent projects, more difficult enrichment worksheets, and more special assignments and reports.

Another study placed observers in 46 classrooms throughout the nation, and the observers found that 84 percent of the activities that academically talented students took part in were the same as those of the rest of the students. A third study followed 300 teachers trained in curriculum compacting. Between one-fourth and three-fourths of material taught to talented students could be eliminated by compacting. This was material the students already knew, material that was redundant, repetitious, and tautological. If what these studies showed was true, that teachers generally do not have the time, the knowledge, or the will to differentiate content for the academically talented students they inevitably will have in their classes, the idea that academically talented students do or can receive a special, differentiated education in the regular classroom is false (Archambault et al., 1993; Reis et al., 1993; Westberg, Archambault, Dobyns, & Slavin, 1993).

These Classroom Practice Studies by the National Research Center for the Gifted and Talented at the University of Connecticut were, at base, depressing. Delisle (1995) criticized them: "And don't even get me started on the National Center for the Gifted and Talented sponsored 'research' that shows that classroom teachers almost never differentiate curricula for their most able students!" (p. 11). Delisle thinks that the studies bash teachers and do not reflect what classroom teachers willingly and eagerly do for their bright students.

Another National Research Center study was reported in 1997 (Westberg & Archambault). This was the Successful Practices Study conducted in 10 elementary schools across the country. Observers sat in on classes and noted what common practices were used in grades three through five to differentiate for gifted and talented students. These districts had won awards and had reputations of differentiating and individualizing for students. These were the common themes among these districts that enabled them to provide for all students: (1) The teachers had advanced training and knowledge, often advanced degrees or extensive workshop training and staff development; (2) The teachers were willing to try new ideas; (3) The teachers voluntarily collaborated with other colleagues at grade level, across grade levels, in and out of school; (4) The teachers were aware that students have different academic needs and tried various strategies including setting high standards, modifying the curriculum, finding mentors, supervising independent projects and studies, and instituted flexible grouping; (5) The schools had respected and innovative leaders both in the superintendencies and in the principalships; (6) The teachers felt they had support for their innovations, and they felt respected. The atmosphere in the schools was warm and pleasant, and the teachers were supportive of able students.

Westberg and Archambault (1997) said that the factors were "linear." That is, when teachers have advanced training and staff development, they become more willing to try change. When they collaborate with others, they hear new ideas and try them out. When schools have strong, respected, and innovative leaders, teachers' ideas are valued and supported. This results in "a belief system and school culture that supports the development of the student's talent" (p. 50).

Resource Rooms

Another common way of dealing with the needs of the academically talented is to have resource rooms. These are sometimes for pullout groups and sometimes for individual students where they can work on projects, continuously progressing academically. The resource room model is derived from special education, where learning disabled and handicapped children receive special tutoring part of the time from a special tutor teacher in the resource room. The use of resource rooms for academically talented students, or the combining of the duties of the resource special education teacher to include helping all talented students, is also sometimes practiced. A caution should be leveled here, and that is that the teacher should have special training in talent development education. The resource room should also contain *resources*, for example, computers with access to databases.

Along with the resource room, there is often a call for a resource teacher to work in the classroom with the regular teacher, to take care of the needs of the academically talented students. While the special resource teacher for learning disabled students can help the students do the regular classroom work, the resource teacher for the academically talented must often provide alternative work for work the student already knows. This is a great challenge, and difficulties may arise between the two teachers regarding "turf." Teaming is presently touted as a real alternative, but teaming often falters because of personality conflicts. Districts should carefully study both the resource room and the resource teacher options before putting students and teachers into these situations (Sapon-Shevin, 1994; Smutny & Blocksom, 1990). Figure 2.3 examines some advantages and disadvantages of resource rooms and pullout programs.

Self-Contained Classes and Special Schools

A very cost-effective way of teaching academically talented students is the self-contained classroom. That few academically talented students have an opportunity to be

Figure 2.3   Advantages and Disadvantages of the Resource Room and Pullout Models

ADVANTAGES	DISADVANTAGES
1. Pullout programs are quite easy to set in motion.	1. Costs more as extra teachers have to be hired and special facilities provided.
2. The teacher in the regular classroom has more time to work with the other students.	2. The regular classroom teachers get frustrated and often feel that students leaving disrupts their instructional plan.
3. Students who are left in the classroom have a chance to shine.	3. Students in the regular classroom might feel resentful.
4. The teacher in the pullout program can focus on critical and creative thinking since the teacher in the regular classroom focuses on the standard curriculum.	4. The academically talented students might have to make up work in the regular class-room while having more work in the pullout classroom.
5. The differentiation of curriculum is separated from the classroom flow.	5. Curriculum may have no relationship to curriculum in the regular classroom.
6. Students receive special help in areas of strength.	6. Students are treated differently according to ability.
7. Teachers can feel as if they have "their" kids.	7. Teachers are isolated from the other teachers.
8. Students can have time with other students to discuss intellectual interests that may not be shared by students in the regular classroom.	8. Students may feel different from the rest of the students in their regular classroom.
9. Collaboration with other teachers is encouraged.	9. Students are academically talented all the time, and not just during pullout time.
10. Small groups of students can do special projects that would not be possible in the regular classroom.	10. Small groups of students may receive special privileges other students don't receive (e.g. access to computers, field trips)
11. Teachers of the talented can provide intensive instruction in areas of expertise (e.g. the arts, foreign language).	11. Turf issues with regular classroom teacher may arise (e.g. homework, lessons and assemblies missed).

in a self-contained setting indicates that districts do not have cost-effectiveness of programming for the academically talented as a major priority. In the self-contained classroom, the students who are identified as talented are placed into a classroom with a teacher who is trained in the education of the academically talented. For a middle-sized district, this could mean one classroom per grade. If 1 out of 10 students is intellectually talented, and there are about 200 students per grade, a classroom of 20 intellectually talented students could be created.

The advantages of the self-contained option are obvious: the students would receive education suited to their intellectual level, they could move through material at a fast pace, and they could experience enrichment, broadening of subject matter, as a matter of course. No one extra would have to be hired, as is necessary when the pullout option is used. Students would be free to be academically talented all day long. The teachers would not have to haul materials from site to site, as they do now in many districts where they have several buildings of pulled-out children.

When self-contained classrooms are proposed, the complaint that "you are taking away my best students; these students are spark plugs" is often heard. Again, the question has to be asked, if not answered. Who benefits from having academically talented students be "spark plugs" for the other students? The other students or the academically talented students? Where are the rights of the academically talented student, the right to have an appropriate education, in this debate? Inclusion for the academically talented should take place in areas of the curriculum other than traditional academic areas: that is, inclusion for the academically talented should take place in the arts, in the physical sciences, in affective education, on field trips, recess, and the like.

When I was the principal of a school for high-IQ children, I noted that there was a qualitative difference in the education that teachers were able to provide in the self-contained class in the special school. The whole tone of the school was different; students proceeded at a rapid pace and photocopy machines rapidly wore out as the students ate up material from books that were advanced for the grade level. Even within the high level of academic achievement, there were differences among students, and teachers had to individualize instruction. Where students would have been permitted to be lazy and careless, getting easy As, being academic leaders in a regular classroom, they were challenged and had to work hard within their own level of academic ability. This led me to conclude that the self-contained option is the most desirable option for high-IQ students with strong academic abilities. The mean achievement scores of students in this school were in the mid-90th percentiles on standardized tests. The teachers covered the required state curricula for any given grade level within a few months and the students were able to advance according to ability without fear of being thought of as weird or strange, and without being thwarted.

Kolloff (1989) conducted a study comparing student achievement. Students in a pullout program were compared with students in a self-contained classroom setting. The students in the self-contained classroom scored significantly higher in achievement, figural divergent production, and critical thinking. Self-concept was a little lower for students in the self-contained classroom. Perhaps this was because they were now with intellectual equals who were able to keep them intellectually challenged. Figure 2.4 examines the advantages and disadvantages of the self-contained classroom.

Inclusion, Intervention, Consultation, Facilitation

School reform efforts in the early 1990s led by Theodore Sizer, Harry Levin, and others have begun to take hold. Two of the models for the education of the gifted and talented are becoming the dominant models in many states. These are cluster grouping and inclusion. Based on the change in the field of special education that promotes the belief that all students deserve to be served in heterogeneous classes, with facilitators, intervention specialists, or special teachers working right along with the regular, or essential, classroom teacher, this model is now becoming predominant. Many districts have phased out the self-contained classroom for the gifted and talented. They have phased

Figure 2.4   Advantages and Disadvantages of the Self-contained Model

ADVANTAGES	DISADVANTAGES
1. Cost-efficient: No extra teachers need to be hired.	1. Self-contained classroom may be called "tracking" with its incumbent accusation of elitism.
2. Students can work at an academic pace consonant with their ability. No need to "wait" or "teach."	2. Student self-esteem may suffer when academic challenge with intellectual peers is present.
3. Students and teachers may experience a lack of community with the rest of the school.	3. Self-contained option may be used as a means of *de facto* racial or social class segregation.
4. Teacher can stay put and not have to move from building to building.	4. Teacher may "settle in" and become stagnant.
5. Students can move easily into advanced programs in high school.	5. Articulation issues may arise when students move schools or grades and they are academically ahead of the others.

out special advanced classes in middle school and high school. They have phased out resource rooms for special students, both for students with low IQs and for students with high IQs. Teachers who are training for special education and for the education of the talented and gifted receive training in collaborative strategies. The three common models in the education of the talented (acceleration, pullout, and self-contained) now include cluster grouping and heterogeneous grouping.

Students who are identified as having special needs because of their intellect or handicap receive individualized educational plans. These plans for the talented are similar to those that have been developed over the past 25 years in special education, as a result of Public Law 94-142. For the talented, such plans are at present less focused on due process, and more on curriculum differentiation to be provided by the essential classroom teacher or by the educational intervention specialist or facilitator for talent development. A case example is given at the end of this chapter.

The Renzulli Schoolwide Enrichment Model (Renzulli & Reis, 1989) seems to be the preferable model in many schools. Type I (schoolwide enrichment), Type II (direct teaching of strategies for creative and critical thinking), and Type III (individual and group special projects) activities lend themselves to this emphasis on heterogeneous grouping. Students are selected via a "Revolving Door" arrangement, with certain students doing projects at one time, and others doing projects at other times. Professor Renzulli was a keynote speaker, presenting the Schoolwide Enrichment Model during the 1997 National Middle School Association conference. A debate with Paul George who believes that all grouping should be heterogeneous created controversy among the participants (L. Beach, personal communication, November, 1997). Renzulli's plan has three service delivery components: (1) the Total Talent Portfolio, a vehicle for systematically gathering and recording information about a student's abilities, interests, and learning style preferences; (2) Curriculum Modification Techniques, including curriculum differentiation, provision of in-depth learning experiences, and integration of enrichment activities; and (3) enrichment learning and teaching through provision of enrichment clusters to multi-age heterogeneous groups of students. The SEM (School Enrichment Model) can serve as a structure for schools trying to develop the talents of all students (Renzulli, 1995).

The facilitator, consulting teacher, or intervention specialist—pick your term—often works with flexible groups of students, perhaps with math or science instruction, perhaps with humanities instruction, pulling the students for special instruction, but always working in consultation with the essential classroom teacher. The number of certified teachers in any classroom is often doubled, tripled, or quadrupled with this model. The teacher who has responsibility for the talented students is no longer isolated and alone, working in her resource room or pullout classroom, with no knowledge of what the students are doing in their home classrooms. She is in partnership, out there in the classroom, collaborating on teams, helping plan lessons that are multileveled. She may teach whole group lessons in creativity training or critical thinking or study strategies. She may work with a high-end reading group or a math group when the class is working in these domains. She may mentor projects and displays, design special learning centers, or plan special trips. This model also has its advantages and disadvantages, outlined in Figure 2.5.

In summary, whatever the district's plan for educating talented children, it is apparent that several options should be made available:

1. Accelerative strategies should be in place, including early entrance, flexible pacing, and special opportunities for students in mathematics, science, and language arts.
2. Individual plans for students, with mentors and seminars, should be available.

Figure 2.5 Advantages and Disadvantages of the Inclusion Model

ADVANTAGES	DISADVANTAGES
1. Students are in community, with no one being singled out for special treatment.	1. Special education teachers no longer have their "own" students or their own classrooms.
2. Teachers are in community, working for all children, planning and collaborating on lessons and activities.	2. Academic standards may lack rigor and be watered down. Pace of instruction especially may be affected.
3. More adult professionals are present in the classroom.	3. Special teachers need different skills and personality attributes when collaborating than when teaching in their own classrooms.
4. "Equity," "diversity," and "cooperation" are emphasized for all students and teachers.	4. The needs of the individual talented students may be subsumed to the group needs. Talented students may have to "wait" and "teach" rather than be challenged and be taught.
5. Interdisciplinary and cross-grade planning teams coordinate the curriculum.	5. The teacher of the talented may feel fragmented, teaching many lessons but no courses or subjects.

3. Opportunities should be made available for talent development in a wide range of areas, especially in the visual and performing arts.
4. Programming should be available for young talented students, with early identification of nontraditional and disadvantaged students.
5. There should be trained teachers.

Do Special Programs for the Talented Have an Impact?

A 1994 study by Delcourt, Loyd, Cornell, and Goldberg looked at 14 school districts and over 1,000 elementary school students in grades 2 and 3. They found that "in terms of achievement, gifted children attending special programs performed better than their gifted peers not in programs" (p. vii). Students in special schools, separate classes, and pullout programs achieved much higher than students served in regular classroom programs. In their attitudes toward learning, students in special schools were highest; that is, they viewed their classroom as student-centered. Students in separate classes were most dependent on teachers for guiding their assignments and work. Overall, the study showed that "no single program fully addresses all the psychological and emotional needs of students" but in terms of high achievement and academic self-concept, "the concept of specific programming for the gifted is clearly valid" (p. 79).

TEACHERS OF THE TALENTED

Many studies have focused on the qualities necessary for the teacher of the talented, but many have skirted the obvious question that the teacher of the talented asks himself or herself: "Am I talented? Do I need to be gifted and talented in order to teach gifted and talented students?" Once the potential teacher has answered these questions to his or her own satisfaction, and has answered a related question, "Are my own children talented?" (for many teachers of the talented started their interest in the field through being parents of the talented), the task of teaching talented children can be undertaken.

The answer to this question need not be that the teacher has a high IQ, or that the teacher's children are talented, but that when ego is put aside, the teacher can settle down and be a professional. Many successful teachers of the talented would not have qualified for the program for the academically talented when they were in school, but they have the personal characteristics of charisma, excitement, drive, and interest that all good teachers have.

For subject matter specialists, though, it is advisable that in-depth knowledge of the subject matter field be present. Talented students are quick to spot phonies and fakes who say "I don't know" one time too many, or who say "Look it up" once too often. Good spelling is also recommended, because students often giggle and hem and haw when the teacher can't spell. One of the main qualities that we looked for in the self-contained school for the academically talented was that the teachers had a breadth of interests; that is, they knew about literature, the arts, and contemporary culture—as participants and spectators. They went to the theater, they read books, they traveled, they talked about their experiences.

Rubin (1983) called for artistry in teaching. Teachers who use artistry are able to excite their students. They use worthwhile ideas; they are ingenious in finding ways for students to examine these ideas; they are skillful in pursuing these ideas. Teachers who use artistry have four attributes: (1) they make their teaching decisions intuitively; (2) they have a strong handle on their subject matter and do not have to grope for relationships between ideas; (3) they have confidence in their teaching ability; (4) they are exceedingly imaginative. While teaching, they can make instructional decisions rapidly, thinking on their feet; they try to accomplish several purposes at the same time; and they have "pedagogical intelligence." That is, they are able to draw on their experiences and come up with something new. While Rubin's suggestions about artistry in teaching are not specifically for teachers of the talented, they seem to apply, as talented students are often challenging and difficult to keep interested.

Olenchak (1989) focused on the backgrounds of successful teachers of the talented in order to provide a composite portrait. What was their academic preparation? What were their reasons for selecting talent education as a focus for their teaching? Olenchak said that having had previous role models was the most salient characteristic; admired teachers inspired teachers of the talented. Academic background was not as important; more than 70 percent of the teachers had themselves had inconsistent academic careers. The teachers were realistic about the amount of work it takes to be a teacher of the academically talented, and they were able to absorb huge workloads. They also chose to be teachers of academically talented students because they felt that there was a real lack of opportunity for such students, and they felt a social mission to change this, and to provide opportunities. Teachers of the talented must like talented students; they must gravitate toward them and be ready to advocate for them.

Armenta (1997) used the word "passion" in describing why people decide to become involved in the field of the education of the gifted and talented. She surveyed 20 professionals in the field—scholars and graduate students. They were average age 36 and had at least a master's degree. She found that they identified with the gifted students, and many of them had had negative school experiences because of their own "lack of appropriate opportunities and services" (p. 105). They recalled being bored and misbehaving. The reasons they chose the field were (1) the field appealed to them; (2) they were touched by gifted children with special needs; (3) they were moved by their own experiences as gifted children; (4) they were interested in learning and intelligence; (5) they thought the field would be challenging; (6) they were parents of gifted children; (7) they saw that there were possibilities for jobs in the field; (8) somebody else who is in the field encouraged them to enter the field. Like Coleman's (1994) study, this study by Armenta (1997) concluded that the teachers identify with their gifted students. "The empathy of the participants toward gifted children often developed into the altruistic decision to help gifted children and youth" (p. 100) and they entered the field with passion and determination.

In my experience in a state with funding for the education of the gifted and talented, and the necessity for those teachers to be licensed, I have noticed that many teachers enter the field accidentally; that is, there were jobs, they had been substitute teaching or had been geographically stuck or had spent many years out of the field at home raising children. The altruistic reasons that Armenta (1997) and Coleman (1994) found are not as common as other reasons. That is not to say that altruism doesn't take over once the people enter the field. However, it is just as common for teachers, once they have been in the field for awhile, to take a regular classroom or to leave the field. The field is also a means of entrée for women into administrative positions as teachers become coordinators and coordinators leave the central office and become building principals, moving up the line in administration. This happened to many of my colleagues, students, and friends over the years. It also happened to me.

Another study of the personalities of teachers of the talented showed that on the Silver and Hanson Teaching Style Inventory (theoretically based on the Myers-Briggs Type Indicator-MBTI), they preferred intuition (N) over sensing (S) (Howell & Bressler, 1988). Preference for intuition is also a characteristic of intellectually talented and creative youngsters (Myers & McCaullay, 1985; Piirto, 1992a/1998).

Reis and Renzulli (1988) recommended that when a person is applying for a teaching or coordinating position in education of the talented, certain questions be asked up front, including the following:

1. Is this a new program at this school?
2. Has one existed in the district or county before?
3. If a program is already in place, what are its strengths and weaknesses?
4. How do administrators, parents, classroom teachers, and students feel about the program?
5. Has it been evaluated? If so, what were the results?
6. Whose idea was it to start the program?
7. Has a district-wide committee been established to make decisions about beginning the program?
8. Have a definition, identification system, and programming model been selected yet?
9. Does the idea for a program have the support of central office administration, building principals, instructional staff, and parents?
10. Will I coordinate and teach in the program and what percentage of time will I spend doing each?
11. Will other teachers of the talented be hired and if so, when?
12. If other program teachers are to be hired, will I have some input into their selection?
13. What is the budget for this program?
14. What kind of formal inservice has the faculty received?
15. Who is my supervisor? (pp. 67–69).

In addition, Reis and Renzulli recommended that if there is more than one teacher, someone should be appointed as coordinator. This prevents arguments and philosophical disagreements. New teachers should be asked the following questions:

1. Does the candidate have an interest in working with very able students? Why?
2. Does the candidate have any background or course work in education of the gifted and talented? If not, is he or she willing to pursue course work or attend seminars or conferences?
3. Does the candidate have a similar philosophy toward education (in general) as the program espouses?
4. Can the candidate stop teaching and be a resource (if the program is based on a resource room model)?

5. Does the candidate agree philosophically with the district definition, identification system, and programming model?
6. Can the candidate get along with other staff members (classroom teachers and administrators) in the gifted/talented program?
7. Does the candidate have special talents, interest areas, and skills that are especially desirable for a gifted/talented teacher? (p. 69).

Invitational theory is important for intervention, consulting, or facilitation teachers. This system was developed by William Purkey and J.M. Novak (1983). A teacher of the talented should, because of the reasons mentioned earlier—negative perceptions of talented students and their teachers—proceed in an invitational way. The teacher should not call himself/herself nor be called the "gifted teacher" but "teacher of the talented." The teacher should not purport to be *the* expert but should invite other teachers who work with the students to participate in planning for the education of talented students, and should recognize that, in pullout situations, these teachers have the students longer than the teacher of the talented. The teacher of the talented should invite participation by parents, community members, and other educators, not close the door and cringe. Openness and invitation breed openness and invitation.

In summary, teachers of the talented must like and be able to work with talented students especially, and with all students as well. As with all teachers, they must honor and affirm their students' abilities. They should receive special training in the education of the talented, whether or not there is a state mandate to do so. Such training often takes the form of staff development that is conducted within the school itself, and not in the form of special course work at the university. The Richardson study (Cox, Daniel & Boston, 1985) made several recommendations for such staff development, emphasizing that teacher support is especially important for teachers of able students. In fact, Shore et al., (1991) in *Recommended Practices in Gifted Education,* noted that "trained teachers tend to be more supportive of gifted students and programs, and teachers without special training have been apathetic and even hostile" (p. 37), but that it doesn't seem to matter whether the training is college course work or inservice at the school.

PROGRAM EVALUATION

How will a district know a program is effective? The goals that are set after the philosophy and the needs assessment are completed should be evaluated to determine whether or not they have been met.

Borland (1989) cautioned that program evaluation should include more than Scriven's (1967) "formative" and "summative" evaluation. Nevo's (1983) functions of "psychological or sociopolitical function" and "administrative function" should also be taken into account. *Formative evaluation* is diagnostic evaluation. Data are collected throughout the year, and the staff continually modifies and changes the program as the diagnosis indicates. *Summative evaluation* is targeted for the community. Is the program effective? The program has been in place for a certain amount of time, and now the question is asked, did it work? Formative evaluation is used for developing and improving programs; summative evaluation is used for program accountability.

The *psychological* or *sociopolitical function* of the evaluation should also be considered. Is the evaluation being conducted to advertise or promote the program, or to get rid of the program? Often the presence of programs for the talented in a district is noted as the lodestar of a district's overall quality; real estate agents in particular may use the presence of a program for the talented in order to sell in a certain neighborhood. Or the evaluation might show a lack of services, and this too can serve a political purpose for the state organizations for talented students; the lack might demonstrate a need for more funding or more programming. Evaluation can also serve an *administrative function*; for example, when a teacher uses a grade to show a student who's boss, the grade is being used administratively; the evaluation is being conducted for reasons other than the quality of the student's work.

Evaluation can also serve to confirm what one already knows because the initial questions were not valid. Many programs give out survey questionnaires to the participants as an evaluation measure. Often the questionnaires ask whether or not the participants "liked" the program. If they "liked" it, the program is deemed to be effective and the evaluation shows that the program was successful. Asking the right questions, questions formed by the goals, should be a primary step in conducting a program evaluation.

Thus, evaluation procedures, like other procedures, should ideally be in place before the program is instituted, and these should be guided by the goals and by the desired outcomes. Unfortunately, evaluations are often conducted hurriedly and in a slapdash manner, and thus the evaluation is neither as organic nor as effective as is desirable. One of the major challenges for the field of the education of the gifted and talented is for constructive evaluation to take place. After all these years we still don't know whether programs work.

VanTassel-Baska and Avery (1997) recommended that multiple sources be consulted when a program evaluation is conducted. These are (1) a review of program documents; (2) focused interviews with principals and other selected program staff; (3) classroom observations in both classes for the gifted and talented and in regular classrooms; (4) surveys of parents, educators, and students; and (5) focus groups of stakeholders to hear their issues and concerns.

David Fetterman (1993), a past president of the American Evaluation Association, wrote a paper for the National Research Center on the Gifted and Talented about how to evaluate programs for the gifted and talented. An expert in qualitative research, he suggested that programs first do self-evaluation much as accrediting agencies require. Self-examination will permit "early detection" of problems. Besides collecting documents and conducting surveys as is usually done in an evaluation procedure, Fetterman recommended that evaluators try to be nonjudgmental, that they seek the views of insiders, and that they triangulate their data; that is, that they confirm every opinion through several other data sources.

Few programs seem to conduct regular evaluation; few states require program evaluation; and few program administrators seem comfortable in doing either self-evaluation or arranging for external evaluation. And even when a district invites an external evaluation, the data may not be valid for very human reasons. In one case, a district volunteered to be evaluated in a state-wide effort to encourage evaluation. When the graduate student sent by the outside evaluator came, she was dressed inappropriately, too casually, for the standards of this suburban school district. She admitted to the parents, administrators, and teachers in meetings that had been set up especially for her that she had never been employed by a public school system and so she was not sure what questions to ask. As she left, the superintendent told the consultant that the information gathered would not be viewed as valid, as telephone calls from worried participants had told him that the evaluator had no credibility with the stakeholders in the district. Such a seemingly small human foible may have interfered with validity. This is always a danger when outside evaluators conduct evaluations. Knowing the culture, the dress code, and the socioeconomic demographics of a school system being evaluated is important for outside evaluators.

Using Longitudinal Data for Evaluation

One way to conduct an evaluation is to compare students who qualified for a program but did not enroll in the program with students who qualified for the program but who did enroll. Alexander (1997) found that 63 students who did enroll had "long-term positive effects as measured by achievement, educational and career choices, and perceptions as students reflected back after graduating from high school and in some cases, college" (p. 169). Three studies conducted in Ohio showed varying results. Utilizing a survey I developed, three of my graduate students found that on the whole, programs for the academically talented do have positive effects in rural and urban schools.

In a medium-sized industrial city, students who had attended a magnet elementary school for gifted students obtained several hundred thousand dollars more in scholarships for college, were the valedictorians of three of the city's high schools, and were accepted at competitive universities such as Stanford, Northwestern, and the University of Chicago. The students who qualified for the program but who chose to attend their neighborhood elementary schools spent more hours in high school working rather than participating in extracurricular events, went to state universities instead of nationally competitive universities, and were not in the honor society as often as the students who did attend the magnet elementary school (internal study conducted by Arturo Hernandez, 1995).

Solars (1995) found that students who attended a one-day a week pullout program for 15 students from grades 4 through 6 did not achieve any differently from the students who just missed the cutoff for the program. The students who just missed the cutoff were the valedictorian and the salutatorian of the high school class in a small midwestern college town of 25,000 people; the students who did not attend the special pullout program also went to more competitive colleges, had more awards, more extracurricular activities, and more sports participation. Solars concluded that the pullout group was too exclusive but that it did provide a refuge for very high IQ students, who viewed their experience in the program positively.

Widman (1997) found that students who qualified for a program but did not attend did not view learning as positively, or with as much curiosity as those who had attended the program. Those who participated had more leadership positions in the school and community and participated more in activities that required performances.

A checklist for program planning is presented in Figure 2.6.

Figure 2.6   Program Planning Checklist for Local Districts

Program Planning Checklist	Begun	1 yr. Short-term	5 yr. Long-term	Meets State Guide-Lines
1. Catalyst: Get permission for pilot study/obtain state funding/ reason for beginning to plan has occurred.				
2. Review literature on G/T.				
3. Get training (workshops, college courses, etc.).				
4. Visit other programs.				
5. Develop awareness in administrators.				
6. Develop awareness in board.				
7. Develop awareness in community.				
8. Develop awareness in teachers.				
9. Select planning committee.				
10. Get training (workshops, college courses, etc.).				
11. Note state and regional consultants who can help.				
12. Do needs assessment with administrators.				
13. Do needs assessment with board.				
14. Do needs assessment with community.				
15. Do needs assessment with teachers.				
16. Determine available space/transportation/staff.				
17. Analyze present programs for G/T components				
18. Develop a prototype definition of giftedness/talent for district.				
19. Develop a prototype philosophy based on definition and needs.				
20. Establish program goals and objectives.				
21. Write a tentative plan based on information gathered. Circulate through levels to superintendent. Revise with feedback obtained.				
22. Present proposal for program to board.				
23. Get board approval for program.				
24. Get financial (staff, materials, facilities) allocation from board.				
25. Begin to seek other financial resources (grants, gift, state allocations).				

(continued on next page)

Figure 2.6 *Continued*

Program Planning Checklist	Begun	1 yr. Short-term	5 yr. Long-term	Meets State Guide-Lines
26. Plan program:				
a. Determine relation to regular classroom.				
b. Determine grouping options: self-contained; pullout; regular classroom; cluster.				
c. Add career/college planning component.				
d. Add personal counseling component.				
e. Develop continuum of services for all pre-K–12 gifted and talented students:				
• Early childhood component				
• Elementary school component				
• Middle school component				
• High school component				
27. Decide who will be served in order of program development.				
28. Plan identification process:				
a. Select identification team if different from planning team.				
b. Research literature and best practices on identification.				
c. Obtain training/college courses.				
d. Make commitment to identify poor, culturally different, visual and performing arts talented, handicapped, twice-exceptional, and highly creative talented students according to district demographics.				
e. Determine multiple criteria for each area of giftedness and talent.				
f. Screen for the following:				
• High IQ/ intellectual				
• Specific academic				
• Visual and performing arts				
• Other (creative/leadership/athletic)				
• Other				
g. Select first students (for the short range).				
h. Inform stakeholders (parents and students and teachers).				
i. Encourage formation of parents' or parent/teacher group.				

Figure 2.6   *Continued*

Program Planning Checklist	Begun	1 yr. Short-term	5 yr. Long-term	Meets State Guide-Lines
29. Plan staff needs based on students identified:				
a. Determine ongoing regular classroom teacher and administrator training needs.				
b. Determine intervention specialist needs/certification/licensure/ according to state requirements.				
c. Determine books/resources/materials/technology needs.				
d. Determine joint/team planning needs.				
e. Determine schedule/load needs.				
30. Determine space/rooms/labs/transportation/facility utilization.				
31. Determine individual educational plan policy:				
a. Determine IEP protocol/format.				
b. Determine who will receive IEPs (twice-exceptional, very high IQ, all?).				
c. Determine who will administer IEPs.				
d. Determine consultation, conference, possible legal issues, who is on IEP team, etc.				
32. Determine curriculum based on five precepts for curriculum:				
a. Based on learning characteristics of students in domains of strength.				
b. Possessing academic rigor.				
c. Thematic and interdisciplinary.				
d. Curriculum orientation decided upon by curriculum planning team.				
• Curriculum as personal relevance				
• Curriculum as academic rationalism				
• Curriculum as (a) social adaptation or (b) social reconstruction				
• Curriculum as technology				
• Curriculum as process				
• Curriculum as insight				
• Curriculum with postmodern elements				
e. Curriculum balanced and articulated.				

(continued on next page)

Figure 2.6 *Continued*

Program Planning Checklist	Begun	1 yr. Short-term	5 yr. Long-term	Meets State Guide-Lines
33. Program evaluation:				
a. Conduct formative evaluation process.				
• Seek the views of administrators, parents, teachers, and students.				
• Conduct interviews and value others' perspectives				
• Contrast program goals with actual performance				
• Utilize multiple sources of information; do not rely only on interviews.				
• Use observations to document changes in the program.				
• Seek depth of understanding gained from looking at student participation in classroom activity, extracurricular activity, home activity, faculty meetings, and school board meetings.				
b. Conduct summative evaluation:				
• Decide, based on formative data, what should stay, what should change, and what should go.				
34. Other				

Adapted from Reichert (1990, October). .

CASE EXAMPLE Four Years as a Consulting Teacher for the Gifted and Talented

by Peggy Hirzel, Medina Schools, Ohio *(Used with permission of author)*

As I sat in the first meeting of the new consulting teacher program I felt overwhelmed. I was the "new kid on the block," having been hired just days before. I had been a substitute teacher in the district for six years, but this was a leap into uncharted waters. As the meeting progressed, I realized even the most experienced teachers there were also treading on unfamiliar territory.

Our director of instruction led the meeting. She explained that our current program for the gifted and talented was not consistent with the new goals of our district. "Success for all" was a central theme of our philosophy and "success for some" no longer fit. Our job would be to create an inclusionary program that would provide enrichment for the greatest number of students possible. We could no longer use only an IQ score to measure a student's talent. We needed to look at children in terms of multiple intelligences and find ways to help classroom teachers challenge all kids. As I sat nodding in agreement, inside I wondered if it was possible for such an ideal to become a reality. We laid out the beginnings of a basic framework for the program, but I left feeling very unsure of my direction.

The first few months were both exciting and very difficult. I worried about developing relationships with classroom teachers. How could I keep that delicate balance of being readily available without being pushy?

My first attempts were met with polite skepticism. When I offered to meet with teachers to plan differentiated units, I was met with comments like "Well, I'm not sure if I need anything now, but I'll let you know." I knew I had my work cut out for me.

Finally, the sixth grade teachers were receptive to working with me. They were happy to have another hand in the classroom and were my greatest supporters. We worked together on fiction studies, math enrichment, social studies projects, and science experiments. They truly helped me get started and gain the confidence I needed to progress with the other grade levels.

As the months went by, I began working more with the fourth and fifth grade multiage teachers. They were looking for math problem-solving activities, so I began teaching weekly whole class lessons. I offered the same service to the other fourth and fifth grade teachers. Two of them used me occasionally and two of them never used me. Fortunately, these two teachers did not have any identified gifted children in their classrooms. I periodically asked if there was any way I could help and provided biweekly challenge activity packets, but my services were not used in these classrooms. Although this was disappointing, my time was being filled to capacity with the other classrooms and an inservice program with which I was involved.

The first year was filled with confusion, frustration, and long hours resulting in exhaustion. However, there was also a great deal to be positive about. I developed many strong relationships with other teachers. Ten out of twelve teachers were using my services. More importantly, though, I felt the program was off to a successful start because I had affected many children. I was able to work with many more children who needed enrichment than I would have in a traditional gifted program.

As Year Four progresses, I am amazed how much has changed. I am no longer devising ways to make myself available to classroom teachers. Rather, I find myself spread too thin and know I need to cut back on my teaching schedule.

The sixth grade was moved to the middle school and with rapid growth in our district, the consulting teachers began serving grades 3, 4, and 5. I now have 16 teachers to whom I am accountable. We have estimated that a consulting teacher should serve 10 or less teachers for optimal service. Needless to say, I am feeling a bit overloaded.

Many positive changes have happened over the past four years. I have developed good working relationships as well as personal friendships with many teachers in my building as well as with the coordinator of services for the gifted and talented and the other five consulting teachers at the other five elementary schools. Four years of experience have also helped me to develop confidence in my abilities as a consulting teacher. I enjoy the flexibility of working with students in a variety of ways—whole class lessons, individual research, small groups in my room, or cluster groups in the regular classroom. Every day is different, which suits my personality. There are still frustrations which I assume will always be part of the job. There are still a few teachers who are resistant to inclusionary services for talent development. When the third grades were added last year, it was in many ways like starting all over again. I needed to build relationships with a new group of teachers. I found this more difficult than in the first year because my time was more limited due to fourth and fifth grade activities and whole school projects.

When teachers ask me for services, I find it very difficult to refuse. Unfortunately, I have reached a point where I need to do that. I am also spending too much time teaching math (I have 15 math classes a week). I would like to spend more time on language arts and science.

Although the consulting teacher job is not an easy one, it is rewarding. I feel that I am reaching many children who would not receive enrichment with a traditional program for the gifted and talented. I teach an afterschool hands-on math and science class with a fifth grade teacher. Only five of the 27 students are identified as gifted, but almost all of these students are incredibly insightful and inquisitive in the area of science. These students help to remind me that there are many more ways of displaying intelligence than IQ tests. The consulting teacher program helps to provide enrichment to kids who need it, whether they test well or not. It makes the work worth it.

Figure 2.7   Consulting Teacher Services

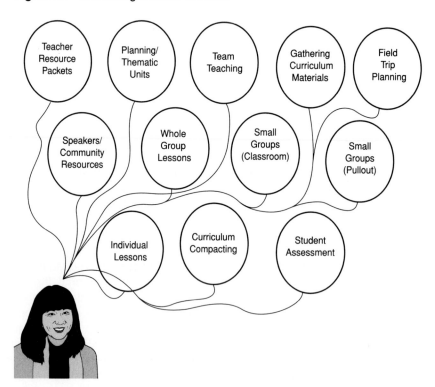

SUMMARY

1. Most states now have provisions for the education of talented students.
2. A district planning a program for the talented should plan for administrator awareness. This awareness should include a knowledge of state and federal provisions and legal issues related to talented students.
3. A district planning committee should be constituted and they should first conduct a needs assessment to learn what is already being done; new ideas should be considered.
4. Among the first tasks should be a written philosophy.
5. The district may choose among several commonly used models for gifted education, including the pullout model, the self-contained model, and various forms of grouping.
6. Choosing the teachers for the talented is very important. Teachers of the talented should have several special qualifications, such as interest in and liking for talented students, and special training in the education of the talented.
7. Program evaluation should be formative, summative, and should take into account political, psychological, and administrative functions. Evaluation outcomes should be guided by good evaluation questions based on the goals.
8. A typical inclusionary program is described in the case example.

3 IDENTIFICATION OF THE ACADEMICALLY TALENTED: HIGH-IQ TALENT AND SPECIFIC ACADEMIC TALENT

FOCUSING QUESTIONS

1. Look at a nearby program for talented children. How do they identify their students?
2. Discuss the concept of identifying talent *potential*.
3. Consider the giftedness construct with relationship to high IQ.
4. Why is it necessary to have a guiding theory in the identification of the talented?
5. Discuss how the challenges of identification obsess educators of the talented.
6. What are the advantages and disadvantages of using multiple means of identification?
7. When would a district sacrifice efficiency for effectiveness? When would a district sacrifice effectiveness for efficiency?
8. How is nomination affected by the state of the curriculum and the training of teachers?
9. Look at how matrices are used in identification in a district with which you are familiar. Comment on their use.
10. What is the difference between an SAI and an IQ?
11. You are a consultant for a school district. How would you identify high IQ or general intellectual ability and specific academic ability?
12. You are a consultant for a school district. How does the concept of *predictive behaviors* affect the identification of students?

Figure 3.1 Overview of Chapter 3

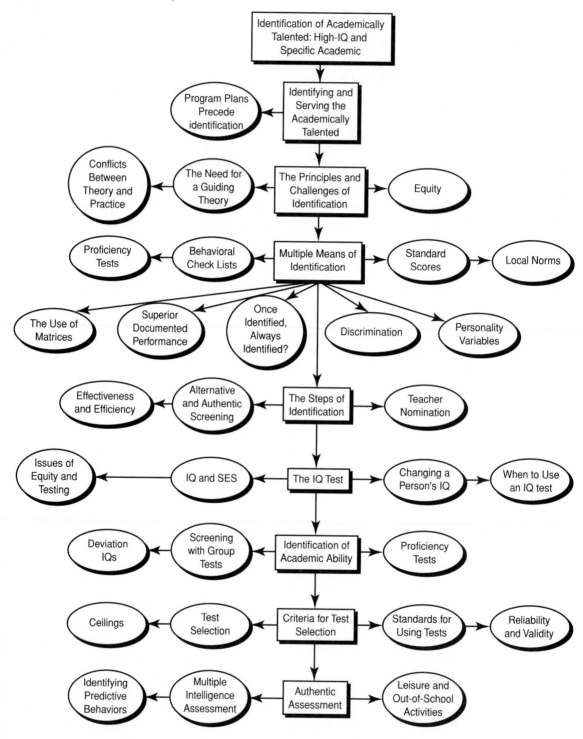

It was just a neighborhood gathering, a birthday party for someone's fortieth birthday. The neighbors were sitting in the backyard, eating hot dogs, and one of the new people asked Marilyn Potter what she did for a living. Marilyn said, "I teach academically talented children." Then a discussion very familiar to teachers of the academically talented began. "How do you find academically talented children?" was the first question. "How do you know they are talented?" "What do you do with academically talented children?" "Aren't all children talented?" Marilyn was used to this kind of attention; she had been an educator of talented children for 10 years now, and she herself had seen the definition of *gifted* change to *academically talented*, the dimensions of giftedness refined, and the identification processes standardized in her state. By now she had answered all the questions people could think up. Parents of young children were especially interested in talented children. Some of them thought they had an academically talented child, and some of them were glad they didn't have an academically talented child.

Marilyn often felt that she was like the doctor or lawyer at the cocktail party who gets asked for medical or legal opinions. Marilyn took a deep breath and listened to the questioner, whose name was John. "How do you identify academically talented children?"

"Well," Marilyn said, "there are guidelines in our state for how to identify the different types of talented children."

"There are different types of talented children? Didn't they used to call them gifted children? I hate that word, gifted."

"Well, we are trying not to use the word 'gifted' as much nowadays," Marilyn said. "And the reason is that it sets people off—people like you."

"OK. I thought gifted children are those with genius IQs and talented children are those who are good at skills, like athletics or art."

"Well, high-IQ kids are most recently called *academically talented*, but there are other children who are talented also. There are children who do well on a standardized achievement test—kids with high IQs do well on aptitude tests. Aptitude tests are supposed to show different abilities than achievement tests do; aptitude tests supposedly show the child's potential, while achievement tests show what the child knows, or has achieved. However, in practice, these are often the same children, especially if the requirement for being academically talented is to score high in *both* reading and math, for example. Our state recognizes that a child may be talented in one area, for example, mathematics, and not be talented in another area, for example, language arts. Most people are talented in this way—they are good in one specific area and may be average in other areas. An IQ means that a quotient has been calculated, and in order to get a high IQ, a student must be high in all areas."

"And then," Marilyn continued, taking another breath, "there are the kids who are talented in the visual and performing arts, who may get average scores on intelligence and achievement tests, but who possess extraordinary potential for achievement as artists, dancers, actors, or musicians. Our state calls these children talented also."

"That makes sense," John said. "Are there any other kinds of talented children?"

"Well, some states identify children who are creatively talented, although our state doesn't."

"Creatively talented? You mean, good in art or good in writing?"

"No. They mean good in fluency and flexibility and things like that. That's a hard thing to do, because every child who hasn't been abused is probably creative in kindergarten," Marilyn said. "But they use creativity tests and checklists. Some experts think that you can't be talented unless you're a creative producer, or that creativity underlies all expressions of talent, and trying to identify students who have creative ability might not be such a good idea. It's so nebulous, creative talent."

"Well, you're the expert," John said. "You lost me there. I bet they try to identify them because they're afraid they're going to miss someone."

"The whole identification idea is to identify the kids who have the *potential* to become talented adults," Marilyn said. "We sort of give it our best guess. We say, because you have these characteristics as a child, we *guess*, we *predict* that you're going to be a talented adult. The test scores are just good guesses. High test scores and good grades say you'll probably do well in school, and if you do well in school, you'll get into college and if you get into college you'll get a decent job and do well in life."

"Well, my IQ is only 115," John said, "and I've done all right in life. I wasn't gifted, though. I always got As and Bs. I went to law school, graduated, and the practice is doing just fine."

"But there are other, more important factors that make for high achievement in life," Marilyn said. "You had the family backing and the motivation, didn't you?"

John nodded. "Any other kinds of talent? This is really interesting."

"Well, some states identify leadership talent, although our state doesn't. Those kids are the ones who have been leaders and who have the potential to be adult leaders. And, of course, there are the athletes. Varsity athletes could be called talented children, too, talented in psychomotor areas."

"Well, I know about talented athletes," John said. "Did you watch the World Series last fall?"

"Yes. And when you think of how we educate athletes in realizing their talents, you have the ideal program, if you think of it," Marilyn said. "We hire specially trained teachers for them to coach them in the development of their talents. We have a special budget for their education. We find their level of competition, even if it's across town or in the next county, and, if they are good enough, we have state and national tournaments so they can play at their levels of competition. We build special facilities for them and buy special equipment so they can realize the fulfillment of their talent. If we did that for the others, for the high-IQ or general intellectual high-IQ kids, for the specific academic talent kids, for the visual and performing arts kids, for the kids with talent for inventing or for visual arts, we'd have quite a program for talented students."

"Impossible," John said. "That's a pipe dream." His eyes wandered off. "Can I get you another hot dog?"

➤ ➤ ➤ ➤ ➤ ➤ ➤ ➤ ➤ ➤ ➤ ➤ ➤ ➤ ➤ ➤ ➤ ➤

This vignette illustrates that there is great interest in talent development and also that there is confusion about where talent is manifested. Most people have quite a narrow view of giftedness and talent, believing that gifted children are those who score high on an IQ test. In fact, this belief is so pervasive, Tannenbaum (1986) said that while most experts on giftedness say that defining giftedness as high IQ is too simple, they then go on to discuss giftedness "on the basis of studies of high-IQ children." He cautioned that such presuppositions and generalities will trap educators forever in the "giftedness-equals-high-IQ myth" (p. 394). For many years in the field of education of the gifted and talented, people argued about the best means for identification of academically talented children. Today, various states have written guidelines for identification. Few argue that students with great school-related ability, however defined, should receive a special education from the schools.

In 1997, James Borland of Columbia University commented on recent developments. He said that most programs are too inclusive; that is, they include too many students. He called it the "roach motel phenomenon—kids check in but they don't check out." Students are admitted early and then more students are added. Students are rarely removed from programs. This is similar to the Lake Wobegon Phenomenon, where "all the students are above average." The cause of this is that programs are seen by parents as status symbols. The parents advocate for their kids forcefully and persistently, and the administrators cave in under the onslaught (J. Borland, personal communication, College of William and Mary National Curriculum Conference, March 1997).

IDENTIFYING AND SERVING THE ACADEMICALLY TALENTED

As noted in Chapter 2, before identifying students, the district, community, region—whatever body is doing the identifying—must agree on what talents they are going to identify. What is the school's job? Should the school identify and serve all of the various types of gifted and talented children that are listed in the federal definition of giftedness and talent, the Marland definition? Is it the province of the school to serve the creatively talented, or the visual and performing arts talented, or the leadership talented? Should the school emphasize all eight of Gardner's intelligences and identify talent potential in them? Or what about the up and coming theory of Sternberg (1997)? Should the schools identify creative, executive, and practical information-processing intelligence as Sternberg pervasively suggests? It is certainly the province of the schools to serve the academically talented. But can the schools serve *very* high-IQ students appropriately?

What is appropriate for the school? Some theoreticians such as Borland (1989) argue that the school properly should have in its target population students who have a need for programming in the high-IQ or general intellectual and specific academic ability areas. He said that the schools should be in the business of training intellectuals, and that the schools should be wary of programs for the talented that do not serve their needs. He said these programs should be in the business of "preparing the students to dedicate themselves to the life of the mind, or at least to hold it in special esteem" (p. 36). He indicated that too many students are being identified for programs for the academically talented (Borland, 1997).

Students are usually identified for their intellectual potential as indicated by test scores. The program for the education of the talented should be designed to challenge the talented who have shown predictive behaviors for realization of talent in certain domains that are appropriate for the school to foster—academic, athletic, vocational, and the arts.

Program Plans Must Precede Identification

I may be belaboring the point, but when identifying talented children, there is one major corollary principle that must be kept in mind. As discussed in Chapter 2, identification must be paired with programming. Programming must be congruent with the type of talent that has been identified. This seems very logical, but in reality, programming for talented children often has nothing to do with the strengths of the identified child. For example, a child may have been identified as having strong mathematical abilities, and the program he or she is put into emphasizes the reading of the classics. This is not to say that the reading of the classics is not desirable or necessary for the student who is strong in mathematics, but often this child desperately needs a fast-paced, in-depth program in mathematics, above and beyond what is being provided in the regular classroom, where the mathematically talented child is bored and dulled by the repetitious drill that the rest of the students need. This child may have been identified as talented in mathematics and then be put into a situation where his strengths are not developed.

Elementary school programming for the academically talented often has as a weakness an overemphasis on language arts at the expense of mathematics and science. The reason may be that elementary school teachers are often unsure of themselves in mathematics and science; in fact, they often became elementary school teachers because of their hesitations about their math abilities back when they were making career decisions. On the other hand, elementary school teachers are often enthralled with reading and with children's literature, and are stronger in verbal skills than in mathematics. When elementary teachers think of enrichment for the academically talented students in their schools, they often prefer to teach to their own strengths, which are often strengths in the verbal areas. If the teacher of the academically talented is weak in mathematics, programming in these cases should involve special teachers who specialize in mathematics and science in order that the young talented learners who are identified can be adequately served.

Often children who have been identified for different kinds of talent are put into the same class for special programming. Identification must be followed with suitable programming that speaks to a student's talent area.

THE PRINCIPLES AND CHALLENGES OF IDENTIFICATION

The most influential nationwide report on identification was the Richert, Alvino, and McDonnel assessment in 1982. In this report, the authors said that the identification of the talented must follow six basic principles:

1. *Advocacy*—the identification procedures should be for the benefit of all students.
2. *Defensibility*—the best research should be used.
3. *Equity*—the civil rights of all students should be safeguarded and disadvantaged talented students should be identified.
4. *Pluralism*—a broad definition of talent should be used.
5. *Comprehensiveness*—various kinds of talented students should be identified and served.
6. *Pragmatism*—the district should be permitted to make local modifications of the guidelines and tools.

Equity

The major challenge of identification is the challenge of equity. That the tests easily identify children who are from the middle and upper middle socioeconomic classes is a given. Jamieson McKenzie, in a 1986 study, showed that significant relationships existed between participation in gifted and talented programs and the variables of race, per-pupil expenditures, assessed property value of the districts, and socioeconomic status. The richer districts spent more money on gifted and talented programs, and had more programs.

In the late 1980s and early 1990s, the U.S. Department of Education Office of Educational Research and Improvement granted several million dollars for the Jacob K. Javits Gifted and Talented Students Education Program, seeking to find alternative means of identifying underserved gifted and talented children. Projects were funded in order to develop assessment instruments to identify talented African-Americans, Native Hawaiians and Filipinos, limited English proficient (LEP) Hispanic students, economically disadvantaged students, handicapped students, rural students, underachieving students, Native American students, learning disabled students, young students, and migrant students. Standardized tests have historically not identified as many disadvantaged children, and these federal projects sought alternative ways to do so. Many of these are described in this book.

However, standardized tests should not be burned like the books in *Fahrenheit 451*. Though the charges that the tests are biased against minority and economically disadvantaged groups have been loud, many statisticians and testing experts note that the validation efforts and reliability studies have indicated that the tests are more well constructed now than ever and most evidence shows that they are not so biased (Anastasi, 1989).

For example, look at the Metropolitan Achievement Tests, Seventh Edition (1993). This test was standardized in a very thorough way (Finley, 1995). First a review and analysis of widely used school textbooks was conducted. State and local curricula and objectives were consulted. Aims of the professional organizations of teachers such as the National Council of Teachers of English, of Mathematics, for the Social Studies, and the National Science Teachers' Association were considered. The items were then written with the goal to assess higher-level thinking skills in these content areas. Fourteen levels of the test were developed and the items were classified according to whether they focused on knowledge, comprehension, or thinking skills.

The people who wrote the items included former teachers who were independent consultants and freelance writers. The tryout books contained 22,500 items. Teachers' reactions to the items were solicited.

About 750 students at each grade level tried out the items during one 15-day period. The students also took the Sixth Edition of the Metropolitan Achievement Test so that the test-makers could scale the old and new editions. A stratified random sample of 197 districts from 39 states and the District of Columbia participated. A panel made up of African-Americans, Hispanics, Asians, and a women's issues advocate reviewed the results. They pinpointed items that showed gender, ethnic, socioeconomic, cultural, or regional bias, as well as items that showed stereotyping.

The final items selected reflected certain criteria such as whether the content was appropriate, difficult enough for the grade, interesting, absent of bias, and showed a difference between the highest and lowest scorers. The items were balanced so that the cognitive skills were represented across all the grades and subtests. Then a spring and a fall standardization were conducted. Over 230,000 students participated. Again the sample was stratified according to socioeconomic status, geographical distribution, and urban/rural/suburban, public and nonpublic schools. This information came from the 1990 U.S. Census. If a school refused to participate, a comparable school was chosen from a matching stratified random sample. The students were also administered the companion group aptitude test, the Otis-Lennon School Ability Test, in order to confirm that the tests were comparable. Separate, smaller studies were conducted with third graders, with students using calculators, and with the National Assessment of Educational Progress (NAEP) tests. From this impressive description of how a popular and widely-used standardized test is, indeed, standardized, one can see the expense and the care that it takes to make one of these tests, and those who suspect bias should take into account that such deliberate processes were used to avoid bias. Many of the checklists and "quickie" intelligence tests that are in common use have not been developed with such a large norming group.

There are other reasons for bias in identification of minority and economically disadvantaged (the "children of the dream," as discussed in Chapter 12). One is the referral process. Teachers underrefer students who are culturally diverse. A second is academic expectations. Teachers seem to have lower academic expectations for these students. A third is attitude. Usually schools have been taught to focus on deficiences and not on strengths. (See the Case Example in this chapter on p. 130). Some students were, shockingly, called culturally *deprived*, or even worse, culturally *deficient*. St. Jean (1996) said that the focus on deficiencies "has made it difficult to recognize the strengths of these children, and has been criticized because it has diverted attention away from students who have achieved, despite the characteristics of cultural differences" (p. 1).

Other alternative methods for identification, besides group-administered standardized tests, are the administration of individual tests, the case study, the forming of a broad talent pool, the use of local norms, seeking information from parents and community, noting leisure interests, and the observation of predictive behaviors.

Moon, Feldhusen, and Kelly (1991) suggested that a case study approach is the best way to identify disadvantaged children. Borland and Wright (1992a, 1992b, 1993) utilized two Javits grants in identifying young gifted children in one of the poorest schools in New York City. The results were mixed due to family instability and other variables. Richert (1990) recommended that schools should seek to name, in screening, 25 percent of children in any school in the first steps of identification. Howley, Howley, and Pendarvis (1986, 1995) advocated the collection of local norms for disadvantaged populations. They said that the very purpose of trying to find culture-fair assessment instruments is to give children from all the subgroups instruction that is suitable to their cognitive levels. "It seems reasonable to look to artifacts of culture and of testing to explain the lower mean performance of blacks and other minorities (notably the poor) on standardized tests" (1995, p. 39). If one believes that talent is found equally in all ethnic and cultural groups, one must carefully view the fact that the tests continue to identify predominantly mainstream children.

However, with the current rush for total "inclusion," with the call for "equity" in "detracking America," that is, to do away with all ability grouping (see Chapter 2), educators and policymakers must not forget that a substantial proportion of students could be called academically talented, and whether or not their least restrictive educational environment can happen in a full-inclusion classroom should be considered very carefully. Even within the heterogeneous classroom there is ranking and differentiation among individuals and groups. A study by Cohen and Lotan (1995) pointed out "educators have already discovered that they have exchanged severe problems of status differences between tracks and ability groups for equally severe problems of status differences within classrooms." They went on to say, "Many perceptive teachers have also found that cooperative learning techniques so widely recommended for this setting do not solve these status problems" (p. 118).

The Need for a Guiding Theory

The theoreticians in the field of talent education debate endlessly. What theory of intelligence, what theory of creativity, what theory of genius should guide our identification of talented children? Since much evidence is available that high-IQ children have a good chance of becoming productive and successful adults, the high-IQ theory prevails in the schools. The high-IQ theorists, Lewis Terman and his colleagues (1925, 1930, 1947, 1959), who conducted the most important longitudinal study of high-IQ people, and Harris (1990), who followed the students studied by Leta Hollingworth (1926, 1942), as well as Subotnik, Kassan, Summers, and Wasser (1993), who followed up the students at the Hunter College Elementary School, found that people with high IQs have generally successful lives. Other theoreticians about intelligence are Howard Gardner (1983), who said there are eight different kinds of intelligence. Gardner advocated that each intelligence be looked at directly, and that the identification tasks not be verbally biased. He predicted that few children would turn out to show "all high or all low scores across the intelligences" (Kirschenbaum, 1990b, p. 27). Both Renzulli (1988) and Gardner (in Kirschenbaum, 1990b) viewed the identification of talent in childhood as the identification of potential.

In the SOI theory, giftedness is evident in a score in the high 90s on any one of the 26 subtests (Meeker, 1969). Another theoretical example is the triarchic theory of the information-processing theorists such as Sternberg (1985), who said that intelligence has three components. Psychosocial theorists such as Tannenbaum (1983, 1997) and Renzulli (1977) said that adult potential achievement occurs when several test, personality, and behavioral factors are present. Renzulli said a talented adult needs above-average general intelligence or IQ, creativity, and task commitment. Gagné has proposed a frank difference between gifted aptitudes and talent abilities. Feldman has proposed a developmental theory called nonuniversal theory that would be encompassing enough to provide a context for all the variables in considering giftedness and talent (Feldman, 1997; Feldman, Csikszentmihalyi, and Gardner, 1994). My Pyramid of Talent Development and the inclusive giftedness construct (Chapter 1), where high IQ is nice to have but not absolutely necessary, also attempts to provide a context for many variables (Piirto, 1994, 1995a). In fact, the discussions about identification are so endless as to be boring. A look at the program of any conference about educating talented children has a sizable proportion of the sessions devoted to identification. Veteran practitioners in the field are often heard to say "Let's get on with it. Enough, already," especially when most of the "new" methods are really "old" methods recycled and recast into the IQ test mold.

Conflicts Between Theory and Practice

Various theoreticians insist that their own theories are the ones that capture what true talent potential is, and they suggest various means of identifying talent. However, schools generally find these means too complicated. Gardner's theory, for example, requires documented observations of small children interacting with materials, tasks, and with each other, and Sternberg's theory requires a new test that has been in development but that doesn't have the years of validation that the current tests have. The schools want a quick, foolproof, and cheap system for identifying talented students. The conflict between theory and practice is great. Some of the issues follow:

1. *Theoreticians* say that the use of individually administered intelligence tests is the best way of finding talented children. *Schools* say they cannot afford to test each child individually with the long, complex tests that seem to be necessary to determine academic talent.

2. *Theoreticians* say that the present individual intelligence tests are inadequate, because they only measure a few aspects of what we now consider to be intelligence. *Schools* say that these intelligence tests have been around for years, and if the tests are inadequate, they are still the best we have.

3. *Theoreticians* say that much testing, for example proficiency testing, is foolish, that no one has unequivocally proven that the tests have predictive validity; that is, that the tests find children who become successful adults. *Schools* say they need numbers and accountability, and that administering tests is the best way to get the numbers and to show they are accountable; that they are doing their jobs.

4. *Theoreticians* say that portfolios, auditions, and past performance are the best way to find children with talent in all areas, as is done for the visual and performing arts. *Schools* say that they do not have the trained personnel, nor the time, to collect portfolios or to conduct auditions; besides, anecdotal records are illegal in some districts.

Unfortunately, as with most large institutions, entrenchment and inertia are two hallmarks of the educational establishment. In fact, few if any changes have occurred during the past 15 years of so-called school reform, and the ideals of Goals 2000 are far from being met; this also applies to those of us who have a part in identifying and educating the potentially talented. Much of the literature in the field essentially rehashes familiar ideas.

MULTIPLE MEANS OF IDENTIFICATION

The most prevalent identification models being used call for multiple means of identification, so that children won't be labeled by means of a single score on a single test on a certain day. It is illegal in some states to use a single test score to place a child, but often this is only lip service because the individualized intelligence test score is often the justification used for placing a child in a special program. If a child scores above 130 on a Stanford-Binet intelligence test, and the child has poor grades and poor test scores on the standardized achievement test, we say that the child is an *underachiever*, and we implicitly believe the Stanford-Binet score is the true score.

Tests measure different things, yet the assumption is often made that tests are related and reliable indicators of giftedness and that giftedness is indicated by the test score. Test scores vary depending on the test given. A study by Tyler-Wood and Carri (1991) showed that it *does* matter which test is used. Different tests identify different children. They administered the (1) Otis-Lennon School Ability Test (OLSAT), a group test; (2) the Cognitive Abilities Test (CoGAT) group test; (3) the Stanford-Binet Intelligence Scale: L-M individual test; and (4) the Stanford-Binet Intelligence Scale: Fourth Edition individual test to a group of 21 randomly selected talented students with an average age of 9 years 6 months. They found that there were significant differences in the students' scores. The students scored significantly lower on the Otis-Lennon School Ability Test than on the Stanford-Binet Intelligence Scale: L-M and the Stanford-Binet Intelligence Scales: Fourth Edition tests. Scores on the Stanford-Binet Intelligence Scale: Fourth Edition were significantly lower than scores on the Stanford-Binet Intelligence Scale: L-M tests. Although the students had all met their state's requirement for inclusion in talent development education programs, only five of them would have qualified if all four tests had been administered, and 17 would have been eliminated if one or another test were the only one used.

Proficiency Tests

Currently many states have begun to require proficiency tests. The commonplace use of standardized achievement tests is diminishing. If the mandated state-wide proficiency tests, which usually measure floors and not ceilings of achievement, can be used to identify academically talented students, much money will be saved and students will not have to submit to multiple days of testing. However, a caution should be issued: the studies have not been done to determine a relationship between the particular state's proficiency test and scores on standardized achievement tests at the high levels. What do the proficiency tests measure and how is what they measure similar to what is being measured on common standardized tests?

Behavioral Checklists

Other kinds of information collected on a child are gleaned from behavioral check-lists given to teachers, parents, and peers. These checklists are often variations of the Renzulli, Smith, White, Callahan, and Hartman (1976) Scales for Rating Behavioral Characteristics of Superior Students. There is a Learning Characteristics Scale on which the teacher, parent, or peer rates a list of items using the following choices: 1—Seldom; 2—Occasionally; 3—Considerably; 4—Almost always. Some items are long and the length of the item might be a problem. A weighted total is often computed for such behavioral checklists, which may also be problematic.

However, the checklist approach is pedagogically justifiable, because talented adults were most often talented children, and they demonstrated behaviors predictive of their adult gifts (Piirto, 1992a, 1992b, 1992c). The more specific the checklist, it seems, the better the predictions. For example, writers were often voracious, independent, compulsive readers, as in the Case Example at the end of this chapter.

Thus standardized assessment for personality traits should be avoided, as should checklists purporting to identify young students for special programs by checking off such behaviors as "has a sense of humor" or "is curious." Don't all children exibit these behaviors? Howley, Howley, and Pendarvis (1995) noted: "Many such check-lists (rather than describing observable behaviors) merely implement a system for recording subjective judgments about undefined personal characteristics" (p. 90).

Superior Documented Performance

Grades and scores on other tests, such as tests of critical thinking or problem solving, tests of creativity, teacher-made tests, and competency tests, are also often included in the multiple means called for by most state laws. These are often placed on a matrix such as Baldwin's matrix (1984) where the various kinds of information are weighted and tallied, and then the children are ranked. It usually turns out that the children with the highest IQs and the highest achievement test scores get the highest tallies, because of the weighted scores.

The Use of Matrices

A *matrix* is a chart used to enter different kinds of data about the same person. Matrices are often added up using weighted totals. Figure 3.2 shows an example of a matrix.

Critics of matrices point out that matrices falsely report the data, because even a five-point differential can hide significant differences in children. Feldhusen and Baska (1985) cautioned about combining assessment data. Feldhusen, Baska, and Womble (1981) said that standardizing different data should take place, perhaps by using standard scores or T scores. Borland (1989) cautioned users of matrices, saying "I fear that in most cases they are misused and may be doing more harm than good" (p. 106). The "fatal flaw" in their use comes when one computes the final index, because it is impossible to say what the final index represents. Borland said:

> In the Baldwin Matrix . . . one is asked to add together IQ, achievement test scores (double weighted due to the inclusion of a composite score), four disparate subscales from an un-validated teacher nomination form, other teacher recommendations, peer nominations,

Figure 3.2 Example of a Matrix

Name _____

Date _____

_____

W.I.N.G.S. Identification Matrix

_____

Matrix I (Initial consideration)

WISC-R	_____ Points	127–130	131–133	134–137	138–140	140+
or CSI/CAT	_____	2	4	6	8	10
Composite	%ile Points	95	96	97	98	99
	_____	1	2	3	4	5
Reading	%ile Points	95	96	97	98	99
	_____	1	2	3	4	5
or Language	%ile Points	95	96	97	98	99
	_____	1	2	3	4	5
Renzulli-Hartman Creativity	Points	26–28	29–31	32–34	35–37	38–40
	_____	2	4	6	8	10

Total Score _____

_____ Qualifies for second phase   _____ Doesn't qualify

_____ Needs WISC-R   _____ Further testing refused

_____ Needs W-J

(continued on next page)

and some unspecified index of psychomotor ability. What is the result? One ends up with a melange, a hodgepodge whose meaning is unclear. This is analogous to combining a family's income, home equity, number of children, average height, and number of food-processor attachments in order to derive a "quality of life index." (p. 108)

Matrices provide a false illusion of fairness. Students have to jump over many hurdles that are seemingly unrelated to what the programming will be. Adding unreliable data such as checklist data to reliable data such as an individually administered achievement or ability test just doesn't make good pedagogical sense. Matrices should be used to point out strengths, even if in just one area, and should not be added or totaled.

Figure 3.2 *Continued*

W.I.N.G.S. Identification Matrix

Matrix II (Second round of qualifications)

WISC-R	_____ I.Q.	127-130	131-133	134-137	138-140	141+
or CSI	_____ Points	4	8	12	16	20
Woodcock-Johnson Reading	%ile Points	95	96	97	98	99
	_____	3	6	9	12	15
Woodcock-Johnson Writing/Language	%ile Points	95	96	97	98	99
	_____	3	6	9	12	15
Renzulli-Hartman Creativity	Points	24-28	20-31	32-34	35-37	38-40
	_____	2	4	6	8	10

Total Score _____

Method of Qualification:

_____ General Intelligence Ability   _____ Doesn't qualify
(IQ+Ach/Comp+Doc/Sup/Perf)

_____ Specific Academic Ability
(95th %ile+Doc/Sup/Perf)

Additional performance data _____

_____

_____

From *The Wellington Schools Identification Matrix* by C. W. Little, 1992. Unpublished document.
Copyright 1992 The Wellington Schools, Wellington, Ohio. Reprinted with permission.

Use of Multiple Means Can Be Discriminatory

Most of the literature in the field indicates that multiple means should be used to identify students in order to be more fair. However, Richert (1990) warned that using multiple methods for identification can also be detrimental to poor children, because the types of multiple methods are often biased toward identifying white, middle-class children, giving a disproportionate weight to standardized tests. Richert said multiple measures tend to reinforce the conception that being gifted is having a high score on a standardized test, and thus multiple measures "actually exacerbate elitism in identification."

Users of matrices have often intended their use to permit inclusiveness rather than exclusiveness, reasoning that more information is better. If one takes Richert's argument (and Frasier's (1991)—see Chapter 12) that even one type of information should be considered as qualification for the talent pool, and that the requirement to have many scores is discriminatory, one must ask the question of which score, which information? Richert's argument was that this one indication should be enough to have the child considered for placement in a program. One indication such as this gives a hint for the identifiers. The case study at the close of this chapter is an illustration. This is referral by *predictive behavior*. In summary, the use of matrices should be viewed with skepticism if the totals are derived from weighted categories. They are valuable, though, in showing where talent may lie. That is, one should not total the matrix by adding up the weighted scores; one should just look to see where strengths lie. One strength is enough for curriculum differentiation. If a child is strong in mathematics, mathematics should be looked at for differentiation. It is not necessary for this child to be strong in reading also.

The Use of Standard Scores

Feldhusen, Baska, and Womble (1981) advocated the use of standard scores, which would correct for and show the differences discussed in the previous section. A standard score is a score that is expressed as a deviation from a population mean. No matter what standardized test a student takes, the score can be put on a distribution chart in what are called *standard deviations*. A standard score indicates how far from the mean, or average, the student's score appears. The advantage of standard scores is that they are based on measurement units that are equal and, thus, they can be averaged. For example, a deviation IQ is a standard score. The mean is 100, and one standard deviation above the mean is 115, while two standard deviations above the mean is 130. Students who score two standard deviations above the mean score are in the 98th percentile. Figure 3.3 gives an indication of how the use of standard scores would equalize the information. The scores should be traced vertically, from top to bottom, to indicate comparisons.

One fact has surfaced in all these years of striving to equitably identify talented children, and that is that the unfairness is vested on poverty-stricken, culturally penalized children of whatever ethnicity. Certainly, ethnicity is not a primary discriminator among children when considering their performance on tests. Children from poor families whose parents are well educated (for example, families of struggling artists or actors) do not score lower. The influence of a lack of early childhood intervention in areas such as nutrition, mental stimulation, and safety, and not only of poverty, should be considered in identifying talented children. Early childhood identification and an enriched preschool education should be priorities (see Chapter 5), especially in economically heterogeneous districts.

In economically homogeneous districts, identification by means of test scores is more accurate. In a one-company mining town such as my hometown, for example, where most of the families work for the company, and where the highest incomes in town may be those of certain merchants such as car dealers, test scores and grades can be used with greater certainty that the children could benefit from special programming for the talented. In a multicultural urban environment, the students may come

Figure 3.3   Normal Curve and Derived Scores with Application to the Talented

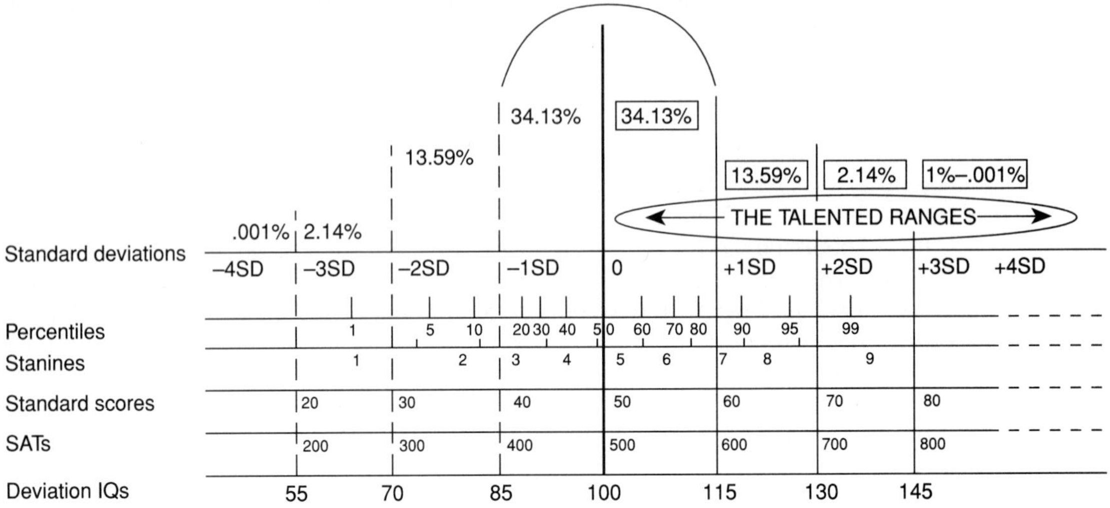

from homes of greater differentiation in terms of income and privilege. Some students may spend their weekends at their country homes or skiing in Aspen, and others may spend their weekends watching crack dealers sell drugs. Such districts should, even must, collect local norms and conduct case studies, choosing students for special talent programming by using unconventional means, even if these means cost more.

The Use of Local Norms in Identification

The U.S. Office of Civil Rights has approved a process that uses the collection of local norms to prevent inequity. Few school systems use local norms, but the practice should become more prevalent. If a disproportionate number of white, middle-class students is being chosen for special education for their talents and potential, the school district should look at test scores and select, for each group (by advantage, disadvantage, race, cultural, ethnicity, or gender), the top percentage of students. The school system should collect this data for several years, and establish the cutoff scores for the number of children (Richert recommended the top 25 percent) the district wants to include in its talent pool. The district should establish norms for the top 25 percent poor African-Americans, poor whites, poor Latinos, poor Native Americans, poor Asians, etc.

Pendarvis, Howley, and Howley (1990) said that the collection of local norms at least uses standardized and validated instruments rather than the commonly used and misused behavioral checklists, creativity tests, and nonverbal tests, which are often poorly validated and not reliable. Howley, Howley, and Pendarvis (1995) also said, "By establishing local norms, by using tests normed on minority groups, and by implementing quotas, schools can ensure that gifted programs serve poor and oppressed groups much more equitably than they now do" (p. 93).

However, Mills, Ablard, and Brody (1993) cautioned that using local norms should be done carefully: "Local norms certainly appear preferable for use with minority and disadvantaged populations, but only for local programming purposes." In collecting local norms, decision makers must take care that the students come from similar backgrounds; Mills, Ablard, and Brody said districts should not "make comparative judgments across populations" (p. 184).

Nevertheless, in striving for a broad pool of potentially talented children, the district should not lose sight of the easily identified children and should not, in the interests of fairness, refuse to serve those children who are obviously talented and languishing in boredom in the regular classrooms, enduring drill, practice, and repetition *ad infinitum* of what they already know or knew when they entered the class. They should not refuse to serve those children already sitting in the heterogeneous classroom as miniature teachers, patiently explaining last night's or tonight's homework to slower classmates. They should not refuse to serve those children who are clapping the erasers or running errands to the office while waiting for others to understand what they already do. They should not refuse to serve those children who are reading their lessons upside down or cross-eyed to diminish boredom. While accepting the challenge of identifying all talented children, the district should be sure to accept the challenge of serving those children it has easily identified. The challenge of *excellence* is a stirring challenge, as well.

Another use of local norms has been in districts that have a large population of students who would qualify for special education because their scores are in the high ranges. Some districts believe they are serving most students with low and moderate academic talent quite adequately with the programs currently offered, and so they collect local norms to determine who, in the district, scores highest and should be considered for rapid acceleration, early entrance to college, grade-skipping, and other special options that should be part of the education of the academically talented. The problem with most standardized tests is that they do not have norms within norms— that is, on the highest ends, there are few ways to differentiate among high-scoring students. A student who scores in the 97th percentile and above should be retested out of level. Shore et al. (1991) cautioned, "we want to be able to distinguish among gifted children as well as between them and others because each individual has a different pattern of abilities to be addressed" and they said that tests that have high ceilings should be used: "Formal tests should have high maximum scores, and the average scores of exceptionally able persons should not be close to the maximum" (p. 59).

Identifying Personality Variables

Another challenge of identification is identifying and considering personality variables in students. With the use of the Pyramid of Talent Development, people wonder how personality attributes can be emphasized. Young children should generally not be assessed for personality variables, as these are often undifferentiated (Murphy, 1995). The validation of group and individual tests has improved, but still and rightly, many testing experts caution against using alternative methods that are not reliable and not valid. The potential identified by high academic test scores requires other, nonacademic abilities (Goleman, 1997; Piirto, 1995a).

These are most commonly listed as creative ability and intrinsic motivation, though I would add intuition, perceptiveness, self-efficacy, resilience, discipline, passion, risk taking, and the like (see Chapter 1). To realize the potential identified by high test scores, a child must also have an environment—at home, at school, and in the community—that encourages the potential. Genetics, gender, and chance also operate. How do we develop personality attributes in children who have high test scores? How do we include children with the personality attributes who do not have high test scores, but who have high potential for life achievement?

Some programs use a criterion such as *task commitment* or *persistence* (Renzulli, 1977) in their identification models; that is, they want children in their programs who are *already* motivated to achieve and to learn. Others argue that it is not legitimate to demand such personality attributes from a child before the child enters the program; the program should develop these attributes within the child after the child has demonstrated the potential by having high test scores. How to identify personality traits such as motivation is the challenge for educators, because most available instruments are suitable for research purposes only, and are not considered by many test reviewers to be sufficiently valid or reliable for widespread use in making decisions about children's lives.

However, without going so far as to give personality tests to young children, such attributes can be developed through curriculum for all children (see Wilkes' Case Example in Chapter 1 on p. 40). Goleman (1995) has suggested several programs that seek to develop emotional intelligence.

Once Identified, Always Identified?

A related and sticky problem is that some children are identified by their test scores one year and then the next year their test scores slip and they no longer qualify according to the identifying criteria. Another related, and again sticky, problem is that some children may have high test scores, may get into a program, and may not perform according to the standards set by the teachers in the program. Educators of the talented have different responses to these difficulties. Some say that children should be reevaluated and re-placed regularly, that participation in the program for the talented should not be an entitlement but a privilege, not a right but a reassessable decision. Others say that the highest test score is the truest test score and that the child is merely underachieving for reasons that may have to do with the program or that may have to do with the child (Silverman, 1989; Tolan, 1992a, 1992b). They say the reason for underachievement should be pinpointed and the child should not be removed from the program.

Regular reevaluation and re-placement seems to be the most fair course. If this is stated up front, at the beginning, and everyone expects this, then adequate warning has perhaps been given that underachievement is understood but not accepted in the program for the education of the talented. A child should also be able to reenter a program. These policies must be made clear *before* placement. Shore et al. (1991) said "It may be wise to risk error on the side of inclusion rather than exclusion in order to avoid litigation by disappointed parents" (p. 44).

Another problem is that of social continuity. If a child does not qualify from one year to the next and the child is removed from the school or the program, how does the child feel, when his or her social group is removed also?

THE STEPS OF IDENTIFICATION

Most identification procedures have several steps. Tannenbaum (1983, 1986) compared these steps to a funnel (Figure 3.4). At the wide end is *screening*, at the middle is *selection*, and at the narrow end of the funnel is *differentiation*. Screening is a fast,

Figure 3.4 Steps Toward
Identification

Based on information in *Gifted Children: Psychological and Educational Perspectives* by A. Tannenbaum, 1983. New York: Macmillan.

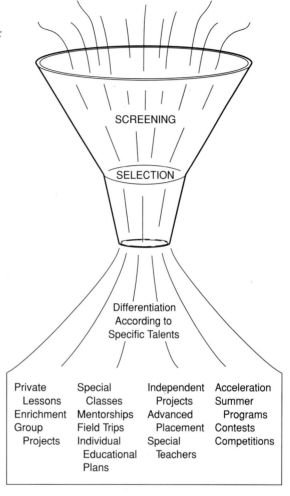

SCREENING

SELECTION

Differentiation
According to
Specific Talents

| Private Lessons Enrichment Group Projects | Special Classes Mentorships Field Trips Individual Educational Plans | Independent Projects Advanced Placement Special Teachers | Acceleration Summer Programs Contests Competitions |

efficient measurement for a large population to identify individuals who may deviate in a specified area, such as the incidence of maladjustment or readiness for academic work. Screening should include "even those children who only show vague hints of giftedness" (1983, p. 365). Selection includes chances for the children to "prove themselves in real and simulated enrichment activity to show how well they respond to the challenge" (1983, p. 370). This concept of having children prove themselves *before* selection should be more widely used. Differentiation sifts and sorts "potential mathematicians from potential literary critics, engineers from composers, historians from scientists, and so on, until the student's performance at school becomes more aligned with intelligent career choices" (1983, p. 371).

Borland (1989) said there should be *screening* and *placement* in the identification flowchart shown in Figure 3.5. Existing records, group tests, and referrals lead to the screening, from which the candidate pool is selected. Additional testing is performed,

Figure 3.5   Flowchart Representing the Program-Planning Process

Reprinted by permission of the publisher from Borland, James H., *Planning and Implementing Programs for the Gifted.* (New York: Teachers College Press, © 1989 by Teachers College, Columbia University. All rights reserved.) Figure 5.1, page 99.

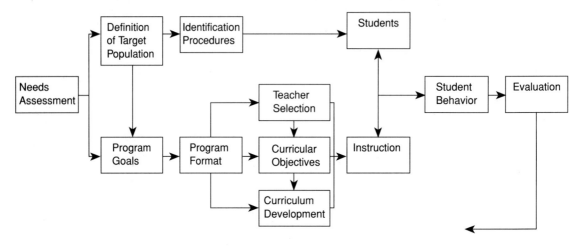

and a selection formula is used by the selection committee. Some students are selected for the program, and those who are not are put back into the candidate pool for future consideration.

Alternative and Authentic Means of Screening

Other means of screening besides the use of tests include the use of portfolios, folders, grades, and letters and nominations from the community, teachers, and parents. These have the advantage of being focused on the individual child and his or her demonstrated superior performance. Parents are a good and underutilized source for information about children's work and interests. The use of parent information should be part of the screening process. Peer nomination, community nomination, and self-nomination should also be included. (See the parent nomination form from Javits Project SPRING in Figure 3.7 on p. 128). The point of screening is to cast the widest net, to include rather than exclude, to inquire rather than close off. If a child wants to be considered for the program for talented students, the child should be permitted to apply.

Too often in the schools we do things *to* students, rather than *with* students. In fact, testing is not as "objective" or "quantitative" or mathematically reliable as we would like. But tests are a primary means of screening and should not be discarded. The National Research Center on the Gifted and Talented site at the University of Virginia in Charlottesville, Virginia, has published a monograph, *Contexts for Promise: Noteworthy Practices and Innovations in the Identification of Gifted Students* (Callahan, Tomlinson & Pizzat, 1993), that details innovative practices currently being used in identifying students throughout the United States.

Feldhusen and his colleagues (Feldhusen, Asher & Hoover, 1984; Feldhusen & Baska, 1985; Feldhusen, Hoover & Sayler, 1990) have done much work on identification. They say there are five steps in identifying the talented. Identification systems used in gifted education are similar to these five steps:

1. In the *Nomination Phase*, students who score above the 90th percentile on the Iowa Test of Basic Skills and above 120 on the Cognitive Abilities Test (CoGAT), who were nominated by teachers in the regular classrooms, who were nominated by teachers of the talented, and/or who had participated in gifted/talented programs in the past are in the initial pool. Collectors of local norms would simply choose the students who scored the highest for their particular subgroup.

2. In the *Data Gathering Phase*, teachers fill out the Scales for Rating the Behavioral Characteristics of Superior Students (SRBCSS) (Renzulli et al., 1976). They used the Learning, the Motivation, and the Creativity Scales.

3. In the *Data Synthesis Phase*, all the above information is put onto a chart that contains all the information for at least 12 children, for purposes of comparing data.

4. In the *Diagnostic Assessment Phase*, professional judgment is emphasized. A district-wide selection committee is formed, consisting of teachers, administrators, and specialists. For borderline cases, appropriate school personnel should be consulted. Relying on this committee to select the children makes the selection process more fair and equalizes the chances of all nominated children being selected. Disadvantaged children, the authors felt, are also given more of a chance when the professional judgment committee looks at the data as a whole. The committee should also write guidelines for exit processes for students who want to leave the program. Exit guidelines are extremely important; usually these require parent permission and a conference.

An alternative to using a committee is to use a formula. However, formulas that purport to be mathematically valid are often falsely so, just as matrices are falsely objective. The use of a committee to choose students who will be served in a special program puts the decisions where they belong—with the good judgment of the profesional educators.

5. In the *Validation Phase*, the staff reviews the identification procedure at staff meetings. An independent outside consultant could be hired to look at the identification procedures, using both quantitative and qualitative measures. Since the program will be questioned and the identification procedures will also be questioned, both should be looked at by someone who is not emotionally or professionally involved. Regular evaluations and reports by outside experts should be included. Any district that utilizes a procedure for identification such as that described here can be assured that the proper care is going into the process.

Effectiveness and Efficiency

Students can be nominated for the program for talented students by teachers, peers, parents, people in the community, or by themselves. Most districts prefer teacher and parent nomination. The principles of *effectiveness* and *efficiency* should guide the identification process.

Effectiveness

The first, most important principle to guide the nomination is that the nomination process should be *effective*. That is, it should include *all* of the children who will meet the criteria for talent in that particular area. The nominations should effectively include *all* of the children who have high IQ or general intellectual ability, or *all* of the children who have specific academic ability, or *all* of the children who have visual and performing arts ability, or *all* of the children who have creative thinking ability.

Efficiency

A corollary principle to guide the nomination is that the process should be *efficient*. That is, it should include no students who will not meet the criteria in that particular area of talent. The nominations should efficiently *exclude* the children who do not have high IQ or general intellectual ability, *exclude* the children who do not have specific academic ability, *exclude* the children who do not have superior visual and performing arts ability, *exclude* the children who do not have creative thinking ability, or *exclude* the children who do not have leadership ability.

Of course, given the fact that identification procedures deal with children and with potential, perfect effectiveness and efficiency are unachievable. However, Pegnato and Birch (1959) found that using a group IQ test cutoff of 115 on the Otis-Lennon was 93 percent effective in identifying students for intellectual ability, and using a group test IQ cutoff of 130 was 55 percent efficient. Teacher judgment was 45 percent effective and 26 percent efficient; honor roll placement was 73 percent effective and 18 percent efficient. Their research indicates that screening should include students from about one standard deviation above the mean; these students should then be considered for selection.

The Hazards and Benefits of Teacher Nomination

Although most districts prefer teachers to do the nominating, one reason that teachers may not be effective nominators is that most teachers have not had formal training in talent development education. Most undergraduate teacher education preparation programs may include only a cursory mention of the needs of talented children. The mandatory course on exceptionality may, because of time constraints, only include handicaps and mental retardation, and may give short shrift (usually about one or two clock hours) to the education and characteristics of the talented. Teachers may presuppose that talented children are only those girls who dress prettily and wear patent leather shoes, or are only those boys with thick glasses, red hair, and freckles, or are only the highly motivated children who get all As. Inclusion of pedagogy about the needs and characteristics of the talented in undergraduate and graduate education courses should be a given.

Nomination by trained teachers can be beneficial. Most teachers improve significantly in their ability to identify talented children effectively after they have had some training. All educators should have one three-hour course in talent development education as a bare minimum. When teachers have training in the characteristics of talented youth, and in programming for talented youth, they are quite reliable as nominators. Why aren't teachers effective as nominators without some training? Teachers are likely to overlook talented students who do not conform to the rules of the classroom, who do not do their homework, or who are culturally different. One of the criticisms of the Terman study (begun in 1922) has been that the students were first screened for getting IQ testing by teacher nomination. Howley, Howley, and Pendarvis (1986) said, "reliance on observed class work may cause teachers to refer average students instead of talented students" (p. 28). Who was missed because of this first screening for the Terman study being done by teachers? What became of them? Perhaps they were the ones who reached the eminence none of the Terman population reached.

A chilling study was reported (Peterson & Margolin, 1997) in which teachers in two middle schools were asked to nominate students for a new program, a discussion group for gifted students. The district had sizeable Latino and African-American populations. The teachers did not receive a definition of giftedness. They spoke confidently about the students they believed were gifted. The teachers mentioned traits they believed gifted students had: "Good behavior"; "High academic achievement"; "Hard-working, going beyond on projects"; "Competitiveness"; "Highly organized"; "Good performance in all academic areas"; "Leadership"; "Being well-rounded"; "Verbal strengths"; "high motivation"; "Goal orientation"; "Winning awards"; "Perfectionism"; "Great kid"; "nice, good" (p. 88).

Only three minority students were nominated—Latino brothers whose mother was Anglo, and an African-American described as "highly acculturated" (p. 89). The teachers nominated students who were, like themselves, white, middle-class, and "good"—that is, the students represented the teachers' ideal selves. The teachers believed that they were being objective, that there was no implicit bias in their nominations, that they were not showing favoritism. The researchers concluded that the nomination process for gifted children illustrates "that the dominant culture is not easily thwarted," and that "positive sorting" is disciminatory as well as "negative sorting" (choosing students for remedial programs). Peterson and Margolin noted that when certain intelligence tests were declared invalid in California in 1979, the reason was that they were selecting a disproportionate number of minority students for classes for the "educable mentally retarded" and not for selecting a disproportionate number of minority students for programs for the gifted.

The use of portfolios, the inclusion of data from parents and the community, as well as peers, should be encouraged as alternative ways to achieve effectiveness. These means may not be very efficient; that is, they take a lot of time and are "messy" in administration and in evaluation. Most research has continued to show that the most efficient and most effective way of identifying *high-IQ* or *general intellectual ability* students and *specific academic ability* students is by using standardized tests, and that is why standardized testing will not disappear soon. However, the urgent need to include students from all populations within a district, and the fact that some standardized tests do not effectively identify them, means that the messy and human process of looking at other kinds of data, authentic data, must begin to prevail.

Ford (1996) spoke strongly about teachers and their record in nominating black students for special talent development education programs. "A primary factor in the successful identification of gifted Black students is teacher attitude ... teachers frequently emphasize such behaviors as cooperation, answering correctly, punctuality, and neatness when identifying gifted students" (p. 27). Ford pointed out that these may not be the behaviors that minority, underachieving, creative, or nonconforming students demonstrate. The same lack of training about identification of culturally different or even traditional talented students exists for school counselors and school psychologists.

THE IQ TEST

One reason for the persistence of the IQ test in schools has been that it does succeed at globally predicting school and job performance. That is, a high IQ generally predicts high grades in school, and high grades in school predict entrance into a good college, or any college, and achieving a college degree leads to a good job and a higher income. Some four-year colleges select all of their students from those who score in the top 10 percent on intelligence tests (Herrnstein & Murray, 1994). Having a degree from a college, a good job, and a high income are often results of having academic talent. Therefore, one definition of academic talent is having a high IQ, two standard deviations above the mean, or approximately 135 and above. While many critical theorists point out that the intelligence quotient is discriminatory, and based on class differences (see Kincheloe, Sternberg & Gresson, 1996), it is still a good predictor of school and job achievement. Weinberg (1989) went so far as to say, "Many would, in fact, offer the intelligence test as the major achievement of psychology in guiding everyday practical affairs" (p. 100).

Shall we continue to use tests as the primary means of identifying the academically talented? An article by Humphreys (1986) stated that, indeed, the presence of academic talent is indicated by the use of intelligence tests. However, the issue of equity in testing is as pertinent now as it was during the early days of testing in the United States Army and in the testing of would-be immigrants. That people of color, Jews, and Italians were found to be mentally deficient and thus deportable is today laughable, as all ethnic groups have displayed intelligence and have assumed prominence in the society in all areas.

IQ Tests and Socioeconomic Status (SES)

Moreover, intelligence scores do not follow socioeconomic status (SES) as closely as has been stated. The development of high IQ or general intellectual talent has to do with what happens to the child after birth. Thus, the presence of intellectually talented children in all socioeconomic groups is explained. Humphreys said, "The gifted children who were born into the most unlikely environments, as gauged by the usual indicants of privilege, cannot be explained by measurement error. Environmentalists must look at subtler factors in the home than level of SES" (p.154). Humphreys also stated that using differential identification measures for different races or socioeconomic group necessarily waters down the types of education that will be offered to them.

Howley, Howley, and Pendarvis (1995) pointed out that IQ tests may be misused. Teachers and parents may use an IQ score to explain why a student is or is not doing well in school. Another misuse occurs when we predict how students will perform in school by means of their IQ score. IQ test scores do not show whether the child had an equal opportunity to learn what the test is measuring. Therefore, the scores are misused when such assumptions are made. They said, "We conclude that comprehensive, individually administered intelligence tests and high-ceilinged achievement tests can serve selection procedures fairly... . Extremely high scores on any of these standard measures should qualify children for dramatic modifications in their schooling" (p. 93).

Ford disagreed that innate aptitudes are measured by IQ tests. Ford (1996) said, "In essence, students' performance on standardized tests do not measure innate aptitudes. To interpret IQ scores and test results in this manner is a dangerous method of social and educational oppression" (p. 192). Ford concluded, "Traditional standardized tests show little criterion validity relative to Black students, and their utility for making consequential decisions about Black students' futures is questionable" (p. 22).

Weinberg (1989) said that the tests themselves should not be blamed, for performance on intelligence tests "is influenced by a variety of motivational and personality variables that have little to do with formal cognition or achievement" (p. 100). He went on to note that the tests have been greatly improved and that they do indeed predict how well a child will do in school: "it is ironic that tests have been outlawed for the very purpose for which they were designed—to prevent subjective judgments and prejudice from being the basis for assigning students to special classes or denying them certain privileges" (p. 101). The outrage in the educational establishment produced by *The Bell Curve* (Herrnstein & Murray, 1994) shows that the debate is far from over, and in fact, political correctness nowadays would frown on the use of an IQ test to choose a child of whatever gender, race, or economic situation for special treatment.

Can We Change a Person's IQ?

How malleable is the IQ? *If* the IQ is malleable, doesn't the use of the IQ discriminate against those whose early childhoods were not enriched? Is that which is inherited immutable, unchangeable? Can genetics be changed? Scientists struggling to answer these questions have come up with some general results.

First, the IQ is malleable: able to be changed, or molded, to a certain extent. This is called *trait plasticity*. Experts say that the IQ is malleable by about 20 points. Plomin (1986, 1997) has estimated that about 50 percent of intelligence is inherited, and Bouchard et al. (1991) and the twin studies people go higher, saying that twins reared apart show about 72 percent of heritability. These twin studies have been done on adults, and an adult twin shows more similarity to her reared-apart twin than she would have as a child. That is, the similarities between twins who are reared apart manifest in adulthood more than in childhood. In childhood, the environment plays more of a part than in adulthood. We do not know which factors of environment are surely predictive of having a high IQ, though one would suspect the factors would be in the home, the community, and in the school.

Leaving heredity aside, however, prenatal environment is also crucial. Fetal Alcohol Syndrome (FAS), for example, and the birth of babies with AIDS, cocaine, or heroin addiction affects those babies' lives no matter what their genetic makeup. It has been estimated that intervention (or education or environment) can change a person's IQ 20 to 25 points (Zigler & Seitz, 1982). This is good news for educators, because if one is a teacher, one must believe that a person's intelligence can be changed. The deterministic view that you are what you are born with should have no place in education, especially in the field of talent development education. Why even teach if one believes a child cannot be changed?

When to Use an IQ Test

Freeman (1986) said that at the high ranges of IQ, above 135, it seems that what IQ tests measure is not ability that is inborn, but ability fostered by environment. Shore et al. (1991) said that while IQ tests should not be the sole means of identification, there is "a useful place" for them in an identification plan. In their book on best practices, they recommended that "when no other direct index leads to the identification of a child's high ability, the addition of an IQ test might be helpful" (p. 55).

The Intelligence Quotient, or IQ, is a thing of the past, say the latest researchers and thinkers on intelligence (Gardner, 1991; Kincheloe, Sternberg & Gresson, 1996; Sternberg, 1997). The IQ test is discriminatory against poor people and minorities, the critics say. The schools disagree, at least as far as their practice is concerned. Applied psychologists are in demand. The most commonly used individually administered tests that yield IQs are abilities tests such as the Wechsler Intelligence Scale for Children-Revised (WISC-R); the Stanford-Binet Intelligence Scale: Fourth Edition (S-B4); the Kaufman Assessment Battery for Children (KABC); the Woodcock-Johnson Psychoeducational Battery-Aptitude (W-JP-A). Appendix A offers a comparison of many available standardized tests.

An IQ is the score obtained when a battery of ability tests is administered and mathematical manipulations are performed to yield a quotient (intelligence *quotient*). Some subtests are often weighted more than others. Originally, the IQ was formulated by subtracting the mental age from the chronological age but this was modified in the early twentieth century by William Stern who suggested that the the mental age divided by the chronological age multiplied by 100 would yield an *intelligence quotient.* One can get a quotient from any battery of tests, and what is tested by one battery is often different from what is tested by another battery. A few validation studies have compared what the tests measure, but once that holy number, the IQ, is obtained, the people using that number may not stop to think about what the battery of tests measured.

The sanctity and persistence of the IQ has to do with its ease of explanation. No one who has found out his or her IQ will ever forget it. The number is branded in the brain. If the IQ is high, the person feels smart. If the IQ is low, the person feels dumb. No one questions the battery of tests that went into obtaining that number. Because people who are employed in the field of the education of the talented are expected to be cognizant of intelligence testing, they should be aware of the pros and cons of using such tests. Lawsuits about the use of IQ tests for special educational placement [*Larry P. v. Riles* (1979). No. C71-2270 RFP (Calif.)] have led, in some districts, for example in Chicago [*Parents in Action on Special Education v. Hannon* (1980). No. 74 C 3586 N.D. 111], to the use of nonverbal tests such as the Raven's Progressive Matrices (Baska, 1986).

Critics of IQ tests say that these behaviors in no way approximate what intelligent behavior is. Supporters of IQ tests say that the tests have worked quite well in predicting school success. Salvia and Ysseldyke (1991) said that "intelligence tests are simply samples of behavior. And different intelligence tests sample different behaviors. For that reason it is wrong to speak of a person's IQ. Instead, we can refer only to a person's IQ on a specific test" (pp. 171–172).

Issues of Equity and Testing

Saccuzzo and his colleagues (Johnson, 1994a, 1994b; McLaughin & Saccuzzo, 1994; Saccuzzo, Johnson & Guertin, 1994a, 1994b) in the San Diego Javits grant did much comparative testing of thousands of students who had been referred as being potentially gifted. Through use of the WISC-R, they found that "children who are in the process of becoming bilingual demonstrate their giftedness through performance-based tasks, such as quantitative/math type skills in order to compensate for their verbal disadvantage" (p. 100). Johnson (1994a) found that the WISC-R was "biased in favor of Caucasians and Asians, and biased against African-Americans and Filipinos" (p. 69). Different strength patterns appeared for each ethnic group. "No way was found to use the WISC-R to select a proportionately balanced population." She went on to strongly say, "The use of the WISC-R in diverse populations as the primary selection device for gifted programs is an inappropriate use of the test" (p. 70). The researchers tried out the Standard Raven Progressive Matrices Test (RPM) as well (Saccuzzo, Johnson & Guertin, 1994b). They stated, "Considering only children referred for giftedness testing, the RPM produces far better equity for all ethnic backgrounds when compared to the WISC-R." The Raven "overselected" whites, but far less so than the WISC-R (120 percent to 200 percent proportionate to their numbers in the population). The RPM proportionately selected Native Americans, Pacific Islanders, and Indochinese, but underselected African-Americans and Latinos. It predicted language achievement for African-American and white students, and math achievement for whites. It is highly correlated with the *g*-factor of Spearman.

However, the Raven selects different children than the WISC-R, and so if the district's definition of giftedness is what the test selects, this will be problematic. Verbally advanced children are selected by both tests. Students selected only by the WISC-R are verbally advanced and highly motivated. While young, they have high IQs on the WISC-R, but as they get older their IQs regress to the mean because of the unreliability of the test at ceiling levels. Those students who are selected by the RPM have high potential but average or below-average school achievement. Low motivation is also often evident. "This type of student is not always accepted by teachers as gifted" (Saccuzzo, Johnson, & Guertin, 1994b, p. 42). The researchers concluded "We are convinced that as traditional tests are presently used, there exists not a single one that would produce an equitable selection for gifted programs." The researchers noted that the multiple intelligences approach currently being used is one option in achieving equity. Another is using portfolios and other subjective data, which "face numerous obstacles in terms of objectivity, reliability, and predictive validity." They concluded that using traditional standardized tests with "local-ethnic norms" and using "traditional tests in creative ways" are two options that should be tried, given the fact that traditional tests are at least more objective than the other options.

THE IDENTIFICATION OF ACADEMIC ABILITY

The most common way to identify specific academic ability, such as ability in mathematics or reading, is to use standardized achievement tests, which yield scores in various achievement areas. However, while identifying high IQ needs an IQ test, identifying specific academic ability does not need a standardized test. That is, an IQ is defined by a test and does not exist apart from the test from which it was scored.

Group Tests Used for Screening

The use of standardized group achievement or ability tests for identification is a widespread practice that has some difficulties. For example, a group test is rarely as accurate as an individually administered test. A teacher standing in front of a group of children reading directions and then roaming the rows with a stopwatch is supposed to notice the child who is just filling in any old bubble, or the child who is on the wrong starting line. Often the teacher does not notice this. The younger the child, the less accurate the group tests are. Teachers often receive little or inadequate training for administering group tests. Individually administered tests, even if administered by someone with little or inadequate training, are more desirable, simply because the administrator is facing the child being tested, flipping pages, marking boxes, and interacting with the child.

A group test is supposed to be merely a *screening* device, part of the district's strategy for casting the widest net. Often the child's score on the group test is itself the criterion, and a child enters or is not permitted to enter the program on the basis of a score on a group test. This may be efficient practice, but it is not effective practice. The best way to use the scores on a group test is to include all students who score above a certain cutoff, for example, one standard deviation above the mean minus the standard error of measurement. These children should then be looked at further and perhaps administered individual intelligence tests.

Deviation IQs

A deviation IQ is a standard score with a mean of 100 and a standard deviation of 15 or 16. Many intelligence and achievement tests yield a deviation IQ sometimes called a School Ability Index (SAI). For the Otis-Lennon School Ability Test, the choice of terminology was made to "emphasize that performance reflects learned abilities relating to school achievement and to reduce possible misrepresentation of the concept of IQ" (Dyer, 1985, p. 1107). A deviation IQ is not a "true" IQ (if a "true" IQ exists, it is "true" because it was derived from a standardized *ability* test and not from a standardized *achievement* test). The score is numerically rendered into a standard score. Oakland (1985) said, "The use of the School Ability Index rather than IQ is appropriate to denote abilities learned in part by experience and schooling rather than presumed primarily unvarying and innate" (p. 1108). However, the test publisher was criticized for not providing a reason for the change: "Is the SAI [on the Otis-Lennon] measuring intelligent behavior or is it measuring school achievement?" (p. 1108). Oakland says the publishers try to have it both ways; that is, they say it is equivalent to an IQ but that it is also a measure of ability for school learning. The question to ask is How highly correlated is the school ability test with achievement tests which would also seem to show school ability? If it is highly correlated, then why give two tests?

The definition of an achievement test is that it is a test used to measure knowledge, abilities, understanding, or skills acquired from academic work; that is, achievement is what has been learned from instruction. The definition of an ability test is that it is a test that measures several of 23 aptitude factors listed by the Educational Testing Service (ETS). The factors commonly assessed are combinations of several of these: Flexibility of Closure, Speed of Closure, Verbal Closure, Associational Fluency, Expressional Fluency, Figural Fluency, Ideational Fluency, Word Fluency, Induction, Integrative Process, Associative Memory, Memory Span, Visual Memory, Number, Perceptual Speed, General Reasoning, Logical Reasoning, Spatial Orientation, Spatial Scanning, Verbal Comprehension, Visualization, Figural Flexibility, and Flexibility of Use.

Often districts do not administer a separate *ability* test. Instead they use the *derivation IQ* projections they get from group *achievement* tests (for example, the California Achievement Test, the Metropolitan Achievement Test, the Iowa Test of Basic Skills). This practice saves the district the cost of administering a separate test. Does using an achievement test to identify ability work? Are the same children identified using an achievement test as would be identified using an abilty test? One must look at the studies that have been done that show how well the tests are correlated, how consistently they measure the same thing.

The district must also look at the content validity of these tests and determine whether the same things are being measured. A group achievement test usually measures such things as spelling, mathematics computation, and factual knowledge. A group ability test usually purports to measure abilities in spatial reasoning, or verbal reasoning, or general reasoning. An ability test claims to measure *potential* for knowing while an achievement test measures what is *already* known. An ability test is mystical, somewhat deterministic, even Calvinistic; an achievement test is practical, based on reality. However, some ability tests and achievement tests seem to be highly related; that is, achievement is related to ability; if the tests are highly related, why not save money and use the achievement test? A caution: This would prevent the district from identifying students who score high in abstract abilities but who don't know the facts measured in achievement tests. (These students are usually called *underachievers*.)

Although ability and achievement tests are highly correlated, the purpose of the achievement test is to measure past mastery, and the purpose of the ability test is to predict future academic success. Past success predicts future success, true, but the tests were designed for different purposes. Thus the SAI derived from an achievement test is an achievement index, not an ability quotient; it is a *deviation* score (for example, see the normal curve in Figure 3.3 on p. 106). This confuses many people new to testing. Just remember that the SAI is based on what the student already knows; the IQ is supposedly based on the student's so-called potential, or raw brain power in a few ability factors.

Proficiency Tests

Many states are now using proficiency testing at certain grade levels, and educators of the talented are asking whether proficiency tests can be used to identify academically talented students. The answer is yes and no. Remember that the definition of academically talented is slippery, that there is no absolute standard for what academic talent is. It seems reasonable to say that if the school's (or the state's) definition of academic talent is that those students who scored in the 95th percentile and above on the state proficiency test have "it" (academic talent), then the proficiency test can be used. If the school's (or the state's) definition of academic talent is something else, some objective standard such as knowing the 50 states and their capitals by age 7 or being able to write compound-complex sentences by age 10, and the proficiency test doesn't measure that, the proficiency test should not be used.

All humor aside, the proficiency tests are new, and the validity work has not been done, especially on the high end, where scores are usually attenuated because of fewer items to show differentiations among levels of high performance. A further caution is that proficiency is just that, knowing enough to get by, competence and not expertise. Interestingly enough, the perception has been that proficiency merely shows minimum competency, but a student told me that in her school, only one of the 24 students who had been identified for her program by means of a standardized achievement test would have been chosen for the program for the academically talented if the proficiency test had been the standard, as only one student passed the proficiency test at the highest level on all four subtests, which is the standard the state had set for using proficiency tests to identify for talent development education programs. Obviously the proficiency test and the standardized achievement test are not correlated; that is, they measure different things, and the standard for measuring academic talent is relative and not fixed.

CRITERIA FOR STANDARDIZED TEST SELECTION AND STANDARDS FOR TESTING

The practitioner in talent development and gifted education will be expected to know about testing because most academically talented students are identified by means of tests. Therefore, the practitioner should be aware that certain criteria should be used in selecting tests. Use of the reviews in the *Mental Measurements Yearbooks* is one necessity. Another necessity is to read the test manuals.

Is There Adequate Reliability and Validity?

First, the test should have acceptable reliability and validity. *Reliability* refers to the test's comparability and consistency over time and in relationship to other, similar tests. Reliability is the extent to which a test is dependable, stable, and consistent when administered to the same individuals on different occasions. Technically, this is a statistical term that defines the extent to which errors of measurement are absent from a measurement instrument. The person in charge of choosing tests should consult the technical manuals that test reviewers provide as well as the test reviews to determine the size of the groups and the types of people that the test was normed on, and how comparable the test is to other tests. Consulting someone who has a good background in testing—a school psychologist, for example—is also crucial.

Validity

Validity refers to how appropriate the test is for the use to which it is being put. Validity is the extent to which a test measures what it was intended to measure. Validity indicates the degree of accuracy of either predictions or inferences based upon a test score. Is the test valid for assessing a child's academic talent?

Content Validity For an achievement test, content validity can be determined by looking at current textbook content, academic skills developed in that grade, and diversity of potential errors. Items that are more difficult for one group than for a comparison group are eliminated. A reviewer (Harrison, 1989) criticized the makers of the Wide-Range Achievement Test-Revised (WRAT-R) for claiming content validity from looking at items in dictionaries, correlating with items on the Woodcock-Johnson achievement subtests, and having an administration format similar to classroom activities. "None of this evidence supports content validity," said Harrison (p. 904).

A second concern when looking at content validity is whether the test has an adequate number of items, and whether those items measure knowledge in the domain that is to be assessed. Longer tests are more valid than shorter tests. The more items per content area, the more likely the test will show what the student knows or what the student can do.

Another concern of content is cultural. Many tests have been called culturally unfair, and in the past, "culture-fair" tests such as the "chitlings test," which used black slang for the vocabulary section, were developed to show how biased the tests were. A child from the inner city may not know what a septic tank is. A child from a rural area may not know what a subway is. However, while admirable in intent, these tests have often not been valid.

It is an unfortunate fact that establishing reliability and validity for a test is time consuming, expensive, and labor intensive, and groups and individuals without the backing of the big business test companies often have difficulty in establishing their tests as suitable for use by large numbers of school systems. This also holds true for creativity and critical-thinking tests, motivation and self-esteem questionnaires, and checklists. However fun it may seem to give a child a questionnaire, a checklist, or an inventory, the fun must stop when decisions about the child's life are made on the basis of such instruments that have questionable validity and reliability. This cannot be stressed enough. Figure 3.6 gives a list of criteria that should be used for test selection.

Concurrent Validity This determines whether the test is related to other tests to see whether they assess the same skills. A high coefficient score (from 0.7 to 1.0) indicates the two tests are highly related. A low coefficient score (from 0.1 to 0.4) shows they are not well related. If an ability test and an achievement test are highly related, one may want to ask, why give both tests? Again, the samples must be comparable (i.e., random) in order for scores to be reliable.

Construct Validity *Construct validity* means, does the test measure what it says it measures? Is there such a construct—pattern or model—in the world? Construct validity is most difficult to establish. What is intelligence? What is achievement? What is creativity? These are the questions one must ask, and one must formulate a theory as to what these are and then make a test that measures that belief. Harrison (1989) criticized the WRAT-R test makers for claiming construct validity because the raw scores increased with age, and the items were internally separated. These are "necessary but insufficient" for construct validity, she said (p. 904).

Reliability

Reliability is consistency. A test may be reliable but not valid. Both validity and reliability are important, but validity is the most important. Current-day critics of standardized testing have said that most commonly used achievement tests and ability tests published by large, research-based companies are reliable but not valid. There have been at least five methods of determining whether a test is reliable:

1. *Test-retest reliability.* The technical manual should indicate whether or not individuals with the same ability were retested at least twice and the same scores were obtained. Retests should be undertaken. For younger ages, Cronbach (1985) said the manual should indicate that retests were made at 100 cases at each early age and at spaced later ages.

2. *Equivalent forms reliability.* Two or more parallel alternate forms of the test should have been made so that an individual taking one form would score the same on the second form.

3. *Split-halves reliability.* Since making equivalent forms is difficult, split-halves reliability is often substituted. This consists of taking the test and cutting it into two or more parts and having the individual take them separately but score the same.

4. *Reader reliability.* If there are open-ended questions, usually essay questions, in a test, each essay should be read by at least two readers. They should agree. If they don't agree, the answer should be read by a third reader.

Figure 3.6 Criteria for Test Selection

1. Is there a justifiable reason for testing the student? (Has the school consulted the code of Fair Testing Practices in Education [1968]?)
2. Does the person or committee choosing the test have expertise in testing?
3. Is the person who will give the test skilled in test administration? (Is training conducted with teachers?)
4. Is the test normed on a large enough population comparable to that to which the student(s) belong(s)?
5. Is the behavior that is being tested adequately sampled on the test itself?
6. Does the test measure what it says it measures?
7. Does the test predict observed future behavior of successful people in the field?
8. Does the test manual adequately and clearly provide the information needed for questions 3, 4, 5, and 6?
9. Have the Buros *Mental Measurements Yearbook(s)* and *Tests in Print* been consulted for test reviews from independent reviewers? (Buros Institute of Mental Measurements, 135 Bancroft Hall, University of Nebraska, Lincoln, Nebraska 68588-0348)
10. Is there a compelling reason to use a group test?
11. Is there a compelling reason to use an individual test?
12. Does the test have high enough ceilings for assessment of talent?
13. Does the test have scoring that is relatively easy to accomplish, or is it relatively cost-effective to send it away to be scored?
14. What information does the test protocol give? Is this information sufficient for interpretation, placement in a program, or communication to parents?
15. What is the optimal group size for administering the test?
16. What is the length of sitting for the test to be administered? (Thirty minutes for primary, 40–60 minutes for intermediate, and 90 minutes for junior and senior high)
17. How will the school convey the test information to the parents?
18. Will the test be used for diagnostic/prescriptive reasons or for placement?
19. Will the test be placed in the student's permanent record?
20. How will the school convey the test information to the student?

5. *Examiner reliability.* The test should be administered according to test directions each time it is administered. The examiners should be trained and regular reviews of how to administer the tests with consistency should be conducted.

Are There Adequate Ceilings?

In testing lingo, a ceiling is the upper limit of ability that can be measured by a particular test. The ceiling effect is especially essential in considering tests for academically talented students. Children who score at the 99th percentile, "topping out" the test, are in danger of having their abilities underestimated. Also, at the highest extremes, even small percentile differences indicate large differences in the group; for example, on some tests of, say, 60 items, students could get 40 items right or 58 items right and still achieve a score in the 99th percentile. Some scores are reported as composite scores. Composite scores combine all three subtests in reading, say, or in math. The composite score is a quotient derived from the subtest scores. Composite scores have little or no use in educational planning, especially if they are high. Subtest scores should be used and out-of-level tests should be applied until useful diagnostic information is obtained. Several thinkers in the field prefer the Stanford-Binet L-M for the reason that its ceilings are higher than those of its successor the Stanford-Binet Fourth Edition (Silverman & Kearney, 1992).

Standards for Teachers Who Use Tests

The teacher of the gifted and talented is more likely than many other teachers to use standardized tests. A standardized test is a form of measurement that has been normed against a specific population. Standardization is obtained by administering the test to a given population and then calculating means, standard deviations, standardized scores, and percentiles. Equivalent scores are then produced for comparisons of an individual score to the norm group's performance. With that in mind, Appendix A lists the professional standards that should be observed by educators who use such tests.

AUTHENTIC ASSESSMENT

Authentic assessment of educational achievement looks directly at what a student actually can perform in the specific subject matter area. Standardized tests, on the other hand, measure indirectly or not at all, as they filter the knowledge through the test format and the student's ability to read. Authentic assessment is also called *performance assessment, alternative assessment,* or *direct assessment.* Authentic evaluations include a variety of techniques such as written products, portfolios, checklists, teacher observations, and group projects. Most authentic assessment should be able to be summarized numerically or put on a scale to make it possible to combine individual results. Authentic assessment was developed in the arts and apprenticeship systems. Writing is now almost always assessed authentically rather than through multiple choice tests, and open-ended mathematics, science, and social studies assessment is also becoming common. In many communities, development of the process of authentic assessment includes the parents, administrators, university faculty, and the community. Their participation helps to assure that racial and cultural biases are minimized. Authentic assessment can be used to find talented students.

Here are common current uses of authentic assessment: (1) the New York Regents exams, parts of which have included essay questions since their inception—and which are scored locally (while audited by the state); (2) the Advanced Placement program, which uses open-ended questions and tasks, including not only essays on most tests but the performance-based tests in the Art Portfolio and Foreign Language exams; (3) statewide writing assessments in two dozen states where model papers, training of readers, papers read "blind," and procedures to prevent bias and drift gain adequate reliability; (4) the National Assessment of Educational Progress (NAEP), the Congressionally-mandated assessment, which uses numerous open-ended test questions and writing prompts (and successfully piloted a hands-on test of science performance); (6) newly-mandated performance-based and portfolio-based statewide testing in Arizona, California, Connecticut, Kentucky, Maryland, and New York. Wiggins (1992) said, "Genuine accountability does not avoid human judgment." Judgment of products can be improved through training, through the use of exemplars, through mandatory evaluation audits, and through the use of disinterested evaluators reviewing the work "blind," as in the case of academic, artistic, and athletic peer review.

Authentic assessment helps parents and the community to actually see what the students are producing, and to compare the products of those whose products were judged more highly than others.

An ERIC Digest by Grant Wiggins (1992) gave a series of comparisons of authentic assessment and traditional standardized tests, which are listed in Table 3.1.

Rubrics should be created for the assessment of performances, portfolios, and other authentic displays of student strengths. Multiple Intelligence (MI) assessment has been developed through several Javits Projects. Gardner (1995a) indicated several criteria for the assessment of multiple intelligence projects in the following list on p. 126. These criteria could be transferred to other kinds of project assessment for alternative assessment for identification purposes.

Authentic assessment includes a writing portfolio.

Table 3.1   A Comparison of Authentic Assessment and Standardized Tests

Authentic Assessment	Traditional Standardized Tests
Students show knowledge they have acquired.	Student shows recognition, recall, and the ability to "plug in" what was learned out of context.
The student demonstrates the tasks that mirror instructional activities: conducting research; writing, revising and discussing papers; providing an engaging oral analysis of a recent political event; collaborating with others on a debate, etc.	Usually limited to paper-and-pencil, one-answer questions.
Shows whether student can craft polished, thorough and justifiable answers, performances or products.	Asks the student to select or write correct responses—irrespective of reasons. Once the answer is chosen, time usually does not permit revision or reasons for choosing certain answers.
Validity and reliability achieved by emphasizing and standardizing the appropriate criteria for scoring such (varied) products.	Standardizes objective "items" and, hence, the (one) right answer for each. Validity on most multiple-choice tests is determined merely by matching items to the curriculum content (or through sophisticated correlations with other test results).
Involves "ill-structured" challenges and roles that are more similar to the ambiguities of adult and professional life.	Often assess static and arbitrary, discrete and simplistic elements of drill-like activities.
The essential challenge is known in advance— the upcoming report, recital, presentation, project, performance, etc. The standards for evaluating are also known in advance.	Usually requires complete secrecy for validity, making it difficult for teachers and students to rehearse and gain the confidence that comes from knowing their performance obligations. How questions are chosen is often secret and mysterious and thus not open to public scrutiny.
Scoring is expensive when compared to multiple-choice tests (about $2 per student vs. 1¢) but the gains to teacher professional development, local assessing, and student learning are many.	Tests mislead students and teachers about the kinds of work that should be mastered. Norms are not standards; items are not real problems; right answers are not rationales.
Learning is viewed as a process and assessment is organic as the student matures within the learning situation.	Students come to believe that learning is cramming; teachers come to believe that tests are after-the-fact, imposed nuisances composed of contrived questions—irrelevant to their intent and success.
Students, community, teachers, and administrators come together in deciding what makes up effective academic performance.	Multiple-choice tests can be valid indicators or predictors of academic performance. It is the form, not the content, of the test that is harmful to learning. People are led to believe that right answers matter more than habits of mind and the justification of one's approach and results.

Information from Wiggins, G. (1992). The case for authentic assessment. ERIC Digest ED328611.

Multiple Intelligence Assessment of Projects—Dimensions

1. Individual Profile
   - Look at what the project reveals about specific cognitive strengths, weaknesses, and proclivities of student (linguistic, logical-mathematical, spatial, bodily-kinesthetic, musical, intra- and interpersonal)
   - Also consider disposition and attitude toward work (perseverance, risk taking).
2. Mastery of Facts, Skills, and Concepts
3. Quality of Work (employ the criteria of specific genre)
   Innovation and Imagination:
   - Aesthetic judgment and technique
   - How well is the concept showcased?
   - How well is the performance executed?
4. Skill in Communication of the Results
5. Reflection (metacognition about project)
   - What does the project mean?
   - What to do next time?
   - What was done well?
   - What can be improved?
   - How does it relate to past and future work?
6. What Does the Project Reveal about the Student?
7. Did the Project Require Collaboration or Cooperation? Should It Have?
   - Many students need to have help on formulating and executing projects: parents, community, teacher, peers. (Gardner, 1995)

Identification of Predictive Behaviors

The nomination process, including the screening by tests, may ignore what some people in the field (Renzulli, 1988) called *gifted behaviors*, which here are perhaps more accurately called *predictive behaviors*. Often, for culturally different children, identification cannot be made by means of standardized tests, but only by means of observation of predictive behavior. Predictive behavior is behavior that is typical of those who have talents in certain areas. For example, one of the surest ways of recognizing young artistic or musical talent is that the young artist draws and the young musician evidences musical interest through singing, drumming, tooting, or pausing to listen to music for longer periods of time than other children. The person talented in this area oftentimes demonstrates this predictive behavior compulsively and repetitively. The young inventor Henry Ford began by taking apart clocks and then machines and buggies. Many inventors began in rural areas, especially on farms, where they began to fix things and then to improvise new machines.

The young researcher constructs incipient research projects. One student finished all the science courses in his high school by his sophomore year. When he was but seven years old, he had a plot of land roped off on his family's property where he collected, tallied, and noted the species and moisture, and tallied the occurrence of various phenomena (J. Blair, personal communication, 1992). The young gardener gardens. I know a Ph.D. plant geneticist whose predictive behavior was apparent in the backyard garden of his suburban Detroit home, where he experimented with cross-fertilization. The young writer reads and reads and reads and writes. The young mathematician does math, thinks in mathematical terms, dreams in matrices. The teacher who observes such compulsive and repetitive predictive behavior often can identify a potentially talented adult without the use of tests. Such observation is especially necessary when the child may be culturally different, and when the test scores may not be high enough to identify the student by commonly used methods. At the end of this chapter, there is a Case Example of just such a culturally different child.

Tolan asserted that having scored high on a test is enough and no concomitant achievement is necessary (Tolan, 1992b). Tolan said that such traits as advanced vocabulary, playing with toys for older children, preferring to talk to adults, heightened moral sensitivity, and the like "are generally considered qualitative and subjective" (p. 15). These are precocious asynchronous behaviors that are common to students with high IQs, signaling that the child needs advanced level educational opportunities and perhaps counseling intervention. She said that parents are often not asked about their children's predictive behaviors, and if they are, their observations are not taken seriously by school personnel (personal communication, October, 1992).

Leisure and Out-of-School Activities as Predictive Behaviors

Leisure activities have predictive value for later career choice and adult accomplishment. People choose what they do in their leisure time, and students choose what extracurricular activities in which they want to participate. If they participate in certain leisure activities or extracurricular activities for a number of years, there is a good chance the activities are interest-driven and not chosen for social or popularity reasons. Throughout the world, researchers have pointed out that talented people can be identified by looking at what they do outside of school, during their leisure time. (Baird, 1985; Kerr, 1985; Milgram & Hong, 1993; Milgram, Hong, Shavit, and Peled, 1997; Perleth, Sierwald & Heller, 1993). Figures 3.7 and 3.8 are examples of nomination forms that allow the parents and community to provide information about a student's out-of-school activities for use in selecting participants in a program for talented students.

Milgram et al. (1997) said, "The predictive validity of IQ/achievement test scores with reference to adult accomplishments is modest at best" (p. 111). They did a study with 91 high-IQ male Israelis, having followed them from 1982 into adulthood. They found that 45 percent of the students had participated in teenage activities that related to their adult choices of vocation. Out-of-school interests can be viewed as strong predictors of adult domain-specific behaviors and even accomplishments in later careers. This finding, in a Western-oriented country with similar child raising practices to the United States, has implications for the disadvantaged. Milgram et al. said that out-of-school domain-related activities are commonly encouraged by middle-class families, but may not be encouraged in disadvantaged families. "Accordingly, in the same way that educational planners concern themselves with providing special, formal educational opportunities for the disadvantaged, they might consider how to expose disadvantaged youngsters to the kinds of stimulation that might lead them to engage in challenging leisure activities" (p. 118).

Figure 3.7   Sample Parent Nomination Form

Parent Information

Rationale:

Data about potentially gifted students collected from outside school settings from parents and other adults can provide information that may be unknown or unobserved by teachers in an educational setting.

Objectives:
  1. To identify behaviors and skills that are not visible in the classroom.
  2. To collect information about in-depth interests.
  3. To collect evidence of nonverbal abilities.

Parent information about the student and his or her capabilities at home and in the community can be invaluable when accompanied by examples. The identification committee for special gifted students can evaluate the information in terms of age levels and abilities.

Parent Information Survey

Student Name _____ Date _____

Parent Name _____

Directions: If your child has special talents or interests in any of the areas on this form, please fill them out. Fill out only the categories that fit your child. Return this form to your child's teacher by _____. Thank you for your help.

My child

  1. Fixes things: _____yes _____no

     If yes, what kinds of things? _____

     _____

     _____

     How long has he/she done this? _____

     _____

     _____

     Can you remember (and tell us) any stories about this? Or send a sample to

     school? What is it? _____

     _____

     _____

Figure 3.7 *Continued*

2. Makes things: _____ yes _____ no

If yes, what kinds of things? _____

_____

_____

How long has he/she done this? _____

_____

_____

Can you remember (and tell us) any stories about this? Or send a sample to

school? What is it? _____

_____

_____

3. Collects things: _____ yes _____ no

If yes, what kinds of things? _____

_____

_____

Can you remember (and tell us) any stories about this? Or send a sample to

school? What is it? _____

_____

_____

4. Writes things: _____ yes _____ no

If yes, what kinds of things? _____

_____

_____

How long has he/she done this? _____

_____

(continued on next page)

Figure 3.7   *Continued*

Do you have some samples of work that you can send to school? _____

_____

5. Reads a lot: _____ yes _____ no

   If yes, what kinds of things? _____

   _____

   _____

6. Is really interested in: What? _____

   For how long? _____

   Do you have any samples? _____

7. Something that hasn't been mentioned that I would like to tell you about my

   child: _____

   _____

   _____

   _____

From "Project SPRING," Indiana University and Bowling Green State University, 1990–1993, part of a Javits Act federal grant. Used with permission.

CASE EXAMPLE: Jose

by Sylvia Rodriguez-Mylinski *(Used with permission of author)*

This study was done by Sylvia Rodriguez-Mylinski, an English as a Second Language (ESL) teacher, for a first course in the education of the talented in a medium-sized northern U.S. city.

I believe Jose is a talented student, even though he has not been identified as such. I first came to these conclusions shortly after I became Jose's ESL teacher. When I first met him, when he was 10 years old, I noticed he was very curious. He kept asking me questions, and during reading he would always add new information to the stories we had read. He did very well in reading class; however, he was flunking everything else. I talked to several teachers about him, but no one would confirm my observations that he was very bright, especially since he was doing so poorly. When I got his CTBS (Comprehensive Tests of Basic Skills) scores back, my suspicions were confirmed. His Cognitive Skills Index was 126, even though his grades were low. His highest scores were in Reading Comprehension and Language Expression, his lowest in Math Computation.

Last year I had contacted Jose's mother because I was very concerned about Jose's grades. The children had been taken out of the home and placed in a home under the care of Children's Services because it was suspected that the children were physically abused. When I spoke to Jose's mother about this, she became angry because she felt that the school and the social services had interfered with her methods of discipline. At that time, she was hostile to my approach and was reluctant to speak to me.

As part of my case study, I finally went to Jose's home. The house was located in a low-income area. It was sparsely decorated and neat. The rooms were quite dark, so I asked Jose's mother whether she would turn on the lamp. She apologized and said it did not work. Three smaller children (Jose's brother and sisters) were playing in the kitchen. There are seven children in the family, ages 2 to 14

Jose was identified by his ESL teacher's observation of his predictive behavior of constant reading.

years. At age 11, Jose is the second oldest. His oldest sister is living with his grandmother. Jose's mother said his infant physical development was normal, that he walked at about age 1, and talked at about age 1 year 6 months. She said that she taught him to read in Spanish at age 4. He was only her second child and she had more time to devote to him.

Jose's parents are divorced. According to Jose's mother, Jose's father drank, used drugs, and was abusive. They moved to our town from Chicago after the divorce, and she does not know where he is. At the time of the case study, she was living with a man who was not Jose's father. He was unemployed and had his own apartment, although he spent a lot of time with Jose's mother. Jose's mother alluded to the fact that her male friend was an illegal immigrant from Mexico, and asked that I keep this confidential. She said that he had attended college in Mexico, but she did not know what he had studied. Her male friend enjoys reading and they are both very active in their church, and spend much time reading the Bible.

Jose's mother is from Nicaragua. When she was 16 years old she came to the United States for economic reasons. Her parents had a poor marriage and her mother was the main provider. They were very poor. At the age of 12 she was working in a drugstore delivering messages and medicine. The owners told her she was very bright and hoped that she would continue with high school. She was unable to finish high school and wishes that she had done so and had gone to college. She has six brothers and sisters. A younger brother and a younger sister did go on to college. They live in California and she has lost track of them. One of her cousins is an author, and she is very proud of him. She spoke briefly of her suffering in Nicaragua.

Jose's mother understands English; however, she feels embarrassed that she cannot speak English well. She would like to go back to school to learn English, but she has no one to take care of the younger children. Besides, she does not trust anyone else with her children. The family attends church three or four days a week. The members of the church and of her family have often commented on how bright Jose is. Jose has had a chance to travel to Mexico with the pastor of the church.

Jose's Predictive Behaviors

Jose spends most of his time at home reading, drawing, and watching television. Ever since he was young, he has been able to entertain himself. Jose's mother said that she rarely has any problems with him, except that sometimes she wishes he wouldn't spend so much time reading. She can't get him to do anything else. When he was in his room supposedly doing his homework, he would be reading, and she would assume that he was doing his homework. She also said that many times Jose knows how to do something, but says he doesn't just to get out of doing it. She thinks this is laziness, and that his constant reading is his way to be lazy.

When I asked his other teachers about Jose, his principal said, "Oh, he's the one who is always reading." I interviewed his teachers. His present teacher said, "Jose could be a good student if he did his work. He is always reading. Once he asked to go to the restroom. He took a long time so I sent in another student to get him. He was sitting in the john reading." Then his teacher gave me a picture that she had taken away from him. He had been drawing when he was supposed to be doing his work.

I asked his last year's teacher about him. She said, "Jose was always reading. I could never get him to do his work. He was well behaved, except when he stood up for his friend Carlos, who was always getting into trouble." His classmates also noticed his behavior. His teacher said that they were talking about the meaning of the word *bookworm*. The children said, "Oh, you mean a person like Jose?"

I shadowed him in school for two days, and I took photographs of him in various situations. During the free breakfast program, Jose was reading. Before school, Jose was in the library, looking for a book to read. During lunch, Jose was reading. During a class break, Jose was reading while everyone else was talking. Walking down the hall, Jose was reading. Waiting for an interview with me, Jose was reading. During recess, among all the students playing games, Jose was standing at the side of the playground, reading. After school, sitting on the gym floor waiting for the bus, everyone was talking. Jose was reading.

In my class, we do a lot of reading and writing, and Jose is the most advanced writer. When he went to Mexico with his minister, he got very interested in Mexican folk tales, and combined three of them in this story:

How the Sun, the Moon, and the Stars Got into the Sky

Once upon a time there were no people, but there were gods. Once they thought about making something that would live on earth, and so they made a man. But they so liked the man that they made more. Now men were hungry, so the gods made animals. But still there was something wrong. So one of them went to earth in the form of man. He went to the oldest of them all, and asked why men were sad. The man, not knowing he was talking to a god, said, "Well, men are lonely on this earth." When the god heard this, he went back to where the other gods were and he told the others, so then they thought about making women. So they did. Men were glad and they gave thanks to the gods and went home.

Now there was a woman who was mean. Everyone knew her. She wanted to know about the gods in the sky. So she climbed in a big tree that touched the sky. There she hid in a cloud and went to the house of the gods. There she saw a big pot of fire and she stole it. The gods immediately found out about it and turned her into a witch! She hid her ugliness in the mountains.

Now there was no sun, no moon, and no stars (so people could see each other, they used fire). But the witch didn't need anything like that because of the fireball she had in the pot. Also, animals knew about this too. They were afraid of her. But a coyote had an idea. He went to the mountains where the witch dwelled, which was named Witch Mountain and he sat by the bottom. On the other side was the witch with a club!

The witch said, "If you try to steal my fireball you are going to be hit by this club. The coyote, who was smart, said, "Why would I try to steal something of someone so beautiful and young like you?" She said, "No one has said that I was beautiful and young before." He said, "Look in the pool of water in front of you." She bent down and looked, but she forgot about the pot that was unguarded. Then the coyote seized the pot by the handle and ran. The witch screamed when she found out. But it was too late. He was gone. While he ran, the pot shook so much that pieces of fireball broke off and got stuck in the sky and became stars. The biggest one became known as the Moon. Coyote ran until he got to the highest mountain and there he hung the pot, which turned into the sun. The people thanked the coyote. The gods made him into a god and took him into the sky. He lived there happily and was glad that he had helped the people.

This story was written in English. I have corrected a few spelling and grammatical errors, but this was essentially what Jose wrote. I was interested in whether Jose was reading Spanish or English, and whether he thought in Spanish or English. I asked him several questions:

How do you remember things?
  Like words? Well, I know Spanish better than English. If there is a word in English and it is hard to pronounce, then I read it in Spanish instead. If I forget a word like "guitar," I think of the things that are in my church and then I remember it.
  What language do you read better in?
  I read better in Spanish.
  How else do you remember?
  I feel my books.
  Where do you get the books you read?
  From the library at school, or from my teacher.
  If you could invent something, what would you invent?
  I would invent a robot so he could help me clean my house and do my homework so I could have time to read.
  What country would you like to visit?
  I would like to visit Nicaragua because my mom is always talking about how different it is there.

During this interview I uncovered an amazing fact. Jose has never been to McDonald's or Burger King. He has only been to one movie, and has been to a museum once, that time with his class. For fun his family goes to the park, and to church where "we study the Bible." Jose's lack of exposure to the artifacts of the culture such as fast food, movies, and museums is quite common among many of my ESL students. He is an example of a talented student whose behavior, rather than test scores, shows his talent. I have referred him to the gifted program coordinator, although I don't have much hope that he will be served. I will continue to ask him about his reading, and to help him with his writing.

➤ ➤ ➤ ➤ ➤ ➤ ➤ ➤ ➤ ➤ ➤ ➤ ➤ ➤ ➤ ➤ ➤ ➤

SUMMARY

1. Identification of academically talented children usually means identification of high IQ or high achievement by means of standardized tests.
2. Before collecting information on certain tests and certain steps in the process of identification, the school system must make a commitment to programming for the academically talented student, wherever that student is found.
3. While many academically talented students will be found through the means of achievement and intelligence tests, some will not be. These are the ones that are worrisome to school districts.
4. Several steps are commonly taken in the identification process in most school districts: nomination and screening, selection, and placement.
5. The identification of academically talented students should also be attempted by local norms, case studies, authentic assessment, academically related common, nontested predictive behaviors, and leisure interests.

IDENTIFICATION OF CREATIVITY

FOCUSING QUESTIONS

1. Look at the creativity education component in a nearby program for the exceptionally talented and discuss it.
2. Trace the history of the psychometric creativity testing movement.
3. What social forces and reasons are most important in discussing the emphasis on creativity?
4. Discuss the transfer of creativity training.
5. Can a person's life be called his or her creative product? Why or why not?
6. Does a creative product have to be tangible? Why or why not?
7. What are some of the cautions that must be observed when considering creativity testing?
8. Discuss validity and testing for creativity.
9. Discuss reliability and testing for creativity.
10. How does "significance" play a part in considering which tests to use?
11. Why should portfolio assessment be part of the assessment of talent?
12. Discuss why or how a student's product shows his/her creativity.

Figure 4.1   Overview of Chapter 4

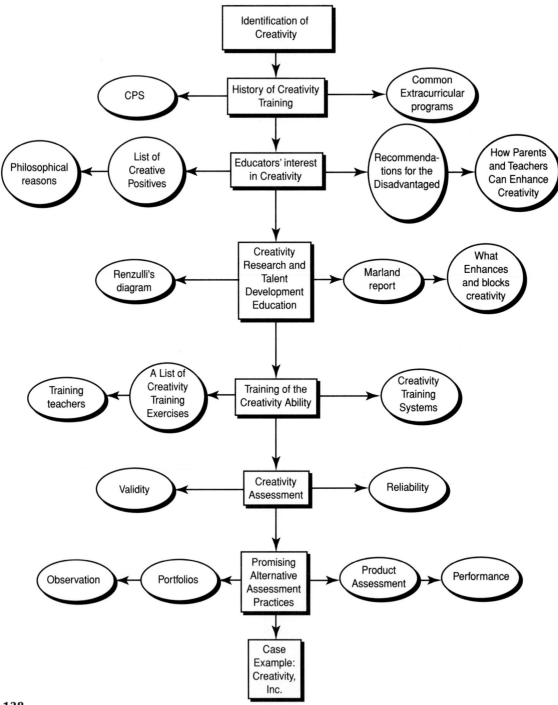

Chris Wiley entered his classroom for the first time. He had just been hired to teach talented students in the fifth and sixth grades. Chris had been an English major in college, and had graduated with a 3.9 average in his major. He had been in the honors program and wrote a senior thesis on Thomas Wolfe. He had taught high school English last year, but he had been riffed over the summer, and last week the superintendent had called him and asked whether he'd be interested in taking the district's gifted education position that was partly funded by the state. Dr. Cranshaw, the superintendent, said Chris would have to enroll for at least two graduate classes in gifted education, but that the job was his even though he'd had no training. She told Chris that people had spoken well of his teaching and she was committed to providing good education for the district's talented students.

Chris decided to give it a try, even though he'd never had any experience with elementary school children. Because these were bright children, he thought his high school English background would come in handy. He'd teach them some good literature. He was a little worried about the math and the science, but he'd always gotten As in those subjects in his high school honors classes, and he had taken four years of each, so he thought he'd at least be able to refer the bright young math and science kids to the proper mentors. He wasn't too worried about social studies; history and geography and economics and such were all woven into great literature.

The classroom was bright and looked out over the playground. Dr. Cranshaw said that the former teacher had left all her lesson plans along with the materials the school and the parents' association had bought. Chris spent the afternoon looking over the plans and materials. They all seemed to have something to do with brainstorming, flexibility, fluency, and creativity. For one entire month last year, the files contained black-line photocopies of brainstorming ideas culled from a magazine that catered to teachers of the gifted. What were the students brainstorming about? Ways to buckle coats. Ideas for fall parties. Ways to improve the school lunch line.

Chris decided he had better find out more. He attended a regional meeting of the teachers of the talented and they were all exchanging ideas; the ideas were more about brainstorming and creativity. There was a large room set up where people were sitting at tables playing games and exchanging handouts about creativity. People were dressed in strange costumes. Where was the English? Where was the math? Where were the science and social studies? He studied the course of study for the state. Again, it seemed to emphasize these processes more than subject matter. Chris was beginning to feel he was in the wrong pew. His strong subject matter background, as a trained high school English teacher, hadn't prepared him for all this "process" talk. One of the speakers, a famous scholar in creative and critical thinking, even made a keynote speech in which he said that "process *is* content." Chris thought he had a lot to learn.

Chris's situation is not that unusual. He was experiencing the culture shock that high school subject matter specialists experience when they look at the differentiated curricula of some gifted and talented education programs. Many of these are differentiated with an emphasis on process, rather than on content, and often the processes emphasized are those associated with creativity training. Students who are identified as having high IQs and high specific subject matter achievement are put into the talent development education program and are given creativity training.

HISTORY OF CREATIVITY TRAINING

Teaching gifted and talented students to become more creative has become so commonplace as to not even be questioned. Few even question how elitist this idea is. The notion that only a few students should receive creativity training grew out of the education movement after World War II. How did this come about? Let us try to make some sense of this creativity explosion. In 1955, at the University of Buffalo's Creative Education Foundation, a project was begun in which students were to be taught creative problem solving according to the Parnes-Osborn model. At the end of 14 months, those who had taken the course were compared to those who had not. Those who had taken it averaged "94% better in production of ideas" (Osborn, 1963).

This modest beginning produced a wave of followers and a whole cadre of special creativity teachers emerged, who taught courses, gave speeches, and conducted workshops on the creative problem solving method. By the mid 1970s, creative problem solving (CPS) was being taught to educators of the revitalized gifted education movement (Feldhusen & Clinkenbeard, 1986; Isaksen & Treffinger, 1985; Torrance, 1987a; Treffinger & Isaksen, 1992). Often the divergent and convergent thinking used in creative problem solving was mistakenly called "creativity." Creative problem solving is a formal process, a series of steps, in which the problem solvers use divergent production (brainstorming) and convergent production (criteria setting) to work their way through a thorny situation called a "mess." Figure 4.2 shows a diagram of the CPS process.

This relatively new term, *creativity*, came to mean much to educators of the gifted and talented. As an outgrowth of the social revolution of the 1960s and early 1970s, people have come to believe that the schools stifle children's creativity. An example is the popular Harry Chapin song about a first grade child who could already draw flowers, but who then had to learn how to draw the flower everyone else drew. Stifling children's creativity is, according to some views, necessary, and in other views, evil. Recent editions of widely adopted school textbooks have begun to include enrichment activities that supposedly help children to think creatively. Creativity is "in." A lesson on environmental pollution could, as an enrichment activity, ask students to list things that are green. This is called *brainstorming*. It is an open-ended activity that encourages *fluency* in creativity parlance. *Flexibility* training is also part of creativity enrichment. Teaching children to be flexible is asking them to come up with alternative ways of thinking.

The Necessity for Practice

William Durden, the director of the Center for Talented Youth (CTY) at Johns Hopkins University, has said that creativity training has often missed an important necessity,

Figure 4.2 Steps in Creative Problem Solving

The Steps	What Happens
A Problem Exists	Identify the problem by asking questions: who, what, where, when, why? We need to enhance student ability to recognize or sense problems.
Data Finding (Clarify the problem by collecting information)	We need to collect data in order to improve the understanding of the problem. What is "fuzzy" needs to be made clear. Ask: What are illustrations of the problem? What are things that cause the problem? What are further problems caused by the problem?
Problem Finding (Stating the problem)	Many problems may be imbedded in the original problem. State subproblems, recognize problems *caused* by the problem. A manageable problem is selected and stated in this form: "In what ways might ... ?"
Idea Finding (Generating solutions)	Generate as many ideas as possible for solving the problem. This is a good place to use creative thinking techniques. Brainstorm ideas.
Select a Solution (Decision making)	Choose the most important criteria; use the decision making process and evaluate potential solutions against defined criteria. Ask: What criteria must the solution meet? What solution comes out on top?
Acceptance Finding (Implementing the solution)	Work out the details: Who will do what? How? Where? What should we watch for? How can we convince others? Who else must be involved? Identify "assistors" and "resistors."

Reprinted from Morrison, M., and Duncan, R. (1992). *Model for the Identification of Creative-Thinking Ability* (p. 39). Ohio Department of Education, Research and Demonstration Series in Gifted Education.

which is that the person who is creative must have information (1985). Educators who stress Bloom's higher levels of synthesis, analysis, and evaluation in problem solving and who ignore the lower levels of knowledge, comprehension and application, have "oversold" students. In an editorial written in *Academic Talent* in 1985, Durden said, "the 'lowest' cognitive realms play a key role in nurturing the development of a talented/creative person. The repetitious, the mundane, the traditional, transformed into a celebrated ritual—sometimes secretly and passionately pursued—characterizes the education of countless highly creative and talented persons" (p. 8).

Ghiselin (1952) called this the acquiring of *automaticity*. In his essay on the creative process, Ghiselin said that the creative person, in no matter what domain, must know his of her field well enough to be able to proceed automatically. To know something so well that it can be executed automatically is to have practiced it over and over again so that the execution is almost unconscious. The creator doesn't have to think about the process, the how to. Athletes practice for hours on end, shooting baskets, pitching baseballs, lobbing tennis balls. Musicians practice. The pianist Gary Graffman titled his 1981 autobiography *I Really Should Be Practicing.* Writers practice. The juvenilia of such writers as Virginia Woolf and the Brontes, or the voluminous adult production of Joyce Carol Oates, all attest to the need to keep writing, no matter what. *Understanding Those Who Create* (Piirto, 1992a/1998) details other creators' attention to practice. Visual artists practice. Van Gogh, in his final days, estimated that he had created thousands of works. Picasso kept working into his eighties. Scientists and mathematicians begin publishing at early ages and most of those who have an impact on the world keep on experimenting and publishing. Simonton (1986, 1988, 1994) has detailed this. Asian cultures such as the Japanese and Chinese understand this and approach training for creativity from quite a different perspective; repetition and automaticity are prerequisites for the risk taking necessary in creating something new.

Durden in his 1985 essay also noted that creators need good memories: "And memorization—that lowly beast—how does one account for its presence early in so many highly talented persons' lives, and yet its almost total absence in the directives of contemporary education?" (p. 8). He said that people who have made significant accomplishment in fields such as science, medicine, letters, and the arts, did so because they had information: "Creativity needs information," Durden said. The schools should realize that "disciplined attention at an early age" is more important than premature focus on "global issues, creativity per se, problem solving, the future, infinity, dismissing any trace of constraint, routine, discipline, or tradition" (p. 8).

Special educators of academically talented youth are sometimes reluctant to ask their students to practice, to memorize, and even to acquire background knowledge. They may jump straight into process and forget content. They may use creativity training as the main differentiation of curriculum for the academically talented. However, not many of the commonly used creativity training programs, packages, and systems focus on discipline-based creativity. The specialists who usually teach talented visual and performing artists or talented athletes rarely use such techniques as CPS. Some widely used programs do have components that encourage creative behavior within domains—after the student has acquired some knowledge.

Celebrations such as Young Authors Fairs, where children write their own books, or Odyssey of the Mind (OM) events, where teams of children compete in categories of problems to make new products, or Invention Conventions, where children invent new doodads (some of which are bought by businesses), or Future Problem Solving (FPS) contests, where children use the CPS process after studying about a certain world problem, or History Day competitions, where students choose historical situations for projects, or science fairs, where students do science projects, have components that can contribute to the necessary gathering of information a creator needs. These competitions are modeled after the sports model, the team model; and while they can be fun and exciting—or even disappointing to those who lose—educators of the talented should also note that creative behavior also occurs in solitude, in meditative thought, when one is all alone and thinking.

Invention Conventions and similar events encourage creative behavior using a competition/team model.

Creativity came to be called an *ability* quite recently—after 1964. An *ability* is a special skill or talent. The talent to be creative, then, is *creativity*. To be an expert on creativity is to be an expert on those who make something new, or to be an expert on teaching people how to make something new.

EDUCATORS' INTEREST IN CREATIVITY

There are six reasons why creativity is of such interest to educators of the talented (Piirto, 1992a/1998): These are (1) reasons of quantity—we want more creative products; (2) reasons of quality—we want better creative products; (3) philosophical reasons of the pursuit of freedom and of mysteriousness; (4) reasons of equity—we want to identify children with creative potential who might not be identified as having academic talent or visual and performing arts talent; (5) reasons of nationalistic pride—we want more creative individuals so that we can compete internationally in inventions and business; and (6) to prepare for the future. Schools have concern with items 4, 5, and 6: equity, nationalism, and preparation for the future.

Torrance made a list (published in 1969) of *creative positives* by which disadvantaged children might be recognized. Torrance's list (see Figure 4.3) has 100 items in 18 clusters. Feldhusen (1992b) said a number of these items "are useful in assessing specific areas of strength or talent" (p. 17).

Note that many of the creative positives in Torrance's list have to do with aspects of personality or general behaviors and not with behaviors within a domain, because disadvantaged children may not have had an opportunity to be exposed to domains where creative production is generally sought in the school setting. The list was generated to be used with disadvantaged children (Feldhusen, 1992b), and the purpose was to try to find predictive behaviors without overly emphasizing behaviors within domains where people are creative.

The Place of Creativity in Education

Few even question whether the enhancement of creativity is the proper province of the schools. Some might say that to identify a child who has creative talent may require the use of means that have nothing to do with what schools are supposed to do: teach children to fit into society by civilizing them, and by teaching them to read, to write, and to figure—that is, to make them literate. They may say that the schools today have their hands full doing both tasks, although some would argue that teaching children to be more creative enhances their self-esteem and thus helps them to learn the basics more easily. Others argue that high self-esteem comes from working hard on a project or program, that self-esteem comes from overcoming adversity and achieving, that many programs for enhancing self-esteem fail to address the necessity for hard work and overcoming difficulties.

Creative talent is currently called a form of giftedness in the schools of the United States and Canada. Pragmatists say that since creativity is written into federal definitions, creativity thus becomes a concern of the schools. Creative thinking is currently called an ability that is separate from talent in specific domains such as visual arts or writing or music. It is the ability to produce something new—if not to the world, to the person doing the producing. Whether creativity *is* actually a measurable ability, a separate construct, has been debated and questioned. The concept of creativity has been invested with a lot of serious interest and research in various disciplines in the last 40 years. Whereas Guilford in 1950 said he looked for research on creativity and had come up with only a few articles, now there are thousands of experts, thousands of speakers at conventions, thousands of people doing research. No wonder there is so much confusion about creativity. Many theories have been espoused by many theorists.

The creativity literature is filled with comments by people in one field or another disagreeing about so and so's ideas. Creativity is a vital concern of thinkers in such diverse fields as business (entrepreneurship), the arts, philosophy (aesthetics), medicine (research), and psychoanalysis (genius and madness).

Runco (1992), in a position paper for the National Research Center on the Gifted and Talented at the University of Connecticut, said that creativity education should be a vital part of education in general, especially for disadvantaged students. Since the potential for creativity is not dependent on income or on ethnicity, educators can be optimistic: "Creative potential seems to be very widely distributed," said Runco. Students' grades have no relationship to their creative potential, nor does their attitude

Figure 4.3 Torrance's Checklist of Creative Positives

1. Ability to express feelings and emotions
   ____ Expresses feelings and emotions facially
   ____ Expresses feelings and emotions by body gestures
   ____ Expresses feelings and emotions in writing
   ____ Expresses feelings and emotions in discussions
   ____ Expresses feelings and emotions in role playing
   ____ Expresses feelings and emotions in dramatics
   ____ Expresses feelings and emotions in dance and/or creative movement
   ____ Expresses feelings and emotions in visual art media
   ____ Expresses feelings and emotions in music and rhythm

2. Ability to improvise with commonplace materials
   ____ Makes toys from commonplace materials
   ____ Uses commonplace materials to modify toys
   ____ Makes games from commonplace materials
   ____ Uses commonplace materials for school purposes
   ____ Uses commonplace materials for home purposes
   ____ Uses commonplace materials in "inventions"
   ____ Uses commonplace materials in role playing and creative dramatics

3. Articulateness in role playing and storytelling
   ____ Role playing becomes very involved and lifelike
   ____ Expresses ideas in role playing
   ____ Responds at empathic level toward others in role playing
   ____ Becomes very involved in storytelling
   ____ Engages in fantasy in storytelling

3. Enjoyment of and ability in visual art
   ____ Experiences real joy in drawing
   ____ Experiences real joy in painting
   ____ Experiences real joy in sculpture
   ____ Experiences real joy in other visual art activities
   ____ Understands subject matter by "drawing it" (illustrating stories, illustrating history, drawing biological objects, making maps, etc.)
   ____ Communicates skillfully through drawings
   ____ Communicates skillfully through painting
   ____ Communicates skillfully through sculpture
   ____ Makes others see something new through visual arts

5. Enjoyment of and ability in creative movement, dance, dramatics, etc.
   ____ Experiences deep enjoyment in dance and/or creative movement
   ____ Experiences deep enjoyment in creative dramatics
   ____ Becomes completely absorbed in dance and creative movement
   ____ Becomes completely involved in creative dramatics
   ____ Can interpret songs, poems, stories through creative movement
   ____ Can elaborate ideas through creative movement and/or dance
   ____ Movement facilitates learning and understanding ideas, events, concepts
   ____ Creative dramatics facilitates learning and understanding ideas, events, concepts
   ____ Creates own style of movement, dance, etc.

6. Enjoyment of and ability in music, rhythm, etc.
   ____ Writes, moves, works, walks with rhythm
   ____ Rhythm facilitates learning of skills
   ____ Rhythm facilitates learning and understanding ideas, events, concepts
   ____ Creates songs
   ____ Creates music
   ____ Can interpret ideas, events, feelings, etc., through rhythm
   ____ Can interpret ideas, events, feelings, etc., through music

7. Expressive speech
   ____ Speech is colorful
   ____ Speech is picturesque (suggests a picture, etc.)
   ____ Speech includes powerful analogies, metaphors, etc. *(continued on next page)*

Figure 4.3   *Continued*

_____ Speech is vivid (lively, intense, penetrating, etc.)

_____ Invents words to express concepts new to him/her

8. Fluency and flexibility in verbal media

_____ Produces large number of different ideas through drawing

_____ Produces large number of ideas with common objects

_____ Produces large number of ideas through creative movement/dance

_____ Produces large number of ideas through music and rhythm

_____ Produces large number of ideas in play situations

_____ Produces large variety of ideas through drawings

_____ Produces large variety of ideas through dance

_____ Produces large variety of ideas through music

9. Enjoyment of and skills in small group activities, problem solving, etc.

_____ Work in a small group facilitates learning

_____ Tries harder in small groups

_____ Produces ideas in small groups

_____ Becomes more alive in small groups

_____ Skillful in group organization

_____ Highly aware of feelings and skills of others in small groups

10. Responsiveness to the concrete

_____ Ideas start flowing when concrete materials and objects are involved

_____ Uses concrete objects and materials to generate ideas, solutions, etc.

11. Responsiveness to the kinesthetic

_____ Movement stimulates ideas

_____ Movement communicates ideas

_____ Skillful in interpreting meaning of movement

12. Expressiveness of gestures, body language, etc.

_____ Expresses ideas powerfully through gestures, "body language"

_____ Body says the things words do not say

13. Humor

_____ Portrays comical, funny, amusing in writing

_____ Portrays comical, funny, amusing in role playing

_____ Portrays comical, funny, amusing in drawings

_____ Makes humorous comic strips (original)

_____ Portrays comical, funny, amusing in dramatics

_____ Makes people laugh in games

_____ Makes up humorous jokes

_____ Makes people laugh (not make fun of) in discussion

_____ Tells his/her experiences with humor

14. Richness of imagery in informal language

_____ Makes others see pictures when telling a story or relating personal experiences

_____ Makes people see a picture when describing something in a conversation

_____ Makes people see pictures in role playing and dramatics

15. Originality of ideas in problem solving

_____ Produces solutions that others do not think of

_____ Produces solutions when no one else can

_____ Solutions are unusual, unconventional

_____ Stories have unusual endings

_____ Stories have unusual plots

_____ Comes up with inventions to solve problems

_____ Innovates with commonplace materials to produce solutions to day-to-day problems

16. Problem-centeredness

_____ Doesn't give up, keeps trying to solve problems

_____ Shows concern and tries to solve problems of others

_____ Is hard to distract when he is concerned about a problem

_____ Keeps seeing relevance of new information to problems of group

17. Emotional responsiveness

_____ Responds emotionally to stories, events, needs of group members, etc.

18. Quickness of warm-up

_____ Always ready to go: may get tired of waiting and become "turned off"

From Torrance, E.P. (1969). Creative positives of disadvantaged youths. *Gifted Child Quarterly,* 13(2), pp. 71–81.

toward school. In fact, creative students may have a negative attitude toward the conformity required in the institutional school setting. Motivation to create is most important, and there are many ways to be creative. Runco said, "educators can do quite a bit with it simply by manipulating incentives and rewards. They do, however, need to ensure that they do not undermine the intrinsic motivation of students."

Students should see the educators modeling and demonstrating independence of thought, spontaneous activity, and valuing originality. Runco listed six behaviors that educators should avoid in teaching for creativity (see Figure 4.4).

Figure 4.4   Runco's Recommendations for Enhancing Creativity in Disadvantaged Students

AVOID	ATTEMPT
1. Avoid relying on verbal materials; use a variety of materials; tap various domains (e.g., music, crafts, mathematics, language arts, physical education).	1. Allow independent work, and not just where it is easy (e.g., while working on crafts or art projects).
2. Avoid relying on verbal rewards. Concrete reinforcers may be best for many disadvantaged students.	2. Discuss creativity with students; tell them why it is valuable. Be explicit about how and when to be original, flexible, and independent.
3. Avoid overemphasizing structure and curricula with predictable outcomes. Ask questions that allow students to follow their own (potentially divergent) logic and thinking, even if unpredictable. Plan to follow students' own interests part of each day.	3. Monitor your expectations; be aware of potential halo effects.
4. Avoid prejudging students who are nonconforming and students who find their own way of doing things.	4. Recognize the multifaceted nature of creativity.
5. Avoid suggesting (even implicitly) that your own way of doing something is the best or only way.	5. Recognize that creativity is a sign of and contributor to psychological health.
6. Avoid going overboard.	6. Work to appreciate what children find for themselves; give both helpful evaluations and supportive valuations.
	7. Inform parents of what you are doing, and why.
	8. Read the creativity and educational literature and work with others who study and value creativity.

From Runco, M. (1992). "Creativity as an Educational Objective for Disadvantaged Students." University of Connecticut: National Research Center on the Gifted and Talented.

Figure 4.5 How Parents and
Teachers Can Enhance Ceativity
in Children
From Piirto, J. *Understanding Those
Who Create.* (1992a/1998). Tempe,
AZ: Gifted Psychology Press.

1. Provide a private place for creative work to be done.

2. Provide materials (e.g., musical instruments, sketchbooks).

3. Encourage and display the child's creative work and avoid overly evaluating it.

4. Do your own creative work and let the child see you.

5. Pay attention to what your family mythology is teaching.

6. Value the creative work of others.

7. Avoid emphasizing sex-role stereotypes.

8. Provide private lessons and special classes.

9. If hardship comes into your life, use the hardship positively to encourage the child to express himself/herself through metaphor.

10. Emphasize that talent is only a small part of creative production and that discipline and practice are important.

11. Allow the child to be "odd"; avoid emphasizing socialization at the expense of creative expression.

12. Interact with the child with kind humor.

How Teachers and Parents Can Enhance Creativity

Teachers and parents can work in partnership to enhance creativity. First of all, creativity is affective—the necessary risk taking and sense of openness to experience, or naiveté, required demand a safe environment in which to explore. Both the home and the school should try to provide such. Trust is also important; that is, someone who is trying out creatively should not be put down, and should be permitted to fail as well as to star. (The Case Example at the end of this chapter on p. 181 discusses the affective approach to creativity training in more detail.). A person who tries out creativity should have a safe group (the class, the family) with whom to be. In my book *Understanding Those Who Create* (1992a/1998), there are 12 suggestions for teachers and parents to enhance creativity. The suggestions are listed in Figure 4.5.

CREATIVITY RESEARCH THAT HAS INFLUENCED THE FIELD OF TALENT DEVELOPMENT EDUCATION

The psychometricians' influence on our understanding of creativity has been great. One can see this influence in the evolution of the term *creativity*; in recent dictionary definitions, creativity is called an *ability*. If something is an ability, it is logical that attempts would be made to measure this ability or to find what factors it possesses. That is the job of psychologists called *psychometrists*. To set the record straight, and to detail the pervasive influence of psychology on the field of the education of the talented, a historical summary is warranted. Such a summary follows, and one might call this the "old" paradigm of creativity. The tendency to call creativity an ability began during the 1930s and culminated in large grants from foundations and the government being awarded to major universities in the 1940s after World War II. These grants were given so that researchers could find the means of identifying creative potential. Table 4.1 lists some of the major studies or projects in creativity assessment and research. See also Piirto (1992a/1998) for an overview of creativity studies.

In 1971, the Marland report from the federal government education office listed "creative or productive thinking" as one of the six types of giftedness. The Javits Gifted and Talented Students Education Act of 1988 retained the word *creative*, saying that gifted and talented students have high potential to be high performers in "areas such as intellectual, *creative*, artistic, or leadership capacity or in specific academic fields." The 1993 definition also retained the word *creative*. Specifying creative *capacity* remains quite confusing to practitioners, however.

As late as 1991, researchers divided students into "high creatives" and "low creatives" and "high intelligence" and "low intelligence" in order to show some obscure aspect of divergent production improved with training (Carroll & Howieson, 1991). One can understand why this was done; as Baer (1991) noted, "Research on creativity requires some kind of assessment procedure. This is an obstacle that has plagued the field" (p. 25). In conducting a study, one needs quantifiable pre- and post-measurements.

Such studies demonstrate an underlying prejudice that is similar to that discussed in Chapter 1. Studies of intelligence take high scores on an IQ test as comparison measurements. Studies of creativity take high scores on divergent production tests such as the Torrance Tests of Creative Thinking (TTCT) as comparison measurements. Then the researchers call the subjects highly intelligent or highly creative, making the jump from assessment to assumption of *intelligence* or *creativity*. That is why some psychologists have said, "Intelligence is what intelligence tests measure." It does not follow that creative capacity, or even creativity, is what divergent production tests measure.

The Separation of Creativity from Talent

As mentioned in Chapter 1, Marland postulated a talent called *creativity*. Following up on studies such as those by Getzels and Jackson (1962) and Wallach and Kogan (1965), schools came to define *creativity* operationally as scoring above average on an IQ test, and having some measure of creative potential, such as ranking high on a creativity checklist or scoring high on a standardized divergent production test. They separated creative talent from IQ. This is called the *threshold theory*, the theory that creative people have above-average IQs, but not necessarily the highest IQs.

Table 4.1   Creativity Assessment Reseach

Study and Dates	Researchers and Publications	Findings
Institute for Personality Assessment and Research (IPAR), 1950s–1960s, University of California at Berkeley	Frank Barron (*Artists in the Making; Creativity and Personal Freedom*); Ravenna Helson (gender differences in creativity); Harrison Gough (personality preferences of creative people); Wallace B. Hall and Donald MacKinnon, (*In Search of Human Effectiveness*, 1978)	Method of personality assessment developed: Personalities of creative architects, writers, mathematicians, inventors, engineers, research scientists are remarkably similar. Created many instruments such as Barron-Welsh Art Scale, and Adjective Check List
Air Force Aptitudes Project 1950s–1960s, University of California at Los Angeles	J.P. Guilford (*The Nature of Intelligence,* 1967)	Factor analysis to verify Structure of Intellect cells; Divergent production tests created
Research Conferences of the Identification of Creative Scientific Talent, University of Utah, 1955, 1957, and 1959	Calvin Taylor	1. Brought together thinkers at conferences, generated research proposals at many universities 2. He also was an early advocate of talent development. His Talents Unlimited program is nationally disseminated
University of Chicago Studies of Creativity and Talent Development, 1960s to present	1. Jacob Getzels and Philip Jackson (*Creativity and Intelligence: Explorations with Gifted Students*, 1962) 2. Michael Wallach and Nathan Kogan (*Creativity and Intelligence in Children*, 1972) 3. Jacob Getzels and Mihalyi Csikszentmihalyi (*The Creative Vision*, 1976) 4. Development of Talent Project: *Benjamin Bloom and colleagues* (*The Development of Talent*, 1985) 5. Mihalyi Csikszentmihalyi (*Flow*, 1991; *Creativity*, 1996)	1. Defined "creative" students as those who scored high on a divergent production test, though they had above-average IQs. Beginning of consideration of "threshold" theory 2. Suggested that creativity can be stifled by fear of evaluation and lack of motivation. This followed their replication of the Getzels and Jackson study, *Modes of Thinking in Young Children* (1965). 3. Classic study of problem finding (as opposed to problem solving) with fine arts students at the Art Institute of Chicago 4. Studies of creative musicians, athletes, physicians, researchers, mathematicians, and patterns in their lives. 5. Studies of creative process in regular people and in eminent creators

Table 4.1   *Continued*

Study and Dates	Researchers and Publications	Findings
Creativity Studies Project, 1953 to present, State University of Buffalo	1. Alex Osborn (*Applied Imagination*, 1953) 2. Sidney Parnes (*Creative Behavior workbook*, 1967) 3. Donald Treffinger (*Handbook of Creative Learning*, 1982) 4. Scott Isaksen (*Frontiers of Creativity Research*, 1987) 5. Treffinger, Isaksen, Gerard Puccio (1995)	Brainstorming and the Creative Problem-Solving Process (CPS); assertion that creativity can be developed and trained An ecological approach to CPS, taking into account personality assessment
University of Minnesota and then University of Georgia, 1950s to present	E. Paul Torrance (many articles and books about enhancing creativity in school children)	Took Guilford battery of divergent production tests and developed *Torrance Tests of Creative Thinking*
Brandeis University and Harvard University, 1980s to present	Theresa Amabile (*Social Psychology of Creativity*, 1983)	Research on intrinsic motivation for creativity: Creative people have domain-relevant skills, creativity-relevant skills, and task motivation
Harvard University, 1980s to present	1. Project on Human Potential: Howard Gardner (*Frames of Mind*, 1983) 2. Project Zero: David Perkins (*The Mind's Best Work*, 1981)	1. Research on multiple intelligences and on problem solving in the arts 2. Research on selection and inventiveness as part of creativity
Yale University, 1980s to present	Robert Sternberg (*The Triarchic Mind*, 1985; editor of *The Nature of Creativity*, studies of insight, etc., National Research Center on Giftedness)	The intelligent person has creativity as well as practicality and executive ability.
Tufts University, 1986	David Henry Feldman (Nature's Gambit, 1986) with Lynn Goldsmith	Research on prodigy and creativity; co-incidence theory of development
University of California (Davis), 1980s to present	Dean Keith Simonton (*Greatness*, 1994; editor of *Journal of Creative Behavior*)	Statistical historical work on world class creators and leaders; chance-configuration theory; historiometry
University of California at Fullerton, (1990s)	Mark Runco (many books; editor of *Creativity Research Journal, Encyclopedia of Creativity*)	Studies of divergent production; studies of development of adult creativity

Renzulli's Definition

Renzulli, as mentioned before, came up with a definition of giftedness that meets in a Venn diagram, at the intersection of creativity, above-average intelligence, and task commitment (Figure 1.3 on p. 26). Renzulli is the only current theorist whose work has been adopted by the public schools to any great degree who insists that the gifted person must have something called the creativity ability. Renzulli also subscribed to the threshold theory, saying that the student's measured intelligence need not be the highest measured intelligence, usually operationally defined as being two standard deviations above the mean on an IQ test. In 1992, Renzulli published an elaboration of his theory of creative production called "A General Theory for the Development of Creative Productivity Through the Pursuit of Ideal Acts of Learning." This theory links the teacher, the learner, and the curriculum, insisting that creativity is manifest in a student's pursuit of interesting products within a domain. Other theorists such as Sternberg (1988b) and Feldman (1982), who have also said creativity is a necessary aspect of giftedness, have not seen their theories receive much practical application in schools. Schools have difficulty declaring that creative potential is *measurably* separate from having academic ability or high academic achievement, for how does one measure creative capacity before the creative act takes place? What is a capacity for creativity? Doesn't everyone have such a capacity? Isn't that part of being human? These are some of the questions the critics ask. Do some children have more capacity for creativity than others?

The Existence of a Creativity Ability

For the reasons just discussed, educational practitioners came to follow a somewhat controversial pedagogical practice in attempting to identify creativity ability by means of tests or behavioral checklists.

In addition, what is measured and touted as being related to creativity ability is quite nebulous. The ability to generate many alternatives (flexibility) or to list many items (fluency) may be helpful to the creative person, but tests that measure such abilities have been called reductive and inaccurate by critics such as Sternberg (1988b), Gardner (1982), and Borland (1986a). For example, take writing ability. Poets are called the most creative of writers (Gardner, 1983), yet in a writing creativity test, fluency is often the means of determining a high score. A high score means the person has more potential to be a creative adult; thus the person supposedly has more creative ability. The more words, the more fluent. But poets distill experience into a few words. Poetry is the art of codifying intense observation of the world into words. Poets would probably not score well on tests that emphasize fluency, although what they say may have the greatest resonance to the audience.

Educators who believe that divergent production tests are related to real-life creativity should at least look at the tests and see what they intuitively think about what the tests are asking. Sometimes educators have a naive trust in the mystery of the test. Treffinger (1986) called this the *creativity quotient fallacy.* He said "it is unrealistic to expect that there will ever be (or that there should be) a single, easily administered, simply scored test booklet that educators can use to decide who is at least one standard deviation above other students in creativity" (p. 16). Runco (1993) stated it well:

> There is also a need for tests which involve skills like those actually required in the nat-
> ural environment . . . . Clearly divergent thinking involves more than productivity and
> ideational fluency. If we know how fluent a child is with ideas, what do we really
> know? Just that the child can be fluent with ideas. To understand creative children we
> need to know many other things—about domains of interest and affective tendencies,
> to name just two examples (p. 21).

Yet there is a need for numbers, for accountability, in the schools, and this need has driven the practice of using tests and checklists to identify creativity.

To confuse the matter more, Marland's fifth type of giftedness was giftedness in the visual and performing arts: painting, drawing, acting, music, dance, sculpture, etc. These abilities are more usually called *talent* and are identified by experts and professionals evaluating a person's performance by means of a portfolio or an audition. That visual and performing arts talent is different from creative ability is sometimes difficult to understand. Aren't certain actors creative? Aren't dancers creative? Aren't certain musicians creative? Aren't certain visual artists creative? Or for that matter, aren't certain scientists creative? Aren't certain mathematicians creative? Aren't writers creative? Scientists, mathematicians, and those with writing talent are generally identified in the "academic talent" portion of identification matrices (see Chapter 3).

Marland's 1971 definition of giftedness and Bloom's 1985 definition of talent also listed psychomotor ability, athletic ability, or the ability to move one's body kinesthetically in space. Guilford (1967) called it *figural* ability; Gardner (1983) called it bodily-kinesthetic intelligence; Bloom (1985) called it athletic or *psychomotor* talent. Aren't athletes and dancers creative? When the soccer player is charging down the field darting here and there, sneakily looking for the surprise shot to the goal, isn't he creating as he goes along? Sportscasters call it a "play," as in the comment, "Let's look at that sensational play that so-and-so just made." Spontaneous, or free, play is intrinsically creative. Isn't the dancer creating as she extends her limbs in relation to the music? Of course.

Whether or not there is a separate ability called *creativity* that can be measured is the all-important question that the schools face. Perhaps the state of the art of measuring creativity is not advanced enough as yet. Or perhaps we should abandon such efforts and just concentrate on creating the emotional climate in our classrooms and in our homes that enhances creativity. Studies have indicated that creativity is enhanced or blocked by certain emotional, or affective, conditions, listed in Figure 4.6.

Figure 4.6 Creativity Blocks and Enhancements

What Blocks Creativity?

Situational Factors

1. Overemphasis on verbally-oriented, logical-analytical, cognitive ways of educating
2. Tendency of teachers to punish students who show evidence of emotional sensitivity, intellectual skepticism, playfulness, guessing, idealism
3. Undue emphasis on practicality and usefulness
4. Socioeconomic blockages
5. Pressure tactics by parents and teachers to produce conforming behaviors
6. Time limits
7. Performance pressures
8. Doing work one hates
9. Organizational rules and regulations
10. Overemphasis on neatness, cleanliness, order, discipline
11. Lack of appreciation of the importance of creativity in everyday activities

Internal Factors

1. Undue concern with the opinion of others
2. Deeply rooted internal prejudices
3. Freezing of behavior into rigid patterns
4. Turning the wish to be creative into a fantasy
5. Fear of risk taking
6. Psychopathology
7. Overly evaluative attitude; desire for a "quick" solution; unwillingness to "sleep on it"
8. Excessive involvement with others; neglect of own needs
9. Intolerance of playfulness, unwillingness to admit play into life of self and others
10. Worries, anxiety
11. Internal dialogues with foes, real or imagined
12. Constant interruption

What Enhances Creativity?

Situational Factors

1. Group atmosphere that is playful, gamelike, noncompetitive
2. Group atmosphere that is not overly evaluative
3. Conditions and materials that facilitate (make it easy)
4. Motivation that is related to the situation
5. No time restraints or stopwatches, untimed condition
6. Avoidance of interpretation
7. Mutual trust
8. Privacy
9. Mild stress
10. Process rather than product orientation
11. Solitude
12. Meditation, thinking time
13. Encouragement of intuitive perception

Internal Factors

1. Receptivity to new phenomena
2. Ability to let capacities flow of themselves, without effort
3. Lowering of defenses and inhibitions; lack of rigidity (flexibility) in gender roles
4. Understanding self-awareness
5. Realistic self-appraisal
6. Self-discipline ("95% work, 5% talent")
7. Wide interests, rejection of external restraints
8. Ability to elaborate
9. Ability to transform
10. Ability to improvise
11. Ability to show humor
12. Ever-increasing self-expression with materials
13. Background knowledge in the domain where creativity is being attempted

TRAINING FOR THE CREATIVITY ABILITY

The practice of training for the creativity ability was researched at the State University of Buffalo. Through the years, since the Creative Education Foundation was begun in 1953, researchers developed two levels of creativity training in their Creativity Studies Project. Level I was termed *tools* level (Treffinger, 1986), which involved activities such as brainstorming, attribute listing, morphological analysis, forcing relationships, synectics, and the like. Students were taught these tools separately, through workbooks and exercises. The teaching of these tools still takes up a major portion of the time spent in many classes for the education of the gifted. The second level of creativity training is the application of these tools in the Creative Problem Solving process (CPS), or the Future Problem Solving process (FPS), or in such programs as the Odyssey of the Mind (OM).

Creativity Training Systems

Many packaged creativity training programs exist, some of which are useful in improving divergent production if that is what is desired. The assumption is an old one in education: Special training in a certain way of thinking will transfer and will help a person use that way of thinking when doing specific tasks within a domain. For example, it is hoped that teaching a person to think deductively, to use logical propositions, will help that person to make logical decisions when it comes time to vote for one city council candidate over another. However, it must be emphasized and reemphasized that transfer is specific, rather than general. Some of the most commonly used creativity training programs are described in Figure 4.7.

The teacher training plan for Project Vanguard is shown in Figure 4.8. There are many other creativity training systems. As one teacher said, it seems as if there's a new catalog of creative thinking materials in the mail each week. Few of these programs, except for Edwards's and Goldberg's, feature creativity within a domain—Edwards for drawing and Goldberg for writing. Therefore, transfer of skills learned would have to be emphasized to students, as most creativity is practiced within domains.

Teachers Benefit from Creativity Training

Some studies do show that teachers benefit from creativity training. McDonnell and LeCapitaine, in a study called "The Effects of Group Creativity Training on Teachers' Empathy And Interactions With Students" (1985), showed that 13 teachers who received 40 hours of group creativity training at Synectics, Inc., in Massachusetts, had statistically significant increases in empathy compared to a control group. The teachers also reported that the training helped them to be more open with their students, to listen intently to student responses and ideas, to reinforce students, and to allow students to experiment more. There is nothing in the training of fluency, flexibility, elaboration, and originality that justifies it as the special province of classes for high-IQ children. The fun, laughter, easy atmosphere, charged climate, and productivity that result from creativity training should be available to all children. Another study, Project Vanguard (Morrison & Dungan, *Model for the Identification of Creative-Thinking Ability*, 1992), found that teachers who had creativity training were better

Figure 4.7 A Sampling of Creativity Training Programs

Divergent Production Testing

These tests and the pros and cons of their usage have been described in Chapter 3. The practice of testing for divergent production cognition has continued out of a concern for inclusiveness. The problem of "false negatives," or elimination of those who are really creative because they scored low on such tests, is one of the main difficulties. The inclusion of those who score high but who have no creative products or other indicators is a plus, as the high score indicates they are able to function divergently. In 1993 Runco stated that "divergent production tests are very useful estimates of the potential for creative thought."

Creative Problem Solving (CPS)

This is the granddaddy of all creativity training and it is a foundation, or basis, for such programs as Future Problem Solving and Odyssey of the Mind. People work in groups and solve a "mess" through divergent and convergent processes such as "problem finding" and "solution finding," "criteria setting" and finally focusing on the one best answer. Treffinger, Isaksen, Feldhusen, and colleagues have produced many training materials. So has Doris Shallcross (1985). Each summer they hold an international creativity conference in Buffalo. Thousands of people attend.

Gordon's Synectics

Synectics is putting unlike objects together to form a new object. There is a training center where people learn this. It is also a popular teaching technique in textbooks about models of teaching.

Meeker's Divergent Production Exercises

These exercises are found in Meeker's *Sourcebooks* (1973; Meeker & Meeker, 1976). There are basic and advanced levels that contain exercises in all of Guilford's divergent production factors.

Torrance's Programs

Many programs, workbooks, and other materials are available at the Torrance Center for Creativity at the University of Georgia, many of them developed by Torrance's graduate students and colleagues over the years. A typical book, developed after Torrance wrote extension exercises for a Ginn textbook series, is *Incubation Teaching: Getting Beyond the Aha!* (by Torrance and Safter, 1983).

Taylor's Talents Unlimited

Taylor (1969) identified nine talent totem poles: academic, productive thinking, communicating, forecasting, decision making, planning and designing, implementing, human relations, and discerning opportunities. This program was validated by the National Diffusion Network and is widely used in schools.

Williams's Ideas for Thinking and Feeling

Williams (1970) created exercises following the Guilford divergent production aspects.

Samples's Metaphorization

Samples (1976) suggested ways to help people form metaphors, noting that almost all theory-making in science is metaphoric.

Figure 4.7   *Continued*

Eberle's Work

Eberle (1982) wrote exercises in creative visualization. He also invented the term SCAMPER, as a code for teaching creative thinking. (S-ubstitute C-ombine A-dapt M-odify P-ut to other uses E-liminate R-earrange).

Future Problem Solving

This international competition is based on the Osborn-Parnes model of Creative Problem Solving. Students do research and propose solutions for world and community problems.

Odyssey of the Mind (OM) Competitions

Odyssey of the Mind is an international competitive program where teams of students invent and create according to certain problems all have been given.

Edwards's Drawing on the Right Side of the Brain

This technique (Edwards, 1979) uses upside-down drawing so people can see holistically and not form brain codes.

Rico's Writing the Natural Way

Rico (1983) pioneered the now widespread use of "webbing" to generate ideas and organizational structure. Computer software exists to help in this process.

Invention Competitions

These are commercially run by various groups, including Invention Museums.

deBono's coRT Lateral Thinking

Lateral thinking is a packaged program used in thousands of schools internationally (deBono, 1978). Six "thinking hats" are taught.

Davis's Personal Transformation

The Davis program (1981) emphasizes the affective as well as the cognitive aspects of creativity enhancement.

Bagley's and Hess's Guided Imagery

This popular book (1983) has many guided imagery scripts, useful in all curricular areas.

Crabbe's and Betts's Creating More Creative People

These are books (Crabbe, 1990; Crabbe & Betts, 1990) written for the Future Problem Solving program, with an emphasis on getting more creative people by means of creativity training. These are exercises designed in similar ways to those above.

Cameron's The Artist's Way

A 12-step program (1992) by a creative writer which combines "morning pages" with meditative techniques. Twelve weeks of exercises about "recovering": "Recovering a Sense of Connection"; "Recovering a Sense of Autonomy"; "Recovering a Sense of Faith"; this program speaks to the mid-1990s obsession with dysfunction.

(continued on next page)

Figure 4.7 *Continued*

Goldberg's Creativity Exercises

A series of exercises (Goldberg, 1986) to help creative writers break through their blocks to writing, including such techniques as "writing practice" and writing in public places. This extremely popular program for writers has applications in other fields, just as Edwards's drawing program does.

UCONN Confratute

An annual summer conference called Confratute held at the University of Connecticut has a creativity strand. Hundreds of teachers attend and learn how to differentiate their curricula and infuse aspects of creativity into their daily work. The work of Renzulli, Reis, and colleagues is published by Creative Learning Press and is the most widely adopted plan used by schools. Many books written by teachers are available.

Project Vanguard

A 30-hour teacher-training project in providing creativity training for teachers in order that they may be able to adequately identify students with creative potential. Teachers receive training in morphological analysis, synectics, metaphors, analogies, visualization, attribute listing, "what ifs," inferring, random input, forced input, criteria finding, and the creative problem-solving process.

Reynolds's Creativity, Inc.

This is a high school extracurricular creativity program, utilizing affective techniques and art enhancement exercises to help students probe into their inner selves in order to reach their truly creative cores. It has the advantage of cutting to the emotional, as a way of reaching the creative. We have used this program at our summer institutes for talented teens. The students respond very positively. (See the Case Example at the end of this chapter.)

---

able to identify children who demonstrated creative behaviors (see Figure 4.8). Much more research needs to be done in this area, but it would seem logical that trained teachers would be better able to emphasize creativity in their teaching. Teachers who take creativity courses in our graduate licensure program report great affective insights, a fresh and open look at tired old ways of doing things, and improvement in their risk-taking capabilities.

The training of creativity should be a part of every staff development plan. People can be taught to be more creative and less fearful. If school districts are serious about effectively teaching creative thinking, they must provide the necessary backup training. There are many commercial programs available and many trained people who can provide creativity training to school districts. School districts also should provide rigorous instruction in the fields in which the creativity training can be applied.

Many opportunities exist for teaching students to be more creative. Some of these are extracurricular, and some of these are curricular. Starko (1995) has written a book that helps teachers infuse creativity into their regular curriculum. Few schools offer special classes in how to be more creative, and so the technique and lessons must be integrated

A student's creative ability is enhanced by projects that require a creative problem-solving process.

and incorporated into the courses as they are taught. Every school has experts who can help the student who is creative in some domain to be nurtured in that domain.

Many people do not believe that the school is the place to work to enhance student creativity, and in fact, they doubt whether any such exercises do really train people to be more creative. I am of mixed opinion on this; on the one hand, doing such exercises can make people aware of what goes into creativity, if the exercises are based on the research about creative people. These would be likened to the drills that athletes practice or the scales that musicians practice or the skills that one seeks to acquire to get automaticity in an area in which one wants to be expert. On the other hand, perhaps such exercises are too abstract to promote transfer.

After all, does practice in risk taking encourage the risk taking that creative people must have in doing their creative work, as well as in pursuing their careers? Is risk taking teachable through a creativity enhancement exercise? If one begins to think about this, though, one realizes that the "ropes courses" through which many businesses send their employees to build a sense of trust in each other also encourage physical risk taking as a "safe" rehearsal for "dangerous" life. With these caveats in mind, teachers could use a list of possible activities to construct educational experiences for their students in the hope that they will learn to be more creative (Figure 4.9). Ultimately, the purpose of such training is to free the inner person through imagery. Colleagues who teach in our program use fingerpainting, storytelling about ancestors, clay, construction paper to make each person's personal monster, singing, and other means to encourage the students to express themselves through metaphor.

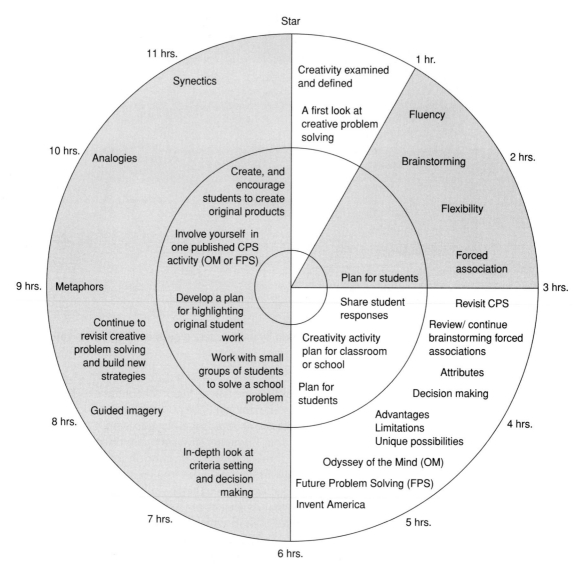

Figure 4.8   Project Vanguard Teacher Development Program Plan

Reprinted from Morrison, M., and Dungan, R. (1992). *Model for the Identification of Creative-Thinking Ability*, (p. 37). Ohio Department of Education, Research and Demonstration Series in Gifted Education.

I have taught a creativity course that utilizes exercises in risk taking, trust building, and the cultivation of an attitude of openness, or naiveté. The students also try exercises in cultivating self-discipline. They work daily in creativity Thoughtlogs. We work with the five I's: (1) *Imagery*, including guided imagery and film script visualizing; (2) *Imagination*, including storytelling; (3) *Intuition*, including the intuition probe, psychic intuition, and dreams; (4) *Insight*, including grasping the gestalt, going for the *aha*, and Zen sketching; and (5) *Inspiration*, including the visitation of

Figure 4.9   Less Linear, Organic, Approach to Creativity Enhancement

Working on Core Attitudes
- Cultivating risk taking
- Cultivating naiveté
- Cultivating self-discipline
- Cultivating group trust (if in a group)

Thoughtlogs

The Five I's

1. *Imagery*
   - 10-minute movie
   - Guided imagery

2. *Imagination*

3. *Intuition*
   - Intuition probe, psychic intuition
   - Dreams and intuition

4. *Insight*
   - Grasping the gestalt, Aha, Zen sketching

5. *Inspiration*
   - Visitation of the muse

Creativity Rituals
- Solitude
- Creating ideal conditions
- Using background music

Nature
- I am a naturalist
- This is the day the Lord hath made

Meditation
- Meditate on beauty, meditate on the dark side, meditate on God

Improvisation
- Jazz, theater, word rivers, writing practice, creative movement, rhythm and drumming, scat singing, doodling, dancing to rock 'n' roll

Use of Humor: telling Jokes

Synaesthesia
- Seeing, hearing, smelling, tasting, touching

Exercise
- A walk, a run, aerobics, a team game

Conversation: A Salon

A Visit to a Bookstore/Library, a Museum, a Concert, a Play, a Movie, a Reading or a Lecture, a Place (Travel) the muse, creativity rituals such as solitude, creating ideal conditions, and using background music. We imitate those creative people who treasure nature and its contents, making naturalist notations and drawings. There is an exercise called "This is the day that the Lord hath made/Let us rejoice and be glad in it." We try meditation, meditating on beauty, on the dark side, on God. We do improvisation with jazz, theater, word rivers, writing practice, creative movement, rhythm and drumming, scat singing, and doodling. We try to see the humor in everything. We tell jokes. We cultivate all five of our senses and also blend them for a sense of "synaesthesia." We vigorously exercise so endorphins will kick in. We try to find our domains of passion by noticing when we go into a state of flow. We try to answer to our *daimons*. We explore the joys of good conversation and start a monthly salon at my house. We visit a bookstore, a library, and a museum in order to honor the creativity of others. We attend a concert, a play, a movie, a poetry reading, or a lecture.

The culmination of the course is an individual creativity project. The students may not use already existing kits or molds, and must avoid the "season curriculum"— Christmas decorations, Hallowe'en pumpkins, or St. Patrick's Day shamrocks. One wrote a poem when we visited the art museum, and it became the lyrics for the first song she composed. Other individual creativity projects have included an autobiographical video ("My creative self"); performance of an original song; performance of an original radio play; design and modeling of an original dress for a sorority formal; a plan for an advertising campaign; a synchronized swimming routine; a grunge rock band audio tape; a photographic exhibit; an exhibit of original artworks; a reading of an original short story; an autobiographical multimedia presentation; a translation into English of Chinese, Greek, or Spanish literature; an original dance routine; a new recipe for scones; an original afghan; designs for costumes for a play; a reading of original poetry; a business plan for a new business; a music video; *a capella* singing; an original rock 'n' roll song; philosophical musings about the meaning of life; and display and demonstration of a particularly creative Thoughtlog. One football player, a defensive back, took all the game tapes for his entire college career, spliced them together to show himself in the improvisatory acts of dodging, running, and hitting. Projects are evaluated with a holistic scoring system, and we are often so moved at the projects that we weep. At the end of the course, most agree that, indeed, creativity can be enhanced through direct teaching.

Teaching Elaboration for Transfer

It would be logical that such exercises would be more transferable if they were conducted within various domains where creativity is sought. For example, I have done extensive work with the Poet in the Schools program as a practicing artist, working with students and adults on writing. One of my favorite activities is to help students with what in Guilford lingo is called DMU, the *divergent production of semantic units* (or story writing) by helping them to elaborate. I often use slides and we practice close observation. One slide is of a butterfly, enlarged. We talk about the butterfly: the patterns, the colors, the powdery fragility, light and dark. I read to them from such master prose works as Darwin's descriptions of Argentina in *The Voyage of the Beagle* (1845/1906), and Diane Ackerman's *Natural History of the Senses* (1990). These are sample passages to illustrate elaboration in writing:

Ackerman on vanilla:

Walk through a kitchen where vanilla beans are basking in a loud conundrum of smell, and you'll make some savoring murmur without realizing it. The truth about vanilla is that it's as much a smell as a taste. Saturate your nose with glistening, soulful vanilla, and you can taste it. It's not like walking through a sweetshop, but more subterranean and wild. Surely this is the unruly beast itself, the raw vanilla that's clawing your senses. But no. The vanilla beans we treasure aren't delectable the way we find them in the jungle. Of all the foods grown domestically in the world, vanilla requires the most labor: Long, tedious hours of hand tending bring the vanilla orchids to fruit and then the fruit to lusciousness. Vanilla comes from the string-bean-like pod of a climbing orchid, whose greenish-white flowers bloom briefly and are without fragrance. (Ackerman, 1990, p. 159).

Darwin on fireflies:

At these times the fireflies are seen flitting about from hedge to hedge. On a dark night the light can be seen at about two hundred paces distant . . . the light has been of a well-marked green colour . . . I found that this insect emitted the most brilliant flashes when ir-ritated: in the intervals, the abdominal rings were obscured. The flash was almost coin-stantaneous in the two rings, but it was just perceptible first in the anterior one. The shining matter was fluid and very adhesive: little spots, where the skin had been torn, continued bright with a slight scintillation, whilst the uninjured parts were obscured. When the insect was decapitated the rings remained uninterruptedly bright, but not so brilliant as before: local irritation with a needle always increased the vividness of the light. The rings in one instance retained their luminous property nearly twenty-four hours after the death of the in-sect. From these facts it would appear probable, that the animal has only the power of con-cealing or extinguishing the light for short intervals, and that at other times the display is in-voluntary (Darwin, 1845/1906, p. 29).

Another example of elaboration could be used with students in music composi-tion, or an improvisation class. One could tell the story of Andre Previn hearing Art Tatum play "Sweet Lorraine":

At fourteen he [Previn] heard a scratchy recording of "Sweet Lorraine" by blind black pi-anist Art Tatum, and he just "fell apart. It was unbelievable." Previn scoured the stores for sheet music to "Sweet Lorraine" and found that it was just a "pleasant, folksy little tune." Wondering where all the notes on the record came from, he realized that Tatum himself had added them. "He'd taken that puerile thirty-two bar melody and made ingenious music out of it." (Bookspan & Yodkey, 1981, p. 103).

Art Tatum had elaborated a simple melody and created a classic jazz piece. Elabo-ration as a divergent production technique could be taught through the visual arts as well; students could create a design and then embellish it using a computer graphics program. Elaboration in mathematics, science, drama, and dance could also be taught by people who know these domains.

Perhaps this is key: The person doing the teaching of creative techniques should have more than a passing knowledge of the domain. I feel quite comfortable teaching people how to be divergent in the writing domain; I would not, however, feel comfortable teaching in the visual arts domain or the music, mathematics, sci-ence, or other domains.

Creativity Since the Marland Report

Since the Marland Report and its huge impact on practitioners in the field of gifted education, many researchers have attempted to define creativity. Because of the difficulty in translating theory to practice, educators of the gifted were interested in what the researchers were finding. A somewhat uneasy marriage has taken place between psychometricians, psychologists, and educators of the gifted. Again, educators have focused on the psychologists' research, because of the close connections between psychology and education. The "stars" of the conference circuit in the world of the education of the talented and gifted are psychologists, researchers, and theoreticians who call psychology their domain. Seldom is the keynote speaker a creator in a traditional domain—a writer, artist, musician, scientist, mathematician, actor, dancer, architect, or inventor. The "stars" are those who study about creators. In fact, the cognitive scientist David Perkins (1981) said that anecdotal accounts of the creative process and what goes into it are not reliable, implying that the scientists who study about creativity know more about creativity than the creators themselves, who, according to this kind of thought, wander around blind and deaf to their own processes, and so perhaps it is warranted that speakers at education conventions are psychologists, and not educators or creators.

It is time to consider that creativity underlies all manifestations of talent. The scientist formulating his theories and the mathematician formulating her theorems are creative. The visual artist finding a visual problem is creative. The poet who chooses words that signify feelings is creative. The dancer who extends her limbs to music is creative. The actor who creates a character is creative. The musician who plays a piece masterfully is creative. The composer, the choreographer, and the engineer are creative. Also, with a bow to Maslow (1968), the person who is self-actualized is creative. The mother designing a new dress for her daughter is creative. The carpenter making blueprints for a new project is creative. Can we identify their creative *potential* early? Probably not, at least not by the means available to us today, by the creativity tests and the creativity checklists and the teacher nomination forms. Each is creative at something. Each is creative doing something. A product is necessary, and what Chris Wiley, the new teacher of the talented we met at the beginning of this chapter, found in his new classroom were, perhaps, empty processes divorced from content.

Creativity is the underpinning, the basement, the foundation that permits talent to be realized. Creativity is in the personality. Most creative people are just generally creative, and not only creative in their domains. They live creatively, divergently (Pirto, in press). What does this mean for the schools? Is there enough hard evidence to warrant the identification of creative thinking as an ability in itself? Are the presently available instruments for doing so valid and reliable for use with young school children? Are the time, effort, expense, and difficulty efficient and effective?

The schools seem to have little time, will, or propensity for providing such intensive knowledge and training, except in academic fields. The schools do have as their undisputed province the development of talent in certain domains. Writers, speakers, mathematicians, and scientists who are creative have obtained most of their creative knowledge through intensive study in school. Vocational talents are taught to and enhanced in special vocational schools or in programs in comprehensive high schools. However, at young ages, artists, musicians, certain kinds of athletes (for example, gymnasts, tennis players, and ice skaters), actors, and dancers usually have to obtain their special training elsewhere. Special high schools, with specially trained teachers, exist to develop the talent creativity of these students, but if a parent wants a child to receive special training in one of these talent domains early, special lessons and teachers outside of school are necessary.

Therefore, the emphasis of creativity training should not be solely conducted in the program for the education of the talented. Schools that want to emphasize creative thinking in their programs for the education of the gifted may want to look at this requirement and focus on developing the student who is creative *at* something. A creative thinker who has nothing to think about is not creative. Training in creative thinking should be viewed as what it is—process training—an aspect of the curriculum, but not the content of the curriculum for the talented.

The intensive "coach" model of athletics, music, dance, and the studio training of the visual artist are models that may be useful. Perhaps this model should be looked at with a view toward the education of divergent production abilities in the talented. With the emerging focus on "inclusion" and the diminishing emphasis on "pulling out" students from classrooms, perhaps creativity training should be conducted with all students, and educators of the talented should focus on specific individual plans for developing specific talent in the individual talented student, including out-of-school private lessons from specially trained coaches, if necessary.

CREATIVITY ASSESSMENT

The assessment of whether someone is creative or whether their product is creative is problematic. Tests have been made. Rubrics have been drawn up. Judges have been chosen. How do we assess creativity?

Reasons for Measuring Creativity

Why try to *measure* creativity? Treffinger (1987) gave seven reasons: (1) to focus on the strengths of individual students; (2) to recognize that IQ and achievement testing are limited; (3) to help schools, which must be practical, in obtaining data so that they can make comparisons between themselves and others on standardized norms; (4) to expand the basic profiles of students to include new information that is creativity oriented; (5) to help teachers find that they themselves possess creative talents; (6) to contribute to research about nurturing creative behaviors; (7) to refuse to view creativity as something mysterious but as something that can be understood.

Two Schools of Thought

There seem to be two schools of thought on the value of testing for creativity. The psychometric approach, testing, has met with criticism. The practice of testing for divergent production cognition has continued out of a concern for inclusiveness, however. Cramond (1994) defended the use of divergent production tests, saying "why not use any and all methods available to ascertain where children's strengths lie?" (p. 70). Others have called attempts to measure creativity by giving people paper and pencil tests not rich or complicated enough (Baer, 1991, 1993/1994, 1994; Baird, 1972b, 1985; Borland, 1986a; Eysenck, 1990; Gardner, 1982, 1983, 1993; Stein, 1987; Sternberg, 1988b).

Torrance came up with a definition of creativity as a process. If creativity is a process, then normal, everyday people could enhance their creativity by knowing what the process is. Torrance defined this creative process as follows:

> ... becoming sensitive to problems, deficiencies, gaps in knowledge, missing elements, disharmonies, and so on; identifying the difficulty; searching for solutions, making guesses, or formulating hypotheses about the deficiencies; testing and retesting these hypotheses and possibly modifying and retesting them; and finally, communicating the results. (Torrance, 1974, p. 8)

To do this, he developed tests with names such as Ask and Guess, Unusual Questions, Product Improvement, Unusual Uses, and Just Suppose. The tests were scored for Guilford's divergent production aspects of fluency, flexibility, and originality. The results of these subtests were factored into something called a *Creativity Index,* similar to a quotient.

The Torrance Tests of Creative Thinking (1966) began to be widely used in schools. The implication became that the higher the score, the more potentially creative the child was. In attempting to show that paper and pencil testing of aspects of the divergent mode of intellect can truly identify creative potential, Guilford, Getzels and Jackson, Torrance, Wallach and Kogan, and others began a controversial practice that still continues today. Mainstream educators of the gifted and talented have continued to attempt to identify creative potential by calling *creativity* a separate type of talent, an ability, rather than a necessary aspect of the realization of talent potential. Their reasons for doing so have to do with a need to be inclusive. That is, those children who have creative potential may not be found by other means, but they may become included in programs by the use of paper and pencil vehicles such as tests and checklists. This has led to much confusion in the practitioners' sector.

Motive to Create

Psychologists trying to find the secrets of creativity, and ways to make people more creative, have discussed motivation. Perkins (1988) called for the inclusion of motivation in the assessment of creativity. After all, what are people creating for? Why does the writer write, the painter paint, the inventor invent, the scientist experiment? He said that the creativity testing of people may be off base: "Whereas testing for creativity typically emphasizes flexibility, fluency, and similar indices, values and patterns of deployment seem to offer the best predictors of creativity" (p. 380). That is to say that motivation to do creative activities must be taken into consideration.

In fact, it would seem that motivation to create is the major factor in being creative. If a person wants to study, practice, and develop automaticity so the performance of the creative activity is easy and almost unconscious, it would seem that half the battle is won. Consider the parents of young gymnasts or ice skaters, of young musicians or actors; a common thread in many of these parents' tales about the development of their children's talents is, "She *wanted* to do it. I just helped her." The need for expression of emotion through the metaphoric media of visual arts, poetry, dance, theater, and the like speaks to the primacy of motivation. One doesn't create unless one wants to create.

Hennessey (1997) summarized the research she has conducted with Theresa Amabile on the necessity for intrinsic motivation in creating. Of the three components they say are necessary for creativity (domain skills, creativity skills, and intrinsic motivation), "intrinsic task motivation is considered by Amabile, myself, and others to be the most important" (p. 284). Hennessey said that further experiments had shown them how to inoculate children from toxic evaluative environments. "Expected reward, expected evaluation, and other extrinsic constraints can have a negative impact on both students' motivation and their creativity" (p. 287). Teaching students to approach tasks playfully and with an attitude of risk taking seems to help them. Simply encouraging children to take pride in their accomplishments, avoiding undue competitiveness in the classroom, giving students choices about assignments, encouraging them to be independent learners, showing them how the teacher herself values creativity, are all strategies Hennessey suggested to increase intrinsic motivation in students.

Evaluating Creativity Assessment Instruments

Amidst all this controversy is the bewildered professional responsible for educating the talented, whose state department may have a requirement that children with creative thinking potential be identified using creativity tests or checklists. The busy educator often does not have the time nor the propensity to wade through the research evidence, and the research itself is often done by the people who can benefit most from showing that their own tests and checklists have validity and reliability. The validity and reliability of such tests and checklists should be considered seriously by the practitioner.

Validity

Validity is best described as the test's truthfulness. That is, does the test measure what it says it will measure? The three types of validity are: (1) content/construct validity; (2) criterion validity; and (3) concurrent validity.

Content/Construct Validity of Creativity Tests *Content*, or *construct, validity* is necessary in order to determine whether the test has indeed measured what it says it measured. To determine whether a creativity test is valid, one must look at what it measures. Divergent production is not creativity, and creativity is not only divergent production. The lack of a universal definition for creativity and the complexity of what creativity is are the major problems in developing any test or measure. Some researchers take one aspect of creativity, for example, divergent production of figural units, or free drawing within circles and squares, and then state that people who were pretested and posttested on that one test improved their creativity. That is certainly not so, and that is where consideration of the content of what is measured is important. Creativity is too complex to be measured by a simple five-minute test, or even an hour-long test.

Researchers develop tests continuously and seek to validate them. People using tests that proclaim to be "creativity" tests should look carefully at the content of the test. Is filling in blanks or drawing within boxes creative? Even if the tests are called *divergent production* tests, does divergent production, by implication, translate itself to creativity?

Is there a separate creativity construct, a creativity ability? How is this construct or ability related to tested intelligence? The difficulties of separating the factors of fluency, flexibility, originality, elaboration, and such in the operation of divergent production present an ongoing problem. Some researchers have made construct validity studies of the divergent production tests and found them wanting (Baer, 1994; Borland, 1986a; Hocevar, 1980; Runco, 1991).

Criterion Validity of Creativity Tests *Criterion validity* refers to whether or not test scores predict performance later on in life or in other areas. This could be called the *transfer* ability discussed earlier in this chapter. For example, does a high score on a creativity test given in elementary school predict that a person will be a true creative achiever when he or she is in high school or is an adult? Criterion validity is also called *predictive validity.*

If a creative ability test does not predict future performance in fields needing the creative ability, why test? Torrance has spent a lifetime testing children, following up on them, trying to find out whether their scores on such tests as his Torrance Tests of Creative Thinking have predictive validity. Sorry to say, the answers are mixed (Hocevar, 1980; Torrance & Safter, 1989). While independent reviewers and researchers do some validation work, much of it is done by the test makers, who may commit what literary critics call "the pathetic fallacy": they may design studies that reflect their drive to prove that their test works.

Concurrent Validity of Creativity Tests *Concurrent validity* establishes whether the test measures what real people in the field supposedly being measured really do. Khatena, Torrance, and colleagues have attempted to establish the validity of inventories they have devised that purport to show that certain childhood behaviors predict for future adult creativity (Morse & Khatena, 1989).

Is the Threshold Theory Valid? Runco and Albert (1986) said that the threshold theory—that one needs above-average intelligence to be creative—is incorrect. Some of the studies done on creativity and its relationship to intelligence have used IQs derived from ability tests, such as the Stanford-Binet. Other studies have used IQs derived from achievement tests, such as the California Achievement Test (CAT). The Stanford-Binet and the California Achievement Test are thought to measure the same things, but they don't. Because researchers assumed that they were measuring the same things, they conducted experiments based on false initial assumptions caused by differences in the tests. Thus, statements that one must have above-average intelligence in order to get a good score on a creativity test are false.

In summary, the results of validity studies of divergent production tests have shown that they are not as strong as desired, and that, therefore, their presence in an assessment package should probably be put into the category of experimental.

Reliability

Three interrelated types of reliability must be considered by the person using creativity testing: (1) stability; (2) equivalence; and (3) internal consistency. Is the test stable? If a person takes the test early in the day, and then takes the test again later the same day, will the results be relatively the same? The best way to assure this is to administer equivalent alternate forms of the test, which is why most standardized tests have Form A or Form B. The idea is that a person taking Form A will score the same on Form B, thus assuring that the score in each case is equivalent and, therefore, stable and consistent. However, in the field of creativity testing this is very difficult, because of what is being measured. An analogy would be to compare the scoring of a multiple-choice test with the scoring of a divergent production test. It is easy to mark a multiple-choice test. But when the person has an open-ended format with no right answers, it is very difficult to make items equivalent. Is asking a person to list unusual uses for a ball equivalent to asking a person to list unusual uses for a bat? Another way to establish equivalence is to split the test in half, and see whether the scores from each half are about the same, using odds and evens or other ways of splitting the test. Does the test have internal consistency? This is called *split-half reliability*. Again this is difficult in testing for creativity.

The reliability of tests can be increased by administering the tests in a standardized way, by using objective scoring measures, by having item difficulties that are equal (again, is listing unusual uses for a ball easier than listing unusual uses for a bat?), by having the test measure only one aspect of creativity, and by increasing the number of items on the test. Administering the tests in a standardized way and scoring them objectively is particularly difficult for divergent production tests.

Administering Divergent Production Tests Reliably Test administration conditions are a challenge for reliability. Lissitz and Willhoft (1985) found that the TTCT were highly sensitive to how the directions were given, or "experimenter manipulation" (p. 1). After finding that such differences in giving directions changed the results, they cautioned other researchers that "studies using the Torrance Tests should be viewed with extreme caution" (p. 10).

Runco (1986, 1987) also found that encouraging children to be original increased their fluency, or the number of responses they gave. Since fluency is always a large proportion of the total score given in such divergent production tests, increasing the fluency raises the child's test scores. But if some test givers tell the children to be original and some do not, the test scores will be changed and, therefore, not comparable.

Scoring Divergent Production Tests Reliably Scoring is also a challenge to reliability. Scoring is not merely marking which multiple-choice questions the student answered correctly or incorrectly. The responses are as varied as the people taking the test, and they have been codified into classes, so that a trained scorer can recognize certain patterns. For example, a response is called original if it only occurs once or twice in a group of 30 people. The scorer must remember who has done what and how many times it has occurred. It is better to have several people score the same tests independently. When several people score the same tests independently, they are called *interraters*. If they come up with similar scores, the scoring is said to have high *interrater reliability*. Another way to score such difficult tests is *wholistic scoring*. Several people score the same test, and the scores are averaged, throwing out the highest score and the lowest score. This is the manner in which Advanced Placement Program (AP) tests such as the AP Composition tests are scored.

Independent researchers (Halpin & Halpin, 1973; Heausler & Thompson, 1988; Rosenthal, DeMers, Stilwell, Graybeal & Zins, 1983) have found that scoring the tests presents difficulties of overrating and underrating the test information, or of giving the same student high scores, but for substantially different reasons. This means that even if scorers are highly trained there still will be differences that affect the final scores in the areas of originality, say, or in elaboration.

To summarize, teachers and other educational practitioners are often not well trained in administering creativity tests and checklists. Also, school districts often do not check into the research base that went into the checklist or creativity test. Perhaps this is because the research is confusing, since validity and reliability are so complex and inadequately understood by practitioners who choose tests.

The predictive validity of divergent production (often called creativity) tests is most difficult to establish because the tasks on the tests have little relationship to real-life creativity. The scoring of these tests is also difficult, because the scoring requires subjective judgment and scorers must be trained. When a person is reading the results of studies that say the treatment made the group "more creative," she should see whether or not that meant more fluent, flexible, etc., and decide whether fluency and flexibility are the outcome behaviors sought by the educational experience that is being given to the children. Is making children more fluent and more flexible making children more creative? Or is creativity more complex than that? Doesn't creativity take into account more personality qualities and require more commitment?

Studies of Significant Results

Beyond the concern of whether tests are valid and reliable comes the consideration of whether or not the results are statistically significant. If the results are "significant," people in the schools decide to pay attention. But "significance" is an area where college professors and statisticians play. The level of significance is shown like this: (1) $p < 0.05$, which means that the results are due to nonchance factors 95 percent of the time; (2) $p < 0.01$, which means that the results would occur 1 percent of the time, or less, by chance; and (3) $p < .001$, which means that the results would occur less than one time out of a thousand, by chance.

Many of the studies of creativity testing are *correlational*, which means that they compare one test with another to see whether the tests are related. If they find the tests to be related, the results are "significant." But only a few researchers question whether the tests are in fact measuring creativity, whether the tests have construct validity. Other studies try to isolate the factors being measured on the tests. If the researchers find that the factors are, indeed, separate and isolatable, the results are "significant." These studies are theoretical and they are necessary—but they're not immediately very helpful to the practitioner.

Also, even if the study is not correlational or factorial, but experimental, and the results are "significant," what does that really mean? Even if they did become significantly more fluent, flexible, or more elaborative—even more original—what is the *transfer* of fluency, flexibility, and originality to real-life creativity, and then, if it transferred, how did we measure it? By giving more divergent production tests, or looking at real-life creative products? Did those who scored significantly higher in verbal fluency go on to write mammoth, many-paged novels, a new *War and Peace*, or a many-paged scientific research project report? (Remember that transfer transfers to like tasks.)

To use a significant increase in fluency as a measure of whether or not the people who received the educational experience became more creative, or even more "divergent," is not the right answer to the question of whether the participants bene-fited. What does it mean to "increase" one's creativity?

The Normal Curve Assumption

When we give a test we make the assumption that the test results can be plotted into a normal curve, with 68 percent in the middle and 16 percent on either end. Al-though one can derive a normal curve from any test, the underlying assumption that there is a normal curve of creativity, or, to put it another way, the underlying as-sumption that some people have a fuller cup of creativity than other people, has not been proven. Likewise, when some people talk about giftedness, their underlying as-sumption is that a person with a high IQ is gifted, that the person has a fuller cup of giftedness than a person with a lower IQ.

This assumption is an important issue when talking about creativity testing, because it assumes that the person taking the test has "more" creativity if he or she gets a higher score, and that a person has "less" creativity she gets a lower score. When using divergent production tests, school districts often establish a cutoff score and admit the highest scorers to the program for those who have creative potential. The assumption that people are distributed along a normal curve of creative thinking is operational here. Thus the person who is most fluent, or gives the most answers, will get a high score. Divergent production tests are given and then creativity training is undertaken. After that children are retested on the divergent production tests to see if they are more "creative." If they score significantly higher, the program is deemed successful.

Many researchers, practitioners, and readers believe in the mystical power of testing and lose their powers of logical thinking when they see significance correlations.

One study of dancers—who are physically, kinesthetically talented—gave them paper and pencil tests of Guilford's figural operations to see whether they became better on paper and pencil tests of figural operations after having dance lessons (Alter, 1984). The research question seems to beg the question. Dancers should be measured by dancing, and not by divergent production tests.

Checklists and Questionnaires

Checklists are very popular, except among those who review them for the *Mental Mea-surements Yearbooks (MMY)*. The reviewers often find them wanting in both validity and reliability. The numbers of people used to derive the norms, whether or not the sampling was truly random or similar to that of the people being tested, and whether the statistics show how the tests are correlated with other tests are often criticized. Table 4.2 summarizes some of the research about commonly used creativity tests and checklists.

A careful person can see that some difficulties arise when using checklists and tests to identify and select children for special programs. Checklists serve another purpose, however, and that is one of description. To use a checklist to select for a program is one thing; to use a checklist to describe a person is another. Whether or not one subscribes to the theory behind the checklist is also important. The Myers-Briggs Type Indicator (MBTI) is one example. If one has doubts about the Jungian theory of personality types, the information gleaned from the checklist about the personality of the person may not be seen as valuable information. The Adjective Checklist (ACL) is another example, as is

Table 4.2 Commonly Used Creativity Tests and Checklists

Name of Instrument	Reasons to Use	Reasons Not to Use
Williams Creativity Assessment Packet (CAP)		1. Manual not written well; validation data scanty and poorly documented (Damarin, 1985) 2. Contains "a technically uncertain set of instruments whose usefulness is limited by a lack of appropriate information as to validity and reliability" (Rosen, 1985, p. 412)
Renzulli-Hartman *Creativity Characteristics Scale* in the Scales for Rating the Behavior of Superior Students (SRBSS)	1. "A shining example of on-target efficiency" (Davis, 1997) 2. "Face validity, stability, and retest reliability for fifth graders seemed all right" (Rust, 1985) 3. "Strengths include their conceptual formation and their ease of administration" (Rust, 1985, p. 1210)	1. Validity was determined by comparison with the Torrance Test of Creative Thinking (TTCT) and correlated with verbal subscales but not with nonverbal subscales (Arguliewicz, 1985) 2. The references in the manual seemed outdated; concurrent validity was "untested" (Arguliewicz, 1985) 3. There is "a verbal bias in the Creativity Scale items and suggests that caution should be exercised in using this scale to identify students for programs that emphasize nonverbal creativity" (Renzulli et al. 1976, p. 9). 4. Length of the stem is confusing to raters (Piirto, 1994a,1992a/1998)
Renzulli-Hartman Scales for Rating the Behavior of Superior Students (SRBSS)—Scales for *Artistic Characteristics* (Part V), for *Musical Characteristics* (Part VI), for *Drama Characteristics* (Part VII), and for *Communication Characteristics* (Part VIII)	Focuses directly on creativity in domains	1. Catalog still advertises the 1976 version 2. Weighted totals often operate against minorities and disadvantaged children (Frasier, 1991)
GIFT (Grades 1–6) GIFFI I and II (Grades 7–12) PRIDE (preK and K) self-report inventories	Content validity of GIFT—items similar to established instruments (Rimm & Davis, 1976)	Expensive and secret (Callahan, 1991; Piirto, 1992a/1998)

Table 4.2   *Continued*

Name of Instrument	Reasons to Use	Reasons Not to Use
Adjective Check List (ACL) Creativity SubTest	Based on real characteristics of creative producers. Adjectives describing a creative personality are "adventurous, ambitious, artistic, assertive, clever, complicated, curious, energetic, enterprising, imaginative, independent, initiative, intelligent, interests wide, inventive, original, progressive, resourceful, self-confident, temperamental, and versatile." Creative personality high scorers are "venturesome, aesthetically reactive, clever, and quick to respond." Intellectually, they have such characteristics as wide interests, mental ability, and fluency of ideas.	1. Confusing as to which characteristics are most salient 2. Not useful for children as their personalities are not developed
Torrance Tests of Creative Thinking (TTCT)	1. Extensive research base available where researchers have used it in pre- and posttesting situations 2. May help to find "false negative"—a person not thought to be creative who scores high	1. Scoring requires extensive training for reliability 2. Measures a limited divergent production definition of creativity 3. Predictive validity not convincingly established
High School Personality Questionnaire (HSPQ)	1. Large research base 2. Second-order creativity score possible to obtain	1. Creativity score based on research using teacher selected "creatives" and not on adult creatives (Piirto & Fraas, 1995) 2. Psychological training needed to interpret and administer
Myers-Briggs Type Indicator (MBTI)	1. Large research base with theoretical orientation	1. Psychological training needed to interpret and administer 2. No "creativity" profile
Overexcitability Questionnaire (OEQ)	1. Theoretically based 2. Finds psychomotor, sensual, imaginational, intellectual, and emotional overexcitabilies	1. Difficult to code and rate 2. Psychological training needed to interpret and administer 3. Small research base using children

(continued on next page)

Table 4.2 *Continued*

Name of Instrument	Reasons to Use	Reasons Not to Use
SOI Creative Thinking Test	1. Easy to administer 2. Company will score	1. Measures a limited divergent production definition of creativity 2. Predictive validity not convincingly established
SAGES—Screening Assessment for Gifted Elementary Students; two forms, Elementary and Primary	Comprehensive packaged identification system with ongoing validation efforts	Assesses only divergent production

the California Psychological Inventory (CPI) and the Minnesota Multiphasic Personality Inventory (MMPI), the 16 Personality Factors (16PF) Inventory, and many others.

Many of the major studies of creative people used these checklists, with varying results, according to the type of creative person being studied. Note that the persons were studied according to the *domains* in which they were creative, and not for some postulated "ability" to be creative (Piirto, 1992a/1998). Davis (1989) said "In order to more accurately identify creative persons, for example, for participation in G/T programs, a recommended strategy is to use both types of tests, divergent thinking tests to evaluate some cognitive creative abilities and personality/biographical inventories to assess affective, motivational, and experiential factors" (p. 258).

PROMISING ALTERNATIVE ASSESSMENT PRACTICES

The use of personality checklists filled out by the students is entirely different from using those checklists filled out by the school system, which supposedly show that the student possesses certain researched characteristics and thus is potentially creative.

Interrater Reliability on Storytelling

Hennessey and Amabile (1988) came up with another method, not using testing, that can be used to assess verbal creativity in elementary students, and that is storytelling. Children told stories that were rated by teachers. The procedure was simple. Children were asked to view a book with no words, think up a story, and then tell the story aloud, telling one thing about each page. Three teachers with no special training then rated the tape-recorded stories on *creativity, liking, novelty, imagination, logic, emotion, grammar, detail, vocabulary,* and *straightforwardness.*

Their ratings were very similar, giving high interrater reliability. The experiment had proper controls and the results of the children's stories results were compared relative to each other, so there was no confusion with IQ testing. This shows there are many other ways to assess creativity than paper and pencil tests.

Performance Criteria

Project Vanguard (Morrison & Dungan, 1992) found that performance criteria should be used along with divergent production tests and creativity checklists. The researchers looked at the creativity components in such contests as Odyssey of the Mind, History Days, science fairs, Future Problem Solving, and math and writing contests, and they recommended that schools who need to identify children with creative potential consider what the children are already doing in these arenas. Figure 4.10 shows the components needed in identifying unique ability in creative thinking.

Observation of Creativity

There are several ways to conduct observations of creative behavior, to try to notice those children who demonstrate creative behaviors within certain domains. A multifactored identification matrix, shown in Figure 4.11, was developed by Project Vanguard.

Who should make the observations to look for creativity in students? The *Model for the Identification of Creative Thinking Ability* (Morrison & Dungan, 1992) stated: "Since we are looking for patterns of behavior over time, the observations should be made by those who are in an ongoing relationship with the child, and may also be made by an older child him/herself" (p. 103). Observers can include adults such as parents and friends, as well as teachers of special subjects and coaches in competitions that involve creative thinking, such as Odyssey of the Mind, Future Problem Solving, and science fairs. Some experts believe that behavioral checklists should be filled out by adults or by students themselves, and not peers, because of the possible confusion of popularity with

Figure 4.10   Performance-based Assessment for Gifted Identification in the Area of Creative Thinking

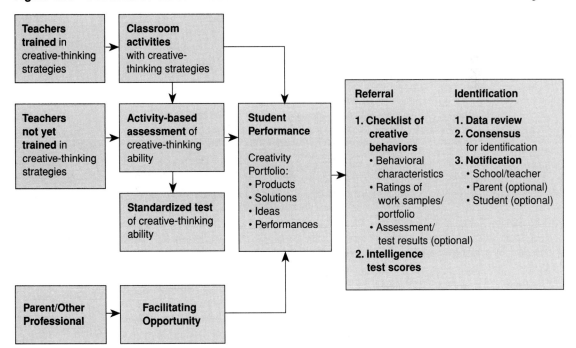

Reprinted form Morrison, M., and Dungan, R. (1992). *Model for the Identification of Creative-Thinking Ability*. Ohio Department of Education, Research and Demonstration Series in Gifted Education.

Figure 4.11   Multifactored Identification of Unique Ability in Creative Thinking

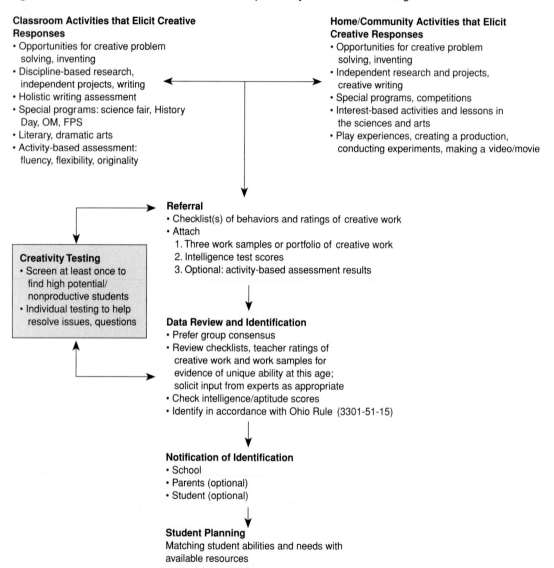

Classroom Activities that Elicit Creative Responses
- Opportunities for creative problem solving, inventing
- Discipline-based research, independent projects, writing
- Holistic writing assessment
- Special programs: science fair, History Day, OM, FPS
- Literary, dramatic arts
- Activity-based assessment: fluency, flexibility, originality

Home/Community Activities that Elicit Creative Responses
- Opportunities for creative problem solving, inventing
- Independent research and projects, creative writing
- Special programs, competitions
- Interest-based activities and lessons in the sciences and arts
- Play experiences, creating a production, conducting experiments, making a video/movie

Referral
- Checklist(s) of behaviors and ratings of creative work
- Attach
  1. Three work samples or portfolio of creative work
  2. Intelligence test scores
  3. Optional: activity-based assessment results

Creativity Testing
- Screen at least once to find high potential/ nonproductive students
- Individual testing to help resolve issues, questions

Data Review and Identification
- Prefer group consensus
- Review checklists, teacher ratings of creative work and work samples for evidence of unique ability at this age; solicit input from experts as appropriate
- Check intelligence/aptitude scores
- Identify in accordance with Ohio Rule (3301-51-15)

Notification of Identification
- School
- Parents (optional)
- Student (optional)

Student Planning
Matching student abilities and needs with available resources

Reprinted from Morrison, M., and Dungan, R. (1992). *Model for the Identification of Creative-Thinking Ability.* Ohio Department of Education, Research and Demonstration Series in Gifted Education.

creativity. Several adult observations should be solicited, and if the child is old enough, a self-report should also be included.

Where should observations be made? The school is often not the ideal setting for the observation of creative behavior, given the necessities for classroom control and for group discipline. Observing that a certain child is rebellious or is a "class clown" is not enough information to make the intuitive leap that the child is creative. Home and extracurricular settings are ideal, as are field trips for competitions, private lessons, and enrichment settings. Summertime observations should be included as well. Such behaviors as independent research based on interest and elaborate play activities such as theaters in the backyard and imaginative fantasy play on the computer or with friends in the neighborhood should be included in the assessment.

A behavioral checklist may be utilized, but caution should be used, so that what is on the checklist is related to actual behaviors that creatively productive people exhibit. A caution about "amount" of characteristics is necessary here, because often the temptation is to check a number of items, put them on a matrix, and add them into a weighted total. One item checked may indicate creative potential just as well as several items checked. Figure 4.12 is a behavioral characteristics list developed by the State of Ohio (Morrison & Dungan, 1992). The Ohio checklist for Project Vanguard was developed under a $100,000 grant and the materials are in the public domain.

Schools will become more cautious about identifying creative potential, as lawsuits and fuzzy validation efforts become more publicized. Karnes and Marquardt, in a 1989 monograph written for the Indiana Department of Education, stated, "Almost certain to generate litigation during the next decade are the procedures used for selection of participants in gifted education" (p. 16). Since creative potential is such a nebulous concept, and since most of the instruments used are still in the category of research instruments, schools should be quite careful about whom they name—and more to the point—whom they do *not* name as being talented in creativity.

The assessment of creative potential has many pitfalls, but careful, thorough, and informed people can sidestep these pitfalls with proper attention. One of the ways to sidestep is not to identify for the "creativity ability" but to identify for talent—specific talent. Another is to judge products for their creativity.

Identifying Creative Potential by Product Assessment

A bonus baby for the Cleveland Indians can throw a ball 95 miles per hour at the age of 18. His uncle observed him throwing rocks at an early age and could hear the whiz of the rocks flying by him. The speed was already there. His "product," a fast ball, was obvious, and its speed could be measured. So, too, it may be with the assessment of creative potential. Such assessment has been called *portfolio assessment.* "Portfolio" has become a popular and amorphous term in the past decade. Portfolios are used in various systems of what has come to be called *authentic assessment.* Several states, including Vermont, have revised their assessment procedures of students to include student portfolios. A 1997 evaluation of the Rochester, New York, alternative assessment program showed that "gender, socioeconomic, and racial inequities persist even with authentic assessment, although alternative assessments have a smaller gap between Blacks and Whites, and a larger one between the genders than do standardized tests" (Supovitz & Brennan, 1997, p. 472). That is, authentic assessment is no panacea for the ills of society visited upon the schools, but it is worth trying.

Portfolios

A portfolio is not just a folder containing a student's homework; rather, portfolios are made for certain purposes, and the purpose will determine the content and shape of the portfolio. Here is the Northwest Regional Laboratory definition of a portfolio:

Figure 4.12 Behavioral Characteristics Related to Creative Thinking

Student's Name _____ Date _____

Age _____ Grade _____ School _____

Person completing: _____

Relationship to child: _____ **Phone** _____

Characteristic	Observed		
In relationship to other children this age:	Consistently	Now and then	Not yet
1. Has wide range of interests across many subject areas and topics, including some that are stereotypically held by opposite sex			
2. Less interested in facts and details			
3. Discovers or notices important problems; finds problems to solve			
4. Is open to new and varied experiences in many areas such as fantasy, feelings, ideas, aesthetics, values, actions			
5. Takes intellectual risks; choice of topics/problems reflects potential for failure; enjoys working on the edge of competence			
6. Uninhibited in behavior; spontaneous			
7. Categorizes ideas differently, more broadly; can see more linkages between ideas and things than other students			
8. Is confident of abilities and ideas; may seem overly confident			
9. Becomes intensely involved in creative problem-solving activity			
10. Enjoys complexity, ambiguity in ideas and situations			

Reprinted from Morrison, M., and Dungan, R. (1992). *Model for the Identification of Creative-Thinking Ability.* Ohio Department of Education, Research and Demonstration Series in Gifted Education.

A portfolio is a purposeful collection of student work that exhibits to the student (and/or others) the student's effort, progress or achievement in (a) given area(s). This collection must include:

1. Student participation in selection of portfolio content;
2. the criteria for selection;
3. the criteria for judging merit; and
4. evidence of student self-reflection. (Arter, 1990)

The fact that the student participates in the formation of the portfolio, the fact that something is not being done to the student, but being done with the student, is a new feature in the world of assessment. With an emphasis on portfolio assessment, students have a voice in creating the pictures of themselves they want to present.

What content should a portfolio represent? The purpose of the creative products portfolio is to assess creative potential. Thus creative products should be included. These can include writing, music, art, mechanical, oral presentations (for example, recorded on audio or videotape), presentations, science projects, inventions, and mathematical problems solved or attempted with a view to the originality, the imagination, the uniqueness represented by the attempt. Clubs and groups that deal with creativity and competitions and contests participated in should be included also. But these should not be weighted more strongly than solitary pursuits done while waiting for mom and dad to get home from work. Books read and modifications made should also be noted.

The cognitive characteristics of creativity, flexibility, fluency, elaboration, and originality may be ways of assessing portfolio data, but poets may write few words and not be "fluent," and musicians may compose in standard song form, and not be flexible. These cognitive aspects should not be the main criteria for assessing a portfolio as being particularly strong, but should be included in the assessment. Younger students should have as strong a voice as older students in creating their own portfolios in order to be named as having creative potential and being able to participate in special activities designed for children with creative potential.

Johnsen and Ryser (1996) studied whether portfolios were valid in predicting primary students' success in programs for the gifted and talented. Teachers rated the portfolios and classroom performance of 120 students. Portfolios contained "drawings, paintings, scrap art, made-up stories, work with numbers, tapes of reading or musical skills, photos of three-dimensional items, certificates or awards, or sports or dance descriptions" (p. 257). The criteria for rating the portfolios were (1) *high-quality work*; (2) *advanced vocabulary*; (3) *leadership skills*; (4) *in-depth understanding*; (5) *advanced work*; (6) *detailed presentation*; (7) *creative responses*; and (8) *keen sense of humor*. The teachers rated whether the quality was present or absent. The researchers found that the portfolios did predict who would be chosen for programs for the talented later on in elementary school. Johnsen and Ryser said that "the use of product portfolios [is] . . . . a fairer, less biased approach in identifying students from racial and ethnic minorities. . . . The portfolio may indeed provide an avenue for greater inclusion of underrepresented groups in gifted programs" (p. 266).

Reis and Renzulli in 1991 presented a validated Student Product Assessment Form that is very helpful, not only in finding creative potential, but in evaluating student products once the potential is found. Bessemer and Treffinger in 1981 developed the Creative Product Analysis Matrix, which was revised in 1987. Torrance and his colleagues have also developed various forms. Such forms are valuable tools in helping students to improve their products, and in providing quality services to talented students. Figure 4.13 is another Project Vanguard form, Teacher Rating of Creative Work. The field of talent development education has begun to collect research and to validate that research so that optimum development of students' talents can take place.

Figure 4.13   Teacher Rating of Creative Work

Work Sample or Student Portfolio

Please attach this rating form to the work sample or student portfolio.

Student Name _____ **School Year** _____ **Grade** _____

Teacher _____

1. What was the problem/assignment/discipline area?

2. Time span of activity: From _____ to _____

3. Briefly describe the *planned* outcome/product/solution:

4. Not all plans result in satisfactory outcomes, although the work completed during the project may have been approached in a very original way. Was this outcome successful? _____ yes ____ no
   If not, please explain.

In comparison with other students with whom I have worked, this product/idea/solution shows evidence of:	5 Exemplary	4 Excellent	3 Adequate
1. Unique point of view; novel or original solution; unusual perspective	startling	unusual	adequate
2. Valuable and appropriate contribution for this age	very valuable, appropriate	valuable, appro-priate	adequate
3. Inner drive; sustained effort to completion	overcame many obstacles	stuck with it over time	adequate time spent
4. Increase in, and application of, knowledge as a basis for creating unique solutions	read, learned in tangential fields	read widely	read adequately
5. Choice of topic/problem that reflects potential for failure; working on the edge of com-petence; personal risk taking	took great amount of risk in choice of topic	moderate risk	some risk

Reprinted from Morrison, M., and Dungan, R. (1992), *Model for the Identification of Creative-Thinking Ability*. Ohio Department of Education, Research and Demonstration Series in Gifted Education.

CASE EXAMPLE: Creativity, Inc., A Program for Developing Creativity in Adolescents

by F. Christopher Reynolds, Teacher, Berea, Ohio and Singer/Songwriter *(Used with permission of author)*

My Foundation as a Songwriter

I grew up in a family where music was a natural part of life, but my own songwriting needed more than safety. It needed to be perceived and cultivated. Today, I am a songwriter because at critical points in my development, I was given a bit of help (Christopher, 1997). I later developed my program, Creativity, Inc., based on the help I received in high school.

I can recall several powerful crystallizing experiences in my songwriting development. The first was at a very young age. I was at my grandfather's house in Cincinnati, at the age of six. I took a toy harmonica behind his big couch. I played a mournful song about the end of the dinosaurs. "What became of the dinosaurs?" I would sing a few lines and then play that harmonica. This song was so sad to me that I cried. Behind the couch as I composed my first song, I entered an oceanic state of expanded awareness. I lost track of time and place. A few days later, I tried my song again, but it never worked again in the same way. I didn't have that kind of experience again until I was a teenager.

At age 13, I was beginning to learn to play the guitar. I just figured out a new chord that I would learn later was Esus4. That chord moved me into a mood and I began to write another song. This one was about a boy who killed his father and ran away. I entered the oceanic feeling again. It was another sad song about what was gone. What strikes me now is the melancholy. To this day, I think I'm still enamored by my own sorrow and how it is enlivened when it's put to music.

The following year, I saw *A Hard Day's Night*. I knew then that music was the kind of power that I wanted to develop. Maybe it's every teenage boy's dream to be chased by thousands of girls who want to rip his clothes off, but for me, I felt I actually had a shot at doing such a thing because I was the best guitar player my age at the time.

My friend Randy and I began passing lyrics back and forth. We were trying to write songs and we kept a folder of all of our work. We had a band the next year and had composed two songs, one about the sea and another about drifting through space. Then we met Big Dave Kerchner. He was a divorced man who lived above the skating rink in town in a small room. He became our encourager. He was especially important for me because he always focused in on the original work. He told me that any future in music would be carried by original compositions. He encouraged the whole band to be as creative as possible. His inspiration was a large influence on me when I developed Creativity, Inc. We spoke for several years about making a special school for artists.

One night, he took us to see a psychic. We got there about midnight and stayed until 4 a.m. It was remarkable for all of us. I walked away from that with a sense of calling. That call stays with me to this day. My call, my *daimon*, is one of making a music that touches the soul and of educating individuals in a way that they realize how their creative act has a one-of-a kind impact on the world.

One last part of my foundation as a songwriter is the role that making music played in my dealings with the traumas of life. At 19, when my best friend Dale was killed, it was music that brought me through. I wrote a song for him that I played over and over as I wept. When I got up the composure to play the song for my parents, I told them, "I know that I'm a songwriter now. I will never stop making music."

The Development of Creativity, Inc.

After I had been teaching French in the Berea Schools for a few years, I saw that the artistically and creatively inclined students had few outlets unless they were in formal music programs or formal art programs. When I saw the need for a more inclusive program for the artistically gifted, I designed Creativity, Inc. Its design was inspired by the mentoring I received during my own adolescence. The course is a series of ten 2^1/$_2$ hour sessions in which students focus on creating in a number of media as well as in the media of their choice. Students become peer mentors, which means that they learn how to respect and encourage the often fragile originality of the other students. They also make connections to the larger community of creative individuals that includes former "graduates" of the program and artists in the local community.

The power of Creativity, Inc. is that it helps the adolescent gain confidence during a time in life when many experience a sort of "midlife crisis," as they decide whether or not to develop individual creativity. The program makes clear the connection between self-expression in the arts and the affective domain. Drawing on techniques of expressive therapy in sculpture, painting, poetry, music, acting, dance, guided imagery, and creative writing, the students learn through experience the enriching, integrating effects that working with the imagination brings. The result is, regardless of future success, the adolescent knows that beauty and the arts are always a means to work things out.

Over the ten-week period, student work alternates between personal creative endeavors and preset activities. The central focus is always on the image and the imagination. When images are shared, they are met with imagination. This means that discussion is less about probing the artist's intent than about a personal response. Here is a typical dialogue among the young creators:

Individual 1: "This area of the painting looks like a coyote."
Individual 2: "To me, you've painted a picture of lungs."
Teacher: "Yes, I see the coyote and the lungs. There's a butterfly there, too."
Artist: "I see that. Let me think. It's reminding me of the freedom to breathe, like being out West. Looks pretty good to me right about now!"

The students learn how discussion of images moves best in this fashion from quality to quality, by likenesses. Following is a sketch of the ten sessions of Creativity, Inc.:

1. *Earliest work.* Students bring in what remains of their earliest creativity. In sharing, they are reminded of the freedom to create that was childhood. This sets the tone for the course in which the goal will always be on positive critique, on what is liked in each work.
2. *Finger painting.* Where have you been dwelling? Students are given large sheets of paper and finger paints and they express what psychological, symbolic place in which they have been living lately.
3. *Latest work.* Students bring in and share what they've been working on lately or they bring in an idea that they are going to develop over the next few weeks.
4. *Music.* Students bring in lyric sheets and copies of their favorite songs. Discussion is about which images resonate within the others and on which part of the song is particularly touching to the student who brought the song in.
5. *Sculpture.* An organic whole. Show the students a tree. Comment on how all the parts of the tree form a greater whole. Have the students make a clay image that shows the organic whole of their lives, how the different extensions are related.
6. *Poetry.* Students bring in a piece of their own poetry to be read and shared. Discussion that follows is always a personal response to the images in the work.
7. *Where were you hurt?* Stories from the body. Students take five minutes to remember places on their bodies where they have been hurt. They are then placed in pairs and given several red strips of crepe paper. Students take turns telling body stories. At the completion of each story, the listener ties a red strand to that part of the body. Students share stories with the larger group. Muse on the miraculous fact of surviving the many traumas of life.
8. *Latest work.* Students share again an original work that is completed or in progress.
9. *Guided imagery.* Students visit a house in the woods by guided imagination. The images are interpreted and the activity of dreaming is discussed.
10. *Putting it all together.* Give each student a cardboard box. They then put together all of the images generated during Creativity, Inc. Give each student a candle to place in the center of the personal images. Visit each box as a group. Discuss it as a work of art like before. The candle represents the fact that while images are helpful in self-knowledge, there will always be part of us beyond our self-images.

Creativity, Inc. has been in existence for about seven years, and has worked with students from middle school age to graduate students. Most creativity training programs focus on a more linear approach, but it is my belief that creativity springs from deep within, in an atmosphere of trust, caring, and valuing of that small, timid venture that is a person's first expression of the creative wish.

➤ ➤ ➤ ➤ ➤ ➤ ➤ ➤ ➤ ➤ ➤ ➤ ➤ ➤ ➤ ➤

SUMMARY

1. People believe that schools should do more to nourish creativity in children.
2. The term *creativity* has recently evolved from its roots in agricultural terms.
3. There are many reasons for the emphasis on creativity. Some are reasons of quantity, quality, equity, national competition and pride, and freedom.
4. Confusion exists about how creativity relates to talent. Creativity underlies all expresssions of talent.
5. "Creativity" testing is often divergent production testing and the tests are often questionable in validity and reliability.
6. Creativity is often shown in creativity *at* something, *in* something, or *with* something, even at young ages.
7. Many checklists have questionable validity and reliability. The closer the questions on a checklist are to actual creative behaviors in a domain, the more reliable they are.
8. Some personality questionnaires give valid descriptions of creative people.
9. Promising practices must include performance assessment in fields transferable to the domain where the creative production is expected.
10. Creativity training should be considered for all students, not just the identified talented students.
11. Creativity, Inc. is a creativity training program for adolescents and adults, featured in the Case Example.

PATHS OF TALENT
DEVELOPMENT

CHAPTER

5 THE YOUNG TALENTED CHILD FROM BIRTH TO GRADE TWO

Characteristics of Young
    Academically Talented Children
Factors That Enhance or Inhibit
    Young High-IQ Talent
Identification of Young
    Academically Talented Children
Choosing a School
Curriculum for Young
    Academically Talented Children
Case Example: A Plan for Scott

FOCUSING QUESTIONS

1. Why is there a risk that young academically talented children will learn to underachieve?
2. Discuss precocious reading and its relationship to verbal talent.
3. What have researchers learned about the infancy of academically talented children?
4. What have researchers learned about the toddler stage in academically talented children?
5. What does dyssynchrony have to do with assessing the abilities of young academically talented children?
6. How is mathematical ability exhibited in young academically talented children?
7. When and how should young academically talented children be identified as such?
8. Compare and contrast the Hunter College Elementary School model and the Project Spectrum model for identification.
9. How do Piagetian tasks and creativity tasks help identify young academically talented children?
10. Look at some preschools in your area. Which would you recommend to parents of precocious children? Why?
11. Look at the curriculum given in this chapter for kindergarten. How does this differ or how is it similar to the kindergarten curriculum in your school district?
12. Look at the mathematics examples and science scope discussed in this chapter. How do these differ or how are they similar to what your school district teaches?

Figure 5.1 Overview of Chapter 5

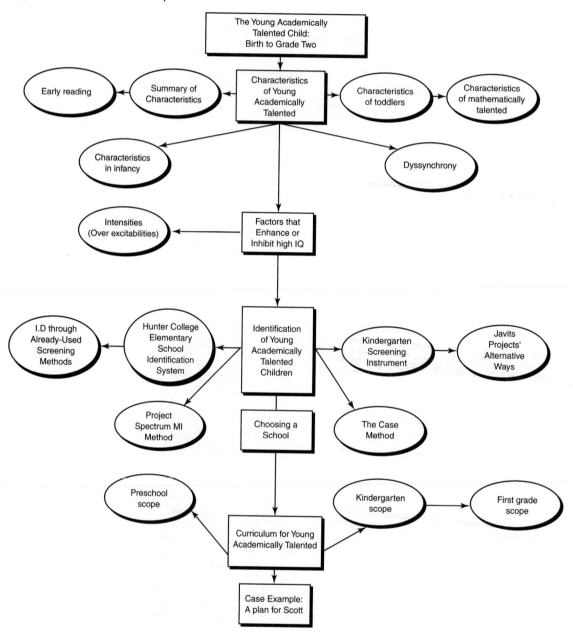

Four-year-old Maria has been waiting and waiting to go to school. She plays school all the time. She is the teacher, and her dolls are the students. At her day-care center, she is the one who always leads the other kids in games, because she is the only one who can read. The other kids look up to her, except when she tries to make them do things they really don't want to do, such as count by twos. The day-care center teacher told Maria's mother that Maria was very bright. She was told the same thing when Maria went for her preschool screening, and the district recommended that Maria be tested by the school psychologist. The school psychologist told Maria's mother that Maria had an IQ of 145 on the Stanford-Binet Intelligence Scale: Fourth Edition test, which put her into the 99th percentile. This would qualify her for the program for academically talented children in a few years. The program for the academically talented didn't start until fourth grade, although they did have enrichment lessons in first through third grade.

Finally, it is the first day of school. Maria just turned 5 in August, and she has her new dress on and her new shoes. Her mother braids her hair and fastens it with new barrettes. When she gets to school, she is anxious for her mother to leave, yet still she feels shy, with all these kids here. Half of them are crying as their parents leave them. Maria looks around the room and sees a shelf of books. She always reads when she doesn't know what else to do, so she goes over to the shelf and waits for things to calm down. After all the parents have gone, the teacher tells the children to sit on a line painted on the floor. As the children have come into the room, they have been given large name tags. The teacher sits on a small chair with the children in a semicircle around her and says, "My name is Mrs. Miller, boys and girls. Welcome to kindergarten. In kindergarten, we will learn our letters and our numbers so that we can learn to read in first grade."

"I can read already," Maria says, jumping up.

"That's nice," says Mrs. Miller. "Maria, when we want to talk, first we must stand, and then we must wait until Mrs. Miller calls on us."

"But I can read already!" Maria's voice gets petulant, and tears start in the corners of her eyes.

"Maria, that's nice," said Mrs. Miller. "But in kindergarten, we will learn how to read right. Please sit down now."

Maria is chagrined. She feels shame and embarrassment. She sits down. She has taken the first step to underachievement. Underachievement is the prevailing situation in the education of academically talented young children in most schools today. By the time she has been socialized into the kindergarten milieu, Maria will have learned to keep quiet about her abilities, and even to suppress that she can read. In first grade, she will comply with the reading tasks in order to fit in. By second grade, even though she will be getting all her work right, she will have learned that she doesn't have to put forth any effort in school in order to be the best student. By third grade, she will have learned that boredom and laziness are the hallmarks of school work. By fourth grade, when she gets into a pullout program for academically talented students, she will resent it when the teacher of the academically talented tries to challenge her, and in challenging her, stretches her capabilities. Maria, unfortunately, is a typical young academically talented child who enters the public school system.

One of the education goals for the year 2000 states that all children must come to school ready to learn. The push and the emphasis behind this goal has been to increase spending for Head Start, and for compensatory programs at the preschool level. At major national conferences on the education of young children, very few sessions consider the needs of young academically talented children. Much help and support has been directed at socially and mentally disadvantaged young children, as well it should be.

In the meantime, however, the educational needs of young children who are bright have been overlooked. In most certification programs for the early childhood education, the needs of young academically talented children are given short shrift. When these children enter school they are enthusiastic and capable, but soon they find themselves forced to conform and to hide their academic talent. By the time they do get into even the minimal programs being provided to academically talented children, which usually begin at third or fourth grade, they are often confirmed underachievers. The Howleys and Pendarvis (Howley, 1992; Howley, Howley, and Pendarvis, 1995) have suggested that acceleration for academically talented young children should begin with early entrance to school. Saying that such practice is "essential," "legally defensible," and good pedagogical practice, they suggested that early entrance to kindergarten or early entrance to first grade should be considered by parents of precocious youngsters and by the schools. An edited book on young gifted children was published in 1998 (Smutny). This contains articles by many of the thinkers in the field of the education of the gifted and talented combined with the expertise of early childhood specialists (see Cummings & Piirto, 1998).

CHARACTERISTICS OF YOUNG ACADEMICALLY TALENTED CHILDREN

Maria may be beginning, with her first encounter with formal schooling, a life of underachieving. She possesses two of the characteristics that are hallmarks for identifying the young academically talented child: (1) She has a high IQ on an individually administered test; and (2) she could read before going to school. Of the second characteristic, about half of cognitively gifted young children read before they go to school, and half do not.

Early Reading

Children who begin to read on their own, without special teaching or drill, seem to be those who will be deemed academically talented. Mills and Jackson (1990) did a study of 10- to 12-year-olds who were able to read at ages 5 and 6 and found that these students were still above average in reading comprehension. Jackson (1988) said that the deep comprehension needed for advanced reading takes verbal intelligence, and children who read exceptionally early have a certain adeptness at code breaking, especially the code of print. However, the children who do not read precociously soon catch up. Burns, Collins, and Paulsell (1991) found that when academically talented eight- and nine-year-old students from supportive home environments who had been reading at age 4 were compared with students who had not been reading at the same age, the early readers were still reading at higher levels in word attack and dictation subtests, though the other students who had not been reading at age 4 were their equals in comprehension and word recognition.

Jackson (1992) has followed precocious readers. She has found that those who are age 2 or 3 when they learn how to read without instruction may be exceptional in knowledge acquisition and in general intelligence, but they may not go on to develop this verbal intelligence; rather they may go into other fields that require high general intelligence. She said that those who become misplaced are often those who had high word identification abilities but moderate general intelligence, and that "precocious reading often may be their last remarkable accomplishment" because the schools don't present them with opportunities that require rapid learning and manipulation of new symbol systems.

Judith Dolgins, learning consultant at the Hunter College Elementary School for high-IQ students, said that about one-third of their kindergartners come to kindergarten reading with high level comprehension. About half are reading books like *The Cat in the Hat.* Another one third are reading "The cat is red." The teachers can start teaching for comprehension because the students are ready. By halfway through kindergarten half are reading. Usually more than half leave reading. For a handful, the reading "light bulb" goes on in first grade. Dolgins said that if there's a learning disability, you can usually tell in first grade (personal communication, September 1997).

Reading is the precocious behavior that is noticed most. Those disadvantaged young children who happen to be early readers are the ones, in disadvantaged groups, who are usually identified. Children who are not disadvantaged, who are taught to read with parental support, are sometimes called "hothouse flowers," but the Mills and Jackson study showed that these children also continue to be good readers even five and six years later. Nevertheless, with careful observation, it is possible to recognize a young academically talented child who does not have the ability to read, and without the use of an individualized IQ test. Shaklee and her colleagues at Kent State University used videotapes and computer analysis to find examples of behaviors and identifiers indicated by minority and disadvantaged children grades K–3. The project was called Early Assessment of Exceptional Potential and Cooperative Alliance (EAEP) and it was a Javits grant funded by the Office of Educational Research and Improvement, U.S. Department of Education, in the early 1990s (Shaklee & Hansford, 1992; Shaklee, Whitmore, Barton, Barbour, Ambrose & Viechnicki, 1989).

It is necessary to attempt to identify talented children at a young age; if the identification is careful and thorough, the effects of a disadvantaged environment can be mitigated. A summary of the characteristics of young talented children follows:

Characteristics of Young Talented Children

1. They are precocious, regardless of the talent area. Some may demonstrate precocious behaviors in several talent areas.
    a. Verbally talented children acquire vocabulary and speak in sentences earlier than age-mates. They can break letter codes and make abstract verbal connections.
    b. Mathematically talented children acquire numeration and number concepts sooner than age-mates.
    c. Musically talented children may often sing on key, demonstrate an interest in the piano or other musical instruments, and stop what they are doing to listen to music.
    d. Children talented in visual arts demonstrate artwork that is similar to that of older children.
    e. Kinesthetically or psychomotor-talented children demonstrate advanced motor ability.
    f. Spatially talented children may want to take things apart to see how they work, and demonstrate an understanding of mechanics that is advanced for their age.
    g. Children talented in the inter- and intrapersonal areas will demonstrate advanced understanding of social relationships, and demonstrate emotion about such things that age-mates will not perceive.
2. They have excellent memories.
3. They concentrate intensely on what interests them, for longer periods of time than age-mates.
4. Dyssynchrony (asynchrony) is obvious, especially in high-IQ children.
5. Affective precocity may lead to the assumption of leadership roles and to preferring older companions for play.

Characteristics in Infancy

A few studies have been conducted of academically talented children who had been studied since infancy (Lewis & Louis, 1990; Lewis & Michalson, 1985). Lewis and Louis (1990) listed several cognitive characteristics that can distinguish a potentially academically talented child in infancy. A high-IQ child will become bored quickly with old stimuli, even at the age of 3 months. It is as if—even at such a young age—the child is curious and wanting to explore new horizons. Lewis and Louis said that cognition for infants is made up of the ability to hold attention, of curiosity, and of a good memory.

Even newborn infants who turned out to have high IQs would stop crying to pay attention to something they heard, would get quiet when they heard a voice, were not cuddly but resistant, and would respond to stimuli in their cribs when they were not being held. Their parents said they were independent, intense, and difficult in temperament. Infants who turned out to have high IQs were selective in their oral behavior, reacted negatively when they were constrained or when they were pulled up, could remain awake without crying, seemed to have the sight and hearing of older infants, seemed to show more emotions that were related to the movements they made, actively responded to stimuli, and were frequently active and tense (Lewis & Louis, 1990; Lewis & Michalson, 1985).

The child's *primary behavioral style* and the environment in which the child be-haves probably predict development more than either heredity or environment, Lewis and Michalson thought. Attempts to give infants IQ tests have failed to predict reliably which babies will have high IQs later on, because environmental factors will generally determine how the potential is developed. However, other observational data seem to have more promise. The infant's cognitive traits of curiosity, attention, and memory seem to have some relationship to future high IQ. The infant's *rate of disinterest* is also predictive. If a child becomes rapidly disinterested in old stimuli, the child must re-member having seen that stimulus before in order to become disinterested.

Another predictor of high IQ is the child's verbal development. High-IQ children made earlier sounds resembling words and speech, read at an early age, often without formal teaching, had advanced vocabularies, asked many questions, and had good au-ditory memories and good memories for information. In fact, the high verbal intelli-gence shown in early readers has been found to be a consistent predictor of potential academic talent. Young academically talented children are advanced, compared to their age peers, in the verbal areas of talking, of writing, and of reading. The mother of a young academically talented child said that her son, at the age of 16 months, had a vocabulary of about 200 words, and was able to put two words into a sentence: "We go," or "Daddy, up!" where the average two-year-old has a vocabulary of about 50 words. The child was identified as gifted soon after he entered school and in second grade was reading at a level comparable to sixth graders.

Characteristics of Toddlers

Other characteristics besides this advanced verbal ability were noted by White (1985). Among these are the ability to notice discrepancies, including discrepancies in time, in perceptions, and in logic. A young academically talented child is also better able to think about the future and to deal with abstractions such as love and peace. She is less egocentric than her age-mates, and may ask questions about the well-being of creatures around her. She makes associations that are quite original and may amaze people with the connections she makes. She is more capable than her age-mates at planning and at carrying out activities that have several steps, and she can see how tools and other resources are used to carry out these activities. A particularly noticeable trait of young academically talented children is their ability to concentrate for longer periods of time than nonacademically talented age-mates.

Affectively, young academically talented children often have difficulty with their nonacademically talented age-mates, because the talented child will often direct the games and activities and assume leadership roles the other children might not un-derstand or like. "Bossy" is an epithet often given to such children, and they often can't understand why the other kids don't follow them with aplomb. This does not seem to affect their self-concepts, however, because their advanced social skills are often appreciated by older children, and the older children will let them play. In fact, one way to recognize a young academically talented child is to look at his interac-tions with older children. If the older children let him play, or talk to him as an equal, accepting his suggestions and his participation, chances are that the child has advanced social skills.

Another affective quality of young academically talented children is that they *like* to learn things. They show persistence in learning, and can concentrate longer on learning tasks than other children. They learn with intensity and with retention. Parents are often surprised at their retention. One mother of a young academically talented child told this story (Piirto, in press): Stacy's mother said that Stacy was early in all her developmental milestones. She walked at eight months and was an early talker. Stacy read some before she came to school.

Stacy was "so curious about everything. She liked to be talked to, she liked to be read to. She was into everything. She really made sure that we knew what she wanted." Her mother is a special educator and she did language samples on Stacy, recording her mean length of utterances from an early age. She didn't want to "get too clinical with my own child," but she found it fun to see a child developing typically, and not atypically as in the students she taught. Stacy's parents provided lots of exposure to language and books, and they took her everywhere. She had been enrolled in preschools and day care since the age of 18 months and she was always very interested in being with other children. Stacy had a sight word vocabulary—street signs, logos—by the time she was four years old. She retold stories rather than read them.

Stacy's good memory was apparent early. At age 3, when they were returning from a visit to relatives, Stacy said, "Daddy, I really don't think we should take the Waterson Expressway. I think we're going to run into too much traffic around Exit 34. I think it's a better idea to get off and take Route 7." Stacy had "mentally choreographed in her mind exactly how to get from point A to point B." Stacy's much-admired grandmother in Cleveland also read to her, talked to her, and sent her tapes of books she had read aloud; then Stacy would read along to her grandmother's taped voice.

Stacy's father was an architect, and her mother a college professor who taught teachers to work with mentally handicapped children. Stacy was the oldest sister of a younger brother and a preschool sister. When Stacy was asked when she knew she was smart, she responded with what is probably an apocryphal story in her family:

> Probably when I was two, because I first saw my mom, and I kept watching her dial the phone number to my grandmother's house, who lives in Cleveland. I was living in Kentucky then. I memorized it and just practiced it in my room, and one day I picked up the phone and dialed her, and she was surprised to hear a two-year-old talking on the phone. She asked, "Is your mommy there?" and I said, "No, Mommy's outside." She said, "How did you know how to dial?" I said, "I practiced." So, after that, my mom knew that I was really smart, so she started teaching me my ABCs, and I knew them when I just turned three, and I could count and all that.

Another advanced cognitive skill possessed by young academically talented children is a good memory.

Lewis and Michalson (1985) noted that the above characteristics hold true for children who turned out to be academically talented in *verbal* ability. This is an important point to note.

Mathematical Ability

Children who turned out to be academically talented in mathematical ability were "undistinguishable from other infants" (Lewis & Michalson, 1985, p. 53). Thus,

Lewis and Michalson called for a skills approach to the identification of very young academically talented children. For example, Edward Teller, the theoretical physicist, told an anecdote about his own early life, saying that he would put himself to sleep by reciting mathematical tables. His mathematical interest was a characteristic even before he went to school (Blumberg & Panos, 1990). A graduate student told about her mathematically talented son who loved to read the telephone book and would focus on the page numbers when being read to (J. Walker, personal communication, 1993). As always, when discussing academic talent, even in young children, the practitioner must ask, "academically talented in what?"

Blackshear (1979) administered the Comprehensive Test of Basic Skills (CTBS) and a divergent production test to primary students and found that the standardized achievement test mathematics subtests worked well to identify young children academically talented in mathematics. Bowie (1979) administered the short form of the Stanford-Binet Intelligence Scale: L-M to 77 first and second grade students and found that mental age was the best predictor of arithmetic reasoning ability. Assouline and Lupkowski (1992) extended the out-of-level testing model used by Johns Hopkins University to identify mathematically and verbally academically talented seventh graders to the identification of young academically talented mathematics students. They tested students as young as six years old on the Secondary School Admissions Test (SSAT), eliminating the ceiling effects of grade-level tests (Lupkowski & Assouline, 1992; Lupkowski-Shoplik & Assouline, 1993, 1994). The point is that specific abilities tests administered out of level should be used to find mathematically talented young children.

Dyssynchrony

Another characteristic that should be noted in the early development of talents is that the child will probably be more advanced in one area than in others. This is called *dyssynchrony*. It can be characterized as uneven development. One-half to two-thirds of verbally academically talented children are reading by age 5, but they are often unable to do handwriting because their fine motor skills are not developed. Terassier (1985) pointed out that verbally talented young children score four to six years above their age level in the Analogies section of the Wechsler Intelligence Scale for Children (WISC), while in their Vocabulary, Information, and Arithmetic they are two to three years above their age level.

Porath (1991) found, in comparing two groups of six-year-olds who were academically talented in verbal intelligence and academically talented in spatial intelligence with eight-year-old mental age peers, that the verbally talented children performed verbal tasks similar to the eight-year-olds and the spatially talented children drew pictures similar to the eight-year-olds, but that in physical development they were more similar to other six-year-olds than to the eight-year-olds. Six-year-olds who were advanced in both verbal and performance areas performed similar to the eight-year-olds on both the balance beam and in verbal tasks. This is another example of what could be called dyssynchrony. Morelock (1992) discussed a similar lack of fit, and used the term asynchrony to describe the emotional depth of such precocious high-IQ children. This will be discussed further in Chapter 11.

FACTORS THAT ENHANCE OR INHIBIT YOUNG HIGH-IQ TALENT

What are the factors that can enhance or inhibit optimal intelligence for preschool students? Feldman (1982), in a follow-up study of the famous Quiz Kids who were on television in the early 1950s, said that in each case, early on, at least one parent shared an interest with the child, gave the child much attention, provided appropriate materials and tools for the child, and gave much encouragement and praise. Others have pointed out that parents read aloud to the child and interacted with their young children about what they were reading. One young writing prodigy said that her mother read Shakespeare to her, "the real stuff, not the watered-down stuff" at an early age (Piirto, 1992b; 1992a/1998). The poet Dylan Thomas's father, a teacher, also read Shakespeare to his young son (Fitzgibbon, 1965). Another factor that can enhance early academically talented is birth order. Firstborn and only children seem to get more attention from parents and this seems to result in more firstborns turning out to be intellectually talented or to become creative producers (Simonton, 1988).

Lewis and Louis (1990) cited several factors that can inhibit the development of intelligence. Among these are early trauma such as the death or divorce of parents, hospitalization for illness or surgery, deprivation of food, shelter, or safety, and general loss and separation. Maslow's hierarchy of needs applies. A human being must have certain basic needs met before talents can develop.

Intensities (Overexcitabilities) as Characteristic of Young Gifted Children

Case studies have been done of young gifted students ages 4 through 6 in which they were analyzed using Dabrowski's overexcitabilities: Psychomotor, Sensual, Imaginational, Intellectual, and Emotional (Howard, 1997; Tucker & Hafenstein, 1997). Classroom observations and parent questionnaires were used. Sensual overexcitability was noticed in their dictated poetry and "their notice of color, movement, beauty, touch, an unusual word" (Howard, p. 84). Aspects of sensual overexcitability studied were stroking behavior with different textures, and an appreciation of the sensory aspects of experience. Psychomotor overexcitability was observed in their marked enthusiasm, rapid speech, surplus of energy, and impulsive actions. They showed emotional overexcitability in their "deep sensitivities to the feelings of others in the class and to world situations they wanted to discuss" (Howard, p. 84). Emotional overexcitability is characterized by concern for others, timidity and shyness, fear and anxiety and difficulty adjusting to new environments, and intensity of feeling (Piechowski, 1992). They showed intellectual overexitability through their "extraordinary curiosity"; one girl dominated group discussions "with sophisticated information on the topic far beyond the understanding and patience of most children in the group" (Howard, p. 84). Intellectual overexcitability is demonstrated through asking probing questions, problem solving, and theoretical thinking. Imaginational overexcitability was observed through fantasy play, animistic and imaginative thinking, daydreaming, and dramatic perception (Tucker & Hafenstein, p. 70). Sometimes the manifestations of overexcitabilities resemble Attention Deficit/Hyperactivity Disorder (ADHD), but the difference is the young gifted child focuses and directs the energy and is able to concentrate on matters of interest.

IDENTIFICATION OF YOUNG ACADEMICALLY TALENTED CHILDREN

Early identification is essential. Parents and other adults seem to be good identifiers. At the Hunter College Campus Schools, about 50 percent of those who are referred by parents for IQ testing at a young age are usually found to have very high IQs, while most of the others have high IQs. About 800 Manhattan children ages 3 and 4 are tested on an individual test each year, and about half of those do have IQs in the 99th percentile. The same has been found to be true in Seattle, at Rutgers University in New Jersey, and in Illinois (Robinson, 1987). Linda Silverman in Denver has also reported similar percentages (personal communication, 1991). This indicates that parents are indeed aware of their children's precocity.

Louis and Lewis (1992) found that parents' implicit beliefs about their children's ability levels were closely related to their actual tested IQs. Parents were especially accurate in their assessments of creative thinking and abstract thinking abilities, and in their assessments of memory abilities. Parents who choose to have their children tested because they think they have high IQs are more often right than not. Among the behaviors that parents noted were that the children seemed to be ahead of their peers, were curious, were aware of the environment, had an early interest in books and reading, recognized words and symbols, listened to music, had advanced abilities in art, showed leadership and advanced socialization abilities with peers and with older children, and had a long attention span.

Attempts have been ongoing to identify young children with the potential to be academically talented adults. One of the oldest schools for academically talented children is the Hunter College Elementary School, where young academically talented children have been identified since 1941, and which uses IQ tests to screen for young talent. Among the newest attempts have been Project Spectrum at Harvard University and the DISCOVER Project in New Mexico, both of which use multiple intelligence (MI) approaches to finding young talent. These two represent poles of difference, as discussed later in this chapter.

Other districts have gradually developed their own assessment instruments, based on necessity and follow-up research. Some research has been done in identifying children through the Head Start program (Karnes & Johnson, 1987). The Kindergarten Screening Instrument (Rivers, Meininger & Batten, 1991) of the Lincoln, Nebraska, Public Schools is one such instrument that need has dictated. Many other such attempts have been made. The Early Assessment of Exceptional Potential (EEAP) Javits project (Shaklee & Hansford, 1992) came up with a list of primary identifiers not usually picked up on tests. Case studies were used in other Javits programs, Project Synergy and Project START. All these will be discussed here.

The Hunter College Elementary School Identification System

The Hunter College Elementary School in New York City admits children ages 4 and 5. The admission process has been modified, depending on current admissions pressures, but essentially the school has always used individual intelligence test scores to admit children of all races and ethnic groups, although the whites are primarily

Jewish (Subotnik, Karp & Morgan, 1989). Because the school is tuition free, and because it provides a high-quality elementary school education, New York City parents are anxious to have their children admitted. One version of the procedure was validated (McCarthy & Navarre, 1985; McCarthy, Rosenfield, & Navarre, 1984).

Children ages 3 and 4 are tested with the Stanford-Binet Intelligence Scale: Fourth Edition (SB4) or the Wechsler Intelligence Scale for Children III (WISC-III). This individual IQ test is the preliminary screening for admission, and potential students have to score above the 97th percentile. Annually, from a pool of about 300 young children who meet the cutoff score on the tests, 16 nursery and 32 kindergarten students are eventually selected. First all high scorers go through a second round of testing conducted by consultants, teachers, and psychologists who come in for one week.

The students are observed in the second round during 90-minute sessions. Group observations consist of tasks that simulate classroom situations. How students behave is observed in these situations. Collaborative activities, where a group of students is given something to do, are offered. Consultants note how the students relate to the teacher and to each other as they observe them interacting in free play. Students do individual tasks in memory and classification, sorting, following directions, comparing, and the like. These tasks are different from those on the Stanford-Binet. "The emphasis is on what is expected of children at Hunter, what skills and talents are most desirable for this setting," said Polly Breland, Director of Admissions (personal communication, September 24, 1997). "We look at what skills and talents are most desirable for this particular school setting. The ability to communicate effectively and relate to others is especially important to us."

The selection is done by teachers. Identities are coded, and pseudonyms are assigned instead of numbers. First, the genders are balanced so there are equal numbers of boys and girls. Ethnically, the children resemble the population of Manhattan. Ethnic and economic factors are often inferred rather than asked directly. "We know the ethnicity if the family reports it; we will know whether or not the family has been to preschool; whether or not the family qualifies for waiver of the fee," said Breland. What quartile of the birth year is also considered, so that the children are balanced for age throughout that year. Recently the cutoff date was changed, moved up to be earlier, as the nursery children were often immature. This change of a few months has helped instruction immensely, said nursery teacher Nancy Torres (personal communication, September 1997).

In one study, about half of these students went on, after six or seven years, to score very high on the Hunter College High School Admissions Test, administered to about 3,000 sixth grade students from all five boroughs of New York City each January (Piirto, 1990c). The Hunter High School Admissions Test is psychometrically similar to the Scholastic Aptitude Test (SAT) (McCarthy & Navarre, 1985). In order to qualify to take the Hunter High School Admissions Test, these 3,000 sixth graders had scored in the 94th percentile in both reading and mathematics on the standardized achievement test administered in their home schools. Of these 3,000, the 180 highest scorers on the Hunter High School Test were ranked and were admitted to the Hunter College High School.

Half of the Hunter College Elementary School students who had scored high on an IQ test administered before preschool, did not, in sixth grade, meet the cutoff above which the 180 admitted youngsters scored. They were also admitted to the Hunter College High School without regard to their scores. A follow-up study (Piirto, 1990c) found that this half of the elementary school students also continued to demonstrate significantly lower grades, achievement, and aptitude test scores while attending the Hunter College High School. They had experienced a very enriched elementary school curriculum in a special school, but they achieved lower than students who entered the school from all over the city. One could interpret this study by speculating about the worth of a special elementary school education for the academically talented, or one could note that the Hunter College High School only admitted the top 180 scorers out of 3,000 high achievers, and therefore it served the very highly academically talented, that the half who continued to achieve lower than these students would, in any other high school, have been in programs for the academically talented and would have done exceptionally well. One could speculate that half the admitted preschool students were *false positives* (children who really have high IQs but later do not), although an internal study showed that a similar group of children attained even higher IQs than when admitted when retested in second and third grade (Rosenfield, 1987).

As Robinson and Chamrad (1986) said, it is much more difficult to achieve a false positive score than a false negative score: "rarely can a child attain a score higher than the level of which he or she is capable" (p. 161). False negatives are easy to attain. "Fatigue or illness, discouragement, resentment, poor reading skills, insufficient acquaintance with English, underlying depression," and other problems such as emotional and behavioral problems are common causes of attaining a false negative score, especially when the test is a group test.

The fact remains that identifying by use of an individual intelligence test score is still about the most reliable way of identifying young, potentially academically talented students from the middle and higher socioeconomic classes. Kaufman and Harrison (1986) pointed out that the trained psychologists who are licensed to administer such tests "may thus identify academically talented cognitive behaviors in a child even when the obtained IQs or standard scores are below the established cutoff points" (p. 156). They also asserted that giving individual intelligence tests may be the most fair way of identifying students who are not academically talented in stereotypical ways, or who might go undetected because they are poor—economically disadvantaged.

Kaufman and Harrison (1986) also said that individual intelligence tests are the best predictors of school achievement and of ensuing life achievement and that the various subtests should be used to identify nontypical academically talented children, that is, high scoring children as well as children with special abilities who may not score high in all areas and thus not rate high in general ability. Roedell, Jackson, and Robinson (1980) said, for example, that mathematics subtest scores should be used to identify students with potential mathematical ability. This sounds logical, but many schools require a high general ability score and do not look at subtest scores for placement.

The use of standardized individual intelligence tests is still a relatively sound pedagogical practice in identifying young academically talented students who come from backgrounds where there has not been trauma. Robinson and Chamrad (1986) gave three reasons why this is so: (1) young children need a global measure because they are not yet sharply differentiated in abilities; (2) the tests have been developed for a wide range of ages and therefore the young student will be able to "top off" on a subtest and a level for the child can be obtained (this is not true for grade-level tests for many academically talented children, who score in the 99th percentile; therefore, they should be tested on the next highest level); and (3) it has been shown that intellectual ability is an "essential ingredient of children's high academic attainment" (p. 161).

All experts caution, though, that the earlier the test is given, the less stable it is. For example, Stanford-Binet tests given to the same children at ages 3 and 6 showed a 0.59 correlation between scores, "a substantial correspondence but not of sufficient strength to serve as a base for long-range planning" (p. 161). This indicates that retesting should be a part of programs for young children if they are to be served properly. Silverman (1986) said that "the younger the child, the more valid is a global [IQ] assessment; the older the child, the more differentiated are his or her abilities into specific aptitudes" (p. 139).

Another New York City program for academically talented youngsters is the Hollingworth Preschool. They also use individual intelligence tests as a first screen, and children who score three standard deviations above the mean are treated as being academically talented. Borland (1986b) said, "We have not yet figured out how to explain away such a result; chance and 'overachievement' appear to us to be rather feeble explanations" (p. 166). They also conduct other testing in observational situations. They have found few false positives, but quite a few false negatives, children who first scored between 110 and 125, or above average, who upon retesting later, turned out to experience "significant increments" in their test scores.

Identification Through Already-Used Screening Methods

Many schools use the Brigance K & 1 Screen prior to students' entering kindergarten. Two studies, one a Javits project, explored how this test can be used to identify potentially gifted students. Feiring, Louis, Ukeje, and Lewis (1997) described the method used in the Newark, NJ schools in the Minority Gifted Children project. There were three steps: (1) children who scored above the 85th percentile on the Brigance were further tested with a specially developed gifted screening; (2) gifted screening was similar to the Wechsler Preschool and Primary Scale of Intelligence and the Stanford-Binet, Form L-M; (3) final assessment was done with the McCarthy Scales of Children's Abilities. The project identified 2 percent of the kindergartners in Newark. Glascoe (1996) also used the Brigance Screens. She established cutoffs for each subtest above which students later tested as gifted on the Slosson Intelligence Test-Revised (SIT-R) and the Woodcock-Johnson Psychoeducational Battery Tests of Achievement-Revised (WJ-R). The cutoff scores identified two-thirds of the students later found to score in the gifted ranges on these two instruments. (*Note:* The Slosson test was deemed to have validity problems in Mental Measurements Yearbooks (MMY) reviews).

The Project Spectrum MI Model of Identification

Some researchers doubt that a global intelligence score has much usefulness, especially with young children. One alternative approach was Harvard's Project Spectrum. "We do not dispute the value of considering IQ as one factor in the identification and placement of a gifted individual; we do suggest that other factors deserve to be taken into account as well," the project's proponents said (Ramos-Ford & Gardner, 1997,

p. 57), and they asked the question, "Gifted in what?" (Hatch & Gardner, 1986). Based on Howard Gardner's multiple intelligence theory, first explicated in his *Frames of Mind,* (1983) the project eventually developed an approach to assessment that is different from traditional paper and pencil testing. The assessment method involved four features: (1) *continuous assessment:* "an examination of progress and learning (or lack thereof) should occur every time an individual is involved in a domain" (Ramos-Ford & Gardner, 1997, p. 58); (2) *ecological validity:* assessment should take place in a situation similar to actual working conditions of people who work in the domain; (3) *intelligence-fair assessment:* the tasks look directly at the intelligence and do not confuse them by filtering through logical-mathematical or linguistic intelligence; (4) *working style assessment:* the person being looked at is also judged for how engaged, persistent, and distractible he/she is. The results are compiled into a narrative profile rather than a numerical score. They formulated 15 different ways of finding out what a preschool child's strengths were. They also discovered about a dozen working styles (Ramos-Ford & Gardner, 1990, p. 60; 1997, p. 61).

The domains of knowledge examined in Project Spectrum and the 15 ways to determine a child's strengths were as follows (Ramos-Ford & Gardner, 1997, p. 61):

Domains of Knowledge Examined In Project Spectrum

Domain: Language
1. Invented narrative measure   Storyboard
2. Descriptive narrative measure   Reporter activities

Domain: Movement
3. Creative movement measure   Creative movement curriculum
4. Athletic movement measure   Obstacle course

Domain: Music
5. Production measure   Singing activity
6. Perception measure   Pitch discrimination

Domain: Mathematics
7. Counting/strategy measure   Dinosaur game
8. Calculating/notation measure   Bus game

Domain: Visual Arts
9. Art portfolios (including structured drawing activities)

Domain: Social
10. Social analysis measure   Classroom model activity
11. Social roles measure   Peer interaction checklist

Domain: Science
12. Hypothesis-testing measure   Sink and float activity
13. Logical inference measure   Treasure hunt game
14. Mechanical measure   Assembly activity
15. Naturalist measure   Discovery area

Project Spectrum also identified working styles that showed the children's strengths and weaknesses, using a trait structure approach (Ramos-Ford & Gardner, 1990; 1997):

Working Styles of Preschool Children

Child is:

Easily engaged ◄—► Reluctant to engage in activity
Confident ◄—► Tentative
Playful ◄—► Serious
Focused ◄—► Distractible
Persistent ◄—► Frustrated by task
Apt to reflect on own work ◄—► Impulsive
Apt to work slowly ◄—► Apt to work quickly
Conversational ◄—► Quiet

Project Spectrum also noted whether or not the children showed the following working style traits:

1. Child responds to visual/auditory/kinesthetic cues.
2. Demonstrates planful approach.
3. Brings personal strength/agenda to task.
4. Finds humor in content area.
5. Uses materials in unexpected ways.
6. Shows pride in accomplishment.
7. Is curious about materials.
8. Shows concern over "correct" answers.
9. Focuses on interaction with adults.
10. Transforms task/materials.

The researchers emphasized that the children were evaluated in relation to their development at a particular time, and that the children had to be reevaluated periodically and regularly as they developed. They believed that such assessment would yield what they called "a more capacious view of giftedness." Ramos-Ford and Gardner (1990) felt that the multiple intelligence's approach to identifying preschool precocity "will identify many more children as being 'at promise' than the traditional methods of the past" (p. 65).

The Kindergarten Screening Instrument

Other individual school districts have attempted to develop ways of finding young academically talented children. This could be called the local solution, and must be looked at as not meeting the standardization requirement that large national norming procedures have set. Over the years, the Lincoln, Nebraska, schools have attempted to identify, in an equitable way, academically talented students who are entering kindergarten, without regard for disadvantage. They have developed a Kindergarten Screening Instrument that assesses conservation of number, mathematics reasoning, and language development. Their research has shown that the instrument they have developed predicts quite well which children will qualify for the academically talented program when they are tested in second and third grade on the California Achievement Test, or when they are referred for individual testing on the Stanford-Binet Intelligence Scale: Fourth Edition at the end of first grade (Rivers, Meininger & Batten, 1991).

Two young children experiment in the movement domain.

Storytelling is used to provide the language sample. The student is tape recorded while telling a story about a picture supplied by a teacher. In assessing the results, the scorers noted the students' use of prepositions, pronouns, demonstratives, articles, verb forms, and plurals. (Hennessey & Amabile (1988) also used storytelling to identify children with potential for creative thinking.)

Some work has been done on the Piagetian developmental levels of young academically talented children, and it is known they perform substantially differently on preoperational and conservation tasks than do nonacademically talented children (Robinson & Chamrad, 1986). The mathematics conservation tasks screen for equality, conservation, countersuggestion, and quotity.

Javits Projects: Alternative Ways to Identify

In addition to these methods, the U.S. Office of Educational Research and Improvement has committed several millions of dollars to alternative ways to identify young outstandingly talented students. These are called Javits grants, and Table 5.1 summarizes their approaches. The alternative ways of assessing young talent seem to be working; the investment seems to be paying off. The research shows promise (Callahan, Tomlinson, & Pizzat, 1992; U.S. Department of Education, 1994). Figure 5.2 shows the 18 identifiers that were used by the Kent State University project listed in Table 5.1, the Early Assessment for Exceptional Potential (EAEP) project.

Table 5.1   Javits Projects for Identifying and Serving Talented Young Children

Title	Program Type	Identification
Early Assessment for Exceptional Potential in Young Minority and/or Disadvantaged Students (EAEP) Kent State University, OH Contact person: Beverly Shaklee	Demonstration teaching in primary social studies and science lessons	• Portfolio assessment process using 18 primary identifiers • Observational data collected on videotape
A Model Program for Identifying Young Underserved Gifted Students Montgomery County Schools, MD Contact person: Waveline T. Starnes (Obtained second grant for multiple intelligences assessment 1993–1995)	Small and large group instruction; specialized nurturing in small group, pullout, and enrichment classes; multiple intelligence pullouts	• Multilayered identification incorporates multiple criteria • Multiple intelligence checklist • Diagnostic Battery Program of Assessment Diagnosis and Instruction (PADI) • Identification through teaching
The Full Potential Program for Underserved African-American Students—Supporting Early Education and Development (SEED) Atlanta, GA Contact person: Thelma Mumford-Glover	Special curriculum including enrichment and specific academic areas in grades 1–5; infusion of African-American history and culture	• Behavioral rating scales designed to rate culturally appropriate expressions of outstanding talent in African-American students • The Optimal Performance Locator for Teachers • The Optimal Performance Locator for Students
Spotting Talent Early in Minority Students: Project STEMS in Howard County, MD University of Virginia Contact person: Paula M. Pizzat	Teachers trained to observe talent traits among minorities during specialized curricular activities taught by G/T resource personnel	• STEMS observational checklist including ten behavioral indicators • STEMS teacher questionnaire (pre and post) surveys teachers prior to inservice training and following the yearly program
DISCOVER (Discovering Intellectual Strengths and Capabilities while providing Opportunities for Varied Responses) University of Arizona Contact person: C. June Maker	Training observers and raters to watch students while they solve problems of several different types working alone and in groups	• A continuum of problem types from well-structured to ill-structured, with activities from linguistic, logical-mathematical, and spatial domains
Project START (Support To Affirm Rising Talents) Charlotte-Mecklenburg Board of Education & University of Virginia Contact person: Anne Udall	K–3 economically disadvantaged family outreach, curriculum modification, school selection, mentor programming	• Case studies and other alternative ways of identifying young gifted children

Table 5.1 *Continued*

Title	Program Type	Identification
Minority Gifted Children: Early Identification and Education for Gifted Minority Students in Grades K–2 in Newark, NJ Contact person: Candice Feiring	Training of regular classroom teachers	• Multiple-entry screening and assessment procedure
Ohio Comprehensive Inservice Training Program for Identifying and Providing Services to Young Gifted Children Who Are Economically Disadvantaged. Ohio Dept. of Education Columbus, OH Contact person: Dan Tussey Received refunding in 1996	Inservice training model to improve methods for identifying young, economically disadvantaged gifted students	• Intensive training to building and community teams on identification by alternative and other methods
Pittsburgh K–3 Gifted Project Pittsburgh Public Schools Contact person: Janice Matthew	Kindergarten through grade 3 model field testing screening and identification practices	
Project SEARCH (Selection, Enrichment, and Acceleration of Rural Children) South Carolina Dept. of Education Columbia, SC	Kindergarten through grade 2 to increase number of disadvantaged students in state-funded programs	• Language development through literature, drama, and hands-on teaching
Identifying and Nurturing Early Mathematical Talent University of Washington, Seattle, WA Contact person: Nancy M. Robinson	Focus on unmet needs of children ages 4 to 6 who have advanced mathematical reasoning	• Develop a battery of quantitative and qualitative measures to identify and assess mathematically talented children
Project Discovery: Nurturing Giftedness in Young Students Through Investigation Ohio Valley Educational Cooperative LaGrange, KY Contact person: John Rosati	Teacher training to involve young students in making independent investigations and creating new knowledge for K–3 rural disadvantaged and economically disadvantaged	• Seek to reach children before they are "labeled"; use regular classroom activities to identify; teachers serve as "talent scouts"

(continued on next page)

Table 5.1 *Continued*

Title	Program Type	Identification
Project First Step San Diego City Schools Contact Person: David Hermanson	Trains teachers to integrate higher-level thinking; encourages parents; readies students for formal identification in second grade	• Train teachers to recognize children who are African-American, Hispanic, limited-English-proficient Hispanic
The Javits 7+ Program Community School District #18 Brooklyn, NY Project Director: Joyce Rubin Grant received twice	Designed to identify and serve students who are traditionally underserved; staff and parent development to individualize and nurture children's multiple intelligences	• Interdisciplinary, theme-based, multiple intelligence curriculum • Identification matrix based on MI strengths and characteristics

The Case Method for Identifying Extremely Poor Students

Project Synergy also developed a method of finding poverty-stricken gifted kindergarten children (Borland & Wright, 1992a). The researchers emphasized that *site-specific* and *site-appropriate* methods should be used, that children should be looked at in the context of their surroundings, and that the use of matrices or the manipulation of test scores by using so-called "culture-free" testing instruments have not proved to work. The goal was to place the children in transitional settings so that they would be ready for placement in classes for the talented within a certain period of time.

Before the screening began, the researchers first sat in the kindergarten classes for several days, to become familiar with the milieu, with the procedures used in the classes. Screening was conducted in several phases. For standardized test data, they used the Test of Early Mathematical Ability (TEMA), 2nd edition, the Test of Early Reading Ability (TERA), 2nd edition, and the Peabody Picture Vocabulary Test-Revised. They used the latter because its manual says it is suitable for identifying children with limited English proficiency, but the pre- and posttest results cast some doubt on its veracity. Nontraditional assessment through classroom observation was another method. They focused exclusively on each child for 15 minutes, keeping a running record of the child's behavior, noting especially the evidence of the ability to concentrate, to solve problems, and demonstrated memory.

Project Synergy staff also exposed the children to multicultural, curriculum-based enrichment activities. For example, they read a story featuring African-American children and presented activities in art, mathematics, and language, noting the children's behavior. This served to focus the teachers on behaviors that might be called "gifted."

Figural, or nonverbal, assessment was also part of the screening. The students completed the Draw-a-Person Test, to provide insight about figural creativity. A portfolio assessment was also completed, using student products, with parents completing a card called "Let Me Tell You About My Child," and teachers completing a card called "Notable Moment Cards."

Figure 5.2   Identifiers of Young Talent from the EAEP Project

1. *Exceptional learner* (acquisition and retention of knowledge)
   a. Exceptional memory
   b. Learns quickly and easily
   c. Advanced understanding/meaning of area

2. *Exceptional user of knowledge* (application and comprehension of knowledge)
   a. Exceptional use of knowledge
   b. Advanced use of symbol systems: expressive and complex
   c. Demands a reason for unexplained events
   d. Reasons well in problem solving: draws from previous knowledge and transfers it to other areas

3. *Exceptional generator of knowledge* (individual creative attributes)
   a. Highly creative behavior in areas of interest or talent
   b. Does not conform to typical ways of thinking, perceiving
   c. Enjoys self-expression of ideas, feelings, or beliefs
   d. Keen sense of humor that reflects advanced, unusual comprehension of relationships and meaning
   e. Highly developed curiosity about causes, future, the unknown

4. *Exceptional motivation* (individual motivational attributes)
   a. Perfectionism: striving to achieve high standards, especially in areas of talent and interest
   b. Shows initiative; self-directed
   c. High level of inquiry and reflection
   d. Long attention span, when motivated
   e. Leadership: desire and ability to lead
   f. Intense desire to know

From Shaklee et al. (1989). *Early Assessment for Exceptional Potential.* Washington, D.C., U.S. Department of Education.

Teachers were then asked to nominate children who should be looked at more closely. The researchers did not use a checklist, since they believe that "none of the available checklists" are "convincingly validated, but that their use restricts the teachers' attention to a limited list of predetermined traits and behaviors" (Borland & Wright, 1992a, p. 16).

A pool of children was developed, and diagnostic assessment was employed. Dynamic assessment by means of Vygotsky's and Feuerstein's notions of scaffolding and assessment of what the child is about to be ready to do was employed. A matrix task was used that is similar to that on the Standard Raven Progressive Matrices (RPM) in which students employed both inductive and deductive reasoning to come up with answers. Other nontraditional assessments—for example, literature-based activities—were employed. Not all children received the TEMA, the TERA, and the Peabody. This screening narrowed the pool.

The Project Synergy researchers then chose children through discussion by committee, and not through composite scores or matrices. Borland and Wright said, "Although quantitative data are included in each file, no attempt is made to assign a single composite score to each child. The wealth of information that has been so painstakingly collected over two months is too valuable to be lost by placing it on a matrix or attempting to sum nonadditive data" (p. 21). They noted that strong yeses were immediately apparent, as were strong noes, and that the bulk of the committee's time was spent with the maybes.

Validity data were gathered as well, and it was found that of the 18 children identified, seven were accepted at a school for the talented after the transitional services were provided. The vagaries of life in such a situation were apparent in whether these children continued in the research project.

A modified case study approach was used by Sandel, McCallister, and Nash (1993) to identify preschool children. First students were referred, then they were screened through interviews with parents, teachers, and the student to see whether further cognitive testing was warranted. Most of the preschoolers referred were white females, indicating that people's perceptions of what is "gifted" include the color of their skin, their gender (at least at a young age), and their ethnicity.

DISCOVER Assessment

Maker, Rogers, Nielson, and Bauerle (1996) of the University of New Mexico described the DISCOVER (Discovering Intellectual Strengths and Capabilities while providing Opportunities for Varied Responses) assessment process for young Hispanic and American Indian children developed under Javits grant funding. This assessment process is based on Gardner's Multiple Intelligences (MI) theory (1983) and on Shiever and Maker's problem continuum (1997). Students are observed problem solving using spatial, logical-mathematical, and linguistic intelligences. Teachers trained in the implementation of the problem continuum taught using it. Students were observed in the fall and in the spring by four individuals per classroom. Bilingual Spanish observers were included as observers and directions were given to the students in both English and Spanish. The experiments are showing that young outstandingly talented students can be identified using these observational techniques while they do regular classroom work based on the problem continuum.

In 1997 Maker reported that validation studies have shown that the DISCOVER assessment checklist is valid; that is, the instrument measures what it says it will measure. An interesting finding had to do with persistence (one of the personality attributes mentioned as being common in the talented). Maker said, "the one behavior most frequently checked across all activities and for students at all levels of ability was 'follows through to completion'" (p. 5). She thought this indicated that the tasks were interesting and engaged the students. The follow-up studies have also shown no gender bias overall. The assessment seems to find students in numbers commensurate with their demographics and numbers within the communities: "The identified gifted students have linguistic, economic, and educational backgrounds like other children in their schools' communities" (p. 7). Maker concluded that these preliminary results are very encouraging to schools who seek to identify young talent but that more research was underway.

However, young academically talented children also need a special curriculum and special arrangements at school.

CHOOSING A SCHOOL

When the time comes for precocious youngsters to go to school, either preschool or kindergarten, parents of such children have difficulty choosing. Special schools that welcome and nurture precocious children may be nonexistent. However, other schools can contain within their philosophies and educational frameworks suitable settings for bright children. The parents of the bright child should look beyond the surface, however. One family, whose father is a scientist and mother an artist/writer, thought the Waldorf Schools, with their multigrade philosophy and warm environment, would be ideal for their dreamy boy. Then they read about Rudolph Steiner, whose philosophy of science is taught in this system. The science taught in Waldorf Schools was diametrically opposed to what the family wanted the child to learn about the universe. They kept him in the public schools and made extra efforts to take family trips to museums and natural areas.

Smutny, Veenker, and Veenker (1989) listed several qualities of schools that would be suitable for talented students (and all students). Among these were the presence of teachers who welcome bright children and who have had some training in how to educate them and how to recognize their characteristics. The teachers should be "facilitators who encourage independent thinking" and the curriculum should include "learning by sensing, feeling, and intuiting as well as academic instruction" (p. 101). If the school sends home many worksheets, which indicate that the students are doing lower-level thinking, if only teachers speak and children listen, if materials such as paper and books are not available, or only are available at certain times, if the walls are boring and not ripe with color and records of activities, parents should probably look elsewhere. A school that has the following features will probably be a suitable environment for a precocious child (Smutny, Veenker & Veenker, 1990):

1. Offers open-ended opportunities in which multiple answers/questions are acceptable.
2. Introduces new concepts; brings in ideas and materials from outside the classroom.
3. Encourages (but does not insist upon) participation. (Even the very young gifted need time to pause and reflect . . .)
4. Offers independent study, allows for individual learning styles, and provides specific opportunities for individuals.
5. Is positive, accepting, open-minded.
6. Makes blank paper and writing materials available at all times.
7. Makes allowance for some noise during group projects.
8. Provides activities in a variety of settings—tables, bookshelves, learning or resource centers, out-of-doors areas.
9. Has child-centered bulletin boards displaying children's works.

10. Encourages mentors, senior citizens, parents, grandparents, community volunteers to visit and assist.
11. Encourages peer praise and positive interaction.
12. Encourages creative expression, fantasy, imagination, original art, stories, and other works (pp. 98–99).

Meininger (1991) provided a theory for the education of young academically talented students. These are the implications that should follow the identification of talent in young children:

1. There are internalized expectations of what the learning environment should be to meet their needs. The closer the match between expectations and the environment, the more rapidly and *efficiently* cognitive development will proceed.
2. Young gifted children expect to be challenged and to be actively involved in the learning process.
3. Young gifted children need access to learning activities beyond their cognitive developmental stage.
4. Young gifted children need opportunities to interact with and manipulate a variety of symbol systems.
5. Young gifted children require concrete experiences appropriate to their developmental stage to acquire and apply rules of the stage.
6. Young gifted children have uneven patterns of development and expected responses should vary depending on task demands.
7. Young gifted children need to control their learning through self-selection of contents, products, and processes.
8. Young gifted children need to have their abilities verified both by recognition of abilities by others and by opportunities to use their abilities.
9. Young gifted children need to feel inclusion with their age peers to provide psychological safety.

A special school for the academically talented should be sure to include these situational and environmental surroundings. Such a school is the Hunter College Elementary School in New York City, which welcomes high-IQ children beginning in preschool.

CURRICULUM FOR YOUNG ACADEMICALLY TALENTED CHILDREN

An optimal preschool, kindergarten, and first grade program for academically talented children includes affective and physical components as well as cognitive components.

Preschool Curriculum Scope for Academically Talented Children

The curriculum (Piirto, 1988) should be both enriched and accelerated, and should emphasize the child first and his or her intellectual talent second. The dysynchrony referred to above is especially obvious with academically talented preschool children, some of whom may be reading, but who may have trouble buttoning their buttons. Youngsters should be introduced to an environment in which they are encouraged to learn from each other as well as from their classroom teacher and support staff. Class size should be no more than 16 children, with a full-time aide. Children should be encouraged to develop further their love of learning, their analytic ability, and their curiosity about people, objects, and ideas in the world around them.

Basic content skills should be introduced when the students demonstrate the readiness to read, write, or count. The development of listening and speaking skills should be integral to the curriculum. Music, art, foreign language, and science should enrich each week's lessons.

Process—thinking skills—should also be emphasized, including analysis and abstract reasoning. The children will probably be moving from preoperational to concrete operational stages later on in the year. Students should be exposed to rudimentary brainstorming, observing, comparing, classifying, imagining, planning, and problem solving. Research skills should be introduced and career awareness can begin. Parents can visit the class and speak about their careers also.

Play should be an integral part of the preschool curriculum for the academically talented. Dramatic play should be encouraged, and performances should be given to other classes throughout the year. Special projects such as "Forest Animal Day" can also be undertaken, featuring mathematics activities, writing activities, art activities, and songs about animals found in nearby forests. Each preschool unit should have writing, arts, affective, and informational components. The project-based curriculum is a long-time strategy of progressive education, and such emphasis is a hallmark of the Reggio Emilio school in Italy, where students use art and other interdisciplinary activities as outcomes and catalysts for what they learn.

Preschool and Kindergarten Curriculum Scope

Administrative Requirements

A kindergarten for academically talented children should have no more than 18 children, with a full-time aide. The room should be large and airy, with attractive learning centers. The room should have a sink and a bathroom, with cubbies for the children's possessions. Full-day preschool and full-day kindergarten should be the norm for young academically talented children, with adequate mats and comfortable places to put them, for periodic rest times.

Procedures

Procedures in preschool and kindergarten should include grouping the academically talented children according to their skill levels in reading and in mathematics, with many activity centers that are individualized to meet the demands of the various levels of the students. The instructional time should be allotted so that the children can experience a variety of activities in visual, tactile, and auditory modes. Children should work in both small and large groups as well as individually. Teachers should prepare some formal, whole group lessons, but there should be plenty of child-directed, free-choice activities as well.

Interdisciplinary Learning

In the preschool and primary curriculum for academically talented students, interdisciplinary learning should be emphasized, with the language arts feeding the social studies, with music enriching the arts and mathematics, with science piggybacking on foreign language. Darlene Freeman (personal communication, August 1993) brought in a professor of urban history to lead the children on walks through various neighborhoods in Manhattan, with various styles of architecture and longer or shorter histories. The deep knowledge of the speaker was tried and challenged by the high-IQ youngsters, who avidly asked questions at a surprisingly abstract level. Not only was connectedness demonstrated in such thematically structured classrooms, but students with different abilities or different interests had opportunities to research and explore (even among students with high IQs, there are many different needs and competencies). The students had research partners and made projects based on their explorations of home, neighborhood, and community.

Self-expression through storytelling, listening skills, sequencing, narrative development, identifying the parts of a story, recognizing similarities among stories, and predicting cause and effect should be part of the language arts curriculum. Creative writing and storytelling through the use of puppets should also take place.

For example, Lisa Castillo, a teacher of the academically talented, emphasized myths and fairy tales as the cognitive backbone of her class of high-IQ kindergartners. Several versions of each myth and fairy tale were read to the children. They discussed the stories in depth. For example, one day they discussed the role of deception in *Hansel and Gretel*; another day they discussed the role of greed in *Rumpelstiltskin*. Analogy construction in young children has a specific developmental path. Castillo (1994) said that first, talented children (and all children) "should be given many opportunities to construct analogies based on themselves. For example, when studying botany, 'person:arm::tree:branch' is relevant; when studying transportation, 'person:feet::car:wheels.' After they have gained experience with self analogies, they can branch out to more distant comparisons" (p. 64). Domain analogies such as "sail:boat::wings:plane" can come next, and then cross-domain analogies such as "yolk:egg::filament:lightbulb" can be attempted. Talented children can soon master cross-domain analogies, while other children may be limited to self analogies, and others to domain analogies. Resource Module 5.1 presents a classroom snippet using analogical thinking from Amy Liebov's kindergarten for high-IQ students.

Resource Module 5.1   Classroom Dialogue in the Second Week of School with High-IQ 5-Year-Old Students

The classroom is remarkably quiet for 8:45 A.M., just before school starts. Children are clustered around computers, talk quietly, look at learning centers. There are 20 children, one teacher, and one aide. Walls are almost empty because Dr. Liebov only puts up children's work, not adults' work. Animals sit on a shelf. There are many books, a block corner, geometric shapes, tables. It is the second week of school and the students are just beginning with analogical thinking. The first task is to work with similes. Yesterday the students worked with "red." The flip chart shows these similes:

Ann's dress is as red as

lipstick	nail polish
fire	a sunset
blood	Superman's cape
Mars	a heart
a rose	a tomato
an apple	

Dr. Liebov: Now I need you to listen. I have an important lesson. Yesterday we were talking about similes. Michael remembered those special sentences. Who remembers what we wrote about the other day? What do similes do? Anna?

Anna: It has to be "as" or "is."

Dr. Liebov: Michael? I'll tell you a simile. Ann's dress is as red as lipstick. What word did I use?

Michael: Like.

Dr. Liebov: What did we do in this sentence? Similes do what? Do you remember? We were doing it in a special way. We were comparing. Do you remember? Kate, in these similes we were comparing what?

Kate: Ann's dress with something else.

Dr. Liebov: Perfect! Do you have any idea why we use a simile? Kareem?

Kareem: It helps you remember what's in the book.

Dr. Liebov: Can you think of anything else a simile does? Hannah?

Hannah: It helps you to see.

Dr. Liebov: Right. It helps you to see something better. I'm going to read a poem to you.

What is yellow?

Yellow is the color of the sun, the feeling of fun, the yolk of an egg, a duck's bill, a daffodil, summer squash, chinese silk, the cream on top of Jersey

(continued on next page)

Resource Module 5.1   *(continued)*

milk, dandelions … yellow blinks on summer nights in the off and on of firefly
  lights … yellow is topaz, a candle flame … Yellow is the color of happiness.
  The sun is as yellow as . . .

Jessie, read it … "The sun is as yellow as …" This is the beginning of what kind of
  sentence? Let's see who can finish that for me. Tyler, can you tell me an ending?

Tyler: The sun is as yellow as a daisy.

Another child: The sun is as yellow as a duck's bill.

Kayle: As a chick.

Dr. Liebov: Kate noticed something as I was writing on the board.

Kate: You're making it like a sun.

Dr. Liebov: That's a simile: "like a sun." Think of things that make you think of
  yellow. Think of things that are always yellow.

A child: As yellow as a light.

Another child: But these lights are white.

Dr. Liebov: Light bulbs are usually yellow. So we'll write "as yellow as . . ." Hanna?

Hanna: As blonde hair.

Another child: Like me!

A child: You don't have blonde hair!

Another child: You have dark blonde hair.

Another child: As yellow as a yellowjacket.

One child: The sun is as yellow as a banana.

Another child: The middle of the circle is like a sun, and the words are like the
  rays.

Dr. Liebov: Good noticing.

Stephanie: A peach.

Dr. Liebov: Peaches are yellow with another color.

A child: Red.

Another child: The inside of a melon.

Another child: A bee.

Dr. Liebov: Think of the sun.

A child: As yellow as a sunflower.

Dr. Liebov: The seeds are dark but what color's always on the outside.

A child: Those are the petals.

Henry: As yellow as the yolk of an egg.

Dr. Liebov: I have a question. Many times when we read stories in the classroom, a lot of times the authors write with similes. I'm going to describe
  Hanna. (She pulls Hanna up and turns her to face the circle of children.)
  Hanna's hair is as yellow as the sun, and her shirt is as red as a tomato. Can
  anybody think of a simile to describe Hanna?

Resource Module 5.1   *(continued)*

A child: Her shoes are as white as a piece of paper.

Dr. Liebov: You don't have to use colors.

A child: Her socks are as red as a tomato.

Michael: Her pants are as blue as a sky.

Gabriel: As a night sky.

A child: Hanna's sneakers make her run as fast as she can.

Dr. Liebov: Is that a simile? I can't imagine how fast.

A child: As a rabbit.

A child: As a cheetah.

A child: As fast as a subway.

Dr. Liebov: That's a great comparison. Make a simile about a peacock's colors and the colors of Hanna's pants? When Michael said, she could run as fast as a train, …

Henry: Her pants have as many colors as a peacock.

Dr. Liebov: Like a rainbow?

Henry: Her pants have as many colors as the rainbow.

Dr. Liebov: Then you would be comparing her pants to the rainbow.

A child: The white on her pants is as white as the stars.

A child: I just noticed, she has some colors on her pants the same as her shirt. She has red on her pants. Her headband is as yellow as the sun.

Dr. Liebov: Good noticing.

Tony: And her headband is as circly as the sun.

Dr. Liebov: Tony wasn't comparing the color of her headband, he was comparing the shape. Good job, guys.

Mathematics

Among the mathematics goals in kindergarten is that the child should understand the meaning of numbers in the real world. The concept of symmetry should be introduced. Whole numbers through 20, sorting by attributes, tallying and organizing information, graphing, picture graphs, bar graphs, estimation, comparison of sets, number patterns, introduction of addition and subtraction algorithms, addition facts to 10, and counting by numbers other than 1 should be part of the kindergarten mathematics curriculum for academically talented children.

In mathematics, preschool and kindergarten academically talented programs should begin teaching the students sorting, ordering, one-to-one correspondence, awareness of numbers in the environment, concrete operation, counting, comparing, seeing patterns, recognizing attributes, problem-solving skills, and logic.

Dr. Amy Liebov sings a song to her kindergarten class of gifted and talented students.

Manipulative materials should be used, including balances, attribute blocks, Unifix cubes, Cuisenaire blocks, Legos, pattern blocks, tangrams, and inch blocks (Mason, Fogler, Yost, Stearns & Gottling, 1988).

Science

In kindergarten science, the curriculum should emphasize the study of the self in relation to others and in relation to the environment. Included should be the study of the five senses, living and nonliving things, and of life cycles in the natural world. Students should be introduced to the scientific method: questioning, hypothesizing, observing, evaluating, recording, and concluding. The following curricular science areas should be emphasized: living and nonliving, change, categorization, ourselves, the plant world, and light and heat. Materials used for science study should include plants, water, animals, magnets, simple machines, scales, microscopes, cooking utensils, magnifying glasses, rulers, and the like.

Social Studies

In social studies, young students should begin to understand social values such as the importance of caring for others, of feeling good about oneself (self-esteem), of having respect for others' property, of taking responsibility, of noticing the world outside the home, of recognizing it's all right to be different, of listening to other people's opinions. Slides, videos, filmstrips, discussion, guest lectures, independent study, and field trips should be used (Freeman, Holder & Varlese, 1988). Figure 5.3 lists "favorite books" for academically talented students in preschool through second grade.

Figure 5.3   Mrs. Brauer's Favorite Books for Pre-K to Grade 2

Favorite Books for Academically Talented Students, Pre-K to Grade 2

Aardema, Verna. *I Know Why Mosquitoes Buzz in People's Ears*. Dial Press. 1975.

Alexander, Lloyd. *The House Gobaleen*. Dutton. 1995.

Allard, Harry. *Miss Nelson Is Missing*. Houghton Mifflin. 1977.

Appelt, Kathi. *Bayou Lullaby*. Morrow. 1995.

Bemelmens, Ludwig. *Madeline*. Puffin Books. 1939.

Bunting, Eve. *Dandelions*. Harcourt. 1995.

Byars, Betsy. *The Golly Sisters Ride Again*. Truesdell. 1994.

Cecil, Laura. *The Frog Princess*. Greenwillow Books. 1995.

Cohen, Miriam. *Will I Have a Friend?* MacMillan. 1967.

Daly, Niki. *Not So Fast, Sonpololo*. Atheneum. 1985.

De Regnier, Beatrice. *May I Bring A Friend?* Atheneum. 1964.

Flournoy, Valerie. *The Patchwork Quilt*. Dial Books for Young Readers. 1985.

Fox, Mem. *Tough Boris*. Harcourt. 1994.

Friedman, Ina R. *How My Parents Learned to Eat*. Houghton Mifflin. 1984.

Goble, Paul. *Beyond the Ridge*. Bradbury Press. 1989.

Griffith, Helen V. *Georgia Music*. Greenwillow Books. 1986.

Griffith, Helen V. *Grandaddy's Stars*. Greenwillow Books. 1995.

Han, Suzanne Crowder. *The Rabbit's Escape*. Holt. 1995.

Hoffman, Mary. *Amazing Grace*. Dial Books for Young Readers. 1991.

Lionni, Leo. *Swimmy*. Random House. 1963

London, Jonathan. *Like Butter on Pancakes*. Viking. 1995.

Mahy, Margaret. *The Rattlebang Picnic*. Dial. 1994.

McClosky, Robert. *Blueberries for Sal*. Viking Press. 1948.

Meddaugh, Susan. *Hog-Eye*. Houghton. 1995.

Moss, Lloyd. *Zin! Zin! Zin! A Violin*. Simon and Schuster. 1995.

Ness, Evaline. *Sam, Bangs, and Moonshine*. Holt, Rinehart, and Winston. 1966.

Nolen, Jerdine. *Harvey Potter's Balloon Farm*. Lothrop. 1994.

Pinkley, Dav. *Hallo-Wiener*. Scholastic. 1995.

Polacco, Patricia. *The Keeping Quilt*. Simon and Schuster Books for Young Readers. 1988.

(continued on next page)

Figure 5.3   *Continued*

Priceman, Marjorie. *How to Make an Apple Pie and See the World.* Knopf. 1994.
Rathmann, Peggy. *Good Night, Gorilla.* Putnam. 1994.
Rathmann, Peggy. *Officer Buckle and Gloria.* Putnam. 1995.
Reiser, Lynn. *The Surprise Family.* Greenwillow Books. 1994.
Say, Allen. *Grandfather's Journey.* Houghton Mifflin. 1993.
Sayre, April Pulley. *If You Should Hear a Honey Guide.* Houghton. 1995.
Schwartz, Amy. *Annabelle Swift, Kindergartner.* Orchard Books. 1988.
Shoenherr, John. *Rebel.* Philomel. 1995.
Shelby, Anne. *Homeplace.* Orchard Books. 1995.
Silverman, Erica. *Don't Fidget a Feather!* MacMillan. 1994.
Slobodkina, Esphyr. *Caps for Sale.* Harper and Row. 1968.
Seuss, Dr. *If I Ran the Zoo.* Random House. 1950.
Van Allsburg, Chris. *Jumanji.* Houghton Mifflin. 1981.
Viorst, Judith. *Alexander and the Terrible, Horrible, No Good, Very Bad Day.*
 Atheneum. 1972.
Waber, Bernard. *Ira Sleeps Over* (series). Houghton Mifflin. 1972.
Waddel, Martin. *When the Teddy Bears Came.* Candlewick. 1995.
Wild, Margaret. *Our Granny.* Ticknor and Fields. 1994.
Williams, Vera. *A Chair for My Mother.* Greenwillow Books. 1982.
Woolridge, Connie Nordielm. *Wicked Jack.* Holiday. 1995.
Zolotow, Charlotte. *When the Wind Stops.* HarperCollins. 1995.

This list is reprinted with permission from Regina Brauer, the long-time librarian at the Hunter College Elementary School for high-IQ students in New York City.

First Grade Curriculum Scope for Academically Talented Students
Social Studies

The grade 1 social studies program for academically talented students could focus on helping students realize their roles as members of a family and school community. The development of identity and social interaction skills should be stressed. The student should explore self, family, and school in social, political, economical, geographical, and historical contexts. The grade one program should emphasize interdisciplinary learning to assist in developing content knowledge and process skills (Piirto, 1988).

Language Arts

Language activities for academically talented students, as in all first grades, emphasize receptive and expressive language: getting ideas, listening, observing, identifying main ideas in reading, understanding sequence, following directions, drawing inferences, making generalizations, and arriving at logical conclusions. Conversation, discussion, storytelling, and creative dramatics are used as oral arts; for writing, dictation, copying, cooperative dictation, writing of poems and stories, and independent writing are begun (Piirto, 1988).

Science

Mason, Halkitis, Cruz, and Arafat (1988) detailed a program for science at the Hunter College Elementary School. Some of the topics in their program are shown in Figure 5.4, which illustrates what a grade 1 curriculum in science and technology should contain.

Figure 5.4   Topics for Grade One Science Curriculum for Academically Talented Students

Topic: Motion

What is motion? Understanding falling motion: Do all things fall at the same speed? What is the role of air in falling motion? How do gravity and weight affect motion? How do we make a simple scale? How do we use the spring scale to measure weight and force of gravity? What is the effect of air on falling motion? How can we create a parachute out of everyday materials? How does friction vary on different surfaces? How much force is needed to lift? How does an inclined plane affect lifting? What is swinging motion? What is spinning force and centrifugal force? How do we use "animotion" to make flip-its?

Topic: Sinking and Floating

How do we test for sinkers? How do we test for floaters? How do we make a sinker float? Do all objects float similarly? How do objects float in different liquids? How do we create a hydrometer? How do we design a raft?

Topic: Electricity

What is static electricity? How does a light bulb work? What is current electricity? How do we create a circuit? What is a conductor? What is an insulator? Let's create a quiz electric game.

Topic: Buildings

What are types of buildings? What kinds of homes do animals have? What are the elements of buildings? What materials do people use for building? How do we use bricks to make walls? Let's make a structure from straws and pipe cleaners. Let's design a house for the "Three Little Pigs."

Topic: Matter

Let's describe what "properties" are. What are solids? What are liquids? What are gases? What is evaporation? What is condensation? What is melting? What is freezing? How does matter change with temperature? How do we measure temperature?

From Hunter College Elementary School, New York City, NY.

Mathematics

Mathematical goals for academically talented first graders should include set concepts, whole numbers through 50, counting objects and grouping, ordering numbers, even and odd numbers, basic facts in sums, the role of zero, subtracting whole numbers, concepts of fractions (halves, fourths, eighths, thirds), geometric terms such as *vertical, horizontal,* and *angle,* properties of solid figures such as cylinders and pyramids, measurement in money, time, and temperature, algebraic sentences, and statistical concepts such as tallying and collecting data.

In fact, Nielson (1992) has suggested that the models provided by existent classrooms for young academically talented children could be looked at by all educators. In an ethnographic study of several primary classrooms for academically talented students, she noticed that the teachers shared certain beliefs. Among these were that they believed the students were capable of and could work independently; that there were routines and procedures so that the children felt safe and the routine was predictable; and that competition was deemphasized and assignments were individualized. The classrooms were designed so that the desks were movable, the walls were covered with student work, and numerous interest centers were evident. Direct teaching lasted no more than 15 or 20 minutes. The pace was accelerated and thus children had time for exploratory activities. Teachers used open-ended questions and there was much peer interaction among the students as they discussed. Parents were evident in the schools, helping in the classrooms and volunteering in the library or the lunchroom. In other words, there was no magical formula, no mysterious key, in the education of young academically talented students. The learning environment was just a good learning environment, period. Education for young academically talented students should not be denied because of lack of resources or of time.

To conclude, the needs of the young academically talented child are those of all children: warmth, acceptance, love, trust, and a feeling of competence. Unfortunately, educators have often ignored the cognitive needs of young academically talented children, thinking that they can wait until the rest of the class catches up. The period of several years of valuable educational time is often essentially wasted for these children. Academically talented children deserve a challenging educational environment suitable to their learning characteristics of rapid processing, good memory, intense concentration, and broad and unusual interests.

CASE EXAMPLE: A Plan for Scott

By Teri Manion

Scott was a student at the Primary Enrichment Center, a multiage program for gifted learners in kindergarten through second grade in a midwestern urban school district with an enrollment of 4,500 students. Students qualify for the program based on scores achieved on standardized ability and achievement tests. Scott qualified for the program based on his IQ score of 147. During the first week of kindergarten, Scott was given the Ekwall Reading Inventory to determine his reading level. His reading level was similar to that of third graders. He was placed in a group with three other students who were also reading at the same instructional level, one a kindergartner and the others first graders.

Scott would be assigned an independent reading contract to complete. He would be allowed to choose a book at his instructional level that he would like to read based on his interest. Then he would complete the higher level thinking products that go along with the reading contract.

Another area of the curriculum that was differentiated for Scott was spelling. Because of his advanced reading ability, Scott's classroom teachers agreed that he should begin formal spelling at the second grade level. On Mondays he was to be given a pretest. Then he would only be tested on the words he missed on the following Friday.

Scott used the workshop designed for kindergartners. The workshop encouraged students to become self-directed through stimulating and purposeful activities. Activities were based on academics and student interests and were structured to allow students to experience a variety of activities in visual, tactile, and auditory modes. It would also assist him in his fine motor skills, helping him learn how to tie his shoes and with letter formation.

In mathematics, kindergartners were instructed using the Houghton Mifflin First Grade Mathematics Series. Scott was not challenged. After two weeks, Scott was given the end-of-the-level first grade math test. He was able to complete the entire test independently and missed one problem out of 24. He was placed in the math group being instructed at the second grade level. He was also involved in a math program that allowed him to work at his own pace. Pretests and posttests determined the level of mastery for each student. Teachers acted as guides, helping students as requested.

In mathematics class he demonstrated quick retention of mathematical concepts and easily solved problems that were frequently considered difficult by his peers. He often found insightful shortcuts when problem solving and used his mathematics talent in places other than in math class. He demonstrated his understanding of time and of fractions quite readily. He continued to work independently, demonstrating 80 percent mastery or better on the modules for the math program. By the end of the year he was in level four, the only kindergartner in the history of the program to do so. Multiplication and division were challenging him by the end of the year. Scott commented that IMS (Independent Math Study) was his favorite time of the day.

Because of his difficulty with fine motor skills, Scott was placed in the writing group designed for kindergartners. Here, correct letter formation would be emphasized, along with sentence and story writing with teacher guidance. Flexible grouping would be utilized so if he was no longer being challenged, he would be able to move to a more challenging writing group.

While Scott's teacher moved at a fast pace in reading, he pressured her to move at an even more rapid rate. Often he would know a particular skill without ever having been taught it. About mid-November, after finishing the first and second grade reading skills and completing one-half of the third grade basal reader, Scott's teacher began teaching the skills from the fourth grade basal reader to his group. This seemed to be challenging enough for Scott. Occasionally he had difficulty decoding a word and he would often ask the meaning of a word not reviewed as part of a vocabulary lesson. Furthermore, he sometimes found it difficult to locate words in each chapter. In independent reading, Scott finished the books rapidly and became engrossed. He needed no assistance in answering comprehension questions. He completed each contract in a short time.

Scott was an outstanding speller. He would become very upset with himself when he did not pass a pretest. His teacher would remind him that it was OK not to pass a pretest. On Fridays he always received high marks on the regular words and on the challenge words. By December he had mastered most of the kindergarten skills. He moved to first grade workshop board where the activities included journal writing, editing sentences, dictionary skills, counting money, brainstorming, art appreciation, critical-thinking skills, and skills centers. He worked from this board until the end of the year, working at a fast pace, completing many activities each day.

Scott had quite an imagination. During story writing time, he had many creative ideas and soon improved his writing skills so that he could write his ideas coherently. He also completed two group science contracts. He worked quickly and was completely focused. He would read and share with the students and with the teacher. He was able to absorb and retain a vast amount of information at one time, sharing it as if he were reading it directly from the book instead of repeating what he had read a few minutes or a day before. Each science provided about 15 activities, and Scott completed activities centered around the themes of the body, magnets, plants, and simple machines.

The Primary Enrichment Center's year-long theme was the study of Japan. Students learned about its geography and compared it to the United States. They wrote *haiku,* made a rice cookbook, and learned to count and write the numbers 1 through 10 in Japanese. They practiced calligraphy, read Japanese stories, and made a *sumi* painting. The students also designed kimonos and wore them while performing *kabuki.* Scott showed much enthusiasm about studying Japan. He often brought books to school about Japan that were on loan to him from the school's and city's libraries, and he liked to share the information he learned.

The affective education component was called "Chair Chat." Lessons focused on the four affective areas of self-concept, interpersonal relationships, responsibilities and decision making, and aesthetic education. Lessons on cooperation, tolerance, and conflict resolution were specifically planned for Scott and several other students, as these were areas of weakness. Scott did well during group lessons but had difficulty transferring what he learned to real-life situations. Oftentimes his teacher had to help him and another student resolve a conflict. Scott became stubborn and was difficult to deal with even when his teacher tried to be a mediator. After a certain period of time, Scott would cooperate and the problem would be resolved.

A follow-up interview with Scott at the end of the year revealed that he was very aware of his precocious behaviors. He understood his need to be in the program. He had a positive attitude about school and had a strong desire to learn and to be challenged. He explained that his favorite subject was mathematics, yet seemed to enjoy all subjects.

➤ ➤ ➤ ➤ ➤ ➤ ➤ ➤ ➤ ➤ ➤ ➤ ➤ ➤ ➤ ➤ ➤

SUMMARY

1. The main characteristic of young talented children, regardless of the domain of their talent, is precocity.
2. Infants with academic talent often demonstrate alertness, restiveness, and curiosity.
3. Toddlers with talent are advanced in comparison to age-mates.
4. An early environment that is nurturing and safely permissive enhances precocity.
5. Factors inhibiting the development of early talent are traumas such as divorce, health problems, poverty that deprives shelter or safety, orphanhood, abuse, and excessive authoritarianism.
6. Parents and primary caretakers are good identifiers of early talent in all areas.
7. Individual intelligence tests are good identifiers of early academic talent.
8. Project Spectrum, Head Start, and other programs have provided alternative, contextual ways of finding and nurturing young talent.
9. Curricular practices for young academically talented children should be based on the progressive education/enrichment model. with strong emphasis on concrete experiences and interdisciplinary activities that are intellectually challenging, with low student-to-adult ratios. Individual, continuous progress should be stressed.
10. A rich, free, play life is essential for the optimal development of young talent.

CHAPTER

6   THE ELEMENTARY AND MIDDLE SCHOOL TALENTED CHILD

FOCUSING QUESTIONS

1. How are the characteristics of high-IQ children similar to those of children talented in other domains?
2. What, to you, are the most interesting characteristics of young scientists?
3. What, to you, are the most striking characteristics of young mathematicians?
4. Why should reading be predictive for verbal talent?
5. What are other professions, besides writing, in which verbal talent is necessary?
6. What school activities would show science talent?
7. What school activities would show mathematics talent?
8. Why do you think young actors have often been overlooked in school?
9. What would you tell a child who wants to dance but who is overweight?
10. Look at the biography of an entrepreneur. Were there behaviors in childhood that were predictive?
11. Why are inventors often rural?
12. Discuss gender differences in talent in elementary school.

Figure 6.1 Overview of Chapter 6

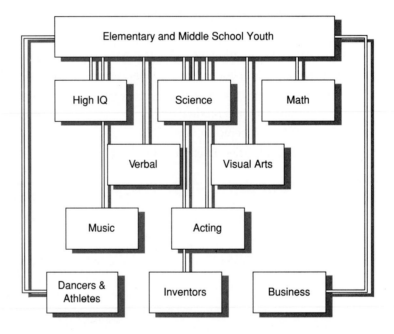

Suzanne is nine years old. She has been in the program for the academically talented since she took her first standardized test in second grade. Her teachers also nominated her because she is responsible, clean, and helpful, as well as getting all As on every assignment she is given. She often helps slower children with their work after she finishes her work. Her father and mother are teachers in a neighboring district, and they like the fact that she is considered a top student. She began to read as soon as she entered kindergarten, but didn't make a fuss over it; she just let the teacher teach her what an "A" is and what a "K" is. She enjoyed practicing her letters over and over again, and she enjoyed the praise she has always received. She reads at least six books a week. The Baby-Sitters and the Sweet Valley girls are her favorites, because she can read them rapidly, and she has reread the Laura Ingalls Wilder books every year since she was seven. She also likes to read books about heroines such as Clara Barton.

Kevin is nine years old also. He has been in the program for the academically talented since he took his first standardized test in second grade also. His teachers have always thought that he is one of the smartest kids they've ever taught. Kevin doesn't like to read fiction much; he likes to read nonfiction, especially nonfiction about astronomy, and he is crazy about old cars. He has several books about old cars and he can tell you the date of any model from the Model A to the latest Lexus. He is best at science and math; he is so good his teachers often don't know what to do, because he grasps the principles they are teaching almost before they can get them out of their mouths. He is quick, no doubt about that. He's "truly gifted," the principal says. He's also opinionated and hates to do his homework.

These two high-IQ children are typical of children with academic ability. Such children are the ones most often identified and served by talent education programs, and their characteristics are often the ones that are checked on checklists. Many experts have listed characteristics of high-IQ, academically talented children (Clark, 1992; Davis & Rimm, 1989; Eby & Smutny, 1990; Gallagher, 1985; Hollingworth, 1926; Kitano and Kirby, 1986; Parke, 1989; Pendarvis, Howley & Howley, 1990; Renzulli et al., 1976; Sternberg & Davidson, 1985; Tannenbaum, 1983; Terman, 1926). Two methods are used to find academically talented children. The first is by testing, discussed in Chapter 3 in the summary of commonly used identification procedures; the second is by observation. These methods are usually combined.

PREDICTIVE BEHAVIORS AND COMMONLY OBSERVED CHARACTERISTICS OF HIGH-IQ CHILDREN

The main trigger that brings these characteristics to the attention of parents and teachers, as stated in the previous chapter on young academically talented children, is the fact that these children are *precocious* in intellectual development. Precocity includes abilities for retention and transfer and precocity occurs in all spheres or areas of talent.

The high-IQ student is precocious in different areas than is the child precocious in physicality. The high-IQ student is precocious in areas measured by such tests as the Stanford-Binet Intelligence Scale: L-M or IV, or the Wechsler Intelligence Scale for Children. These areas are (as measured by the Stanford-Binet Fourth Edition): (1) *Verbal Reasoning* (Vocabulary, Comprehension, Absurdities, Verbal Relations); (2) *Quantitative Reasoning* (Quantitative Number Series, Equation Building); (3) *Abstract/Visual Reasoning* (Pattern Analysis, Copying Matrices, Paper Folding and Cutting; (4) *Short-Term Memory* (Bead Memory, Memory for Sentences, Memory for Digits, Memory for Objects). The physically precocious child is precocious in areas related to balance, dexterity, coordination, the elements of physical talent depending on the sport or physical activity. When precocious high-IQ students take such tests as mentioned above, their IQs will possibly come out in the top ranges, approximately two standard deviations above the mean, about the top two or three percent, meaning they do very, very well in all three areas (if not, their scores would not come out so high, as the scores are averaged and made into a composite score, placed onto a normal curve, and converted to a deviation IQ). Gallagher and Lucito (1960) found that children with high IQs performed well in the Similarities, the Vocabulary, and the General Information subtests, and children with low IQs had higher scores in the subtests in the performance area on the WISC.

Sternberg and Davidson (1985) made the point that intellectually talented children are those with general intelligence, and may have different characteristics than talented children of other types: "general intelligence is one of the mind's capabilities; creativity, musical ability, and artistic ability are other examples" (p. 43). The problem with this is that general intelligence is often confused with these other abilities, as stated in Chapter 1: The question that should be asked is, "What is the *minimum* IQ necessary for achievement in other areas?" Predating Sternberg and Davidson, Freehill (1961) said, "after a certain point, the linear relation between IQ and success may break down" (p. 58).

Nevertheless, it is the duty of the schools to notice precocious children and to provide for their education, as much as it is the duty of the schools to provide for all others. The following is a discussion of some of the salient characteristics of such children during the elementary school years. Most lists are similar to the list that Terman came up with in 1925. The students were predominatly from white, middle- or upper-class California families. However, one 1992 study (Scott, Perou, Urbano, Hogan & Gold, 1992) has shown that white, Hispanic, and black parents show remarkable agreement in voicing which characteristics they felt were indicators of academic talent.

The prevalence on checklists of an item that says, "shows a good sense of humor" is really an indication that the child has advanced verbal ability, because the types of humor that are most often noted are puns, quips, twists and turns of words and phrases. Besides precocity with its concomitant characteristics of transfer, memory, and rate of learning, high-IQ children also have an ability to generalize. They can be observed to demonstrate a willingness to intellectually explore and to invent. They have obvious curiosity, forethought, and judgment, and they are original. They are prone to self-criticism and moral anxiety. They are able to persevere. They are often eager for acceptance by adults, and demonstrate social conscience. These characteristics or variations of them are found in all the literature about high-IQ and academically talented children. Sometimes checklists are used that have lists of characteristics similar to these, and totals of check marks are added in order to assign the dimension of "amount" of characteristics—often to the detriment of children who may have been deprived of a rich early environment.

Rather, educators should observe that students are precocious; that is, they are intellectually ahead of their age-mates in one or several of these characteristics. To add up scores of such observational checklists might miss children who have not had the rich early environment or the setting in which to show their intellectual abilities. Frasier et al. in 1995 proposed 10 core characteristics for the gifted and talented listed in Table 6.1. As you can see, some of these are not mentioned in the Terman list (1925) nor on the list generated by Hispanic and African-American parents in a 1992 study (Scott et al.) that are also included in the table for comparison.

Table 6.1   Comparison of Characteristics

Terman High-IQ Children	Frasier et al. Cross-cultural Synthesis	Hispanic & African-American Parents Study
Retentive memory	Memory	Good memory
Desire for knowledge		
Unusual vocabulary		Good vocabulary
Can carry on an intelligent converation	Communication skills	Talked early
		Early reading
Makes rapid progress at school		Learned quickly; performs above peers
Grasps and understands new ideas quickly	Insight	
Has keen general interests	Interests	
Can reason rapidly		
Spoke early	Reasoning	
Ability to accomplish difficult things	Motivation	
Keen observer	Problem solving	
Has a range of general information		
	Imagination/creativity	
Asks intelligent questions		
	Humor	
	Inquiry	

Consider, for example, the highly successful A Better Chance (ABC) program, which has successfully identified poor children in deprived settings. The organization has "scouts" in several hundred schools and school districts, and their scouts are trained to observe children and to focus on those who may have one or several personality characteristics. As Judith Griffin (1992) said:

> We look for the child who has a strong sense of self, pride, and worth. We look for the child with an independent mind—the child who can resist peer pressure and other typical negative social conditioning—the child who, on occasion, can even resist the teacher. We look for the child who, at critical points in his or her development, is prone to asking questions such as "Who am I?" or "Where am I going?" We look for the child who believes that her self-determination, creativity, and hard work will pay off. We look for the child who can channel his anger at being disadvantaged into strategic action to change his situation. And at ABC we especially look for the child who is willing to take a risk. One who is willing to endure the anxiety, suspense, disappointment, and humiliation inherent in experimenting with new behaviors and situations. One who can persevere. (p. 128)

As one can see, most of the characteristics that A Better Chance notices are characteristics of *personality*—self-determination, creativity, flexibility, resilience.

A Paradigm Shift

These by now common observations about the limitations of definitions of giftedness, which state that to have a high IQ is to have giftedness, have led to a sea change, a paradigm shift, in the field of talent development education. In 1992, the editor of the *Gifted Child Quarterly*, John Feldhusen (1992a), made a landmark statement in his editor's column:

> There is certainly a great deal of interest among researchers and developers in gifted education in finding ways to identify youth who might otherwise not be found. I believe, however, that it is a great mistake to search for generally gifted youth in these special populations [minorities, underachievers, disadvantaged]. The better approach is to search for special talents, aptitudes, or abilities from a more diagnostically oriented point of view. All systems of identification for all youth would do well to reorient themselves to the diagnostic approach which seeks to assess youths' special talents, aptitudes, or abilities, but the need is particularly acute when we are assessing youth from special populations who might have suffered severe restrictions in their development of general, all-around giftedness.
>
> Most current identification systems call for multiple measures which are added up to a single composite index of giftedness. Many youth from special populations have not had the broad opportunities to develop such a broad pattern of giftedness, but they have often developed special talent within a particular domain. The identification process should be designed to find the special talent. Subsequent educational service should focus on facilitating growth in this talent area. (p. 123)

This landmark statement, by the editor of the most widely read journal in gifted education, heralded a departure from the years and years of concentration on the intelligence quotient. Feldhusen then went on to say that using a talent identification approach—"Talent Identification and Development in Education (TIDE)"—would forever abolish the charges of elitism and the difficulties of labeling "the gifted few." The process should be called "diagnostic selection" and programming would follow according to the diagnosis. Feldman, quoted in Chapter 1, also signaled a paradigm shift in 1991 and 1992. Treffinger (1991) also hailed a basic change. Treffinger and Feldhusen, two long-time leaders in the field of the education of the gifted and talented, joined Renzulli in making overtures to general education and attempting to minimize differences. I am among these thinkers. Feldman in 1997 called for a "Pax gifteana" as practitioners and thinkers seek reconciliation. Talent development practitioners seek to identify and serve students in many domains; the high-IQ practitioners seek to protect the needs of these special verbally and mathematically precocious children who score three standard deviations and above on an IQ test, but are not opposed to considering that talents are present in many domains.

What are the characteristics of other talented children who may or may not score very high on an IQ test—the young musicians, writers, artists, scientists, mathematicians, actors, dancers? I have approached creativity by looking at characteristics of students by creative field or domain (Piirto, 1992a/1998). Let us consider the predictive characteristics of elementary school children with talent in such domains.

PREDICTIVE CHARACTERISTICS OF CHILDREN TALENTED IN SCIENCE

Science "talent" may not be the right term, since "talent" is often assumed to be inborn and not acquired, and science ability relies more on intellectual factors that may be acquired than on physical factors that are often inherited. For example, physical coordination is needed for "talent" in dance and in acting; thus dancers and actors are called "talented." The predisposition for achievement in science may or may not be inborn. However, the term *science talent* has been in use for awhile, as in the decades-old Westinghouse Science Talent Search, and the term continues to be used. Science talent seems to have components of verbal, mathematical, and prior science interest and achievement (Lynch, 1992).

Gardner (1983) in his Multiple Intelligence theory (MI) included science talent within his category of "logical-mathematical intelligence." Today science talent is often thought to be the same or almost the same as mathematical talent, but scientists use mathematics as a tool for their experiments, and mathematicians use mathematics to display the beauty of the elegant proof (mathematics talent is discussed later in this chapter). Logical-mathematical intelligence underlies both science and mathematics.

Piaget (1947/1960), a biologist, said that logical-mathematical thought formulates theories and then seeks to prove them. Logical-mathematical intelligence is the ability to deduce and then to apply. Piaget showed that children may experiment with simple objects and manipulations and note patterns. He called this formal operational thought, and said that it emerged about the age of 10 or 11. Later validation studies have shown that formal operational thought may never emerge, and that it often emerges later. Piaget was himself a scientist, and his predispositions may have influenced his own deductions, causing him to overgeneralize for all children when what he was observing were children precocious in logical-mathematical talent.

Most of the creativity literature of the 1950s and 1960s may have overgeneralized also. Such world leaders in creativity as Calvin Taylor conducted several world conferences on creativity at the University of Utah, bringing researchers together to talk about finding children with the ability to be creative. The creativity talked about there was creativity in science. Theoretical physicist and historian of science Thomas Kuhn was asked to present a paper at the Third University of Utah Research Conference on the Identification of Scientific Talent, held in 1959. Calvin Taylor and his colleagues had been trying to gather knowledge about how to identify potential scientific talent—as a result of the Cold War and the aftermath of World War II. In the paper he delivered there, Kuhn described the "essential tension" between the convergent production of scientists and divergent production of scientists, and asserted that the scientific process has evolved so that great convergent production is necessary for any meaningful divergent production to have effect. (Kuhn later said that writing the 1959 paper provided his basic impetus for further thought about the nature of scientific paradigms (Kuhn, 1977).) Kuhn's 1952 book on scientific thought continues to be influential.

Reminding the participants at this conference that all scientists learn from textbooks—books written especially for students—and that the textbooks contain the currently fashionable paradigms of scientific knowledge, Kuhn showed that scientific advance generally comes from people steeped in current paradigms:

> These books exhibit concrete problem solutions that the profession has come to accept as paradigms, and they then ask the student, either with a pencil and paper or in the laboratory, to solve for himself problems very closely related in both method and substance to those through which the textbook or the accompanying lecture has led him. Nothing could be better calculated to produce "mental sets" or *Einstellungen*. (Kuhn, 1977, p. 228)

Kuhn then wondered why such a tradition produces new paradigms—*novelty* production is often a definition of creativity—saying that the typical scientist aims "to elucidate the tradition in which he was raised rather than to change it" (p. 234).

New theories thus emerge from old theories, and the innovators are often steeped in the tradition rather than apart from the tradition. Saying that this is true even for most inventors, Kuhn said that Edison's "oddball" personality in actuality "barred him from fundamental achievements in the basic sciences," and further, that Edison, as well as Tesla and Gramme, "advanced absurd cosmic schemes that they thought deserved to replace the current scientific knowlege of their day" (p. 238). Saying that the scientists gathered at the University of Utah in 1959 might be in search of the inventive personality that emphasizes divergent thinking, rather than the basic scientist who works within the convergent tradition, Kuhn implied that paradigms change gradually, and are accepted gradually, and not suddenly.

If the reader will refer to the observed characteristics of high-IQ children discussed above, you will see that characteristics such as curiosity, the ability to see the underlying structure of problems, intuition, the ability to read well, to decode symbols, are all characteristics of high-IQ children. In fact, science talent may be one of the results of scoring well on an IQ test. Scientists need high IQs. Roe (1953), in studying adult scientists, noted that their average IQ was 166. Simonton (1984, 1988), in reanalyzing Cox's data (Cox, 1926), noted that the IQs of theoretical physicists are higher than IQs of other types of scientists, with social scientists having the lowest of the high IQs. Therefore, the observable characteristics of high-IQ children would perhaps also help find children with science talent. However, Tannenbaum (1983) said, "The relatively modest relationship between ranking in science and in other tested abilities, particularly intelligence, suggests that this aptitude [science aptitude] is partially independent of any other. Even the overlap between science and mathematics scores seems less than is often expected" (p. 136). It is easier and more cost-effective to give a child a test than to make close observations, and a difficulty with observational data collected from elementary students is that their abilities have not been developed, and at best, observers are making only educated guesses. Of course what is a test but an educated guess? Most of these guesses should probably be based on the demonstrated science interests of the children, for a predictive behavior of young scientists is that many of them were interested in science from an early age.

Fliegler's Checklist

Another early source, Louis Fliegler (1961), cautioned that finding potential science talent is a precarious business. He said that standardized tests are helpful; science achievement tests measure accomplishment and thus may unearth students who know more about science than the curriculum has been able to show; and interest inventories may be valuable for use with younger children. He pointed out that science talent may not be "always a function of intelligence as measured by the usual I.Q. tests." High math ability might be present, "but not always." High verbal ability might be present, "but not always." Science ability may not and probably does not have anything to do with a student's social skills, leadership ability, or athletic ability. Fliegler came up with a checklist that still seems apt:

1. Interest in science during the preschool years
2. Curosity as to what makes things work
3. Ability to understand abstract ideas at an early age
4. Strong imagination in things scientific
5. A love of collecting
6. Abundance of drive—willingness to work on a science project for long periods of time in the face of difficult obstacles
7. Better-than-average ability in reading
8. Better-than-average ability in mathematics
9. Unusual ability to verbalize ideas about science
10. High intelligence, IQ of 120 or more
11. Tendency to think quantitatively—to use numbers to help express ideas
12. Willingness to master the names of scientific objects
13. Willingness to pass up sports and other games in favor of scientific pursuits
14. Tendency to relate stories about science, including the writing of science fiction
15. Creativity in science projects, including writing
16. Evident discontent with reasons that other children readily accept for things scientific
17. Unwillingness to accept explanations about things scientific without proof
18. Exceptional memory for details
19. Willingness to spend long periods working alone
20. Ability to generalize from seemingly unrelated details
21. Ability to perceive relationship among the various elements in a situation

As can be seen, these items are *science*-specific. Number 2 could apply as well for inventors (who, as scientists such as Kuhn are quite ready to say, are often not scientists). Numbers 3, 7, 8, 18, 20, and 21 are functions of high IQ, *general* ability. Number 5, the love of collecting, is found in most children. However, the nature and organization of the collection is important to note. Many children collect rocks; science-talented children collect rocks in categories and organize their rock collections in sophisticated ways. As a child, one future metallurgist worked at rockhound shows helping local rockhounds organize their exhibits and read widely in geological science books that his teacher considered too technical and too advanced for his age (K. Rundman, personal communication, 1974).

Biographical Examples of Science Ability

A look at selected biographies of people who became scientists is instructive as to their predictive behaviors. Biographies present interesting case studies. While one would need to quantify from many biographies as the Goertzels (1962, 1978) and Simonton (1984, 1988) did, in order to formulate generalizations from biographies, biographies of adult achievers present illustrative material of points already made.

Francis Galton

The young Francis Galton provides one example. Galton, at the age of 8 in 1830, knew the phyla and order of insects; that is, he had interest-driven advanced science knowledge, just as many budding scientists today do. This advanced knowledge is included on behavior checklists. Galton's father wrote a diary entry on April 4, 1830:

> I read him an extract about locusts in Peru and Violetta said she'd seen lots at Ramsgate.
>
> **Francis:** "Oh, those were cockchafers."
> "Well, said Violetta, "they are the same things."
>
> **Francis:** "Oh no, they're quite different, for the cockchafer belongs to the order Coleoptera but the locust belongs to the order Neuroptera." (quoted in Forrest, 1974, p. 7)

Marie Curie

Two-time Nobel prize winner Marie Curie was the daughter of teachers. Her father taught physics and prided himself on keeping up on the latest research. Eve Curie's 1937 biography of her mother described this incident about her superior memory and her curiosity about science from Marie Curie's early life in Poland in the 1870s:

> Hung on the wall was a precision barometer mounted in oak, with its long gilt pointers glittering against the white dial; on certain days the professor regulated and cleaned it minutely in front of his attentive children. The other was a glass case with several shelves laden with surprising and graceful instruments, glass tubes, small scales, specimens of minerals and even a gold-leaf electroscope... . Professor Sklodovski used to take these objects into his classroom, but since the government had reduced the hours devoted to science, the glass case was always shut.

Manya [Marie] could not imagine what these fascinating trinkets were. One day, straining on the tips of her toes, she was contemplating them with bliss when her father simply told her their name: "Phy-sic app-a-ra-tus."

A funny name.

She did not forget it—she never forgot anything—and, as she was in high spirits, she sang the word in tune. (Curie, 1937, pp. 15–16)

Albert Einstein

The theoretical physicist Albert Einstein had a friend of the family, a medical student, Max Talmey, who took an interest in him and who gave him, at the age of 12, some books to read. Einstein demonstrated early a delight in reading about science:

He showed a particular inclination toward physics and took pleasure in conversing on physical phenomena. I gave him therefore as reading matter A. Bernstein's *Popular Books on Physical Science* and L. Buchner's *Force and Matter*, two works that were then quite popular in Germany. The boy was profoundly impressed by them. Bernstein's work especially, which describes physical phenomena lucidly and engagingly, had a great influence on Albert, and enhanced considerably his interest in physical science. (Talmey, quoted in Clark, 1971, p. 15)

Talmey also gave Einstein Spieker's mathematics textbook, *Liehrbuch der ebenen Geometrie*, and once a week Einstein would show him the problems he had done the week before. Actual accounts of Einstein's childhood interests and activities are few, and probably inaccurate, but Talmey's reminiscence is considered to be true.

Early older friends or adult role models are thus shown to be important. While young scientists may be conforming and have self-discipline, they also have been found to have been interested in science early; to have had collections of rocks, insects, spiders, and the like; to have had a parent, a relative, a family friend, or a teacher who encouraged them and who talked to them about their interests; to have had a sense of wonder about nature and its manifestations. John-Steiner (1985) said that young scientists have "informal apprenticeships of the mind" (p. 176).

Parallel Childhoods: Einstein and Teller

The childhoods of Einstein and of Edward Teller were remarkably similar, although Einstein was born in 1879 in Germany and grew up there, and Teller was born in 1908 and grew up in Hungary. Teller, like Einstein, was thought at first to be mentally slow. Einstein did not speak well until about age 6, and Teller did not speak until about age 3. When Teller was four years old, in 1912, according to his biographers Stanley Blumberg and Louis Panos (*Edward Teller: Giant of the Golden Age of Physics,* 1990), "The words gushed forth in polysyllables, understandable phrases, complete sentences" (p. 5). Before age 6, Teller showed his precocity in mathematics by putting himself to sleep with multiplication problems, asking himself the number of seconds in a minute, hour, day, week, year?

Einstein showed his precocity in mathematics by the age of 9. Both boys were musical. Einstein started the violin at age 6. Teller started the piano at the same age. Before long, he was playing the piano so well that his mother, who was talented in music, began to hope that he might become a concert pianist. Both boys were readers. Teller especially liked Jules Verne's science fiction, hated Latin, and was bored in math. Teller's biographers said, "His keen interest in mathematics had propelled him into the realm of basic algebra, and he was so far ahead of the class that he seemed apathetic" (p. 18). His grade school teacher ignored him when he tried to answer questions. Teller was so advanced that the teacher thought Teller was repeating the class, and that's why he knew all the answers. (It is an odd fact that there were several other Hungarians who grew up along the same river valley in Hungary at the same time of political unrest. These boys didn't know each other then, and later, when they met, they said they must have come from Mars. Others were Eugene Wigner, a 1963 Nobel Laureate; Leon Szilard, who in 1942 with Fermi produced the world's first controlled nuclear reaction; Theodor Von Karmann, an aeronautical engineer; and John Von Neumann, considered one of the finest mathematicians in the world. All these boys came from families that were close, who valued education and who provided a stimulating intellectual atmosphere in the home.)

Students who have talent in mathematics and science often become interested early in the mathematical structure of music and of chess. Teller, for example, early "sharpened his zest for mathematics, chess, and the piano, often becoming engrossed for hours at a time in the sonatas and fugues of Bach, Beethoven, and Mozart" (p. 21). Einstein was 14 when he discovered the mathematical structure of music through the works of Mozart.

Both boys had the influence of a university mentor. Einstein's parents took in a boarder, Max Talmey, a medical student who wrote the memoir quoted above. Talmey called the Einstein home "happy, comfortable and cheerful":

> After a short time, a few months, he had worked through the whole book of Spieker. He thereupon devoted himself to higher mathematics, studying all by himself Lubsen's excellent works on the subject.... Soon the flight of his mathematical genius was so high that I could no longer follow. Thereafter philosophy was often a subject of our conversations. I recommended to him the reading of Kant. At that time he was still a child, only thirteen years old, yet Kant's works, incomprehensible to ordinary mortals, seemed to be clear to him. (Clark, p. 16)

Teller's father feared that his love of mathematics would lead him to be a poorly paid and low-status mathematics teacher. However, he contacted a mathematics instructor at the University, Leopold Klug, who appraised Teller's aptitude for mathematics. Klug brought Edward a copy of Euler's *Geometry*, and discussed the book with him. After several visits, Klug told Teller's father that "Your son is exceptional." For Edward the meetings were inspirational and he began to want to emulate Klug. At age 14 he plunged into Einstein's book on relativity. Both boys wanted to be physicists but their fathers were afraid they wouldn't be able to make a living, and so they persuaded them to enroll in engineering school. Both were from Jewish backgrounds that were not particularly religious. Both fled the Nazis to come to the United States during World War II.

Though both these boys, who became theoretical physicists and chose science, some research has shown that young mathematicians and young scientists differ (Bloom, 1985; Tannenbaum, 1983). Both need a certain threshold of general intelligence, and

Tannenbaum (1983) said: "After the scientist's first job, IQ influences positional recognition directly, regardless of first job prestige, educational background, and scholarly performance" (p. 134). Simonton (1984, 1988) said that people in the physical sciences have the highest IQs, with the physics Ph.Ds having IQs of about 140. Biologists prefer hobbies and books related to nature. Young physical scientists often like to work with mechanical toys and gadgets, and young social scientists are often spellbound readers. Terman's follow-up studies showed that scientists had an early and persistent interest in science. Science students were interested in the causes of things, were daydreamers, liked to solve mental puzzles, and liked art that was symbolic and music that had classical structures. They liked to read science books, to build models, and to take walks in nature. Often solitary, their interests in high school tended to emphasize science clubs, science experiments, and they liked to solve scientific problems. Science teachers often had great influence on them (Brandwein, 1955). These teachers were themselves science achievers, active professionals in their learned societies, active in curriculum writing, and had hobbies associated with science, such as memberships in hiking clubs or birdwatching societies.

Margaret Mead

Margaret Mead, the social scientist and anthropologist, was also the child of a teacher. Her father was a college professor and her mother a researcher. Margaret demonstrated early the anthropologist's ability to classify and also an early interest in ritual, according to biographer Jane Howard (1984):

> By the age of ten Margaret had meticulously divided her room "into a pagan half and a Christian half; the pagan half held the Aurora by Guido Reni and a small replica of the Venus de Milo for which I had saved my allowance for a whole winter." In the Christian half were "madonnas, a beautiful carved old prie dieux [sic] bought by accident at an auction, and a small clay jar made from earth from the Holy Land. Around the top were rotogravure reproductions of the murals in the State Capitol depicting the religious sects of Pennsylvania." (p. 32)

These interests and predictive behaviors of scientists emerged early in their development, during their elementary school or early middle school years. One of the difficulties that schools have in finding talent is that much of the talent is manifested at home, in the activities the child does out of school, and that is why talent observation in schools should be in partnership with parents. Another difficulty is that so much depends on the home environment as an actualizer of future scholastic achievement. If the child has had a home environment that does not permit scientific exploration or wondering, the background knowledge that is necessary for future science exploration will not be present. Sosniak (1985b) noted similar characteristics of research neurologists in their first 13 years. The young scientist is most often an older or only child, and most often male, though concerted attempts are being made to interest more females in pursuing science. We don't fully understand the reasons that women don't pursue science, though Subotnik's longitudinal study of Westinghouse winners has indicated a problem in college and in doctoral studies having to do with mentoring.

CHILDREN TALENTED IN MATHEMATICS

Of course, the predictive behaviors that could be observed about children interested in science, in literature, or in mathematics are similar, because children should not be expected to demonstrate focused interests so early. The fact that Einstein, who later became a scientist, also read in advanced mathematics books, is a clue. Young mathematicians will likely score high on the mathematics portions of standardized tests. Mathematicians do, however, reveal mathematical interests in their early childhood. Talent in mathematics is readily apparent to teachers and to parents, more apparent than talent in philosophy or in writing novels. Mathematics is one domain in which prodigies regularly appear (Feldman, 1986). Those who proceed to develop mathematical talent have high IQs, and mathematical ability has a strong relationship to the g-factor (general ability).

Kruteskii (1976), a Russian researcher, studied 200 students to try to find out what constitutes what he called "a mathematical cast of mind." He investigated how they gathered mathematical information, how they processed that information, and how they retained it. The researchers found eight predictive behaviors of mathematical ability:

Predictive Behaviors of Mathematical Ability

1. The ability to grasp the formal structure of the problem
2. The ability to be logical in numerical and spatial ways, utilizing symbolic information such as numbers and letters, and to think with mathematical symbols
3. The ability to generalize rapidly using mathematical objects, relations, and operations
4. The ability to learn efficiently by abbreviating and shortening steps in mathematical processes
5. The ability to be flexible in solving problems, to shift strategies, and to take different roads to the desired end
6. The ability to appreciate parsimony (simplicity or economy) and elegance (grace and richness) in solutions to mathematical problems (note that this ability may be a main difference between those who become mathematicians and those who become scientists)
7. The ability to reconstruct problems, to reverse the steps in the mental process
8. The ability to remember the main features of mathematical problems and solutions, and to store mathematical information

Mathematical ability of the highest sort, according to Kruteskii, combined strong analytical ability with strong spatial ability and strong verbal ability. Kruteskii excluded both rapid calculating ability and superior rote memory for such things as mathematical tables, saying that average calculating ability and average rote memory were enough. To have analytical ability was most important. Later in the chapter (p. 257), Figure 6.2 includes a teacher's list of predictive behaviors for talented mathematics students.

Gardner (1983) said that mathematical ability falls within his category of "logical-mathematical intelligence" and stated that, "quite possibly, the most central and least replaceable feature of the mathematician's gift is the ability to handle skillfully long chains of reasoning" (p. 139). Mathematicians have to think so hard their heads hurt. What Gardner called logical-mathematical intelligence, Guilford (1977) called "symbolic" intelligence. People with superior symbolic intelligence are able to understand symbolic information.

Gustin (1985) studied 20 highly regarded research mathematicians in the Development of Talent Research Project (Bloom, 1985). Their early years were similar to the young scientists' early years, except that the young mathematicians had a decided interest in solitary learning and in solitary pursuits. Gustin said, "Research mathematics tends to be a very intense solitary activity. Even as young children many of the mathematicians were content to play alone for long periods of time" (p. 294). The young mathematicians also read, made models, and did other independent projects. They also were good students, but their elementary school years were barely remembered.

Unlike the research neurologists, the research mathematicians didn't particularly like to follow the instructions given with their models and kits. Like the research neurologists, they read a lot and indiscriminately. Their parents knew that they were unusual children and treated their questions seriously, teaching them how to find the answers.

Biographical Example of Mathematical Talent

Bertrand Russell

The brilliant mathematician and philosopher Bertrand Russell, whose *Principia Mathematica,* written with Alfred North Whitehead, is a classic work of logic, was orphaned by the age of 2 and he and his older brother lived with their grandparents. In the first volume of *The Autobiography of Bertrand Russell* (1967), Russell recalled:

> Throughout the greater part of my childhood, the most important hours of my day were those that I spent alone in the garden, and the most vivid part of my existence was solitary. . . . Throughout my childhood I had an increasing sense of loneliness, and of despair of ever meeting anyone with whom I could talk. Nature and books and (later) mathematics saved me from complete despondency. . . .
>
> At the age of eleven, I began Euclid, with my brother as my tutor. This was one of the great events of my life, as dazzling as first love. I had not imagined that there was anything so delicious in the world. After I had learned the fifth proposition, my brother told me that it was generally considered difficult, but I had found no difficulty whatever. This was the first time it had dawned upon me that I might have some intelligence. From that moment until Whitehead and I finished *Principia Mathematica,* when I was thirty-eight, mathematics was my chief interest, and my chief source of happiness. (p. 38)

Russell had difficulty with algebra at first, "perhaps as a result of bad teaching," for he had to memorize rules and when he couldn't remember them, his tutor threw the book at his head, "which did not stimulate my intellect in any way." His grandmother did not believe that he should spend too much time at his lessons, but he was so curious that he would sneak and read by candlelight, ready to jump into bed if someone came and told him not to read. His second favorite subject was history. Of his intellect, he said, "As soon as I realized that I was intelligent, I determined to achieve something of intellectual importance if it should be at all possible, and throughout my youth I let nothing whatever stand in the way of this ambition" (p. 39). Russell's solitary childhood and early love affair with the beauty of mathematics is typical of the development of mathematical talent in the early years.

Inventors

A pervasive youthful predictive behavior of those who became inventors was their propensity for tinkering. Over and over in the biographies of inventors, one sees that they were predominantly of rural background, and they loved to take things apart and put them back together. Henry Ford grew up on a farm outside Detroit and he was always known as the neighborhood clock fixer. Thomas Edison grew up in rural midwest towns and he could always find a better way to do something. Colangelo (1991) studied inventors in Iowa and found that most of them had grown up on farms and that their inventions came about from thinking about improvements of existing inventions. Colangelo has also developed a scale for identifying mechanical inventiveness. Other useful lists of behaviors common to inventors are available in the Strong Vocational Interest Inventory and various state and federal vocational talent and interest programs. Many states have computerized searches and talent lists available in most guidance counselors' offices.

Business and Entrepreneurial Talent

There is some evidence that the biographies of entrepreneurs also show that they exhibited behaviors predictive of their later success. Henry Ford, for example, guarded his pennies carefully and shepherded his clock business so that he could save to buy necessities. The rags to riches themes of such heroes as Horatio Alger are also common themes in American writing. Thomas Edison published a newspaper and sold it on trains when he was very young. John D. Rockefeller was a successful speculator in oil and minerals, but before that he had his own small businesses when he was a young man in Cleveland. Bill Gates began as a math prodigy, got a perfect 800 on his math SAT, went to Harvard, but dropped out before graduating to concentrate on his entrepreneurial career in computer software.

CHILDREN TALENTED IN WRITING OR LITERARY SCHOLARSHIP

In looking back, adult writers and people who went into such professions as teacher or professor or scholar of literature have noted that among their predictive behaviors was that they were voracious readers when they were young (Piirto, 1987, 1989a, 1989b, 1991a, 1992a/1998, 1992b). This reading was early and passionate. The writers encountered the written word with intensity and enjoyment. Reading was often used as escape from the world. Their work also has certain qualities. Children with verbal talent often score well on standardized test sections for reading comprehension and on other indicators of verbal ability. They also exhibit certain characteristics in their writing such as imagination and use of unusual syntax. Following is a poem by a nine-year-old girl who was enrolled in a school for academically talented children, but her ability far surpassed those of her academically talented peers. A letter from her mother in 1990 said that she was in high school now, writing novels. This writing continued into college.

Sweet aromas fill the stallion's heart
Eyes of blue, hide of white
Glimmering with its sweat

On the run, under burning sun.
As quick as a shimmering, sunny stream.
Panting wildly, wildly panting
Suede rabbit hops in its way.

This poem illustrates unusual linguistic precociousness in the repetition of consonant and vowel sounds (*assonance* and *consonance*), the sophisticated *rhythms* ("Eyes of blue, hide of white"; "on the run, under burning sun"; "Panting wildly, wildly panting"); the improbable *images* ("suede"). "Sweet aromas" in the horse's heart creates an initial *paradox*. It is not known, nor logical, that there would be aromas in a horse's heart. This girl pays no attention to the logic. The second line uses the repetitive device of *parallel structure* to create a rhythm. The third line sets up a *visual image* that is answered in line 5—"glimmering" and "shimmering." In the fourth line, the letters "r," "u," and "n," are repeated in various *melodic combinations:* "run", "under", "burning," and then, the "run" is resolved into "sun," which is repeated in the next line, in an *alliterative* phrase, "shimmering sunny stream." The urgency of the *reversed phrases* in the fifth line, "Panting wildly, wildly panting," keeps the excitement of the poem. Then, when a "suede" rabbit hops, we can feel the danger inherent in that ordinary situation. The *unusual adjective,* "suede," used to describe a rabbit is in no way the usual cliche that people come up with when they refer to rabbits.

At least 16 qualities are shown in the writing of young children who display extraordinary talent (Piirto, 1987, 1989a, 1989b, 1992a/1998, 1992b):

Qualities Found in the Writing of Children Who Display Extraordinary Talent

1. The use of paradox
2. The use of parallel structure
3. The use of rhythm
4. The use of visual imagery
5. Unusual melodic combinations
6. Unusual use of figures of speech—alliteration, personification, assonance
7. Confidence with reverse structure
8. Unusual adjectives and adverbs
9. A feeling of movement
10. Uncanny wisdom
11. Sophisticated syntax—hyphens, parentheses, appositives
12. Prose lyricism
13. Displaying a "natural ear" for language
14. Sense of humor
15. Philosophical or moral bent
16. A willingness to "play" with words

Prose Talent

What about prose? Does extraordinary talent exist in prose writing, and what are some of the characteristics of such writing? Exceptional childhood achievement in poetry is more common than exceptional childhood achievement in prose (S. Tolan, personal communication, 1991). However, exceptional talent does show up in children's prose writing. Consider this example, written by an eight-year-old, after church and before dinner, in a small rural town in northwest Ohio in 1977:

The Dog Who Stayed With Me

Jimmy, me, and Carol were excited today. It was time to meet under my apple tree. We often, after we met, played in the empty house next door (which was for sale), and brought Teddy to play too. It was one Sunday morning, a chilly one, too. We hardly met that day. But we met inside my house instead of under the frozen, cold apple-tree, pale blue frozen sky, cold icicles of sun falling on us. We were very chilly as we instead went into the empty house with Teddy, who was kept overnight by Carol. "Rudy!" Ma yelled at me, "Get away. Here comes the moving truck." I didn't have time to ask questions. I just ran in to get Teddy if dad meant moving in the empty house. Carol said, "Rudy! Look!" A little setter, just a baby, leaped out of the car (behind the moving truck) and ran to my arms. "Why, hello, there!" Carol said, scratching the setter puppy's red-shining back, "Rudy, ball time!" I chattered my teeth, as another sun-icicle fell on my head. The wind furiously blew, and almost knocked the puppy out of my arms. "Come on, puppy!" and I tried to run without jolting the puppy. But I was so cold I couldn't help it. "Rudalas, come!" Dad yelled, and he saw the puppy. "Bring it in, but hurry!" I flung open the door and put the setter down upstairs in my warm bedroom. I ran downstairs, and the puppy followed. I got some meat scraps and a small, low bowl of milk. I teased him and held out the meat. He didn't need teasing, though. He followed me anyway. "Come on, Caboose." I began to call him Caboose. "Little Red Caboose," I often said. He followed me like a caboose and was fed. I went to bed, and below my bed I heard Caboose lapping up the milk and snapping the meat. I fell asleep at last, for Caboose's lullaby of panting was wonderful. His panting was like a lullaby. Next morning was school. I flung up my coat, and caught it. Last of all, I patted Caboose. But every time I turned my back, he whined. He leaped up and followed me. I didn't even know until I entered the school, for the marble-tile on the halls made Caboose's claws go click, click. When I got to school, Mrs. Dainty, my fourth grade teacher, just about died. "Don't you ever bring pets to school without my permission," she said.

This prose piece by an eight-year-old displays remarkable use of syntax. The sentence, "We often, after we met," shows an understanding of grammatical apposition. The use of parentheses "(which was for sale)" and "(behind the moving truck)" is unusual. The use of the hyphen in the words "apple-tree, "red-shining back," and "marble-tile" is unusual. These words may or may not be hyphenated in common usage, and in fact their hyphenation suggests that the writer has read prose works where the hyphen, the parenthesis, and the use of apposition is common, perhaps nineteenth-century or early twentieth-century novels? The lyricism of the child's words, "under the frozen, cold apple-tree, pale blue frozen sky, cold icicles of sun falling on us," and "lullaby of panting," is adult in quality, only many adult professional writers strive for such lyricism, whereas this child effortlessly wrote this way. "I chattered my teeth," again suggests that she knows that teeth chatter, but not that they do so by themselves. The "lapping" and "snapping" of the dog show a sense of parallel structure and prose rhyme.

There is another characteristic of good literature that is most difficult for children—uncanny wisdom or any "wisdom" at all. This is the quality that we look for in the literature that we read, and this is the reason that we don't give credence to literature by children. What wisdom can children have? Wisdom is acquired by experience. The subject matter of the poems and stories by children is usually childlike. The plots of the stories are predictable, with space ships for the boys and mysteries for the girls. There are monsters and fantasies. The poems are also about the concerns of the children writing them. Maturity is essential in literary quality. No Nobel prize for literature will, nor should it, go to a child, or even a young adult of prodigious talent. But the talent does exist, and sometimes children display wisdom not won by age.

Characteristics of outstanding prose writing by children were also listed by Kough in 1960, one of the early pioneers in the education of the talented:

Characteristics of Outstanding Prose Writing

1. Can develop a story from its beginning through the build-up and climax to an interesting conclusion
2. Gives a refreshing twist, even to old ideas
3. Uses only necessary details in telling a story
4. Keeps the idea organized within the story
5. Chooses descriptive words that show perception
6. Includes important details that other youngsters miss, and still gets across the central idea
7. Enjoys writing stories and poems
8. Makes the characters seem lifelike; captures the feelings of his characters in writing (Kough, 1960, p. 27–28)

Most such lists contain similar items. The point is that the child with creative writing talent manifests that talent by doing writing. The writer writes.

Characteristics of Children with Writing Talent

What characteristics do children with such talent have in common? A survey of adult, published poets and young, unpublished poets about their youth (Piirto, 1987), showed that (1) they all read—a lot; (2) their parents read to them—a lot; (3) they admired words and expression by words (One nine-year-old girl said that writing "is a sometimes better way to express feelings than words and actions. It also helps me to think logically."); and (4) they read early. Research on early readers has shown that they have parents who answered their questions, who spent much time with them, reading to them, and who were readers themselves (Roedell, Jackson & Robinson, 1980).

The verbally talented engage the written word with fervor and with a qualitative difference that is hard to miss. With relationship to the Dabrowski theory of overexcitabilities (Piechowski & Cunningham, 1985), it would seem that incipient writers engage the written word with an intensity that is often interactive, almost physical. One example is a young writer in a study of creative adolescents (Piirto, 1992b), who spoke out loud to the characters when reading an exciting book.

Whether or not these young writers will become well-known novelists, poets, or essayists is impossible to say. Chance plays a large part in the flowering of creativity. What makes the difference between a verbally talented child who will be a creative writer, and a verbally talented child who will be a teacher, a scholar, a professor, or an editor? Little work has been done in this area. One would venture to say, though, that emotional need to write in a certain genre (poetry, fiction, drama) would play a large part in what career a verbally talented child will choose. Many academic departments—English, history, humanities, drama, philosophy, political science, and the like—are filled with verbally talented people who have chosen the road of teaching or scholarship and not creative writing in typical genres.

At young ages, the verbally talented should be recognized for their abilities and nurtured. They should be given many opportunities to write in all sorts of genres, as well as develop research and critical thinking abilities. Nevertheless, the opportunity for the nurturing of such talent is there, once the talent is discovered. A look at the juvenilia and early life of a sample of prominent writers, using a biographical approach, is illustrative that many prominent writers displayed predictive behaviors in writing and reading.

Biographical Indicators of Verbal Talent

George Eliot (Cross, 1903), Stephen Crane (Berryman, 1950), Jane Austen (Halperin, 1986), Dylan Thomas (Fitzgibbon, 1965), Thomas Wolfe (Nowell, 1960), Virginia Woolf (Bell, 1976; DeSalvo, 1989), Tennessee Williams (Spoto, 1985), the Brontë family—Emily, Charlotte, and their less famous brother and sister, Branwell and Anne— all were early and voracious readers in houses that had books. Hinkley (1945) described the long sagas that the Brontës wrote about the magical kingdoms of Angria and Gondal. The four Brontë children (two other Brontë children died young) were the children of a clergyman. Their mother died young. He raised the children, speaking to them as adults and giving them free range of reading material around the home. Hinkley said, "The young Brontës never played with other children. They were touched by no other adult influence in these plastic years" (p. 16). They read and wrote and drew. "The growing imaginations were never shocked or shackled because no one hinted they ought to be" (p. 19). Their youth helped them develop "an incapacity for being shocked at words, and a zest for fearless scrutiny of events and characters" (p. 19). By the time she was 24, Charlotte had written more than 20 novels of about 60,000 words about the characters in the mystical land of Angria. Radford (1990) discussed the early lives of Alexander Pope, Samuel Johnson, Thomas Chatterton, and Daisy Ashford (who wrote a critically acclaimed novel in 1890 at age 9, and stopped producing at age 13), and their early interaction with books was also apparent.

When selecting students for special programs requiring verbal talent, perhaps their reading activity should be considered, as well as whether or not they write on their own. Self-selection based on motivation should also be a part of creative writing identification. Does the child want to be a writer, want to write?

CHILDREN TALENTED IN VISUAL ARTS

Because one cannot produce a work of visual art without talent, it is logical that early talent would be recognized and nurtured and predictive behaviors noted. Visual arts talented children may or may not have high test scores on intelligence and achievement tests. They will, perhaps, score high on the spatial portions of ability tests. Visual art talent is made up of visual-figural intelligence in both Guilford's terms and spatial intelligence in Gardner's terms. Guilford (1977) said that figural intelligence is "concrete intelligence" (p. 16). Gardner (1983) said that spatial intelligence is necessary, but not sufficient for visual arts achievement. Spatial intelligence is necessary in the sciences and in mathematics as well as in visual arts. The person with spatial intelligence possesses the ability to see imagery. In fact, chess ability is the "single area" most illustrative of the need for spatial intelligence. Gardner said, "The ability to anticipate moves and their consequences seems closely tied to strong imagery" (p. 192). Feldman (1986) also discussed chess ability and chess prodigies. The spatial ability necessary for visual (plastic) arts seems to be a "sensitivity to composition" found in both connoisseurs of arts and artists themselves (Gardner, p. 195).

Al Hurwitz (1983), himself a visual artist, noted that certain behavioral and work characteristics are common for visual arts talented children. The following list gives the predictive behaviors of visual arts talent:

1. *Interest:* Interest in visual arts begins early, and emerges through drawing.

2. *Precocity:* The young visual artist often moves through the stages of drawing rapidly, just as young musicians move through the mastery of music rapidly. This is called precocious development, and when the child is between 9 and 11, she often begins to become frustrated with her development, as she begins comparing her efforts with images from mass media.

3. *Ability to concentrate:* Another behavioral indication the young visual artist displays is the ability to concentrate for a long period of time on an artistic problem, as well as a preference for being alone while doing art.

4. *Works on own time:* The child is self-directed, and does art on her own, away from the art room.

5. *Draws for emotional reasons:* Hurwitz (1983) commented that the visual arts talented person may not fit the common perception of creative people, especially with regard to the personality aspect of risk taking, for the talented young person has "invested a great deal of themselves in developing mastery" and thus, "they are unwilling or unable to experiment in new areas" (p. 34). The child may use art as a retreat, drawing for comfort.

6. *Fluency:* There is also an indication of fluency in the talented young artist, that is, the child often has more ideas than there is time to enact them. The work has details that other children miss, and the child will often do multiple drawings.

7. *Communication:* The child may use a drawing to illustrate a point, because drawing to the talented young visual artist is like talking or writing to the verbally talented student.

Characteristics of Artwork of Visual Arts Talented Children

Winner (1996) said that "the core ability of the visually artistic child is a visual-spatial precocity that makes it possible to capture the contour of three-dimensional objects in two-dimensional space" (p. 74). Their drawings are like those of older people in these ways: (1) shapes that are recognizable; (2) lines that are fluid and confident; (3) volume and depth; (4) drawing objects in difficult positions; (5) composition shows dynamic proportion; (6) realism; (7) an ability to master the drawing customs of their own culture; and (8) ability to tell stories in pictures. Hurwitz (1983) also listed the characteristics found in the artwork of visual arts talented children:

1. *Realistic representation,* or *verisimilitude:* Talented young artists also are able to control their compositions, blending and mixing colors, and consciously linking forms and experimenting. Junior and senior high school students will begin to surpass their teachers in realistic representation; they may draw detailed comic strips with narrative structure.

2. *Use of detail:* Even in young children, the use of detail in drawings is extraordinary.

3. *Visual and kinesthetic memory:* They use their visual memories to enhance the artwork they make. Their extraordinary visual and kinesthetic memories show up at an early age, and they are able to use such recall in filling three-dimensional space, as when playing with clay.

4. *Use wide variety of media:* Talented young artists practice for hours, and use a wide variety of media, not just pencil and paper. They are curious about the possibilities of other media.

5. *Improvisation:* They are doodlers, improvising with shapes and lines, seeing patterns that appear from negative space. Hurwitz said, "Art functions as an extended conversation between form and imagination" (p. 57).

Like Gardner (1983), Hurwitz (1983) also differentiated between visual arts talent and critical sensitivity to the arts, saying that the latter is also a visual perception talent, but that it relies more on verbal ability.

Interest in the identification of artistic talent began early. In 1926, Florence Goodenough theorized that intelligence can be measured by drawing. In 1939, Norman Meier wrote a monograph on factors in artistic aptitude. Other researchers have been Clark and Zimmerman (1983, 1984, 1986, 1987). Clark, in 1989, published his Drawing Abilities Test. The point is that the children are identified by behaviors related to the talent. The researchers have also advocated the use of observation, portfolio, nomination, and interviews. Clark and Zimmerman were awarded a Javits grant in the mid-1990s to continue their work in identifying and serving visual arts talent. The project was called Project ARTS.

Identification of these youth should be keyed to the characteristics discussed in this section. The drawing production tests mentioned earlier can also be administered. No IQ cutoff score should be required.

CHARACTERISTICS OF CHILDREN TALENTED IN MUSIC

Musicians practice. They take private lessons. They play alone. They play in groups. Even if they are in school groups, choirs, bands, or orchestras, they must take private lessons in order to further themselves in their music. Schools have the responsibility to identify students who are musically talented, and to serve them in music programs, but no child who has musical talent will proceed very far unless she has private teachers. This could be said to be true for visual arts talent as well, though nowadays few young talented visual artists take private lessons. Today, few young talented creative writers take private lessons from writers. Few young talented scientists and mathematicians take private lessons, although all young people who are talented in music must, and do.

Much has been written on musical talent, and much of that has been autobiographical and biographical. Gardner in 1983 named musical intelligence one of his "frames of mind." Musical intelligence is a cast of mind that requires acute hearing ability, or *audition*, as well as the ability to understand the organization of rhythms. Many have associated musical intelligence with mathematical intelligence, but Gardner said that this ignores the emotional impact of music, and of the musically talented person's ability to evoke emotion.

Musical talent often shows up early, and if a family has a keyboard instrument, the musically talented child will probably be picking out tunes at a young age. Musical prodigy, or the ability to perform at an adult professional level, shows itself as more complex and more advanced at a young age than simple musical talent. Winner (1996) noted these characteristics of young music precocity: (1) a "rage" to make music; (2) astonishing memory for music; (3) improvisational behavior; (4) making the work harder by challenging oneself; (5) early and strong pleasure in music; (6) ability to transpose music; (7) ability to change focus while interacting with music, from listening to one's own playing, to the notes on the page, to the whole sound of the group if one is in a group, to paying attention to the whole structure of the piece.

Japanese and Chinese Views of Musical Ability

There are cross-cultural differences in attitudes toward talent. In Japan, for example, talent is not thought of as arising in a child; talent is trained. Shin'ichi Suzuki, in *Nurtured by Love* (1983), advocated that musical talent could be trained from early infancy, in a system of talent education called the Suzuki method. He wasn't interested in definitions of talent: he said any child who learns to speak can learn music. Repetition, as in learning a foreign language, is necessary—he said, "ability is one thing we have to produce (or work for) ourselves. That means to repeat and repeat an action until it becomes a part of ourselves."

With the Suzuki method, a parent, usually the mother, works closely with the children in the acquisition of the rudimentary musical skills necessary to play the violin. Mothers of infants are first taught to play one piece, and the children listen to recordings of the piece. The children do not play; the mother plays on a small violin. The child then asks for the violin, and the training begins. The more the child practices, the better the child gets. The first song is "Variations on Twinkle, Twinkle Little Star." This, it is to be emphasized, is a training method, and follows the philosophy that musical intelligence can be taught. Asian education utilizes drill and practice to the point of mastery, and Westerners might wonder whether such education creates automatons or maestros.

Suzuki called such practice essential to the development of talent: "If you compare a person who practices five minutes a day with one who practices three hours a day, the difference, even though they both practice daily, is enormous. Those who fail to practice sufficiently fail to acquire ability" (p. 97). He went on to say that the person who practices five minutes a day will have to work for nine years to accomplish what the person who practices three hours a day accomplishes in one year. He also advocated memory training early in a child's schooling. He said, "Children of high scholastic standing at school are simply ones whose memory skill is unusually well developed, and I believe that inferior students are merely ones who have not acquired memory skill" (p. 92). For example, even in preschool, children are taught to memorize 53 *haikus* in the first term, 64 *haikus* in the second term, 45 *haikus* in the third term. He said, "Children who at first could not memorize one *haiku* after hearing it ten times were able to do so in the second term after only three or four hearings, and in the third term only one hearing" (p. 93), and such memorization enabled the children to "spontaneously" made up their own *haiku*, "expressing things they have noticed."

This cross-cultural difference applies in other domains and in other Asian countries as well. Gardner, in a 1989 article called "Learning Chinese Style," spoke about observing art education in China. He noted that young students were taught calligraphy, repeating over and over certain patterns and figures. The differences between U.S. education and its emphasis on early exploratory activities in art and early Chinese art education were so great, he wondered whether the Chinese children would be able to transfer their training to freehand drawings, and so he asked them to draw a portrait of him with their calligraphy brushes. They were able to do so, with several of the 10-year-old students making recognizable portraits. Gardner said, "Chinese children were not simply tied to schemata. They can depart from a formula when so requested."

Characteristics of Music Talent in Children

The western way is to notice, to observe, whether a child has certain characteristics. Following are some common predictive behaviors and characteristics of early musical talent, adapted from the *Music Educators' Journal,* (March 1990):

Characteristics of Musically Talented Children

1. Spontaneous response to rhythm and music
2. Love for singing familiar and made-up songs
3. Relative or absolute pitch and strong feelings for tonality
4. Highly developed ear
5. Ability to associate pitch with visual symbols
6. Memory for music heard
7. Chooses music to express feelings
8. Ability to match pitch
9. Appreciation for the aesthetic structure of music
10. Ability to discriminate among contrasting phrases and sections of song and musical compositions
11. Wants to take music lessons or play an instrument
12. Concentrates on music; stops to listen to music

Schools should never use IQ tests as a screen in identifying music talent, but should use the musical aptitude measures that have been validated over the years. These can be used to identify talent in youth from musically deprived families, where the school is the agency that identifies the child. In the United States and Great Britain, standardized tests have been developed to identify music talent in young people. These are such tests as the Seashore Measures, which were developed for the Eastman School of Music in 1919, the Gordon Musical Aptitude Tests (MAP), the

Gordon Primary Measures of Music Audiation (PMMA) developed in 1979, and the Gordon Intermediate Measures of Music Audition (IMMA) developed in 1982. Haroutounian (1993) listed other measures, but these are the most commonly used. The Musical Characteristics scale of the Scales for Rating the Behavioral Characteristics of Superior Students (SRBCSS) also point out domain-based predictive behaviors and characteristics of musical ability.

Bamberger (1986) said that young musically talented children go through a "midlife crisis" in their adolescent years. Young musically talented children approach music wholistically, using many strategies quite naturally as they approach music. Bamberger said, "For these younger children, internal representations of musical structure are not yet fixed in their attachments to the conventional meanings associated with external notation systems" (p. 411). The crisis comes when the child comes to consciousness, becomes more self-critical and reflective about music. This time is a "period of serious cognitive reorganization." She said that "there can be neither return to imitation and the unreflective, spontaneous 'intuitions' of childhood, nor a simple 'fix-up'" (p. 411).

This transition from the promise of prodigy to the artistry of the adult musical artist is developmental, and Bamberger likened it to Piaget's concept of disequilibrium falling to equilibration and then to a reorganizing of schemata. She said that the midlife crisis is a process of reorganizing, during which the child learns to analyze and synthesize musical knowledge. Feldman (1986), in discussing musical prodigy, showed that even though prodigies perform at an adult level of competence, stepping into an adult career, with all the savvy that entails, is a different story.

Examples and Studies of Musical Talent

Sosniak's study (1985a) of concert pianists in the University of Chicago Development of Talent Project showed several predictive behaviors and characteristics of the development of musical talent in the early years:

1. They came from homes where music was respected, even valued, and often there were amateur players in the household.

2. Music lessons were considered a necessary part of growing up, and the children were expected to take lessons. Their parents scheduled lessons for the children, and the children went.

3. The teachers were such that the children liked going to music lessons. The families chose teachers who were good teachers, who conveyed a love of music to their students.

4. The families expected the young musicians to practice, to spend time in preparing their piano lessons. It was part of the family script, the "family mythology" (Piirto, 1992a/1998, p. 296). Once the commitment was made, and the students were found to be talented, the family expected they would practice. Other children of their ages spent a lot less time at lessons. The students also liked the piano and liked practicing. Often siblings were also given music lessons, but the ones with the most drive were the ones who achieved the most.

5. The lessons began early enough that the routine of practice had been made part of the family schedule before the other activities normal to young children came up, before the scout troops and the sports teams and the other lessons. Their practice was already a set part of their days.

6. The young pianists were called such, and got the label of "pianist" by their friends, by adults in the community, and by audiences, even before they were teenagers.

Sosniak pointed out the importance of these early years in developing habits of motivation, discipline, and self-concept in the young pianists. Their aspirations to become pianists had a foundation in the family commitment to the playing of the piano as worthwhile and valuable, and in the family's physical and financial and psychological support of that commitment.

Rock and popular musicians also followed this developmental path to some extent. Boyd (1992) interviewed 75 contemporary musicians for her study, *Musicians in Tune*. B.B. King, the blues guitarist, grew up in poverty in the Mississippi Delta. Boyd said, "music was integral to the rural African-American culture from which B.B. King emerged" (p. 26). King said, "For some reason I was always crazy about the guitar," and by the time he was a teenager, he played with several quartets and sang gospel. He also listened to his aunt's records of blues artists. The Irish singer-songwriter Sinead O'Connor came from a musical family, as did the songwriter Randy Newman, the new age flutist Paul Horn, the drummer Terri Lyne Carrington, and the rock singer Rod Stewart. Some musicians can switch easily from classical to popular, for example, the Indian sitar maestro Ravi Shankar, who also comes from a musical family. The Marsalis family of musicians is world renowned. Aretha Franklin sang gospel in the choir in her father's church. Country singer Hank Williams was the father of country singer Hank Williams, Jr.

The classical pianist Gary Graffman is another example of a musician who came from a musical family. His parents were Russian immigrants who left Russia during the Russian Revolution and who, like many Russian Jews, finally ended up in New York City. His father was a violinist who had attended the St. Petersburg Conservatory with Jasha Heifetz and Dmitri Prokofiev, and who became a faculty member at the Mannes School of Music when he got to the United States. Gary's father started him on violin at age 3, but then switched him to piano, where he demonstrated his ability early. The famous piano teacher Isabelle Vergerova, who had also attended the St. Petersburg Conservatory, took him on as a student. By the time he was eight years old, he was giving several recitals a year. Of his father, he said, "He knew that just because I happened to play extremely well for an eight-year-old, it was by no means ordained that I would therefore grow up to be a concert pianist," and so his father made sure that Gary had a good general education so that "when I finished school I would have options" (p. 46). By the age of 12, Graffman was able to give a concert at Town Hall.

In identifying those with musical potential, the schools should rely on experts in music, and those who are identified should be encouraged to seek private study. Scholarships should be made available for those who have potential and not enough money. Special schools that emphasize musical education exist in many large urban areas. These are both public and private. A family might consider moving if a child has demonstrable talent.

CHILDREN TALENTED IN ACTING AND DANCING

Two of Gardner's "frames" of intelligence (1983) are *bodily-kinesthetic* and *intrapersonal,* and these are what actors and dancers exhibit. Guilford called these abilities *figural* and *behavioral.* Athletes exhibit bodily-kinesthetic intelligence also, but the intrapersonal intelligence is what enables actors and dancers to interpret the world through their bodily actions. Actors also have talents in the use of the voice to mimic and to project. Bodily-kinesthetic intelligence is "skilled use of the body," which has evolved in humans over millions of years. Westerners have divorced the mental from the physical, and have spoken of the body as separate from the soul, or the heart. Recent thought has attempted to reconcile the two, as people have been urged to exercise, and research has shown that physical activity is positively related to longevity.

Actors

The most admired and highest paid creative people are certain movie stars, some of whom command millions of dollars for a few scenes in a motion picture. Yet one of those, Marlon Brando, has been quoted (Schickel, 1986) as saying he thinks acting is not even a profession worthy of a man. Other actors have been more eloquent about what comprises their creativity. Like singers, their instruments are their voices and their bodies, but unlike singers, their material is other people, and not notes on a page.

The director Peter Brook, in 1969, said: "Acting begins with a tiny inner movement so slight that it is almost completely invisible" (p. 225). He went on to say that stage actors have an awareness of this tiny inner movement because of what is required with a live audience, but film actors often have to act with a camera as an audience. This is why stage actors can be film actors, but film actors often have difficulty becoming stage actors. The camera lens is able to pick up the tiny inner movement much more acutely than a live audience is.

Brook said that this flicker, this tiny movement, is often present instinctually in young actors. Child actors "can give subtle and complex incarnations that are the despair of those who have evolved their skill over the years." Then something happens, and later on, the child actors "build up their barriers to themselves" and find that touching the essential is difficult if not impossible (p. 226). This would seem to relate to Bamberger's developmental theory of music talent fulfillment, and the presence of the "midlife crisis" in adolescent performers, as discussed earlier.

Special schools for the arts have auditions for young actors, and there are some audition-related tests, but there are no known tests such as divergent production tests that are any good for the unearthing of such talent. Again, the quality, the spark, seems to be recognizable by experts. When I was a principal of a school for intellectually gifted children in New York City, casting agents would often visit. They liked the verbal precocity of intellectually talented children, and were often there seeking a particular "look" in a child. They would peek from the doorway room to room, and they would point at a child who had the "look" they sought. A talented child who didn't have the right demeanor would not be invited to audition. They would contact the parents to see whether they would permit the children to audition. The "look" came first; then the assessment of potential talent followed. This was true for theater, film, and television casting.

Theatrical children often come from theatrical families. The Redgraves, the Fondas, the Bernhardts, and the phenomenally successful Macaulay Culkin are examples. Again, the home milieu is a prerequisite for the nurturing of the predisposition for talent, and the skilled expert is necessary for the identification of potential. Most often, however, the child actor does not become the gifted adult actor. What should also be considered here is the "stage mother" phenomenon. Many parents impose upon their children their own desire for fame and fortune by submitting them to auditions and try-outs. Judy Garland's mother is an example; she permitted Judy to be administered amphetamines and depressants in order that movie schedules be met (Edwards, 1975). Patty Duke's parents are another example. They changed her name from Anna to Patty in order to conform to studio wishes (Duke & Turan, 1987). Both actors suffered from mental difficulties later on in life.

What do biographies show about the childhoods of people who became known as actors during their adulthood? The actor Marlon Brando has been recognized throughout the world as both the consummate stage actor and the consummate film actor. His role as Stanley Kowalski in Tennessee Williams's *A Streetcar Named Desire* framed the role for all actors for all time. His role as the Godfather in the movie of the same name did the same. Brando was born in Nebraska and after the family moved several times, to California and back, they settled in Libertyville, Illinois. His father was a salesman and his mother was active in community theater in Nebraska, and Henry Fonda, who acted in the same community theater, commented on her talent. Brando had two older sisters who were also inclined to follow the arts. Brando was a rebellious child, and had difficulty getting along with teachers and others in authority. His biographer, Bob Thomas (1973), said, "In his early years, Marlon displayed an actor's sense of mimicry. 'Who can sound the most like a train?' he would ask at the dinner table, and then provide the best imitation" (p. 8). He was very competitive with his sisters, and would often run away when they took care of him. One of his friends in Evanston, Illinois, where they lived for a few years, was the child Wally Cox, who also later became an actor. Thomas said, "Wally and Marlon formed a friendship that would extend for a lifetime. They shared a common fear of being uprooted from friends and family surroundings; Cox's family moved many times before he was grown" (p. 10). In one of his movies, Marlon Brando said of his character's childhood [which Bates (1987) said paralleled Brando's own childhood], "My father was a drunk, a screwed-up bar fighter. My mother was also a drunk. My memories as a kid are of her being arrested. . . . I can't remember many good things" (p. 63).

The actor John Wayne's family also moved often, as did the playwright Lavonne Mueller's, whose father was in the military. Biographies of actors often show they had childhood turmoil and no special academic oustandingness, perhaps because teachers didn't care for their attitudes (Piirto, 1992a/1998). In *The Way of the Actor* (1987), Brian Bates said that actors, when they are young, often adopt the role of humorist to deal with taunts and teasing. Many adult actors experienced, in their youths, frequent changes in their lives such as moving, divorce, and illness. Bates said actors' stories of their youths often "have in common the experience of being an 'outsider.' Different. Struggling to belong. And while it would be facile to accept them as representative accounts of the actors' childhoods, it is striking that they have such a similar theme" (p. 50). The "outsider" role could be imposed from without or within; the actors could have been conscious rebels, such as Marlon Brando or Jack Nicholson, or could have been painfully shy and rejected by peers, as were Meryl Streep and Dustin Hoffman.

Bates said that traditionally actors have been, by definition, outsiders: "In traditional societies, being an outsider was not only a common experience for the future actor. It was obligatory. . . . People who became shamanic actors had one thing in common. They invariably had a difficult time growing up; and troubled childhood and adolescence" (p. 51). The young actor may act as a way of healing hurts.

Kough, in 1960, came up with a list of characteristics that may mark acting talent in elementary school:

Characteristics of Dramatic Talent in Young Children

1. Readily shifts into the role of another character
2. Shows interest in dramatic activities
3. Uses voice to reflect changes of idea and mood
4. Understands and portrays the conflict in a situation when given the opportunity to act out a dramatic event
5. Communicates feelings by means of facial expression, gestures, and bodily movements
6. Enjoys evoking emotional responses from listeners
7. Shows unusual ability to dramatize feelings and experiences
8. Moves a dramatic situation to a climax and brings it to a well-timed conclusion when telling a story
9. Gets a good deal of satisfaction and happiness from play acting or dramatizing
10. Writes original plays or makes up plays from stories
11. Can imitate others; mimics people and animals (p. 20)

Renzulli et al. (1976) also made a Dramatics Characteristics scale in their Scales for Rating the Behavioral Characteristics of Superior Students. This contains 10 characteristics such as "Volunteers to participate in classroom plays or skits," and "Handles body with ease and poise for his particular age," or "Is able to evoke an emotional response from listeners—can get people to laugh, to frown, to feel tense, etc." This is a Likert scale, with a weighted total.

Dancers

The life of the ballet dancer is brief, a flame ignited before adolescence, at the age of 8 or 9, and extinguished in her twenties or thirties, when, if she has had any success at all, she goes back home to the Midwest and opens a ballet school in her hometown to teach the hopeful children with the same dreams she had. Of course, there have been exceptions, such as Martha Graham, who didn't dance until she was in her twenties. Modern dancers seem to have longer professional lives than classical ballet dancers. Some continue dancing through their forties and into their fifties.

Walter Terry (1971), for many years *The New York Times* dance critic, called dance an art of danger in which we, as spectators, participate vicariously. The *aesthetic* of dance is kinesthetic, and we "journey with the dancer along the paths of adventure created by the choreographer" (p. 14). The philosopher Susanne Langer (1953) called dance a phenomenological art, an art that exists in the moment, that is apprehended in the moment. Dance provides an illusion of force through the skill of the dancer, who uses her body to provide that force implicitly. Even more than the actor, who has voice and speech, the dancer must rely on gesture, extension, and physical being to tell a story. The music is the framework, but the dancer is the frame.

The ballet, begun in the sixteenth century, is the most formal form of dance in the Western world. The dancer needs a classic body, a certain shape of neck and curve of the arch of the foot. The dancer must not be too tall or too short, although those limits currently are being stretched. The product of the actor is a role. The product of the dancer is a role. The product of the musician is the performance of a piece. The role, in order to be enacted with perfection, demands that the person enacting it has been trained, and training in dance is difficult and demanding, as it is in all creative domains.

Potential for dance achievement is recognized by experts in the domain. Body type, strength, and determination are the keys. Perhaps the latter is the most important for realization of dance ability. The gymnast Olga Korbett came to the United States in the early 1990s to train U.S. gymnasts. Her assistant said that Korbett had great skill in "finding the fire." When asked what "fire" is, the assistant said that it is the determination, the will, the discipline to practice and to succeed. If a young gymnast has the talent and not the fire, there is little chance she will become very successful. The same is true for dance. Suzanne Farrell, a dancer with the New York City Ballet from the 1960s through the 1980s, is an example. In her 1990 autobiography, *Holding on to the Air,* she described this.

Farrell was born and raised in Cincinnati, in a family of women. Farrell described her life with her two older sisters as being the life of a daring tomboy. She lived in a small four-room house, and for play, would walk the beams and pipes of the construction site of a nearby subdivision being built. This was a girl slated to become one of America's premier ballerinas.

She started dance lessons at the College Conservatory of Music in Cincinnati. Her two sisters also danced, but Suzanne was early recognized as having a unique talent. The three girls shared a bedroom, and one of their favorite games was called "Ballet." One would be the Teacher, one would be the Mother, and Suzanne would be the Student.

What she liked about her early ballet lessons were the acrobatics they did for the first 15 minutes, and the tap dancing for the last 15 minutes. Farrell said that early on she "loved the way the clicks and the rhythms overtook my body and made it move." She also had a girlfriend who was as obsessed about dance as she. The two girls would call each other up on the phone and give each other combinations to do, writing them down in the dark, using flashlights: "Glissade, jete, glissade, jete, pirouette. . . . and then we'd both put the receiver down and get up and slide, jump, slide, jump, turn before reconvening on the phone to discuss the difficulties and changes necessary" (p. 32).

School was not her favorite activity, and she said, "I wasn't stupid, but I had a hard time sitting still in class and was always being reprimanded for fidgeting. Nonphysical concentration was simply boring." A few years later, she was chosen to be the girl in the *Nutcracker,* and was noticed by Diana Adams, a New York City Ballet scout for George Balanchine. Her mother took her and her sister to New York City when Suzanne was 16, and Suzanne attended two high schools, but her dance schedule at the New York

City Ballet was so strenuous and the tour schedules were so demanding that she never did graduate from high school. She said, "I have never felt lonely when I was dancing, even dancing by myself." Farrell's life as a ballet dancer was typical of that of many. The concentration and dedication necessary must come early.

A study by Zakrajsek, Johnson, and Walker in 1984 describing and comparing the learning styles of dancers and physical education majors found that there were no significant differences between the dancers and the physical education majors, and that both preferred to learn in concrete ways. There were also no gender differences. The researchers used the Kolb Learning Style Inventory. Both groups tended to be concrete, or dependent learners, needing personalized feedback, and preferring to work with others. They were not interested in self-directed learning through printed materials or books. This would seem to indicate that those who seek to identify young dancers should not focus on paper and pencil tests, but rather include concrete experiences.

GENDER DIFFERENCES IN TALENT DEVELOPMENT

Even in elementary school, gender differences become apparent. Dance is more often thought to be appropriate for girls, and getting good grades in science and mathematics are expectations for boys. Students themselves assimilate gender expectations early. These expectations are amalgamations of expectations and observations that students make. Eccles and her colleagues (1985a, 1985b; Eccles & Howard, 1992) have studied gender socialization and found that parents and teachers had different gender socialization. Boys were socialized early more toward math and science and sports such as baseball, football, and soccer, and less into drama, art, and music. Girls were socialized early into verbal areas and into drama, dance, art, and music. Their parents support them once they do make these choices. And there is even less basis if these socializers actively discourage such consideration.

Thus it is evident, as Gruber and Davis (1988) found, that the seeds of adult achievement are within the youth. The predictive behaviors of these youth were evident early. Young creative writers read and write; young visual artists think visually and draw; young musicians demonstrate their auditory talents; young dancers and athletes like to move; young scientists have oddly classified collections; young mathematicians often think in algorithms. Young inventors tinker. Young entrepreneurs are enterprising. Young actors would seem to be the ones in whom it would be most difficult to find predictive behaviors, although the two checklists mentioned earlier seem helpful. Family support and approval is necessary in the families of all these talented youth. Tying the identification measures more closely to the specific domain behaviors expected would seem to be the logical choice for school districts who want to identify those with talent. However, personality traits are extremely important in the realization of potential, so it would seem, at the elementary school level, that the development of personality traits such as risk taking, assertiveness, androgyny, flexibility, imagination, and intuition should be part of the curricular agenda. How to develop such aspects of personality is the instructional challenge.

But noting who is talented is just the beginning. After these behaviors are duly noted and recognized, individual programs for talented youth should be created. These may take the form of special pullout options for small groups of children of like talent, but the basis for the educational intervention should be a detailed look at the strengths of the individual child. The days of placing children with verbal or art talent into an accelerated class for mathematically precocious youth, just because they are identified as talented, should be long past.

MULTIPLE INTELLIGENCE IDENTIFICATION AND REPORTING

Several Javits projects used the Gardner classification of intelligences in trying to make programs more equitable. Among them was the program in the Montgomery County Public Schools in Rockville, Maryland. They developed a checklist for identifying learning strengths according to multiple intelligences. The checklist shown in Figure 6.2 was used for elementary school children to grade 5.

Another Javits project that focused on multiple intelligences was the Javits Seven+ project in Community School District 18 in Brooklyn, New York. Students were identified by checklist through observation. Parents also received report cards based on their students' progress according to the multiple intelligences. Figure 6.3 illustrates the report card.

THE MIDDLE SCHOOL CHALLENGE

In recent years, the education of talented youngsters has undergone a change (Piirto, Cassone & Wilkes, 1998). Several studies have indicated that the goal of success for all students may give short shrift to the goal for "all" if the "all" includes academically talented students. Tomlinson (1994) said, "Gifted middle school learners are at special risk in the absence of appropriately challenging instruction" (p. 178). She noted "boomerangs" in curriculum for these students. Among these is the conclusion that concrete learning is what middle school students need. Tomlinson noted that many academically talented middle school students are able to think at highly complex and abstract levels. When all the instruction is targeted for the concrete and the hands-on approach, these students may suffer the very apathy and disengagement that is common for at-risk learners. Self-esteem is tied to accomplishment, and when accomplishment is easy or not struggled for, apathy can result.

Vars and Rakow (1993) advocated an integrative curriculum. Other terms that seem synonymous with *integrative* are *interdisciplinary, correlated, unified, fused, holistic,* and *core* curriculum. The purpose of such approaches to teaching content is to enable the students to make connections between knowledges common to the separate domains. This is often done through scheduling innovations such as block schedules or other ways of viewing school time and through manipulating sequence so that, for example, students in social studies may read literature that is applicable to the topic being studied in social studies. Such integrative curriculum requires common planning time and deep subject matter knowledge on the part of the teachers, as well as a compatibility of personality and philosophy. Teachers should make "use of a judicious mix of heterogeneous and homogeneous groupings" so that the students can have the experience of working with others of unlike ability and interest as well as the experience of working with intellectual peers.

Figure 6.2   MI Checklist for Identifying Learning Strengths*

Child's Name _____   Teacher _____

Grade _____   Date _____

Write the number (1-5) that most closely represents your overall observations of this child in each intelligence. You may check any behavior(s) you feel is (are) particularly strong for that child. Please add any comments you believe will help another teacher plan for this child.

> 1 - You have not observed these behaviors.
> 2 - You have occasionally observed them.
> 3 - You have usually observed them.
> 4 - You almost always or always observed them.
> 5 - No opportunity to observe these behaviors

LINGUISTIC _____ (overall rating)

1. _____ Enjoys word play; chooses to memorize and recite poems, tongue twisters, puns, riddles, etc.
2. _____ Starts conversations or discussions on his/her own
3. _____ Expresses ideas easily either orally or in writing; is a good storyteller or writer
4. _____ Can give several meanings when describing an object or idea (e.g. how an object looks, how it's used)
5. _____ Remembers and describes new ideas
6. _____ Readily verbalizes background knowledge and factual information
7. _____ Asks many questions
8. _____ Talks through problems; explains solutions
9. _____ Shows verbal ability in English, considering another language is used in the home
10. _____ Uses advanced vocabulary for age

LOGICAL-MATHEMATICAL _____ (overall rating)

1. _____ Chooses to play or work with number activities
2. _____ Finds number patterns or geometric patterns in the environment (e.g., tiles, flowers, leaves)
3. _____ Joins smaller ideas into larger ones
4. _____ Can provide specific examples to support a generalization
5. _____ Finds ways to work through an unfamiliar number problem using own plan or strategy
6. _____ Is able to plan or describe steps or events in order
7. _____ Groups objects and ideas in a variety of ways: finds similarities and differences
8. _____ Uses a systematic approach to problem solving
9. _____ Assembles puzzles with skill and enjoyment

BODILY-KINESTHETIC _____ (overall rating)

1. _____ Chooses motor skills (e.g. skipping, balancing, jumping)
2. _____ Mirrors or repeats movements easily

(continued on next page)

*Note: This checklist was made before Gardner added the naturalist intelligence.

Figure 6.2 *Continued*

3. _____ Readily masters hand (clap) patterns or steps
4. _____ Develops large muscle (gross motor) skills easily (e.g. roller skating, jumping rope)
5. _____ Develops small muscle (fine motor) skills easily (e.g. tying shoes before kindergarten, draws unusually well for age)
6. _____ Tries to master a new physical skill independently
7. _____ Prefers to touch and explore the shape of objects in order to learn about them

SPATIAL _____ (overall rating)

1. _____ Chooses to express ideas through visual media or through interactions with objects in the environment
2. _____ Constructs and designs visual patterns
3. _____ Puts things together imaginatively to form a construction (e.g. collage, sculpture)
4. _____ Shows an understanding of physical perspective
5. _____ Takes things apart and can put them back together (e.g. puzzle or mechanical objects)
6. _____ Can organize and group objects
7. _____ Shows artistic appreciation; responds to color, line, texture
8. _____ Carefully plans use of space on paper
9. _____ Puts relevant details in drawings

INTERPERSONAL _____ (overall rating)

1. _____ Eager participant in group activities
2. _____ Initiates or makes offers of peer tutoring
3. _____ Meets own needs through adults and other people
4. _____ Expresses feelings to others
5. _____ Shows leadership; organizes activities including other children
6. _____ Chosen by others to help or join a group
7. _____ Easily builds relationships with others
8. _____ Shows strong sense of fairness in the interest of the group

INTERPERSONAL _____ (overall rating)

1. _____ Self-motivated, independent, and resourceful
2. _____ Accepts ownership for one's behavior
3. _____ Self-confident
4. _____ Empathizes with other children
5. _____ Has sense of humor
6. _____ Can laugh at oneself
7. _____ Sticks to one's beliefs
8. _____ Takes risks
9. _____ Concentrates on topics or tasks
10. _____ Plays creatively
11. _____ Persistent in self-selected activity

MUSICAL _____ (overall rating)

1. _____ Chooses musical activities
2. _____ Reproduces a newly heard melody or rhythm
3. _____ Composes rhythms, patterns, melodies

Figure 6.2   *Continued*

---

4. _____   Sings on key
5. _____   Identifies musical instruments heard in a musical composition
6. _____   Plays musical selections by ear
7. _____   Sings or hums melodically during independent activities
8. _____   Experiments with objects to create different sounds

Comments:

_____

_____

_____

However, Tomlinson (1994) said that the thematic approach common to middle school curricula falsely assumes that the academically talented learners will have their needs taken care of because higher-level thinking skills, creativity skills, and critical thinking skills will be folded into the thematic units. That all students need to do higher-level thinking is a given, but the question of pace and depth is still not answered, and academically talented middle school students are fast learners who can master the knowledge (if that is, indeed, the goal of the school) in much less time than it takes most middle school students. Tomlinson (1994) made several recommendations for middle schools in including instruction for their academically talented students:

1. Acknowledge that there are academically talented learners in the middle school, and note that they do have cognitive and affective differences.
2. Plan for the learning needs of these students; consider a coaching model.
3. Include flexible grouping; do not insist on heterogeneous grouping for all learning tasks.
4. Prepare the teachers to be able to work with students in groups.
5. Define the curriculum that is suitable for these learners.
6. Utilize many learning strategies to encourage higher level thinking in all students, but don't assume that because these are included that academically talented students' needs are taken care of.
7. Help teachers to plan for diverse needs of all students, including the academically talented.
8. Conduct staff development and encourage college courses in curriculum differentiation for academically talented learners.

Students are able to decide for themselves what kinds of education they prefer, and Armstrong (1989, 1994, 1995, 1997) has worked on a method for having them do so. It is called Q-sort. Students sort cards with items based on best research practices in the field (Shore et al., 1991). Cassone (Piirto, Cassone & Wikes, 1998) used this with middle school students in one city in the midwest in order to determine program options. Armstrong's list is presented in Figure 6.4.

Figure 6.3   Javits Seven+ Report Card*

Pupil _____	ID# _____		
Ratings Used		**Marking Periods**	
E = Excellent G = Good			
S = Satisfactory N = Needs Improvement	1	2	3
I. SPECIAL SKILLS			
A. Fluency			EGSN
1. Frequently responds to questions	EGSN	EGSN	
2. Comes up with many ideas	EGSN	EGSN	
B. Flexibility			EGSN
1. Sees things from different points of view	EGSN	EGSN	
2. Suggests/tries alternate ways of working with materials	EGSN	EGSN	
C. Originality			EGSN
1. Presents ideas in new or unusual ways	EGSN	EGSN	
2. Expands on his/her and others' ideas	EGSN	EGSN	
II. INTERPERSONAL/INTRAPERSONAL INTELLIGENCE			
A. Citizenship			EGSN
1. Cooperates with adults and classmates	EGSN	EGSN	
2. Carries out responsibilities	EGSN	EGSN	
3. Demonstrates leadership qualities	EGSN	EGSN	
4. Shows self-control	EGSN	EGSN	
5. Works well independently	EGSN	EGSN	
6. Shows respect for and demonstrates an understanding of the needs of others	EGSN	EGSN	
B. Social Studies			EGSN
1. Has an awareness of the community	EGSN	EGSN	
2. Recognizes patterns and connections with other cultures	EGSN	EGSN	
III. SPATIAL INTELLIGENCE			EGSN
Expresses ideas through artwork	EGSN	EGSN	
Uses materials in new and unusual ways	EGSN	EGSN	
IV. LINGUISITIC INTELLIGENCE			
A. Reading			EGSN
1. Learns new words	EGSN	EGSN	
2. Reads with understanding	EGSN	EGSN	
3. Shows an interest in reading	EGSN	EGSN	
B. Oral Language			EGSN
1. Listens actively	EGSN	EGSN	
2. Initiates and/or participates in discussions	EGSN	EGSN	
3. Expresses thoughts clearly	EGSN	EGSN	

*Note: Naturalistic intelligence was not included.

Figure 6.3   *Continued*

C. Written Language				EGSN
1. Writes picture/word stories	EGSN	EGSN		
2. Expands on his/her or others' ideas	EGSN	EGSN		V.
LOGICAL-MATHEMATICAL INTELLIGENCE				
A. Mathematics				EGSN
1. Demonstrates ability to solve computational problems	EGSN	EGSN		
2. Demonstrates problem-solving skills	EGSN	EGSN		
3. Shows understanding of math concepts	EGSN	EGSN		
4. Shows ability in using manipulatives to represent mathematical concepts	EGSN	EGSN		
B. Science				EGSN
1. Wants to find out the how and why of things	EGSN	EGSN		
2. Observes, interprets and evaluates information carefully	EGSN	EGSN		
VI. MUSICAL INTELLIGENCE				EGSN
Exhibits a sense of auditory awareness	EGSN	EGSN		
Shows and creates rhythmic patterns	EGSN	EGSN		
Appreciates varied musical expressions	EGSN	EGSN		
VII. BODILY-KINESTHETIC INTELLIGENCE				EGSN
Shows an ability to create patterns through movement	EGSN	EGSN		
Demonstrates coordination and control of physical movement	EGSN	EGSN		
Participates with interest in varied physical activities	EGSN	EGSN		

CASE EXAMPLE: The School, the Parents, and the Girl

By Rachel Wilkes, Age 17, Extended Essay: International High School, Eugene, OR

My interest in girls' self-esteem began in ninth grade. One Sunday night at an International High School student government meeting, our adviser told us that she had just finished reading a new book called *Reviving Ophelia* (Pipher, 1994). She enjoyed it and suggested that we should take the time to read it. I jotted it in my notebook and didn't think much about it. Later that year, I finally bought the book and was intrigued by all the case studies of girls my age. I followed *Reviving Ophelia* with *SchoolGirls* (Orenstein, 1994), about a reporter who spent several months in two radically different California middle schools. Interested even more, I decided I wanted to write my senior paper about girls' self-esteem.

Some researchers advocate an integrative curriculum for academically talented students, to enable students to make connections among content from various domains.

"I don't raise my hand in my classes because I'm afraid I'll have the wrong answer."
  "Boys are less afraid of being wrong."
  "Boys do better in math."
  "I hate school now. I'd rather work."
  "I have really started to doubt myself academically."
  "Either way I lose. If I make a good grade my peers are mad. If I make a bad grade, they spread it around that even I can screw up."

Unfortunately, these are not fictional quotes. They are real comments made by teenage girls, and they support research done by the American Association of University Women (AAUW) indicating that girls suffer a drop in academic self-esteem during adolescence. Additional research suggests that boys' self-esteem goes up in adolescence while girls' goes down (Orenstein, 1995). I was interested in finding out whether my female peers had also experienced this decline. I administered a 21-question survey to 69 girls from coeducational high schools and eight girls from a private, single-sex school. Thirty percent of girls in coeducational schools lost academic self-esteem in middle school and 36 percent lost self-esteem in high school. In the specific areas of math and science, 27.5 percent of girls lost self-esteem in middle school, and the number leapt to 39 percent in high school girls as girls tackled more advanced classes.

Figure 6.4   Student ADAPT Classroom Cues Record Form

Student's Name: _____

Teacher: _____   Date: _____

**How do you think you learn best? You can tell us by sorting
the cue cards and recording your ideas on this form.**

Directions

Each of the 40 cue cards has one idea about how students might learn best. To tell
us about what ways you think you would like to learn, you should:

1. Sort the cue cards into three groups:

    Group A: I would really enjoy learning this way.
    Group B: I do not feel that this is either a good or a bad way for me to learn.
    Group C: I would prefer **not** to learn in this way.

2. Then put an **A** by the number of each statement that you prefer (the **A group**).
    Put a **C** by those you would rather not do (the **C group**). You do not need to
    record the numbers for the statements that you feel are neither right nor wrong
    for you (the **B Group**).
       There are no right or wrong answers. Your answers are your opinions.
       If you do not have the cue cards to actually sort, just look over the statements
    attached to this form and put an A or C as described above.

Examples

___A___ 1. I should be expected to do high quality work.
_____ 2. I would like to learn a lot about fewer topics instead of learning a little
             about a lot of topics.
___C___ 3. I would like to do independent studies with some guidance.
_____ 4. I would like to learn how to be an independent learner.

Student ADAPT Classroom Cues Record Form

Put an "A" in the space for each idea that you think is a good way for you to learn
and a "C" in front of each idea that you do not feel is a good way for you to learn.
You do not need to put a letter in each blank.

_____ 1. I should be expected to do high quality work.
_____ 2. I would like to learn a lot about fewer topics instead of learning a little
             about a lot of topics.
_____ 3. I would like to do independent studies with some guidance.
_____ 4. I would like to learn how to be an independent learner.
_____ 5. I would like to learn how to feel good about myself.
_____ 6. I would like to be in special classes or programs that are especially
             right for me.
_____ 7. I would like to understand what my special classes or programs are
             trying to teach me and why that is important.

(continued on next page)

Figure 6.4 *Continued*

_____ 8. My creative abilities should not be ignored or abused.

_____ 9. I would like to broaden my interests.

_____ 10. I should not be forced to agree with others.

_____ 11. I would like to be able to learn things in an earlier grade or at a younger age than I normally would.

_____ 12. I would like to spend some of my time working with the rest of the class but I would also like opportunities to work independently.

_____ 13. It would be fine with me to work with other children who are not my age if we have similar interests and abilities.

_____ 14. I would like to study some interesting things that are not already part of my regular classes.

_____ 15. For at least some of the time, it is important to me to be in classes with students whose ability matches mine.

_____ 16. I would like to study things that are of particular interest to me.

_____ 17. I would like to work with people who really know a lot about the subjects they teach.

_____ 18. I would like to be actively involved in learning; I like to be in classes where we do more than listen to the teacher.

_____ 19. I would like to combine study in several subject areas at the same time.

_____ 20. I would like to understand more about my feelings and opinions.

_____ 21. I would like to learn about different careers.

_____ 22. I would like to do more art, music, or plays.

_____ 23. I would like to be asked to read things that make me think, not simple things that expect me just to give answers memorized from the book.

_____ 24. I would like to learn with computers.

_____ 25. I would like to learn more about what things might be like in the future.

_____ 26. I would like to learn about famous people.

_____ 27. I would like to learn in ways that take into account the ways I learn best.

_____ 28. I would like to learn research skills.

_____ 29. I would like to learn how to communicate more effectively.

_____ 30. I would like to learn to think in both organized and creative ways.

_____ 31. I would like to learn ways to work better with others.

_____ 32. I would like to learn by going on field trips.

_____ 33. I would like to learn how to plan better by learning how to set goals.

_____ 34. I would like to learn about how I learn.

_____ 35. I would like to learn by asking questions, doing experiments, and solving problems.

_____ 36. I would like to learn how to find solutions to real problems.

_____ 37. Teaching other children is a good way for me to learn.

_____ 38. I would like to learn at my own rate, even if it is faster than the other children in the class.

Figure 6.4 *Continued*

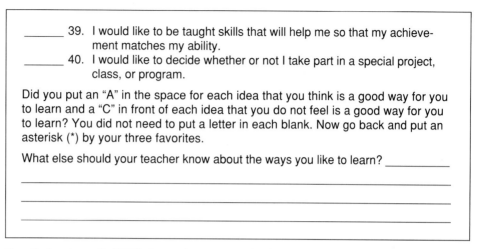

_____ 39. I would like to be taught skills that will help me so that my achievement matches my ability.

_____ 40. I would like to decide whether or not I take part in a special project,
class, or program.

Did you put an "A" in the space for each idea that you think is a good way for you
to learn and a "C" in front of each idea that you do not feel is a good way for you
to learn? You did not need to put a letter in each blank. Now go back and put an
asterisk (*) by your three favorites.

What else should your teacher know about the ways you like to learn? _____

_____

_____

_____

From D. Armstrong, D. (1989). Appropriate programs for the gifted: An analysis of gifted elementary students' perceptions. *Journal for the Education of the Gifted,* 12 (4), 277–292. Used with permission.

There are three factors which determine whether the girl will be swayed by other influences, or whether she will be resilient and self-confident throughout adolescence. The three most important factors for a girl to maintain her academic self-esteem are (1) the quality of the academic setting; (2) the personality and learning style of the girl; and (3) the level of parental involvement.

Responses to my surveys were divided on the issue of equal attention in the classroom. In the responses to the question, "Do you think teachers call on girls the same as boys?" there was no glaring evidence of sex discrimination. Some of the girls responded that since boys are more aggressive or outspoken, they dominate classroom discussion. One girl said, "I did an experiment with my (male) literature teacher last year, and he called on the same five boys 60 times while he only called on the girls 10 times."

The girl is the vital "leg" in the concept of the "three-legged stool." Even if the academic setting is bias-free and parents are supportive, there are no guarantees a girl will have a positive academic experience: part of the responsibility rests on her shoulders. Although schools are essential in cultivating and enriching a girl's intellectual life, the girl must possess certain traits to be successful. Pipher (1994) discusses traits such as resilience, optimism, and androgyny. I administered surveys to teachers representing all grade levels and asked them to list qualities of girls who do well in school. Some answers included self-discipline, organization, self-esteem, a sense of humor, a willingness to take risks, eagerness to please, cooperativeness, inquisitiveness, and being hard working. Sadly, these are traits which Pipher claims girls generally lose in adolescence. Teachers seemed to like the fact that these girls are eager to please. Pipher argues that girls lose their "true selves" in their attempt to please others (p. 37).

Piirto (1994a, 1995a) agrees that these characteristics, as well as others, are crucial to an individual's success. In fact, personality attributes make up the "base" of her Pyramid. The attributes include imagination, self-discipline, leadership, resilience, androgyny, passion, tolerance for ambiguity, persistence, self-esteem, drive, aggressiveness, self-efficacy, naïvetè , and compulsiveness. A study of talented high school students (Piirto & Fraas, 1995) showed that talented students of both sexes display more androgynous characteristics. The females were dominant with a need to achieve, while the males were more sensitive to aesthetic values than other males. Given these facts, the importance Pipher placed on retaining preadolescent androgyny and "tomboy" behavior was right on the mark.

Piirto's Pyramid goes against the normal explanation of IQ as intelligence. Piirto suggests that a person needs a certain minimum IQ to be successful (the center of the Pyramid), but that the minimum IQ needed varies from profession to profession. The individual also possesses a specific talent in a domain (the top of the Pyramid). While the Pyramid represents the individual, various "suns," or influences, act upon him or her: chance, home, school, gender differences, and community and culture.

An 18-year-old piano protegé I read about in an article in the newspaper is an example of how the Pyramid works. She has innate talent (the tip of the Pyramid); she works hard, practicing hours every day (the base of the Pyramid); her parents signed her up for lessons when they realized she was gifted (the "sun" of home). Her IQ was not mentioned because although she is very gifted, that specific number does not matter in the domain of music.

What significance does the Pyramid of Talent Development have in regard to teenage girls? If girls are losing the very characteristics which are necessary for success, something must be done. Girls need to lose the misconception that "I'm not smart enough for that" or "I'll never get good grades." Rather than focusing on IQ, qualities such as hard work and self-motivation should be encouraged. Some highly capable students are lazy and, therefore, not as successful; conversely, some students are at the top of their class not because of innate genius, but because of persistence and drive. Girls need to find areas in which they are talented, and need to be encouraged to cultivate those talents to their fullest. The suns of home and school are key influences. Parents and teachers must teach girls how to develop these traits in their preteen years so they will not give them up during the challenges of adolescence.

In conclusion, an unbiased academic setting is not always enough. To succeed in school, a girl must also possess certain personality traits. Teachers and parents are crucial in encouraging these traits in children. Girls should be taught, both in school and at home, that intelligence is not measured by IQ; it is what is done with innate talents that determines success. When the personality attributes of the Pyramid of Talent Development are cultivated and praised, girls will enter adolescence prepared to weather any storm. With the three-legged stool intact, American education will be at its best: parents, teachers, students, and society will benefit.

> > > > > > > > > > > > > > > > > >

SUMMARY

1. Experts in various creative fields can recognize those with creative potential. Both behavioral inventories and tests are also appropriate for identifying talent.
2. Young scientists often have an early interest in science and join science groups, have extensive collections, and exhibit certain predictable behaviors.
3. Young mathematicians often have an early interest in the structure of music and of chess and exhibit certain predictable behaviors. Mathematical talent is required for many adult professions.
4. Young inventors often like to fix things and to tinker.
5. Young entrepreneurs like to concoct business schemes and can handle money.
6. Young writers often have uncanny wisdom, an ability to use words almost as music, and are voracious readers. Verbal talent is required for many adult professions.
7. Young musicians often evidence a love for music and rapid progression in music lessons. Family commitment to the musical talent is also in evidence.
8. Young visual artists often draw to communicate and evidence their early talent in drawing that is advanced.
9. Young dancers have certain body frames and kinesthetic talents.
10. Gender differences show up early, and are often enhanced by the socialization patterns of teachers, parents, and peers.
11. The middle school model often overlooks the academic needs of talented students, especially their needs for advanced material in a belief that heterogeneous grouping is socially and emotionally best for students of this age.

CHAPTER
7   HIGH SCHOOL AND COLLEGE TALENTED YOUTH

FOCUSING QUESTIONS

1. How do verbal ability and mathematical ability differ? How are they the same?
2. What is the importance of having a good memory for various kinds of talents?
3. What would you, as a teacher of high school and college youth, do to enhance memory in subject matter?
4. Obtain your own personality preferences on the Myers-Briggs Type Indicator. How would you as a teacher have to modify your preferred teaching and learning style for your talented students?
5. Discuss how a student's family background affects the development of his or her talent(s).
6. Look at a standard biographical work about Nobel prize winners Albert Einstein or Barbara McClintock. Are there any gender differences in salient events in their adolescent and college years? How did their adolescent and college years point the way for their future careers?
7. What is the importance of the social milieu in the development of talent?
8. What is the role of the teacher of performers? How does this differ from the role of the coach of performers?
9. Discuss the development of talent in adolescent musicians.
10. How important are personality factors in the development of talent in dancers, musicians, and actors?
11. What qualities do leaders need? Discuss the identification and development of leadership ability.
12. What is tacit knowledge and how would a high school counseling office make students aware of it?
13. How should colleges change the way they counsel students in order to include tacit knowledge within the students' majors?

Figure 7.1   Overview of Chapter 7

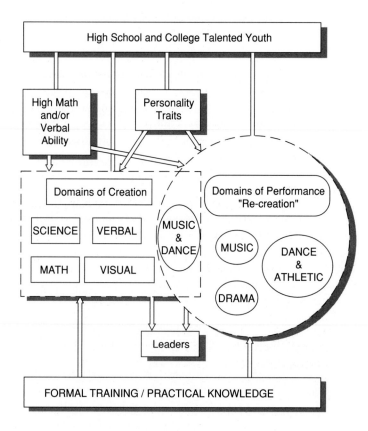

Alexis had moved to town during her seventh grade year. Her mother was a professor of harp at the local university's music department. Her father was a professor in the chemistry department. As soon as she arrived in the college town, the school system knew there was something unusual about Alexis; Alexis's mother confessed that Alexis had skipped third grade, which accounted for her small size. But her test scores, both the achievement test and the individual intelligence test routinely given to new students in the district, indicated that Alexis scored in the 99th percentile in all areas, even for the seventh grade level, although she was 11 and not 13, as are many seventh graders. Alexis's mother asked the school system whether they would put Alexis into the eighth grade. This would mean that she would have skipped two grades. Alexis was brought into the discussions, and she said, "Why not? If I know what is supposed to be taught to me in seventh grade, let me go into eighth grade, where I will learn new things." The school system, used to having quite a few bright children because this was a university town, concurred. Alexis, age 11, entered the eighth grade.

A few months later, the local coordinator of programs for the academically talented notified Alexis's parents that Alexis's test scores showed that she qualified for the Talent Search, and that she might want to sign up to take the Scholastic Aptitude Test (SAT) with the rest of the seventh graders who had qualified by scoring in the 95th percentile in both reading and mathematics on their standardized group achievement test. The reason for giving the SAT to these young students prior to their taking such subjects as algebra and geometry was that their mathematical analysis ability would show up more clearly before they had taken such courses. Alexis signed up to take the test, and when the results came back, she found that she had scored above 460 on the SAT-Verbal portion of the test, and 520 in the SAT-Mathematics. This placed her in the same range as the average high school senior. She was just going to turn 12.

The university wrote her a letter, inviting her to participate in a three-week summer program in mathematics. Alexis's mother and father were enthusiastic about this opportunity for their only child, and they pooled their finances and sent her to the program, where she completed the equivalent of one year of high school mathematics. The test scores showed that she had mastery comparable to high school sophomores. The school system permitted her to test out of algebra and to enter an advanced algebra class, but they wouldn't accept the credit from the summer program. Nonetheless, she still met school criteria, because she had three Carnegie units of math by the time she graduated. She took Advanced Placement courses in BC calculus, chemistry, English, and history. Her high school counselors made an arrangement with the university for her to continue her studies on a cooperative enrollment plan, but the state department of education said that she couldn't graduate from high school because she hadn't taken state history and four years of physical education. Alexis and her parents sued the state department and won. She graduated as valedictorian of her high school class, and went on to the academically competitive state university.

When she got there, she pursued her interest in math and science, and continued to get As in her classes. She had trouble picturing herself as a researcher, though. She told her friends, "I'm just a hard worker; that's why I get good grades." Her boyfriend, Kurt, was majoring in political science and wanted to go to law school. They studied together and partied together and spent almost all their time together. When Alexis turned 20, they decided they wanted to get married. Alexis and her mother began planning a lovely wedding with music by her mother's colleagues. Alexis told one of her chemical engineering professors, during a lab class, and he looked at her rather strangely, and said, "Serves you right. We lose all our best girls to marriage. I thought you were going to go to graduate school and get a Ph.D." This was the first time a professor had ever spoken to her personally about her career plans, and Alexis was taken aback. She hadn't thought that she had enough talent to pursue a Ph.D. and become a researcher. She was in her senior year in college. Her high school counselors and teachers had encouraged her and pointed her to a good college and to an interesting major with career potential. But no one in her college had taken an interest in her career development. She had trouble imagining herself as a successful professional. She remembered this professor five years later, when she began her master's degree program in math education.

The paths of development of academically talented and other talented people begin to diverge in high school and college; that is, they begin to take on the characteristics of career development within certain fields. To predict which path a child will take, it is sensible to look at a child's interests. What a young person is interested in and the extracurricular activities in which he or she participates are remarkably predictive of later talent development across the years. Community theater activists often participated in theater in high school and college. Scientists had scientific interests as youth; in fact, Terman (1965) commented that the interests of the academically talented men who became scientists changed little over the course of 40 years. Mathematicians, likewise, had mathematical interests as young people. Few well-designed studies about the influence and longevity of interests exist, but anecdotal and biographical evidence abounds.

For another clue, what do tests tell us about the nature of youths such as Alexis? Detailed analysis of test scores of youths who scored better than one in 1,000 on such tests as the SAT and their parents by Camilla Benbow (1992) has shown that academic talent shows up on tests as precocity. This was found to be true for those who scored highest on the verbal portion as well as the mathematical portion. Precocity means having the characteristics of those who are older. Of course, many older people never score as high on these tests as talented youth, so precocity would have to be showing the characteristics of *academically talented* older students.

There were differences in the scores between the high verbal and the high mathematical, though. Colangelo and Kerr (1990) and Benbow and Minor (1990) found that these were two distinctive types of academic talent. The high *verbal* youth scored best on general knowledge and verbal tests, and the high *mathematical* youth scored best on nonverbal reasoning, spatial ability, and memory. The high mathematical youth were also faster, and so speed was a major factor in their scores. High mathematically talented youth are predominantly male; that is, "the gender difference in mathematical talent is quite stable and robust" and is not attributable to bias in test items (Benbow, 1992, p. 100).

This gender difference was as true for the American College Test (ACT) as for the Scholastic Aptitude Test (SAT). (These studies and the social-emotional nature of such academic talent are also discussed in Chapter 11.)

COGNITIVE COMPONENTS OF HIGH ABILITY

How do the talented youth who score high on such tests process information? Prior knowledge is an important factor. In other words, background knowledge in a field contributes to better scores on tests in that field. High scorers on such tests as the SAT and the ACT are able, however, to abstract, to analyze, and to make inferences, whereas low scorers are prone to try to remember details and to apply them directly. The high scorers are able to find the principles that underlie the problems presented to them. Young test-takers in the Talent Searches do not have much background knowledge, however, because they have not been exposed to the courses that students who take the test in high school have taken. What accounts for their performances being similar to those of seniors in high school? Benbow (1992) said that students who score exceptionally high in mathematics had "superior general problem-solving ability," what she called "somewhat better procedural knowledge in mathematics than students talented in other domains" (p. 102).

The cognitive skill of *memory* is also different between verbally and mathematically talented youth. Verbally talented youth are able to access long-term memory; mathematically talented youth can do a better job in working with and updating what is in short-term memory. Not surprisingly, "mathematically talented students performed better when the stimuli to be represented were digits and possibly spatial locations, while the verbally talented performed better in remembering words." (Benbow, 1992).

Besides being precocious and different in their ability to formulate equations (procedural knowledge in mathematics), young and older adolescents with verbal and mathematical abilities have been found to have different brain hemispheric functioning than students of average ability. Both verbally and mathematically precocious teens have been found to have enhanced right-hemisphere functioning. The characteristics that have been thought to describe talented youth are also the characteristics that have been used to describe the right hemisphere's functions. Benbow commented that "it is interesting to note that some of the characteristics that have long been found to describe intellectually talented students . . . are also thought to characterize the cognitive functions or contributions of the right hemisphere to problem solving (e.g., see things holistically, deep comprehension, advanced moral reasoning, and humor)" (p. 104). Dark and Benbow (1994) also noted that verbally and mathematically talented people also seem to perform better when a task is new and novel.

These students generally have scored high on IQ tests as well as achievement and aptitude tests. Verbal and mathematical ability (or both) are strong components of the intelligence quotient. Students who score high on IQ tests are generally high achievers in school (except for underachievers, as discussed in Chapter 11). In fact, that is what IQ tests predict: That those who score high on them will do well in school, and then get into college, and then into a good job. But do students who do not score high on IQ tests do well in school, get into college, and then get good jobs? It depends on the field that is studied. However, realistically, the main factor is that the student graduate from college, not that the student graduate with the highest grades in college, unless the career path suggests graduate school. Many core contributors to various disciplines did not even graduate, for example Bill Gates, the software entrepreneur, and Steve Martin, the actor.

Leonard Baird (1985), in a study for the Educational Testing Service (ETS), reviewed many studies of the relationship between scores on ability and achievement tests, grades, and future accomplishment. Put simply, he concluded that there is a small positive relationship between academic achievement and life accomplishment. In reviewing the Berkeley studies at the Institute for Personality Assessment and Research, he noted that there were "essentially no differences between the academic ability or intelligence of the creative and uncreative groups; the major differences between the groups seemed to be personality measures" (p. 72).

In reviewing studies of scientists, engineers, and physicians, studies of National Merit Scholars, studies of managers and business people, Baird found that there were "scattered correlations," which was not surprising "considering the diversity of criteria and samples" (p. 72). Baird found a trend that showed that scoring high on a specific skill test, for example, a biology achievement test, is related to later achievement in biology, and is "more predictive of success in those fields than tests of general academic ability" (p. 73). In reviewing the Terman longitudinal studies, he concluded that "comparisons of 'successful' and 'unsuccessful' members of the sample demonstrated essentially trivial differences in test scores, but showed the importance of personality in this very highly selected group" (p. 72). (Baird's and the IPAR studies contributed to the development of my thought in formulating the pyramid in Chapter 1; that is, that personality is more important than test scores; that achievement in specific talent domains is more important than general intellectual ability.)

Baird said, however, that high academic ability did not guarantee high attainment. In fact, he concluded that while high ability in academics is a condition necessary for entering certain upper tier occupations and careers, there is a similarity among people in these careers in "a number of other talents and traits as well as in academic ability" (p. 76). This makes it hard to differentiate. Therefore, it is difficult to distinguish among the effects of academic ability, personality traits, practical knowledge of how to get along in a profession, and even gender. Baird said that "Although a certain level of academic ability is required for entrance to the training demanded of people in the occupation, it would be very difficult to demonstrate a high correlation between ability and success within these occupations" (p. 76). That is, while having academic ability has some role across occupations, the role of academic ability within occupations has not been determined. The work of Subotnik and Arnold (1996) on talent development in high-ability females has shown that gender is also a contributing factor in the realization of talents; while the women they studied had high ability and achievement, life factors later on in college and early adulthood contributed more to their dropping out of the pipeline in science and mathematics than did their ability or lack of it.

What these studies imply for the educational professional at the high school or college level is that high academic achievers (or students with high specific abilities) and high aptitude test scorers (or students with high IQs) often go on to high-level college and professional positions, but that having a high test score on an achievement or ability test is not sufficient. Benbow and Lubinski (1995) said that "we can identify at age 13 most students who have the potential to become our nation's great scientific achievers" (p. 388). But personality traits, extracurricular activities, past accomplishments, and practical, tacit knowledge about how to further one's chances of successful entry into a profession also play a large role in whether a student will go on to show substantial adult performance. Baird (1985) said that within groups of creative professionals, intelligence test scores are not very different. However, those who are most creative and productive have large and constant differences in their *personalities* and in their *values*. This suggests possible research areas for researchers into talent development.

PERSONALITY ATTRIBUTES

Long lists of personality attributes that aid or detract from the realization of potential have been compiled. Studies of mathematically talented students at age 13 note that such personality attributes as endurance, motivation, achievement, maturity, leadership, self-control, theoretical and aesthetic orientation, and creativity (Benbow, 1992; Benbow & Lubinski, 1997) were present in these students. Renzulli (1977) emphasized task commitment. The studies of writers, architects, inventors, mathematicians, and scientists at IPAR at Berkeley found that these effective people had "a strong need for independence and autonomy; a high acceptance of impulse; high personal dominance; rejection of conformity pressures in thinking; a detached attitude in interpersonal relations; risk taking; and a liking for order and method combined with a fascination with disorder and exceptions" (Baird, 1985, p. 17).

Taylor (1965) listed motivational characteristics for people who achieve in creative fields. These were "intellectual persistence, liking to think, liking to manipulate and toy with ideas, need for recognition for achievement, need for variety, need for autonomy, preferences for complex order and for challenges therein" (p. 60). People who were achievers also had a "tolerance for ambiguity." They resisted early closure when solving problems; they had the patience needed to master a problem. Teachers of academically talented students have often said that some of the students don't want to be told the answer; they want to figure it out for themselves. High achievers also liked to put things into mental order, and liked to make improvements on what already existed. They were energetic, productive, and disciplined. These creative persons were autonomous, self-sufficient, and "more independent in judgment (contrary to group agreement, if needed, to be accurate)," as well as being "more open to the irrational in themselves, more stable, low in sociability, more interested in unconventional careers" (Taylor, 1965, p. 60). The males were more feminine, and the females were more masculine, in other words, they tended towards androgyny. They exhibited dominance, aggressiveness, self-assertion, unconventionality, and adventurousness, combined with self-monitoring, internal control, emotional sensitivity, and introversion.

Holland (1961) found that scientists were emotionally stable, friendly, and thoughtfully introverted, while those in the arts were more depressed, more androgynous, and even more introverted than the scientists. As far back as 1958, Drevdahl and Cattell commented that "it seems that personality decidedly exceeds intellect in importance. Therapists and teachers have long been familiar with the fact that emotional conflicts and frightening inhibitions can confuse intellectual operation. There can be little doubt that many potential geniuses (as far as intellect alone is concerned) have been cowed into impotence by unfavorable environments" (p. 109).

The influence of environment on the shaping of personality is extremely important. Baird (1985), in commenting on the usefulness of the Terman studies for uncovering which factors lead to adult achievement—IQ score, personality, socioeconomic status, and/or level of educational attainment—said, "Perhaps the most striking aspect of these results is the expectedly small role of intelligence scores, compared to the influence of social class, educational level attained, and personality traits reflecting personal stability, social impressiveness, and ambition" (p. 71). Baird noted that the typical Terman study subject has not turned out to be "a genius," but rather "a healthy, prosperous middle-class professional," and he cautioned about using the longitudinal results of the Terman study to assess the effects of having a high IQ unless there is a suitable comparison group of "accomplishments of individuals who obtained the same educations but who had lower intelligence scores" (p. 71). The personality traits that distinguished the Terman "A" group (those who had more success in life) and the "C" group (those who had less success in life) were "prudence and forethought . . . self-confidence . . . will power and perseverance . . . integration toward goals . . . absence of inferiority feelings" (p. 71). More recent studies (Csikszentmihalyi, 1995; Gardner, 1993; Simonton, 1995) on extraordinary creativity confirm the presence of these or similar personality attributes.

It is possible to obtain a high score on an achievement or ability test without such personality traits, but it doesn't seem to be possible to be considered a creative producer within any specific field without certain personality traits valued in that field. For example, a scientist probably needs skepticism; a mathematician probably needs intuition; a musician needs discipline; a writer probably needs humor; a visual artist probably needs a love of solitude, whereas a dancer might not. Rather, a dancer probably needs extraversion, as does an actor. Cox (1926) found that geniuses needed personalities that showed persistence, confidence, and character strength. McClelland (1961) coined the term "need for achievement," a trait that people who attain have. Need for achievement is nurtured by parental and school expectations for excellence, and by the rewards and punishments a person receives. Simonton (1995) even conjectured that historical periods have personality characteristics: "Some eras desire elegance and restraint; others value fanciful elaboration and virtuosity; still others call for emotion, depth, and power" (p. 283). Those who are deemed creative and talented in any era are those able to "create artistic translations of the group mind" (p. 283).

Motivation to achieve is another personality factor that those with adult attainment have. There have been two types of motivation stressed in the literature: intrinsic motivation and extrinsic motivation. Those who attain seem to have greater intrinsic motivation (Amabile, 1983; Hennessey, 1997).

The HSPQ and Academically and Creatively Talented Adolescents

Cattell, Cattell, and Johns, in discussing the high school form of the 16 Personality Factors test, the High School Personality Questionnaire (HSPQ) (1984), noted several personality characteristics of students with high IQs. They seemed to have better morale, more persistence, and greater school interest, were popular as work partners, well adjusted to school, and showed leadership. A look at the 10 test items in this scale shows they are analogies, and so to generalize so greatly about students who got them right seems perhaps a little frivolous.

However, a 1997 study using the HSPQ showed that 125 students who were identified as gifted and talented scored significantly higher than a comparison group on this factor, Factor B, showing the Factor is related to tested intelligence and achievement (Piirto, Hohman, Nickle & Ryan, 1997). The academically talented students also were more conforming, more sensitive, more bashful and introverted, and more self-sufficient. They also had higher need for achievement, creativity, independence, and leadership.

Gender differences on the HSPQ were found also, between students identified as artistic and creative and a comparison group (Piirto & Fraas, 1995). The creative males were more sensitive and nonconforming than the comparison males. The creative females and the comparison females showed no gender differences. Both the academically and creatively talented girls and the comparison girls tended toward androgynous characteristics such as tough-mindedness, tough poise, dominance, and aggressiveness. The talented boys tended toward androgynous characteristics as tender-mindedness and sensitivity. While the girls were aggressive, they were less aggressive than the talented boys and the talented boys were more tender-minded than both the talented girls and the comparison girls. Both the talented girls and the talented boys showed similarities in the dimensions of leadership, need for achievement, and creativity, with no significant differences apparent. However, the talented boys showed more creativity than either the talented girls or the comparison girls. This could be an indication of the fields in which the talent was displayed: musical theater, creative writing, and visual arts. When a young man decides to attend a summer institute in these nontraditional fields, he has already indicated self-sufficiency and nonconformity, more so than the girls who decide to do so.

Our recent studies confirmed a study by Porter (1964) using students with IQs higher than 130 and above-average achievement that showed that the boys and girls who were good students had high scores in conformity. The boys were self-sufficient and less sensitive, while the girls were more warm, more bold, and more self-disciplined. The girls who were high achievers were also low in dominance. Another study using the HSPQ with high-IQ (between 130 and 160) high school students showed that the males were less warm and apprehensive, and were dominant, withdrawn, self-sufficient, and self-disciplined. Likewise, the females were withdrawn; however, they were also less conforming and more cheerful (Werner & Bachtold, 1969).

Myers-Briggs Type Indicator (MBTI) and Talented Adolescents

A study done with 100 talented adolescents and a comparison group showed that there were also gender differences between the two groups. The hypothesis of androgyny in the personalities of the talented was again confirmed. The study "Thinking Girls and Feeling Boys: Educating Talented Adolescents" (Piirto, Gantz, Ramsay, Steele, Tabacca & Fraas, 1997; Piirto, 1998a) found that the group of talented adolescent girls preferred Thinking (T) to a greater degree than in the normal population. It also found that a greater number of the talented adolescent boys preferred Feeling (F) than in the normal population. The overwhelming preference of the talented adolescents on the Intuition-Sensing continuum was for Intuition (N). The implications for curriculum design should be explored, as the study confirmed what other studies (see Myers & McCaullay, 1985) have found.

A high-IQ group of males preferred INTP (I, Introversion; P, Perceiving); for high-IQ females, the preferences were INFP (Myers, 1962). More than 80 percent of the academically talented females preferred Perceiving over Judging (J). Both males and females preferred the perceptive attitude. Perceptive types with strong preferences "may see even modest structure as unduly restricting" and "probably like a flexible, spontaneous way of life better than a planned, orderly way" (Myers & McCaulley, 1985, p. 54). The perceptive attitude is "spontaneous, curious, and adaptable, open to new events and changes, and aiming to miss nothing" (p. 14). The intuitive attitude, which both males and females showed, "permits perception beyond what is visible to the senses, including possible future events." These adolescents may "become imaginative, theoretical, abstract, future oriented, or creative" (p. 12).

In looking at students' scores on the SAT, the researchers found that introverts were the highest scorers on the SAT-Verbal and that J types have higher grades, while P types have better aptitude scores. T types do better in science and mathematics. Introverts and extroverts had no significant differences in their aptitude scores. Intuitive types (N) did score significantly higher than Sensing (S) types in measures of abstract thinking and verbal ability, but the differences were smaller, but still significant, when practical skills were tested. There were few significant differences in aptitude between Thinking and Feeling types, or between Judging and Perceptive.

Introverts do better on untimed tests and Intuitives do better on timed tests. Myers (1962) said, "introverts use their minds, including their intuition, in a way that is different and advantageous for dealing with the intricacies of thought and language" (p. 37).

Students who prefer Judging (J students) were described by faculty as "thorough, responsible, dependable, good on details, performs up to capacity, meets deadlines, works steadily, fond of work, industrious, and completes undertakings" (Myers & McCaulley, 1985, p. 99). Better grades are given to J types than to P types, regardless of their aptitude. J types also are able to focus their energies, which permits them to apply their learning. Thus, the trends for grades among bright high school and college students went this way: Is scored higher than E's, N's higher than S's, T's and F's had no clear differences, and J's got better grades than P's. Myers and McCaulley said, "The J types consistently achieve higher grades for a given amount of aptitude; that is, they overachieve. The P types get grades lower than expected for their level of aptitude; that is, they underachieve" (p. 106). (See Chapter 11 for a discussion of the counseling issues of overachievement and underachievement.)

Academic Self-Esteem in Young Women

Another study of high-ability young women was done by Callahan, Cornell, and Loyd (1992). The young women were enrolled in a special program that permitted them to earn both a high school diploma and a college diploma in six years. They administered the young women personality instruments and found that, compared with a comparison sample of high-ability girls who were not accelerated, these young women demonstrated somewhat greater psychosocial difficulties. The young women from families that "valued having established rules and structures" were the most well liked and had the highest self-confidence (p. 254).

Another study looked at 400 females in grades 9 and above in special residential schools for the sciences and mathematics (Callahan et al., 1996). Their mothers had a more important role in initially encouraging them to enter the special schools and after attending for awhile, many of them felt trapped, because their academic progress was such that they could not return home as their home schools would not be able to offer courses they could take. The students experienced extreme emotional stress, and the workload was such that their social lives and the possibilities of participating in extracurricular activities were drastically attenuated.

DOMAIN-SPECIFIC TALENTS

By this time, it is quite clear that the most efficient and effective way to approach talent is to consider the specific talents that talented youths possess. While many colleges give preference to students who have high composite scores on such college entry examinations as the SAT and the ACT, recent definitions of intelligence would indicate that considering *specific* types of talent would yield more accurate results. Considering multiple intelligences theory (MI), for example, Gardner's (1983) "frames of mind" would be a place to start: academic talent is most often linguistic intelligence and/or logical-mathematical intelligence. Naturalistic, spatial, musical, bodily-kinesthetic, interpersonal, and intrapersonal should also be considered. Sternberg's (1985, 1997) practical, creative, and executive aspects of intelligence in his triarchic theory should be appraised.

Academic Strengths, Interests, and Self-Concept

A 1990 study by Colangelo and Kerr considered students who had perfect scores on the ACT. Of the 729,606 high school juniors and seniors who took the test during 1985–86, there were 6,706 students who obtained perfect scores in one or more of the areas. More students scored perfectly on only one scale (5,615) than scored perfectly on all four scales (3). This indicates that academic talent is more likely to be concentrated within specific domains than spread out among several. Composite scores wash out specific academic talent. A related issue is that of academic self-concept. Students who feel they are good in one area are more likely to continue to take courses in that area (Marsh & Young, 1997). Interest and success in an academic area often depend on how well a person perceives he/she can achieve in that area.

When scores on several subtests are added and then divided to get a quotient or composite score, the students with strong academic talent in one domain of knowledge may not be noticed. Colangelo and Kerr stated unequivocally, "Looking at the comprehensive scores of the ACT was not a good indicator of extreme talent" (p. 406). This study confirms that good pedagogical practice in talent education would be to look at domain-specific talent rather than general academic ability. Colangelo and Kerr said, "It seems possible that students with extraordinary abilities in a specific area could 'fall through the cracks,' failing to be admitted to an institution or honors program where appropriate challenge existed in his or her area" (p. 407).

What were the specific profiles of extremely talented perfect scorers in each domain? The perfect scorer in English was likely to be a white female, who did not plan to major in English, but who planned to major in medicine, engineering, or the social sciences. She wanted to go to professional school after college. Girls were twice as likely to obtain perfect scores in English. This upholds the "robust" findings that girls score higher on verbal areas, findings that earlier researchers on sex differences such as Maccoby and Jacklin (1974) reported.

Perfect scorers in mathematics, natural sciences, and social sciences were likely to be white boys, who did not plan to major in these academic fields, but like the girls who scored perfectly, had plans of majoring in applied fields such as medicine, engineering, or the applied social sciences. These boys had extracurricular interests in instrumental music, departmental clubs, and intramural sports. They also wanted opportunities to be in honors programs and to pursue independent study. Minorities, except for Asian-Americans, were underrepresented in the group of perfect scorers. The researchers said that it is disconcerting that these students with such extreme academic talent were not choosing to go into academic and scholarly fields, but into applied fields. "Outstanding students in mathematics and science exacerbate this situation each time they choose studies in careers outside their exceptional strengths" (Colangelo & Kerr, p. 408). Colangelo and Kerr also enjoined schools and counselors to encourage such students to participate in contests and activities that especially need that type of academic talent, such as Westinghouse Science Talent Searches, or mathematics, science, and English competitions and clubs. If such students receive recognition for their special abilities, the likelihood that they will want to pursue studies in the domains of these abilities is increased.

The gender and ethnic differences were also clear, with most girls excelling in only one of the academic areas. The propensity for girls to steer away from high-level academic courses in the natural sciences and in mathematics is well known. It is also known that Native Americans, for example, are the least likely to take college preparatory courses of study, and African-Americans are second least likely. Taking courses is the way to achieve, and to gain background knowledge necessary for entering high-level studies. Again, counseling students for suitable course taking is a necessity.

Family Background of Students with Talent

While it is commonly known that parents' educational level is predictive of a child's educational level, not many researchers have noted that a child is likely to follow a path of development that parents approve of and in which at least one parent has an interest. André Agassiz's father was a tennis coach; Agassiz became a world-class tennis player. Gary Graffman's father was a violinist; Graffman became a concert pianist. Vincent Van Gogh's family was in the ministry and he had uncles who had an art gallery; Van Gogh first decided to become a minister and then an artist. Darwin's grandfather Erasmus Darwin was a scientist; so was Darwin. Michael Redgrave was an actor; so are his daughters, Vanessa and Lynn. The Fonda family and the Sheen family are also examples. John Cheever was a fiction story writer; his children Susan and Ben are writers also. The playwright Russel Crouse married the daughter of a novelist and their children are the actor Lindsay Crouse and the writer Tom Crouse.

Karl Menninger, his brother Will, his nephews Roy and Walt Menninger, his grand-nephew John and grandniece Liza are all psychiatrists. Richard Petty and his sons Kyle and Lee are auto racers. The politicians Albert Gore and Robert Kennedy, Jr., came from political families. The Marsalis family is a family of musicians.

In some families, one's profession seems destined by environment and interest on top of biological predisposition (Brophy & Goode, 1988; Feldman & Piirto, 1995). Jamison (1995) showed the darker side—the passing along, in first-degree relatives, of predispositions to mental illness and bipolar disorder in many writers, artists, and musicians (Piirto, in press).

An example from Susan Cheever's memoir, *Home Before Dark* (1984), illustrates how interest was developed in the children of a writer:

> Every Sunday after dinner, we each recited a poem for the rest of the family. It began with sonnets and short narrative verse, Shakespeare and Tennyson, but soon we were spending whole weekends in competitive feats of memory. My father memorized Dylan Thomas's "Fern Hill," my mother countered with Keats's "Ode to a Nightingale," I did "Barbara Fritchie," my father did "The Charge of the Light Brigade," and so forth. Ben, who was eight, stayed with shorter poems." (p. 107)

Birth order is also important. Sulloway (1996) did an extensive study of rebellious and creative later-borns: "most individual differences in personality, including those that underlie the propensity to rebel, arise within the family" (p. xiii). He said that firstborns, who are often high achievers in conventional ways, "lead fashionable re-forms, populist revolutions, and orthodox science," while later-borns, if they go into politics, are "radical revolutionaries, fostering protest long before it is stylish to do so" (p. 351). Later-borns advocate unpopular causes, "such as abolition, socialism, anarchism, and atheism." In science, later-borns typically support unconventional ideas. Sulloway said, "They work hard to precipitate crises on their complacent elder siblings, who generally see little reason to abandon the status quo" (p. 351).

Another effect that parents have on their children is what Simonton (1984) called "the orphanhood effect." A parent's death seems to provoke children to become achievers. The mother of Jane and Peter Fonda committed suicide. So did the mother of the surrealistic painter René Magritte. Edgar Allen Poe's mother died and he and his sister were in the room with her body for several days. Terr (1990) speculated that this precipitated Poe's fascination with death and horror. The actor James Dean is another example. He was extremely close to his mother, who died when he was nine years old. Sent to live with relatives back in Indiana, Dean began to focus on drama and acting. When he talked about his mother, he said, "She left me while I still needed her." One large study of 700 eminent people showed this: 61 percent lost a parent before the age of 31, 52 percent before the age of 25, and 45 percent before the age of 21 (Goertzel, Goertzel, & Goertzel, 1978).

The family's lifestyle is a great influence on a child's and a teenager's talent de-velopment and school achievement. Nontraditional lifestyles do not seem to affect achievement as much as one would think. Rather, it is the closeness of the family and the degree to which the family considers itself a family that is important. One study (Weisner & Garnier, 1992) showed that academic achievement is not nega-tively affected when a child is in a one-parent family, a low-income family, or a

family with "frequent changes in mates or in household composition" if one particular factor was present: if the family chose the lifestyle because it had an intelligible
and clear meaning for them—for instance, a religious choice leading to home-
schooling—but if the nonconventional family emphasized achievement as important, the children did not experience a lowered achievement pattern.

The variable that was important was that the parents were committed to the
lifestyle and to the importance of school achievement. One thinks of the "aging hip-
pies," the "bohemian actors," and the "poor struggling artists in garrets" as being in
this category. While poor, or in unconventional living arrangements, their children
are often high achievers who follow in their parents' footsteps, just as children from
families with more conventional lifestyles.

Behavioral Rating Scales

Identification of talent potential should be an ongoing operation in schools. Identification that occurs too early and too rigidly, as Useem (1992) noted in speaking of
mathematical ability, may lead to a shrinking of talent pools and talent development
programs just when a larger pool is needed.

Schools and researchers have pursued the route that Holland (1961) took, and
have sought to validate rating scales that secondary schools—and perhaps colleges—can use. Among these are Feldhusen, Hoover, and Sayler (1990), who made
and validated the Purdue Academic Rating Scales and the Purdue Vocational Talent
Scales. They made and validated rating scales in these areas:

1. Purdue Academic Rating Scale: Mathematics
2. Purdue Academic Rating Scale: Science
3. Purdue Academic Rating Scale: English
4. Purdue Academic Rating Scale: Social Studies
5. Purdue Academic Rating Scale: Foreign Language
6. Vocational Agriculture Talent Identification Scale
7. Business and Office Talent Identification Scale
8. Home Economics Talent Identification Scale
9. Trade and Industrial Talent Identification Scale

Feldhusen (1986, 1992a, 1992b, 1992c) identified three major domains from which
talent should be sought at the secondary level: (1) *academic-intellectual talents*, in
such areas as science, mathematics, English, social studies, languages, and computers; (2) *artistic-creative talents*, in such areas as music, dance, drama, graphics,
sculpture, and photography; and (3) *vocational talents*, in such areas as home economics, trade and industrial, vocational agriculture, and business and office.

SCIENCE TALENT DEVELOPMENT

Recent studies have shown that less than 6 percent of high school students plan to major
in the sciences in college, and of that number, about 50 percent change majors. This
leaves 3 percent of students who continue with their science majors (Green, 1989;

Tomlinson-Keasey, 1990). What are the characteristics of youth who initially have an interest and talent in science, and is 3 percent enough? Are there jobs and positions for the scientists who do make it through the highly structured and competitive science education system?

As shown in the last chapter, scientists as children demonstrated an early interest in science topics, in classification and classification of collections, in reading non-fiction. They received high scores on IQ tests. Their families were relatively stable, and their fathers were present and involved in decisions about their educational and personal lives. In high school, these interests continued and were nurtured by science clubs and science teachers. They pursued hobbies that were focused on science such as ham radio or bird watching, trail hiking or weather watching.

Sosniak (1985b), in her study of research neurologists, said that they came from "active, academically oriented families" (p. 350). The parents were busy and interested in many things; they were active in the community and active in their careers. Most of their fathers had professional careers; a little over half of their mothers (11 out of 20) had careers as well, and they were also active in the community. The scientists grew up in families where children were expected to go to college; this was part of their family mythology (Piirto, 1992a/1998). The families did not often specify that the children were expected to go to college and major in the sciences, but several of the research neurologists, when they decided to change majors—to major in philosophy, or in economics—were told of their families' disappointment. Their families wanted them to major in medicine and had groomed the students this way all along. They had all along the way internalized their families' expectations and seldom had conflicts with their families about such expectations. "They seldom pressured their children in any way—because they didn't have to" (p. 392).

The scientists exhibited several commonalities on their paths through adolescence to careers in science:

1. They were good students in all subjects, and were as likely to take advanced English courses as advanced science courses. They were not at, but were near, the top of their high school classes. Most of them attended good academic comprehensive high schools, with classes that had hundreds of students. They were in the "honors" classes.

2. They had science projects at home, and were provided with materials, kits, and laboratory equipment if they wanted it. They may not have entered the science fairs, but they still had home experiences in the sciences. Several of them said they especially liked to read *Scientific American*, a magazine to which their families subscribed.

3. Their extracurricular activities were both more and less indicative of their future career choices. Most of them were heavily involved in a variety of extracurricular activities, in which they took leadership roles. Being president of the biology club and president of the student body were equally as common. Their major extracurricular activity in high school was athletics, and in college, they were involved in fraternities and student government. In college they realized that their athletic talent, while good enough for high school, left them "out of their depth" and they limited their athletic participation to intramurals.

Advanced Placement classes are often taken by academically talented students in high school.

4. They didn't generally remember particular science teachers in high school, but took the courses because they were expected to. The teachers they did remember were those, in whatever field, who were demanding and had high standards. One remembered a biology teacher who wouldn't give an "A" on laboratory notebooks and another remembered an English teacher who set high standards on the acquisition of standard English grammar, punctuation, and spelling.

5. All along they had scientific interests that were outside of school. As in other fields, their out-of-school interests were a significant indicator of their future direction.

Although they were considered "well rounded" in both high school and college, these future scientists knew what counted most. Their studies came first and partying and politicking second. All along the way, the personalities of their teachers were quite influential in helping them decide on ways to pursue science. One noted that if he had met a chemistry teacher who inspired him, he would have been just as likely to take more chemistry classes as biology classes.

How did they become researchers? Overwhelmingly, they found their first experiences with research "fun." One traced this interest to his high school years:

> A couple of years it was astronomy. So we got a cheap telescope and I got into that, and then I wanted to take pictures, so I rented a cheap camera . . . Then it would be, I got interested in microscope work. I would do things like that. Do them for a couple of years, intermixing with sports or other things . . . I was into growth hormones for awhile. Because I got into this in biology. So I started reading about it. And there was this plant hormone . . . that people were studying. So I sent away for the patent. I synthesized it and started putting it on plants and stuff. I used to enjoy stuff like that. It never went anywhere. I never discovered anything with it, but it was fun (Sosniak, 1985b, pp. 371–372).

Biographical Examples of Science Talent Development

Albert Einstein

Biographical information on specific scientists is also available. Einstein, for instance, in his high school (*Gymnasium*) and college years, had an unusually disrupted life, compared to other scientists. Born in 1879 in Ulm, Germany, his family moved to Munich when he was young, and he entered the Luitpold Gymnasium in Munich in 1889, where he attended school for six years. He resented the militaristic attitudes and the discipline, and his biographer Clark (1971) said the teachers there "had made him detest discipline; but . . . they had taught him the virtues of self-discipline, of concentration, of dedication to an ideal, of an attitude which can be described as firm or relentless" (p. 21). He pursued his goals with single-minded determination. At the *Gymnasium* he was not interested in studying the classics but was "increasingly able" in math, and was "precocious" in philosophy. His father's business failed again, and the family moved across the Alps to Milan, Italy, when Albert was 15. He was boarded out to a distant relative and exhorted to finish the course at the *Gymnasium* so that he could become an electrical engineer, the profession his father had chosen for him as being practical and likely to have employment for him. He stayed behind for six months and then went to Milan to join his family. Some stories say he was expelled from the *Gymnasium*; others say he had a nervous breakdown. Clark said, though, that it is likely that he was a brash, sarcastic, "precocious, half-cocksure" young man who "knew not merely which monkey wrench to throw in the works, but also how best to throw it" (p. 20).

This move halted his formal education, for there is no record of him attending school in Milan, although his sister and brother did. For the year and a half that he later called the happiest of his life, he was in Italy, first in Milan and then when his father's business failed again, in Pavia. He traveled on his own and enjoyed Italian culture. The "precariousness" of the family's financial life made it necessary that he begin to prepare for a career. His father was adamant. Forget this philosophical "nonsense" and get a degree in something practical, Albert was told. He had no *Gymnasium* certificate, and thus could not enter a university. Then his father heard of the Swiss Federal Polytechnic Institute in Zurich, Switzerland. A *Gymnasium* certificate was not necessary. Albert had a letter from a teacher at the *Gymnasium* asserting that he was very talented in mathematics. He also presented a paper that he had written when he was 16. It was called "Concerning the Investigation State of Aether in Magnetic Fields" and it was later called a "pointer" for his future direction in theoretical physics. "At the age of sixteen Einstein had discovered a paradox by considering what would happen if one could follow a beam of light at the speed of light—the result being 'a spatially oscillatory electromagnetic field at rest'" (Clark, 1971, pp. 22–23). He applied to the Swiss Federal Polytechnic Institute in the fall of 1895. He was 16 and a half years old, two years younger than most university entrants. They let him take the entrance examinations, and he passed in mathematics but failed in knowledge of zoology, botany, and modern languages.

His father made arrangements for him to attend a boarding school at Aurau, Switzerland, to try to eliminate his deficiencies. This school was a favorite of his, run by a kindly, avid ornithologist who took the students on long mountain hikes, and who had a different classroom in his home for every subject, so that the materials could stay and the experiments didn't have to be taken down. Fellow students later described Einstein as being arrogant and prickly, "sure of himself," with "a restless spirit," a young man of whom it was said, "nothing escaped the sharp gaze of his bright brown eyes. Whoever approached him immediately came under the spell of his superior personality. A sarcastic curl of his rather full mouth . . . did not encourage the Philistines to fraternize with him" (p. 26). In fact, Clark theorized that if he had not had the intense scientific interest in the mystery of the universe that he had developed, he might have become a "model iconoclast."

Einstein liked Switzerland so much that he renounced his German citizenship in 1896, at the age of 17, and applied for Swiss citizenship, which was not granted until 1901. He passed his examinations in 1896 and began a four-year course of study that was aimed to "qualify him for a post on the lowest rung of the professional teacher's ladder" (p. 29). He took lodging at several boarding houses; he ate frugally; he took weekend trips to hike in the mountains or to sail on the lake; he visited his family; he played the violin at musical evenings with friends. His life during this time was typical of Zurich student life. He was studying to be a teacher of mathematical physics, and studied such subjects as differential calculus and definite integral theory. He took electives in gnomic projection and exterior ballistics, as well as anthropology and mountain geology, banking and business, and philosophy, with a special emphasis on the philosophy of Goethe.

However, he was drawn to the natural sciences more than mathematics, to physics more than geology. He liked laboratory work and said later that he was "fascinated by the direct contact of the experience." He liked theoretical physics best. Einstein was studying physics at precisely the time in the history of science "when physics was about to be revolutionized but when few students were encouraged to be revolutionaries. Without his own basic dissenting spirit he would have got nowhere" (Clark, 1971, p. 36). He did just enough to get by in his formal course work, and in his private life, in his private studies, he did his real work. He didn't like the traditional and conforming approaches of his physics professors and began to intensely read and study on his own. He studied people considered to be scientific revolutionaries such as Kirchhoff, Helmholtz, Hertz, Maxwell, Mach, and the mathematician Poincaré. These he later acknowledged to be major influences. He became known to his professors as a student who might never graduate, a student who was "a great deal of trouble."

He hated examinations so much that after taking one he later said that he could not have a decent scientific thought for at least a year. But he did graduate in 1900, and his reputation for being difficult preceded him. He was not offered a beginning post as a teacher at the school, as others of his class were. He wrote to a friend that he felt "suddenly abandoned by everyone, standing at a loss on the threshold of life" (p. 40). He went back to his parents' home in Milan, and began to write letters looking for employment. He had no offers. He presented himself for the required three months of military service in Switzerland, and was rejected for flat feet and varicose veins. "Shocked and distressed," he began to try to publish so that he would have a better chance for a job offer.

Einstein's adolescent and college years showed little to indicate his future genius, except for the personality traits of stubbornness, arrogance, and curiosity and dedication to scientific ideas. The fact that he was productive, that he was writing scientific papers is also significant. Also, his deficits in standard subjects and his precocity in subjects in which he was interested also seem to be indicative of his future path.

Holland in 1961 published a study of high achievers who had achieved National Merit Scholarships. Although this was a very restricted sample, he attempted to differentiate within that sample between students who would be adult creative producers and those who were merely high academic achievers. He asked the students for information on their products on a "Creative Science Scale":

Holland's Creative Science Scale

1. Gave an original paper at a scientific meeting sponsored by a professional society
2. Won a prize or award in a scientific talent search
3. Constructed scientific apparatus on own initiative
4. Invented a patentable device
5. Had scientific paper published in a science journal

Although Einstein was attending college 60 years before Holland's scale was derived, one can see that Einstein may not have been picked out as having potential science talent, because of the public nature of four of the achievements listed above. Einstein had written an original paper but it was not published. He had made his own scientific apparatus, but had seriously injured a hand doing so, in a typical act of rebellion against authority—while tearing up an order that told him to do it one way and not another. The existence of such scales as Holland's points to the necessity for looking at the behavior and interests of the youth who will be a scientist as there are often clues in the youthful and college behaviors of such youth that they will become scientists.

Subotnik and Steiner (1994) have conducted longitudinal research on 94 students who were winners in the prestigious Westinghouse Science Talent Search in 1983. Each year 300 high school students are named as semifinalists, based on a technical paper about a science or mathematics project. Most of them finished college, but 35 percent of them had not pursued science or mathematics majors. Those who made other choices cited four basic reasons: (1) they had experienced science instruction that was not exciting; (2) they had developed interests in other fields; (3) they did not find the scientist's lifestyle appealing; and (4) they realized they had been channeled into science by teachers or parents when they really didn't want to be scientists. One person said:

> I came into MIT with the desire to win the Nobel prize in chemistry, become a prof at MIT, Cal Tech, Harvard, or Stanford, and do this real pioneering fundamental chemical research. . . . I started looking at what interests I had not pursued for years and years. The scientists that I saw that were successful did not have these interests. They were not interesting people. I was beginning to find scientists really dull and selfish in the sense of individual responsibility (Subotnik & Steiner, 1994, p. 11)

There were no gender differences between those who chose to continue in science and those who did not, although the females were more "wistful" in describing their experiences in science, and viewed the mentors they had as more important than did the males.

Mentors are crucial in the development of a science career. They perform four functions for their mentees: (1) being role models; (2) being someone with whom to speak intellectually about issues related to science; (3) being emotional supports; and (4) being able to provide the student with contacts in the field. Low salaries for science researchers, the necessity to understand how to function as a political animal in a science department, and the necessity to seek grants constantly to fund research were reasons not to pursue science. Subotnik and Steiner said that their longitudinal research highlighted "the unfortunate picture" of the state of the development of science talent in the United States. Even the most talented science students seem to suffer from institutional neglect in college. And then when or if they did graduate with their Ph.D.s, there were no jobs to support them as the funding of basic research had almost dried up.

Women in Science

One of the challenges in the fields of science and mathematics is the challenge of bringing women into the field. Both fields are essentially populated by men. The National Association for Women in Science and Mathematics has published many brochures, pamphlets, and studies about this challenge. Many of these focus on the necessity for mentoring for high school, college, and adult women scientists.

Barbara McClintock

The Nobel prize-winning U.S.-born plant geneticist Barbara McClintock was born at the turn of the century to a family that valued learning. Her father was a physician and her mother an independent thinker. From an early age she developed in herself what she called, "a capacity to be alone" (Keller, 1983, p. 20). The third child in a family with four children, Barbara and her siblings were encouraged to explore and to take chances. Barbara herself was known as a good athlete in the neighborhood. Once, when the boys in a nearby neighborhood wouldn't let her play in a baseball tournament, the other team arrived with one member short, and she helped the rivals win.

She was closer to her father and her uncle than to her mother. Keller (1983) said, "Throughout adolescence it became increasingly clear that she was committed to 'the kinds of things that girls were not supposed to do.' The passion for sports gave way to the passion for knowledge" (pp. 25–26). She loved facts, information, knowing things. At Erasmus Hall High School in Brooklyn, she became very interested in science. McClintock said, "I would solve some of the problems in ways that weren't the answers the instructor expected . . . I would ask the instructor, 'Please let me . . . see if I can't find the standard answer' and I'd find it. It was a tremendous joy, the whole process of finding that answer, just pure joy" (p. 26).

Barbara graduated from high school and went on to Cornell University, which in 1919 had the reputation of being hospitable to women who wanted to go to college. She enrolled in the College of Agriculture, which had free tuition. She also was interested in a lot of other things, and she had trouble focusing. She would sign up for a class that interested her, and if it didn't fulfill its promise, she would stop going, and collect a Z grade.

She became interested in genetics during her junior year, and started focusing on plant breeding. She decided to major in the subject. Her career path was not similar to those of male scientists. Instead, Keller (1983) said, "at the end of a particularly exciting course (in genetics), her own interests in the subject were further encouraged by a special invitation from the professor to take the graduate course in genetics" (p. 35). The plant breeding department didn't admit women to the graduate program, so she registered as a graduate student in the botany department, and audited courses in plant genetics. Keller said that the personality characteristics that were predictive of her single-mindedness in trying to get a graduate degree in plant genetics were apparent even early on: "As a child McClintock had a striking capacity for autonomy, self-determination, and total absorption. But what was truly exceptional was the extent to which she maintained her childlike capacity for absorption throughout her adult life" (p. 36).

Evelyn Fox Keller

The theoretical physicist and historian/philosopher of science, Evelyn Fox Keller, in speaking with journalist Bill Moyers in 1990, believed that science itself is propelled by the masculine, by ideas of masculinity: "The central metaphor for the scientific revolution was a marriage between the mind and nature that was modeled on a particular kind of marriage, a patriarchal marriage, the purpose of which was the domination of nature" (p. 74). She traced the history of thinking objectively and of excluding feeling and emotion to the growth of the scientific revolution. The effect, in the history of science, was to exclude women: "The domain of science was restricted to men, and to a particular world of men, and the development of science was deprived of a pool of talent. It also meant the exclusion of certain kinds of talent in the men who did not become scientists" (p. 75).

Keller first got interested in science when she was assigned a paper for a composition class, and she read George Gamow's books: "I fell in love with physics. I fell in love with the life of the mind." Keller said that she still finds physics a "deeply satisfying inquiry into reality." She said, however, "my career in physics was thwarted by my being a woman":

> I was a graduate student in physics at Harvard in 1959, and that was extremely painful—in effect, it was impossible. I was one of three women in a class of a hundred. I could not get my professors to speak to me. I was scrutinized, laughed at, and humiliated. I came with a reputation of being very smart and so I was an object of enormous curiosity. It was terrible. And very lonely. I couldn't take it. I did actually get my degree in theoretical physics, but only after leaving the actual premises to do my dissertation on molecular biology. (Moyers, 1990, p. 80)

Keller has gone on to a career in an interdisciplinary field—a joint appointment in women's studies and the history of science at the University of California-Berkeley.

Tales of humiliation and discouragement were also told by a woman who went to college to study geological engineering in the 1960s. Now a teacher of the academically talented, Ruth Huber's story is told in the Case Example at the end of Chapter 8.

MATHEMATICS TALENT DEVELOPMENT

The development of mathematical talent is also at a critical state in the United States, with most Ph.D.s in mathematics going to students who are foreign-born. Useem (1992) cited studies that seem to show that one of the reasons is the rigid and early practice of ability grouping for mathematics in schools. When schools group for mathematics too early, only including students who are early achievers, the "late bloomers" or those who have not realized their potential because of early environmental or genetic influences will never receive mathematics at a challenging enough level.

The key course for mathematics achievement is calculus. Calculus is the gatekeeper, or flunk-out course, in many programs in mathematics in higher education and in engineering. Useem (1992) thought that taking calculus from high school teachers seems to provide a better educational experience:

> The high school classes are usually smaller and more personal, the teachers assigned to them are often the best in the department, the classes meet more frequently than college classes, material is explained in more detail, and the teachers are more available to students for extra help. College classes, especially those in large universities, tend to be larger, less student centered, and often taught by foreign-born graduate students or professors whose English is more limited. While teaching calculus is viewed as an attractive opportunity for high school teachers, college professors shy away from teaching such an introductory level course. (p. 329)

Students who take calculus in high school are also more likely to pass calculus in college. Having taken calculus in high school signals to admissions officers that a student is "a member of the academic elite" (p. 329).

Useem found a startling array of policies that admitted students to the fast track in mathematics, eighth grade algebra culminating with twelfth grade calculus, the recommended path for achievement in mathematics. Students were found overwhelmingly to come from homes with parents who had college educations. This sorted out students from working class and lower socioeconomic backgrounds, providing a "class" distinction among mathematics achievers and those who were relegated to taking regular classes. The beliefs of the mathematics administrators were a major factor as well. If a mathematics administrator believed that mathematics talent arises early and is "just there," and a student can be placed by seventh grade into a track that will lead to Advanced Placement (AP) calculus senior year in high school, that is what happened in the school district. If the mathematics administrator believed that late bloomers and others should be included in the track to calculus, the courses were opened up to many more students than the top 5–6 percent. One such administrator said:

> It is better to have more kids in the middle grade accelerated math because once they are cut out, it is extremely hard to get back in . . . Many are late bloomers . . . They are bright but are not ready at that time but are ready two years later and you have cast a lifetime sentence on them. Some baseball players make the major leagues who never made little league . . . It is easier to have homogeneous grouping and restrict the numbers in eighth grade algebra but the harm that that does to the other 20–30 percent is unforgivable philosophically. (Useem, 1992, p. 340)

Useem noted that the department chairs and coordinators were not likely to lose their jobs or move jobs, and so their beliefs affected district policy "indefinitely."

The policies for grouping students in mathematics were so varied as to beg serious intervention from higher administrators or parents. But rarely did they notice or complain. Some districts had quota systems; only a certain number of students could get into eighth grade algebra and the rest, no matter what their achievement, had to be in other classes. Others chose students as early as second grade based on reading scores or IQ tests. Others only permitted students who had been in pullout programs in elementary school to be in advanced mathematics. Others did not permit students who moved into the district to participate in advanced courses. Useem (1992) said that these districts used "factors other than students' prior mathematics achievement level" in placement. These tended to be lower socioeconomic districts, where parents were not likely to raise a furor, but believed that the school knew what it was doing. In more affluent districts, there were also variations.

Perhaps educators of the academically talented should look at how early they are sorting children and should consider the consequences of such sorting. The widely published and well-researched Study of Mathematically Precocious Youth (SMPY) and its Talent Search has the goal of sorting children in seventh grade to identify those with extreme mathematical talent. Those with less extreme talent also have potential, as Benbow (1992) was careful to note. But early experience and identification mean something, for Swiatek and Benbow (1991) found that "students who participated in fast-paced mathematics classes . . . were most likely to be in math/science career tracks ten years after the classes were conducted. Their subsequent achievement in high school and college also tended to be higher" (in Benbow, 1992, p. 116).

Feldhusen, Hoover, and Sayler (1990), in the Purdue Academic Rating Scale: Mathematics, noted 15 behaviors that are common in students with mathematical talent (Figure 7.2). Perhaps a rating scale such as this could be used along with standardized test data to broaden the pool of those with mathematical talent.

Figure 7.2 Purdue Academic Rating Scale: Mathematics

Student: _____

Grade: _____ Date: _____

Teacher: _____ School: _____

Read each item and rate the student according to this scale:

1 Rarely, seldom, or never   3 Quite often or frequently
3 Occasionally, sometimes   4 Always or almost always
DK Don't know or have never observed

_____ 1. Generalizes mathematical relationships, relates concepts in various applications
_____ 2. Organizes data to discover patterns or relationships
_____ 3. Persistent in learning math, concentrates, works hard, motivated, interested
_____ 4. Analyzes problems carefully, considers alternatives, does not necessarily accept first answer
_____ 5. Resourceful in seeking ways to solve a problem
_____ 6. Interested in numbers and quantitative relationships, sees usefulness or applications of mathematics
_____ 7. Learns math concepts and processes faster than other students
_____ 8. Good at verbalizing math concepts, processes, and solutions
_____ 9. Identifies and restates problems, good at formulating hypotheses
_____ 10. Reasons effectively
_____ 11. Enjoys trying to solve difficult problems, like puzzles and logic problems
_____ 12. Visualizes spatially, can create visual images of problems
_____ 13. Develops unique associations, uses original methods for solutions
_____ 14. Sometimes solves problems intuitively, then cannot always explain why the solution is correct
_____ 15. Recalls relevant information or concepts in solving problems, recognizes the critical elements

Used with the permission of John Feldhusen.

Gustin (1985) described the middle years of exceptional research mathematicians. In high school they began to focus on mathematics rather than on science, finding mathematics intrinsically more interesting, although almost all of them were like the young scientists in Sosniak's study; they did science experiments and projects on their own, at home. One said:

There was a formula for determining the trajectory of a rocket and the range. It is a trigonometric formula with the sine 2x, and I wanted to let x be equal to 75 degrees. So that means that you have to compute the sine of 150 degrees. Well, the tables only go up to 90 degrees, and I didn't know how to compute. So I had to look at my brother's trigonometry book and I decided then that the mathematics was more interesting than the physics. (Gustin, 1985, p. 299)

The mathematically talented were more interested in physical science than biological science, and they also had a pattern of reading ahead in their mathematics books and reading more advanced mathematics books on their own. They liked to work alone, not in groups, and they learned to be independent learners through their curiosity about what comes next in math. Gustin (1985) said, "Nothing that went on in school was more interesting than what they were learning on their own" (p. 302). One said that he slept through math because his school believed in heterogeneous grouping and the pace was that of the slowest student. Most of them were recognized as having mathematics talent and were on math teams, participated in the Westinghouse Science Talent Search, and attended special summer programs. These activities were important, because math became special, and "by excelling in contests and fairs the mathematicians discovered the excitement of doing something well and being recognized for it" (p. 308).

Most of these young mathematicians were accelerated. They chose their colleges not for their mathematics departments but for other reasons, for example, "Everyone in our family goes there." In college, they experienced the typical path of talent development. They looked to their mathematics professors as role models. They formed informal groups with like-minded mathematics majors to discuss problems. They began to plan to go to graduate school. Gustin (1985) quoted one mathematician speaking of his passion for mathematics:

> First of all, I was fascinated by it. It's just beautiful. I liked it. I liked the order, here was something unquestioned. It had worth, you couldn't argue about it. Everything else you could. There was just endless debate about this or that. But here there were no two ways about it. I remember thinking this stuff has worth. And that was it.
>
> You have to have the sensation that you want to know . . . You do it because it's fun. You have a good time. But you cannot make yourself work hard enough to do a really hard problem unless you want to know why it works.
>
> I can tell you quite frankly when I first decided I'd stop playing and really work at mathematics. I was about second or third year in college. I'd been playing at it. I'd learned. I'd read and all this, but that's play, that's passive. And then I did nothing else but mathematics for many, many, many years. It's impossible. I don't know anybody who does first class mathematics who doesn't work all the time. Your world becomes very small. (p. 321)

As mentioned before, mathematicians sort themselves out from scientists by their aesthetic feelings and respect for the beauty of mathematics and for the intrinsic joy they find in doing mathematics.

VERBAL TALENT DEVELOPMENT

People with verbal ability have less sculpted paths than do those with science and math talent. People with verbal abilities are both writers and speakers. Some are good at both; others are good at one or the other. The professions that require verbal ability are fewer than those that require spatial ability, for example. Professions that primarily require verbal ability are writer, preacher, teacher, actor, politician, lawyer, therapist, public speaker, and the like. Professions that require spatial or figural ability are most physical labor professions and occupations, several thousand of which are listed in the U.S. *Directory of Occupational Titles*. These range from hairdresser to mechanic. Yet verbal ability is what is tested on tests and valued in school. The great value placed on verbal ability is necessary, because verbal ability can contribute to success in all careers and professions.

Writers were often early readers and voracious readers; they had often experienced childhood trauma and were prone to depression, even in adolescence; they used their writing ability to escape; and they used writing and reading to express their emotions. They also had high conceptual and verbal intelligence on tests, and on personality inventories they showed themselves to be similar to other creative people, except for their tendency for depression. Verbal ability is enhanced through study, especially study of literature, history, philosophy, and the humanities. Many people with strong verbal ability go into professions that require incisive and critical minds honed by discussion and training in academic fields (Piirto, 1991a, 1992a/1998, 1995c, 1995d).

Schools need to provide advanced work in literature and in the humanities to students with strong verbal ability. This work should include expository writing and criticism, analysis of literary form, study of foreign languages, and in-depth work in multicultural areas. The exclusive study of what some have called D.W.M. (Dead White Male) has given way to new curricula and to the resuscitation and discovery of works by women, minorities, and other-than-Western thinkers. This academic consideration of expressions of multicultural verbal talent has become commonplace in all current textbooks in the United States. The social studies—economics, political science, history, sociology, anthropology, psychology, education—domains that deal with the study of people and how they live together, also require strong verbal ability.

Feldhusen, Hoover, and Sayler (1990) called verbal ability "English" and "Foreign Languages" and constructed two scales to help in finding these students. However, their social studies scale also contains verbal items, as do their science, mathematics, business and office, home economics, vocational agriculture, and trade and mechanics scales in the Purdue Academic Rating Scales. This indicates that verbal ability is a necessary indication of talent in many areas. Two typical questions that appear on all or most of these scales are "Asks appropriate or insightful questions to clarify a task or project" and "Is able to present ideas about a project clearly and effectively." To do both these tasks requires verbal ability.

Besides clear ability in verbal areas, those who become writers and critics in literary areas display the requisite passion for literature, and they choose friends who have similar passions. The friendships of Allen Ginsberg, Jack Kerouac, Neal Cassady, and other writers who would come to be called "Beat" led them to much discussion and reading of their own and other contemporary writers' work. Eileen Simpson detailed the college friendships and later relationships of other writers in the 1950s in her memoir called *Poets in Their Youth* (1982). The importance of friendships among talented people with like minds cannot be dismissed. These people became friends because they were passionately and emotionally involved in the same pursuits. They had common ground and became friends because of their common interests. In fact, one non-negotiable requirement in the development of programs for the talented should be that students of like minds and interests should have an opportunity to be together.

Biographical evidence throughout the ages indicates the importance of shared passion with like-minded friends. The banding together of young verbally talented youth to publish underground newspapers that shock their elders; the existence of coffee houses for poetry readings and literary discussion; the proliferation of small presses to publish each others' work; the sharing of good books and the worshipful admiration of literary mentors; the attending of writers' conferences and the almost messianic attention to certain books and writers among the young verbally talented students attest to the importance of interest—indeed, passion—in the written or spoken word.

Few verbally talented students do become writers, however. The function of education in verbal areas is also—perhaps, primarily—to produce connoisseurs, people who enjoy and appreciate the written word and who can evaluate arguments, see logic, and appreciate the aesthetics. These people often become academics, teachers, professors, critics. Their function is to keep the flame of quality strong and clear. Many people who study for Ph.D.s in literature, history, sociology, philosophy, theater, and other fields in the humanities and social studies are those who have great talent in criticism, judgment, and objective viewing of texts. These talents were honed by specific training in the disciplines, by wide and voracious reading, and by a deep interest in and passion for their fields of study. Policy analysts, lawyers, political scientists, advisers to politicians, and politicians themselves also have verbal talents that are nurtured through close study of text and thought. The aspects of critical thinking that are taught in high school and college are equally as important for verbally talented as for other talented youth, because being able to decide on the validity of an argument affects citizenship. The ability to judge propaganda, to use logic, to critique arguments are all important curricular components necessary for all students, not only the talented. The talented are, however, better at such intellectual exercises and should be challenged.

EDUCATION OF PERFORMERS

The three paths described thus far, those of science, math, and verbal talent, rely on high academic ability and are the natural and just province of the public school. Students with exceptional ability in academic areas deserve education that emphasizes course taking, rigor, and a broad preparation for an unknown career. There are other talented students as well, and these are the ones who will be performers: musicians, actors, dancers, and athletes. James Sloan Allen (1992), the Vice President for Academic Affairs for the Juilliard School in Lincoln Center, New York City, made useful differentiations between those who are preparing for careers in fields in the traditional professions—doctor, lawyer, scientist, academician—and the education of those who are studying to be performers. He said that to educate artists is not an easy task. He differentiated between two types of artists—the creators and the performers:

> Creators, or "creative artists," are the writers, painters, sculptors, composers, choreographers and others who freely invent artworks. They, not performers, have inspired most theories of art, artists, and creativity; for they have license to see the previously unseeable, hear the hitherto unhearable, imagine the heretofore unimaginable, and they have the magical talent to lend these artistic form. There is much to be learned from creators, but there is not much to teach them, save "background" knowledge and a certain facility of execution (no mean task).
>
> Performers, or "recreative artists" as they sometimes label themselves, share with creative artists the gift of an unteachable talent for artistic expression, and like all artists, they are afflicted with ambivalence over displaying that talent in public, relishing acclaim, apprehensive of rejection. Yet creative artists retain the prerogative of privacy (they may be nowhere in evidence when their artworks appear). Performing artists, on the other hand, live constantly under the critical eyes of teachers, critics, audiences, and peers, who tend to equate performers with performance. (p. 200)

Mainstream educators of the talented are often required to identify performers but they leave their training up to experts in the domains of creative performance. One main difference between performing artists and creative artists is that "whatever their innate talent, most performers . . . depend equally on teachable skills" (Allen, 1992, p. 200). Schools for the performing arts owe their existence to this need for expert training. There is a distance between the composer and the choreographer, the playwright or screenwriter and the actor, and that distance is marked by the necessity for performers such as actors and dancers to combine bodily intelligence and emotional intelligence. Allen commented on the necessity in all performers to have physical dexterity and extreme discipline:

> Performing artists must make the fingers move with flawless precision, the voice perfectly hit the note, the body move fluidly, the limbs fly, breathing come at will, tear ducts submit to command. And their polished performances can be astonishing; the pianist whose hands race across the keyboard capturing every harmonic nuance and never missing a note; the dancer who spins blindly *en pointe*, then soars as if suspended in air to land on a dime; the actor who dissolves the stage and enfolds the audience in a drama of verisimilitude; the singer who holds F above high C until the house comes down. So demanding are the physical expectations of performance as to remove performers from the guild of artists and send them into the ranks of athletes. (p. 201)

Allen (1992) compared performers and athletes. Both need original endowments of great physical talent and they depend on health professionals to keep them in physical shape for their performances. Both athletes and artists "play," "train," "exercise," "drill," "practice," "compete," and study with "coaches." Both are called "players." Both have mentors who exert phenomenal influence on them. Both must be able to work with groups and must understand teamwork: "However intensely performers study individually, they usually consummate their artistry collectively, in ensembles—the true solo is a rarity" (p. 201). Both athletes and performers show their mettle in competitive situations. Performing in competitions is their reason for being—the performance. "A performance is a test of capacities between what the creator has created and what the performer can perform," Allen said (p. 202).

Performers must also have good memories. This is not required of creators to the degree that it is required of performers. Creators might have good long-term memory for digits or words, but performers have what is called *active memory*. While memorizing has lost its emphasis in most of education, performers must know how to memorize, for "who but a performer has to memorize anything like the score of a symphony or a concerto, the choreography of a ballet, or the role of Hamlet?" (Allen, 1992, p. 202). The performer begins with the work, and the license to embellish or to improvise is a limited license, because the original work is always there, and straying too far from it negates it: "Although a performer can stamp a work with an individual performance style and surprise a creator with performing insights, the work is almost always there, waiting to be learned and performed" (p. 203).

To put the work into active memory, the performer must practice, in order to acquire automaticity. Arduous practice and rehearsal are required. Intense concentration is required. Musicians respond intuitively to sounds, actors to emotional innuendo, dancers to spatial patterns. They may thus become preoccupied with the "how to," with the practicality of technique, and may become quite narrow in their orientation to the world. That is the challenge of the educator of performers.

Development of Musicians

Kogan, in her 1987 discussion of the life of students at the Juilliard School, described the intense competition among students—for teachers, for practice rooms, for recognition, for auditions, for places in performing groups. She described the intense relationships between teachers and their students: "The teachers seem godlike. Some of them are world-famous performers and others are world-famous teachers. Some are pure inspiration, and others are consummate trainers . . . . The student never forgets that he is the apprentice at the feet of the master" (p. 85). The student is regarded as a "vessel," a "puppet," a "lump of clay," an "apostle."

Allen (1992) also said that the critics and the scholars also view the performers as "vessels," the vessels of the creative artists. The young performing artists often view the critics and the scholars as beside the point. They admire performance, not blather about performance. Allen (1992) said that these performing artists are different from adolescents at the liberal arts college in degree—degree of "artistic talent, strength of their self-discipline, and the clarity of their professional concentration" (p. 205). They may be brilliant intellectually, but the true "gyroscope of their existence" is how they can get better at their performance. They can be accused of vocationalism, for they ask of any abstract idea, "What good is that?" "How can that help my performance?" The result of the self-discipline and passion for performance is the product of the role, and the presence of constant practice, which is "the key element in all considerations of the creative product."

Teachers in general education at such special schools for performers often must justify and relate the material being taught so that the performance students will see a reason to learn it, to remember it, to fill their memories with it instead of the work they are learning to perform. Many students of the performing arts don't want to take the liberal arts classes unless they can see a clear reason that relates to learning their craft. Teachers of such classes must rely on teaching techniques—pedagogical expertise—in order to keep their talented youth learning. Performers are themselves training to become educators—educators of sense, emotion, imagination, and intuition—the great values of the arts. The challenge of teaching performers is to help them see the value of learning, of getting "these unapologetically vocationally minded students to read, discuss, and comprehend challenging books in reference to lived experience" (Allen, 1992, p. 208).

The path of music talent development has three stages. The middle stage, as described by Sosniak (1985a), is characterized by a concentration of effort in the direction of developing the musical talent and "for closing the doors to most alternatives" (p. 57). The family often assists in this concentrated effort, sometimes to the point of moving closer to a desired mentor/teacher/coach. Practicing and learning the profession is "equivalent to a half-time job. For some it was much closer to a full-time job" Sosniak said (p. 57). Peers are found with whom it is possible to talk, play, and live the music. Gary Graffman described his high school friends in his book, *I Really Should Be Practicing* (1981):

> Gradually, though, I began to spend more time with another gang, in some ways rougher and tougher than the Hornets [his childhood friends]. They were my fellow piano students, and instead of stickball we played our current repertoire for each other. The rules of this game involved criticism with no holds barred. . . . So we met often for marathon playing sessions at which we requested and received the uninhibited comments of our peers . . . Many evenings we met at my apartment and played far into the night. When our solo repertoire was exhausted, we read four-hand music of all description . . . Some nights . . . we would pile into the subway and emerge in Greenwich Village, establishing ourselves at an informal nightclub called the Salle de Champagne, which had a good piano. There . . . we would continue our performances and discussions, giving not only ourselves but innocent paying customers insights into the various interpretive possibilities of Brahms' *Variations and Fugue on a Theme by Handel.* (pp. 55–57)

Such passionate interest in the domain is common in all creative lives during adolescence and into college. Margaret Mead and her college friends at Barnard called themselves the Ash Can Cats, and they passionately argued, read, and hung about together, supporting each other in their intellectual interests all their lives. When Mead was in American Samoa on her pioneering anthropological study of adolescence among the Samoans, she would receive, periodically, hundreds of letters from her friends at one time, and she would spread them about the narrow bed she slept in and savor them slowly (Howard, 1984).

Development of Dancers

Barron (1972) studied 32 dance students at a dance school. Twenty-seven of them planned to dance professionally. They had already experienced years of rigorous professional training, had "made the cut" so to speak, in being encouraged to continue to study dance and to fulfill their aspirations. They were flexible, spontaneous, and had what Barron called "a lot of steam" (p. 111). They had high standards for themselves and their work, and expected their teachers to set such standards. The most respected teachers were those who had solid knowledge and background in dance, teachers who loved teaching and the dance, teachers who were interested in the students and who interacted with them, but who were still very strict, perfectionistic, and demanding.

A good dance class was, likewise, "demanding, arduous, and challenging" (p. 90), leaving the dancer with fatigue, exhilaration, and a sense of accomplishment from having a "thorough workout," increasing body strength and skill. Good dance students were those who were self-critical about their dance, students who were able to work hard, long, and with great perfectionistic demands on their abilities. Discipline was a trait that the dance students admired in each other.

When asked the question "Why dance?" the dancers expressed that dance gave them a feeling of joy and elation and an uplifting release of emotions. They liked that they could use their bodies for self-expression; that they had honed their bodies to such responsiveness that they could express complex emotions with small movements. They also liked to dance because their dancing gave pleasure to others: "Some students felt as though they were giving a gift to others; they liked to make people happy, to create beauty for others, and to please" (Barron, 1972, p. 94). Dance was closely connected with emotion: "whatever mood was experienced, it seemed to carry over into the dance, expressing, relieving, or changing the dancer's original state of mind, making dance more enjoyable" (p. 94).

Physical factors affected their dance; when they were tired or sick, their dancing was less resonant. The dancers said that their extensions were not as high, their limbs didn't respond to their minds, and they were more prone to injury, with a result that they experienced "an overall loss in creativity, bounce, and eagerness" in their dancing. Tension in their outside lives also affected their dance, and they often experienced "deficits in control and concentration" (Barron, 1972, p. 96). However, several of the dancers said that dancing even when fatigued or under tension created a release of these and a feeling of well-being after the dance class. Barron said that the young dancers were very intrinsically motivated and viewed dance as necessary for their very existence.

Dance students considered dance a form of art that helps society and helps the dancer to creative expression: "The purpose of art in general and dance in particular was to provide forms for the expression of universal principles of life, oneself, spirituality, that would allow the artist to share his [sic] experiences with others, enriching their lives as well as his own" (Barron, 1972, p. 110).

Gender differences in dancers revealed that the female dancers were open, generous, energetic, and quite excitable, while the male dancers were even more so: "he is much like his female counterpart, though more complicated, conflicted, and flamboyant" (Barron, 1972, p. 111). Male dancers were more "impulsive," more "show-off," and their humor sometimes had a "hostile quality," while their external behavior was "mischievous, rebellious, zany, frank, flirtatious, and pleasure-seeking." They were also good-looking. "Both male and female dancers were quite ambitious"; they both described themselves as "determined, ambitious, and capable," with a need to succeed.

Biographical Example of Talent in Dance

Autobiographical accounts by dancers are interesting evidence of the rigor necessary for achievement in dance. Gelsey Kirkland, who followed Suzanne Farrell as a lead ballerina for George Balanchine's New York City Ballet, began in 1969, at the age of 17, to be partnered by such dancers as Peter Martins, Mikhail Baryshnikov, Jacques D'Amboise, and Ivan Nagy. Like Farrell, Kirkland dropped out of high school in order to dance with Balanchine's company. She wrote her autobiography, *Dancing on My Grave*, in collaboration with her husband, Greg Lawrence, in 1986. In describing the influence of Balanchine's body standards on the development of ballet in America, Kirkland said that Balanchine insisted he "must see the bones":

> I was less than a hundred pounds even then. Mr. B. did not seem to consider beauty a quality that must develop from within the artist; rather, he was concerned with outward signs such as body weight. His emphasis was responsible in part for setting the style that has led to some of the current extremes of American ballet . . . He did not merely say, "Eat less." He said repeatedly, "Eat nothing."
>
> The physical line of a ballerina seemed to have been ordained. A thin body carried the most definition. A slender figure was supposed to be the prerequisite for movement . . . Mr. B's ideal proportions called for an almost skeletal frame, accentuating the collarbones and length of the neck. Defeminization was the overall result, with the frequent cessation of the menstrual cycle due to malnutrition and physical abuse. A fulsome pair of breasts seemed the only attribute with which a ballerina could assert her sexuality." (p. 56).

Kirkland said that she herself had silicone implanted in her breasts during her teenage years, and noted that the Balanchine standards "have been adopted by virtually every ballet company and school in America." Those who refuse to go along are more likely not to find employment as dancers or teachers. Kirkland said that a "concentration camp aesthetic" was emphasized, and said that many of the dancers she knew abused diet pills, went on "quack" diets, and became anorexic, bulimic, or both.

Another caution that Kirkland made to dancers was about the dangers of narcissism that came from staring at oneself in the dance studio mirror. During her early career, "the mirror was my nemesis, seductive to the point of addiction." In the mirror, she found "a double who exposed all of my flaws and pointed out all of my physical imperfections," a person incapable of meeting the "refined ideal of physical beauty" (p. 72):

> As a primary teaching tool for dance, the mirror fosters the delusion that beauty is only skin-deep, that truth is found only in the plasticity of movement. It seems preferable to imitate rather than to create. Imitation can be varied to create the impression of originality. There are endless possibilities for breaking the human mold into novel patterns. To be daring in dance no longer involves risk, virtuosity, and strength of conviction. The dancer can win approval for steps that require no real decision in creative or compositional terms." (p. 73)

Kirkland found that when she devalued the mirror and worked without it, she was able to get past the fascination with her image and to create more original steps and dances. She said, "Classical virtuosity is more than technique, line, proportion, and balance." The spectator and the dancer must come together, holding "a bird with a broken wing," and the bird is healed when the performer achieves "empathy through move-ment." This requires of the dancer "the most demanding kind of inspiration," the inspi-ration of love felt by both performer and audience (p. 72).

Development of Actors

Special high schools exist for the performing arts, in which acting is one of the specialties that students might emphasize. At LaGuardia High School for the Performing Arts in New York City, students who are emphasizing acting take such courses as makeup, pantomime, and movement, as well as traditional general education courses. College majors in theater are also common, with opportunities for partici-pation in all levels of acting performance. Sometimes a potential actor may have a choice between attending a large school where he might study with someone famous, or a small school where he might have a chance to perform in a large number of shows. Auditions for roles at large schools are highly competitive, and the student might make a choice to go a place where there is opportunity for many roles rather than the chance for a few bit parts.

Of course, the time comes when the actor graduates and the move must be made to a center where theater is practiced. This is usually an urban center, with Los Angeles and New York City being the two cities in the United States where actors gather. Chicago, Minneapolis, San Francisco, and Toronto are also lively theater centers for aspiring actors. Many actors continue taking lessons from drama coaches. The struggle to make a living is a real one in the young actor's world, and many of the good-looking waiters in New York City, if asked, are really struggling actors.

There are two major schools of thought about what the actor must learn in studying acting, the "Method" and the "English" styles of acting. Yet no matter which style one studies, the actor is both a performer—of someone else's words, and a creator— of a character who lives the playwright's words. Bates, in *The Way of the Actor* (1987), believed that actors must be both extroverts and introverts: "Actors are required to be absorbed in self-understanding and simultaneously, yet paradoxi-cally, oriented toward the outer world, social stimulation, audiences, both to a greater degree than almost any other group of people" (p. 54). Actors have had reputations as being unstable, but Bates quoted Lynn Redgrave, who said that actors have to be incredibly emotionally stable, but the employment patterns of the profession are so unpredictable that insecurity is quite common. At any one time, about 90 percent of actors are unemployed, and while "sudden and frequent unemployment is endemic to the actor," the nature of the unemployment is also frightening, for "when actors do go to work, to audition or be interviewed for a role, it is a more stressful experience than most job applications because the work is so indivisible from the person" (p. 57).

Bruce Dern was quoted as saying, "Obtaining work and being rewarded for it has much more to do with being in the right place, at the right time, with the right contacts, than it does with talent" (Bates, 1987, p. 57). Why some actors make it and some actors don't is a matter of marketing and not of training. The tacit knowledge of how to get along in the acting profession is not taught in the acting classes to aspiring actors. Many actors thus feel a lack of control over their lives when they enter the profession. "The extremely high-risk, freelance nature of the work is something few people could survive happily" (p. 58). A safety move would be to become active in regional theater, or community theater, or return to school and try to enter a university theater community.

Development of Athletes

Athletes are not generally included in talent development education thinking. One reason is that athletics are well supported by school systems. Teams of athletes get special uniforms, coaches, facilities, buses, and can compete at the levels at which they will be challenged. The community comes out to cheer them on. The boosters raise money and elect school board members based on their support of the teams. The schools have "spirit." That athletes are respected talents is not in doubt. However, athletes, especially those with talents in areas that are not necessarily well supported by the school system, deserve the best that the school, home, and community, gender, and chance can give. Athletes are as much performers as are the actors and musicians. What is the dramatic spike of the ball in the end zone; what is hanging on to the rim of the basket just for a millisecond? Performing for the crowd.

Personalities of dancers and athletes are similar in that they like the concrete, the physical, the hands-on rather than the abstract. Athletes also may suffer permanent injury from sports played while in school, just like dancers. The reason that personality difficulties in athletes may not be as well known as those in writers or actors may have to do with a halo effect. Anderson, Denson, Brewer, and Van Raalte (1994) indicated in a study of personality and mood disorders among athletes that their aberrations are often tolerated by the public and by their institutions because they are so talented. If they come to practice late, they are barely chastised. If they get into trouble with the law, fines are paid. The two most common personality disorders among athletes are narcissism, a state of excessive self-admiration, and antisocial personality disorder. In the latter disorder, the athlete has a history of behavior that violates the rights of others. Of the antisocial athlete, the authors described a typical case:

> A male football athlete has been arrested for vandalizing another athlete's car. The incident occurred in a parking lot at a local tavern and seemed connected to an argument over a female. There were several witnesses and an arrest occurred soon after the incident. The athlete had been drinking. This is not the first time the athlete has blown up. He once threw his roommate's tape deck out a fifth floor window because he did not like the rap music. There is also a long history of scrapes with the law such as petty larceny and drug possession while in high school. Hot-tempered incidents in the locker room have occurred and there are hints of continued substance use. Again, as with the narcissist, he is gifted and tolerated . . . At the hearing, the victim agrees not to press charges if the athlete agrees to pay for all the damages.

Athletes usually "underutilize mental health services" because they don't want to admit weakness and want to maintain autonomy. They fear being teased and ridiculed by teammates.

Several studies have shown that male and female athletes at elite levels (on national teams) are remarkably similar in personality. They have high achievement motivation, high tolerance for pain, are highly competitive, and are able to train with great intensity.

A study by Anshel and Porter (1996) of elite Australian swimmers indicated that there were more similarities than differences between genders. While the males were more willing to sacrifice their recreation time to practice, especially after a disappointing performance, the females also trained extremely hard. Wittig and Shurr (1994) said, "successful female athletes tend to be more assertive, dominant, self-sufficient, independent, aggressive, and achievement oriented and to have average to low emotionality " (p. 324). They resemble the average successful male athlete. Sex role orientations among female athletes showed higher femininity scores for females who performed in individual sports, and more androgyny in females who performed in team sports. Male athletes showed no differences between team and individual sports.

The androgyny may come with some cost. Wildenhaus (1996) indicated "the recognition and development of athletic ability in females may be hampered by the role conflicts that young girls experience with regard to sport" (p. 339). He also indicated that homophobia in the society at large may operate against athleticism in women: "women's athletics is held hostage to fears of lesbianism" (p. 340). Like male dancers, female athletes must operate against the stereotypical gender expectations of the society at large and this may hamper the development of their talents.

VISUAL ARTS DEVELOPMENT

Visual artists also exhibit passion. Georgia O'Keeffe and her fellow students at the Art Students League often went together to see the latest galleries and shows, and this is how she met Alfred Stieglitz, her future husband, when she was 20 and he was 44. When she came back to New York several years later to study to be a fine arts teacher with Alon Bement at Teachers College, she and her friends continued to be avidly interested in art. In the 1989 biography, *Georgia O'Keeffe: A Life*, Robinson said:

> Outside Teachers College, Georgia plunged into the absorbing and stimulating New York art world. Not only the new art: Arthur Dow had traveled on a painting exhibition to the Far West, and his paintings of the Grand Canyon were shown at the Montross Gallery in 1914; both Anita [O'Keeffe's friend, Anita Pollitzer] and Georgia saw them. That year, "291" showed the works of Constantin Brancusi and Francis Picabia, and in December and January, Georgia made trips to the gallery to see the drawings by Braque and Picasso . . . In the spring, she and Anita went to the John Marin exhibition. (p. 103)

Visual artists have a specific path of development in their middle years, and this often takes them to special conservatories of art or to the college of art in the larger university. Summer programs for young artists at Governor's Institutes and such programs as that at the University of Indiana at Bloomington are also important in finding and nurturing young artistic talent. One necessity in the recognition of such talent is the development of a portfolio. There are also tests that have been successfully developed and used in finding visual arts talent. These are the Clark Drawing Abilities Test (ARTS Publishing Co., Inc. Bloomington, IN) and the Visual Memory Drawing Scale (Guip & Zimmer, University of Toledo, Toledo Museum of Art). However, looking at what a student has done and applying principles of development in art talent is a more sure way to identify talent (Winner, 1996).

304

A student demonstrates her creative ability in the domain of visual arts.

In the middle years, the visual artist often comes to a realization that the talent is there. Sloan and Sosniak's study of sculptors in the Development of Talent Research Project (1985) showed that many times their talent was not recognized in high school; in fact, some of the sculptors took no art in high school. Specialists in the field had not noticed them. Their serious study of art began in college with a "hazy goal" of doing something in the arts. They had been building, sketching, drawing, molding throughout their adolescent years; these predictive behaviors alone differentiated them and foretold that they would go on to study art. "Making art was a natural part of their lives" (p. 117). They had been recognized by peers and adults for their competence, and had built a sense of self-esteem about their talent. They had not become enamored with anything else, and may not have felt especially competent in any other areas.

The sculptors were late to come to art, and had undergone a process of self-scrutiny before deciding to study art seriously. They began to encounter teachers who were also artists, and this had a profound effect on them. One artist said, "He was an artist first, and he did teaching second. He was treated like an artist. Somehow that appealed to me" (Sloan & Sosniak, 1985, p. 121). Their teachers were "absolutely committed to what they were doing" (p. 121). They influenced their impressionable students to work with intensity and commitment. The young artists acquired peers who were as intense as they were, and the path of their development had crystallized. They learned the language, the vocabulary of art; they learned to function in the competitive climate of art school; they learned what it took to market their work. They learned to be professionals.

DEVELOPMENT OF LEADERS

The old saw that "leaders are born and not made" has some germ of truth. That is, if a student says, "I want to be a leader when I grow up," the student must necessarily have what Gardner (1983) called "personal intelligence," especially interpersonal intelligence, or knowledge about how to get along with other people. Gardner defined it thus: "Interpersonal knowledge permits a skilled adult to read the intentions and desires—even when these have been hidden—of many other individuals and, potentially, to act upon this knowledge" (p. 239). Such knowledge can be acquired, but often it is an uncanny ability to know what other people want and to have the ability to help them get it. Theories of leadership have emphasized the behavior and traits of leaders, as well as situations that call for various kinds of leaders (Karnes, 1991). Leadership styles have been described as autocratic versus democratic; oriented to tasks versus oriented to relationships; prone to use pressure tactics to gain their ends (Theory X) or prone to use convictions, or persuasion, to gain their ends (Theory Y); or they have been described as emphasizing production or emphasizing relationships (Bass & Barrett, 1981; Blake & Mouton, 1964; Fiedler, 1967; Lewin & Lippitt, 1938; McGregor, 1960). Bass (1985) has written about leaders who are transactional (favoring rewards and negative and positive reinforcement) and transformational (favoring organizational change through institutional change).

Karnes (1991) said that "education toward leadership is probably the most controversial of all the components of gifted education" (p. 125). The task of identifying students who have leadership potential is a mushy one, at best, and the instruments used for such identification have had limited predictive validity. Karnes said that adolescents who have the potential to be leaders seem to have these characteristics: "The desire to be challenged, creative problem-solving ability, critical reasoning ability, initiative, persistence, sensitivity, self-sufficiency, the ability to tolerate ambiguity, the ability to see new relationships, and enthusiasm" (p. 125).

Identification for leadership potential should be ongoing, as youthful leaders may not become adult leaders, and adult leaders may not have been leaders in their youth. However, there seem to be some patterns of continuous leadership among student leaders, who were often in the student council or student government in high school and also in college. Various means of identification should be used, including self-nomination, sociometric inventories, peer nomination, and standardized personality inventories or self-esteem inventories. Past leadership roles also seem to predict future leadership roles.

Commonly used instruments with reasonable validity are the Leadership Characteristics scale on the Renzulli et al. Scales for Rating the Behavioral Characteristics of Superior Students (1976), the Roets Rating Scale for Leadership (Roets, 1986), the High School Personality Questionnaire (HSPQ) (Cattell, Cattell, & Johns, 1984), and the Myers-Briggs Type Indicator. Sample items from the Leadership Characteristics Scale of the SRBCSS were "Participates in most social activities connected with the school; can be counted on to be there if anyone is" or "Seems to be well liked by his classmates." The HSPQ has a leadership potential score that is standardized as a self-rating instrument.

Cattell, Cattell, and Johns (1984) differentiated between leadership and popularity: Popularity is related to "how many friends or dates one has or by listing the persons one would want to spend time with" and leadership is indicated by "the performance of an individual within a group" (p. 53). In looking for leadership potential, these questions should be asked: Who are the people who influence you to work toward the goal? Who are the people who are repeatedly elected to offices? Who are the students who are chosen to be captains of the teams by other students? In their validation studies of the leadership scale, Cattell, Cattell, and Johns found that leaders were less warm, more intelligent, less dominant, "more conforming," and more self-sufficient. The image of a student leader that emerged was that the leader was "a no-nonsense, competent person that is, on the one hand, flexible, and on the other hand, able to stick with a task to its completion" (p. 54).

Karnes (1991) advocated that leadership be taught in separate courses, at retreats, and in special programs, as well as being included as an aspect of curriculum in the social studies. Students interested in developing their leadership skills should make personal plans for how they will do so. These should include finding a mentor or asking the school to find one, and performing internships with leaders in all sorts of fields, in all sorts of situations. The theater student could intern with a manager or a director; the young political leader could intern with a politician; the educator could intern with a school administrator. There is some evidence that planning to be a leader and training to be a leader can lead to better leadership.

THE IMPORTANCE OF PRACTICAL (TACIT) KNOWLEDGE

One truth about helping the talented adolescent and young adult in high school and college is that a significant component of such help must be helping the student to acquire the practical knowledge, the tacit knowledge, of how to succeed in their chosen professions. The gender differences that are blatantly showing by the end of college will be discussed further in the next chapter. But one reason for these differences has been indicated by studies such as Arnold's of high school valedictorians from Illinois (1993).

In 1980, the researchers identified 81 high school valedictorians (46 women and 35 men) from geographically and demographically distributed schools in Illinois. They have been following them for 15 years. They have found that most of the valedictorians attended and finished college with grade point averages of 3.6, but that while the men continued to view their abilities as high, the women "lowered their estimate of their intelligence over their college years" (p. 9). They also found that the women had a persistent concern over how to combine career and family, while the men did not voice such concerns. A third difference between the men and the women valedictorians over the years was that they diverged in their career plans: "By their senior year of college, two-thirds of the women valedictorians planned to reduce or interrupt their future labor force participation to accommodate child-rearing. All of the men planned continuous, full-time labor force participation" (p. 10).

The most striking difference was that, somehow, the young women did not achieve career focus during their college years: "Women tended to report a general career field . . . whereas men listed an occupation, level, and professional setting" (Arnold, 1993, p. 10), and women were also more likely to list several career possibilities during their last year of college. More women went on to get degrees, but 10 years after high school graduation, Arnold found that the women had somehow, during college, missed out on learning what was necessary for moving along in a profession. The implications for higher education were four:

1. Even the top women did not have practical knowledge about how to manage a career; Arnold said, "Mastering subject matter and earning academic distinction is insufficient for guaranteeing the translation of academic achievement into career attainment" (p. 30).
2. Faculty have extreme power in forming the careers of undergraduates and graduates.
3. Transmitting tacit knowledge about career management is often handled best in informal mentoring situations—in the lab, in the poetry club, in the geological field trip van.
4. "Students not only lack tacit understanding about their careers, they are often unaware of the existence and importance of such practical knowledge about their fields" (p. 30).

Arnold quoted a female valedictorian and a male valedictorian to bring home the difference in experiences. The females had to plan "an extra stage" in their lives: One woman, called Ellen, said:

There's a few things I know I want. I know I want to get married. I know I want to have kids. I know I want to have a career. I don't know how much weight I want to put on my career. I don't know how long I want to work. One thing that angers me is that as a woman I have to plan this. (p. 29)

Arnold quoted another valedictorian, named Len, who contrasted his career perceptions with those of the talented young women he knew:

My theory is, I guess, that they [the women] were expected to, or no one minded for them to do very well in high school, in terms of grades in high school math and things like that, but that didn't immediately, directly translate into career ambition. Whereas for me, one just seems like a perfectly logical outgrowth of the other. You do your best in a high school class and you get an 'A.' You do your best in a college class and you get an 'A,' you get admitted to law school and you do your best and you get an 'A' and then, based on that you get a job as a law clerk and you work very hard and do a good job in that and make a reputation for yourself and it all kind of naturally follows. I assume that it must be the case for some people that you got an 'A' in Miss Coopersmith's English class really bears no connection to how ambitious you are for yourself in your career. (Arnold, 1993, p. 31)

Thus the talented adolescent grows to adulthood where the talent becomes fully realized. The formal schooling is done, and the real work begins: the work of proving one's talent. This will be the subject of Chapter 8. However, it is necessary to reflect on some of the common features of the development of talent in the adolescent and college years. In all of the talent fields, one thing has stood out: there were mentors. The mentors chose the students or the students chose the mentors, but wiser minds shared their knowledge with attentive and interested youth. Youth apprenticed themselves to knowledgeable elders. Knowledgeable elders chose or didn't choose promising young followers to be potential colleagues. The mentoring function in the development of all talent can and should not be underemphasized.

Another point should be made, and that is that this chapter has not taken into account all or even very many types of talent that the schools nurture through the process of course taking. There is talent in business, talent in athletics, talent in engineering and the applied sciences, talent in vocational and technical areas, talent in various medical areas, talent in the social sciences, talent in managerial areas. All these and others are appropriately developed in the school setting, and should be considered by those concerned with talent development at the high school and college level. Experts in the development of such talent are resident in most schools. Gagné (1990, 1992), Feldhusen (1992a, 1992b), Renzulli (1992a), Renzulli & Reis, (1991), Useem (1992), and others have proposed a broader model of talent development than previously seen. This chapter, in its limited space, has discussed a few types of talent that illustrate that concept.

CASE EXAMPLE: Predictive Behaviors and Crystallizing Experiences in Three Artistic Male College Students.

Some research we have been doing (Piirto, 1992a/1998, 1994b; 1998b; Piirto & Fraas, 1995; Piirto, Gantz, Ramsay, Steele, Tabacca & Fraas, 1997; Piirto, Hohman, Nickle & Ryan, 1997) has indicated that males in the visual and performing arts have a very strong commitment to their art that begins quite early. For example, we found that high school boys at a Governor's Institute for musical theater, writing, and the visual arts were more tender-minded, showed less tough poise, and were more creative on the High School Personality Questionnaire (HSPQ) than a comparison group of high school boys. They were less conforming and more committed to their art even in high school:

The talented boys, on the other hand, were already nonconforming by the very act of attending a Governor's Institute in musical theater, writing, and visual arts. Males in the arts have already gone against gender stereotypes and may affect a bravado-based swashbuckling "gentleman pirate" demeanor and make a strong emotional commitment to the art in order to even pursue it. (Piirto & Fraas, p. 39)

The notion that people, in choosing a field to pursue, have "crystallizing experiences" has been propounded (Feldman, 1974). The idea that there are "predictive behaviors" for entrance into a talent field or domain has also been propounded (Piirto, 1994a).

With these ideas in mind, I decided to ask three of my students in a course called "Creativity and the Creative Process" about "crystallizing experiences" and "predictive behaviors" in their own lives. One was a junior and a guitarist in the most popular rock band in the area; one, a senior, was a full scholarship theater major who spent a semester in Ireland studying at the Abbey Theatre; one was a junior majoring in visual arts education. I asked them the following questions:

1. What were predictive behaviors and crystallizing experiences in your elementary years that led you to become an artist?
2. What were predictive behaviors and crystallizing experiences in your high school and college years that led you to become an artist?
3. Have you experienced a feeling of "outsider"ness because of your decision to become an artist?
4. What do your parents think about your decision to become an artist?
5. Can you describe your emotional commitment to your art?

In the answers that these three young men gave, it appears that there have been crystallizing experiences, predictive behaviors, and a sensitivity that is typical of men in the arts.

The Musician

In my childhood, for me, the dream wasn't anything that any American kid doesn't dream of—being a rock star. My two brothers and I would find athletic equipment—tennis rackets—and something to beat on and be a band in the bedroom. We got into Michael Jackson and stuff like that that wasn't guitar-driven at all. My older brother was into Jackson Browne and the Rolling Stones, The Who, bands like that. I'd just sit around and imagine. My dad used to play in a band and he was a left-handed guitarist so I couldn't learn from watching him.

I can remember the day I got my guitar. I still have it. I had a buddy who taught me chords and I just took it from there and really kind of developed my own style. I kind of regret not taking lessons so I could read music. I wish I would have taken lessons as far as soloing goes. I can read a little bit of tablature. Solo-wise I could use lessons, but rhythm-wise, as far as just constructing a song, I have no problem with that. It comes really easily. That carried on up through high school. I always used to lie in bed and listen to music and imagine that being me, playing the guitar and singing. My brother D_____(his twin) and I really started hitting it hard in our sophomore year in high school. It was fun, more than anything, because we were just trying different things. We played in a few little bands in high school, had a few shows. I was really scared, though, that whenever D____and I went to different schools it was going to end.

I came here to run track, and he went to another school, where our brother had gone. I wanted to be closer to home and my girlfriend. My brother and I would call and then we'd go home and just play, play, play. When we got home we just played it to death. We started writing material and making things up. When we first started playing we did other people's stuff until I could structure songs. I met the bass player, after I had roommate problems and moved out of my room into his, and we would just constantly play. I just played music all the time.

When I came here, out of high school, I was going to act. I loved theater. I was a theater major for half a semester. Also that year, after I switched from theater to radio/tv, I had a chance to just play my guitar, trying to get better, and I was playing every night, for about three hours. I have a CD collection; I'd put all of them in and just play with them and just go, go, go. I thought, "Why do I even want to act? It's not what I really love to do. I love to make music." I kind of just cut all connection to acting. I even stopped watching movies for awhile, it was that hard. I just picked my guitar up every night and played. I just took my frustrations out on the guitar and made up a lot of new stuff. My frustrations of looking back and knowing something I loved just wasn't there. It kind of really was indirect, I guess, after spending all that time with my guitar, just playing, just listening. I was talking to D_____ and said "I've got to get something going. I need to play in a band and make music." I can just remember looking back and playing my guitar. It was sickening how much I played, you know? It really was. That was probably the crystallizing experience.

I'll tell you this: when it's just us four in a room together, it doesn't matter whether there's five people watching or five hundred; it's going to be the same. I don't care what I look like, because I know what's coming out through me is more than I ever dreamed. I just wish that I could go back to my sophomore year in high school, I could tell myself, yeah, in 1995 you're going to be playing in a band and you're going to record, and you're going to put out a CD too and I would just be— you're crazy, you know? We have a long way to go; it's not going to happen overnight; it's going to take awhile. After graduation here, what's going to happen? I've been through it before in the transition from high school to college, but there's something about being in a band that you can't relate with being on a football team or any kind of group of three people, four people, five people. When I can look at D____ and he can look at me and everyone else and we know what we're going to do before we even do it—you can't practice that; you don't teach it, you just do it. So we're looking back at the circumstances that caused us to meet and play together—it couldn't be written better in a movie, it really couldn't.

People can't talk to me when I have a guitar in my hand because I won't listen. The other guys in the band kind of joke around because they try to talk to me but I just won't. Basically, if I had to do whatever it took, if it meant forsaking friends, family, anything but God, I'll do it. It's spiritual.

Predictive Behaviors:

- *Imagining* himself as a rock star
- Obtaining a guitar and learning to play it
- Joining a band
- Practicing constantly
- Experiencing the "flow" state while playing alone and with the band
- Passion for playing and music
- Interacting with musical father

Crystallizing Experiences

- Roommate problems caused him to meet the other members of the band
- Gaining regional fame and notoriety as being the lead guitar in the best band around

The Actor

Back when I was a little kid, when we moved to our house, I was six—the neighbors across the street didn't know my real name for about two months, because every day I'd walk outside—I'd get up in the morning—I was a new person. I'd pick a look and be a new person. I'd pick a name and that was who I was. The neighbors were real confused. I'd say, "Today, my name is Albert." And I'd do the things that Albert would do. Some days Albert was really fast, and I'd do really fast things. I did that for years. I just liked to do that.

And then in high school—we'd moved to Texas and then we moved back, and I didn't know anybody, so my older brother was taking a theater class just for some extra credits. And we were put into a play, and I only had a couple of lines, but it was fun. I got a big old rush out of it. And then the tryouts came up for the next play, and I tried out, and I got the lead! That was another big step, but I wasn't committed to it or anything. But then one night, one of the actors forgot a line and threw in a line that was in the back. I started this whole new dialogue that threw us back to where we were—it was a good scene and it worked twice—and finished the show, and I thought, "Wow, we screwed up but we got through it. I made things work!"

"The next night it went perfectly. And then people came up to me who had seen the show both nights and they said, "We're really sorry you goofed tonight. You didn't do that one scene where you said this and that happened. I noticed that, I liked that scene." That was the time that I thought, "You know what?" I didn't know what I was going to go to college for. "I think I'll go to college for theater." My parents are teachers and are very supportive and my whole family is artistic—no matter what their job is they do art—my uncle is a pianist. My grandpa didn't get a chance to express himself artistically and he arranges fruit and designs the windows for the store. My older brother is an art professor and does freelance stuff.

After I came here, my freshman year as an actor was great. Then, my sophomore year, somewhere in my development as an actor I started hitting my head against the wall. It got frustrating. It went on for a year! Then I got to do Iago in *Othello*. When I first started acting, that character was the end-all, be-all. My high school teacher was a really great teacher and she was giving me scripts all the time, and when she gave me *Othello* to read over, I just fell in love. Wow! That was what I wanted to do. Then I was given the opportunity to do it; after four or five years of thinking about this play, of imagining what it could be, it was a disappointment. Anything would have been a disappointment. So I dropped my major and went to Ireland.

Why was it such a disappointment? Have you thought about it?

Yeah. I've thought about it a lot. I'd built up the idea of what that could be and because anyway, I was disappointed that I wasn't advancing anywhere; I had hit a wall. So I went to Ireland and hung out at the Abbey Theatre. I thought maybe I'd find it there. I student-directed one of Brian Friel's plays, *Philadelphia, Here I Come*. I was the American. What a surprise. I lost my desire to do it. It's just a job anymore.

The only people in the world who know me are my mother, my girlfriend, and my two best friends. I please everybody. Whatever you want to see, that's what I'll give you. Whatever the group is, I will fit in, because that's what I learned to do as a kid, going outside, pretending I was Albert. I'll even change the clothes.

If I would have pursued acting, I would have gone to Chicago. New York is just musicals. LA has beautiful people. Minneapolis and Chicago have real theater, not a bunch of people singing and dancing and smiling big. It's quality. But I don't want to spend the next 20 years being a waiter.

Predictive Behaviors

- Early playacting
- Growing sense of competence in his craft
- Perfectionism about his craft
- Sense of being a chameleon
- Passion for theater
- Growing tacit knowledge and ensuing doubts about the career path of an actor
- Interacting with artistic family

Crystallizing Experiences

- High school acting experience
- Sense of control over acting process
- College acting role as Iago

The Visual Artist

In my childhood I was the worst artist in the class. I was out of the lines; I didn't do what all the other kids did. I didn't draw well. I remember in first grade I went to a private school where there were a lot of Vietnamese and Oriental guys and they were a lot better than me and I always wanted to be like them and I was never able to. That was the crystallizing experience. I wanted to be them. And so my mom started feeding me sketchbooks. That's just what I wanted to start doing. It was fun.

The frustration we're talking about happened to me in junior high—when hormones made it a blank—there was this caste system and I was not a part of this caste system. I was not the outsider but I was definitely the satellite that moved with the group. One group would alienate me and I'd say no big deal, and I moved where I needed to go. I became very aware of myself, very introspective, very introverted, like that. I would think about me over anybody else.

I think a lot of that frustration came out in my sketchbook. My sketchbook was where I was and they weren't. That was me. That was my friend. I originally started out with comics. Because comic book characters had super powers. They could get away from THEM, they could destroy THEM if they wanted to. So it became me drawing these super heroes that if you looked at them had a characteristic of my being. Something that I would have on me was in that picture. It was a way of just destroying the guys that had the pain that was coming at me. So that became my world. Eventually I got out of comics. I kind of grew up. I swore to myself that I would always collect comics, but then artists and writers became like major league baseball.

But all my energy and my feelings were spilling out onto this—onto the white pages, onto the sketchbooks. I wasn't doing anything of real quality, something you could hang up. I was working in sketchbooks. That was me practicing, running the races, getting things done. I'm now putting out artwork that you can hang. Artwork that I can give my parents and say; "If you want to mat this, go ahead." The other stuff is just garbage; I don't want you to have that. That's my diary—and I don't think it should be hung up. It's just not what I want on the wall.

I think high school was another crystallization. I was finally in the scene, people finally knew who I was. I had a lot of friends, but it was more like—he was so weird—he's that art guy—we can get him to do the pictures. I was the class artist. That was fine. I knew who I was. I just wanted to be part of the group. That's all I really wanted. And so I kept moving on. I had an art teacher who was just a big piece of crap, really. I don't want to be this guy. This is an ideal any young person has—they don't want to be this, or be that. They just put that suit on, "the I don't want to be" guy.

I don't want to be that lax guy who hit on the girls and did jack for art work. I had to go to take precollege art at the local university because I needed something else. So once I was getting stuff like that, my name was built. I went to the high school and won some prizes there. I think that's my focus; this revenge mission I have for this teacher—and me.

Predictive Behaviors

- Early sketchbooks
- Desire to draw

- Feeling as if he were expressing his *true* self through drawing
- Growing sense of competence in his craft

Crystallizing Experiences

- Becoming known as the class artist
- Winning contests
- Taking advanced classes because of disappointment with his teacher

What kind of family do you have?

Musician: Very stable family.
Actor: Basically I lived with Ward and June Cleaver. We moved a lot but the family was stable.
Visual artist: Basic white-bread America, basic nuclear family, me, my mom and my dad.

Do you think you're different from other guys your age?

Visual artist: There's a tough guy image that I portray sometimes that is just a front. You don't call yourself a visual artist. You say, "I draw pictures," because everyone thinks you're gay.
Actor: In theater, that's even quicker. So I put up a rough exterior, which is no big deal. It's another role.
Visual artist: It just kills me the way that people thought that. My parents support me in being an artist, but they guided me towards my option, that is, doing my own work, but teaching other kids about it. They told me not to be a fine artist, because that's the tough part. They said, "Why don't you try teaching?" And they're very supportive in that respect.

When I was doing my education experience last year, I was wearing my earrings, even though I probably shouldn't have, because I like to look as professional as possible, and the teacher introduced me to the class, and she said, "Can anybody guess what Mr. ———'s field is?" And the kids said, "Oh! He's an art teacher!" It wasn't a smiling thing, it was a laughing thing that—you're different, you're an artist, and we're going to show you. It bothers me a lot. Or in the movie *St. Elmo's Fire,* where he doesn't get asked by the prostitute because she thinks he's gay.
Musician: The singer gets the girls. But for me, everyone focuses on "1st and 10, let's do it again" and I'm focusing on "Let's have a song. Let's make another one."

These interviews with three young male visual and performing artists confirmed that they had both predictive behaviors and crystallizing experiences along their paths. They are poised on beginning or deciding on not beginning careers in the arts. They demonstrate passion, tacit knowledge, and the "gentleman pirate" image that Barron discussed in *Artists in the Making* (1972).

Implications for educators of the talented are obvious. Talented students can be identified by means of such predictive behaviors (Piirto, 1992a/1998, 1992b, 1994a, 1994b, 1995a, 1995b, 1995c, 1995d, in press, in preparation.) Their families were supportive and stable, letting the young men choose their own paths and supporting them in their efforts (Feldman & Piirto, 1995). Chance and planning both played a part in their lives.

SUMMARY

1. High school interests and extracurricular activities are predictive of college majors and occupational choices.
2. Verbal talent and mathematical talent are distinctive types of academic talent, although they both have superior access to right-hemisphere functioning.
3. Cognitively, high test scorers in mathematics have good background knowledge, superior problem-solving ability, procedural knowledge, and access to short-term memory.
4. Cognitively, high test scorers in verbal areas have good background knowledge and superior access to long-term memory.
5. High academic ability has influence across occupations but perhaps not within occupations.
6. Personality characteristics such as autonomy, risk taking, dominance, and androgyny are important in determining successful life achievement, but may not be helpful in determining academic achievement.
7. Studies using the Myers-Briggs Type Indicator have been indicators of personality traits of people with various kinds of talent.
8. Behavioral rating scales used to place high school and college youth into talent development programs should focus on specific aspects of the talent dimension.
9. Scientist were good students, in honors tracks, school leaders, and had extracurricular activities in science and athletics.
10. Women who majored in science described difficulties with professors and male peers.
11. Mathematics talent may be too narrowly and too early defined in the United States, leading to an ultimate shortage of U.S. born Ph.D. candidates.
12. Verbal talent is an underlying necessity for many professions, fields of advanced study, and college majors.
13. Performers need a different emphasis in their education than creators do. Physical dexterity and memory are among the necessities for performers.
14. Musicians and dancers experience a narrowing of educational options during high school and college due to the extreme demands of the development of their talents.
15. Visual artists often begin to be regarded as talented in high school and college, even though the talent was there earlier; they often attend special art schools and many go on to receive terminal M.F.A. degrees.
16. The cultivation, noticing, and development of talent is highly dependent on various mentors, from teachers to practitioners in the talent field. At some level, mentors choose mentees, rather than vice versa.

CHAPTER

8 TALENTED ADULTS

FOCUSING QUESTIONS

1. What factors enter into adult achievement?
2. Why is Simonton's quantitative work important in studying eminence and leadership?
3. What are your thoughts about elementary school achievers in adult life?
4. What are adult scientists apt to do?
5. What is the importance of gender in adult achievement?
6. Compare and contrast musicians and mathematicians.
7. Compare and contrast visual artists and creative writers.
8. Compare and contrast scientists and musicians.
9. Compare and contrast mathematicians and visual artists.
10. What are the interpersonal and intrapersonal concerns of high-IQ adults?
11. Why hasn't spiritual growth been emphasized in the education of the talented?

Figure 8.1 Overview of Chapter 8

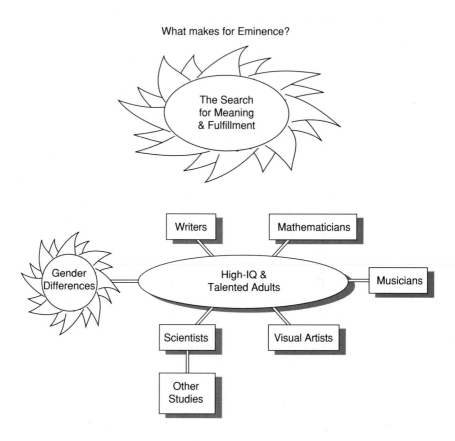

Phil and Marnie looked around the room. They had organized the event and people had indeed come. There, in small groups, were visual artists, composers, musicians, athletes, political leaders, community leaders, scientists, professors from the university, novelists, poets, journalists, actors, dancers. The gala benefit for the cause of universal inoculation for children had brought them all out to this fund-raiser. This certainly was a group of talented adults.

What were they really like, down deep inside? What had they gone through to get here, to the state capitol, to the Museum of Art, contributing hundreds of dollars each to the cause?

Let us summarize what we know about talented adults—adults who have been academically talented, performing arts talented, and talented leaders.

HIGH-IQ AND ACADEMICALLY TALENTED ADULTS

High-IQ adults were probably academically talented children, although "late bloomers" do exist. Late bloomers are well known to college professors, who have been heard to say that their best students are returning adults who have chosen to go to college later on in life, after working for awhile or raising families. These adults regularly "blow the top off" tests, and set academic standards for younger college students, often while keeping up full lives as parents and workers. These adults realized their academic talent late and often go on to assume positions of professional prestige. There is little written about them in talent development literature.

On the other hand, what happened to the academically talented people of the Terman study, those high-IQ children who Terman began to study in the early 1920s? The Terman data are still being analyzed. The research shows that scoring high on an IQ test is not a sure-fire way to guarantee educational or professional achievement, nor does potential in the cognitive area guarantee personal success and fulfillment. Studying 1,069 men and women who were in the original group and who have been followed for 60 years, the researchers made several conclusions (Tomlinson-Keasey & Little, 1990).

First, the home environment in which the child was nurtured is crucial. This home environment seems to be particularly important for the future success of boys, but less important for girls, for reasons unknown. To be well adjusted (not necessarily academically achieving), the home environment for boys included mothers with intellectual interests and proclivities, in which independence was encouraged. These homes were also active, with many activities going on, and the parents did not overly esteem (or "spoil") their children. Negative home environments where the child's needs for safety, shelter, and warm love were problematic, were shown to have a long-term impact. Wallerstein and Blakeslee (1989) showed that children whose parents are divorced seldom recover completely, while the numerous help groups for the adult children of substance abusers testify to the long-term impact of parental substance abuse on children.

A second major influence on whether a person achieves as an adult is personality attributes. Tomlinson-Keasey and Little (1990) said, "The childhood traits . . . diagnostic of future success were persistence, intellectual energy, originality, and ambition"

(p. 443). Other characteristics are "unusual motivation, self-confidence, and strength." The overwhelming research evidence that certain personality attributes are essential for the development of talent led to my placing them as the base of the Pyramid of Talent Development.

A third major influence is socioeconomic class. "High levels of education, occupation, and income among parents predict intellectual achievement of children with amazing regularity," said Tomlinson-Keasey and Little. Parental levels of education seem to be the best predictors of socioeconomic status and thus of adult realization of academic talent. Thus the "chance" or "luck" of being born into a family with educated parents was added as an environmental "sun" on the Pyramid of Talent Development.

Tomlinson-Keasey and Little formed a model. The following eight predictors affected the outcome of occupational achievement in adulthood on the Terman high-IQ group: (1) social responsibility; (2) intellectual determination; (3) sociability; (4) parental education; (5) family harmony; (6) educational attainment; (7) intellectual skill; and (8) personal adjustment. Personal adjustment was influenced by family harmony. Intellectual skill was influenced by parental education, intellectual determination, and family harmony. Educational attainment was influenced by social responsibility, sociability, and parental education (see Figure 8.2). Interestingly enough, Tomlinson-Keasey and Little found that sociability had a negative effect on the development of intellectual skills. It seems that people who chose to develop their social skills chose not to pursue the development of their intellectual skills: "In other words, children who were popular, enjoyed good health, radiated physical energy, and maintained a cheerful and optimistic attitude were less likely to maintain their intellectual skills as adults, whereas less popular children were more likely to evidence intellectual interests as adults" (p. 452).

These findings were corroborated in the study of talented teens by Csikszentmihalyi, Rathunde, and Whalen (1993), in which the students who were most likely to develop their talents were more isolated students, who did not date much, and who were not social leaders in their high schools. It seems that somewhere, some students make a decision to "fit in" (or the decision is made for them by factors such as acceptability, social graces, and peer acceptance), and when they do, they must sacrifice to some degree a goal orientation toward development of talent. One study in the synthesis of research that became the best-selling book *Emotional Intelligence* (Goleman, 1995) indicated that those who become "stars" in large corporations are no longer the lone wolves, but those who are able to create friendship and sharing networks across departments of the corporation.

Feelings of childhood isolation seem to steer children toward intellectual development. Biographical data seem to bear this out. For example, as mentioned in Chapter 6, the mathematician and philosopher Bertrand Russell recalled his childhood solitude. He said in his *Autobiography* (1967), "The early years of my childhood, however, were happy, and it was only as adolescence approached that loneliness became oppressive" (p. 31). Carl Jung, the psychoanalyst, also experienced isolation during his school years, and wrote about them in *Memories, Dreams, Reflections* (1965). Jung's childhood isolation led him to read widely and voraciously and he felt depression and loneliness, which led him early to theorize about people having multiple personalities:

> I used my father's library for these researches, secretly and without asking his permission
> . . . I also began reading German literature, concentrating on those classics which school,

with its needlessly laborious explanations of the obvious, had not spoiled for me. I read vastly and planlessly, drama, poetry, history, and later natural science. Reading was not only interesting but provided a welcome and beneficial distraction from the preoccupations of personality No. 2, which in increasing measure were leading me to depressions . . . Other people all seemed to have totally different concerns. I felt completely alone with my certainties. More than ever I wanted someone to talk with, but nowhere did I find a point of contact; on the contrary, I sensed in others an estrangement, a distrust, an apprehension which robbed me of speech. That, too, depressed me. I did not know what to make of it. Why has no one had experiences similar to mine? Why is there nothing about it in scholarly books? Am I the only one who has had such experiences? (p. 63)

WHAT MAKES FOR EMINENCE?

Whether or not the high-IQ person will become an eminent person is in question. Certain other variables besides scores on an intelligence test are operational, and important. Whether or not eminence is even the goal should also be considered. The term *eminence* is often used to denote extreme fame in domains that are thought to contribute to the good of humankind. A Nobel prize winner, a classical violinist, or a statesman is *eminent*, while an Academy Award winner, a rock and roll star, or a politician is merely *famous* (Pendarvis, Howley & Howley, 1990). VanTassel-Baska (1989) described several varieties of eminence in her essay, "Characteristics of the Developmental Path of Eminent and Gifted Adults." She noted that eminence can be a relative condition; a person may be eminent within his or her own professional

Figure 8.2   Paths to Occupational Achievement and Educational Attainment in the Terman Study High-IQ Subjects

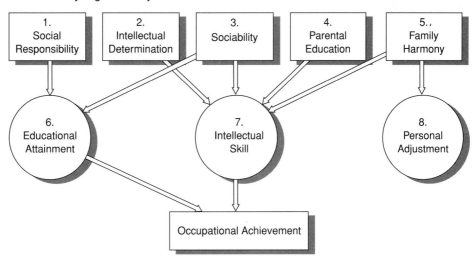

From "Predicting Educational Attainment, Occupational Achievement, Intellectual Skill, and Personal Adjustment among Gifted Men and Women", by C. Tomlinson-Keasey and T.D. Little, 1990, *Journal of Educational Psychology*, *82*(1), pp. 442–455. Copyright 1990 *Journal of Educational Psychology*. Adapted by permission.

group, and therefore eminence should not be confused with fame: "Eminence is related to the furthering of knowledge and, as such, possesses substantiation beyond the phenomenon of name recognition" (p. 147).

The high-IQ people in the Terman study, if this definition is to be used, did achieve eminence within their own groups, or within their cities or geographical areas. Van-Tassel-Baska said the three factors that produce eminence are: (1) being born into the type of family that values knowledge and education; (2) being precocious; and (3) being focused and self-directed. We cannot predict who will be eminent, based on childhood characteristics alone, because these factors overlap and take into account the society, the psychological factors, and the mental qualities of the person.

THE QUANTITATIVE WORK OF DEAN KEITH SIMONTON

Much of what we know about adult creative-productive talent in fields as diverse as music and leadership has been synthesized by the historiometric social psychologist, Dean Keith Simonton (1984, 1988, 1992, 1995). Utilizing a statistical technique called *historiometry*, Simonton has looked at eminent persons and geniuses. Historiometry is a quantitative technique that seeks to discover generalizations about the paths of human life. Utilizing biographical data from such researchers as Cox and the Goertzels, Simonton has conducted studies and reevaluated studies of eminent adults. Following are some of the conclusions he has reached:

1. Family influences such as birth order, loss of parents, and coming from a famous family have much to do with becoming an eminent adult.

2. Role models and mentors have an intergenerational influence on the development of adult eminence; the role models and mentors should be about 20 years older than the mentees or protegés: "Ideas impinge on other ideas across generations" (1984, p. 40).

3. The personality traits and character of eminent adults seem to have been more important than their intelligence. Versatility, or the ability to operate in several different fields, and the need for achievement and power are particularly important in the development of leadership. Leaders also need intellectual complexity rather than dogmatism. Many revolutionaries fail to succeed once they take power because they lack intellectual complexity. The need for power is positively related to leadership achievement.

4. Creative adults have more psychopathology than adults in the rest of the population. Mental difficulties in creative adults may come from having their highly original work go unrecognized and unappreciated, but genetic factors also seem to be involved. Simonton said, "Sometimes intemperate madness is an unsought penalty for genius" (1995, p. 311).

5. The individual personality preference of political leaders has a lot of influence on the decisions they make; dominant and extroverted personalities prefer actions that are dominant and extroverted; reclusive and introverted personalities prefer containment actions.

6. Moral improprieties or styles of life are much less tolerated in leaders than they are in creators in adulthood.

7. The level of education, for creators such as poets, artists, and performers, peaks in its utility somewhere about the junior year of college. "Curiously, creators

with doctorates tend to be slightly less eminent than those with little formal education
. . . That is, the most famous scientists, philosophers, writers, artists, and composers
tend to complete their junior year but not their senior year in college" (1984, p. 66).
The more formal education the creator has, the more dogmatic he or she becomes.
However, illiteracy or little formal education also lead to dogmatism. The ideal of
cognitive flexibility is reached between the junior year and early in graduate school.
Even "truly revolutionary scientists may display [educational patterns] not unlike
those found for artists" (1984, p. 69).

8. Celebrities, on the other hand, such as performers, athletes, entrepreneurs,
mystics—those with ephemeral fame—have different educational paths: "the more
education they have, the greater their fame is likely to be" (1995, p. 71).

9. The best predictors of adult eminence are nonacademic activities and extracurricular activities, and not scholastic honors such as valedictorian, Phi Beta
Kappa, and the like. Self-education, voracious reading across disciplines, and the
ability to synthesize are generally more important than academic honors, though
many eminent achievers, especially in the sciences, were also academically excellent and received honors for such.

10. Productivity is the best indicator of adult eminence. The three factors that
lead to productivity are precocity, rate of productivity, and longevity. Quality arises
from quantity. The earlier a person begins to produce, the more cumulative advantage his or her product will have; that is, if she or he publishes in prestigious journals
early, prestigious journals will be more likely to accept future research publications.
This was called the *constant probability of success* model (Simonton, 1988).

11. Peak productivity falls in different places on the creator's or leader's age
curve, depending on the domain in which the person practices. This holds true for
literary creators as well as scientific creators, musicians as well as leaders. Simonton
(1975, 1984) found that literary prose writers peaked at age 43, and poets peaked at
age 39. Mathematical creativity peaks earlier than creativity in geologists. Political
revolutionaries are younger than statesmen. Founders of religious movements were
generally in their thirties, but elders head religious denominations. These age trends
are intrinsic rather than extrinsic to the creative process. However, according to Simonton, the potential for creative contribution need never vanish.

12. Charisma, the elusive something that a leader has, has also yielded to historiometric analysis. Preliminary investigations of charisma show that it is irrationally perceived by leaders' constituents. Often the leader is perceived to have sexual as well as
social power. Simonton noted a "surprising paucity of homosexuals among the world's
great leaders," perhaps because a leader is expected to prove his virility by producing
offspring. The image "alpha male," or the most powerful male in a primate group, was
invoked by both Gardner (1995a) and Simonton (1995) when referring to leaders'
power and sexuality. Simonton said "alpha males in human societies are virile, tall, and
violent" (p. 39). Women have been alpha males as well ("Queen Isabella of Castile,
Elizabeth I of England, Catherine the Great of Russia, Maria Theresa of Austria, and the
Empress Dowager CiXi, Queen Boudicca, Joan of Arc"), and when they exercised their
power they were indistinguishable from men.

13. The theory that the *Zeitgeist*, or the temperature of the times, governs which
genius will arise to what acclaim or immortality, is arguable because of the production
of multiples. However, along with the production of multiples, the eminent genius

also produces solo: "Einstein's relativity theory was his alone. So was Planck's quantum theory" (Simonton, 1995, p. 122). Simonton said, "the eminent genius is a mere mouthpiece for the age, or a funnel in which diverse sociocultural causes are collated and concentrated" (1984, p. 146).

14. Civil disturbance, political violence, and international war are precursors of periods of creativity. One generation usually passes after the disturbances before the creative products are fully developed and presented to the world.

15. The lifetime output of creative adults has as many hits as misses. Simonton said, "Clearly this pattern of behavior implies that geniuses must be phenomenal risk-takers. Only a willingness to go for the long shot gives geniuses the chance to win big, yet this very proclivity brings with it an even larger accumulation of creative catastrophes" (1992, p. 292).

16. There is a life span developmental path in adult achievers that can be looked at, generalized from, and modeled. This path begins in earliest childhood and impinges on the choice of a creative field as well as the predictive probability of success. Both genetic and environmental influences are responsible.

Simonton's work continues as his astonishing rate of productivity accumulates more studies and more articles. The scholar and those curious about the development of talent should consult Simonton's research.

ADULT ACHIEVEMENT OF YOUNG ACADEMIC ACHIEVERS

The Hunter Group

Terman's study of high-IQ students who grew up on the West Coast has been compared with high-IQ students who grew up in New York City. Researchers (Subotnik, Karp & Morgan, 1989; Subotnik et al., 1993) looked at 156 men and women who had graduated from the Hunter College Elementary School in the 1940s and 1950s. The Terman group had a mean IQ of 148 and the Hunter group had a mean IQ of 159. Subotnik and colleagues administered the Terman midlife questionnaire to people who had graduated from Hunter and who were in their thirties and fourties. The findings were similar to those found by studies of the Terman group (Terman & Oden, 1959):

1. *Marital status*: Similar profiles, with about 10 percent remaining single, and more of the Hunter people having divorced, probably due to the increase of divorce in general.

2. *Religious affiliation:* A disproportionately large number of Jewish people in both samples.

3. *Highest degree attained:* More than 40 percent of the Hunter and Terman men pursued terminal degrees (medicine, law, Ph.D.s). Six percent of the Terman women and 67 percent of the Hunter women had Ph.D., M.D., or LL.B. degrees.

4. *Occupations:* Terman men had more of a variety of careers, both professional and semiprofessional. The highest percentage (8 percent) were executive managers. Of the Hunter men, 20 percent were lawyers, 18 percent were physicians, 14 percent were college teachers, 8 percent were professionals such as dentists or psychologists, and 8 percent were writers. Of the Terman women, 50 percent were housewives, 7 percent were executive business managers, and 6 percent were teachers below

college level. Of the Hunter women, 16 percent were college teachers, 12 percent were professionals such as psychologists, and 11 percent were writers.

Income differences between Hunter men and Hunter women, even with the large number of terminal degrees among the women, were great. The mean income for Hunter men was $105,000 (median = $75,000; range was from $5,000 to $505,000) and the mean income for Hunter women was $47,391 (median = $40,000; range was from $11,000 to $180,000). Subotnik, Karp, and Morgan (1989) said, "The income discrepancies remain constant even when matched by profession. Higher degrees and comparably high intellect did not assure gifted women of equitable financial rewards for their professional efforts" (p. 141).

5. *Feelings about one's present vocation:* Both groups expressed great satisfaction with their careers.

6. *Political self-rating and affiliation:* Statistically significant differences between the groups were found, with the Terman group rating themselves as more liberal. The Hunter group was overwhelmingly Democratic (71 percent), and the Terman group had more Republicans (44 percent) than Democrats (30 percent).

7. *General health:* At midlife, both groups described their health as good to very good.

8. *Mental health and general adjustment:* Fewer than 10 percent of both groups (about that in the normal population) described themselves as having difficulty with their mental health. High-IQ women in the Terman sample seemed to have more mental difficulty.

9. *Factors furthering and hindering life accomplishment:* The Terman group regarded mental stability as necessary in achieving life goals, while the Hunter group thought that persistence and personality were necessary. Terman people felt more dissatisfaction with themselves as far as obtaining educations (they grew up during the Depression and World War II), and Hunter people felt that failing to realize their potential was caused by factors such as luck or the actions of other people. Both groups felt they had experienced more helpful factors than hindering factors in their paths to life accomplishments.

10. *Living up to one's intellectual abilities:* The Hunter group felt that it had done well; the Terman group felt fulfilled if they achieved a comfortable income and desired social status.

11. *Sources of satisfaction:* Men in both groups rated their work first, in ranking sources of satisfaction. Children were ranked second for both groups of men, and third was marriage and hobbies. The Hunter women had similar rankings, while the Terman women chose children, marriage, and social contacts as providing sources of satisfaction.

12. *Definition of success:* Both groups described success as having family love, an adequate income, satisfying work, and being able to help others. Peace of mind was ranked relatively high as well for men and women in both groups.

Subotnik, Karp, and Morgan (1989) concluded that the most striking differences were between the two groups of gifted women. Having a high IQ seemed to predict for success in academic professions but not in aesthetics or the arts. The researchers said, "Like the Terman group, none of the members of the Hunter group has [yet] achieved the status of a revolutionary thinker" (p. 143). Such innovative and radical thought usually emerges out of obsession and idealism, and the Hunter group expressed wistfulness for lost idealism, but they remained relatively conservative and pleased with their conformity. The belief, or charge, that high-IQ students are our "future leaders," seems not to have been supported by either the Terman or the Hunter group. Although the Terman people were not placed in special educational settings, the Hunter students had attended a special elementary school and many of them attended special high schools. There were few differences among the groups, despite the differences in their educational interventions.

The Hollingworth Group

Harris (1990) published a study of the students studied by Leta Hollingworth of Teachers College, Columbia University, in the mid-1920s. These students had been placed in a special program at P.S. 208 in rural Brooklyn, P.S. 500 (Speyer School), and P.S. 165 in Manhattan. The program consisted of special enrichment such as foreign language and music appreciation, but the children were not placed in special classes or in a special school. Sixty-four participants in these special programs for high-IQ children were tracked down in the late 1980s. Interviews were conducted and the group completed questionnaires. Several categories of answers were collected:

1. *Personal:* Both men and women were still in good health. Women had higher rates of divorce than men. This could be because of "the rise of feminist consciousness with its increased societal flexibility for intellectually gifted females," Harris said (p. 219).

2. *Educational:* Harris studied only the educational level of spouses, and found that the men tended to marry women who had less education, while the women tended to marry men who had more education.

3. *Vocational-professional:* Most of the males became professionals, whereas the women did not. Females stated they had experienced financial satisfaction through their work, and their interviews indicated that they had experienced sex bias that prevented them from rising as high as they might have.

4. *Avocational:* They all had a large number of hobbies.

5. *Achievement:* While they listed having children and personal satisfaction as achievements, they had also received honors and awards. The 25 women had achieved one Phi Beta Kappa, seven listings in *Who's Who*, listing in the *Poets and Writers Directory*, a Fulbright fellowship, a National Science Foundation fellowship, and other fellowships, writing awards, and prizes. They had published 11 books and 62 professional articles. One had achieved a juried gallery art show. The 39 males had received two Sigma Xi honors, one Phi Beta Kappa, 15 *Who's Who* listings, two *American Men of Science* listings, two Fulbright fellowships, two National Science Foundation fellowships, two American Academy of Arts and Sciences fellowships, two Guggenheim fellowships, two National Endowment for the Arts fellowships, and more than 30 other awards, prizes, medals, and honorary degrees. They had written 44 books, four novels, and 382 professional journal articles. Clearly, the men had achieved more honors than the women, though not that many more.

6. *Adjustment/fulfillment:* Life satisfaction, like that of the Terman and Hunter groups, was clearly evident: "On the whole, the Hollingworth group appeared to

have attained a great degree of cumulative satisfaction in all areas of life" (p. 221) with the women experiencing satisfaction with friends and the men experiencing satisfaction with their careers.

Kathi Kearney and Rose Rudnitski have also interviewed surviving attendees at the Speyer School (personal communication, November 1997). The school was a major positive influence on their lives and many of them credited this experience for beginning their life's success. One man who attended the school said on his death bed that he could not have done what he had accomplished as a businessman and political leader without having been plucked from his poor neighborhood in the Bronx and sent to the Speyer School (P. Johnson-Kwartler, personal communication, November 1997).

ADULT TALENT DEVELOPMENT BY DOMAIN

Beyond looking at what has happened to people with high IQs, or the academically talented, it seems that one of the themes of the latest thought in the field of talent development education is to look at talent by domain; in other words, what paths have been taken by people who have achieved in the various fields of creative excellence? Are there any common themes within these domains?

Multipotentiality is a characteristic of people with high IQs and people with academic talent. A chosen field is chosen not only because one likes it, but because one has passion for it, a need to do it. John Dos Passos, in his memoir *The Best Times* (1966), talked about his resistance to becoming a writer. He said:

> I had come back from the war and the Near East [1922] not quite sure whether I wanted most to paint or write but with no idea of making a career of either one. I had a faint hankering for the theater. All I knew was that I wanted to get a lot of things off my chest. As one book led to another the plan to take up architecture gradually faded, but I couldn't abide the notion of setting up as an author. I was damned if I'd let anybody classify me on that index card. At least not yet. I was planning to write novels, but on the side. (pp. 130–131)

The novelist Gore Vidal in a 1992 interview said, of his own multipotentiality:

> In those days (1936), I was not only the Boy Airman of the newsreels, but a Renaissance talent . . . I drew, I sculpted, I wrote, I read nearly a book a day, and I saw the movies, and understood from them the world . . . Small talents often come in a cluster, and there are numerous cases of the writer who can draw and the painter who can write and the composer who can do logarithms. In youth, I was the repository of a myriad of mediocre talents. . . . (p. 21)

These "small talents," as Vidal called them, often become hobbies, and the talented adult comes to focus on one domain as a profession.

Personality type preferences of effective adults seem to be similar across domains, however. This may indicate that the multipotentiality is based in personality and that career choice is a matter of interest or passion rather than ability. Donald MacKinnon (1978) reported on the results on the personality inventory, the Myers-Briggs Type Indicator (MBTI), at the Institute for Personality Assessment and Research (IPAR) in their studies of architects, mathematicians, writers, and research scientists. He said that most of the architects, mathematicians, and writers were perceptive (P) types, and "only among research scientists do we find the majority to be judging (J) types" (p. 62) but that even the scientists judged most creative had more preference for P. The IPAR group also found that the effective people studied also showed a decided preference for intuition (N): MacKinnon (1978) said, "In contrast to an estimated 25 per cent of the general population who are intuitive, 90 per cent of the creative writers, 92 per cent of the mathematicians, 93 per cent of the research scientists, and 100 per cent of the architects are intuitive" (p. 63). Writers preferred feeling (F) over thinking (T), while the mathematicians, research scientists, and engineers preferred thinking. Architects were split fifty-fifty in the thinking-feeling dimension. About two-thirds of the creative professionals were introverted (I), although MacKinnon said, "there is no evidence that introverts as such are more creative than extroverts" (p. 63).

Interests and values were also similar across domains. In interests, the creative adults were alike in being "relatively uninterested in small details, or in facts for their own sake, and more concerned with their meanings and implications" (p. 64). They were cognitively flexible, skilled verbally, accurate communicators, and they had intellectual curiosity. They were also "relatively disinterested in policing either their own impulses and images or those of others" (p. 64). In values, all the groups were again similar. Their highest values were the theoretical and the aesthetic. MacKinnon (1978) said that these creative adults had "the capacity to tolerate the tension that strong opposing values create" within the psyche, and that their creative acts were often a striving to achieve reconciliation among opposing values (p. 64). Aesthetic values came through as the adults sought to make their produced works elegant or beautiful. MacKinnon said, "For the truly creative person, it is not sufficient that problems be solved; there is the further demand that the solution be elegant. He seeks both truth and beauty" (p. 64). The last commonality among the creative adults was that most of them were able to produce very unusual mental associations. MacKinnon (1978) said that "the unusualness of mental associations is one of the best predictors of creativity" (p. 65). These characteristics appeared in exceptionally talented adults across domains, across ethnic groups, and across gender.

ADULT CHARACTERISTICS OF PEOPLE WITH SCIENCE TALENT

Three of the main studies of those with science talent have been the research neurologists studied by the Development of Talent Research Project at the University of Chicago (Bloom, 1985), Zuckerman's (1977) study of Nobel prize winners, and Simonton's (1988) *Scientific Genius*. Longitudinal studies such as the Subotnik and Steiner (1994) study of Westinghouse winners, discussed in Chapter 7 should also be included in a discussion of science talent (although at this writing these winners are still early in their careers). Many scientists have paths similar to those of the adult research neurologists studied in the Development of Talent Research Project at the University of Chicago. Their characteristics include curiosity, intellectual agility and ability, and high-level educational attainment.

Adult Research Neurologists

Lauren Sosniak (1985b), in the Development of Talent Research Project at the University of Chicago, studied research neurologists. These were scientists who had first gone to medical school. Medicine is one of the most popular career choices for scientifically talented youth (Colangelo & Kerr, 1990). Twenty research neurologists were studied who had met three criteria: (1) they had received National Institute of Health grants for at least five years; (2) their work had been frequently cited in professional journals; and (3) they were well regarded by chairs of departments of neurology.

After the narrowing of their focus in college, when they decided they really liked to do research, and after their application and acceptance to medical school, they decided to focus on neurology, usually around the second or third year. The choice was greatly influenced by the neurology professors they had. They were often chosen by professors, singled out and encouraged. This is a common way that young talent is developed (Zuckerman, 1977). After a certain point, the professors choose the students to mentor; it is seldom the other way around. If a student is not chosen by a desired mentor, the student's career path is decidedly affected. As touched on earlier, Simonton (1988) called it the *constant probability of success* model. To have one's research coauthored by a respected authority is to be put on the fast path, to state to the world that one is part of the authority's "stable." Here is a comment from the research neurologists about the importance of mentors:

> In the middle of my junior year in medical school a neurology department was created, and one of the guys that came is a guy I still work with. And he took an interest in me . . . It was very fortunate. He had time. He had interest in me. And after a year or two I got the hang of doing research and learning methods. . . . In addition to thinking straight [he] was a role model of somebody who really worked hard and enjoyed it . . . If I'd gone to medical school or another residency and had someone who wasn't as talented as [he is], I don't know that I would be as happy with what I'm doing, which is one measure of success. (Sosniak, 1985b, p. 400)

After graduation from medical school, the neurologists typically took postdoctoral positions in medical research, honing their research abilities. They had to learn how to formulate problems and to ask the right questions. They had to learn how to function in the higher levels of the world of scientists. They had to find out how grants are obtained. They had to learn how to meet high standards in competitive situations. They learned to delay gratification and to count on luck and connections.

Simonton (1988) emphasized that personality traits may change or modify throughout a scientist's life; that is, to use personality inventories early on to find potential scientists is not the most accurate way to do so. However, he said that voracious and continuous reading early and throughout one's life leads to creativity as an adult, no matter the field. The type of reading preferred is different. He also noted that adult scientists are very productive; they begin their productivity early and continue until they die. They are often workaholics, finding intense pleasure in the laboratory and in doing experiments. The intense life of the laboratory is often solitary pleasure, although teamwork and collaboration are increasingly necessary. Those who are academics prefer their research to their teaching, though they may be good teachers. There is no indication that researchers are not good teachers.

The physicist Michael Pupin, in his autobiography *From Immigrant to Inventor* (1922/1960), tells how he invented the electrical transmission line that made long-distance telephone possible. He was a professor at Columbia University and had been a mentor of Armstrong, who invented the FM transmitter, illustrating again how the path of adult development often shows a convergence of talents to certain schools and certain people. Pupin commented on the intense pleasure science brings to scientists: an aesthetic pleasure. He said, "The physical facts of science are not cold, unless your soul and your heart are cold. There is white heat somewhere in every physical fact when we decipher correctly the message which it conveys to us" (pp. 379–380). This intense pleasure in immersion in the domain is key to understanding why a person becomes an adult creative producer. (Pupin also noticed that the teaching load was so great that the professors had to do research in their spare time, at night. He was a pioneer in reducing the teaching loads of scientists so that they could do research as part of their workload, and he is credited for the renewed interest in universities for research.)

ADULT CHARACTERISTICS OF PEOPLE WITH MATHEMATICS TALENT

Mathematicians, people who choose to spend their lives solving mathematical problems, differ from scientists, people who use mathematics as a tool, in the sense that mathematicians view their field as composers view their compositions, or as novelists view the making of a novel. The process of solving the problem is as important as getting the product. Mathematics has an intrinsic beauty that can be discovered by the mathematician.

The mathematician and philosopher Bertrand Russell (1967) described his ecstasy in discovering the principles of mathematics. He attended an International Congress of Philosophy in Paris in 1900 in order to read a paper. There he met the philosopher Peano, whose work excited him. Alfred North Whitehead and his wife were staying with Russell and his wife at his estate, Fernhurst, and the two men engaged in long discussions about the new mathematical and logical principles they were thinking. He said:

> It seems to me in retrospect that, through that month, every day was warm and sunny . . . Every evening the discussion ended with some difficulty, and every morning I found that the difficulty of the previous evening had solved itself while I slept. The time was one of intellectual intoxication. My sensations resembled those one has after climbing a mountain in the mist, when, on reaching the summit, the mist suddenly clears, and the country becomes visible for forty miles in every direction. For years I had been endeavouring to analyse the fundamental notions of mathematics, such as order and cardinal numbers. Suddenly, in the space of a few weeks, I discovered what appeared to be definitive answers to the problems which had been baffling me for years. And in the course of discovering these answers, I was introducing a new mathematical technique, by which regions formerly abandoned to the vaguenesses of philosophers were conquered for the precision of exact formulae. (p. 218)

Likewise, in 1992, Professor Jerry P. King of Lehigh University was quoted in an article called "Championing the Philosophy and Beauty of Mathematics" as saying that mathematics "is the loveliest subject on the face of the earth" (Wheeler, 1992, p. A6). King, the author of *The Art of Mathematics* (1992), said that mathematicians know two truths: one is that mathematics flows from a set of a few general principles, and second, that "at its highest levels, it is done for aesthetic reasons. You do it because it's pretty, not because it keeps airplanes in the sky or because it explains the economy" (p. A6).

King called calculus the "gateway into beautiful mathematics." He created two general aesthetic principles that define mathematics' beauty. The first is the principle of minimal completeness: "like a poem with no extra words, a beautiful theorem completely fulfills its mathematical mission without containing any extraneous elements." The second is the principle of maximal applicability, which is that a "mathematical 'notion' can be widely applied throughout mathematics" (Wheeler, 1992, p. A6). Like the best art created by the best artists, mathematics exists primarily in the mind of the mathematician. The question of creating and discovering is key here: If mathematics exists "out there" as physics exists "out there," are mathematicans discovering it or creating it?

Gustin (1985), in his study of 19 male and one female exceptional research mathematicians, showed that in their adult years they worked extremely hard and long. Gustin said that the mathematicians were "nearly obsessive," and that their "motivation became increasingly central." Mathematics was the one thing, for most of them, that they did extremely well. One mathematician said:

> In spite of what my parents would have had me believe, that I could do anything I set my mind to, I came to the conclusion that that was false. At this point in my life there isn't any particular evidence that I could do anything else particularly well. The point is that there is one area, and one area alone, that I know that I can perhaps in a narrow way be doing something that's on the frontier of present knowledge. Here's one area where I've invested so many years and I've had a certain amount of success, enough to make me feel that I'm not wasting my time. That's a lot of motivation to continue. (p. 328)

The motivation to create is evident in the mathematician's statement, as it is in the lives of other adult creative productive people. The mathematicians, Gustin (1985) said, were "enthralled with the excitement of a new result, a solution to a difficult and elusive problem" (p. 329), and, while they worked in a field where only a few people can understand what they're doing—"typically, neither parents, wives, nor friends understand the work of the mathematicians"—they derived great satisfaction, and "a desire to extend our knowledge of what is true" (p. 330).

Math Olympians

Crosscultural studies of people who were top winners in the Math Olympiad competition have also been conducted (Campbell, 1996). Annually, only eight (six plus two alternates) students out of an initial 350,000 students receive the title of Olympian after taking three progressively more difficult mathematics tests. These eight students attend a summer training program that prepares them for international competition. Only two of the 135 students selected since 1972 have been female. Ninety-four former Olympians participated in the study. Most were Caucasian (84 percent) and Asian-American (16 percent) with a disproportionate number of Jewish students as compared to their presence in the normal population. Two-thirds were firstborn children in small families with children spaced widely apart. Their parents were rather well-to-do, with most of them reporting incomes over $65,000 and 92 percent of them owning their own homes. Their parents, both mother and father, had college educations, with almost half having Ph.D.s, law degrees, and medical degrees. Three-quarters of the Olympians played musical instruments.

Their parents (85 percent) discovered their talents prior to their entering school. Most of them attended public schools (82 percent). Almost half were enrolled in special programs for the gifted during elementary school. Their parents didn't pressure them unduly. Campbell said, "Parents tried not to use pressure as a motivating force

Being a television producer requires spatial, verbal, and mathematical talents.

during the Olympians' developing years" (p. 502). He said, "overall, the Olympians' families supplied higher levels of psychological support and intellectual resources and low levels of monitoring . . ." One-fourth of them were class valedictorians in high school, and most of them graduated from high school at age 16 or 17, indicating that they had been accelerated. Their average SAT Math score was about 500, and the SAT Verbal score was 475. They took more than three Advanced Placement courses in high school. Their extracurricular activities included chess, chorus, the student newspaper, church groups, and most sports except for football. They spent a lot of time on the computer. Those who spent the most time had the lowest grades.

They attended elite colleges on scholarship. They graduated and became professors, engineers, scientists, and computer programmers/designers. They had published 435 articles, 15 books, 274 reasearch papers, and held 15 patents. They averaged nine publications per person. Most were below 30 years old when studied, and so their productivity would be expected to increase. They attributed their publication record to the mentoring they received during their undergraduate and graduate years. A second factor that contributed to their productivity was "effort attribution" (Campbell, p. 511). Campbell noted that "computer literacy was negatively related to productivity, which indicates that Olympians in the computer area do not publish extensively" (p. 511). This may be that they are employed outside academe and their promotions do not hinge on their publication records. A third factor in their productivity was their family's SES (socioeconomic status). They were the children of professors who went on to be professors. "The Olympians who came from higher SES families had the highest level of academic productivity" (p. 512).

A qualitative analysis showed 10 themes in their lives: (1) they delayed in realizing their great mathematics talent; (2) they learned to read early and read math books for pleasure "like others read novels" (p. 513); (3) they were able to turn negative school experiences (of boredom and of nonrecognition of their talents) into growth experiences; (4) they were autonomous, a trait that helped them solve mathematics problems; (5) they were flexible and largely self-taught; (6) their parents were resourceful, finding them special programs, special materials, and special schools; (7) they sometimes had difficulties in social relations, and some had been beaten up, taunted, and teased. One said, "A large fraction of students are hostile to a peer for whom a subject (like math) is easy. They feel that they look bad in comparison" (p. 517). Another said, "More frequently I experience ignorance, fear or apathy toward scholastic achievement" (p. 517). (8) They needed more challenge than they received in school; (9) they had an internal motivation derived from their passion for mathematics; and (10) they considered themselves intellectuals from intellectual home environments.

Creative Female Mathematicians

The preponderance of male subjects in the studies done of creative people is overwhelming. Thus it is refreshing to discuss Ravenna Helson's 1983 study of creative women mathematicians. Helson found that creative female mathematicians were essentially like other creative people, especially female and male creative writers. Forty-four women mathematicians were studied at the IPAR Project at the University of California at Berkeley. The women were nominated by peers and listed in directories of Ph.D.s who had completed their degrees between 1950 and 1960. The criterion for calling these women creative was the quality of their work. Calling them "marginal" in the profession of mathematics, Helson noted that several of them did not hold academic posts or posts in research institutions, but did their work at home. Their average age was 41, one-third were Jewish, and foreign cultural influence (European and Canadian) was strong, as it is with male mathematicians. They were administered personality instruments such as the California Psychological Inventory (CPI) and the Minnesota Multiphasic Personality Inventory (MMPI).

The women mathematicians had superior intellect and great perseverance. They were adaptable and sensitive to the new and to the unforeseen. Their temperaments were subdued but still individualistic. The assessment staff did a clinical Q-sort, and several characteristics emerged as descriptive of the creative mathematicians. They were independent and autonomous, taking pride in their objectivity and rationality while still being able to form associations and think in new ways. They were seen as being dramatic personalities, even "histrionic," and as moody and nonconforming rebels.

In addition, a comparison study was done between the creative women mathematicians and other women mathematicians. The creative women mathematicians were found to be performing in a manner superior to the others, in that they received their Ph.D.s earlier, they submitted papers for publication before their Ph.D.s, and they received more fellowships and grants after graduate school. The creative women were higher in flexibility and lower in achievement orientation and in cooperation, showing that they preferred to do things their own way. They did not enjoy the routine details of working in a highly structured environment. The creative women mathematicians seemed to be preoccupied with themselves, showed more autonomy, and could be described as temperamental.

Self descriptions showed that they were more involved in research than the comparison women mathematicians, and their thought processes seemed to be less overtly conscious. They described themselves as "inventive and ingenious" (Helson, 1983, p. 314), and were less interested in salaries, promotions, and teaching. In their leisure time, the creative women had intellectual pursuits such as listening to classical music, taking nature walks, going to the theater, and reading. They seemed to have simplified their lives and did the few things they cared about greatly. Homemaking and research occupied most of their time, while the comparison women spent much time in administrative duties, teaching, political activity, and community work. The creative subjects scored higher on the Terman Concept Mastery Test than the comparison women. Their score was 144. (The Stanford gifted subjects scored 137, industrial research scientists scored 118, and military officers scored 60.) Creative male mathematicians scored 148. In mechanical reasoning, the creative and comparison women did not differ, and they both scored lower than men.

Helson (1983) noted that these women seemed to have identified more with their professional fathers than the comparison group of women. Both groups often came from families of girls, and the creative women seemed to have few brothers. She said "A number of the women mathematicians seem to have been adopted as the 'son' of an intellectual father" (p. 315). The creative female mathematicians differed from the creative male mathematicians studied. The creative males were higher on social ascendancy, or a desire to rise on the social ladder, as well as intellectual efficiency, or how fast and clearly they could express themselves. Helson said:

> The creative men described themselves as having confidence, initiative, ambition, impact on the environment, and intellectual balance and soundness. In contrast, the creative women described themselves as nonadventurous and inner-focused. In the work style of the creative women the self is totally committed, unconscious as well as conscious processes are involved in the creative effort, and emphasis is directed toward developing what is within rather than toward exploring or mastering the environment. (p. 317)

The fact that this study took place in the late 1960s and studied women who received their college education in the 1950s and 1940s may have something to do with the large gender differences found between creative male and creative female mathematicians. However, even recently, Eccles (1985b; Eccles & Harold, 1992) and her colleagues have shown that mathematical attitudes in the family contribute to females achieving less in mathematics. Mothers' attitudes toward the probability of mathematical success seem to be crucial. Mothers may say to their daughters, "Well, I was never good in math either," and to their sons, "Boys are better at math; they have math ability."

Helson theorized that there may be biological or societal causes for the gender differences. She did a comparison study of creative women writers with the creative women mathematicians and found that the two groups of creative women were remarkably similar. Interestingly enough, she also found that the creative male writers were more like the creative women mathematicians and women writers than they were like the creative male mathematicians. This led Helson (1983) to describe the creative male mathematicians as people who stood alone. "They [creative male mathematicians] have a personality in which there is relatively more social assurance and assertiveness and less conflict with conventional channels of expression and achievement" (p. 318).

The male writers, like the females, paid more attention to unconscious processes than to mastery and initiative. However, the male mathematicians and writers both emphasized their ambition to a greater extent than the creative women, who emphasized that they would be willing to put aside other things in order to write or do mathematics. Helson did further studies and came up with the hypothesis that there are two creative styles: (1) high in ego-assertiveness, or the need to push oneself in the world; and (2) low in ego-assertiveness. Women creators seem to be the latter, and men may be either.

The creative women mathematicians worked at home, did not have prestigious academic posts, and did not teach graduate students. In fact, their lifestyles were more similar to those of the writers than of their male mathematical counterparts. The low ego-assertiveness style does not lead to the publishing of many papers, nor is it productive in the way that Simonton said creative scientists must be. Helson (1983) said that the creative women mathematicians may have been more productive, but the institutions had trouble with their ambivalent and aloof personalities. She said "Understanding and experiment are needed on both the institutional side and the individual side" (p. 329). These glaring differences between creative women mathematicians and creative male mathematicians speak to the continuing difficulty of women in achieving in creative fields because of their double bind, the continuing social expectation that they work the second shift at home as well as the first shift at their creative work.

SOCIAL SCIENCE TALENT: CREATIVE WOMEN PSYCHOLOGISTS

Many academically talented women may not go into pure science or mathematics because of the constraints detailed in Helson's study. A study by Bachtold and Werner (1970/1984) looked at women who had mathematical talent and verbal talent which they combined, and who went into the social science of psychology. The study revealed interesting things about female academics in psychology. The researchers compared 124 psychology professors with the general female population, with college women, with successful academic men, and with male psychologists. The women in psychology had significant differences from the other women in 14 of 16 areas. They were more intelligent, they liked words, they liked working alone, they liked intellectual companionship, they were more silent and introspective, they were more serious and concerned, they were more likely to be introverts than extroverts, they were intensely subjective and had rich inner mental lives; however, they were not recluses, and they liked new experiences. They were accepting and adaptable, open, ready to take chances, and inclined to experiment with solutions to problems.

Successful academic women, they were more likely to be assertive and self-assured. Bachtold and Werner (1970/1984) said, "dominance seems to be a prerequisite for analytic thinking" (p. 242). They had exact, calculating minds, and were able to be flexible in their viewpoints. They showed a similarity to the women Helson studied in that they were theoretically, aesthetically, and independently oriented. They were similar to successful academic men in that they were aloof, intelligent, assertive, serious, flexible, adventuresome, adaptable, and self-sufficient. They differed from successful academic men in that they had higher intellectual ability, were more radical, less serious, and had more rigid internal standards.

More of the women were in clinical fields while the men preferred research. The women in counseling and guidance were more group dependent; the women in developmental psychology were more socially aloof and independent; the counseling psychologists were more adventuresome than the clinical psychologists. The clinical psychologists were "less secure" than the developmental psychologists.

The successful academic psychologists who had more publications preferred contemplation over social relationships. They liked working alone and liked rigorous thought. They also liked intellectual companionship. Developmental psychologists had more publications than clinical or counseling psychologists. There was an interesting difference between the academic women who published and those who did not publish. The women who published had diverse activities; they divided their time between teaching and other scholastic activities, while the women who did not publish spent almost all their time on one job activity. In other words, the more varied the woman's activities, the more productive she was. The women who were college administrators had great social alertness and more aloofness, and the women who were college teachers had a psychological dependence on comfortable relationships with people.

Bachtold and Werner (1970/1984) thought that selection of girls for college and graduate programs should be looked at in terms of personality characteristics:

> The great number of significant differences between the personality profiles of the college women and the successful academic women and the lack of similarity between the personality profiles of gifted girls in special education programs and recognized creative people, both men and women, seem to indicate that a selection on the basis of intelligence and achievement tests does not lead to the discovery and encouragement of potentially creative girls in special classes from the elementary to the college level. (p. 343)

They went on to say that for women, as well as men, personality characteristics such as confidence and unconventionality—even radicalism—may be the determinants of successful academic careers for females.

LONGITUDINAL STUDIES OF TALENTED WOMEN

Project CHOICE

Fleming and Hollinger did a longitudinal study of 80 young women (13 percent African-American) in private, parochial, and public high schools (Fleming & Hollinger, 1994; Hollinger, 1996). Called "Project CHOICE: A Longitudinal Study of Career Development of Talented Young Women," it identified the subjects in 1977, when they were high school sophomores. The researchers followed up on them at the 5- and 10-year points. The young women had received a diagnostic-prescriptive program of counseling and intervention focusing on "understanding issues in female socialization; acquiring a realistic assessment of one's interests, abilities, and values; gathering information regarding the requirements and rewards of appealing occupations; engaging in reality testing; decision making and life planning activities" (p. 318). Utilizing contemporary career development theory, the researchers sought to individualize the plans and intervention for each young woman.

Career theorists have come to realize that career development for women must take into account not only the school and the schooling, but the other life spheres, for these life spheres have great impact on women's career development. In reformulating career development theory, these researchers (Astin, 1985; Farmer, 1985; Gottfredson, 1981; Tittle, 1983) "have drawn attention to the interrelatedness and interdependence of multiple life roles on career decisionmaking and development" (Fleming & Hollinger, 1994, p. 5). Women's career development is more complex than men's career development, and career development theorists have recommended that the dimension of relatedness be taken into account when considering women's careers.

Adult women, no matter what their IQ, no matter what their talent, realize that they have to cope with the fact that they are the childbearers. This has profound implications on their career development. Fleming and Hollinger (1994) said that there is a three-way interaction for women. This is the interaction of person, work environment, and relational context. They suggested that intense work also be undertaken with men and boys "if we are ever to expect them to accept, support, and encourage their gifted spouses'/significant others' journey toward realized potential" (p. 340).

The intense intervention in high school helped the young women in the private, public, and parochial schools raise their expectations and aspirations. The young women who attended private and public schools went on to higher education to a greater degree than those from the parochial schools. The former also attained greater career levels than the latter.

The careers ranged wide. The young women were "law partners, physicians, project managers in public and private engineering firms, film/tv producers, concert musicians, systems/policy analysts, philosophers, neuroscientists, graphic and fine artists, horticulturists, and actresses" (Fleming & Hollinger, 1994, p. 338). Like the general population, some of the women who were followed up also had wrestled with substance abuse, divorce, family dysfunction, and financial exigency. However, they attended college in significantly greater numbers than a control group, they graduated from college, and they entered a diverse group of professions in greater numbers than other females in their state.

The wide range of occupational choices among these women attests to the selection procedure that Fleming and Hollinger (1994) used. They identified the young women by talent domain, and not by scores on an IQ test. They said that codifying their subjects' accomplishments at age 15 on a wide range of types "appears to have paid off handsomely in allowing us to follow more diverse accomplishments in adulthood than academic ones alone would have predicted" (p. 18). Again, this study demonstrates the promise for successful career development intervention during the formative years in the educations of young women. Hollinger (1996) recommended that counselors also emphasize the relational imperative with young women as the reality is that women still follow their husbands in their careers and must "compose a life," starting over and over again as the family moves to new places (Bateson, 1989).

Kerr's Study

Barbara Kerr studied a group of women who had been in the Accelerated Learning Program (ALP) in St. Louis, Missouri, from fifth to twelfth grade. Her first look, 10 years after graduation, was published in *Smart Girls, Gifted Women* (1985). She found that these young women were very similar to the women in the Terman study, even though the Terman women were 40 years older. Most of the women in the ALP group, like the Terman women, had chosen to be homemakers and to have careers in traditional female areas such as teaching, nursing, or clerical fields. Most of the women in the ALP group were satisfied that they had made the right choices, and at age 29 they tended to be married, happy, with children. Kerr (1992, 1997) also noted that at the 10-year follow-up, the women "all denied their giftedness; every respondent in one way or another disparaged the construct of giftedness, insisted on average abilities, or deemed the notion of giftedness irrelevant to their lives" (1992, p. 240). At the 10-year follow-up, the ALP women also recounted "a pattern of declining career aspirations and a series of compromises" in order to back their husbands' aspirations and in order to care for their children. Kerr placed these 23 women in four descriptive groups, the homemakers, those with "disposable careers," those in dual career couples, and those who were single achievers.

In 1992 Kerr conducted a 20-year follow-up and was able to reach all 23 of the ALP women. Twenty years after high school graduation, the women were in much the same circumstances, with families that were growing up. They had a lower rate of divorce than the general population. Kerr grouped them into four groups: (1) the Committed Traditionals, who were teachers and homemakers; (2) the Transforming Women, who had changed their lives despite hardship, following their dreams; (3) the Continuing Professionals, who had completed professional aspirations such as medicine and the military; and (4) the Overwhelmed Women, who continued in low-paying jobs, struggling to make ends meet and to meet the demands of their families. Some of the women were, expectedly, experiencing health problems.

Kerr concluded first that "choices made in late adolescence and early adulthood impose clear limits upon adult attainments" and second, "the impact of giftedness on these women's lives is complex and ambiguous." That is, their high abilities enabled them to achieve, in some cases, without formal education—to start businesses, for example; however, having been "labeled" saddled them with a feeling of regret for not having fulfilled the "external expectations" that such a label had put upon them.

THE PATH OF ADULT CREATIVE WRITERS

The path of the person who wants to be a creative writer is somewhat known by now (Piirto, 1992a/1998):

1. The creative writer was most often an avid, voracious, ravenous, passionate reader, in childhood, adolescence, and adulthood, and continues to be so throughout life.
2. Writers seem to have experienced childhood trauma more often and seem more likely to suffer from adult clinical depression.
3. They often used their early reading and their early writing to escape from the world, and to make sense of the world.
4. When tested on standardized tests, they demonstrate high verbal and conceptual intelligence.
5. They value self-expression over pleasing people.
6. They are productive, often working on several genres at once.
7. They are often driven, but are able to take the rejection of their submitted manuscripts time after time.
8. They like to work alone and value solitude.
9. They seem to have difficulty with alcohol, perhaps to a greater extent than the normal population, although no studies have been conducted.
10. They prefer to write as their means of expression of their emotions and feelings. (p. 170)

Literary biographies are rife: one can go to any university library to see shelf after shelf filled with scholarly and critical biographies about writers. Autobiographies also abound. One of the basic themes that emerges from perusing such richness of documentation and speculation about the lives of successful adult creative writers is that they wrote out of emotional need, and not out of wish for fame and fortune. A series of interviews of writers conducted by *The Paris Review* has included most of the contemporary writers of renown. In an interview, E.L. Doctorow (Plimpton, 1988) said, "A writer's life is so hazardous that anything he does is bad for him. Anything that happens to him is bad: failure's bad, success is bad, impoverishment is bad, money is very, very bad. Nothing good can happen." The interviewer, George Plimpton, replied: "Except the act of writing itself." Doctorow responded:

> Except the act of writing. So if he shoots birds and animals and anything else he can find, you've got to give him that. And if he/she drinks, you give him/her that too, unless the work is affected. For all of us, there's an intimate connection between the struggle to write and the ability to survive on a daily basis as a human being. So we have a high rate of self-destruction. Do you mean to punish ourselves for writing? For the transgression? I don't know. (pp. 315–316)

Joyce Carol Oates, in an essay called "Beginnings" (1988) in her collection of essays called *(Woman) Writer*, noted that writers "cannibalize" their own experiences in order to create their art:

> It remains a surprising (and disturbing) fact to many literary observers that writers should, upon occasion, write so directly from life; that they should "cannibalize" and even "vampirize" their own experiences. But this species of creation is surely inevitable? entirely natural? The artist is driven by passion; and passion most powerfully derives from our own experiences and memories. Writers as diverse as William Butler Yeats,

Marcel Proust, August Strindberg, D.H. Lawrence, Ernest Hemingway, even, to a less obsessive degree, Thomas Mann, Willa Cather, Katherine Anne Porter—all were writers of genius, whose imaginations were not constrained but positively energized . . . by specific events in their lives. (p. 6)

Oates went on to say that writers don't know what they think until they write it down; their writing is an act of trying to come to terms with, of trying to understand, life—and especially their own lives in relationship to the world at large. She said that the mystery is why some things and not other things inspire writers to create: "a word, a glance, a scene glimpsed from a window, a random memory, a conversational anecdote, the shard of a dream" may spark the writer to "intense creativity," while other things do not. The study of young verbally talented children (Benbow, 1992, Colangelo & Kerr, 1990) indicated that their long-term memories were more efficient than those of mathematically talented youth. These sparks of memory, of connection, which Oates documented above, become, in the hands of the skilled writer, great or lesser works of literature.

Barron (1968, 1972) noted that in studying creative writers at the Institute for Personality Assessment and Research (IPAR), writers were statistically more likely to engage in what he called "primary process phenomena" in their creative activity. These were phenomena such as dreams, "especially recurring dreams, prophetic dreams, and dreams of a preternatural vividness and intensity." Other phenomena were "precognitions, telepathy, clairvoyance, the occurrence of unusual coincidences, falling in love, mystical experience of oneness with the universe." On the negative side, phenomena such as "total forlornness" were also experienced by the writers (Barron, 1972, p. 144).

The following list gives the observed personality characteristics of the creative writers (Barron, 1972):

1. Appears to have a high degree of intellectual capacity
2. Genuinely values intellectual and cognitive material
3. Values own independence and autonomy
4. Is verbally fluent; can express ideas well
5. Enjoys aesthetic impressions; is aesthetically reactive
6. Is productive; gets things done
7. Is concerned with philosophical problems; for example, religion, values, the meaning of life and so forth
8. Has high aspiration level for self
9. Has a wide range of interests
10. Thinks and associates with ideas in unusual ways; has unconventional thought processes
11. Is an interesting, arresting person
12. Appears straightforward, forthright, and candid in dealing with others
13. Behaves in an ethically consistent manner; is consistent with own personal standards (p. 146)

Barron characterized the writers he studied as "courageous" in their willingness to continue to experience the world in childlike ways. He said that their creative powers, like those of other creators, expand as they grow older and their controversial stands reflect "qualities of freshness and spontaneity that seem more common in children."

In a book called *On Becoming a Novelist* (1982), the widely respected novelist, essayist, and teacher John Gardner characterized writers as having several strengths, among them strong "verbal sensitivity" (p. 3), that may or may not be recognized by their English teachers; this is different in poets, short story writers, and novelists, with poets being more "persnickety," short story writers having a talent for "lyrical compression," and novelists having a talent for fitting language to character and situation. A second characteristic is having a good eye: "the good writer sees things sharply, vividly, accurately, and selectively" (p. 19) and can create "powerfully vivid images in the reader's mind" (p. 27). Intelligence is the third characteristic: "a certain kind of intelligence, not the mathematician's or the philosopher's but the storyteller's" (p. 24). This intelligence has these qualities:

> It is composed of several qualities, most of which, in normal people, are signs of either immaturity or incivility: wit (a tendency to make irreverent connections); obstinacy and a tendency toward churlishness (a refusal to believe what all sensible people know is true); childishness (an apparent lack of mental focus and serious life purpose, a fondness for daydreaming and telling pointless lies; a lack of proper respect, mischievousness, an unseemly propensity for crying over nothing); a marked tendency toward oral or anal fixation or both (the oral manifested by excessive eating, drinking, smoking, and chattering; the anal by nervous cleanliness and neatness coupled with a weird fascination for dirty jokes); remarkable powers of eidetic recall or visual memory (a usual feature of early adolescence and mental retardation); a strange admixture of shameless playfulness and embarrassing earnestness, the latter often heightened by irrationally intense feelings for or against religion; patience like a cat's; a criminal streak of cunning; psychological instability; recklessness, impulsiveness, and improvidence; and finally, an inexplicable and incurable addiction to stories, written or oral, bad or good. (p. 34)

The writer may go into a trance state while writing, a dream state. This involves the fourth characteristic of adult writers, which is "an almost daemonic compulsiveness" which can be exacerbated by psychological wounds, childhood trauma, defensiveness, guilt, or shame. Novelists are often "people who learned in childhood to turn, in times of distress, to their own fantasies or to fiction, the voice of some comforting writer, not to human beings near at hand" (Gardner, 1982, p. 62). This compulsiveness is manifest in the discipline and perfectionism by which the writer keeps on writing, despite rejection and lack of appreciation. To be driven is necessary, and Gardner thought "no novelist, I think, can succeed without it. Along with the peasant in the novelist, there must be a man with a whip" (p. 70). John Gardner said that even if a would-be writer lacks one of these four characteristics, and still wants to write, he or she should be encouraged to start: "In fact, he will anyway," Gardner said.

In a study of 160 contemporary U.S. writers, 80 males and 80 females, Piirto (1995d; 1998; in preparation) found themes in their lives. The themes were: (1) unconventional families and family traumas; (2) incidence of depression and/or self-destructive acts; (3) certain personality attributes such as motivation; (4) nurturing of talents by both male and female teachers and mentors; (5) predictive behavior of extensive early reading; (6) predictive behavior of early publication, keeping journals, writing to make sense of things; (7) residence in New York City at some point, especially among the most prominent; (8) attendance at prestigious colleges, majoring in English literature; (9) being in an occupation different from their parents; (10) history of divorce; (11) feeling of being an outsider, of marginalization and a resulting need to have their group's story told (e.g. minorities, lesbians, regional writers, writers from lower socioeconomic class, writers of different immigration groups); (12) possession of tacit knowledge; and (13) a personal and ritualized creative process. Gender-related themes included (1) conflict with combining motherhood and careers in writing; and (2) societal expectations of "femininity" incongruent with their essential personalities. Results showed that the women writers were not different from men writers except in the gender-related themes. These gender differences seem to be found among women across all professions.

THE PATH OF ADULT VISUAL ARTISTS

After the decision is made to become an artist, after the training needed, after the practice, the visual artist who is to become successful must, as Getzels and Csikszentmihalyi (1976) said, pay attention to the social context in which art success is engendered. Talent is necessary but not sufficient. For visual artists to come to public awareness, for them to sell their works and gain recognition, they must do at least three or four things:

1. They must buy or rent a loft, a studio, a work space, so that they can show their work, socialize, and retreat. The presence of the studio marks the visual artist as "serious" about his or her work.

2. They must begin to exhibit their work. Certain venues have more prestige than other venues. A one-person show in a gallery or a retrospective in a museum has the most prestige. Group shows in galleries are also acceptable. Entrance and exhibition of work in juried contests is necessary. All of these mark the artist as having received peer and expert recognition.

3. They must move to or near an art center, preferably New York City, in the United States. This is so they will be in "proximity" (Simonton, 1988). Visual artists are not taken seriously in the United States unless they have been recognized in the New York City art market, though other urban areas such as Los Angeles, Chicago, and San Francisco are also major centers, and there are regional centers such as Provincetown, Taos, and Boulder that also give the beginning artist a community and some cachet.

4. A safety step is to get an M.F.A. and try to obtain a position in an art school or in a department of art in a college or university. This keeps the visual artist in the business, but may isolate him or her from the current stream of new art.

Getzels and Csikszentmihalyi (1976) also noted that such socially aggressive steps often work against the ingrained personality of the artist, who is often introverted, fond of solitude, and iconoclastic. They noted that the visual artists they studied, those who were able to "find" the problems in their experiment, often experienced trauma when they moved to New York City, and it often took them several years to get back on track with their work. Another necessity they noted was that visual artists needed a source of financial support, a spouse with a regular job or a family with an inheritance, because the career path of the visual artist is rocky, difficult, and the possibility of success is slight.

Barron (1972) noted that the female visual artists he studied were often more practical than the male visual artists, whom he termed "gentleman pirates" (p. 45) in their bravado and swaggering assertions of passion for their work. The females were more likely to settle on majors in art education or commercial art, specialties that pointed them to secure jobs and some economic stability. Barron said that the male students he studied at the San Francisco and Provincetown art schools "seem much more likely to pursue their work in art." The men were more realistic and more passionate. He said, "the women are less likely to display singlemindedness in their commitment to art" (p. 37).

THE PATH OF ADULT MUSICIANS AND COMPOSERS

In adulthood, musicians and composers continue what was begun in their early lives: practice. Like visual artists, they must relocate to or near a center where music is played and performed. Kogan, in *Nothing But the Best* (1987), noted that New York City has many highly trained musicians: after graduation from Juilliard, "now one is one of thousands of musicians living between West Fifty-Seventh and West 110th streets, trying to get by" (p. 232). Kogan said:

> Hardly anyone ends up with a solo career. Some earn spots in orchestras, some in principal seats. Some teach, some free-lance and some do both. Some leave music entirely. Some reach the top and are disenchanted. Some drift into new careers and find contentment . . . Half the battle is persistence . . . The musician who wants a solo career must make a new commitment once out in the real world. The rest of life will be ruled by excessive discipline. The commitment must be seen as something one has chosen. The musician who sees the commitment as a sacrifice will always be bitter. (p. 232)

Some musicians set deadlines for themselves, saying, "If I haven't done such-and-such by such-and-such a time, I will get out of music and take up law." That is what Kogan herself did. The classical music world is fraught with Catch 22s, just as is the world of other performing arts. If one wants to win competitions, one must have experience in concert playing; however, in order to play concerts, one must have won competitions. To get a contract to record music, one must be on the way to fame, if not famous; in order to get fame and recognition, one must have recorded. To be able to play alone with a major orchestra, one must have been a soloist with another major orchestra. Kemp (1982) said that many musicians use their superior intellects to get out of music, to try out other careers.

The situation is often the same for composers of both popular and classical music. However, the reality is not always as depressing; the musician has mastered and embraced a separate language, the language of music, and knowing this language provides an emotional outlet. Boyd (1992) in her discussion of the creative process with 75 popular musicians of the 1960s and beyond, said that they all knew the pleasure they were able to give to their audiences. She quoted Christine McVie as saying, "Music is the most gratifying of all sensory feelings that we have. Everybody gets something from music; not everybody gets something from looking at a painting. It's the passion, it's the spirit of the person; it moves people" (p. 263). Kogan (1987) said that music, for many musicians "is like a religious calling" while others continue to play "because it's all they know" (p. 235). Many musicians end up thinking that "it was all worth it," and they realize, like one former child prodigy did, "the joy music gives him nothing else could. He could find joy in a person, but not the kind he finds in music" (p. 237). The intrinsic reasons for entering and continuing in the music field seem to speak strongly. Suffice it to say that few musicians would say they are sorry they know the language of music.

OTHER STUDIES OF ADULTS

The Importance of Mentors

Kaufmann, Harrel, Milam, Woolverton, and Miller (1986) did a follow-up of 139 of the 604 1964-1968 Presidential Scholars, young academic achievers who scored in the top 0.5 percent on the National Merit Scholarship Qualifying Test. Eighty-eight percent of them had completed graduate degrees, including 28 percent with doctorates, 17 percent with master's degrees, and 12 percent with medical degrees. About 18 percent of them were university professors, 13 percent were in the medical profession, and 10 percent were in law. Others were in business, the arts, service, sales, and graduate school, but about 42 percent were in fields such as homemaker, rancher, counselor, or guru. When asked about who had been their most significant mentors, 66 percent said their mentors had been teachers they had had, especially graduate professors and high school teachers. About 55 percent reported mentors of the same sex, and 45 percent reported mentors of the opposite sex. Most of the women (75 percent) had mentors of the opposite sex. Mentors provided role models, support, encouragement, and socialization into the profession.

The adult talented person often becomes a mentor. Advice from a student was given to prospective mentors (Ambrose, Allen & Huntley, 1994):

Staying away from didacticism, ruling and governing is important. Let them wonder and come to terms with what they need to know. Be completely open to their needs and interests. Guide them. Offer direction, but let the power of their own volition move them . . . . don't see a young person's interest of self-motivation as a threat . . . and do not forget that you can learn as well . . . treat them as human beings, not as students. (p. 133)

Fulfillment of Potential, Life Satisfaction, and Competence in Women

Schuster (1990) compared four studies in midlife of high-IQ women, some of whom had been in the Terman study. These were Birnbaum's study of 1975, Ginzberg's study of 1966, Schuster's study of 1986/1987, and Terman and Oden's study of 1959. These were women who had been born in 1910, 1920 to 1930, and 1940. There were differences in the careers of the 1910 and the 1940 birth cohorts, with the 1940 birth cohorts having spent more time in the work place and having achieved more in careers. This is not surprising. Having been labeled "gifted" affected all the women throughout their lives, with some of them saying the label made them feel "overly demanding and self-critical in adult life," and most of them saying that the label had had "an overall positive effect" (Schuster, 1986/1987 p. 474). Some denial of their abilities was still present, and many of the women did not see themselves as having exceptional abilities, but just the ability to "do things fast" (p. 475).

Most of the women expressed satisfaction with their lives regardless of their birth dates. However, those who had worked in careers outside the homes "perceived themselves as significantly more competent" than those who had stayed homemakers. Yet many of the women who had careers described themselves as socially isolated, better at work than at relationships with people. Schuster (1986/1987) said, "given the aspirations of many bright young women today who want to 'do it all' in career and family pursuits, the health and emotional risks that may be faced by gifted women with high potential need to be studied in greater detail" (p. 477). Walker (1989) expressed similar thoughts when speaking of her follow-up study of graduates of the Hunter College High School. Reis (1996) studied 12 older women, ages 55 to 70. Lynch (1996) studied four Polish women who maintained their prominence both during the Communist regime and during the democratic revolutionary times. Basu (1996) studied 15 Hindu college educated, professional women from India. Bell and Chase (1996) studied 27 women school superintendents. Napier (1996) studied nine women in the American Indian Leadership Program. West (1996) studied seven high-achieving rural women. Kastberg and Miller (1996) studied six women academics with blue-collar backgrounds. All had succeeded in their professional lives. Noble, Subotnik, and Arnold (1996) said:

> Overcoming adversity is a familiar refrain in gifted women's stories, as is the struggle to maintain self-confidence and self-esteem. Gender-role conflict poses significant challenges, from the athlete's and mathematician's encounter with masculine sterotypes, to the research scientist's efforts to combine committed relationships and careers. Institutional obstacles such as gender bias in testing, inflexible advancement tracks in science, and resistance to female leadership in educational administration threaten the achievement of many individuals. Decisive action . . . mentors, models, and allies are central features . . . giftedness, personal motivation and tenacity, the support of allies, and resilience enable the fulfillment of talent among exceptionally diverse women across social groups and domains. (p. 428)

Noble, Subotnik, and Arnold (1996) proposed a model of female talent development. The model takes into account the foundations from which the woman comes. If she is far from the mainstream, she has more difficulty than if she is right within the action. Her personality traits, her family background, and psychological factors such as resilience are also part of her foundation. These are filtered by the opportunities presented to her and by the demands of the talent domains she wishes to enter. The women then realize their potential in any of three paths: (1) in the personal domain through self-actualization; (2) in the public domain through leadership; and (3) in the public domain by attaining eminence (see Figure 8. 3).

Fulfillment of Potential, Life Satisfaction, and Competence in Men

Studies of adult men are not as recent as the studies of adult women. The Terman studies since 1925 have shown that the high-IQ men generally took their place in

Figure 8.3 A New Model of Female Talent Development

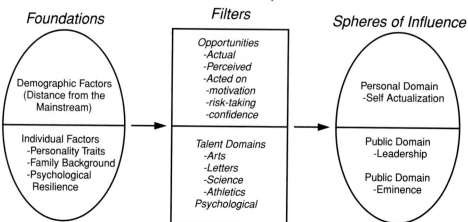

From K.D. Noble, F.F. Subotnik, and K.D. Arnold, (1996). "A New Model for Adult Female Talent Development." *In* K. Arnold, K.D. Noble, and R.F. Subotnik (Eds.), *Remarkable Women: Perspectives on Female Talent Development* (pp. 427–440). Cresskill, NJ: Hampton Press.

society as was expected, in professional positions. They went to college and demonstrated satisfaction with their lives. The follow-up study of the high-IQ students who attended Hunter College Elementary School (Subotnik et al., 1993) also showed that the men had relatively high incomes and liked their lives. One 40-year-old man responded to a question about how happy he was this way:

> I wouldn't trade in the essence of my life. On the other hand, I wish some things would have worked out differently. Law is, for me, a second career. I wish I could have been successful as a professor of sixteenth century English literature. But them's the breaks . . . My parents only now think that I have done something worthwhile [becoming a lawyer]. They did not and do not respect the academic life. I doubt I have the drive to be a superstar . . . nor am I sure that we need superstars. Talented people, sure. Visionaries, absolutely. But there is more than enough focus on individual brilliance in this world. (p. 91)

Subotnik et al. (1993) described the former Hunter students as choosing consciously not to "prove themselves by participating in the exhausting pursuit of revolutionary change" but instead opting for "relatively happy and successful lives" (p. 118). They concluded that personality attributes and personality disposition are the key factors that make the difference between eminence and "mere professional competence." Personality attributes are developed through interaction with life as well as through adversity and strife. They questioned whether education for eminence is even possible by beginning at the elementary school level, and noted that graduates of special high schools such as the University School at the University of Chicago had much greater numbers of eminent graduates.

Studies of eminent men have shown that if they are leaders, they have certain family emotional climates, usually parents who are appositional (warm mother, cold father), according to Gardner (1995a). They have strong verbal talents and the ability to tell a story that appeals to the masses. Simonton (1995) noted the leaders' aggressiveness and persistence as well as their prolificness in publishing and creating their work. They had "genetic endowment; integrative complexity; power, achievement, and affiliation motives; developmental experiences such as birth order, orphanhood, education, and marginality; . . . dogmatism, explanatory style, dominance, extraversion, morality, and psychopathology" (p. 403).

The Blurring of Traditional Gender Lines in Adulthood

Thus it seems that gender issues—that is, being male—are not as important to gifted men as being female is to gifted women, at least in halting their successful drive to eminence. However, a group of writers has been analyzing the roles of adult men and women with the result that the traditional lines between genders are being blurred in an attempt to unify. Writers such as Bly (1990), Farrell (1986), and Keen (1991) talk about what it means to be a man. Writers such as Brown and Gilligan (1992), Belenky, Clinchy, Goldberger, and Terule (1986), and Shepherd (1993) talk about the ways that women develop and grow. Shepherd (1993), a long-time scientist, talked about how she and her colleagues are feminizing science. Both genders emphasize cooperation, relatedness, feeling, the search for self, responsible morality, friendship, and empathy. All the writers are themselves gifted achievers.

Linda Jean Shepherd, the scientist, concluded that doing science needs the deep values and ways of knowing of the feminine:

> I do not believe in spurning technology or think that imposing more bureaucratic layers will solve the problems of science. I see it as a challenge to all individuals to open our minds to new possibilities, to reflect deeply, to reexamine our values, to come to know ourselves, to develop our feeling and intuition to complement thinking and sensation, to integrate the Feminine—to become more whole people. (p. 284)

Sam Keen, a psychologist, concluded that the struggle of the next century will be a struggle "between two tribes with opposite worldviews." The men and the women will be together. Those men and women with a "General Motors mentality" will oppose those men and women who want to save the earth. Keen said, "There is nothing more urgent that men and women have to do together than to redeem ourselves from anonymous organizations, too much television, and fast food, and rediscover the enduring satisfactions that are inseparable from common meals, the communion of friends, and the gathering of community" (p. 230). This blurring of gender lines in responsibility for more than one's own home and family, a lifting of responsibility to the highest levels, seems to be what visionary writers of both genders are saying, despite their differences in development.

COUNSELING ISSUES FOR ADULTS WITH TALENT

Lovecky (1986) focused on the emotional and social needs of adults with high IQs and of adults with personal talent. She found they exhibited five traits that make them at risk for interpersonal and intrapersonal confict. Such people may exhibit what Gardner (1983) called interpersonal and intrapersonal intelligences. These were (1) divergency; (2) excitability; (3) sensitivity; (4) perceptivity; and (5) entelechy. She said that these traits could have positive or negative implications for the talented adults.

Divergency

The ability to be unusual, innovative, inventive, and resourceful is a distinguishing trait of creative adults (Piirto, 1991a, 1992a/1998). These are positive traits, and people who are creative are often regarded as valuable in coming up with new ideas. However, they also may be looked askance at by groups at work; they may be stubborn and hold onto their ideas come what may; they may not "fit in"; they may rebel against the pressure in the work place to conform. Lovecky said divergent thinkers may "experience alienation and eventually an existential depression" (p. 573).

Excitability

Similar to the "overexcitabilities" in the Dabrowski theory (Piechowski, 1979), adults who have high IQs, "gifted adults" in Lovecky's (1986) terms, are excitable in that they are able to concentrate their energies for long periods of time: They are able to "focus their attention and concentration" and "to use their energies productively in a wide variety of interests, and to do many things well" (p. 573). This makes them take risks and lets them enjoy meeting challenges. They are not manic, however, because they can calculate the consequences of the risks, and are not reckless but know how to stop. High production is characteristic of gifted adults. However, they may experience difficulty in regulating themselves as far as the numbers of projects they take on, for they often fear boredom. Craving the new and different, such adults may be unable to finish the projects they take on, but may move to new projects in order to cure their boredom. Lovecky said, "Their dilemma is one of always doing but feeling little gratification because others often reap the rewards accruing from the long-term development of their initial ideas" (p. 573). "Chronic depression" that cycles itself into ever more production may be the result.

Sensitivity

Having a profound regard for others, and experiencing significant and real empathy are characteristic of some gifted adults. "They think with their feelings," Lovecky

(1986) said. "Poets, investigative reporters, Peace Corps workers, and political and religious leaders are often gifted in sensitivity" (p. 573). Piechowski (1992), in his case studies of Peace Pilgrim and Etty Hillesum, said that such people experience "transforming growth" (pp. 180). These people have an inner transformation that leads to a feeling of inner peace and an embracing of a world consciousness. Such people, who have reached the highest levels of human emotional development, form a conviction that "peace in the world will be secure only as each and every one of us works toward inner peace" (p. 183). The Dabrowski Theory of Positive Disintegration, as Dabrowski (1964) called it, has five levels, as shown in Figure 8.4.

This hierarchical theory of adult development has gained popularity in the field of the education of the gifted and talented ever since the late 1980s and early 1990s, when several conferences were held at Ashland University. People began doing dissertations on the topic of overexcitabilities (Ackerman, 1997; Breard, 1996), the part of the theory that focuses on the psychological intensities that gifted people supposedly have to a greater degree than others.

A problematic interpretation of this is the implication that only high-IQ adults can reach Levels IV and V. Silverman (1994) said that having "high moral values requires a complex organism with a facility for abstract reasoning. High intelligence is synonymous with abstract reasoning ability and complexity of thought" (p. 112). She went on: "Gifted children, both male and female, seem to have the moral and emotional sensitivity required to help society evolve from a dominator to a partnership mode." Later on in the same piece, Silverman decried the focus on talent development in the field of gifted education. "In the substitution of a mosaic of talents for children, we have lost the entire moral dimension of giftedness" (p. 113). She then went on to relate the definition of giftedness as asynchrony (see Chapter 5), and asynchrony as manifested in high IQ as found through IQ testing. "The higher the child's IQ, the greater the asynchrony" (p. 114). Silverman went on to equate asynchrony with moral understanding: "Asynchrony, intensity, and moral sensitivity are inherent in the experience of giftedness, whether or not a child demonstrates specific talents in a given domain" (p. 114). She defended the use of IQ tests, saying "even children from diverse ethnic backgrounds stand a better chance of being found on IQ tests than on achievement-based measures, since achievement is more a function of environment than ability. Many extremely gifted African-American children would never have been located without IQ tests" (p. 114).

Tolan (1994) went on with this argument in another article in the same special issue of *Roeper Review*: Whoever gifted adults may be, they are not people with talents that should be developed, but they are people with unusual minds. "Gifted children do not disappear when they graduate from high school or finish college or graduate degrees. They become gifted adults. If they enter adulthood blind to their unusual mental capabilities, they may go through their lives fragmented, frustrated, unfulfilled and alienated from their innermost beings" (p. 137). Giftedness is within, and not without, according to Silverman, Tolan, and Morelock (1996).

Feldman (1997) replied to Morelock (1996) saying, "Yet, there is a sense in which the preoccupations and concerns of those who wish to preserve the place of the extremely high IQ, verbally precocious child at the center of the field have taken their case too far." Feldman named here the primary characteristic of people with extremely high IQs, their verbal precocity, and that is what is problematic about the views of those who say that only people with high IQs can reach Levels IV and V in the hierarchy Dabrowski proposed. If a person is not prominent, eminent, or visible as a leader, how would one know whether Levels IV or V had been reached? That is a question that has been proposed by the thinkers about the theory. If *emotional* development is on a hierarchical continuum, and fewer and fewer people are able to reach the highest levels, tested intelligence may be irrelevant, unless verbal precocity is necessary to emotional development or only to the expression of that development in words and ideas. That may be why Piechowski sometimes uses a modified label for the Dabrowski theory, calling it the "Dabrowski theory of emotional development."

Piechowski expanded the concept of emotional giftedness in a paper in 1997 (Piechowski, 1997b). Emotional giftedness often brings on what Dabrowski called *positive maladjustment*: "It is positive because it means being true to oneself and to the universal ideals of compassion, caring, and to the idea that each individual deserves consideration" (p. 2). The emotionally gifted child or adult is very empathetic, compassionate, and humane. Along with this is an irate or outraged sense of justice: "such stance is often in opposition to others' self-interest, prejudice, and ruthlessness. Therefore, the two terms, *emotional giftedness* and *positive maladjustment,* overlap" (p. 2).

Lovecky (1986) said that such sensitive and peace-seeking, peace-loving adults may also not understand that "others do not feel so deeply or intensely" and thus they may judge others who do not care so deeply to be superficial. Such sensitive adults may also find that other people might be hesitant to share their concerns, and "other people may believe that the gifted adult experiences their pain more intensely than they do, and they may feel robbed of their own feelings" (p. 573). The vulnerability of such adults may lead them to isolate themselves, and to avoid relationships with others.

Perceptivity

Intuition (N) and perception (P) are often preferred modes of acting in talented youth and adults (Myers & McCaulley, 1985). Lovecky (1986) said, "these gifted adults are able to understand the meaning of personal symbols and to see beyond the superficiality of a situation to the person beneath" and may be especially able in helping people to self-understanding. Seeing the lie of social facades, such perceptive adults may be short-tempered with mundane social activity and may be impatient and even intolerant of the commerce of everyday life. Lovecky called this "seeing," and said that "People who are gifted at 'seeing' often seem to have a touch of magic about them. They are able to view their and others' behavior

Figure 8.4   Levels of Emotional Development According to Dabrowski's Theory of Positive Disintegration

---

Level V: Secondary Integration

The struggle for self-mastery has been won. Inner conflicts regarding the self have been resolved through actualization of the personality ideal. Disintegration has been transcended by the integration of one's values into one's living and being. The life is lived in service to humanity. It is lived according to the highest, most universal principles of loving—compassionate regard for the worth of every individual.

   Illustrative quote: *"A magnetic field in the soul."* —Dag Hammarskjøld

Level IV: Organized Multilevel Disintegration

Individuals are well on the road to self-actualization. They have found a way to reach their own ideas, and they are effective leaders in society. They show high levels of responsibility, authenticity, reflective judgment, empathy for others, autonomy of thought and action, self-awareness, and other attributes associated with self-actualization.

   Illustrative quote: *"Behind tranquility lies conquered unhappiness."* —Eleanor Roosevelt

Level III: Spontaneous Multilevel Disintegration

Multilevelness arises. The person develops a hierarchical sense of values. Inner conflict is vertical, a struggle to bring one's behavior to higher standards. There is a dissatisfaction with what one is, because of a competing sense of what one could and ought to be (personality ideal). This internal struggle between higher and lower can be accompanied by existential despair; anxiety, depression, and feelings of dissatisfaction with the self (inferiority, disquietude, astonishment).

   Illustrative quote: "I regard the better but follow the worse." —Marcus Tullius Cicero

Level II: Unilevel Disintegration

Individuals are influenced primarily by their social group and by mainstream values, or they are moral relativists for whom "anything goes," morally speaking. They often exhibit ambivalent feelings and indecisive flip-flop behavior because they have no clear-cut set of self-determined internal values. Inner conflicts are horizontal, a contest between equal, competing values.

   Illustrative quote: *"A reed shaken in the wind."* — Matthew, XI: 7

Level I: Primary Integration

Egocentrism prevails. A person at this level lacks the capacity for empathy and self-examination. When things go wrong, someone else is always to blame; self-responsibility is not encountered here. With nothing within to inhibit personal ambition, individuals at Level I often attain power in society by ruthless means.

   Illustrative quote: *"Dog-eat-dog mentality."*

---

objectively. However, others may then feel vulnerable and threatened" (p. 579). The perceptive gifted adult may hide what he or she has "seen" in order to prevent rejection by others.

Entelechy

Lovecky defined *entelechy* as "a particular type of motivation, inner strength, and vital force" (p. 574). The dictionary definition says *entelechy*, in Aristotelian terms, is the ability to actualize one's beliefs. It is the culmination of potentiality; thus entelechy is the goal of the education of the talented. These adults, Lovecky said, are often "highly attractive to others who feel drawn to openness, warmth, and closeness" (p. 574). However, such adults may also be vulnerable to overextension; to giving too much to others and not nurturing themselves. Lovecky said, "the risk is anxiety about requests from others and avoidance of closeness in interpersonal relationships" (p. 574).

The gifted adult with these characteristics should take care to (1) know oneself; (2) accept oneself; and (3) find sources of personal power by listening to their inner selves. They should also cultivate interpersonal relationships with people who appreciate them and their sensitivities. Lovecky said gifted adults may need to have large numbers of friends, each of whom serves to meet some needs and not others. Different facets of their multidimensionality can be nurtured by the various friends. Lovecky concluded that "gifted adults, perhaps more than any other group, have the potential to achieve a high degree of self-actualization" (p. 575).

Spiritual Growth

Piechowski (1992) said that the highest degree of actualization in such highly sensitive adults is spiritual growth, as Peace Pilgrim experienced it. The phases of spiritual growth are similar to the theoretical structures of various psychologists. For example, for Maslow, the highest plane was reached in peak experiences of self-actualization. For Jung, the highest level was completing one's individuation. For Adler, the framework was topped by struggling to work for the good of others; for Erich Fromm, reaching a loving existence was the ultimate. Piechowski (1992) said that in the fifth level of the Dabrowski theory, people who lead ordinary lives are capable of the inner transformation that leads to inner peace; this is the realization of nonseparateness: "that we are all cells in the one body of humanity, that our destinies are interconnected; and the choices we make—for personal gain or for the good of the whole—shape the world situation toward war or toward peace" (p. 202).

Both Piechowski and Lovecky echoed many other prominent psychological thinkers to imply clearly that the path of the gifted adult leads on from personal achievement in one's profession to a more universal plane. While spiritual growth is not emphasized in talent development throughout the developmental years, it seems to be a goal that adults seek. The key and stumbling block to attaining spiritual freedom seems to be forgiveness. Piechowski (1997b) said, "Even moral exemplars who, inspired by compassion, genuine love for their fellow human beings, and strong religious faith dedicated their lives to helping others, say that they have to make an effort to be forgiving" (p. 6). It seems that once one is able to forgive, one can be what Rubin (1996) called a *transcender*.

Often the process of forgiving comes in working with image, symbol, and metaphor through creative pursuits, especially the arts of writing, music, acting, and the making of visual representations. This seems to be a reason that many creators feel a deep connection to their essential selves while doing their work. Enlightenment does not only come from the "talking therapy."

Case Example: Engineer As High School Teacher

by Ruth Huber *(Used with permission of author)*

Ruth Huber teaches honors chemistry and physics at Medina High School in Medina, Ohio.

I was the older of two girls in a family of two children. Before I was born my father had specifically said that he wanted a girl. I guess that in our society I was unusually lucky, in that as a first child I was not a disappointment because I was a girl. I remember that as a very young child, no more than four, I wanted to be "a boy like Daddy." My mother talked me out of this by telling me that boys didn't wear jewelry and perfume (remember this was about 40 years ago, and back then they didn't). In retrospect, I believe that I realized, even then, that the boys got to have all the adventures and excitement. I know that when I watched the Mickey Mouse Club the characters that I most wanted to be like were the boys. The girls just stood around cheering them on, or being frightened, or whatever. The boys actually got to do all that neat stuff.

I was sort of the boy in the family by default. My father had hoped for a son when my sister was born, and when she turned out to be another girl, I was the one who hung around my father handing him tools and helping. Later, when my interests were more typical of a boy than a girl, my father was always encouraging me. Both he and my mother always told me I could be anything I wanted to be. They encouraged me so much that I was really not aware of sex discrimination. The schools I attended allowed girls to join the science club, etc., so there was no reason for me to believe that other people felt any differently than my parents did. I honestly believed that sex discrimination was something out of the dark ages, and could have no influence on my life in the twentieth century.

The first thing that happened to change my opinion was when I was about 15 years old. I had decided at the age of seven that I wanted to be a geologist. I had taken summer classes at the Museum of Natural History and was, therefore, aware of some of their programs. At that time the government was building the interstate highways through the area. The rock layers that the road was to cut through were known to be a very rich source of fossil material. The museum put out an announcement that they needed teenage volunteers to watch the rock as it was being broken, so that the museum could recover any fossil finds. My mother called the museum to volunteer my time, only to find out that they did not want me, because I was a girl. It seems that the contractors on the project had stated that if a girl or woman walked onto the site, they would walk off. The woman at the museum who was in charge of the find could not even go to the site. At that time, I chalked up the problem to a few dinosaurs from a previous age. I still did not really believe that this was a prevalent attitude.

The next experience, however, convinced me that sex discrimination was alive and well in the twentieth century. I graduated in the top 10 percent of my class a few weeks before my seventeenth birthday. When I went to a prominent university to interview, I was repeatedly told that I did not want to go to there. They said I should go to the local women's college. They never came out and said I couldn't go to the university where I interviewed, but they made their point clear anyway. My father's only comment was that there were bound to be schools that wouldn't want me.

I started college at a liberal arts college instead. After two years I transferred to an engineering school in another state. I graduated from there with a degree in geological engineering. While I was there the discrimination was far more subtle. At that time the ratio of males to females was about 10 to 1. The male students, instead of competing for our attention, would call us "water buffalo" and other equally uncomplimentary names. In labs, if one of us was the only female student, she worked alone. I did very well in my classes, but it was almost as if there was an unspoken curriculum to which I was not privy. The male students seemed to have some source of information about what companies would be looking for on job interviews, what we would actually be doing on certain types of jobs, etc. I often felt incomparably stupid in these situations, because this was not discussed in class, and I didn't know where they were getting all this knowledge of how the world worked.

The discrimination I experienced was not really institutionalized in the schools; rather, it was a product of the society in which I lived. In many ways the attitude of the schools was very liberated, but it did not prepare me for the real world. The world came as a very painful shock.

This was the paper I was going to hand in until I read a book this weekend. Interestingly, the book has nothing to do with feminism, sexism, or women. The book is the memoirs of Richard F. Feynman, winner of a Nobel prize. He worked on the Manhattan Project, and was quite a character. What really caught my interest was his description of his childhood. Oh, how I wish I had known him as a child. His interests and mine had so much in common. We both had laboratories at home. We both read so much on our own that we were embarrassed as college students, because we didn't know how to pronounce the technical words that we knew from print.

I started to wonder why he accomplished so much and I have accomplished so little. He, of course, is brilliant, but I was evaluated by a university psychology department when I was 12 and pronounced well into the gifted range. It isn't that I expected that I would have won the Nobel prize. I feel so often that, even though I love teaching, I am wasting my gifts and education. I feel that since I have been given so much, I should be doing more for humanity.

The more I thought about it, the more I realized there was one huge difference in our upbringing. He took risks constantly. This was not always to his immediate advantage, like the time he set fire to his bedroom, but ultimately it allowed him the self-assurance to take risks professionally and scientifically. He wasn't afraid to make mistakes. Girls, at least when and where I was raised, were discouraged against risk taking. We were constantly warned against anything that might be dangerous. I wasn't allowed to do any of the experiments in my chemistry set that used a flame. I couldn't go exploring by myself. I had to wear dresses, which make all sorts of activities more difficult. By the time I was a teenager I didn't even need to be reminded of all these prohibitions. They were part of my normal behavior patterns.

I can even see from an evolutionary standpoint where it would be an advantage for our species to have the female not take risks. The offspring are so dependent on their mothers that risk-taking in the female could endanger her young. It would, therefore, not be surprising if the male found adventurous females unappealing. The natural imperative to find a mate and reproduce would be very difficult to fight, if indeed the male indicates by his behavior that he does not like females that are risk takers, or that are in competition with him.

I understand only too well how much pressure that can be for a young woman to face. When I was at Tech, I was going with a mechanical engineering student. I was always concerned because my grades were much better than his. He struggled with courses like fluid mechanics, which I adored. I even debated with myself whether I should deliberately lower my grades, so I would not jeopardize the relationship. My own husband (now ex-husband) once told my mother that he was afraid to have his IQ tested because he was afraid it might not be as high as mine. He was always putting me down. In spite of a disastrous marriage, there is part of me that longs even now for a marriage that is a completely equal partnership. Maybe the best way to describe it would be in terms of the movie *Butch Cassidy and the Sundance Kid.* I want to be Butch Cassidy and I want to marry Sundance. Not that I want to go into bank robbing as a career, but I want that kind of equality in a relationship. I have found many men who were willing to treat me equally as colleagues, but once a relationship comes into the picture, they pull back. Maybe it is instinctive in the male to need to be a superior risk taker and therefore more successful than his mate. It isn't right and it isn't fair, but maybe it is just the way things are.

➤ ➤ ➤ ➤ ➤ ➤ ➤ ➤ ➤ ➤ ➤ ➤ ➤ ➤ ➤ ➤ ➤

SUMMARY

1. Studies of the Terman high-IQ group showed that adult achievement was predicted by more factors than grades and school achievement.
2. Eminence and leadership are predicted by family and social factors as well as IQ.
3. Students who attended elementary schools for high-IQ children went on, for the most part, to obtain college degrees and to enter the professions. Women earned far less money than men.
4. Scientists follow a predictable developmental path, influenced by their mentors.
5. Creative women psychologists exhibit tenacity and productivity as well as aggressiveness.
6. Mathematicians and Math Olympians are mostly male. They have high IQs, are highly motivated, and come from small, well-educated families.
7. Creative female mathematicians were more like creative men and women writers than like creative male mathematicians.
8. Career development counseling and intervention with young women of high school age has predictive power for their career development in adulthood; the high schools they attended are also significant.
9. Adult creative writers had social conscience and a need to express their emotions.
10. Adult visual artists often have to enter "the loft culture" in order to have their work recognized.
11. Musicians and composers, like other creative adults, experience stiff competition in adulthood as well.
12. Mentors were recognized as important by Presidential Scholars.
13. Adult talented people experience interpersonal and intrapersonal issues that may be fulfilling or disturbing, depending on the situation.
14. Reaching the highest levels of psychological growth seems to be a need for adults who have interpersonal and intrapersonal intelligence. This is called spiritual growth and may or may not be tied with formal religious faiths.
15. Women may become science teachers instead of scientists because of the vagaries of their lives, marriages, having children, and moving around the country with their husbands.

CURRICULUM, COUNSELING, AND AT-RISK TALENTED STUDENTS

PART

III

CHAPTER
9   PRECEPTS FOR CURRICULUM FOR THE ACADEMICALLY TALENTED

FOCUSING QUESTIONS

1. Why should the curriculum for intellectually talented students be differentiated? What are some reasons why it should not be differentiated?

2. How does the personal philosophy of the teacher, administrator, or curriculum theorizer affect his/her recommendations for curriculum for the intellectually talented?

3. Why should a curriculum for intellectually talented students have the quality of academic rigor?

4. Look at the curriculum of a nearby school's program for the gifted and talented. Evaluate according to the five precepts discussed in this chapter.

5. If you had to choose three precepts to focus on in a curriculum you design, which would they be, and why?

6. The seven orientations introduced in this chapter may or may not be mutually exclusive. Discuss.

7. Discuss the setting of standards for performance assessment and outcomes as they relate to the work of academically talented students.

8. Evaluate the literature unit according to the five precepts. Discuss.

9. Evaluate the probability unit according to the five precepts. Discuss.

Figure 9.1   Overview of Chapter 9

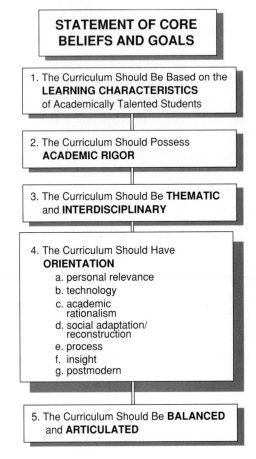

STATEMENT OF CORE
BELIEFS AND GOALS

1. The Curriculum Should Be Based on the
LEARNING CHARACTERISTICS
of Academically Talented Students

2. The Curriculum Should Possess
ACADEMIC RIGOR

3. The Curriculum Should Be **THEMATIC**
and **INTERDISCIPLINARY**

4. The Curriculum Should Have
ORIENTATION
    a. personal relevance
    b. technology
    c. academic
       rationalism
    d. social adaptation/
       reconstruction
    e. process
    f. insight
    g. postmodern

5. The Curriculum Should Be **BALANCED**
and **ARTICULATED**

Dr. Terrence Boyle sat with the others on the board at the long polished table. The motion was made and seconded. The chair said, "All in favor of approving the joint statement of the National Association for Gifted Children and the Council for Exceptional Children—The Association for the Gifted joint statement of core beliefs and goals, say 'aye.'" A chorus of "ayes" followed. There were no "nays."

Dr. Boyle, a professor of curriculum studies at a large university, sat back in exhaustion and relief. Much work for several years had gone into this statement. The two main professional organizations, the learned societies in the field of the education of the gifted and talented, had hammered out the statement following the 1993 federal report, *National Excellence* (See Chapter 1). Now it was approved. The membership had been given a chance to respond and to give feedback. He felt as if all his years on the board were worth it. Now he could teach his curriculum classes with a clear sense of mission, for curriculum is the main reason for the existence of the field of the education of the talented, and this statement gave the theoretical undergirding necessary for curriculum planning. Figure 9.2 contains the Statement of Core Beliefs and Goals.

The next two chapters about curriculum are important reasons for this book, as the very reason for the field is to provide different curricula for students with different learning characteristics. In the education of academically talented children, curriculum ideas have gained currency and lost appeal just as they have in other areas of education. Educators of the academically talented have often been the first to apply, and then to reject or modify, certain "hot" areas of curriculum modification. We have been "hot mamas."

They ("we") were right up there with the latest ideas. They began to talk about "right brain" and "left brain" years before the rest of education used these terms. They delved into learning styles in the middle 1970s, when other fields of education were firmly embracing mastery learning. Guilford's Structure of the Intellect model of multiple factored intelligences, through its adaptation by Mary and Robert Meeker, was being used to assess and prescribe for academically talented youngsters in the late 1970s. Educators of the academically talented studied and discussed Howard Gardner's "frames" of mind and multiple intelligences among themselves as soon as his book came out in 1983. Robert Sternberg's "triarchic" theory of intelligence and Theresa Amabile's social psychology of creativity were the subjects of keynote speeches at national and state conferences as soon as their books hit the bookstores.

This quickness of educators of the academically talented to explore the latest ideas has continued. Yet the curricula being offered academically talented youngsters are often reactive rather than proactive, and often reflect the biases of the administrators and confusion among the educators. This said, curriculum for the gifted and talented has also been profoundly influenced by current education trends, retro as they are, as the field is a part of the whole.

A brief historical overview shows that in the 1980s, several national reports influenced curriculum thinking in the U.S. These were (1) *A Nation at Risk* (1983); (2) *The*

Figure 9.2 Educating America's Gifted and Talented Children: A Statement of Core Beliefs and

A joint statement of the National Association for Gifted Children (NAGC) and the Association for the Gifted, The Council for Exceptional Children (CEC-TAG), 1998.

We believe that:

- Talent comes in many forms and may be manifested in multiple domains.
- Children are individuals who bring to the classroom a diverse set of aptitudes, achievements, and potential.
- Gifts and talents may be developed over a period of time and may manifest themselves at different stages in a child's development.
- The full spectrum of talents are present in every cultural, racial, and socioeconomic group.
- The population diversity that characterizes our schools is a positive source of talent potential.
- The range of aptitudes, achievements, and potential among children suggests a need for varied educational experiences designed so that every child in the classroom is actively engaged in respectful, challenging, and meaningful learning.
- It is the responsibility of educators to design educational experiences to maximize the development of talents in all children.

Therefore, we as organizations join in a common commitment to the highest standards for educational practices in an effort to ensure that:

- Local educational agencies provide a continuum of educational opportunities to ensure that a sufficient variety of options are available to assist each child develop one or more apparent or emergent area of strengths.
- Teachers have the opportunity to learn and are encouraged to implement methods necessary to develop the strength areas within every child, from the struggling learner to those who learn more quickly.
- Every student has access to opportunities to develop his/her full potential through strength-based learning and highly engaging learning activities.
- Educators and related service personnel who work with children in our schools are trained and expected to recognize and develop exceptional gifts and talents in any domain such as the traditional academic areas, the arts, or leadership.
- Curriculum reflects a high level of challenge and is adapted in classrooms to the educational needs of students in that classroom.

To achieve these goals, we envision a partnership based on cooperation, collaboration, and commitment that will result in a common understanding that talent development and enhancement contributes positively to the goal of providing maximum learning for each and every child.

Carnegie Report (1986); (3) The College Board *Project Equality* (1983); and (4) The report of the National Science Commission (1983). All these reports decried the low levels of instruction and mastery of content in the United States. Also in the 1980s, several threads of influence were apparent. Among these were the "neoconservatives," such as Adler's *Paideia Program* (1984), Ravitch's *The Schools We Deserve* (1985), and Hirsch's *Cultural Literacy* (1987). Then there were the neoprogressives (or liberals), including Goodlad's *A Place Called School* (1983) and Sizer's *Horace's Compromise* (1983). Bloom's focus on mastery learning, an approach based on dividing content up into small "teacher-proof" bits, in *All Our Children Learning* (1980), was a thread, and there began a cognitive psychology assertion that students cannot learn unless they are taught to understand; that is, the knowledge must be deep (see Gardner's work since the 1980s and 1990s, after Bruner's focus on this in the 1970s); other psychologists insisted that intelligence is information processing and metacognition about the curriculum content is important (Sternberg's work since the 1980s). Domain- or discipline-based cognitive research also had an influence in the 1990s, with work on the acquisition of expertise utilizing comparisons between experts and novices and research that students transfer information depending on content and context (Corner & Hagman, 1987).

The calls for curriculum reform in the early 1980s led to multimillion dollar projects in math and science curricula in the late 1980s and the early 1990s. Among these were the University of Chicago mathematics project and projects at the National Science Foundation and the American Academy of Science. National reports on how the United States students compare in global achievement, such as the National Assessment of Educational Progress (NAEP), were the focus of curriculum reports. Other trends affecting curriculum thought were the idea that the computer should be a tool of learning for all children in all classrooms, and that students should have an understanding of global issues. The surge in the interest in values education in the 1970s gave way to deep disapproval in the 1990s, with the call by conservative religious groups that such education is not the province of the schools. All these threads have influenced the field of the education of the gifted and talented as shall be seen below. However, the education of academically talented students has often been left to the whims and prejudices of those who think that cream will rise to the top and that these students don't need anything special.

Virgil Ward noted the differences in the way academically talented students learn in *Differential Education for the Gifted:*

> Intelligent children learn more, continue to learn longer, extract more meaning from what they sense, apply and associate more accurately, are interested in ultimates, and learning is a more essential part of their life's need. (1961/1980, p. 154)

Thus it is incumbent upon planners of curriculum for academically talented students to plan carefully and well, and to be sure that the curriculum that is planned is suitable and defensible. This chapter considers several precepts that should improve curriculum planning for academically talented students. First, the *learning characteristics* of the students must be considered in the planning. Second, the curriculum should possess *academic rigor*. Third, the curriculum writers should strive to make the curriculum *thematic* and *interdisciplinary*. Fourth, the curriculum should be written with *seven curriculum orientations* in mind. Fifth, the curriculum should be *balanced* and *articulated* in content, process, and thematic approach.

A DEFINITION OF CURRICULUM

One useful definition of curriculum, and the one to be elucidated here, is from Eisner (1985): "Curriculum of a school, or a course, or a classroom can be conceived of as a series of planned events that are intended to have educational consequences for one or more students" (p. 39). Curriculum thus broadly conceived is made up of planned goals and objectives, and uses materials and activities that lead to the acquisition of those objectives. The educational consequences, in this case, are those for academically talented students; that is, for those who have been identified as having superior cognitive abilities or specific academic abilities. An even wider definition of curriculum will also be considered in this chapter, and that is the definition of curriculum as all the experiences, as a way of being in the schools, "what the older generation chooses to tell the younger generation. So understood, curriculum is intensely historical, political, racial, gendered, phenomenological, autobiographical, aesthetic, theological, and international" (Pinar, Reynolds, Slattery & Taubman, 1995, p. 848).

A historical look at curriculum for talented students must take into account the work of Virgil Ward, James Gallagher, C. June Maker, Joseph Renzulli, Abraham Tannenbaum, Joyce VanTassel-Baska, James Borland, Sandra Kaplan, Jeanette Parker, and others. Arlene Nielson has joined in the latest revisions of Maker's classic 1982 books. All of these have had influence on the field of curriculum for the talented. All say that the main reason for the education of talented students is to provide a differentiated curriculum because the academically talented students learn differently, especially in rate and in ability to think abstractly. All emphasize that curriculum for the academically talented should be different in kind, and in emphasis, and not specifically in type. They call for a "defensible" curriculum that is differentiated.

Borland said, "Curriculum is the essential issue in the field—gifted education exists for one reason—the students exist and require curriculum differentiation because the core curriculum is not meeting their needs." Borland believes that curriculum should be based on a solid scope and sequence, for most curriculum happens at the unit level. Teachers spend a lot of time and effort developing units, and the school district has little or no input into the content of the units, which are, at best, "idiosyncratic." Rarely do districts have a strategic curriculum plan for their talented students. For example, students in a class for gifted and talented students might study presidential politics because it is an election year and not because presidential politics is in the scope and sequence (personal communication, National Curriculum Conference, Williamsburg, VA, March 1997).

Others believe that curriculum for academically talented learners should be mainly enrichment or mainly independent study. But all agree that the student needs should be analyzed and the curriculum should present what those needs are determined to be. Still others wonder whether it is even possible that the curriculum that is written down is the curriculum that is learned by the students.

Whether they know it or not, all experts give curriculum advice based on their personal or academic belief systems about curriculum. Education is not value free, especially the education of special populations. The researchers have come to some agreement: curriculum for the academically talented should be made up of a synthesis of subject matter or content approaches, of skills or process approaches, and there should be some attention paid to products. Lately, thematic approaches to curriculum have held sway. While these are laudable, certain subject matter experts doubt that high-level mathematics, for example, can be taught in the context of themes. Following is a discussion of the five precepts for curriculum development outlined earlier in this chapter.

PRECEPT 1: BASE CURRICULUM ON LEARNING CHARACTERISTICS OF ACADEMICALLY TALENTED STUDENTS IN THEIR AREAS OF STRENGTH

Curriculum theorists in the field of the education of the academically talented say that curriculum developers should always keep in mind that the reason for differentiation is that the basic curriculum is not suitable for the academically talented learner. The curriculum must be modified according to academically talented students' exceptionalities. These include their ability to learn at a faster rate, their ability to think abstractly about content that is challenging, their ability to think productively, critically, creatively, and analytically, and their ability to constantly and rapidly increase their store of knowledge, both knowledge of facts and knowledge of processes and procedures.

Pace

Virgil Ward wrote what he called "General Principles of Educational Design" for the education of the academically talented in 1961, and even then he said that the curriculum should be based on the learning characteristics of academically talented children. All the curriculum thinkers have followed suit. The education of academically talented students should not be entirely different from that of all students. How it is different should be in kind, in quality, and in the level of insight the students are expected to acquire. Ward said, "Curricular adaptations suited to the intellectually superior will often be 'discouraging to slower intellects'" (1961/1980 p. 287). Even before Ward, Leta Hollingworth said, in 1942:

> . . . a child of 140 IQ can master all the mental work provided in the elementary school, as established, in half the time allowed him . . . these exceptional pupils are running errands, idling, engaging in "busy work," or devising childish tasks of their own, such as learning to read backward . . . many are the devices invented by busy teachers to "take up" the extra time of these rapid learners. (p. 15)

Ward went on to say, in his third proposition for the differentiation of curriculum for academically talented learners, that the curriculum should be made up of "economically chosen experiences designed to promote the civic, social, and personal adequacy of the intellectually superior individual." Since students with high IQs seem to transfer knowledge more rapidly and more thoroughly, this ability to transfer should generate innovative curriculum. The curriculum should be both high level and abstract. What thinkers about curriculum for the academically talented are saying today, and what thinkers about curriculum for the academically talented in the 1920s, 1930s, and 1950s were saying, seem to be remarkably similar, for Ward predated Gallagher, Maker, Renzulli, VanTassel-Baska, and Tannenbaum. All say that one of the learning characteristics of academically talented students is that they learn fast, with less repetition and drill. The curriculum should be differentiated to accommodate this ability.

Depth

Curriculum thinkers also say that the curriculum should be different in quality. The administrative arrangements discussed in Chapter 2 need to be accompanied by a reorganization of both materials and methods. Kulik (1992b) reminded curriculum planners that ability grouping should be accompanied by content that is different.

In doing this, the school should promote flexibility in program planning. Curriculum theoreticians in the field of the education of the academically talented have often noted that academically talented students often educate themselves, choosing to get mediocre grades in subjects in which they are not interested, and to pursue with passion subjects they are interested in. Therefore, the educators of the academically talented should have a handle on what subjects the identified subjects are interested in, but should also take care to see that they have a general education as well and don't just focus on their interests to the exclusion of other subjects.

Learning Through Reading

Many experts in the field of the education of the academically talented advocate that learning by doing is the preferred way to teach academically talented students, but Ward said that the very nature of giftedness is that talented students are often self-motivated, and they learn more through reading than through being active with concrete tasks. A look at the biographies of talented adults often shows that they spent many solitary childhood hours reading.

In fact, curriculum for academically talented students can often be enhanced through the teaching strategy of good lectures because students who are academically talented are able to form generalizations and to deduce and to provide examples from stated principles. Ideas should be the "central factor and crucial point" in the instruction of talented students. Ward advocated what he called the "principle of economy" in the curriculum for talented students, saying that teaching the academically talented child or young adult what he or she can learn for him or herself is uneconomical.

Curriculum experts agree that academically talented students should be taught at a faster pace and with more complexity, and said that their achievement should also be evaluated by advanced objectives that use more than just recall, association, or comprehension. Since these students also have a tendency to be creative, they should be encouraged to be so.

Maker's Summary

Maker (1982a; Maker & Nielson, 1997) made a detailed chart that summarized the characteristics known to be common to academically talented children. The content of the curriculum should be modified according to level of abstractness, depth of complexity, scope of variety, quality of organization, economy, the study of people, and methodology used in teaching academically talented students.

Maker and Nielson thought the curriculum should encourage higher-level thought processes, should be open-ended, should emphasize discovery, should teach students how to prove and how to reason, should have aspects of freedom of choice and group interaction, and should be different in pace and variety from the curriculum offered to other students. Products should be emphasized, and these should focus on real problems, be geared to real audiences, should be evaluated according to predetermined criteria, and should involve aspects of transformation. Maker said the learning environment should be open and student centered, encouraging independence of thought. It should be accepting, complex, and afford high mobility for academically talented students.

PRECEPT 2: ACADEMIC RIGOR IN THE CURRICULUM

Robert Sawyer, in a 1988 essay calling for academic rigor in curriculum for the academically talented, said that given these learning characteristics, academically talented students are often mightily disappointed when they receive their education, even in their special classes. He said, "what often greets them is an array of faddish, meaningless trivia—kits, games, mechanical step-by-step problem-solving methods, pseudoscience, pop psychology: curriculum of the lowest level." Sawyer called this "robbery of the gifted."

The call for academic rigor was strong in two articles published in 1991. Donna Harrington-Lueker, in *The Executive Educator*, said that "too much of what passes for gifted and talented education . . . is trivial, faddish, and unlikely to meet the needs of gifted youngsters" (p. 19). Singal, in *The Atlantic*, said that even the brightest students who attend the most competitive universities cannot do the work that was expected of them 10 years ago. He said that literature classes that used to require the reading of one or two novels per week now require one novel every two weeks because the bright students cannot keep up. Underlying all these criticisms is the implicit belief that curriculum for academically talented students should possess more academic rigor. William Durden of Johns Hopkins University's Center for Talented Youth (CTY) even went so far as to say that academically talented students shouldn't have special "gifted and talented education," which is basically a "rip-off," but that the education for academically talented students should be a rigorous liberal arts education (Harrington-Lueker, p. 19). It is obvious that much of what has passed for gifted and talented education has been cutesy, fragmented, and divorced from traditional bodies of knowledge that students should be studying.

There is no need for a curriculum for the academically talented if the level of challenge is not addressed. The watchword and justification for most differentiation of curriculum should be, "If all children can do it, all children should do it." This leaves out field trips or the addition of computers as a means of differentiation. The level of challenge should be such that those learners with the learning characteristics mentioned above will be as challenged as the hard-working "C" student, whose work habits and study habits often outshine those of the academically talented student who has never reached the frustration level in terms of challenging material, and who gets "As" and "smiley faces" without even trying very hard.

Assessment in the Context of Academic Rigor

In the early 1990s, the cognitive psychologists and social reformers of the antitracking variety were leading the debates for changing the means of assessment from standardized, multiple-choice format tests to more authentic means based on students' actual knowledge and performance. In 1991, the *Review of Research in Education*, a publication of the American Educational Research Association, published a review by Wolf, Bixby, Glenn, and Gardner on "new forms of student assessment." In this article, the authors noted that so-called objective tests have proven to be anything but, as our definitions of intelligence have changed from the linear, normal-curve-based definitions to the more fluid, amorphous, and process-oriented findings of cognitive science. How do we measure student understanding, especially the understanding of students with outstanding talent?

The "Dumbed-Down" Curriculum

Another reason talented students may not be nominated by teachers is that some talented students do not respond to the *dumbed-down* curriculum. This is a term used by former Secretary of Education Terrell Bell, and it refers to the recent and progressive targeting of the curriculum level to the lower-ability students in an effort to help them achieve. Also called the *Lake Wobegon syndrome,* this dumbing down has the effect of making all the children "above average." A study in 1979 by the Educational Products Information Institute showed that 80 percent mastery of subject matter was attained by 60 percent of a group of fourth graders when they were tested in September on the material they would be studying throughout the year. A later study (Kirst, 1982) also showed that the levels of textbooks have dropped by two years in the past 10 years. A 1988 study (Taylor & Frye, 1988) demonstrated that most fifth and sixth graders passed the pretests in reading comprehension even before they began basal reading instruction.

Renzulli and Reis (1991) cited these studies and others to show that talented students are not being challenged in the classroom by the current curricula. International comparisons have shown that the best U.S. students score lower than the those in other countries. The Third International Mathematics and Science Study, published in 1997, shows how the best U.S. students compare:

How Do Our Best Students Compare with Others' Best?

Comparisons of averages tell us how typical students perform, but they do not tell us about the performance of our nation's best students—those who are likely to become the next generation of mathematicians, scientists, doctors, and engineers. If an international talent search were to select the top ten percent of all students in the 41 TIMSS countries combined, what percentage of U.S. students would be included?

In mathematics, 5 percent of U.S. eighth graders would be selected. High-scoring nations would have more of their students represented in the "international top ten percent." . . . 45 percent of all Singaporean students and 32 percent of all Japanese students would be chosen in the international talent search in mathematics. In science, 13 percent of U.S. students would be selected, in comparison to 31 percent of Singaporean students and 18 percent of Japanese students.

If the international talent search were to lower its standards considerably to choose the top half of all students in the 41 TIMSS countries, 94 percent of eighth graders in Singapore and 83 percent in Japan would be selected in mathematics, compared to 45 percent of eighth graders in the U.S. In science, 82 percent of the students in Singapore and 71 percent of students in Japan would be selected, compared to 55 percent in the U.S. (Peak et al., 1996, *Pursuing Excellence*)

Preliminary analyses of the results have led to several tentative conclusions. Among them is the fact that U.S. students do more homework, and spend as much time in mathematics and science classes as do students in Japan and Germany (in-depth qualitative studies were conducted for these three countries).

Conclusions

- No single factor can be considered to influence student performance in isolation from other factors. There are no single answers to complex questions.
- The content of U.S. eighth-grade mathematics classes is not as challenging as that of other countries, and topic coverage is not as focused.
- Most U.S. mathematics teachers report familiarity with reform recommendations, although only a few apply the key points in their classrooms.
- Evidence suggests that U.S. teachers do not receive as much practical training and daily support as their German and Japanese colleagues.

Academically talented students may be dulled, bored, reactive, argumentative, and not docile when confronted with the current curriculum. Teachers would be hard pressed to nominate them when their behaviors indicate they don't like the educational environment provided by these very teachers. One teacher, after a lesson in curriculum compacting, went back and gave her third graders the chapter tests in all the subjects. In March, she found that all of them had mastery of all of the material she was supposed to cover (D. Ball, personal communication, 1991).

Many thinkers assert that the standards for such youth (perhaps all youth) are not high enough, that there should be multiple standards, but when multiple standards are suggested, the critics protest that "tracking" is being advocated. National subject matter groups such as the National Council for the Social Studies and the National Council for History Standards, and testing groups such as the National Assessment of Educational Progress have, in the past few years, published tentative grade-level standards for students. Single levels of standards for music for elementary and middle school students were set by the Music Educators National Conference, with two levels for high school students, "advanced" and "proficient" sets, with the advanced level targeted for serious students of music.

These ongoing efforts by professional associations reflect the growing concern in the society for equity. Teachers of the talented with knowledge of the subject matter, and with some idea of what rigor in subject matter means, may find the standards that their national groups set are too low for the abilities of their students. In a speech in 1997, VanTassel-Baska said that the more national standards are translated to state standards, the more the translations in state and local levels are watered down (personal communication, College of William and Mary, March 1997).

The major subject matter fields have made some shifts in philosophy, content, and methodology. For example, Table 9.1 shows the mathematics shifts.

What the TIMMS Studies Showed

In 1995, the Third International Mathematics and Science Study (TIMSS) tested the mathematics and science knowledge of a half-million students from 41 nations at

Table 9.1   Shifts in Mathematics Curriculum

	Old	**New**
View	Drill and Practice View	Problem-Solving View
Research Base	Behaviorism	Cognitive Science
Goals of Math Instruction	Mastery of isolated facts and skills	Understanding of mathematical concepts to apply to new problem situations
Goals of Learning	Applying computation skills and memorizing math facts to get the right answer	Problem solving, understanding the conceptual nature of the problem, knowing when to employ skills and facts as tools to solve the problem
View of Learner	Passive; vessel receiving knowledge from external sources	Active; connecting intuitive and prior knowledge to new formal knowledge

five different grade levels. In addition to tests and questionnaires, the TIMSS included a curriculum analysis, videotaped observations of mathematics classrooms, and case studies of policy issues. Twenty-six nations participated in the fourth grade assessment (Peak et al., 1997). Figure 9.3 shows the results for fourth and eighth grades. Conducted by the U.S. Education Office of Research and Improvement Educational Statistics Department, TIMSS called itself "a fair and accurate comparison of mathematics and science achievement in the participating nations." The study did not compare all United States students with the best students from other countries, but the sample was randomly selected and overseen by an international technical review committee to make sure that strict research standards were met.

The researchers analyzed videotaped lessons from Germany, Japan, and the United States from the eighth grades. They made a few conclusions about the students and the teachers based on surveys they conducted. Teachers in Japan and Germany have extended supervised internships before they are permitted to teach. In the United States, the supervised internships are often a short eight weeks. Japanese teachers have more opportunities to discuss teaching-related issues than do U.S. teachers. U.S. teachers have more college education than their colleagues in all but a few TIMSS countries. Student diversity and poor discipline are challenges not only for U.S. teachers, but for their German colleagues as well. Japanese eighth graders are preparing for a high-stakes examination to enter high school at the end of ninth grade. The results of the TIMSS eighth grade study are shown in Figure 9.4.

U.S. teachers assign more homework and spend more class time discussing it than teachers in Germany and Japan. U.S. students report about the same amount of out-of-school math and science study as their Japanese and German counterparts. Heavy TV watching is as common among U.S. eighth graders as it is among their Japanese counterparts. The researchers concluded that no single factor can be considered to influence student performance in isolation from other factors.

Figure 9.3   Results of TIMSS Fourth Grade Study

	Mathematics	Science
Achievement: National rank	U.S. fourth graders perform above the international average of the 26 TIMSS countries. U.S. students are outperformed by those in 7 countries and outperform those in 12 countries. Among our major economic partners who participated in the study, our students' scores are below those of Japan, not significantly different from those of Canada, and are significantly higher than those of England.	Fourth graders in only one country—Korea—outperform U.S. students in this subject. U.S. students outperform those in 19 countries. Among our major economic partners who participated in the study, our students' scores are not significantly different from those of fourth graders in Japan, our students outperform those in England and Canada.
Achievement: Content	In mathematics content areas, U.S. fourth graders exceed the international average in five of the six areas assessed. These five areas are: whole numbers; fractions and proportionality; data representation, analysis, and probability; geometry; and patterns, relations, and functions. The U.S. average is lower than the international average in the content area of measurement, estimation, and number sense.	In science content areas, our fourth graders' performance exceeds the international average in all four of the areas assessed. In three of these content areas—earth science, life science, and environmental issues and the nature of science—U.S. fourth grade students are significantly outperformed by only one or two other nations. In physical science, five other nations perform significantly better than the U.S.
Achievement of academically talented students	If an international talent search were to select the top 10 percent of all fourth grade students in the 26 countries, in mathematics 9 percent of U.S. fourth grade students would be included.	If an international talent search were to select the top 10 percent of all fourth grade students in the 26 countries, in science 16 percent of U.S. fourth grade students would be included.
Gender	There is no significant gender gap in fourth grade mathematics achievement.	In some content areas of fourth grade science, U.S. boys outperform U.S. girls.

The content of U.S. eighth grade mathematics classes is not as challenging as that of other countries, and topic coverage is not as focused. The content of U.S. mathematics classes requires less high-level thought than classes in Germany and Japan. U.S. mathematics teachers' typical goal is to teach students how to do something, while Japanese teachers' goal is to help them understand mathematical concepts. In the United States, most of the nearly 16,000 districts design their own curriculum or standards, usually within broad guidelines issued by each of the 50 states. There are many different commercially published textbooks. Because most textbooks are designed with an eye to sales in as many districts as possible, they include the content specified by the guidelines from a number of different states. As a result, textbooks usually contain much more material than a teacher can cover fully in a year. Each of the many different textbooks includes somewhat different topics from which teachers in various districts can choose. Few states or districts closely monitor or enforce compliance with state or district standards, and U.S. teachers usually have the latitude to design the content and pace of their courses to suit their perception of their students' needs. Most U.S. mathematics teachers report familiarity with reform recommendations, although only a few apply the key points in their classrooms. Japanese teachers widely practice what the U.S. mathematics reforms recommend, while U.S. teachers do so less frequently.

Figure 9.4   Results of TIMSS Eighth Grade Study

	Mathematics	**Science**
Achievement: Content	U.S. eighth graders score below average in mathematics achievement compared to the 41 nations in the TIMSS assessment. International standing is stronger in algebra and fractions than in geometry and measurement.	U.S. eighth graders score above average in science achievement compared to the 41 nations in the TIMSS assessment. International standing is stronger in earth science, life science, and environmental issues than in chemistry and physics.
Gender	The U.S. is one of 11 TIMSS nations in which there is no significant gender gap in eighth grade math achievement.	The U.S. is one of 11 TIMSS nations in which there is no significant gender gap in eighth grade science achievement.
Curriculum	• The content taught in U.S. eighth grade mathematics classrooms is at a seventh grade level in comparison to other countries. • Topic coverage in U.S. eighth grade mathematics classes is not as focused as in Germany and Japan. • U.S. eighth graders spend more hours per year in math classes than German and Japanese students.	• In science, the degree of topic focus in the eighth grade curriculum may be similar to that of other countries. • Our nation is atypical among TIMSS countries in its lack of a nationally defined curriculum. • U.S. eighth graders spend more hours per year in science classes than German and Japanese students.
Cross-cultural grouping practices	In the U.S., students in higher-level mathematics classes study different material than students in lower-level classes. In Germany and Japan, all students study the same material, although in Germany, lower-level classes study it less deeply and rigorously.	Eighth grade students of different abilities are typically divided into different classrooms in the U.S., and different schools in Germany. In Japan, no ability grouping is practiced.
Achievement of academically talented students	If an international talent search were to select the top 10 percent of all students in the 41 TIMSS countries, in mathematics 5 percent of U.S. students would be included.	If an international talent search were to select the top 10 percent of all students in the 41 TIMSS countries, in science 13 percent of U.S. students would be included.

The twelfth grade study showed even more dire results for the United States, although Canada scored quite well in international comparison (see Figure 9.5). When the researchers analyzed the content of the twelfth grade assessment in mathematics, they found that for most nations, the content was seventh grade level, but in the United States, the content was ninth grade level. For science, they found that the content was equivalent to ninth grade in most nations, but to eleventh grade in the United States. This relates to the concern among educators of the gifted and talented that textbooks have been "dumbed down." Algebra and geometry topics, chemistry and physics appear later in the curriculum of the United States than in other countries (*Pursuing Excellence: A Study of U.S. Twelfth-Grade Mathematics and Science Achievement in International Context,* 1998).

The question of money spent on education was also discussed. The United States was one of the more affluent countries, with a GNP per capita of $25,860 compared to $17,305 for all 21 countries participating in the general knowledge portion of TIMSS. However, about one-third of the countries had GNP per capita similar to or higher than the United States ($23,500 to $37,000). Similarly, the United States had higher per capita public spending on elementary/secondary education than two-thirds of the other countries. U.S. performance resembled the economically less affluent countries (those with lower GNPs per capita and lower per capita expenditures on elementary/secondary education) participating in the general knowledge assessments, and two of the less affluent countries (Hungary and Slovenia) also outperformed the United States (*Pursuing Excellence: A Study of U.S. Twelfth-Grade Mathematics and Science Achievement in International Context,* 1998).

The proportion of graduating students currently taking mathematics was lower in the United States (66 percent) than the average in all the countries participating in the general knowledge assessments (79 percent). Most of the factors related to students' lives do not seem to account for U.S. students' relatively poor performance either. Among these factors, this is the case for mathematics and science course taking during the final year of secondary school, hours spent on homework or studying, the use of calculators, the use of computers, positive attitudes toward mathematics and science, personal safety in school, television and video watching, and hours spent working at a paid job. Only the percentage of students using a calculator during the TIMSS general knowledge assessment is related to the U.S. performance on the mathematics general knowledge assessment relative to the other TIMSS nations (*Pursuing Excellence: A Study of U.S. Twelfth-Grade Mathematics and Science Achievement in International Context,* 1998).

While most of the student characteristics do not explain U.S. performance relative to other countries, they may still be related to individual student performance within the United States and other countries. For example, although country averages for television watching, homework, and mathematics and science course-taking were not related to average performance, individual students who watch less television, do more homework, and take mathematics and science during the final year of secondary school generally outperform their peers. TIMSS does not suggest any single factor or combination of factors that can explain why the United States' performance is so low. From initial analyses, it also appears that some factors commonly thought to influence individual student performance are not strongly related to performance when comparing average student performance across countries (*Pursuing Excellence: A Study of U.S. Twelfth-Grade Mathematics and Science Achievement in International Context,* 1998).

Dr. William Schmidt, who was the director of the study, said:

> For some time now, Americans have comforted themselves when confronted with bad news about their educational system by believing that our better students can compare with similar students in any country in the world. We have preferred not to believe that we were doing a consistently bad job. Instead, many have believed that the problem was all those 'other' students who do poorly in school and who we, unlike other countries, include in international tests. That simply isn't true. TIMSS has burst another myth—our best students in mathematics and science are simply not 'world class.' Even the very small percentage of students taking Advanced Placement courses are not among the world's best.
>
> U.S. students have been provided with weak foundations for studying advanced mathematics and science. Our high school specialists are ill prepared to gain the most from advanced study. A few grades of weak specialization in high school do not appear able to overcome the weak foundation we lay in earlier grades.
>
> How mathematics and science are arranged in courses also seems to be part of the problem. Better U.S. students study physics in only one or two courses. This is very different from what the students study in the higher achieving countries where physics study begins during middle school and continues throughout high school. Better U.S. mathematics students during high school years take separate courses in geometry, pre-calculus, etc. In most TIMSS countries, students take a course in mathematics—a course which may include studying parts of advanced algebra, geometry, finite mathematics, and calculus at the same time. They may take such courses for several years.
>
> What these results for U.S. high school seniors make clear is that there is no one source of these problems and no one source for their solution. The problem is bigger. It is in our system, not any single part of it. We can waste our time protesting each and every change. We can also waste our time thinking that any one change will solve all our problems. In either case, what we do is waste our time. U.S. mathematics and science education has neither simple villains nor 'magic bullets' to cure our ills. We've failed our tests. Do we want to fail our futures, too? (Schmidt, 1998)

Figure 9.5   Results of TIMSS Twelfth Grade Study, 1998

	Mathematics	**Science**
Achievement: National rank	The results of the TIMSS assessment show that overall, U.S. twelfth graders were below the average of the 21 countries participating in the assessment of mathematics general knowledge. Students in the final year of secondary school in 14 countries (the Netherlands, Sweden, Denmark, Switzerland, Iceland, Norway, France, New Zealand, Australia, Canada, Austria, Slovenia, Germany, and Hungary) scored above our twelfth graders. Students in four countries were not significantly different (Italy, the	The U.S. international standing on the general knowledge component of TIMSS was stronger in science than in mathematics. This pattern is similar to the findings at fourth and eighth grades in TIMSS. On the science portion of the general knowledge assessment, U.S. students scored below the international average, and among the lowest of the 21 countries. Students at the end of secondary school in 11 countries (Sweden, the Netherlands, Iceland, Norway, Canada, New Zealand, Australia, Switzerland, Austria, Slovenia, and

Figure 9.5 *Continued*

	Mathematics	Science
Achievement: National rank *(continued)*	Russian Federation, Lithuania, and the Czech Republic). Students in two countries (Cyprus and South Africa) performed significantly below students in the United States.	Denmark) outperformed U.S. twelfth graders. Students in seven countries (Germany, France, the Czech Republic, the Russian Federation, Italy, Hungary, and Lithuania) were not significantly different. Students in Cyprus and South Africa performed below students in the United States.
Achievement: Content	On "percent of a percent" problems, the international average was 64 percent. The U.S. average was 57 percent. On interpreting a line graph, 85 percent of U.S. students responded correctly in comparison to an international average of 74 percent. In finding the length of a ribbon to go around a box, 32 percent of the U.S. twelfth graders responded correctly to the item, in comparison to an international average of 45 percent.	In science, the United States is one of seven countries where the standing relative to the international average was lower at the end of secondary schooling than it was at eighth grade. The others were former Communist Bloc countries plus Australia and Germany. Students were asked to apply scientific principles to develop explanations, to explain pollution, and to demonstrate knowledge of complex information about the interdependence of life.
Achievement of academically talented students	The performance of U.S. twelfth grade advanced mathematics students was among the lowest of the 16 TIMSS nations that administered the assessment to a comparable population of their advanced mathematics students. Eleven nations outperformed the United States, and no countries scored below the United States.	The performance of U.S. twelfth grade physics students was among the lowest of the 16 TIMSS nations that administered the assessment to a comparable population of their students. Fourteen nations outperformed the United States.
Gender	Apparently there is no gender gap at grade 12. In most of the 22 countries participating in the TIMSS mathematics general knowledge assessment, young men performed significantly better than young women. The U.S., however, was one of three countries (South Africa and Hungary were the others) in which there was no significant difference across gender.	In the United States, there was a gender gap on the science portion of the twelfth grade general knowledge assessment. Excluding South Africa, in all other TIMSS nations, including the United States, males performed significantly better than females on the science general knowledge portion of the assessment.

Academic Rigor: Alternative Assessment

The movement away from assessment in multiple-choice and essay formats to portfolios and assessments of products done over a period of time is still in its infancy. A 1992 RAND Corporation study of the Vermont effort in performance-based assessment showed that teachers did not receive enough inservice for their assessments to be valid cross-district and throughout the state, though the educators themselves felt a commitment to such assessment (Rothman, 1992). A 1997 study showed that portfolio assessment in Rochester, New York, did show differences in results from the standardized tests. First and second grade girls scored higher than boys on the portfolios while boys scored higher on the standardized tests. Black students scored better on portfolios than on standardized tests. Latino students performed better than the black students on standardized tests but not on portfolios. The students who qualified for free lunch and who spoke a language other than English did poorly on both portfolios and standardized tests (Supovitz & Brennan, 1997).

Enthusiasm for the new means of assessment has outpaced research on their effectiveness. It seems that the political agendas of school reformers have harnessed their hopes to alternative assessment and the research is hard put to catch up. Interestingly enough, the "best" schools of the public variety, suburban schools, have been reluctant to jump on many of the reform bandwagons when it comes to giving up standardized testing and assessment, and the "worst" schools, those that are underfunded in urban and rural areas, are those upon which experiments are conducted.

For example, some researchers have noted that verbal ability is even more a factor in portfolio assessment than in traditional assessment. This bodes ill for at-risk students (see Chapter 12). Wolf was quoted (Rothman, 1992) as saying that "Until we break the stranglehold of language on portfolios and open them up, we will again have in portfolios just a different sort of sorting method" (p. 24). How high the standards will be set and what depth of knowledge will be permitted to be shown are also thorny problems. Educators of the talented should be sure that the standards that are set are truly challenging for talented youth. Repeated cautions have been raised stating that grade inflation and an emphasis on mediocrity have been and continue to be the norm for all students, including the talented. One time-tested way of assuring rigor and quality is to make sure that the teacher has a deep knowledge of the subject matter and a knowledge of what can be asked to challenge the talented learner. However, parent, institutional, and student pressures for easy grades have undermined many a teacher's resolve to set high standards. Indomitability, my students tell me, is not welcomed in new teachers without tenure.

The Center for Talented Youth (CTY) has existed for 20 years, providing special programs for advanced learners. Durden and Tangherlini (1993) listed what academically talented high school students should be able to do when they graduate:

1. Express ideas clearly and concisely in Standard Written English.
2. Be able to write a 10-page term paper that is persuasive, supported with relevant evidence, and sensitive to the basics of style and syntax.
3. Be able to understand complex historical, scientific, and technical reading material.
4. Be familiar with the United States' literary and artistic traditions and its African, Asian, and European influences.

5. Have reading knowledge and conversational fluency in at least one foreign language.
6. Be skilled and able to solve problems in algebra, geometry, trigonometry, and analytic geometry.
7. Have a working knowledge of calculus and statistics.
8. Be able to use computers for spreadsheets, fundamental programming, and word processing.
9. Be able to pass Advanced Placement Program (APP) tests in world geography and United States, European, Asian, and African history.
10. Be able to pass an Advanced Placement Program (APP) test in physics, chemistry, and biology.
11. Be able to pass oral examinations as well as written examinations in all these areas.

They pointed out that these are common standards for students in Europe and Asia and that these standards would carry the academic rigor required for the education of the academically talented.

PRECEPT 3: A THEMATIC AND INTERDISCIPLINARY CURRICULUM

What curriculum thinkers have advocated is that with the special learning characteristics unique to academically talented students, an interdisciplinary curriculum should be put into place for academically talented students. In a 1986 article, Jacobs and Borland noted that the usual enrichment curriculum for academically talented students is "little more than a hodgepodge of unrelated topics and activities" (p. 159). They presented an Interdisciplinary Concept Model shown in Figure 9.6.

According to this model, academically talented students should be exposed to the structures, terminologies, and methodologies of various disciplines (p. 161):

1. The empirical methods used to generate scientific knowledge
2. The quantitative methods used to generate mathematical knowledge
3. The esthetic methods used to create meaning in the arts
4. The use of ethical argument to clarify philosophical issues

A diagram of a wheel, with the various disciplines—arts, humanities, mathematics, science, social studies, language arts, philosophy—should be constructed and students should freely associate. What comes up should be placed within the appropriate discipline.

In the mid-1990s, two Javits grants were awarded to develop thematic and interdisciplinary curricula in language arts and in science. Interdisciplinary in this sense means that in literature, all the language arts were included (speaking, writing, reading, etc.). Joyce VanTassel-Baska at the College of William and Mary was the Project Director for these grants. Curricula were developed, piloted, and organized for talented students. The goal of each science unit is to allow students to analyze several real-world problems, understand the concept of *systems*, and conduct scientific experiments. These units also allow students to explore various scientific topics and identify meaningful scientific problems for investigation. Through these units students experience the work of real science in applying data-handling skills, analyzing information, evaluating results, and learning to communicate their understanding to others. Figure 9.7 presents a brief synopsis of the units in the science curriculum.

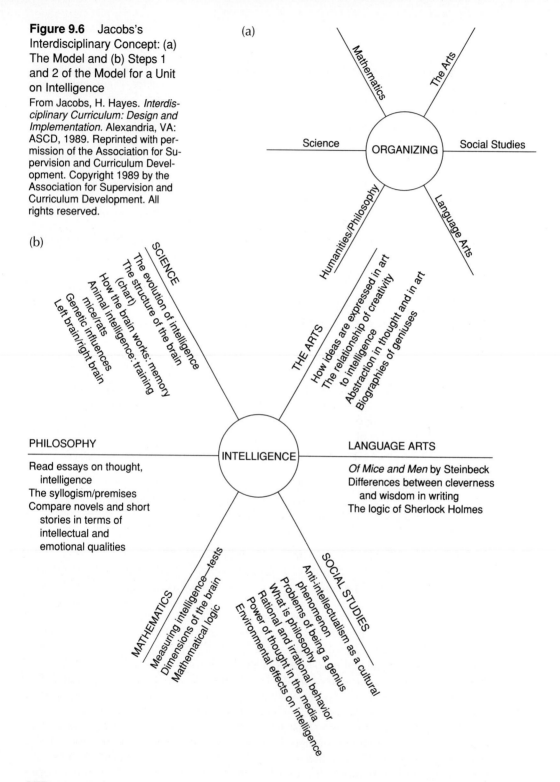

Figure 9.6 Jacobs's Interdisciplinary Concept: (a) The Model and (b) Steps 1 and 2 of the Model for a Unit on Intelligence

From Jacobs, H. Hayes. *Interdisciplinary Curriculum: Design and Implementation*. Alexandria, VA: ASCD, 1989. Reprinted with permission of the Association for Supervision and Curriculum Development. Copyright 1989 by the Association for Supervision and Curriculum Development. All rights reserved.

(a)

Mathematics

The Arts

Science   ORGANIZING   Social Studies

Humanities/Philosophy

Language Arts

(b)

SCIENCE
The evolution of intelligence
The structure of the brain
(chart)
How the brain works: memory
Animal intelligence: training
mice/rats
Genetic influences
Left brain/right brain

THE ARTS
How ideas are expressed in art
The relationship of creativity
to intelligence
Abstraction in thought and in art
Biographies of geniuses

PHILOSOPHY

Read essays on thought,
intelligence
The syllogism/premises
Compare novels and short
stories in terms of
intellectual and
emotional qualities

INTELLIGENCE

LANGUAGE ARTS

Of Mice and Men by Steinbeck
Differences between cleverness
and wisdom in writing
The logic of Sherlock Holmes

MATHEMATICS
Measuring intelligence—tests
Dimensions of the brain
Mathematical logic

SOCIAL STUDIES
Anti-intellectualism as a cultural
phenomenon
Problems of being a genius
What is philosophy
Rational and irrational behavior
Power of thought in the media
Environmental effects on intelligence

Figure 9.7   Science Units from Javits Grant at National Curriculum Project*

Acid, Acid Everywhere (176 pp.)	Presents the structure of systems through chemistry, ecological habitats, and transportation. These structures overlap within this unit to graphically illustrate to students the nature of interactions among systems. This unit poses an ill-structured problem that leads the students into an interdisciplinary inquiry about the structures of and interaction between several systems, centering around the study of an acid spill on a local highway. The systems included in this unit are chemical reaction systems, ecosystems, and transportation systems.
The Chesapeake Bay (192 pp.)	Poses an ill-structured problem that leads students into an interdisciplinary inquiry about several individual systems and their interactions. The content of the unit focuses on the various systems involved in the pollution of the Chesapeake Bay. The systems included in this unit are ecosystems, chemical reaction systems, government systems, and economic systems.
Dust Bowl (176 pp.)	Gives students the opportunity to explore the concept of systems through the study of a model ecosystem. It poses a problem for students to resolve, enabling them to approach the ecosystem study through the eyes of apprentice scientists. To resolve the problem, students must build a model ecosystem and understand the global systems (weather, planetary) that are the bases for the model. This problem gives students a real-world problem to solve that serves as a vehicle for student involvement and enables them to see the complexity of one system in relation to the systems upon which it depends.
Electricity City (184 pp.)	This unit is geared towards allowing students to successfully master the concept of systems in the context of a city's electrical system. This goal is embedded by revealing an increasingly complex problem. Students are engaged in the task of building and wiring part of a local city. Through the process of developing and evaluating possible alternative problem resolutions, students learn that it is essential to understand the complex interactions among systems in order to evaluate the potential success of their solution.
Models: A Study of Animal Populations Grades 7–8	This unit integrates population biology, mathematics, and technology. The ill-structured problem puts students in the stakeholder role of assistant to the mayor of a small town in which residents are demanding that something be done about the deer that are eating their landscaped plants. Throughout the unit, students deal with physical models, conceptual models, and mathematical models as they tackle the deer problem and then the further complication of Lyme disease. (Authors: Dana T. Johnson & Beverly T. Sher)
Hot Rods (248 pp.)	Explores the question of the effects of nuclear power waste. The unit is introduced through the eyes of the mayor of a town in which a nuclear power plant is located who must decide if the facility can expand its waste depository. How safe are the plant's nuclear waste disposal techniques? What are the biological implications of radiation? What are the trade-offs with which society must live as we accept nuclear technologies into our lives? These questions, very much unresolved in the current scientific literature, are explored by students as they prepare to make recommendations about the use of a nuclear power plant in their fictitious town. *(continued on next page)*

Figure 9.7 *Continued*

No Quick Fix (184 pp.)	Uses systems as the fundamental concept to help students understand cell and tuberculosis biology. In a series of widening concentric circles, students learn that the cells are elements in larger systems, such as the immune system, and the even larger system of the human body. Students also interact with the human social systems: health care and public education. Students take on the role of physican and begin to search for the cause and resolution of the problem. While unraveling the interactions among the various systems, students come to appreciate the complexities of staying healthy in the modern world.
What a Find! (184 pp.)	This unit is an exploration of the field of archaeology. Students are put in the role of junior archaeologists at a research museum and discover that construction work has been halted on a new school because of the discovery of historic artifacts. To determine whether or not the dig is important enough to halt building the school entirely, students learn to excavate and actually conduct the dig—carefully seeded with "historic artifacts." Piecing together the meaning of the artifacts becomes the vehicle for learning systems, which in this case, is the system of a family in an historical period of time

*The Science Units are available from Kendall/Hunt Publishing Company, P.O. Box 1840, Dubuque, IA 52004-1840, Phone: 1-800-228-0810 or Fax: 1-800-772-9165. Check their Website at: http://www.kendallhunt.com.

In addition, the Javits grant funded other research and publications; for example, the *Conceptual Overview of Science Education for High-Ability Learners,* which gives an overview of how to organize science instruction for academically talented students. They also published *A Curriculum Framework in Language Arts for High-Ability Learners K–8,* which does the same for curriculum for language arts. Topic papers in the language arts are also part of the grant dissemination materials. In mathematics, the project produced a *Resource Guide to Mathematics Curriculum Materials for High-Ability Learners in Grades K–8,* and in research skills, *A Guide to Teaching Research Skills and Strategies (Grades 4–12).* The Language Arts units feature the overarching theme of *change.* Figure 9.8 presents a list of the units that were developed through the grant.

These language arts units have six goals, listed in Figure 9.9. These units have been developed specifically for academically talented learners, with federal money, and they are open-ended enough so that teachers can individually choose and create but they are rigorous enough so that high academic standards are met in an interdisciplinary and thematic manner.

PRECEPT 4: SEVEN CURRICULUM ORIENTATIONS

Elliot Eisner in *The Educational Imagination* (1979, 1985, 1994) delineated five different orientations to curriculum. Most descriptions of curriculum orientations in academically talented education speak of the content, process/product, and concept

Figure 9.8   Language Arts Units from Javits Grant at National Curriculum Project*

Autobiographies: Personal Odysseys of Change Grades 4–6 (221 pp.)	In this language arts unit, students study the concept of change by reading autobiographies of writers and by looking at change in selected lives. As they examine life stories and self portraits, they also study literature and examine works of art from various cultures. Selected stories from "Junior Great Books" were chosen for their probing issues of identity. In order to gain insight into the development of talent, students should be encouraged to explore their own identities as talented learners through discussions and reflective writing.
Journeys and Destinations: The Challenge of Change Grades 2–3 (184 pp.)	This unit uses an inquiry-based approach to investigate literature in an interdisciplinary, multicultural curriculum. The guiding theme of the unit is the recognition of change as a concept that affects people and their relationships to the world around them. An open-ended approach to the discussion process is emphasized in the search for meaning in literature selections such as *The Green Book, Bringing the Rain to Kapiti Plain,* and *The Ugly Duckling.* Vocabulary development and writing activities support the readings.
Patterns of Change: Cycles in Literature and in the World Around Us (Grades 4-6)	The concept of cyclic patterns of change was chosen as the unifying theme in this unit. Literary works including selected poems deal with cycles in nature, knowledge, history, and human life. In the unit, students are introduced to some of the important approaches and ideas of literary criticism. They are encouraged to use journals, literature webs, essays, and visual projects to organize and express their in-depth ideas on the literature they read. (Author: Mary Pleiss)
Literary Reflections on Personal and Social Change Grades 4–6 (194 pp.)	Even though all four language arts strands of literature, writing, language study, and oral communication are integrated into this unit, the core of the unit involves students interacting with literature while enhancing reading comprehension and textual analysis skills. By reading the literature and engaging in shared inquiry, students should develop an awareness about the nature and importance of change, particularly as it affects people in various circumstances, times and cultures. The literature selections, including *The Secret Garden* and world-class short stories by such authors as Tolstoy and Singer, serve as a basis for discussion. Students engage in writing activities not only by responding to the literature but also by using persuasive writing to express opinions on issues of significance that arise from the literature.
Changing Ideas, Changing Perspectives Grades 5–6 (193 pp.)	This unit highlights persuasion, especially as it relates to oral communication. Emphasis is placed on providing evidence of opinions. Students must cite passages from literature to defend their points of view in discussion as well as written arguments. Literature such as *The Valiant* and "Junior Great Books" stories frame the basis for exploring the reasoning process through analysis and interpretation. Opportunities are presented for impromptu speeches, informative and persuasive speeches, debate, both small and large group discussion, and critical listening skills. Throughout the unit, students work independently on the issue of censorship and present their opinions with supporting evidence at the end of the unit. *(continued on next page)*

Figure 9.7   *Continued*

Utopia: Man's Changing Ideas of the Ideal Grades 7-9	This unit provides an overview of utopia as seen by various individuals, groups, and countries. The unit provides students an opportunity to examine why man's ideas about utopia undergo change. Through the study of literature, art, and music and through other classroom activities, students learn about man's search through the ages for utopia and his struggles to grasp and maintain it on both personal and societal levels. Exploring utopia through personal dreams and goals allows students to more thoroughly analyze the literature read throughout this unit. (Author: Mary Ann Yedinak)
Literature of the 1940s: A Decade of Change Grades 7–9 (197 pp.)	This unit looks at the historical events and social issues of the 1940s through the literature of the decade, including novels, short stories, poetry, essays, letters, and newspapers. Numerous opportunities for reading, writing, listening, and speaking are incorporated into the unit. Each student is required to pose a hypothesis and conduct research concerning some issue of significance that arises from the literature that is studied. Students make both a written and an oral presentation of their research. This unit is rich in materials that highlight the concept of change, including works like Hersey's *Hiroshima, The Diary of Anne Frank,* and McCuller's *Member of the Wedding.*
Threads of Change in Nineteenth Century American Literature Grades 7-9 (205 pp.)	This unit explores five themes in nineteenth century American history through literature of the times: romanticism, transcendentalism, abolitionism, industrialism, and feminism. Each of the five "isms" has its own "literature box" containing appropriate documents to serve as a resource for small investigative teams of students. The "isms" are investigated as change agents in American life through the study of key writings of the period, including selected works of Hawthorne, Melville, Thoreau, and Emerson. Students produce both written and oral presentations of their findings and ideas. Literary works discussed in the unit include *The Adventures of Huckleberry Finn, Billy Budd, Foretopman, Dr. Heidegger's Experiment,* and Poe short stories.
Change Through Choices A Literature Unit for High School Students Grades 10-12	Choices and the consequences of choices that people make have an important impact on life and the success of individuals. This unit, designed for high-ability students, focuses on catalytic choices that determine change in a variety of situations. Rich in content, the world literature chosen can be analyzed and synthesized for depth in understanding cultural similarities and differences. This unit attempts to give the student a chance to question real-world choices and problems and decide what valuable lessons can be learned through careful individual examination of options. (Author: Felicia Dixon)

*The Language Arts Units are available from The Center for Gifted Education, P.O. Box 8795, Williamsburg, VA 23187-8795. Phone: 757-221-2362 or Fax: 757-221-2184. Send e-mail to: cfge@facstaff.wm.edu.

orientations (Maker, 1982a, 1982b; VanTassel-Baska, 1988, 1994). Eisner's orientations provide a different and more comprehensive approach to thinking about curriculum for the academically talented. These are the five orientations according to Eisner: (1) Curriculum as personal relevance; (2) Curriculum as technology; (3) Curriculum as academic rationalism; (4) Curriculum as social adaptation and social reconstruction; (5) Curriculum as the development of cognitive processes. Curriculum should be

Figure 9.9   Goals for Language Arts Curriculum Units from the
National Language Arts Curriculum Project

Goals	Student outcomes/students will be able to:
1. To develop analytical and interpretive skills in literature	1. Describe what a selected literary passage means. 2. Cite similarities and differences in meaning among selected works in literature. 3. Make inferences based on information in given passages. 4. Create a title for a reading selection and provide a rationale for the creation to justify it.
2. To develop persuasive writing skills	1. Develop a written persuasive essay (thesis statement, supporting reasons, and conclusion) given a topic. 2. Complete various pieces of writing using a three-phase revision process based on peer review, teacher feedback, and self-evaluation
3. To develop linguistic competency	1. Analyze the form and function of words in a given context. 2. Develop vocabulary power commensurate with reading. 3. Apply standard English usage in written and oral contexts. 4. Evaluate effective use of words, sentences, and paragraphs in context.
4. To develop listening and/or communication skills	1. Discriminate between informative and persuasive message. 2. Evaluate an oral persuasive message according to main idea and arguments cited to support it. 3. Develop skills of argument formulation. 4. Organize oral presentations, using elements of reasoning as a basis.
5. To develop reasoning skills in the language arts	1. State a purpose for all modes of communication, their own as well as others. 2. Define a problem, given ill-structured, complex, or technical information. 3. Formulate multiple perspectives (at least two) on a given issue. 4. State assumptions behind a line of reasoning in oral or written form. 5. Apply linguistic and literary concepts appropriately. 6. Provide evidence and data to support a claim, issue, or thesis statement. 7. Make inferences, based on evidence. 8. Draw implications for policy development or enactment based on the available data.

(continued on next page)

Figure 9.9   *Continued*

Goals	Student outcomes/students will be able to:
6. To understand the concept of change in the language arts	1. Understand that change is pervasive. 2. Illustrate the variability of change based on time. 3. Categorize types of change, given several examples. 4. Interpret change as progressive or regressive in selected works. 5. Demonstrate the change process at work in a piece of literature. 6. Analyze social and individual change in a given piece of literature.

considered within the context of Eisner's five orientations. The point is that no one is unbiased, and no one approaches schooling with an objective mind. One's belief system informs what one thinks should be taught. Table 9.2 indicates how curriculum thinkers in the field of the education of the gifted and talented might be categorized according to the seven delineations: Eisner's five, Project Zero's teaching for insight, and the postmodernist one.

Table 9.2   Seven Orientations to Curriculum in the Field of the Education of the Gifted and Talented

Orientation	Model (or Aspects of Model)	Relevant Quotation
1. Curriculum as personal relevance	• Renzulli's Enrichment Triad	"Building educational experiences around student interests is probably one of the most recognizable ways in which schoolwide enrichment programs differ from the regular curriculum" (Renzulli & Reis, 1989, p. 230).
2. Curriculum as technology	• Maker's Problem Type Matrix • VanTassel-Baska's various matrices • Tannenbaum's Enrichment Matrix	"Use boxes 1-5 to indicate results; check appropriate box if mastered (use other codes as needed, i.e.: 'N'-not appropriate, 'A'-absent, '1/2' achieved at least half mastery" (Kemnitz, Martin, Hegeman & Hickey, 1982).
3. Curriculum as academic rationalism	• William and Mary Language Arts and Science Models • VanTassel-Baska's "Integrated Curriculum Model" • Talent Search Curricula	"Most of the outcomes that have been officially defined are lacking in specific academic content. This vagueness about content is a continued evasion of our collective responsibility to provide academic guidance. To be genuinely useful, outcomes-based guidelines should spell out . . . by clearly defined grade-by-grade content guidelines for at least fifty percent of the curriculum" (Hirsch, 1993).

Table 9.2 *Continued*

Orientation	Model (or Aspects of Model)	Relevant Quotation
4. Curriculum as (a) social adaptation and (b) social reconstruction	• (a) Javits grant authorization • (b) Postmodern curriculum thinking	(a) Javits legislation reauthorization "targets grants to schoolwide efforts to provide challenging curricula and enriching instruction (often offered in gifted and talented programs) to all students; at least half of the grants will go to high poverty schools" (Elementary and Secondary Education Act, Title IV, Part B, 1988). (b) "An issue of power is who decides? Who decides what learners will learn and what teachers will teach? Does the Advanced Placement Company decide? Does the International Baccalaureate Company decide?" (Piirto, 1997)
5. Curriculum as the development of cognitive processes	• Project Zero's "Teaching to Understand" • Sternberg's "Componential Model" • Taylor's "Multi-Talent Totem Pole" • Maker's "DISCOVER Problem-solving" • Meeker's SOI • Betts' "Autonomous Learner Model" • VanTassel-Baska's "Integrated Curriculum Model"	• "The student will develop Divergent Thinking Processes. 1. The student will develop *fluency*. 2. The student will develop *flexibility*. 3. The student will develop *originality*. 4. The student will develop *elaboration.*" (Ohio Gifted Student Course of Study, 1989) • "The essence of the DISCOVER assessment process is that the children engage in problem-solving activities in their regular classroom setting . . . they use materials that are novel, fun, and versatile, and they interact with their peers while a trained observer records their problem-solving behaviors and describes their products" (Maker, Rogers, Nielson & Bauerle, 1996, p. 9).
6. Curriculum as a means of producing insight	Project Zero's Teaching for Understanding (Gardner, 1991)	"Understandings can only be apprehended and appreciated if they are *performed* by a student . . . students need to begin to 'practice' these performances from the first day of class." Gardner, 1993, p. 191.
7. Curriculum based on contemporary postmodern curriculum thought	"State-organized education is an attempt to create what we have repressed in ourselves. But this act is an act of violence" (Block, 1997, p. 162).	"Many of the common recommendations for curricula for the academically and artistically talented were indeed postmodern: (1) preassessment for individualization; (2) development of student interests; (3) autobiography used to reconceptualize; (4) time as a variable; (5) talent development based on specific talents" (etc.) (Piirto, 1998b, p. 133).

Sawyer's call for academic rigor (1988) speaks to his orientation to curriculum for the academically talented. Renzulli's call for personally chosen projects speaks to his orientation to curriculum for the academically talented (Renzulli & Reis, 1985). Maker's call for high mobility in the classroom speaks to her orientation to curriculum for the academically talented (1982a). VanTassel-Baska's call for the teaching of Latin speaks to her orientation to curriculum for the academically talented (1988).

With a view toward targeting curriculum for all seven areas, the curriculum planner for the academically talented can be sure that the curriculum is comprehensive and can take care that personal biases as to what curriculum should be are balanced with other orientations. Let us take a few examples.

a. Curriculum as Personal Relevance

"What should I teach in my class for the academically talented?" Theresa Avilar, a new teacher for a pullout program of fifth and sixth graders, asked her principal.

"Well, just talk to the regular classroom teacher, and find out what she's doing, and supplement," he said. "What she's doing is fine, but the kids should do extra projects with you, based on their interests. Give them an interest inventory and have them do projects they're interested in, in-depth research on projects they've chosen. You should have seen the project fair last year. What a group!" Theresa Avilar's principal wanted her to teach curriculum that is personally relevant to students.

The 1970s were the decade when "relevance" of curriculum was a key word. In many schools, traditional curricula gave way to mini-courses, and a plethora of subjects grew and gave teachers a chance to teach their favorite, quirky subjects. "Cowboy Songs of the Old West" was as likely to provide credit for literature as "Calculating Percentages for Retail Markdown" was likely to provide credit for mathematics in the high school curriculum. If the knowledge wasn't meaningful to the child, the school tried to change the requirement so that the child would feel as if the knowledge had meaning. The vocationalization of the curriculum also took place as a means for relevance; that the child would need this knowledge in "the world of work" was used as a justification for placing career and vocational content into the curriculum.

In programs for the education of the academically talented, this trend was translated to the practice of insisting that every project the academically talented child did should be of personal interest. Academically talented students should have a hand in planning their own education. Individual plans should be made for individual academically talented students. Academically talented students should also learn to do self-evaluation of their academic work.

As quoted in Table 9.2 on p. 384, Renzulli and Reis also used the orientation of personal relevance in the Enrichment Triad model, in which they insisted that personal interest should be the guideline by which students gain motivation to do Type III activities. The reasons for basing projects on personal interest are obvious. If a child is interested in a topic, she will want to find out more about it. A disadvantage of using student interest is that if a child has not had sufficient exposure to various ideas, the topics of interest might prove shallow. Defenders of the idea that student interest should generate the projects do say that a child who is interested in a topic, say, horses, will of necessity have to learn about other topics. For example, a study of race horses will lead a child to mathematical inquiries, as in learning about speed and rate; to biological inquiries, as in learning about breeding; to social concerns, as in learning about gambling; to historical inquiries, as in learning about where racing horses came from. The student will be interested in pursuing these topics not for their generic interest, but because of her underlying passion about horses.

b. Curriculum as Technology

"What should I teach in my class for the academically talented?" Craig Anderson, a new teacher for a third grade self-contained classroom, asked his principal.

"Well, look at the state curriculum and compact it, making sure they meet all the behavioral objectives and units of performance. Just move through it faster, supplementing along the way," the principal said. "We just have to be accountable for following the state curriculum. What else you do is up to you. We've got a good budget for field trips. Make sure they have mastery, and then you can expose them to more and different experiences. Take a trip to the courthouse and have them see how society really works, and to the art museum to get a little culture."

Another way of viewing curriculum is that curriculum is a technical, scientific, sequential set of steps of mastery of behavioral objectives through technology and contracts. Curriculum technologists such as Ralph Tyler, Benjamin Bloom, and Hilda Taba have advocated this orientation to curriculum, and this is what Craig Anderson's principal thought he should do.

One can see the pervasiveness of the technological approach to curriculum in the writings of curriculum theorists in academically talented education: VanTassel-Baska (1988, 1994) has a chapter on scope and sequence and on developing a unit in her book on curriculum and often speaks of matching objectives to learning characteristics. Renzulli (Renzulli & Reis, 1989) has diagrams of input and output with relationship to curriculum. Maker and colleagues (Maker et al., 1996) created a matrix of five types of problems for the DISCOVER program in Arizona. Williams (1972) made a "morphological paradigm" to implement cognitive and affective behaviors in the classroom for the academically talented. Tannenbaum (1983) made an enrichment matrix that intersected programmatic augmentation with subject matter. The flowcharts, diagrams, and technological terms are pervasive, so pervasive that no one has even questioned their utility. "Curriculum as technology" plans are based on the work of Ralph Tyler (1949) and are known as the Tylerian rationale. Their appeal to educators and curriculum planners has been that they offer a promise of sequential order, of formal organization, of rational thought, much as the assembly line developers and time management specialists have promised. If a curriculum planner designs curriculum according to the tasks set out in the boxes to be checked off, thoroughness is assured, errors can be corrected, and political neutrality is guaranteed. The curriculum as technology designers have sometimes asserted that their plans are "teacher proof."

c. Curriculum as Academic Rationalism

"What should I teach in my class for the academically talented?" Christine Kearney, a new high school teacher, asked the head of the department of English.

"Well, you're even lucky you got the academically talented kids at all, because that's a matter of seniority around here. The most senior teachers used to get the academically talented kids. But since you came with your Ph.D., the principal said you have the subject matter knowledge to teach the academically talented ones. Not that I think a person with a Ph.D. can teach any better than those of us with only Bachelor's degrees," the department head said. He continued, "The principal has me teaching the remedial class this year because he said the best teachers should teach the students who have the most trouble."

"What should you teach? Well, take them through the English lit sophomore anthology, and then supplement with more novels, poems, plays, and essays from the period. Look at the suggested reading list in the appendix."

A third way of approaching curriculum—the academic rationalist view that curriculum should foster intellectual growth in traditional subject matter—is what Christine Kearney's department head believed.

The academic rationalists believe that traditional curriculum has been watered down through synthesis. That is, students no longer study geography or history as separate subjects; they study social studies which supposedly covers history, geography, economics, political science, anthropology, sociology, psychology, and religion, but they don't learn their geography or history or economics or government because the subjects are too interwoven and concepts rather than facts are taught. This synthesis of traditional curriculum has also affected the elementary school, as "language arts" replaced forever the separate study of grammar, penmanship, and literature. Teachers were to be experts in all areas of the broad subject of "language arts," and reading became a subject that was the same as "English." As a result, students came out knowing fewer facts and many concepts.

Core Knowledge

An academic rationalist movement in the 1980s was started by an English professor called Edward Hirsch, Jr. He wrote a book called *Cultural Literacy* (1987), in which he evidenced concern over the "content-neutral conception of educational development" that has triumphed in America because schools of education and education professors have been influenced by Dewey and Rousseau to the detriment of the children's need to know. This has also affected academically talented students and the National Assessment of Educational Progress tests have shown that even the brightest students score lower on fact information than they did 20 or 30 years ago (Piirto, 1989d).

The fact that academically talented students, whose learning characteristics include a good memory, a love for facts, and a rapidity of processing, have also been subject to the decline in general knowledge is deplorable. Teachers of the academically talented often devise cultural literacy activities suitable for academically talented students. They use these not as the complete curriculum but as aspects of the curriculum in their classes for the academically talented. Critics claim that this is study of trivia, but advocates say that most trivia experts have deep knowledge of the fields they're experts in; these activities provide students with background knowledge that enables them to go deeper to insightful knowledge if they wish. It also enables them to talk to their grandparents.

The Core Knowledge Foundation (www.coreknowledge.org/newplans.htm) has lesson plans and units for preschool through grade eight at their Website. For example, the list of reference books for a fifth grade unit on the Renaissance included books that show the academic rationalist point of view of reading classic literature and studying classic historical figures and movements (Resource Module 9.1). The lesson plans and units listed in Resource Module 9.2 illustrate the wide scope of lessons that Core Knowledge teachers have developed utilizing this philosophy.

Resource Module 9.1   Core Knowledge Foundation Fifth Grade Renaissance Unit

Background Knowledge

Bard of Avon: The Story of William Shakespeare by Diane Stanley and Peter Vennema; *Brush Up Your Shakespeare!* by Michael Macrone; *DaVinci* by Mike Venezia; *Lives of the Writers* by Kathleen Krull; *A Medieval Feast* by Aliki; *Michelangelo* by Mike Venezia; "A Midsummer Night's Dream," cassette tape by Mendelssohn; *A Midsummer Night's Dream for Young People* edited by Diane Davidson; *A Midsummer Night's Dream* video from HBO's *Shakespeare: The Animated Tales Series; The Prince* by Machiavelli; *The Renaissance* by Tim Wood; *Renaissance People* by Sarah Howarth; *What Your Fifth Grader Needs to Know* by E.D. Hirsh, Jr.

RESOURCES

Baker, Elaine. *Influential Artists,* Vols. 1 and 2. Dunstable, England: Folens Publishers, 1992.

Bertelli, Carlo. "Restoration Reveals The Last Supper." *National Geographic* Vol. 164, November 1983: 664–85.

Brown, Margaret. *The Important Book.* New York: Harper Trophy, 1990.

Calliope: *Introduction to the Renaissance,* Vol. 4, May/June 1994.

Davidson, Diane, ed. *A Midsummer Night's Dream for Young People* by William Shakespeare. Fair Oaks, CA: Swan Books, 1986.

Folger Shakespeare Library, Volunteer Docents: *Shakespeare for the Young Reader: A Guide to Available Sources.* Washington: 1985.

Garfield, Leon, abr. *A Midsummer Night's Dream* by William Shakespeare. New York: Alfred A. Knopf, 1992.

Heusinger, Lutz. *The Library of Great Masters—Michelangelo.* New York: Scala/Riverside, 1989.

Hirsch, E.D., Jr. *What Your Fifth Grader Needs To Know.* New York: Doubleday, 1993.

Howarth, Sarah. *Renaissance People.* Brookfield, Connecticut: The Millbrook Press, 1992.

Howarth, Sarah. *Renaissance Places.* Brookfield, Connecticut: The Millbrook Press, 1992.

Jeffery, David. "A Renaissance for Michelangelo." *National Geographic* Vol. 176, December 1989: 688-713.

Krull, Kathleen. *Lives of the Writers.* New York: Harcourt Brace & Company, 1994.

(continued on next page)

Resource Module 9.1   (continued)

Larsen, Linda J. *Thematic Unit—Renaissance.* #580, Huntington Beach, CA: Teacher Created Materials, Inc., 1994.

Macrone, Michael. *Brush Up Your Shakespeare!* New York: Harper & Row, 1990.

Moen, Christine Boardman. *Better Than Book Reports.* New York: Scholastic, 1992.

Peppin, Anthea. *The Usborne Story of Painting.* London: Usborne, 1980.

Peris, Carme, Gloria Vergis, and Oriol Vergis. *Journey Through History—Renaissance.* New York: Barron's, 1988.

Polette, Nancy. *The Research Project Book.* O'Fallon, MO: Book Lures, Inc., 1992.

Raboff, Ernest. *Leonardo Da Vinci—Art for Children.* New York: Harper & Row, 1987.

Raboff, Ernest. *Michelangelo Buonarroti—Art for Children.* New York: Harper & Row, 1988.

Reit, Seymour, adapt. "*Don Quixote,* by Miguel de Cervantes." *Boy's Life,* June 1990.

Sabin, Francene. *Renaissance.* Mahwah, New Jersey: Troll, 1985.

Stanley, Diane, and Peter Vennema. *Bard of Avon: The Story of William Shakespeare.* New York: Morrow Junior Books, 1992.

Venezia, Mike. *Getting to Know the World's Greatest Artists—Da Vinci.* Chicago: Children's Press, 1989.

Venezia, Mike. *Getting to Know the World's Greatest Artists—Michelangelo.* Chicago: Children's Press, 1991.

Wood, Tim. *See Through History—The Renaissance.* New York: Viking, 1993.

Other Academic Rationalist Approaches

Other academic rationalist approaches are those of Mortimer Adler, whose Padeia Program (1984) has reached many schools, and of Paul Phenix, whose *Realms of Meaning* (1964) synthesizes great ideas across disciplines. Hirsch and the Core Knowledge Foundation have produced books for the elementary grades called "What Every Third Grader Should Know" and so forth, and several hundred "core knowledge" schools have been founded. As far back as 1961, Ward advocated an academic rationalist approach when he proposed that academically talented students should have instruction in the *Syntopticon* and in the ideas of great thinkers in order to comprehend the magnitude of ideas. He said that instruction in the principles behind these ideas would formulate knowledge in academically talented learners that would encourage them to gain further knowledge. He called this type of instruction "generative."

Resource Module 9.2 Core Knowledge Foundation Lesson Plans and Units

Preschool Lesson Plans and Units:

* Zip to Zowie! Math Exploration, Kindergarten Classroom
* Break Loose With Mother Goose

Kindergarten Lesson Plans and Units

•Spouts Ahoy! •We're Building Heroes •Christopher Columbus •We're Having a Math Circus •Symbols and Silhouettes •Penguins, Seals, and Polar Bears, Oh My! •A Healthy Body Makes Sense •Curriculum Connections Made Easy •Foundations in Art •Around the World in 20 Days •Kindergarten Goes to Kenya! •Once Upon a Time •Rainbows

First Grade Lesson Plans and Units

•Penguins, Seals, and Polar Bears, Oh My! •The Human Body •Classical Music and Composer Wolfgang Amadeus Mozart •Ancient Egypt (1996) •From Colonies to Independence •Exploration, Conquests and Settlement •Ancient Egypt (1997) •Folk Tales from Around the World •Get Your Feet Wet! A First Dip into the Ocean •Animal Habitats and Destruction or Loss of Habitat •Hop Skip and Jump: What Makes Your Body Move? •Matter Matters: Solids, Liquids, and Gases •First Grade Mini Tasks •Out of Africa •It's Positively Shocking! •Where in the World Am I? •Your World, My World, Our World

Second Grade Lesson Plans and Units

•Heroic Scientists in Our World •China •Ancient Greece •Ancient India •The War of 1812 •Up, Down, and Over •We Are a Family •Art and Artists •Our Town •America the Beautiful •Appreciating Art and Artists •Families of Instruments •A Study of Ancient Greece •The Mitchell Trail •Poetry

Third Grade Lesson Plans and Units:

•Let There Be Light! (And Optics!) •The Thirteen Colonies •The Age of Exploration •Vikings: A Link to Our Future •The Vikings: Bad Mannered Barbarians or An Interesting Interdisciplinary Study? •Colonial America: The Original Thirteen Colonies •Native Americans •Art Smart! •Ancient Rome •Astronomy •Discovery: Eastern Woodland Indians and Jamestown Settlement •Geography: World Rivers •Light and Optics •Ancient Rome •Animal Classifications •The Vikings of Scandinavia •Poetry: Developing a Taste •The Roman Civilization

(continued on next page)

Resource Module 9.2 *(continued)*

Fourth Grade Lesson Plans and Units

•Rock My World •Critical Thinking Strategies to Medieval History •American Heroes: Past and Present •King Arthur •China During the Middle Ages •Medieval Life and Times •Caravans •Digging Up the Past •Islands, Adventures, and Adaptations •Early and Medieval African Kingdoms •Star-Spangled Math •Geometry: Beyond Pencil and Paper •Meteorology Matters •Africa: A Cultural Safari •Slip Sliding Through Tessellations Geometry •The American Revolution: An Interdisciplinary Lesson •Where in the World Is Mt. Kilimanjaro? •Your Students Are Poets and They Didn't Even Know It! •Exploring the Middle Ages Through Literature, Science, and Social Studies

Fifth Grade Lesson Plans and Units

•The Age of Exploration •The Spirit of Curiosity •The Commonwealth of Independent States •Flags of the World •Beginner's Chemistry •The Not So Simple Facts About Simple Organisms •Discovering Russia •A Midsummer Night's Dream •Westward Expansion and Spatial Awareness •Understanding World Climates •Westward Ho •World Civilization: A Timeline Approach •What's the Matter? • Chemistry: Matter and Change •Using Media Skills to Travel the U.S.A. •Aztec, Inca, Maya

Sixth Grade Lesson Plans and Units

•It's All in the Genes •The Secret Garden • As the Atom Spins •The Middle East •Beginner's Chemistry •The Wind Blows from East to West •Teaching Ancient Civilizations: Egypt and Greece •The Influence of the Baroque Period on Music, Art & Literature Via Puppet Theater •Capitalism: Roots and Branches

Seventh & Eighth Grade Lesson Plans and Units

•Starting Off the Year on the Same Page •Electricity and Magnetism •Civil Rights Movement

Many debates are raging today about the appropriate academic content for a multicultural world. Social reconstructionists accuse the academic rationalists of omitting the works of women and minorities, and calling "classic" the works of dead white men. In 1988, a social reconstructionist response to the Hirsch book was published. It was called the *Graywolf Annual Five Multi-cultural Literacy* (Walker & Simonson, 1988) and the authors accused Hirsch's list of 5,000 cultural literacy items of being biased toward western culture. The issue is not new. Reading any curriculum subject matter debate will uncover the battles between those who advocate for the "classics" and those who advocate for "relevant" skills and contemporary popular culture.

d. Curriculum as Social Adaptation and Social Reconstruction

"What should I teach in my class for the academically talented?" John Miller asked the programs coordinator for the district.

"Well, we hired you because of your computer background. So teach computer programming, since our kids will need to be on the cutting edges of technology. We've got a new video editing system at the county office, so you might want to teach them video technology, too, and the laser disc system can be used to teach them a foreign language; we've got Spanish on laser disc," the coordinator of programs for the gifted and talented replied. "The main thing is, they've got to be ready for the future, be attuned to the world of work."

A fifth way to view curriculum is that curriculum functions to foster social adaptation and social reconstruction. This is what John Miller's administrator wanted him to teach.

John Miller asked the same question of the county coordinator. "What should I teach my class for the academically talented?"

She was a longtime member of Greenpeace and of Amnesty International, and answered, "Teach them about peace. Teach them about social change. Teach them to be able to reconstruct society as they will have to if we keep going the way we do. There's a neat peace curriculum here at the office that is graded for grades 3 to 8. You might want to take a look at it. Global awareness is another topic you should consider." Relevance is also at issue in this county coordinator's answer to John Miller, though the relevance is not personal but "save the world" relevance. Eisner (1979, 1985, 1994) called this the curriculum orientation of "social adaptation and social reconstruction."

What is socially relevant changes. In the 1950s, one relevance was that the United States had to beat the Russians, and therefore academically talented children were told they should study math, science, and foreign languages. The federal government provided National Defense loans to students who majored in these subjects. In the 1960s, one relevance was that academically talented children should join the Peace Corps and the Teacher Corps and save the poor people of the world, and therefore academically talented children should study humanistic subjects. In the 1970s, students were to focus on inner values, and "clarify" their values so they could be happy. In the 1980s, one relevance was to make money and beat the Japanese, and therefore academically talented children were told they should study business, finance, and law. In the 1990s, one relevance is to save the tropical rain forests and the ozone layer, and to save the world from military destruction, and therefore academically talented children were told they should be preparing themselves for careers that will save the environment. New majors in colleges with the term "environmental" in them became extremely popular. Students could learn to help the environment by majoring in recycling, in environmental politics, environmental biology, environmental chemistry. Other popular majors featured international business, languages, and global cultures.

The social reconstruction view of curriculum has to do with the purpose of the curriculum. In the Goals for Education for the Year 2000, one can see the social reconstruction view in operation. Business views the purpose of the schools as being that of providing workers for business. The society functions to provide workers for business. Social ills are causing the schools to fail in this purpose. Therefore, the schools must first address the social ills. Drug education must be a part of every school curriculum, for all schools must be drug free. The goals were pointed in their omission of the arts and of foreign languages, but they were adamant on the social reconstruction view that schools must teach students not to use drugs.

e. Curriculum as the Development of Cognitive Processes

"What should I teach in my class for the academically talented?" Marissa Snyder asked the principal of the junior high school where she was to teach a special honors class in social studies.

"Teach them to think," her principal said. "Thinking skills, thinking skills, thinking skills. If they can think, they'll be able to make decisions and to function in society. Here's a catalog of materials from *Thinking Your Way to the Top.* They're having a regional workshop in a few weeks, and you should attend that, too. The most famous guru in the thinking skills field will be the speaker, teaching about his special system. We've got money in the budget for you to go. Thinking. Critical thinking. Creative thinking. But on a higher level, for the academically talented kid. That's what to teach."

A fifth orientation is that curriculum should focus on mental process rather than product. In programs for the education of the academically talented this is a common approach, as children learn creative thinking skills such as fluency, flexibility, and elaboration, and critical thinking skills such as analysis and synthesis, often divorced from content. The Anita Harnadek materials (1978) are examples of this, as are the Edward de Bono materials (1970, 1978). This is what Marissa Snyder's principal thought she should teach.

Hands-on math manipulatives help students construct knowledge in a concrete manner.

Educators of the gifted and talented pioneered many of the thinking skills curricula and process instruction. Research and study skills courses are also process oriented. Many teachers use the textbook as their curriculum. Academically talented students should be challenged to organize the material for themselves using general reference books, encyclopedias, and bibliographies, and several texts rather than just one.

This training in research techniques will teach the academically talented child to distinguish between theoretical viewpoints and experiments, between surveys, anthologies, and original reports of data gathering. The academically talented child should learn by browsing, and by rapid surveying of material. Database searches should be common tools for academically talented students. One high school science teacher, conducting a special seminar on marine biology for several academically talented students, asked them to gather their references. One student, whose topic was going to be the interdependence of sea anemones and angelfish, used the computer databases at a nearby major university research center and came up with 1,300 references on sea anemones, 1,100 references on angelfish, and in cross-referencing them, came up with 37 articles that spoke of both. His teacher was providing him with the tools of research. The student was 15 years old. The marine biology seminar then took a field trip to a key off Florida where the students could conduct experiments.

As the teacher observes the academically talented individual seeking to apply knowledge, she can begin to assume that the child understands the idea and is ready for more advanced work. Students should study meaning by studying the etymology of words and by explicating literary works. Slowing down to savor meaning is important. One literature teacher spent the whole semester on one short story, "Araby," by James Joyce. After the course the students felt they finally knew how to read. Academically talented students should also study the argumentative essay, in which essayists expound opposite points of view rather than bland textbooks which purport to "present both sides," for such texts tend to trivialize differences that engage the passions of the populace.

The PIFS (Practical Intelligence For Schools) project funded by the federal government used Robert Sternberg's tripartate theory of how intelligent people process information. In a middle school project, students took courses in how to do a project before they did a project. They learned how disciplines were structured. The pilot elementary/secondary curriculum to help students develop common sense and practical judgment as well as intellect was an interinstitutional effort between Yale and Harvard universities and included Howard Gardner, known for his theory of multiple intelligences.

Critical thinking and creative thinking are watchwords of education these days, but the applications should be stressed more. If a student can write an argumentative essay or construct an argumentative speech about certain concepts she has studied, the application of the critical or creative thinking can be shown. Again, "cute" products are often underevaluated by teachers of the academically talented, who say, "Isn't that creative?" but who may fail to provide helpful feedback in aiding the student to think critically or creatively.

The Renzulli model for enrichment has as one of its types of enrichment Type II (Renzulli & Reis, 1985), or process training. The Schoolwide Enrichment Model lists taxonomies of processes that should be introduced to academically talented students. In a 1991 article, Reis and Burns stated that "many thinking skills activities in academically talented education programs seem to suffer from an abundance of puzzles, games, and worksheets, and a shortage of teaching, transfer, and relevance" (p. 72). They advocated five steps in developing thinking skills components in the curriculum for academically talented students: (1) generating a taxonomy of skills; (2) charting a scope and sequence for the skills; (3) making sure that there is adequate staff development; (4) writing unit plans that infuse thinking skills into the curriculum; and (5) teaching the thinking skills and evaluating the success of the teaching. Figure 9.10 illustrates the Reis and Burns proposed taxonomy of thinking skills necessary for academically talented students.

The days of differentiating curricula for the academically talented by means of infusing process should be long gone. If curriculum developers for the education of the academically talented are still exclusively using the process approach, a study by Schack (1991) should provide a caution. Schack and her colleagues provided 45 lessons in the Creative Problem Solving process and its applications as well as group dynamics, to 214 middle school students in academically talented, honors, regular, and special education. The results showed that "more than identified academically talented students can benefit from process skills taught in gifted programs." An integrated approach utilizing these thinking skills in ways that are related to the content of the curriculum should be the norm for curriculum for academically talented students. Yet the differentiation is often process oriented, so that creative and critical thinking skills are taught separately from content.

f. Curriculum as a Means of Producing Insight

"What shall we teach in our K through 6 magnet school for the academically talented?" the curriculum committee of a large district asked the expert from the university.

"Insight," said the expert. "I've been reading Perkins and Gardner and following the cognitive scientists for years now, and they've finally come up with a dynamite system that will work for all kids, but especially for academically talented kids. If I were your boss, I'd make arrangements to send you to a multiple intelligence school such as those in the Javits Projects to do an observation. You can learn how they do it there and then set up a similar program for your academically talented kids."

The expert continued, "In their Spectrum project, and in their Arts assessment grant, they use projects, apprenticeships, and process-folios to help children make sense of the world, gain deep understanding, and prove they have that understanding through their actions. That's what academically talented students need; they can get the right answers on tests, but do they really understand Newtonian physics?

"You need to have a real hands-on curriculum, with lots of field trips to the museums like the Exploratorium in San Francisco, where they teach the kids deep understanding. And have experts come in—arts companies and the like—but always with a view towards having the students truly understand the concepts. There are

Figure 9.10 A Proposed Taxonomy of Thinking Skills

SKILLS INVOLVING ANALYSIS

Identifying Characteristics and
    Components
Recognizing Attributes and Factors

Conducting an Observation
Discriminating Between Same and
    Different
Comparing and Contrasting
Categorizing
Criteria Setting
Classifying, Outlining, and Webbing

Finding the Main Idea

Summarizing
Seeing Relationships
Ranking, Prioritizing, and Sequencing

Determining Cause and Effect
Completing Analogies
Making Analogies

Predicting
Analyzing
Inferring
Deductive Thinking
Evaluating

CRITICAL THINKING SKILLS

Determining Reality and Fantasy

Determining Benefits and
    Drawbacks
Identifying Value Statements
Identifying Point of View

Determining Bias
Identifying Fact and Opinion
Identifying Exaggeration
Determining the Accuracy of
    Presented Information
Judging Essential and Incidental
    Evidence
Determining Relevance
Identifying Missing Information
Determining Warranted and
    Unwarranted Claims
Recognizing Assumptions
Recognizing Fallacies
Detecting Inconsistencies in an
    Argument
Identifying Ambiguity

ORGANIZATIONAL SKILLS

Mathematical Problem Solving
Formulating Questions
Semantic Mapping
Interpreting Data
Developing Hypotheses

Goal Setting
Decision Making
Planning
Designing
Metacognition
Memory Training
Moral Reasoning

CREATIVITY SKILLS

Deferring Judgment
Considering Alternatives
Problem Finding
Creative Problem Solving
SCAMPER Modification
    Techniques
Attribute Listing
Random Input
Synectics
Guided Imagery
Brainstorming
Fluency
Flexibility
Originality
Elaboration

From Reis, S.M. and Burns, D. (1991). Developing a thinking skils component in the gifted education program. *Roeper Review*, 14(2), pp. 72–79. Used with permission.

some good interactive computer programs out as well. That's what you should teach the academically talented students—well, *all* students—but the academically talented students need it just as much as anyone else."

This university person was reflecting the latest in cognitive scientific thought. Even though a "hands-on" curriculum has been advocated for years, the work of Project Zero at Harvard University has come to emphasize teaching for understanding. This is perhaps within the curriculum orientation of process, but I have listed it separately here. "What is needed is the creation of a climate in which students come naturally to link their intuitive ways of knowing with scholastic and disciplinary ways of knowing" (Gardner, 1991, p. 258).

Teaching for understanding has some parallels with the constructivist method of teaching. The learner is the constructor of his or her own understanding. Teaching for understanding is a concept that portrays teachers as guides, coaches, and facilitators of student learning. Each discipline needs a different analytic style or approach to problem solving (Gardner & Boix-Mansilla, 1994; Perkins, 1991, 1993). Different disciplines call upon different analytic styles and problem-solving approaches, and people need different temperaments and intelligences depending on the discipline they pursue. There are four stages in the development of understanding: (1) intuitive answers and ideas about how the world works; (2) disciplinary thinking; (3) interdisciplinary and transdisciplinary thinking; and (4) personal knowledge. Teaching for understanding has gained a large following among school people.

Gardner's book, *The Unschooled Mind* (1991), discusses how the five-year-old intuitive mind creates schema and paradigms about how the world works that are very hard to break. They are simple explanations for complex phenomena. Teaching for understanding seeks to show students what really is behind the falling of the leaves or the stars staying in the sky.

g. Curriculum Based on Contemporary Postmodern Curriculum Thought

"What shall I teach the academically talented?" asked Mark Hagans of his professor in the curriculum class he was taking for his master's of education degree. "Should I do anything different for them than for the rest of the students?"

"No!" the professor said adamantly. "*With* them, not *for* them. All students should construct their own curriculum. Perhaps the academically talented students will go to greater depth, go at a faster pace, or ask questions that have more scholarly implications, but learning should begin with autobiographical truth, and the student should be assisted by the teacher. The teacher is not a facilitator, however, but is a teacher, a teacher with a vocation to teach (and not to coach). So begin with setting an atmosphere where autobiography can arise naturally. Then take it from there."

Slattery (1995a, 1995b) defined postmodern curriculum thought as that which has risen since the reconceptualization of curriculum in the late 1980s (Pinar et al., 1995). In the last five years there has been a revolution happening in curricular thinking. This revolution has taken on the name of *postmodernism.* Postmodern curricular thought could perhaps be placed in the "social adaptation/social reconstruction" orientation, because it calls for students to begin to change the world beginning with themselves. Postmodern curriculum theory rejects the old scientific approach to curriculum in favor of an approach that starts in autobiography and that takes chaos theory and circular images as framing metaphors. Postmodern curricular thought honors the individual's experience as a starting point for what follows. The discussion of a short story can lead to a re-evaluation of all of literature; the framework of a theme can form the curriculum in all subject matter disciplines as all flow into each other and are melded. Postmodern curriculum is described as what has happened to the world once we were able to truly see how fragile our planet is, blue and green and white, from outer space. This photographic image haunts us all as we strive to create curriculum that values the precarious balance of life on earth. (See the Case Example at the end of this chapter.)

Whether they knew it or not, these advice-givers were giving advice based on their personal or academic belief systems about curriculum. Education is not value free, especially the education of special populations. The researchers have come to some agreement, curriculum for the academically talented should be made up of a synthesis of subject matter mastery approaches, skills or process/product approaches, and the thematic approaches. The days of differentiating academically talented curriculum by means of infusing process without content should be long gone.

PRECEPT NUMBER 5: A BALANCED AND ARTICULATED CURRICULUM

Curriculum balance and articulation is better said than done. What is "balance"? A consideration of each of the above orientations in Precept Number 4 should give an indication of what biases you hold as far as what should be taught. With a handle on your own implicit biases, you can look at what you are teaching to see that you have included other orientations as well. An academic rationalist teacher might seek to "cover" all the novels of Dostoevsky or all the ways to bisect a plane in order to make sure the students are knowledgeable. More is not necessarily better. The U.S. curriculum is "a mile wide and an inch deep" (Peak et al., 1996, p. 35). A process-oriented teacher might seek to teach students to analyze propaganda without any or with trivial propaganda to analyze. How about analyzing the documents and rhetoric that led us to the Gulf War? A personal relevance-oriented teacher—say, a coach of dance, theater, athletics, or music—might permit a student to focus only on areas of intense interest, to focus too early and too soon to the detriment of the acquisition of general knowledge that is necessary for functioning as a citizen of a democracy. A social adaptation or social reconstruction-oriented teacher might use the students to feed the homeless or collect money for the starving, or she might decorate her classroom like a rain forest without intellectual attention to the political and social forces that led to these situations. Awareness of the curriculum orientations should lead to a balance among the orientations.

Articulation is more difficult. Articulation is the planned sequence among and between grade or instructional levels of curriculum materials. Usually in curriculum documents this is noted as "I—"Introduce"; "P"—"Practice"; "M"—"Master." Curriculum articulation assumes that students encounter more complex and higher-level work throughout the grades of school, that one grade level builds on what has been learned before. In observing progressively higher classrooms at different grade levels, I have noticed that teachers repeat material, teaching what was supposedly taught in the curriculum of the grade levels below. This is more than review; it is often unconscious repetition.

As mentioned in Precept 1, one of the characteristics of academically talented learners is their ability to assimilate knowledge rapidly and with good memories. I once asked an academically talented college student how many times he had studied the noun. "About twelve times," he said. "In every grade since first grade." Research is showing what is the optimal time to learn certain things. For example, to learn to speak a foreign language without an accent, one must begin speaking in the early years. One will most likely always speak with an accent if the language is introduced in the high school years. While an articulated curriculum may not always be possible, the planners should try. Content should be articulated so it is progressively more difficult. Process skills should also progress. How many times do students need to learn to brainstorm, or to do the SCAMPER technique? It goes without saying that students should also be assigned products that are of greater difficulty and which require more sophisticated forms of knowing. What is new to the teacher, what has been learned at the last conference or inservice workshop, may not necessarily be new to the students in the class. However, some subject matter needs to be visited more than once; for example, classic works of literature just become more rich upon re-reading.

A balanced curriculum is more than a consideration of curriculum orientations as mentioned in Precept 4. For example, while many elementary school teachers love children's literature, they often find mathematics difficult. They would prefer to teach reading and language arts rather than mathematics. The time spent on literature may slowly get longer and the time on mathematics grow shorter as the year goes on. This may contribute to our nation's lower scores on international mathematics assessments—such as the Third International Mathematics and Science Study (TIMSS), for example. A solution to this would be to just admit it is true: that many teachers in the lower grades do not like mathematics, and to hire mathematics specialists in the elementary schools, people who love mathematics, have taken many mathematics courses, and who have deep knowledge in the subject and know how to teach it. The same goes for music and the arts, for science and for social studies. A balance should be struck among the subject matter disciplines.

Academically talented students should be exposed to teachers who know their subject matter. A special program should not be targeted for advanced reading and ignore the needs of academically talented mathematics students—and vice versa.

Figure 9.11   Practices Addressed by Research in Gifted Education and In General Education

Practices uniquely appropriate to gifted education:
1. Acceleration
2. Career education, especially for girls
3. Program arrangements, influencing academic and affective outcomes
4. Ability grouping
5. High-level curricular materials

Practices needing further research to confirm their appropriateness as unique practices for gifted students:
1. Taking into account cultural and social differences
2. Taking into account learning styles
3. Set an example for affective as well as cognitive growth
4. Highly individualized reading
5. The investigation of real problems and solutions
6. Independent study under competent supervision
7. Gifted children learning by teaching other children
8. Rapid pacing

Practices effective with gifted students but generally applicable to all students:
1. Enrichment
2. Microcomputers
3. Communication skills
4. Humanistic values

5. Creative abilities
6. Inquiry, discovery, and problem solving
7. Gifted historical figures
8. Professional end products as standards
9. Individual programming with a common curriculum
10. A variety of teachers as role models
11. A variety of school and community resources
12. Mentor and internship programs
13. Student-centered pedagogy

Recommended practices for which there is insufficient evidence to make a case for their uniqueness for the gifted:
1. Different grading practices for gifted and for nongifted students
2. Individualization across a student's entire program
3. Assessment of student content interests
4. A broad selection of curricular choices
5. Long and short-term goals that students set for themselves
6. Multidisciplinary curriculum
7. Future-oriented curriculum
8. The arts
9. World affairs and global perspective
10. Extracurricular activities
11. Abstract and basic concepts
12. Thinking skills
13. In-depth investigation of subject matter

From Shore and Delcourt, 1996.

General Education and Gifted Education

Another part of balance and articulation is to decide what curricular and program practices should be advocated for all students, and what should be for academically and artistically talented students. A 1991 study by Shore et al., detailed what research has shown. An update in 1996 by Shore and Delcourt listed these practices which are research based, as shown in Figure 9.11. Most of these are discussed in this textbook.

CASE EXAMPLE A Thought Piece on Postmodern Curriculum:

Twelve Issues for the Education of the Talented*

Jane Piirto

Paper presented at the National Association for Gifted Children Conference in Little Rock., Arkansas, November 9, 1997.

"Modern visions of education as characterized by the Tylerian rationale, behavioral lesson plans, context-free objectives, competitive and external evaluation, dualistic models that separate teacher and student, meaning and context, subjective persons and objective knowledge, body and spirit, learning and environment, and models of linear progress through value-neutral information transmission are no longer acceptable in the postmodern era."
    —Patrick Slattery

"A postmodern world will involve postmodern persons, with a postmodern spirituality, on the one hand, and a postmodern society, ultimately a postmodern global order, on the other. Going beyond the modern world will involve transcending its individualism, anthropocentrism, patriarchy, mechanization, economism, consumerism, nationalism, and militarism. Constructive postmodern thought provides support for the ecology, peace, feminist, and other emancipatory movements of our time, while stressing that the inclusive emancipation must be from modernity itself."
    —David Ray Griffin

Many of the criticisms of the field of the education of the gifted and talented have indicated that the curriculum is good for all students. In addition, Borland (1997) thought that there are too many students being identified for programming, and Winner (1996) thought that the curriculum for the gifted should not be differentiated except for the very high-IQ students. (For other self-critical comments see Callahan, 1996; Gallagher, 1996; Howley, Howley & Pendarvis, 1995; Pendarvis & Howley, 1996.) These thinkers from within our field rightfully ask us to look hard at ourselves, but let me put these critiques into a theoretical framework.

In recent years, a group of educational foundations thinkers known as the curriculum reconceptualization movement (Pinar et al., 1995) called for a rejection of the modernist conception of curriculum as a list of objectives, books, and concepts to be mastered according to the plan set down (and essentially unmodified since he set it down) by Ralph Tyler in 1949. Tyler's four goals for curriculum are essentially unchanged: (1.) What educational purposes should the school seek to attain? [objectives]; (2.) What educational experiences can be provided that are likely to attain these purposes? [design]; (3.) How can these educational experiences be effectively organized? [scope and sequence]; and (4.) How can we determine that these purposes are being attained? [evaluation].

The 1960s civil rights movement, the opposition to the Vietnam War, and the development of the counterculture contributed to a rejection of curriculum as behaviorism, with its "observable" goals and objectives. The rejection of positivism and structuralism led to a crisis of meaning as experiments in the "open classroom," and to neoprogressivist calls to treasure childhood for its own sake, for a more humanistic education with an emphasis on the affective, and on the personal rather than the corporate.

Since the 1970s, the reconceptualization has focused on the dangers of curriculum engineering, emphasizing a focus on freedom and aesthetics, with a call to tie curriculum not to technique but to the human spirit. The reconceptualists have urged educators not to conceive values as goals or objectives, to design an educational environment that values educational activity, to pursue a wider view of what educational activity is, and to foster creativity. They have urged us to value the arts and humanities as well as the sciences and mathematics.

By the 1980s, a move back to the center focused curriculum on stage theories of development, with an emphasis on what was appropriate during various stages. In the 1990s, curriculum showed a fascination with the socialist theory of Vygotsky and the assessment emphasis of Gardner. Higher-order thinking became the emphasis, and at the same time there was a call for going back to the basics. Recent studies such as the TIMSS study, comparing U.S. science and mathematics curriculum (Peak, 1996) with Japanese and German curriculum, have noted that the U.S. curriculum is "a mile wide and an inch deep."

The reconceptualists call for a move from a consideration of curriculum as a set of behavioral goals and objectives; that is, a consideration of curriculum as a field of "design," to a consideration of curriculum from the point of view of *understanding* on a deep level what our in-school, out-of-school, conscious and unconscious curriculum choices and predispositions mean. We need to continue to examine our attitudes toward curriculum, and our ingrown biases, defensiveness, and prejudices. Postmodern curriculum reconceptualists and theorists provide a framework for doing so without resorting to personal attacks or finger-pointing.

I have chosen the omnibus term "postmodern" to define this movement, though others give it names such as "poststructuralist" or "deconstructionist." The postmodern period is variously thought to have arrived after the dropping of the bomb on Hiroshima, after the death by assassination of President John Kennedy, or during the Cold War. The values of postmodernism have been widely discussed in the arts, architecture, and literature, and it is true that the postmodern curriculum theorists often emphasize the aesthetic over the scientific. I have identified twelve avenues, or issues, that might be fertile for our future thinking about who we are and what we do, and provide direction for our discussion and our research.

The twelve issues are (1) issues of time; (2) issues of power and class; (3) issues of the body; (4) issues of the spirit; (5) issues of the canon; (6) issues of justice; (7) issues of diversity; (8) issues of language; (9) issues of discourse; (10) issues of desire and passion; (11) issues of gender; and (12) issues of imagination.

1. Issues of Time

In a critique of the federal report *Prisoners of Time*, Slattery (1995a) noted that contemporary schooling considers time in modernist terms, segmenting and breaking up the whole in a false conception that time is linear. He said that schools and educational researchers falsely assume that curriculum units, grades, grade levels, and classes are neat and pure elements that can be scientifically assessed and applied to other situations if one uses the proper control group. Slattery said, "This philosophy of modernity has resulted in an exaggerated emphasis on manipulation of time: time management, timed tests, wait time, time on task, quantifiable results over time, time schedules, time-out discipline centers, allocation of instructional days on annual school calendars, core academic time, carnegie units, time between classes, year round schooling, and the like" (p. 612). In applying his critique to the field of gifted education, I thought of our emphasis on acceleration. Moving a student fast through the curriculum assumes that there *is* a curriculum, a body of subject matter to be "mastered," when in reality there is not; there are certain school systems' conceptions of curriculum as interpreted by their teachers.

Likewise, the concept of *curriculum compacting,* or *curriculum telescoping,* again to "buy time" for "high-end learners," assumes that there are discrete subject matter "bits" to be learned and "mastered." If a student has read *Romeo and Juliet* in seventh grade, and the eighth grade regular classroom teacher is angry because "we do Shakespeare in eighth grade," two questions need to be asked: (1) how can one "do Shakespeare"?; and (2) did reading *Romeo and Juliet* twice—or five or twenty times—really "cover" the play? Perhaps choosing only one play by Shakespeare, to be read over and over again, will give the student a deeper appreciation for Shakespeare than reading many plays will. Is reading "more" necessarily better than reading "deep"? Curriculum compacting or telescoping seems most appropriate for such a subject as spelling or math facts or definitions, the very lowest levels of learning, the knowledge levels, and not for curricula where higher-level thinking is the norm. We need to redefine our concept of rushing people through.

Social critic and novelist John Ralston Saul, in his 1995 book *The Unconscious Civilization,* also asked a question about our conception of time in relation to schooling. He noted that we have more time than any people throughout history. We organize our educational experiences in a pattern that "increasingly represents a desperate rush, as if driven by the threat that time will leave us behind." The reality is that more and more people have, at the end of their lives, 25 or more years of "retirement," forced idleness. While a few years of retirement is valuable, is 25 years? Saul said, "What this indicates is that, on the conscious level, there is no particular reason, and certainly no practical reason, for us to be front-end loading our lives. Then why does our civilization push us to do so?" (p. 157–158).

Saul's comment made me think about the statement in Goals 2000: "Time is the variable." Presently we want to rush the talented kids through their schooling in order that they can take their places in adult society, and save the world through their great contributions at an early age (see Benbow, 1992; Piirto, 1992a/1998; Simonton, 1994). Considering time from a lifespan perspective, why must we do that? What would maturity do to a person's learning? What about the current emphasis on adult education and the fact that many women stay home to raise their families and then enter careers at a later date? This late entry effectively kills their chances to become world-class, "Big C" creators (cf. Csikszentmihalyi, 1995; Feldman, Csikszentmihalyi & Gardner, 1994), but what if we reconceptualized the timeline of careers, and welcomed mature talented people, mothers, and fathers, into the work force, welcomed their mature insights and contributions? What if we expanded our conception of the talented to include "late bloomers" and focused on them as we do on precocity as shown by behavior or test?

Considering time from a boredom perspective (our kids are bored in school because of the time they spend "waiting"), we have now embraced, as a part of the larger system, the model of inclusion, where classroom pace may be even more slowed down. How can we address this short of home schooling every talented student? How can we balance boredom on the front end with boredom on the back end of life? What is the definition of boredom? There are several types of boredom: one is boredom because one doesn't know the material and another is boredom because one does know the material. Is boredom necessarily bad? Perhaps boredom provides time in which to daydream, to wonder, to wish, to enter a state of reverie where one can think creative thoughts. In our fast-paced, time-conscious field, we may need to revisit our concept of boredom and what to do about it.

2. Issues of Power and Class

The critiques of our field, that we are educating students to duly and without protest assume their roles in society, must be considered. As Kincheloe, McLaren, and Steinberg said, "Education becomes a form of social regulation that guides humans toward destinies that preserve the status quo" (Giroux, 1997, p. x). Are our teachers aware of their complicity with the power structure, their docility in training students toward outcomes that preclude self-examination? Giroux (1997) asked, "How can public school classroom teachers orient themselves to curriculum in a way that acknowledges the underlying ethical and normative dimensions that structure classroom decisions and experiences?" (p. 3).

The illusion of the rationality of the technocratic society pervades our field. While our goal as teachers and professors is to teach students that all beliefs are relative (that is, to bring students to an appreciation of each other's beliefs and views of the world), the postmodern theorists insist that truth is not *relative* but *relational* (that is, what is considered true depends on who is in power, on what the student's and teacher's relation to that power is, and on the *Zeitgeist*). Recently we have seen the Lutheran and Catholic churches of Europe apologize to the Jewish people for their silence during World War II. The churches had thought that if they kept quiet, the Jewish problem would go away. And it did—straight to the ovens. If we stay neutral, we support the power structure. There is no such thing as neutrality, say the liberation theorists such as Macedo and Freire (Lewis & Macedo, 1996; Freire, 1997). This critique needs to be examined by those of us who educate academically talented students. Much of the rhetoric justifying our existence is to "save the world" and to exploit "our nation's natural resources, our bright children." Essentially, we are educating them to assume roles of power and privilege. If someone has power, someone does not, and when the subordinates accept their status as natural, inherent, destined, or random, oppression and power are securely entrenched.

The *National Excellence* report (1993) argues that international comparisons of test scores should drive the education of the outstandingly talented; that is, their "quiet crisis" is that they do not score as high on tests as bright students in other countries. The federal government wrote this report and drives policy toward the achievement of domination by capitalist interests through manipulation of the education of the brightest students in the United States toward achievement on international tests (e.g. TIMSS; U.S. silence about Chinese policy toward Tibet). The justification for these practices is that the United States is "good"; that our capitalist free enterprise system will save the world. At the same time, it destroys indigenous culture: the omnipresence of U.S. products and television in Europe has contributed to a decline in national European cultures (20 years ago, French, or Finnish, or Dutch singers could be found on the juke boxes in European restaurants; these years it is difficult to do so, though there are many American singers). The pervasiveness and popularity of American cigarettes, movies, and M-TV are, in my opinion, effectively commercializing existing national cultures to destruction and death.

On the power issue of social class, bell hooks (1994) noted that when she, as a child of the working class, entered Stanford, she never encountered a professor who was from the working class. Her professors espoused classless values, but were themselves members of the privileged classes. While we in education do not have that situation, for most or many of us are from the working classes—many fathers, like mine, were staunch members of trade unions who sent us to college to fulfill a dream they themselves had—we still behave along lines where class counts. So it is no surprise that we have complied with the implicit goals of this field, to move bright poor students into a higher social class. Or is it? Where are we from? What does that mean for our lives as educators? How have we been silenced? How have we been silenced, in an attempt to "fit in" to the goals of this field, the outcomes? Who better than we to speak up for our own cultures, our own working class values and backgrounds?

Of course, another issue of power is, who decides? Who decides what learners will learn and what teachers will teach? Does the Advanced Placement Company decide? Does the International Baccaulaureate Company decide? Does the college English department decide? Teachers of advanced and honors classes often feel they have so much material to "cover" they cannot breathe, teach, or be free. They feel relegated to positions of "curriculum delivery woman" much as the "milkman" of yore.

Still another issue of power is that of our field within the huge education establishment. We have served as a bellwether; we have pioneered many teaching strategies and philosophies over the years. But we have not received validation or recognition for this, and we have pulled back into our shells, licked our wounds, and whimpered as we were accused of racism, classism, elitism, and test scorism. We slink in a cowardly manner down the halls of our colleges of education. Yet we know we represent a field that has no money, no prestigious following, no government cachet, but which strives toward educating and serving the needs of students who do have learning needs that are different from those of other children. We feel powerless against the onslaught of the criticisms leveled against us. What is our recourse? Perhaps to just continue as we have been, to be the pioneers of innovative educational practice that may begin as education for the talented, but will soon be adopted as education for all. Or maybe our pedagogy of the powerless is not so powerless at all, given our clientele, who can take a gem, a germ, a smidgeon and expand, magnify, and extend.

3. Issues of the Body

In our field we call for the life of the mind. We abhor the anti-intellectualism of current educational curricula, and the undereducated teachers who have no appreciation of "high" culture. Yet cultural critics, multiple intelligencists, and special educators have begun to emphasize that there are many more ways of learning than intellectual ways — that learning gets into the "intellect" through bodily means. Magda Lewis (Lewis & Macedo, 1996) noted, "The body of knowledge that is the curriculum and the body experience of being schooled—learning to be still and be quiet—are not separate from each other in the process of education" (p. 33). On another bodily level, the students on whom we focus are known as "good" (Margolin, 1994). They obey; they are curious and witty and have good memories; they are crowned with halos by adults; they sit politely in classes, helping the slower students without making a fuss, and as such, they may not receive the attention they deserve as frazzled teachers wrestle with the "troublemakers," the physically active students.

On still another level, we advocate that teachers subsume their essential teaching selves from "teacher as interpreter" to "teacher as manager." The model of intervention specialist/facilitation/inclusion that is beginning to dominate how the gifted and talented are taught may mitigate against a close, human relationship between teacher and student. Teaching as "performance" is a bodily act, an act of love and spontaneity. Teachers as "facilitators" may not be able to create the relationships with each individual student that make teaching a theatrical reaching out and coming back. The model dehumanizes the teacher such that the teacher becomes a function and not a person. Teaching is an act of passion and engagement with certain, specific children—"my kids," "my class." On the other hand, the model may encourage such relationships as well.

When we teach as performers, we bewitch our students, and they bewitch us. As a teacher, I am an artist, a dancer; I can change focus from moment to moment; I can read the temperature and mood of my class; I can speak up and say something to make that sleeping student in the back sit up and participate; I can "cover" the material or not, as the moment suits me; every moment of every day in my classroom I am tripping the light fantastic. I am not a "facilitator," a "guide on the side." I am a partner in my students' learning!

bell hooks (1995) noted that the more intellectual the teacher, the more he/she is permitted to deny the body, to be just a mind up there immobile behind the desk or podium in front of the class or lecture hall, proclaiming and personifying the "body" of knowledge he/she holds in the "mind."

4. Issues of the Spirit

Studies by Coles (1991) and Hoffman (1992) have indicated that children have rich spiritual lives. Hoffman said, "Through increasing involvement with young children I saw that some definitely had 'higher' sensitivities for compassion, creativity, or aesthetics. Yet nowhere was this early capability recognized in my textbooks" (p. 15). Hoffman showed that people may undergo experiences that are mystical or spiritual during their childhoods. Our (my students and mine) explorations into the Dabrowski Theory using the Overexcitability Questionnaire (OEQ) have recently unearthed a theme in the questionnaires that focuses on talented students' connection with God. Talented teenagers made such statements as "I love God very much. He has a lot of meaning for me and gives me my most intense pleasure of purity." "God gets my mind going." "God is a paradox I have to think about a lot" (Flint, Schottke, Willmore & Piirto, 1997). The field of the education of the talented needs to address this deep need and curiosity. The deeper question to be addressed in our curriculum thought is, how to engage the deeply spiritual nature of the child? What is spirituality? How can we honor it?

The aesthetic response borders on the spiritual. Likewise, the affective response borders on the spiritual. In these affective and aesthetic explorations we all, both students and professor, are awed by the depth of the spiritual insight gained. We are often in tears from the insights that have pierced us; we are often silent before the wonder of the universe. Both aesthetics and the emotional should be included in any discussion of curriculum for the talented. Music, art, and literature stir us to consider our true selves, our spiritual natures. The curriculum for talented children with their intellectual, emotional, and imaginational intensity must somehow confront the spiritual. The purpose of art is to move us to consider our deepest selves. We should battle, on all fronts, efforts to dismiss the arts as frills and nonessentials. The arts should be infused into every curricular domain.

5. Issues of the Canon

American critic Harold Bloom (1994) discussed the books he believes should be included in the canon. *Canon* is a religious term which has come to mean the inviolable course of study that students should read and discuss in order to become "educated." Mortimer Adler, Robert Hutchins, William Bennett, Diane Ravitch, and others have argued that some books have more value than others as materials to be studied in our classes. Postmodernists argue that popular culture should also be an academic concern. "Who reads must choose," Bloom said. The underlying belief is that if students read "great works" by "great authors" they will become better and finer humans. The definition of "greatness" is that the version of life that has been conveyed in the work is authentic, real, and true. The reader views the work with respect and awe. The danger of using more recent works is that they may present experience that is less respectable for school purposes. Moi (1985) called them "those deviant, unrepresentative experiences discoverable in much female, ethnic and working class writing" (p. 78). What is human is necessarily censored by one's choice of material to include in the canon. The history that is conveyed through these works is most often a "whitewashed" history.

In history classes, students learn from textbooks and get into their minds the timelines and dates so that they can pass proficiency tests. Seldom are they taught critical history; that is, a historical view that critiques what the power structure has done, what decisions it has made. The engagement of bright students in social criticism is not encouraged.

The question arises, What are the basics? Grumet (Grumet & Pinar, 1996) said that the elementary school curriculum has been compressed into "a developmental mythology," where the books we give them must meet the tyranny of DA (developmentally appropriate) guidelines imposed on the elementary school by psychologists and early childhood educators. Grumet said, "In the name of the basics, relation, feeling, fantasy, anxiety, aggression, memory, irony are all banished." Texture and wonder are missing from many of these books; then when students enter high school and college, they are relegated to "ancestry worship, oblivious to the world students actually live in and care about" (p. 17). She said we have focused on ends rather than means.

These are old arguments, and by now, many of us in the field of the education of the gifted and talented have made our own internal answers to these arguments. We may go along with Hirsch (1996), who argued that we must be able to talk with our grandparents, that educational theory has failed, that "skills" divorced from engaging content are useless skills, that the romantic principles on which these theories are based have been just that—well taken, but too romantic—and that a democracy fails if there is not a shared body of knowledge that is conveyed to our students.

Many critics of the canon are themselves privileged and conversant. Then they stipulate that the poor, the disenfranchised, the despairing do not have to be conversant in the canon. On the other hand, to deny a student's worth by ignoring that student's heritage in the name of the canon is also arrogant.

6. Issues of Justice

In an industrial society, how are the economic goods and services and the cultural goods and services distributed? As Donaldo Macedo (Lewis & Macedo, 1996) said, "Where in Goals 2000 are references to educational equity, social justice, and liberatory education? Goals 2000 embraces a corporate ideology that promotes individualism, privatization, and competition" (p. 43). Do we as "objective" educators of the talented, teaching students who have the potential to move from one social class to a higher social class, willfully ignore the huge social problems incumbent upon us in a capitalist system? The reform of welfare, the poverty of children, the increasing disenfranchisement of middle-aged professionals who have been victims of downsizing—are these without cost? Watching the career of Jonathan Kozol, who began writing about the poor students he taught in inner city schools, and who continues to do so with ever more eloquence, is instructive. In *Amazing Grace* (1995), his latest attempt, he called for us to look at our Constitution, the Bill of Rights, and our democratic principles. In desperation he turned to spirituality and sentimentality about the principles of democracy to advocate that we finally, for once and for all, provide equity in our school facilities and faculties. He described how even resilience is turned to political ends:

> I've seen heroic and ephemeral victories of individuals used by conservative sectors of the press to militate against the larger changes it would take to win enduring victories for their communities. [they infer] If only enough children . . . would act the way the heroes do, say no to drugs and sex and gold chains and TV and yes to homework, values, church, and abstinence, and if only enough good parents, preachers, teachers, volunteers, and civic-minded business leaders would assist them in these efforts, we could 'turn this thing around' and wouldn't need to speak about dark, messy matters such as race, despisal, and injustice. (pp. 161–162)

The issue of what our students, called "the best and brightest," will become in terms of their concept of social justice is a real one. Many seem to opt for the best school, the best salary, and the mortgage, the job, and the baby, using their brain power to move into a higher social class and out of their mother cultures. And we encourage this. This is not to say that this is not to be the goal or the outcome for the bright students. Terman's studies showed that no one reached eminence, no one changed the world. They became good citizens, paid their taxes, and collected their salaries. One could almost say that the promise of high IQ seems to be a life of conformity. Yet social issues abound and proliferate. Issues having to do with poverty, disenfranchisement, the environment, racism, still exist and need communal and cooperative solutions.

7. Issues of Diversity

On another note, the purpose of such programs as A Better Chance is to identify bright minority students who are then offered admission to elite private schools to serve as "tokens," vehicles by which the privileged are to be "exposed" to and "educated" about issues of social justice. The challenge of diversity is thus thought to be addressed. Yet is this the case? What is the inevitable consequence, the shadow, the cloud on the horizon for the student who gets the scholarship as well as for the students who are "exposed" to people of different races and social classes? Our field has glossed over this. We are glad that bright students get a chance for social mobility, and we never question whether social mobility is just, or even whether an attention to diversity (relativism) is better addressed in other ways. To stay in the social class one is born into is a sign of failure and not the American way to many families.

Magda Lewis (Lewis & Macedo, 1996) commented that those who are not white, not of the middle and upper classes, those who work with their hands, are marginalized: "If we are not heterosexual, and if we do not embody and display the valued assets of the privilege of Euro-American culture, the school curriculum and schooling experience fling us to the margins" (p. 40). She noted that "successful forms of self-violation are rewarded with credentials." In our education of bright students, we pay scant attention to encouraging our bright students to work with their hands, to be master carpenters, welders, plumbers, mechanics, health care workers, and such, even though such work often has good financial reward and concomitant union job security.

Diversity has complexity that good minds need to address. We have seldom spoken of the fact that white flight by those within the public school system who cannot afford private schools, or who have a commitment to public education, has been flight to our programs for the gifted and talented. A large study reported by Wells and Serna (1996) showed that the resistance to detracking in racially mixed schools was resistance by white parents who fled to the programs for the gifted and talented, creating a class system within integrated schools. A white parent on one of the gifted and talented education computer bulletin boards commented that the academically talented minority students in his district are snapped up by private schools, and the school threatens to shut down its program for the gifted and talented in favor of heterogeneous grouping. "If this is done," he said, "we will form a charter school." If our field does not address the issues of diversity, especially in terms of numbers of students of ethnic and economic minorities served in special programs, the field will be subsumed. This is our most serious challenge. Any district's program for the talented should mirror the ethnic and economic diversity of its community.

An attention to diversity necessarily must value multiculturalism within multiculturalism. Tanya McKinnon (in Freire, 1997), said that multiculturalism is complex even within races. For example, the gender issues for African-Americans include boys who have a "foreshortened sense of the future," as well as "the question of sexuality and high school date rape." Class issues include "the question of African-American and Latino colorism." Essentialism issues include the question of overlapping cultural identities in families who marry cross-culturally but within the race, while the issue of sexism brings up "the question of sexual orientation" (in Freire, 1997, p. 299).

8. Issues of Language

It seems to me fundamental in our field of the education of the gifted and talented that we have a certain language in mind in which these students must speak, write, and think. In fact, we could go so far as to say that our task is to teach that language, the language of the power elite, to our students because they are intelligent, and more likely to be able to move from a lower social class to a higher social class. As a former Hunter College High School (formerly a high school for gifted girls, now co-ed) student said, "I was surprised when I took that test and I scored so high. I took the subway every day from my Irish neighborhood in Brooklyn to Manhattan. They gave us classes in deportment, and in speech, to take the Brooklyn, Queens, and Bronx accents out of us. They took us from our culture and ethnicity and sent us to Harvard." (Personal communication, Marlena Corcoran, Ph.D, Brown University, April 1996.) Have we asked about the cost of this mobility?

On a more philosophical (rather than social justice/political) note, How do we make meaning? We make it with subjectivity. Without going into a discussion of the work of the language theorists and deconstructionists, it is necessary to note, along with Peter McLaren, that "All knowledge is fundamentally mediated by linguistic relations that inescapably are socially and historically constituted" (McLaren, in Freire, 1997, p. 105). The verbally talented should have a taste of such theory as they have minds which can embrace it. When Jacques Derrida came to the Hunter College High School in the late 1980s to give a speech during an assembly, the academically talented high school students followed him as if he were a baseball star. They understood what he spoke about and asked him questions having to do with philosophical truths in the one sentence (from the writing of Immanuel Kant) that he explicated in his whole speech.

I have noticed that many of my students, graduate students learning about the gifted and talented, prefer to read work that is practical and not theoretical, written on roughly the level of children's literature of the middle grades, with lots of pictures or diagrams or lists of hints. Perhaps we in our field should also seek to engage those who will be teaching students advanced in verbal abilities to engage themselves in challenging material that requires advanced reading capabilities. My belief is that any good theory can be explained in common language, but an appreciation of the richness of language is necessary to fully appreciate any written or spoken work.

9. Issues of Discourse

The levels of discussion, or the focus of discussion of educational reform in our field, has been defensive at worst, and conciliatory at best. The rhetoric that says that the nation is at risk and that such and such a model will solve all the problems is simplistic and reactionary, both on the liberal side and on the conservative side. Educational discourse is much more complicated than the latest model or strategy with lines and diagrams within a bound curriculum guide, whether the curriculum is interdisciplinary, thematic, or whatever. The rhetoric often sounds like a pep rally, where we will be number one if we do such and such, as we cheer our team on, the team of the good old USA!, where the bright students will be varsity athletes.

That we think we pose or solve a problem when we discuss a situation, and when we think that problems have solutions, is naive. We have several curriculum models that emphasize problem solving. John Ralston Saul (1995) said, "The desperate need for reason and the accompanying latent addiction to solutions are good examples of the unconscious at work." What have we unconsciously accepted? What have we unconsciously rejected? What are the hidden features, the ways we are compliant, complicit, or blind? All discourse has its hidden, implicit assumptions. Problems "solved" are few. The analysis of the process might reveal where unconscious processes take over, if only for a moment, and where they direct the assumptions that the problem is "solved."

Many of the conversations held between the students and the text are seen in their faces, bodies, and questions, at home and outside of school, and not as seen in their test scores and products judged according to a rubric. Does this matter even though we cannot measure it? Yes. Selection of curriculum materials, modes of encountering the material, value of the material necessarily involves decisions that entail a knowledge of consequences, implied and spoken. Too many of the practitioners in the field of the education of the gifted and talented seek quick fixes, a lesson to do on Monday morning, without engagement in the two critical issues of curriculum: (1) what shall we teach the talented and gifted?, and (2) for what purpose?

10. Issues of Desire and Passion

We as teachers are lovers. We "love" our students in order to engage them in learning. We "love" our subject matter. We "love" our jobs. Passion and desire are all around us. Joanne Pagano (Pagano & Miller, 1996), said, "The educational challenge in the foreseeable future will be to teach people to acknowledge and understand their own passions, their own advocacy positions, without becoming reduced to them" (p. 143). Yet eros has its shadow side as well. Alice Miller, in explicating the place of narcissism in some parents' desires for their children to reflect their own desires and thus lose their true selves (Miller, 1982), has focused on one shadow side of the eros of curriculum. This is seen in the "stage mother" syndrome, similar to the "Little League father" syndrome.

The teacher also can show her shadow side, as was exemplified by the film *Madame Sousatska*, in which a piano teacher sought to prevent students from going to more advanced piano teachers when their growth made moving teachers necessary. This erotic side of our relationship with our students should be acknowledged.

On another level, we should discuss the presence of multipotentiality in our gifted and talented students. What do they love? Hillman's (1996) concept of the *daimon* (after Jung and Plato) is useful in helping a person with multipotentiality. The *daimon* is that which won't let you alone; that which you must work on; that which drives you. The current literature on expertise, on which many thinkers in our field model their work, devalues the place of desire and passion in the acquisition of expertise, focusing on apprenticeship models in which people acquire skills and knowledge. Passion and desire are de-emphasized, probably as they are too messy and emotional. However, without desire, no one will put in the long hours of practice necessary to become an expert in any domain. Every student should be encouraged to answer to his/her *daimon*. I have included the *daimon* in my Pyramid model of talent development as the "thorn" that determines which talent will be developed (See Figure 1.6 on p. 30).

11. Issues of Gender

We are all familiar with the studies of the American Association of University Women (1995) and of Sadker and Sadker (1994) which led to the conclusion that the academically talented female is at risk. Such statements as this by Magda Lewis (1996) are common among talented women:

> In the seventeen years of formal education that preceded my graduate studies I had not studied the history, culture, and political realities of women, of the labouring classes, of racial and ethnic minorities, of gays and lesbians. This is all the more remarkable when I consider that my area of study was the great thinkers of Western intellectual tradition. (Lewis & Macedo 1996, p. 43)

Yet the issue of gender in our field is more than this. The personality characteristic of androgyny is known to be present in creative producers. Yet the presence of gay academically talented and creative students has received no attention in the literature of the field of the education of the talented. The presence of androgyny as a personality attribute common to creative people is sometimes acknowledged (cf. Piirto, 1998; Piirto & Fraas, 1995), but the needs of these students for role models, approval, and humanness are not addressed by educators in our field. However, a consideration of the personality characteristic of androgyny is only a small part of the shame in how we have ignored our talented gays, lesbians, and bisexuals (GLB). The 1997 World Conference and the 1997 National Association for Gifted Children conference posed a beginning as there were several sessions given by parents of gays and lesbians as well as by gay and lesbian teachers.

On another note, the push to engage girls in science and math has not been followed by a complementary push to engage boys in the arts and literature. This has led to a gender-bias that favors scientific and mathematical discourse over aesthetic discourse. One could even say that there is a revulsion toward encouraging male participation in the arts, especially dance.

On still another note, let us look at the makeup of our field itself. The overwhelming number of teachers of the gifted and talented are white women. The overwhelming number of coordinators of programs for the gifted and talented are white women. The lack of presence of men and of minorities must have an unforeseen and unconscious influence on the development and direction of this field. Are there solutions to this latter situation? Probably not, as recruitment of men and minorities seems to fail whenever we try. One fact is that when we do attract men and minorities, they often shoot to the top of the field as we clamor to elect them to offices to indicate how equitable we are.

12. Issues of Imagination

This matter is close to my artist-scholar heart. Along with devaluing the aesthetic experience, the aesthetic way of knowing, the aesthetically and artistically talented, we have also devalued the kind of knowledge they produce. This illusion of rationality has lost sight of the central role of imagination. As Keiran Egan (1997) said, the neoconservatives such as Bloom, Hirsch, and Ravitch and Finn have made the "valuable point that education is crucially tied up with knowledge, and that being educated means, put crudely, knowing a lot." However, on his Website, Egan noted:

> Education is also crucially about the meaning knowledge has for the individual, and that is where the imagination is vital. A person who has meticulously followed the neo-conservative kind of curriculum may still end up among the greatest bores on God's earth. What is absent from those books is attention to, and a clear sense of, how knowledge becomes meaningful in the lives of learners; how we can ensure that students engage . . . in imaginative learning. (Keiran Egan 1997 homepage; see also Egan, 1992)

Using the imagination is risky because there is no right answer. Students often tell me that some of the gifted and talented students they teach are not risk-takers. The older the students are, the fewer intellectual risks they want to take. Having been successful in feeding back what was fed to them, using their memories for facts and details, they may settle into being comfortable and may be reluctant to venture out of this safe realm. Engaging the imagination through metaphor, image, and symbol is necessary for any applicable learning to take place. Imagination is the creative faculty that perceives the basic relationships between things. It is a form of perception that can actively construct mental images of events or objects that illuminate the darkling plain.

While Bloom's taxonomy lists "application" as a middle-level step on the taxonomy, I believe it is the highest step, even after "synthesis" and "evaluation," for being able to apply knowledge takes imagination and creativity. This is crucial in a climate that seeks to devalue the arts and the aesthetic response, and in a field that emphasizes that its students will become "professionals"—those who profess, or who have knowledge they assert in public—scientists, technocrats, business persons, political leaders, and professors. Imagination is a human aptitude that all people need to engage in order to live whole lives.

In addition, the teacher is an imaginative human being, an artist, and not a replaceable mailman with a cunning long leather bag of "tricks" and "strategies" and "skills" in the system of "delivering" curriculum to students. Each lesson, each class, has an unknown story line. Each class period is a novel waiting to be written, a drama waiting to be acted. We often lose sight of the fact that all areas of curriculum are products of human emotions, imagination, passions, and dreams. How did math get here? How did science? Human beings with imagination thought and dreamt, discovered and created these domains.

In Conclusion

While our field has pioneered curriculum such as Creative Problem Solving, Future Problem Solving, Problem-Based Learning, critical thinking, higher-order thinking, Advanced Placement, the International Baccalaureate, Junior Great Books, brain-based thinking, thematic curriculum, interdisciplinary curriculum, and the like, the postmodern curriculum theorists also ask us to engage in understanding *what* we are doing, *why* we are doing it, and *whether* we should continue to do it. This paper has briefly indicated some areas for thought.

SUMMARY

1. Five precepts for curriculum for the talented should be considered:
    Precept 1: The curriculum should be based on learning characteristics of academically talented children in their areas of strength.
    Precept 2: The curriculum should possess academic rigor.
    Precept 3: The curriculum should be thematic and interdisciplinary.
    Precept 4: Seven curriculum orientations should be considered:
    a. Curriculum as personal relevance
    b. Curriculum as technology
    c. Curriculum as academic rationalism
    d. Curriculum as social adaptation and social reconstruction
    e. Curriculum as development of cognitive processes
    f. Curriculum as a means of producing insight
    g. Curriculum based on contemporary postmodern thought
    Precept 5: The curriculum should be balanced and articulated
2. The thought piece in the Case Example for this chapter suggests that curriculum planners consider certain unconscious aspects of the curriculum: Postmodern curriculum theory provides a framework for educators of the gifted and talented to critique the assumptions of the field from within the field. Twelve issues are discussed: (1) issues of time; (2) issues of power and class; (3) issues of the body; (4) issues of the spirit; (5) issues of the canon; (6) issues of justice; (7) issues of diversity; (8) issues of language; (9) issues of discourse; (10) issues of desire and passion; (11) issues of gender; and (12) issues of imagination.

CHAPTER

10 CURRICULUM PRACTICES: IN AND OUT OF THE CLASSROOM

Principles of Curriculum
 Development
Curriculum Practices for
 Academically Talented Students
 in the Regular Classroom
Other Curriculum Modifications
Differentiating Curriculum
 Through Teaching Approaches
 and Techniques: Methods for
 Teaching All Students
Curriculum Outside the Regular
 Classroom
Summary

FOCUSING QUESTIONS

1. Look at and comment on the curriculum plan for academically talented students in a nearby district.

2. Explain how academically talented students' interests often differ from those of other students, and how these interests can be developed through curriculum.

3. Explain how the pace of curriculum can affect the education of the academically talented learner.

4. Explain how enrichment and acceleration are the same. Explain how they are different.

5. Practice making questions geared to Bloom's taxonomy.

6. Describe a teacher you have had who was able to conduct good discussions. What did that teacher do that you, as a teacher of the academically talented, can emulate?

7. Describe the best lecturer you have had as a student. What did that lecturer do that you can emulate as a teacher of the academically talented?

8. Look at and comment on the curriculum offerings for a special, out-of-school program.

9. Look at the elective courses offered in a nearby high school. Comment on their suitability for academically talented students.

10. What qualities of academically talented students are shown in the discussion about Philosophy for Children?

11. Should special programs such as Odyssey of the Mind and Future Problem Solving be only for the academically talented? Discuss.

12. Why is the International Baccaulaureate program suitable as a means of differentiation?

13. Look at an elective class curriculum for advanced students in high school English and discuss it according to the precepts in Chapter 9.

Figure 10.1 Overview of Chapter 10

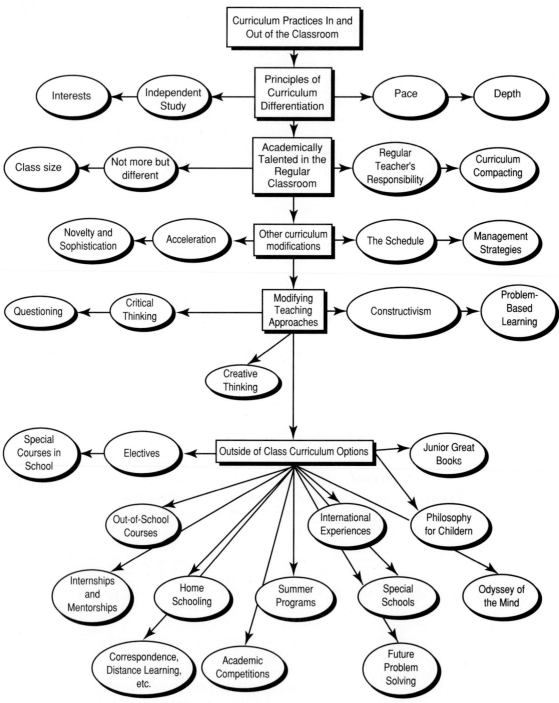

Janet Salvo was confused. She had just been hired to teach in a program for the academically talented at an elementary school, and she had no idea what she was to teach. There was no written curriculum guide for the talent development education program, and when she went into the room where she would be based, and to which the children would come when they were "pulled out" from their classes, she found a mishmash of materials, activities book, and learning centers, but no written curriculum. Last year's teacher had taken a job out of state and no one, including the principal, seemed to know what she had done, but they did know that the kids had liked it, and that they had made inventions.

Janet went through all the boxes of folders and blocks and art materials in puzzlement. She had never taught in a situation where she was supposed to make up the curriculum. In her last school, where she had taught third grade, the curriculum was written down, and when she was in doubt, she'd ask the other third grade teacher across the hall, or just go to the next chapter in the book. But she'd been riffed in that position, and now she felt lucky to get this position. Janet had stayed at home with her kids until all three of them were in school, and now she was trying to re-enter the teaching profession after 12 years at home. She called the county coordinator for help, and they made an appointment to meet for lunch the next day.

"I don't know what I'm supposed to do," Janet said between bites of salad. "What am I going to teach?"

The county coordinator, Marlene Grant, had responsibility for 65 schools in nine districts, and Janet's school was but one of them. The superintendent of Janet's school district was a young man on the way up, using this rural district as a sure way to gain experience in the superintendency while he moved up in the administrative field, and his advocacy of programs for the academically talented came from a realization that the districts he hoped to direct in the future would have this kind of programs.

"We've got a county-wide committee for the education of the talented," Marlene said, "and we're trying to put together a course of study for talent development education for all the county schools. We've been working on it for five years now, and it will probably be finished by January. In the meantime—what grades did you say you'll have?—fourth through sixth?—I thought that's what your school district serves—just do a few units in creative and critical thinking. I've got materials at the county office. Why don't you drive back with me and take a look?"

At the county office, Marlene's cramped office held several bookshelves of books, learning centers, videos, computer software, and other materials suitable for use with gifted children. "Take your time, and take your pick," Marlene said. "I stand ready to help you. Excuse me a minute while I return some calls." Marlene sat at her piled-up desk and began flipping through a stack of pink messages that had come while she had been out.

Janet began looking through the materials and turned to ask, "What subject matter do I emphasize?"

Marlene said, "Well, why don't you try four units, one for September, one for each month until Christmas? Do one math unit, one social studies unit, one science unit, and one language arts unit. Here, look. I've got them arranged by grade level and by subject area." Indeed, Marlene's powers of organization were great, and the materials began to take meaning according to subject matter and grade level. By the end of the afternoon, Marlene had helped Janet pick out materials for each of her three grade levels for September and October. Janet hauled them off, making three trips back and forth from Marlene's office, filling her car's back seat and trunk with materials. The next day she went to her room and began to organize for the kids.

Surprising as the above scenario may seem, it is not unusual for curriculum for academically talented students to be chosen in this way. The curriculum often begins with materials and with suggestions from specialists, and not from any deep knowledge—on either the teacher's or the school system's part—of the curricular needs of gifted children. The aim of this chapter is to provide the reader with principles and suggestions for developing curriculum for gifted students. The lack of a clear, written curriculum may speak to a confusion as to what curriculum is for outstandingly talented students.

Different constituencies of the school view the curriculum in different ways. Their definitions of curriculum might even differ, as elucidated in Chapter 9. These definitions should be synthesized so that a balanced curriculum is planned for the academically talented student.

PRINCIPLES OF CURRICULUM DEVELOPMENT

To recapitulate, there are five precepts in developing curriculum for academically talented students. As discussed in the last chapter, these principles are based on the characteristics of the gifted, and are justified because of the way in which academically talented students learn. Differentiation is necessary for intellectually talented children because of three of their learning characteristics: (1) they often have different *interests* than nongifted children; (2) they have the ability to learn *faster*; and (3) they have the ability to learn in greater *depth*. Academically talented children in all the dimensions of giftedness have these needs, but this discussion will center on the curricular needs of intellectually talented students, who are those with high IQs and with specific academic achievement.

While the last chapter focused on curriculum philosophy that would be suitable for intellectually talented children in self-contained or special classes, this chapter will focus on curriculum with an emphasis on modifications for intellectually talented students who spend the bulk of their time in heterogeneously grouped classes. Parke (1989) and others (Maker, 1982a, 1982b; Maker & Nielson, 1997; VanTassel-Baska, 1988/1994) pointed out that there are three types of curriculum modification that are suitable for intellectually talented learners in the regular classroom: (1) modification according to the interests of the child; (2) modification of the pace, or acceleration; and (3) modification of the depth. Teaching strategies should also be modified for intellectually and academically talented learners.

Special education for academically talented children can be justified only because the school and society recognize that students who are called academically talented need an education that is *differentiated*. Academically talented students need differentiation in their regular classrooms and they need differentiation in their special education classrooms. If academically talented students could be served by the classroom teacher in the regular classroom, there would be no need for the field of talent development education. Unfortunately, it is virtually impossible for the teacher in the regular classroom to meet the needs of all the children, given the usual constraints in the makeup of schools. In the past few years the inclusion of students with behavior, handicapping, and low-IQ conditions has exacerbated the stress on the regular classroom teacher, even though these students are usually provided with an aide. This differentiation should be a difference in quality of curriculum. Because they are *different* in learning characteristics and interests, intellectually talented students require a curriculum that is geared to those learning characteristics. The content of what they learn should be changed—differentiated.

Tomlinson (1995b) listed four characteristics of an effective differentiated classroom:

1. *Instruction is concept focused and principle driven.* Because the instruction is based on concepts, or themes, all students have the opportunity to explore and apply the key concepts of the subject being studied. The goal is that all students come to understand the key principles on which the study is based.
2. *Ongoing assessment of student readiness and growth are built into the curriculum.*
3. *Flexible grouping is consistently used.* In a differentiated class, students work in many patterns and are grouped and regrouped according to task and need.
4. *Students are active explorers with teachers guiding the exploration.* The teacher and student collaborate on goal setting, based on student readiness, interest, and learning profile, and student learning is assessed based on student growth and goal attainment.

Differentiation as a Result of Different Interests

Academically talented students like to think about abstractions; therefore the curriculum should be concerned with general principles and abstractions. They like to deal with complexities; therefore the curriculum may be differentiated by being more complex. For example, the rest of the students may learn about the founding of the nation through reading the Declaration of Independence. The intellectually talented students would be fascinated with the *Federalist Papers* as well, fascinated to learn about the complexities that led to the founding of the nation.

Academically talented children are also able to grasp basic underlying principles and therefore the curriculum should be differentiated in that these principles should be part of the guided discovery process. This should range from revealing the structure of the discipline, in Bruner's (1960, 1983) terms, to being encouraged to use inference and intuition as learning strategies. Repeated studies have shown that intellectually able individuals often prefer, on the Myers-Briggs Type Indicator, the "N" (Intuition) style (Myers & McCaulley, 1985).

The alert teacher will spot these interests in abstractions, in concepts, in underlying reasons. The intellectually talented child often does more than is expected, says more than is expected, and the other students often do not understand what she is driving at during a discussion, because her comments are often higher level than those of her age peers. Peer pressure will often make her lower the level of her comments, and other children may turn away, change the subject, shake their heads, or barely tolerate the intellectually talented child's insights. This is not through perverse dislike, but because the intellectually talented child or the creatively thinking child often says or does things the other students do not understand or find interesting.

Riley and Karnes (1996) assessed the interests of intellectually talented elementary school students. They noted that the interests were "clear and well-defined. They also differed in both depth and breadth from the subjects typically studied within the framework of the regular curriculum" (p. 37). Second and third grade boys were most interested in advanced mathematics, foreign countries, science, zoology, physical science, the history of wars, U.S. geography, acting, and theater. Second and third grade girls were most interested in advanced mathematics, science and zoology, marine biology, computers, physical science, biology, prehistoric times, arts and fine arts, and language arts. Fourth and fifth grade boys were most interested in aerospace, marine biology, zoology, ecology, geography, ancient civilization, astronomy, law, foreign countries, and prehistoric times. Fourth and fifth grade girls were most interested in ancient civilizations, foreign language, ecology, zoology, chemistry, foreign countries, and the arts.

Independent Study as Differentiation

Indeed, some teachers of the academically talented go so far as to say that potentially gifted students can be identified by the fact that they are extremely interested in things that other students do not find interesting. It is a good idea to administer an interest inventory to the whole class and to have them pursue their interests in research. The academically talented student will often use more than the mandatory encyclopedia, and will seek out books and articles that feed the interests. Both Betts' Autonomous Learner Model (1988) and Renzulli's Type III Enrichment (1988) give detailed forms, formats, and directions for conducting independent research.

Differentiation in Pace

Most academically talented students are fast, one-time learners. They are often called precocious, which means "to boil beforehand," from the Latin *praecox*, or "precook." The dictionary translates this as a child's mentality having developed earlier. We say the child is precocious because the child has learned faster and knows more than children of his chronological age. Academically talented children are often one-time learners, who don't need much drill and repetition. Therefore, the curriculum for academically talented children should take into account their precocity and should move at a fast pace, spending only the necessary time in drill and repetition. Moving at a faster pace is called *acceleration*.

Differentiation in Depth

Since intellectually academically talented children can learn fast, they are often able to absorb more factual and conceptual knowledge, and therefore, they can be taught in greater depth. This is the third essential principle in developing curriculum for intellectually talented students. Probing a subject in greater depth is often called *enrichment*. As an illustration, take the usual curriculum requirements for fourth graders in language arts. They read chapter books that contain a certain number of words, a certain level of vocabulary, and require a certain background knowledge. A popular fourth grade language arts chapter book is *The Sign of the Beaver* (Speare, 1983).

Let's take the example of Meredith, a fourth grade girl who is academically talented. Meredith is a student with high cognitive ability, and high reading achievement. If she is interested in the language arts book, she can probably finish it the first day it is presented. While the rest of the class is reading the book chapter by chapter, one day at a time, Meredith is struggling to stay awake, stay interested, and stay in place. She has already finished the book. She knows the answers to all the comprehension questions that the teacher asks. Meredith restrains herself from raising her hand to answer these questions because by now she has learned that the teacher won't call on her but will check the other children to see what they have learned. Meredith needs *differentiation*. This differentiation should be accomplished both by her teacher in her regular classroom, and by the specialist in talent development education in the talent development education classroom.

Tomlinson (1995a) listed the following strategies for differentiation:

Strategies for Managing a Differentiated Classroom

Among instructional strategies that can help teachers manage differentiation and help students find a good learning "fit" are the following:

- Use of multiple texts and supplementary materials
- Use of computer programs
- Interest centers
- Learning contracts
- Compacting
- Tiered sense-making activities and tiered products
- Tasks and products designed with a multiple intelligence orientation
- Independent learning contracts
- Complex instruction
- Group investigation
- Product criteria negotiated jointly by student and teacher
- Graduated task- and product-rubrics

CURRICULUM PRACTICES FOR ACADEMICALLY TALENTED CHILDREN IN THE REGULAR CLASSROOM

Taking into account Meredith's learning characteristics, typical for academically talented students—that she can easily learn at a faster pace, and in greater depth, and that she has different interests than many children—the classroom teacher should be able to differentiate for Meredith. Meredith is probably able to read at a much more difficult level than that of the novel. Meredith is not alone; there is probably another student in the class—Danny—who also finished the book the first day, and who will be struggling to stay awake and interested while the teacher is going over the comprehension questions for others. Danny reads well, but is not the extracurricular reader that Meredith is.

He likes to read technical material, especially the directions for assembling toys and the models he likes to put together. Even though Meredith and Danny are in the most advanced reading group, their level of understanding and comprehension is greater than those in their reading group. What should the teacher do?

The Influence of Class Size

Class size is one reason why academically talented students are *pulled out* from their regular classrooms and served in special programs. The ideal class size would be 15 to 20 students with an aide, with the lower grades having 15 students, and the upper grades having a maximum of 20 students. The regular classroom teacher would be able to handle the curricular needs of all students if this were the case. Such class size rarely happens in schools, and therefore specialists in learning disabilities, handicapping conditions, and talent development education are employed to meet the special needs of children with special needs. Regular classroom teachers rarely have had any training in meeting the needs of their academically talented students. The ideal of having the regular classroom teacher responsible for differentiating and individualizing for each student in her room is an ideal propounded by educational reform movements today. Educators of the academically talented agree that each student should be taught according to his/her needs, and applaud the reform efforts that call for continous pace instruction.

The Regular Classroom Teacher's Responsibility

Beverly Parke (1989), in *Gifted Students in the Regular Classrooms,* said that both the teacher and the child have a responsibility in learning. The teacher's responsibilities are to have an open attitude about adjusting the pace and to create a situation where the pace can be adjusted. This attitude on the part of regular classroom teachers is crucial. If the regular classroom teacher, who has the major responsibility for the education of the academically talented child, feels that the child should teach the others or pass out papers or do as much drill and repetition as slow learners, or make up all the work before he or she is permitted to go to the pullout class, the education of the child will suffer. Unfortunately, many rushed, busy, and distracted regular classroom teachers feel their efforts should be directed at the children who have difficulty learning even the most basic requirements, and they neglect the academically talented children, who they feel can get it on their own. (As a side note, requiring the academically talented student to do two sets of homework, to do more, is a punishment. Many regular classroom teachers believe that theirs is the most important curriculum and the curriculum taught in the pullout classroom is frills. They thus require drill and repetitive homework. This is a real challenge to teachers, and they often go toe to toe on this matter. The principal should step in and make a policy that the students do not have to do two sets of homework. This is no place for a battleground between teachers who often cannot negotiate the situation and thus it is the student who suffers.)

If he or she has time, the conscientious regular classroom teacher—Merediths and Danny's teacher—can locate other resources that Meredith and Danny can use, perhaps by contacting the librarian, or referring to the teacher's manual. *The Sign of the*

Beaver is about a boy who is from a pioneer family in Maine. He and his father have built a cabin on land they have claimed, and the father has gone back to get the boy's mother, sister, and the new baby. The boy is left alone to guard the cabin and the land. He makes friends with a Native American boy. He teaches the Indian to read, and the Indian teaches him to take care of himself in the woods. The teacher and the librarian could perhaps provide the two children with materials about Eastern tribes, about the settlement of the United States before the Revolutionary War, about the westward movement. Providing Meredith with more reading material, since she is a fast reader, will take care of her characteristic of learning at a faster pace, and will give her materials that go into greater depth.

Not More, But Different

Critics might contend that this is the MOTS curriculum—more of the same—and that these two academically talented children should not be required to do more. This criticism is often leveled when the teacher doesn't know what to do with the child who finishes the work fast, and so the teacher gives the child more work—for example, the teacher might say, "Oh, since you finished the odd problems I assigned so fast, do the even ones, too." The trouble with the MOTS curriculum is that it doesn't take into account the fact that the child has already probably mastered the material after doing the first few problems, and that the addition of more problems covering the same skills is needless drill and repetition; indeed, the child is essentially being punished for being fast and accurate.

Winebrenner (1992) listed several strategies for such a situation: among them were to assign the hardest first—the hardest problems, the hardest words—to all students and those who could do them would not have to do the repetitive drill worksheets but could be freed to do other work. (Winebrenner's book has quickly become a classic in the field. In one class of teachers who were given free choice of a book to read as an assignment, one-third chose Winebrenner's book. Her practical suggestions speak to the need for strategies to use in the regular classroom.)

The classroom teacher might also provide the children with other novels about the settling of the eastern United States; for example, *Last of the Mohicans* or *The Frontiersman*. These are challenging reading by James Fenimore Cooper, intended for adults, and written in the literary style common in the nineteenth century. In fact, one good way to differentiate the curriculum for academically talented learners is to utilize original or primary sources such as diaries, letters, newspaper articles, and speeches. Many modern textbooks are "dumbed down" and contain bland, colorless summaries of historical events. Reading the original sources often provides an appropriate challenge and an exciting alternative for readers who are beyond the level where the rest of the class is functioning. Permitting a reader like Meredith to read is not "more," but "better," not punishment, but a treat.

Another set of strategies comes from the problem types listed by Maker (1992). Five problem types are taught using the multiple intelligences as entry points. Figure 10.2 shows a suitable matrix for middle school students based on the topic of "the future."

Figure 10.2 Problem Type Matrix for Middle School Students
Used with permission of Lori Beach.

Theme: The Future Topics: Energy, Population, Space Exploration, & Transportation				
Type I	**Type II**	**Type III**	**Type IV**	**Type V**
Verbal-Linguistic Research people movers or people-moving systems. Write a description of how they work.	Read a classic futuristic novel by Bradbury, Verne, or Asimov. Then read *The White Mountains.* Compare how the two societies are depicted as "advanced."	Write letters to influential people describing your concerns and ideas about a future topic (gov't officials, newspaper editors, school board members, city council members, etc.).	Describe how an airplane with no human pilot would take off from New York City with 250 passengers, fly nonstop across the Atlantic Ocean, and land in England.	Describe your trip to Alpha Pi Space Colony to visit a relative there. Why would you have to stop at a space depot before going to Alpha Pi?
Logical-Mathematical Given population data of major world cities over 100 years, make a multiple line graph of the data to show growth patterns.	Using an astronomy or other reference book, find the distances between earth, the moon and other planets. How long would it take to reach each of them in a space shuttle?	Some scientists feel that we are living in the golden age of planetary exploration. Compare this to the voyages and discoveries of Columbus. What are the similarities? the differences?	You are chairman of the space-program budget committee. How would you spend the money? Include categories and projected project costs.	You have been invited to move to Satellite G1-7 for the next five or six years to be a space farmer. Your personal goods must be transported from Earth to an artificial island for launching, then to a space transfer depot, and then to G1-7. How?
Visual-Spatial Draw a map of your neighborhood and list the population. Assume an increase of 16 percent within 20 years, then draw how the housing might change.	Create a collage to show the kind of changes around you that are related to society's efforts to provide for a population that is growing older.	A sensor is a detector. Some sensors can verbalize needs and problems. Design some sensors for your car or your home that will provide greater safety.	Create or redesign your home to become energy efficient. Include in it as many labor saving devices as possible.	Draw or describe a cartoon that depicts something humorous about cars in the future (e.g., the electric-car salesman reminding people that the extension cord for their car is only 100 miles long).
Bodily-Kinesthetic Choose a computer game with a futuristic setting. Play it, then give an oral presentation on what future aspects were portrayed.	The moon's gravity is one-sixth that of the earth. Role play with a partner how a person would walk, run, play tennis, or other activity on the moon.	Compare the population data for several large cities in your state by designing a human "pictograph" of each of the cities.	Create a dance that depicts a space event, such as the birth of a star, planetary satellite movements, an asteroid belt, etc.	Use your body to create a machine of the future.

Figure 10.2   *Continued*

	Type I	Type II	Type III	Type IV	Type V
Musical	Listen to and list all the changes that will occur "In the Year 2525" (song by Zager and Evans).	Choose among these songs to convey your image of life in 2050: "Theme from Star Trek Voyager," "Also Sprach Zarathustra," or "Theme from Star Wars."	On an electronic keyboard, select sounds that would represent a futuristic traffic jam. Share your composition.	Create an alien love song using synthetic sounds as well as traditional instrumentation.	Compose an aleatory piece of music (one that happens by chance) to depict a futuristic setting you might find on Space Colony Omega.
Interpersonal	Explain how the development of shopping malls has affected city dwellers and their lifestyles.	Develop an opinnonnaire survey with about five or six questions related to specific future-related ideas. Take your survey to friends, family, neighbors, then tabulate their responses.	Canada has discovered new oil fields. How might that affect political or socioeconomic relations between the United States and Canada? What effect might it have on the workers on the Alaskan pipe line?	Discuss with your family how you will adapt to the rising costs of energy. What adjustments will each family member have to make?	Many organizations have opposed certain methods of producing energy. What kind of energy would your class develop that would not evoke protests and criticisms?
Intrapersonal			In order to conserve energy, should the government: restrict auto makers to production of four-cylinder cars, ration gasoline, or have strict enforcement of speed laws? Which do you think would work best and why?	Defend or refute the following statement: Governments should develop legislation to control population increases and to maintain the population at the last census figures.	Because baby boomers are aging, communities with an emphasis on facilities for retired people will be much needed. Plan such a community.

Curriculum Compacting

The major technique for providing appropriate curriculum for intellectually talented students in the regular classroom is often called "compacting." This term was popularized by Renzulli and Smith (1978b). Reis, Burns, and Renzulli (1992) defined it thus: "Curriculum compacting is a procedure used to streamline the regular curriculum for students who are capable of mastering it at a faster pace" (p. 5). Another common term for this is "telescoping" the curriculum. Again, both terms imply that some of the material can be compressed so that the academically able child can do material that is more challenging. The key to successful compacting is pretesting. Here are the eight steps in compacting:

1. Identify the objectives.
2. Find appropriate pretests.
3. Identify students who should be pretested.
4. Pretest students.
5. Eliminate instructional time for students who show mastery of the objectives.
6. Streamline instruction of those objectives students have not mastered but are capable of mastering more quickly than their classmates.
7. Offer challenging alternatives for time provided by compacting.
8. Keep records. (Reis, Burns & Renzulli, 1992, p. 5)

Pretesting

Pretesting is a very simple process, but even teachers with training in compacting often fail to pretest because it is so much trouble. It is just easier to treat all the children the same, and to teach to the lower middle levels. Compacting is done this way: the teacher pretests the children on the knowledge she expects the children to acquire before beginning the unit, the chapter, or the lessons to be taught. If she finds that the children already have acquired most of the knowledge, she arranges to have them learn what they have not acquired, and she can provide enrichment activities rather than have them drill and review what they already know. Sally Reis has said that academically talented students learn new material for one month a year—January—and the rest of the year is spent in boring review (personal communication, May 1989). The first few months are spent reviewing last year and the last few months are spent reviewing this year.

However, the teacher must then be willing and able to provide alternative learning experiences for children who have mastered the content that they are expected to know. The teacher must be supported by the administrative structure. Compacting the curriculum should be part of the repertoire of every teacher. The teacher should be observant and notice students who seem bored, who finish assignments fast, and who get most of the answers correct. These students are probably candidates for compacting. The teacher can interview these students to find areas of interest, or areas of strength, and the students can perhaps be freed to pursue these areas while the other students are learning the spelling words, or practicing the mathematics problems. This takes commitment and time, and so the teacher who wants to compact should start small, with one or two students, in order to get practice in the process. Compacting is often defeated by the large class size and the great diversity of students teachers are required to serve. If class sizes are larger than 20, the teacher must be provided with help in providing for the diverse needs of academically talented students. Many schools have a resource teacher for the purpose of helping the classroom teachers to compact the in-class curriculum, and to provide special enrichment experiences outside the classroom.

Renzulli and Reis (1988), in discussing the types of enrichment to be provided to students who are freed from the routine by compacting, suggest that the school personnel should compile a master list of enrichment and advanced opportunities available in the district and in the community. A child like Meredith, who reads voraciously, and who likes to write, could be encouraged to continue the reading and the writing. Perhaps she could write a story in the voice of a girl of the early 1700s. A child like Danny, who reads well but not as enthusiastically as Meredith, but who is a tinkerer, might perhaps want to study tools of the time, and to make his own replicas. Their point is that the enrichment activities should be directed by the student's interest. It is not uncommon for students who are bored underachievers to get motivated by the reward of being able to do something they are interested in after they have demonstrated mastery of the material the rest of the class is covering more slowly. What has been done with these two precocious students by the regular classroom teacher is *curriculum modification* according to their individual needs and interests.

OTHER CURRICULUM MODIFICATIONS

Other writers about curriculum for the academically talented have urged slightly different modifications. Gallagher (1985) has written that there should be certain types of content modification for the students. He called for differentiation by content novelty, sophistication, enrichment, and acceleration. The first three could be subsumed under the concept of enrichment. To enrich the curriculum according to the principle of content novelty and sophistication is to introduce completely new material that is not usually covered in the regular curriculum. This includes content sophistication, or utilizing students' superior critical thinking abilities to have them do higher-level work based on the principles of the discipline (for example, while the rest of the class is reading *The Sign of the Beaver*, chapter by chapter, Meredith could be studying the causes of the French and Indian Wars). Content enrichment—or giving students content that elaborates on what is already being done (this is the same as modification according to depth)—encompasses novelty and sophistication of material. Content acceleration—or giving students content that is suitable for their achievement and not their chronological age (this is the same as modification according to pace)—is also essential.

Content Enrichment Through Novelty and Sophistication

Many programs for academically talented students choose to modify the curriculum in terms of content novelty. While the rest of the students are learning to comprehend the material, the academically talented students may be working at learning centers on creative thinking or critical thinking that is not part of the regular curriculum. The teacher may order a learning center on space exploration from the county office, place this in the back of the room, and excuse the academically talented student from the drill and practice the other students are undergoing, asking the academically talented student to work through the materials on space exploration. Meredith and Danny would be working at the center on space exploration, and the rest of the students will not have a chance to learn about space exploration. Thus, the academically talented student is exposed to content novelty—new material not assigned to the rest of the class.

Elliot Eisner, in *The Educational Imagination* (1985/1994), noted another reason for including content novelty. He pointed out that there exists a "null" curriculum in our schools, and that is what is never taught, a curriculum that doesn't exist. Saying that the schools presently offer a scientifically biased, business-oriented view of learning, Eisner questioned why so few elementary and secondary schools teach economics, for example, or anthropology, art criticism, filmmaking, or law. The principle of content novelty in the education of academically talented students could embrace these, and other fields that are so new as to not have a place in the traditional curriculum, or that were viewed by curriculum designers as not having enough relevance for students.

The world of knowledge is exploding and a cursory glimpse at the majors offered in any large college's catalog will give a clue about the importance of content novelty. Who said that students should study what a noun is for eight years in a row? Why is knowing what a noun is more important than knowing what a quark is? The traditional "branches" of knowledge taught in the schools have changed little during the past century.

Enriching the content is the most common way of dealing with intellectually talented students. Often this is giving students content that elaborates on what is already being done (this is the same as modification according to depth). This may not be fair, just, or good curriculum practice, but it is a common curricular modification for academically talented students. The rationale often given for including content novelty and enrichment is that academically talented students will probably enter professions where broad knowledge of topics not covered in depth in the school curriculum will be necessary. This reason is also used as a justification for curricular modifications in the pullout program.

To some people, such practice may seem elitist, treating academically talented youngsters as if they should know more than other students. The rationale for providing such enrichment experiences must be that if it is good for the other students, the other students must be permitted to do it also; but if only the academically talented students are capable of doing it, or have the time to do it because they have mastered the material required of the students, it is not elitist. That is, the elitism comes from simple ability, and not privilege. The value of the *time* gained from such practices as compacting or telescoping that free faster students to study other, new subjects cannot be underestimated. Content novelty and enrichment can be explored because time is freed from drill and repetition and the boring spiraling of curriculum concepts.

For example, every social studies book begins with a chapter on maps and land forms. Each year a few new map skills are added, a few new geographical features are added. An intellectually talented child can learn these few new skills and features quickly and well. Time is gained. Perhaps the time can be used to study the geographical features of Neptune as revealed by the NASA space probes. Perhaps the time can be used to look at Buckminster Fuller's Dymaxion Projection Sky-Ocean World Map (Fuller, 1981) and the revolutionary way he proposed of mapping.

Schools often enrich by offering certain subjects to certain students. Foreign language instruction at the elementary school level is now required in many states. This usually takes the form of one year of instruction in the later elementary years. Again, because of their superior memories and analytic abilities, academically talented students are prime candidates for foreign language instruction. Some schools even go so far as to call the foreign language class the means of differentiation for academically talented students, denying the other students instruction in foreign language. This *is* elitism. Academically talented students have no justifiable right to be the only ones receiving foreign language instruction. Rather, they should receive instruction geared to their learning characteristics; the pace of any subject in which they excel should be quickened and the sequence should be modified according to how soon they show mastery.

Content Acceleration

The regular classroom teacher of the elementary student has another option besides differentiation through content novelty. This is content *acceleration*. Acceleration is permitting the child to move as swiftly as possible through the required material. What the classroom teacher decides to do to differentiate for the academically talented student depends on the subject matter. There are essentially two types of curriculum material: (1) that which readily lends itself to enrichment, such as reading or social studies; and (2) that which readily lends itself to acceleration, such as mathematics or foreign language. Subjects that are sequential are candidates for accelerative treatment. In mathematics, a child must learn to add before subtracting, must learn to multiply before dividing. By the time an academically talented child is in the fourth grade, he or she will probably have mastered the skills of reading; enrichment with more difficult reading matter is a way of differentiation. However, in mathematics, the child must be taught, and the sequence of mathematics proceeds from arithmetic to algebra to calculus, etc. Often, one of the most difficult tasks for the teacher of the academically talented is to persuade the administration and fellow teachers that acceleration in mathematics is necessary for the academically talented student, and that that acceleration must take place in the structure of more advanced course taking.

That enrichment and acceleration are two different kinds of curriculum modification is doubtful, according to Southern and Jones (1991). They said that "advanced study in any discipline may entail the kind of activities normally associated with enrichment" (p. 22). Such types of activities are research projects, investigations, considering the social implications of innovations, and using analytical, creative, and evaluative thinking.

Chess is part of the thinking skills curriculum for young academically talented students

Academically talented students often need less explanation; they just need to know the next step. A young academically talented student had attended the Johns Hopkins summer program and had completed the geometry required by his school. He was now interested in fractal geometry. He said all his required plane geometry class was doing was "two points on a line, two points on a line." He sat, bored, during this required class at his school for intellectually academically talented students where testing out of a course was not permitted. The plane geometry class was being offered to eighth graders, where in most schools it is offered to sophomores, but this intellectually academically talented student had already mastered the material. The high point in his day was being able to ask the teacher one or two questions about fractal geometry during the five minutes at the end of the period when the students started on their homework. His teacher kept him pointed in the right direction, and he experimented with fractal geometry on his home computer while having to sit through plane geometry day after day.

Likewise, the student who has a deep and abiding interest and propensity for science will find the elementary school science curriculum nonchallenging and quite frustrating. Generally, elementary school science curricula do not offer the challenge that science aficionados need. A glance at the typical elementary school science scope and sequence shows that the motivated, academically talented science student could probably master all that information in a highly condensed year. Advanced study of science requires mastery of mathematics, for to scientists, mathematics is a necessary tool. Thus, the student who has a propensity for thinking in scientific terms (what Gardner calls logical-mathematical intelligence) should also be accelerated in mathematics.

Southern and Jones (1991) listed 15 types of options that they call acceleration options:

1. Early entrance
2. Grade skipping
3. Continuous progress
4. Self-paced instruction
5. Subject-matter acceleration
6. Combined classes
7. Curriculum compacting
8. Telescoping curriculum
9. Mentorships
10. Extracurricular programs
11. Concurrent enrollment
12. Advanced placement
13. Credit by examination
14. Correspondence courses
15. Early entrance into junior high, high school, or college

Of these, continous progress, self-paced instruction, and curriculum compacting should be considered by the regular classroom teacher.

The Tyranny of the Schedule and the Carnegie Unit

Schools are tied to the convenient administrative idea that "courses" take 180 days, 45 minutes a day, and that students should be tied to this timetable. This is called a

Carnegie unit. Algebra I lasts that long, and so does Algebra II, Geometry, Solid Geometry, and the other mathematics courses. Business-oriented education critics as David Kearns and Denis Doyle (1989) wrote that setting time limits for course mastery has always been "a polite fiction." They said that "self-paced mastery" is called for in school restructuring. "The slow child can work slowly and deliberately. The quick child can move as rapidly as his talent and energy take him" (p. 77).

That academically talented students can master certain course material in a few weeks, as they do in the Johns Hopkins University and the other Talent Search summer programs, is sometimes a rude surprise to school officials. That most intellectually academically talented students are ready for a pre-algebra course by the age of 11 is often thought of as more than an inconvenience; it is thought to be a travesty of developmental propriety. Teachers, in an attempt to deal with the mathematically talented student's speed and mastery, often make that student do extra problems in order to keep her busy. That teacher does not compact. Instead, the teacher should pretest the child, and should provide the child with advanced material, teaching the skills as necessary. Acceleration through subject matter frees the student for more creative work, which is enrichment. Enrichment material is probably more advanced, requiring superior knowledge of the subject at hand. Withholding steps in the process or knowledge from students because "if he knows all the math in fourth grade, and we put him in the fifth grade book in fourth grade, what will we do in fifth grade?" is immoral.

DIFFERENTIATING CURRICULUM THROUGH TEACHING APPROACHES AND TECHNIQUES: METHODS FOR TEACHING ALL STUDENTS

The teacher who is a master in the classroom can differentiate the curriculum just by the way she teaches. Common techniques include questioning techniques, and there is much literature on these approaches and techniques. Common instructional approaches are lecture, direct instruction, using case methods, discovery-based inquiry, simulation and gaming, role playing, problem-centered learning, and problem-based learning. All learning should emphasize inquiry. Inquiry is a process of investigating phenomena, devising and working through a plan, and proposing a solution to the problem. A disposition of inquiry is necessary for successful problem solving. Space permits only a brief discussion on four techniques and methods that can be used with all students within the regular classroom: (1) questioning according to Bloom's taxonomy; (2) Socratic questioning for critical thinking; (3) teaching utilizing creative thinking; and (4) problem-based learning.

Differentiation by Techniques: Questioning According to Bloom's Taxonomy

One way that the regular classroom teacher can differentiate for the academically talented student is in the types of questions she asks. Most teacher education programs do not spend enough time teaching prospective teachers how to question. Observations in classrooms have produced portraits of the types of questions most often asked. Teachers ask questions that require the students to respond with facts;

students ask questions about clarifying the homework assignment. Teachers in general should analyze the types of questioning they do. Teachers of the academically talented, especially, should do so.

The most commonly used hierarchy in formulating levels of questions is Bloom's (Bloom, Englehart, Furst, Hill & Krathwhol, 1956). In this cognitive taxonomy, there are six levels: (1) Knowledge; (2) Comprehension; (3) Application; (4) Analysis; (5) Synthesis; (6) Evaluation. Most questions asked in schools are Knowledge and Comprehension questions.

Knowledge questions often begin with these verbs:

know	recall	name	relate
collect	define	label	specify
cite	enumerate	tell	memorize
repeat	list	recount	

For example, take the story of Cinderella. Examples of knowledge questions about the story are as follows:

How many stepsisters did Cinderella have?
Do you recall what the slipper was made of?

Comprehension questions often begin with verbs such as these:

restate	summarize	discuss	describe
recognize	explain	express	identify
locate	report	retell	translate

Examples of comprehension questions are as follows:

Discuss the events on the night of the ball.
Describe what happened to the pumpkin.

Application questions often begin with verbs such as these:

exhibit	solve	interview	simulate
apply	employ	use	demonstrate
dramatize	practice	illustrate	operate

Examples of application questions are as follows:

Make an exhibit of the ball gowns Cinderella's two sisters and stepmother wore.
Dramatize what happened when the Prince came to Cinderella's house with the glass slipper.

Analysis questions often begin with verbs such as the following:

interpret	analyze	compare	contrast
categorize	classify	group	examine
dissect	diagram	arrange	inventory

Analysis questions would be these:

Compare and contrast Cinderella's treatment by her stepmother and by the Prince.
Examine why the stepmother was so cruel to Cinderella.

Synthesis questions often use the following verbs:

compose	invent	design	create
propose	imagine	predict	improve
produce	formulate	construct	develop

Synthesis questions would be these:

Compose a song that Cinderella would sing while she did her work in the cinders. Design Cinderella's ball gown; chariot; slipper.

Evaluation questions often use these verbs:

judge	decide	appraise	evaluate
criticize	assess	estimate	determine
prove	revise	rate	conclude

Evaluation questions would be these:

Prove that Cinderella deserved to go to the ball.
Determine what would have happened if Cinderella had run away but had not lost her slipper.

The use of Bloom's taxonomy to formulate questions is often suggested when the regular classroom teacher is differentiating for students in her classroom. Academically talented students need few knowledge and comprehension questions, and can swiftly move to application, analysis, synthesis, and evaluation. The classroom teacher with a knowledge of questioning levels can, by asking the right questions, serve all her students according to their abilities. Many other suggestions about questioning have been given by writers in the field of talent development education, but if a teacher begins with a knowledge of Bloom's taxonomy, she will be able to question adequately.

Other Suggestions for Questioning

Given that there are two purposes for questioning—instruction and diagnosis—teachers should ask questions that are prepared in advance, that are clear, and are in logical sequence. Teachers often ask too many questions too quickly, and don't wait long enough for the answers. Increasing the "wait time" to at least three seconds per question permits students to give better answers. Many teachers ask yes or no questions, questions that they have already have an answer for. Questions are used to solicit chorus responses, as if for drill and practice. Asking questions that require deeper thought or that help impel students toward greater understanding are more difficult. Often at public lectures, one hears speakers ask questions that begin with "Don't you think that . . .?," statements of opinion turned into questions.

One recent development that goes along with the increased emphasis on constructivist rather than prescriptive teaching is the advent of student-generated questions, which encourage students to become independent by learning how to learn, how to monitor their own comprehension, and how to make their learning active and focused. Student-generated questions make reading an active process and force the reader to focus attention on the reading material (Cole, 1993; Gillespie, 1991). The manner in which a teacher of the academically talented questions makes much difference. If a teacher can question and encourage student-generated questions, she can serve her academically talented students, can compact the curriculum properly, and can provide differentiation within the regular classroom.

Differentiation by Techniques: Critical Thinking and Socratic Dialogues

Plato (428–348 B.C.) was a philosopher of ancient Greece who was a student of Socrates. After Socrates died of poison in prison, Plato founded the Academy of Athens, the first European university. He lectured to his students without notes, and wrote many dialogues using Socrates as the main character. Socrates would pose problems and the students were to solve the problems through dialogue with Socrates and through research. The Socratic method is a dialectical style of debate: the pursuit of truth through questions, answers, and additional questions. Philosophical ideas are advanced, discussed, and criticized in the context of a conversation or debate involving two or more persons. Socrates, encountering someone who claims to know much, professes to be ignorant and seeks assistance from the one who knows. As Socrates begins to raise questions, however, it becomes clear that the one reputed to be wise really does not know what he claims to know, and Socrates emerges as the wiser one because he at least knows that he does not know. Such knowledge, of course, is the beginning of wisdom.

Socrates affirmed the significance of asking deep questions that probe profoundly into thinking before we accept ideas as worthy of belief. He established the importance of hunting for evidence, of closely analyzing reasoning and assumptions, of examining basic concepts, and pursuing implications not only of what is said but of what is done as well. His method of questioning is now known as "Socratic questioning" and is the best known critical thinking teaching strategy. In his mode of questioning, Socrates highlighted the need in thinking for clarity and logical consistency. Socratic dialogue is but one of 35 critical thinking dispositions advocated by the Critical Thinking Foundation, and presented in Table 10.1. Their Website (www.sonoma.edu/cthink) contains many teacher materials and lessons that have been modified according to critical thinking strategies.

These 35 strategies should always be embedded in content that is taught within the grade level and curriculum. Students who are academically talented will be able to ponder the material at a deep level, but in a democratic society all students need to be taught to think critically, as critical thinking is necessary in order to do the duty of a citizen in a democracy; that is, to vote based on reason and not on emotion and propaganda. Resource Module 10.1 is a social studies lesson illustrating how critical thinking strategies are embedded in a content that is taught to all students.

Differentiating Curriculum Utilizing Creative Thinking

Creative thinking strategies abound and are as close as the catalogs of booksellers at conferences for the teachers of the talented, or as the business or education shelves in a bookstore. Again, embedding the teaching of creative thinking within the content area is extremely important. Often awareness of human creativity is a strategy that can aid students in thinking creatively. Take the omnipresence of metaphor. Metaphor is the use of a word or phrase denoting one kind of idea or object in place of another word or phrase for the purpose of suggesting a likeness between the two. The use of metaphor is commonplace within all academic disciplines and human endeavors. Students often

Table 10.1   Strategy List: 35 Dimensions of Critical Thought

A. Affective Strategies	B. Cognitive Strategies: Macroabilities	C. Cognitive Strategies: Microskills
Strategy 1: Thinking independently	Strategy 10: Refining generalizations and avoiding oversimplifications	Strategy 27: Comparing and contrasting ideals with actual practice
S-2: Developing insight into egocentricity or sociocentricity	S-11: Comparing analogous situations: transferring insights to new contexts	S-28: Thinking precisely about thinking: using critical vocabulary
S-3: Exercising fairmindedness	S-12: Developing one's perspective: creating or exploring beliefs, arguments, or theories	S-29: Noting significant similarities and differences
S-4: Exploring thoughts underlying feelings and feelingsunderlying thoughts	S-13: Clarifying issues, conclusions, or beliefs	S-30: Examining or evaluating assumptions
S-5: Developing intellectual humility and suspending judgment	S-14. Clarifying and analyzing the meanings of words or phrases	S-31: Distinguishing relevant from irrelevant facts
S-6: Developing intellectual courage	S-15. Developing criteria for evaluation: clarifying values and standards	S-32: Making plausible inferences, predictions, or interpretations
S-7: Developing intellectual good faith or integrity	S-16. Evaluating the credibility of sources of information	S-33: Giving reasons and evaluating evidence and alleged facts
S-8: Developing intellectual perseverance	S-17. Questioning deeply: raising and pursuing root or significant questions	S-34: Recognizing contradictions
S-9:Developing confidence in reason	S-18. Analyzing or evaluating arguments, interpretations, beliefs, or theories	S-35. Exploring implications and consequences
	S-19. Generating or assessing solutions	
	S-20. Analyzing or evaluating actions or policies	
	S-21. Reading critically: clarifying or critiquing texts	
	S-22. Listening critically: the art of silent dialogue	
	S-23. Making interdisciplinary connections	
	S-24. Practicing Socratic discussion: clarifying and questioning beliefs, theories, or perspectives	
	S-25. Reasoning dialogically: comparing perspectives, interpretations, or theories	
	S-26. Reasoning dialectically: evaluating perspectives, interpretations, or theories	

Used with the permission of the Center for Critical Thinking, © 1996.

Resource Module 10.1: A Sample Lesson Using Socratic Dialogue
Copyright © Center for Critical Thinking, 1996. Used with permission.

Human Migration

by Chris Langley, Lone Pine USD, Lone Pine, CA

Objectives of the Remodelled Plan

The students will:
- come to understand in detail Baluchi nomadic life, comparing it to their own.
- develop empathy with Iranian nomadic lifestyles, exercising fairmindedness.
- identify complex factors of modern migratory patterns in the United States.
- relate human migration to their personal lives and the future.

Standard Approach

The lesson discusses the reasons people have for migrating, including the search to find food, resources, and better opportunities or because they are forced to migrate. The lesson introduces the concept and vocabulary of nomads. It also discusses historical famines and the effect they had on forcing people to move. The text discusses migration for better opportunities and briefly examines colonization. Forced migrations and the concept of refugees are briefly mentioned, and then the text considers present-day migrations. Movement to cities and warmer climates are mentioned. The teacher's edition suggests discussing modern forced migrations and recalling from the reading some of the facts concerning the reasons for migration given in the text.

Critique

The "Human" Part of Migration

This lesson deals with the reasons for migration. Several theories that are complex in nature are given to the teacher. One concept deals with the idea of "intervening opportunity." It suggests that the ways people look at distant opportunities are affected by the intervening opportunities. A second passage briefly looks at the "push" and "pull" factors. Little effort is made to relate these theories in the text. Rather, simple examples in factual form are listed. Migration is generally pictured in this as negative, only undertaken under duress. An underlying assumption is that migration is either a primitive socioeconomic phenomenon or evidence of poorly-run governments or natural disaster. No effort is made to relate the factors to human lives, to see the multifaceted pluses and minuses in lives, or to ever place the nomadic life in a positive light. The Baluchis of southeast Iran had a semiannual nomadic cycle, where in the winter and spring they tended their

Resource Module 10.1 *(continued)*

herds in the mountains and in summer went to the south to harvest dates. The Shah, and before him his father, saw nomads as an embarrassment to a modern industrial country and they followed a forced plan of resettlement. This resulted in depriving these people of their traditional food sources, and they starved. When they resisted, the government flew in aircraft and machine-gunned them during their traditional migrations.

The traditional pattern of life for the Baluchi was one of pride, grace, and cultural integrity. Living simply and close to nature gave them a way of life without the stress and materialism often associated with modern industrial city life.

The Multiple Perspectives of Colonization

The text makes it sound as if the only motivation for colonization was seeking a better place to live. Little detail about this motivation is given. Nor is any consideration given to the push and pull factors in colonization. Many motivations for countries to support and pursue colonization are ignored. The exploitation of the local peoples, the destruction of traditional life patterns, and the power struggles that resulted between the nations of Europe are overlooked. Instead this migratory pattern is seen simply as people looking for personal opportunities, freedom, and a new way of life.

The Conflicts of Modern Migrations

The text again makes it sound as if the factors in modern migration, the move to cities and warm climates, are simple. People move to cities for jobs, but no mention is made of the negatives in the cities, both historically and today, including high unemployment in cities, lack of training of new workers, and typical urban problems such as crime, overcrowding, and smog. The effect that this migration has on farms and rural areas is not even explored.

Children in my area need to come to terms with these factors. I live in a very rural area that presents excellent living conditions but limited job opportunities. Often the students I work with think simply going to L.A. after graduation will solve all their problems. They often lack the social skills and educational training or perspectives to migrate successfully to the urban areas.

Suggestions for Improvement

Generally the factors discussed in motivating migration are oversimplified, and traditional migration patterns, particularly in the U.S., are seen as simply going from bad economic situations to positive ones. The complexity of the issue is ignored completely.

The remodelled plan is focused on the people of traditional migratory patterns and the nomads. It helps the children to see the qualities of their own lives. In considering modern migration from rural to urban settings, their

(continued on next page)

Resource Module 10.1 (*continued*)

thinking needs to be extended to see the many issues both motivating and limiting these movements.

Strategies Used to Remodel
- S-29 noting significant similarities and differences
- S-3 exercising fairmindedness
- S-21 reading critically: clarifying or critiquing texts
- S-10 refining generalizations and avoiding oversimplifications
- S-24 practicing Socratic discussion: clarifying and questioning beliefs, theories, or perspectives

My remodelled lesson plan basically follows the organization and sequence of the original lesson, but it has two major focuses. The first focus is on the migratory patterns of nomads in traditional society first, and then upon modern migratory patterns that the children would be more familiar with.

The Traditional Migratory Pattern of the Baluchi in Iran

As a Peace Corps volunteer in Iran, I spent much time with the nomadic Baluchi tribes of southeastern Iran and Pakistan. I would begin by showing movies and bringing in various artifacts of the Baluchis, including a wedding coat, a camel saddle bag and articles of clothing. Through discussion and demonstration, I would clarify exactly what a migratory pattern was, in this case a seasonal migration between high pastures and low date palm orchards. I think it is important for the students, by their own examination and discussion, to understand how the lifestyle limits their belongings and how it places certain controls on social patterns including marriage and the education of the children. Once the students had a clear understanding of the meaning of nomads and migration, they would need to examine in detail how the Baluchi life was similar to and different from their own. We would examine some important values in our own culture and compare them to how the Baluchis dealt with similar issues. Of particular interest to these students would be arranged marriages and the youthfulness of the brides, the separation of the sexes, and materialism or possessions. I would stress that models of living and reality itself are complex and self-sufficient, showing how their ways and ours are different but one way is not good and another bad. (S-29) Because the social structure of the Middle East (and particularly Iran) is often viewed negatively here, this aspect will be quite challenging.

Once the students understand this aspect of the lesson, I would take them on to actually act out or plan a nomadic lifestyle. Considering the plight of the homeless might be helpful here if it does not confuse the issue, but I think if the children have any awareness of this social issue, it needs to be addressed. The children would figure out what it would feel like to be nomadic, what belongings they would choose, and what modes of transportation they could adopt. Other social issues could also be experienced, including arranged marriages and separation of the girls from the boys. The goal here would be to have the students understand

Resource Module 10.1 *(continued)*

the lifestyle from the nomadic point of view. Then I would discuss with them the forced settlement plan adopted by the government and have the children see the thinking from the Baluchis' point of view and the government's. (S-3)

By now, hopefully, I would have pointed out some of the positive aspects of the nomadic lifestyle and the children would be ready to critique the text and identify some of the assumptions the text makes. (S-21) This seems very important to me because the students I generally teach seldom consider that a text could be wrong, incomplete or misleading.

The Process of Identifying Migratory Patterns

The process of identifying assumptions would continue on to the second part of this lesson plan considering modern migratory patterns. In particular, we would explore the movement from rural living to urban living. We would need to discover the complexity of this issue, the various factors leading people to move to the city, and what happens to them there. The assumption in my classroom generally, and also, though less so, in the text, is that life is better in the city. Through question and answer and research, the students would come to avoid the oversimplification found in the text. (S-10)

Finally, I would conclude this lesson with a *Socratic discussion* of why people leave Lone Pine (my town) to move to various urban settings (primarily Los Angeles). Important issues to be brought out would be motivation, preparation for a successful move, goals, quality of life, and impact on the city, more so on the local rural areas of the young moving away. Polling the students on their short-range and long-range goals would provide an interesting and enlightening closure activity for the class. (S-24)

study metaphors as a figure of speech in literature class, but they seldom think about the omnipresence of metaphor. The creation of a metaphor is often the way a thinker visualizes the concept she/he is trying to convey. Thus the brain is called a *computer*; the heart is a *pump*; the stock market *crashes*; the immigrants form a *melting pot*; someone in a *white hat* is good; family life is a *circus*; silence has *sound*; time is *money*; people against the Vietnam war were called *doves*; the atom bomb when dropped formed a *mushroom cloud*; slaves escaped through the *Underground Railroad*, etc. The pervasiveness of metaphor can enlighten many a discussion across disciplines (Pugh, Hicks, Davis & Venstra, 1992).

Alternative Representations to Meet Expectations

In teaching for creativity, teachers can emphasize that they value creative thinking by permitting students to do alternative forms of knowledge representation to show they know what is expected to be learned. Rather than the traditional term paper, the traditional multiple choice test, perhaps students could do individual creativity projects that demonstrate their knowledge. Here are some examples of individual creativity projects my students have turned in: an autobiographical video ("My Creative Self"); performance of an original song; performance of an original radio play; design and modeling of an original dress for a sorority formal; a plan for an advertising campaign; a synchronized swimming routine; a grunge rock band audiotape; a photographic exhibit; an exhibit of original artworks; a reading of an original short story; an autobiographical multimedia presentation; a translation into English of Chinese, Greek, or Spanish literature; an original dance routine; a new recipe for scones; an original afghan; designs for costumes for a play; a reading of original poetry; a business plan for a new business; a music video; *a capella* singing; an original rock 'n' roll song; philosophical musings about the meaning of life; and display and demonstration of a particularly creative Thoughtlog. One wrote a poem when we visited the art museum, and it became the lyrics for the first song she composed. One football player, a defensive back, took all the game tapes for his entire college career and spliced them together to show himself in the improvisatory acts of dodging, running, and hitting. Projects are evaluated with a holistic scoring system, and we are often so moved at the projects that we weep.

Direct Teaching of Creative Thinking

Of course, there is a place for the direct teaching of creative thinking. My approach is more "organic," as I call it, consonant with my approach as an artist. The traditional approaches to creative thinking have derived from more linear strategies. Many people feel more comfortable with approaches to the study of creativity in which the lessons are done in lists and the approach is more like "curriculum as technology"; that is, where the lesson has a cognitive purpose and plan. Table 10.2 shows a comparison of three creative thinking overviews: deBono's, Guilford's, and Torrance's (Torrance & Safter, 1989). Figure 4.9 shows my "less linear" approach, as described in Chapter 4. Reynolds' Creativity, Inc., in the case example in Chapter 4, takes almost an art therapy approach to creativity, emphasizing the affective and emotional to a greater degree than my approach or those of deBono, Guilford, or Torrance.

Differentiation by Method of Teaching: Problem-Based Learning

A recent addition to the methodology that is suitable for the regular classroom is Problem-Based Learning (PBL). Medical schools have begun widely using this method, and so have special schools for academically talented high school students such as the Illinois Science and Mathematics Academy, a residential special school. The whole Summer 1997 issue of *Journal for the Education of the Gifted* was devoted to this method (Gallagher, 1997). The curriculum developers at the College of William and Mary provide extensive training on Problem-Based Learning (Boyce, VanTassel-Baska, Burrus, Sher & Johnson, 1997). Focused on learning to understand instead of learning to recall, the students adopt the role of future practitioners of the discipline.

An unclear, or "ill-structured" problem is posed. These problems have four characteristics: (1) the problem cannot be understood without more information; (2) the problem has no one right answer; (3) the problem shifts as more information is obtained; and (4) the answer is not assuredly "right." Educators pose problems that have a curricular purpose; that is, the problems will cover knowledge and concepts that the students will be expected to know within the domain or discipline being taught.

Problem-based learning is experiential; that is, the teacher's role is changed. Table 10.3 shows how problem-based learning differs from the usual way of educating. Problem-based learning is constructivist learning. Constructivism means that the student builds on the known in order to structure the unknown.

Here are examples of ill-structured problems (Illinois Mathematical and Science Academy, 1996, www.imsa.edu):

You are:

1. a scientist at the state department of nuclear safety. Some people in a small community feel their health is at risk because a company keeps thorium piled above ground at one of their plants. What action, if any, should be taken? (Summer Challenge 1992, IMSA)

2. a consultant to the Department of Fish and Wildlife. A first draft of a plan for the reintroduction of wolves to Yellowstone has received strong, negative testimony at hearings. What is your advice regarding the plan? (John Thompson, Ecology, IMSA)

3. a science advisor at NASA. A planet much like Earth has experienced massive destruction of elements of its biosphere. What is causing the destruction of plant life?

Table 10.2   Three Lists of Creative Thinking Skills

Edward de Bono	J.P. Guilford	E.P. Torrance
Getting started	Sensitivity to problems	Finding the problem
Organizing and structuring	Question-asking ability	Producing alternatives (fluency)
Concluding	Perception of what is wrong, minor irregularities	Originality
Focusing	Ideational fluency	Abstracting (highlighting the essence)
Judging evidence	Flexibility	Elaborating
Referring	Elaboration	Keeping open
Detecting what is missing	Synthesizing	Being aware of and using emotions
Judging relevance	Analyzing	Putting ideas in context
Judging importance—priorities	Reorganizing	Combining and synthesizing
Judging strength of evidence	Redefining	Visualizing richly and colorfully
Judging errors and mistakes	Transforming	Fantasizing
Abstracting	Handling complexity	Using movement and sound
Deciding on action	Evaluating	Looking at things from a different perspective
Sequeling—long and short-term consequences	Planning	Visualizing things internally
Knowing the goal		Extending boundaries
Producing alternatives, possibilities		Humor
Planning		Respect for infinity
Producing criteria and judging evidence		
Targeting		
Expanding		
Making rules		
Modifying		

Can new plants from Earth be successfully introduced to help save the planet's environment? (Bill Orton, second grade, Williamsburg, VA)

4. a 36-year-old single working mother with a five-year-old daughter. Upon your husband's death, you receive $20,000 in worker's compensation and $10,000 in stock option shares. How can you invest this money so that by your daughter's 18th birthday, its growth is maximized? (LuAnn Malik, Community College of Aurora, Aurora, CO)

5. a member of President Truman's Interim Committee. What advice will you give the President to help end the war in the Pacific? An atomic bomb has just been detonated at Los Alamos. (Bill Stepien, American Studies, IMSA)

6. invited to participate in a special session of your school board to determine whether *Huckleberry Finn* should be taught in your school district given its inclusion on a state censorship list. (Ed Plum, American Literature, District #214, Barrington, IL)

7. a stockholder of a major oil refinery in Louisiana that has mined oil from wetlands in the southern part of the state. You have received pressure from publicity about the wetlands to make it property of the federal government so that it can be protected. What will you do? (Christine Vitale, 4–5 multigrade, Arlington Heights, IL)

8. the principal of Foggeybottom High School asked by the school board to present a new comprehensive blueprint for all teachers to use at the school. What will your plan look like? What rationale will you give for the plan? (Diana Weidenbacker, Winnacunnet Alternative School, Winnacunnet, NY)

However, Joyce VanTassel-Baska issued a caution about problem-based learning: In order to do it well, schools and teachers need to recognize its complexity and take that into account when organizing curriculum that way or implementing a unit of study already developed using PBL principles. "It takes conversation time and planning time across teachers in order for the beauty of the interdisciplinarity of the approach to emerge and be properly exploited in the classroom. Otherwise, it collapses into one more approach to doing a project without the benefit of content learning going on" (personal communication, November 1997).

Table 10.3 How Problem-Based Learning Compares with Other Instructional Approaches

Curriculum as Prescription	Curriculum as Experience
From the perspective of teacher/expert	From the perspective of student/learner
Linear and rational	Coherent and relevant
Part to whole organization	Whole to part organization
Teaching as transmitting	Teaching as facilitating
Learning as receiving	Learning as constructing

Constructivism as an Approach to Curriculum

Most of the approaches being talked about in the education world feature a Vygot-skian model; that is, students build new learning on learning already begun, using a scaffolding approach as they aid each other in gaining more complex knowledge. This approach is called "constructivist." Figure 10.3 illustrates what the constructivist classroom looks like.

Figure 10.3 Constructivist Classrooms

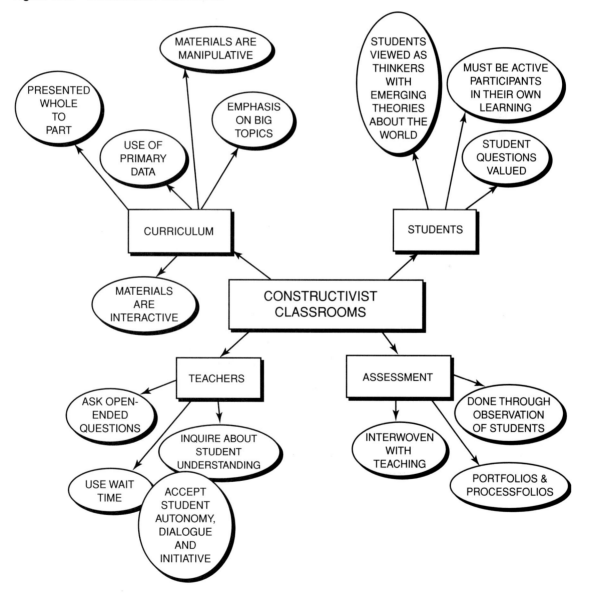

CURRICULUM OUTSIDE THE REGULAR CLASSROOM

The school has walls, fences, yards. Every school is essentially the same, a safe, protected place where children can learn in box-shaped rooms at the direction of well-trained educators. Academically talented students who are placed with other academically talented students in a self-contained school classroom or who are pulled out of their regular classroom for a certain period of time each day or week must have their curriculum modified in ways such as those suggested in this chapter and Chapter 9. There are also options outside the classroom for students. These are of two types—special courses and extra-school options.

Special Courses for Academically Talented Students

Many communities or regions have Saturday programs for students called "Enrichment Academy" or "Super Saturday" or the like. These offer students a chance to explore topics such as acting, or singing, or astronomy, or rocks. Often the teachers for these courses are interested experts who have the detailed knowledge longed for by curious students. Since these are not part of the required curriculum mandated by the state and delivered by the school, such courses are often considered frills, peripherals, or nonsense. However, they offer students a wonderful chance to explore what the Renzulli model calls "Type III" activities. Most of these are not academically rigorous, nor do they demand that the students do in-depth work. But they are good options in assuaging or piquing the curiosity of young probing minds.

Special Elective Courses

As Eisner (1985/1994) indicated, the "null" curriculum is curriculum that is never taught in schools, while most schools teach what a noun is for nine or more years in a row. Once the school is sure that a student has mastered what a noun is, for example, the option of special elective courses should be given. Such courses as broadcasting or theater, statistics or fractal geometry, women's studies or child development, sculpture or classical music could be offered. Students could be freed to explore courses in the vocational track, which are often taught by experts. Auto body repair, carpentry, cooking, or horticulture are all courses that would interest students. Rather than spending their senior year languishing, waiting to take the required government class and waiting to graduate, students could explore electives with time bought after they display mastery of the requirements. A high school of sufficient size could offer such courses, or a regional center could offer them. Full academic credit should be given.

Special, Out-of-School Classes

Aside from the Enrichment Academies and Super Saturdays, which serve the purpose of whetting appetites but not fully satisfying them, children who are academically talented should have an opportunity to take special, in-depth classes from teachers who are specialists. The young, talented artist will benefit from drawing classes. Georgia O'Keeffe and her sisters, in a small town in Wisconsin at the turn of the twentieth century, were all given drawing lessons when they were girls. While Georgia became a famous artist, her sisters became art teachers and all the O'Keeffes were known as talented; some thought Georgia's sister was more talented than Georgia.

There is no record of any accomplished musician who did not have private lessons from a young age, whose only music lessons were those given in school. In fact, the very idea that the school can provide the in-depth attention needed for the development of musical talent is ludicrous. Yet that is what is expected in other areas. The theoretical physicists Edward Teller and Albert Einstein both worked on mathematics with private tutors, besides their work in school. Einstein and Teller, who were a generation apart, had remarkably similar childhoods, Einstein in Germany and Teller in Hungary. Both were encouraged by their fathers to be engineers, and both ended up being theoretical physicists. Both fathers recognized their sons' talents, and obtained help from advanced students while the boys were young.

Young chess players take private lessons; they must, in order to begin to raise their ratings. Among high-IQ students, the private tutor for academic subjects is commonplace in certain geographical regions of the country, especially in the east.

Variations Within the Academically Talented Population and Implications for Curriculum

Again, the nature of academically talented children is such that they achieve more understanding of a subject, at a faster pace. But even among academically talented children there are variations in the ability to master material; therefore, we now discuss curriculum for students with very high IQs.

In a special class for academically talented students in mathematics, William McCandliss, who has coauthored several books on problem solving (*Problemoids*, McCandliss & Watson, 1988), told about the matriculation of a new student. He was teaching advanced fifth and sixth graders advanced mathematical problem solving in a special Saturday class. One day a young boy of six was brought into the class by the administrator of the program. McCandliss said that he thought the material being taught would be too advanced for this 6-year-old. The administrator asked whether the boy could stay in the class for that day. The boy came, sat silently, and at the end of the class was nodding his head. After a few weeks, the boy's understanding had eclipsed the understanding of that of his advanced classmates. His extreme mathematical precocity is rare, but not that rare. For such highly talented children, special tutors and classes are often the best way to go, since the regular school and the special class for others who are talented cannot provide the curriculum needed.

The Study of Mathematically Precocious Youth (SMPY) has studied such students for many years now. Students are administered the Scholastic Aptitude Test (SAT) at about age 11. This is before they have taken geometry. The SAT uncovers mathematical reasoning ability and verbal reasoning ability. Students who score high are often invited to participate in special fast-paced summer programs. Regional talent searches have information about these programs. The Study of Exceptional Talent (SET), a project of the Johns Hopkins University Institute for the Academic Advancement of Youth, identifies students throughout the United States who exhibit extraordinary mathematical or verbal reasoning ability by performing exceptionally well on the SAT before the age of 13. To help its members find appropriately challenging academic opportunities, SET provides personal academic advisement directly and through two publications, *Imagine* and the *Precollege Newsletter*. When members progress onto college, they receive the *Alumni Newsletter*, which focuses on career options, graduate schools, and other related issues.

Winner (1996) went so far as to say that the only students who should receive a special education are those who have very high IQs, and that all education should have its floor raised so that a special education for students with moderately high IQs (125 to 140) can be handled within the regular school program in heterogeneous classes.

Home Schooling as an Option for the Very High-IQ Student

High-IQ students, such as the boy discussed above, often cannot have their needs met by even the most willing school system, because the pace at which they learn is so stupendous. Most high-IQ students thus must be home schooled. There is a network of such students so they can meet and talk with each other, and consultants such as Kathi Kearney and Stephanie Tolan counsel parents of students with high IQs. The Hollingworth Conference for parents, educators, and students is held annually to recognize the needs of those with very high IQs. While many people find the thought of home schooling their bright children frightening, studies are beginning to show that home schooled students score very well on standardized achievement and college admissions tests. Home schooling should take into account a chance for the students to socialize with other students in the crucible of peer relationships, as the protective atmosphere of the home may not provide for the roughness and frankness that all people endure through the process of schooling.

Suitable Special Programs for Academically Talented Students

Over the years, educators of the academically talented have adapted and adopted several commercial programs and used them as curriculum options with academically talented students. Among these are the Odyssey of the Mind program, the Future Problem Solving program, the Philosophy for Children program, and the Junior Great Books program. In addition, academically talented students are often encouraged to enter academic competitions such as the Spelling Bee, History Day, the Invention Convention, Math Counts, Power of the Pen, and the Academic Decathlon. The advantage to these is that they have already been developed, validated, and proved successful. The disadvantage is that they are "packaged" and may discourage creativity on the part of the talent development education professional.

Odyssey of the Mind

This is a worldwide creativity program that utilizes team problem solving and creative thinking. There are three age divisions—grades K–5, grades 6–8, and grades 9–12. Each team has seven members. Each year the director of the program, Sam Micklus, publishes the problems that the teams are to work on. Local, regional, state, national, and international competitions take place. The curriculum orientation, in Eisner's terms (see Chapter 9) is process/product. The Odyssey of the Mind organizers believe that exercising the creative process in making sometimes silly or fantastical products will teach the students to be more creative. The teams are given long-term problems that take months to solve, and during the local, regional, state, national, and international competitions, they solve short-term problems and spontaneous problems.

Following are synopses of the 1997–1998 Long-Term Problems. The time limit given to each team to present its results is eight minutes. Materials used cannot exceed a $100 (U.S.) value.

1. *Balloonacy Cars* (Divisions II, III, IV) This problem requires teams to design, build and run three small vehicles that will break moving and stationary balloons. Each car will carry its own set of cards, which will limit the number of scoring runs it may make. One of these cars will be the carrier, which will be run to transport the other cars, in addition to breaking balloons.

2. *Omerdroid* (Divisions I, II, III, IV) The team's problem is to create and present a humorous performance that includes a team-made Omerdroid (android) that has physical human features. The Omerdroid, designed, built, and operated by the team, must perform human actions during the performance.

3. *Classics . . . Can You Dig It?* (Divisions I, II, III, IV) For this problem the team will create and present a performance about archaeology that includes an act that takes place during an ancient time, in which the purpose and/or use of the artifacts will be depicted, and a modern act, where the archaeologist explains the purpose and/or use of the artifacts based on his or her conclusions.

4. *Double Trouble* (Divisions I, II, III, IV) The team's problem is to design and build one structure that is made up of two individual balsa wood and glue structures. One of the structures will be a beam structure designed to bridge a gap; the other will be a load-bearing structure designed to rest on the beam structure and balance weights. The combined structure will be tested by supporting as much weight as possible. The team members will also create and present a theme for their solution, and will be judged on how well they work togehter during the presentation of their solution.

5. *Heroic Proportions.* In this problem, the team is to create and present a humorous performance that includes a character that has one or more out-of-proportion characteristics, or is extremely large or extremely small. This characteristic will enable the character to do something better, or something it otherwise could not do. The character will use this ability at one time to help a member of its species and at another time to help a member of a different species. All materials used for the team's presentation must fit inside a 4' × 4' × 4' cube.

Information about the Odyssey of the Mind can be obtained from the OM Association, P.O. Box 547, Glassboro, NJ 08028; Phone (609) 881-1603; fax: (609) 881-3596. Website is www.odyssey.org.

Junior Great Books

This widely used program is sponsored by the Great Books Foundation. This is what Eisner would call the academic rationalist approach to learning. In order to teach the Junior Great Books program, teachers must have special training provided by the Foundation. The "Junior" in the Great Books means that excerpts from classical and quality works of philosophy, fiction, poetry, and other literature are read by the students. The approach is called *shared inquiry*. The teachers are taught to question. Shared inquiry is taking a text and deeply reading it, trying to understand what it means. The leader tries to be a guide in helping the participants to reach their own interpretations of the text by raising thought-provoking questions. The text is considered from many points of view, and analysis is done jointly, with everyone's opinion having weight and merit. The leaders of Junior Great Books groups are taught that there are few right answers, and as they study the works, they are urged to read each work at least twice, in order to formulate interpretive questions. The questions they will ask in discussion usually have their origin in one of the following sources:

1. Ideas in or about the book that you consider important
2. Words or passages that you don't understand
3. Passages that have multiple meanings and implications
4. Passages whose truthfulness or application you would like the participants to consider in light of their own experience

A list of the books in the nine series for elementary school students and in the three series for high school students follows in Figures 10.4 and 10.5. While some criticize "great books" lists as being too dictatorial, not representative of multiple cultures, and as elitist, a look at the Junior Great Books list will soon dispell that criticism. Information about this program can be obtained from the Junior Great Books Foundation, 40 East Huron, Chicago, Illinois 60611. Website is www.greatbooks.org/junior.

Philosophy for Children

Philosophy for Children is a validated program available on the National Diffusion Network, and this critical thinking approach is among the best available. This is a curriculum which includes textbooks in philosophy for children, and manuals for teachers. Training is provided by the nonprofit Institute for the Advancement of Philosophy for Children at Montclair State College in New Jersey. Matthew Lipman, the founder, has written novels and manuals. The fictional novels (Lipman, 1974, 1976, 1978, 1980, 1984, 1990) and the accompanying manuals of exercises are designed to foster philosophical discussion among children. The narrator in the novels considers philosophical issues. Each novel considers a branch of philosophy—ethics, aesthetics, logic, metaphysics, and the like. The manuals, designed for teachers, offer teaching suggestions and lists of questions: "Are you the same person if you change your clothes/ if you change your name/ if you change your mind?" Children have the task of "figuring it out." Teachers receive several days of preparation training and then follow-up training in their own classrooms with trainers doing demonstration teaching.

Figure 10.4   Great Books from the Junior Great Books Program for Elementary School

The Happy Lion, Louise Fatio; *The Tale of Squirrel Nutkin,* Beatrix Potter; *How the Camel Got His Hump,* Rudyard Kipling; *Kanga and Baby Roo Come To The Forest, and Piglet Has A Bath* (from *Winnie-the-Pooh*), A. A. Milne; *Arap Sang and the Cranes,* African folktale as told by Humphrey Harman; *Blue Moose,* Daniel Manus Pinkwater; *Anancy and Dog and Puss and Friendship,* West Indian folktale as told by James Berry; *Jack and the Beanstalk,* English folktale as told by Joseph Jacobs; *The Magic Listening Cap,* Japanese folktale as told by Yoshiko Uchida; *The Jackal and the Partridge,* Punjabi folktale as told by Flora Annie Steel; *Nail Soup,* Swedish folktale as told by Linda Rahm; *The Apple of Contentment,* Howard Pyle; *The Red Balloon,* Albert Lamorisse; *The Other Side of the Hill,* Elizabeth Coatsworth; *The Emperor's New Clothes,* Hans Christian Andersen; *How the Elephant Became,* Ted Hughes; *Anansi's Fishing Expedition,* West African folktale as told by Harold Courlander and George Herzog; *The Velveteen Rabbit,* Margery Williams; *The Terrible Leak,* Japanese folktale as told by Yoshiko Uchida; *The Singing Tortoise,* West African folktale as told by Harold Courlander and George Herzog; *Three Boys With Jugs of Molasses and Secret Ambitions,* Carl Sandburg; *Cinderella,* Charles Perrault; *The Mouse's Bride,* Indian folktale as told by Lucia Turnbull; *How Coyote Stole the Sun,* Native American folktale as told by Jane Louise Curry; *The Master Cat,* Charles Perrault; *The Fisherman and His Wife,* Brothers Grimm, translated by Lucy Crane; *The Little Daughter of the Snow,* Russian folktale as told by Arthur Ransome; *The Ugly Duckling,* Hans Christian Andersen; *The Monster Who Grew Small,* Joan Grant; *The Little Humpbacked Horse,* Russian folktale as told by Post Wheele; *Ooka and The Honest Thief,* Japanese folktale as told by I. G. Edmonds; *The Brave Little Tailor,* Brothers Grimm, translated by Ralph Manheim; *Jean Labadie's Big Black Dog,* French-Canadian folktale as told by Natalie Savage Carlson; *Caporushes,* English folktale as told by Flora Annie Steel; *It's All the Fault of Adam,* Nigerian folktale as told by Barbara Walker; *Two Wise Children,* Robert Graves; *The Black Heart of Indri,* Dorothy Hoge; *The Green Man,* Gail E. Haley; *The Mousewife,* Rumer Godden; *The Fire On the Mountain,* Ethiopian folktale as told by Harold Courlander and Wolf Leslau; *Woman's Wit,* Howard Pyle; *The Man Whose Trade was Tricks,* Georgian folktale as told by George and Helen Papashvily; *How the Tortoise Became,* Ted Hughes; *Tom-Tit-Tot,* English folktale as told by Flora Annie Steel; *The Snowman,* Hans Christian Andersen; *Ellen's Lion,* Crockett Johnson; *The River Bank* (from *The Wind in the Willows*), Kenneth Grahame; *The Open Road* (from *The Wind in the Willows*), Kenneth Grahame; *Thank You M'am,* Langston Hughes; *The Water-Horse of Barra,* Scottish folktale as told by Winifred Finlay; *The Story of Wang Li,* Elizabeth Coatsworth; *The Elephant's Child,* Rudyard Kipling; *Vasilissa the Beautiful,* Russian folktale as told by Post Wheeler; *Cedric,* Tove Jansson; *Fresh,* Philippa Pearce; *The Enchanted Sticks,* Steven J. Myers; *Wisdom's Wages and Folly's Pay,* Howard Pyle; *Mr. Singer's Nicknames,* James Krüss; *Alice's Adventures in Wonderland* (selection), Lewis Carroll; *Thunder, Elephant, and Dorobo,* African folktale as told by Humphrey Harman; *The Man With the Wen,* Japanese folktale as told by Idries Shah; *Ali Baba and the Forty Thieves* (from *The Arabian Nights*); *The Goldfish,* Eleanor Farjeon; *Beauty and the Beast,* Madame de Villeneuve; *Prot and Krot,* Polish folktale as told by Agnes Szudek; *The Hemulen Who Loved Silence,* Tove Jansson; *The Devoted Friend,* Oscar Wilde; *The Dancing Princesses,* Walter de la Mare; *Allah Will Provide,* North African folktale as told by Robert Gilstrap and Irene Estabrook; *Mr. Toad* (from *The Wind in the Willows*),

(continued on next page)

Figure 10.4 *Continued*

Kenneth Grahame; *The Further Adventures of Toad* (from *The Wind in the Willows*), Kenneth Grahame; *Charles*, Shirley Jackson; *Ghost Cat*, Donna Hill; *Turquoise Horse, Maurice's Room*, Paula Fox; *Barbie*, Gary Soto; *Lenny's Red-Letter Day*, Bernard Ashley; *The Prince and the Goose Girl*, Lester Mordaunt; *Tramp*, Malcolm Carrick; *Alberic the Wise*, Norton Juster; *Podhu and Aruwa*, African folktale as told by Humphrey Harman; *The Invisible Child*, Tove Jansson; *The Bat-Poet*, Randall Jarrell; *A Game of Catch*, Richard Wilbur; *The Tale of the Three Storytellers*, James Krüss; *Spit Nolan*, Bill Naughton; *The Queen's Care*, Elizabeth Jamison Hodges; *Lucky Boy*, Philippa Pearce; *The Secret of the Hattifatteners*, Tove Jansson, *The Happy Prince*, Oscar Wilde; *Kaddo's Wall*, West African folktale as told by Harold Courlander and George Herzog; *Dita's Story*, Mary Q. Steele; *Oliver Hyde's Dishcloth Concert*, Richard Kennedy; *Mowgli's Brothers* (from *The Jungle Books*), Rudyard Kipling; *"Tiger-Tiger!"* (from *The Jungle Books*), Rudyard Kipling; *Through the Tunnel*, Doris Lessing; *Raymond's Run*, Toni Cade Bambara; *My Greatest Ambition*, Morris Lurie; *A Likely Place*, Paula Fox; *The Mysteries of the Cabala*, Isaac Bashevis Singer; *Bad Characters*, Jean Stafford; *Chura and Marwe*, African folktale as told by Humphrey Harman; *Superstitions*, Mary La Chapelle; *The Last Great Snake*, Mary Q. Steele; *Gaston*, William Saroyan; *Soumchi: the Veldt*, Ray Bradbury; *The White Umbrella*, Gish Jen; *The Parsley Garden*, William Saroyan; *The Secret of the Yellow House*, Anatoly Aleksin; *As the Night the Day*, Abioseh Nicol; *The Summer Book*, Tove Jansson; *The Alligators*, John Updike; *Tweedledum and Tweedle Dee* (from *Through the Looking-Glass*), Lewis Carroll; *The Magic Jacket*, Walter de la Mare; *Props For Faith*, Ursula Hegi; *Letting in the Jungle* (from *The Jungle Books*), Rudyard Kipling; *The Spring Running* (from *The Jungle Books*), Rudyard Kipling; *Harrison Bergeron*, Kurt Vonnegut, Jr.; *I Just Kept On Smiling*, Simon Burt; *At Her Father's and Her Mother's Place*, Natalya Baranskaya; *The White Circle*, John Bell Clayton; *The Zodiacs*, Jay Neugeboren; *End of the Game*, Julio Cortázar; *The Cat and the Coffee Drinkers*, Max Steele; *Anne Frank: The Diary of A Young Girl* (selection); *The Secret Lion*, Alberto Alvaro Rios; *Day of the Butterfly*, Alice Munro; *A Christmas Carol*, Charles Dickens; *Sucker*, Carson McCullers; *The Summer of the Beautiful White Horse*, William Saroyan; *Rules of the Game* (from *The Joy Luck Club*), Amy Tan; *The Destructors*, Graham Greene; *The Watch*, Ivan Turgenev; *Approximations*, Mona Simpson; *The Griffin and the Minor Canon*, Frank R. Stockton; *Star Food*, Ethan Canin; *Winter* (from *The Winter Room*), Gary Paulsen; *High School Graduation* (from *I Know Why the Caged Bird Sings*), Maya Angelou; *Adventures of Huckleberry Finn* (selection), Mark Twain; *Miriam*, Truman Capote; *Zoo Island*, Tomás Rivera; *At The Pitt-Rivers*, Penelope Lively; *New African* (from *Sarah Phillips*), Andrea Lee; *Sponono*, Alan Paton; *Bobby's Room*, Douglas Dunn; *A Bird in the House*, Margaret Laurence; *The Strange Case of Dr. Jekyll and Mr. Hyde*, Robert Louis Stevenson; *The Little Cousins*, Peter Taylor; *The Idealist*, Frank O'Connor; *The Time Machine*, H. G. Wells.

Statistical results of a study conducted by the Educational Testing Service with average children showed significant improvement in formal and informal reasoning ability in a population of 2000 middle school students after they participated in Philosophy for Children curriculum.

Figure 10.5 Great Books from the Junior Great Books Program for High School

Why War? Sigmund Freud
The Melian Dialogue, Thucydides
The Social Me, William James
Rothschild's Fiddle, Anton Chekhov
Concerning The Division of Labor, Adam Smith
Chelkash, Maxim Gorky
How an Aristocracy May Be Created by Industry, Alexis de Tocqueville
Observation and Experiment, Claude Bernard
Everything That Rises Must Converge, Flannery O'Connor
An Essay in Aesthetics, Roger Fry
An Outpost of Progress, Joseph Conrad
On Studying, José Ortega y Gasset
Politics, Aristotle
Of Commonwealth, Thomas Hobbes
Barn Burning, William Faulkner
Of Civil Government, John Locke
In Exile, Anton Chekhov
The Declaration Of Independence, Thomas Jefferson
Equality, Isaiah Berlin
Sorrow-Acre, Isak Dinesen
Why Americans Are Often So Restless, Alexis de Tocqueville
After the Ball, Leo Tolstoy
Habit, William James
The Overcoat, Nicolai Gogol
On Happiness, Aristotle
Habits and Will, John Dewey
Happiness, Mary Lavin
Crito, Plato
On Liberty, John Stuart Mill
Conscience, Immanuel Kant
A Hunger Artist, Franz Kafka
Antigone, Sophocles
Why Great Revolutions Will Become Rare, Alexis de Tocqueville
A Room of One's Own, Virginia Woolf
In Dreams Begin Responsibilities, Delmore Schwartz

For information, contact Institute for the Advancement of Philosophy for Children, Montclair State College, Upper Montclair, NJ. Their Website is www.bgsu.edu/offices/phildoc.html.

Future Problem Solving

The Future Problem Solving Program (FPSP) is a very popular program among the educators of the academically talented. It was begun in 1974 by E. Paul Torrance in Georgia, and it has now been internationally adopted. Based on Osborn's Creative Problem Solving Process (Osborn, 1963), the Future Problem Solving Program involves four-member teams who learn and utilize the FPSP Six-Step Process supported by an FPSP coach. The six-step foundation to creative thinking processes includes:

1. Brainstorming topic-related problems
2. Identifying an underlying problem
3. Brainstorming potential solutions to the underlying problem
4. Developing criteria to judge solutions
5. Evaluating all solutions to determine the best solution
6. Describing the best solution to develop an action plan

Applying the six steps to three annually determined problem topics, student teams write and mail possible solutions at school year intervals to trained evaluators who provide feedback. There are three components: Future Problem Solving, Scenario Writing, and Community Problem Solving. Within each component, there are both Curricular and Competitive Division options. The Curricular Division is designed for grade levels K–12. There are four levels: Primary, grades K–3; Juniors, grades 4–6; Intermediates, grades 7–9; and Seniors, grades 10–12. The Competitive Division, designed for grade levels 4–12, is a statewide, national, and international competitive program. There are three levels: Juniors, grades 4–6; Intermediates, grades 7–9; and Seniors, grades 10–12, and students compete against teams from comparable levels. The 1997–1998 problems were in these areas: Natural Disasters, Freedom, Women in the Workplace, Nontraditional Families, and Medical Ethics.

The Future Problem Solving Program also has a Scenario Writing component. Students develop and submit futuristic scenarios. For the purposes of the Future Problem Solving Program, a *scenario* is a story that might take place as a logical outgrowth of actions or events that took place earlier. It is a prediction of the future and is written as though the future were the present. An FPSP scenario is a short short story in which one possible outcome of the future is developed through character(s) and plot. Each scenario is set at least 20 years in the future and must have a recognizable relationship to one of the Future Problem Solving Program topics for the current year.

The Future Problem Solving Program also has a Community Problem Solving component. Students apply the problem-solving process to real community problems. Through Community Problem Solving, students have implemented a wide range of solutions. The aim is to convert problem solving from the hypothetical to the practical, to help students to become activists in their communities. In Massachusetts, students designed a wastewater plant building, saving the community over $119,500. From raising money to restore the battleship *Texas* to cleaning up hazardous waste in Utah, students use the Community Problem Solving component to help their own communities. The Future Problem Solving Program is at 2500 Packard, Suite 110, Ann Arbor, MI 48104-6827, Phone (313) 973-8781 or 1 (800) 256-1499. The Future Problem Solving Website is www.fpsp.org/toc.html.

Academic Competitions

1. **The United States Academic Decathlon** is a nationwide competition of high school students designed to provide competition and to promote and recognize

academic endeavors. Each team member competes in 10 events: economics, mathematics, social science, language and literature, fine arts, essay writing, interview, speech, and the Super Quiz. The United States Academic Decathlon originated as an outgrowth of the California Academic Decathlon. Each high school enters a team of nine students: 3 "A" or Honor students, 3 "B" or Scholastic students, and 3 "C" or Varsity students. Each Decathlete competes in all ten events. In 1997–1998 the theme was "Looking Outward: Forces Shaping Society," with special emphasis on the Global Economy. Their Website is www. usad.org.

2. **National History Day** sponsors a series of district, state, and national competitions. The program begins in September. The theme for 1998 was "Migration in History." In many states and districts, teachers are invited to workshops where they share ideas about how the year's theme can be most effectively addressed and also receive bibliographies and a list of possible topics. Teachers then introduce the program to their students who, in turn, choose a topic and begin their research. Students are encouraged to choose any topic in local, national, or world history and investigate its historic significance and relationship to the theme by conducting extensive primary and secondary research. Students present their findings in papers, exhibits, performances, and media presentations that are evaluated by historians and educators. National History Day has two divisions: the junior division (grades 6–8) and the senior division (grades 9–12). Some states also sponsor a History Day contest for students in grades 4 and 5. Students can enter one of the following seven categories: individual paper, individual or group exhibit (similar to a museum exhibit), individual or group performance (a dramatic portrayal of the topic), individual or group media (a documentary using either slides, video, or a noninteractive computer program). Groups can consist of two to five students. National History Day can be contacted at 0119 Cecil Hall, University of Maryland, College Park, MD 20742. The Website is www.thehistorynet.com/NationalHistoryDay.html.

3. **Science Olympiad** is a national science competition, with over 12,000 K–12 schools participating across the nation. There are four divisions: A1 (grades K–3); A2 (grades 3–6); B (grades 6–9); and C (grades 9–12). For Divisions B and C, each team is limited to 15 competition members, but many more can be involved in the preparation and building. There are three levels of competition: regional, state, and national. There are 22 events in the B and C divisions, covering all aspects of science, including not only the traditional biology, chemistry, physics, but also engineering, nature, and communication skills. Most of the events involve a team of people (usually two) taking a test, doing a lab, testing a construction, and/or running a contraption. The majority of events test how well students apply the scientific method, as well as their own ingenuity. The address is National Office Science Olympiad, 5955 Little Pine Lane, Rochester, MI 48306. Phone (810) 651-4013; Fax (810) 651-7835. The Website is www.macomb.k12.mi.us/science/olympiad.htm.

4. **The National Geography Bee** is a nationwide contest for schools with any grades four through eight. It is an educational outreach program of the National Geographic Society. With a first-place prize of a $25,000 college scholarship and other prizes in additional scholarships, cash, and classroom materials, the Bee is designed

to encourage the teaching and study of geography. Principals of eligible schools must register their schools to participate. There is a minimum requirement of six students from any of the eligible grades to hold a competition. Principals may request registration by writing to National Geography Bee, National Geographic Society, 1145 17th Street NW, Washington, DC 20036-4688.

5. **The Scripps Howard National Spelling Bee** is one of the oldest competitions. Participants must qualify under two basic requirements: (1) they must not have passed beyond the eighth grade at the time of their individual school finals; and (2) they must not have reached their sixteenth birthday on or before the date of the national finals. Spelling Bee coordinators may, at their discretion, set a minimum age and grade limit. The Spelling Bee's address is P.O. Box 371541, Pittsburgh, PA 15251-7541.

6. **Mathcounts** is a national math coaching and competition program founded in 1983 by the National Society of Professional Engineers to promote seventh and eighth grade math achievement. The Mathcounts format integrates many math subject areas and stresses critical thinking and practical problem solving in addition to computational skills. Mathcounts promotes student interest in math by making math achievement as challenging, exciting, and prestigious as a school sport. Teachers and volunteers coach student 'mathletes' beginning each fall and continuing throughout the year, either as part of in-class instruction or as an extracurricular activity. In 1997–1998, approximately 4,443 schools participated. All Mathcounts materials are created by the National Council of Teachers of Mathematics (NCTM). Mathcounts competitions are designed to be completed in approximately three hours. Competitions at all levels consist of three written rounds (Spring and Target for individuals and Team for all four members) and a fast-paced oral Countdown round for the top 25 percent of students (maximum 10 students) based on individual scores in the Sprint and Target rounds. The Mathcounts Website is mathcounts.org. Write the Mathcounts Foundation, 1420 King Street, Alexandria, VA 22314; Phone (703) 684-2828; Fax (703) 836-4875.

The value of academic competitions such as these for the students is that they get a chance to practice, and to compete with equals. One could call it "varsity" level competition for the mind and brain. Just as athletes compete across schools and regions, so must smart students in order to reach their levels of challenge.

Internships and Mentor Programs

A necessary out-of-school situation for any child in the development of his talent is a mentor. A mentor is a person who provides for the academically talented student a role model and an out-of-school experience in an area that is not available in the school. Usually the goal of this experience is to provide the student with practical knowledge of a certain field or domain, and to provide an opportunity for career modeling.

In certain fields, for example, the sciences, the mentor is crucial. It is no accident that Nobel Prize winners are mentors of Nobel Prize winners. In fact, the young scientist who does not choose his or her mentor well and carefully is often left in the dust when grants, recommendations, and opportunities to learn new techniques come along. Many states and programs for the academically talented provide mentor experiences in all sorts of fields for students. It is incumbent upon the parents, the school, and the academically talented student to participate in these, not only for the intrinsic value of the experience, but for what Simonton (1988) calls the "proximity" value, the value of future connections.

Riley (1992) said that broad-scale and small-scale mentorships can be organized by the school coordinators for their academically talented students. Her guide is a very practical and helpful one. Gray (1982, 1983) has designed a plan for university students to mentor middle school academically talented students in Type III (Renzulli, 1977) independent investigations, and Nash and Treffinger (1986) have also written extensively about the various kinds of mentorships. Mentorships are also discussed in Chapter 11.

International Curricular Experiences

One of the recommendations that came out of the Richardson study in Texas in the early 1980s (Cox, Daniel & Boston, 1985) was a recommendation for more internationalization of the curriculum for academically talented learners. They recommended mastery of at least one foreign language, and an emphasis on being sensitive to foreign cultures. Some urban areas have international schools, of which the United Nations School in New York City and the Denver, Colorado, International School are examples. High school programs such as the International Baccaulaureate are also popular ways of internationalizing the curriculum. The president of the school board of the Princeton, Ohio, schools said that their International Baccalaureate (IB) curriculum for intellectually academically talented high school students is a prime residential drawing card when new professional families move to the area.

The IB academic curriculum meets the condition for academic rigor mentioned in Chapter 9. It is a program for the junior and senior years, in which, of the nine academic credits required, six are traditional courses that are high level and that meet five times a year for a two-year period. There are also three other courses that meet for half that length of time. These courses are selected from six areas: (1) Language A (usually the mother tongue) which requires in depth study of translations of world literature from at least two other language areas; (2) Language B (a second language not studied in such depth—not a mother tongue); (3) the Study of Humankind through one of these: history, geography, economics, philosophy, psychology, social anthropology, business studies; (4) Experimental Studies in biology, chemistry, physics, physical science, or scientific studies; (5) Mathematics; (6) Choice of the following: art, music, a classical language, a second language B, an additional option in social sciences, experimental studies or mathematics, or computer studies.

In addition, the IB curriculum has interdisciplinary courses in the philosophy of learning, and IB students must participate in some form of creative activity. The emphasis here is on international and transnational interdisciplinary learning. Teachers must take subject matter mastery examinations before being qualified to teach.

The curriculum is prescribed and syllabi are precisely followed. One teacher of the IB curriculum at the New Delhi, India, American Embassy School, said that the syllabi were so demanding and packed, that she often felt she had no time to be creative as a teacher because she was preparing her students for the required comprehensive IB examinations when she wasn't teaching the subject matter in the curriculum (personal communication, New Delhi, 1987). A student there, taking the same curriculum, thought it was packed with more information than he could absorb, but that he supposed it was "good for me in the long run." Students who have undergone the IB curriculum have decided advantages in competitive college admissions. The Case Example in Chapter 6, by a student in an International Baccalaureate high school program in Eugene, Oregon, excerpts her senior research paper.

For information, contact International Baccaulaureate North America, 680 Fifth Avenue, New York, NY 10019.

Summer Programs

Many states have Summer Institutes, Governor's Institutes, and Honors Institutes of various configurations, where academically talented and talented students can meet to study and perform. The Johns Hopkins University Center for Talented Youth has special programs for students who score above a certain cutoff on the Scholastic Aptitude Test administered early. Duke University has TIP, for students who score above a certain cutoff score on the American College Test administered early. Many universities offer special summer programs for academically talented and talented youth. These are often thematically oriented.

Special Regional and Residential Schools

Several states have chosen to operate regional and residential schools for academically talented and for performing arts talented students. North Carolina, Illinois, and Louisiana are examples. These schools often produce many National Merit semifinalists and finalists. The advantage to these residential schools is that the students can concentrate and focus on their areas of talent. Special schools that are nonresidential are found in many urban areas. Schools such as those in New York City—the Bronx High School of Science, Stuyvesant High School, Hunter High School, La Guardia High School for the Performing Arts, The High School of Creative Writing—have a long history of providing quality public education to urban and disadvantaged students.

Correspondence, Distance Learning, Independent Learning, and Online Courses

Nowadays it is not necessary to leave the home computer if one wants a truly independent education. Several of the most well-known correspondence courses for academically talented students are the following:

1. **Duke University's Learn on Your Own.** Duke University offers academically talented students the opportunity to take accelerated courses in their hometowns. Courses offered are "English Language: Use and Origin"; "Reflective Writing"; "Microeconomics"; and "Precalculus Mathematics," which consists of four separate courses. Contact Duke TIP, Learn on Your Own, P.O. Box 90747, Durham NC 27708-0747; Phone (919) 684-3847; Website www.jayi.com/.

2. **LetterLinks.** The Center for Talent Development at Northwestern University sponsors the LetterLinks Program for academically talented students. The program provides two options for distance learning: the Center's LetterLinks courses in mathematics, social sciences, and the humanities for students in sixth through twelfth grade, and the LetterLinks/EPGY online math courses for students in kindergarten through twelfth grade. The LetterLinks/EPGY courses are offered jointly by the Center for Talent Development and Stanford University's Education Program for Gifted Youth (EPGY) and provide an opportunity for students to participate in completely computerized mathematics courses that use commonly available personal computer equipment and an Internet e-mail connection. Address: LetterLinks, Center for Talent Development, Northwestern University, 617 Dartmouth Place, Evanston, IL 60208-4175.

3. **Educational Program for Gifted Youth (EPGY).** This is a program from Stanford University. Math studies for students beginning at fourth grade are offered. Contact EPGY, Ventura Hall, Stanford University, Stanford, CA 94305-4115, epgy-info@epgy. stanford.edu.

4. **Virtual School for the Gifted.** This program offers courses in math and science, humanities, and computing, from Europe. Its Website is www.vsg.edu.au/noframes/courses.htm.

5. Advice for the teacher in conducting independent studies is available at a Website called "Students Can Learn on Their Own," at www.erols.com/interlac/index.html.

Thus can the academically talented student be taught according to the precepts in Chapter 9. If the will is there, the way is there. Options ranging from differentiating teaching strategies in the regular classroom, to offering extracurricular competitions and creativity programs, to setting the student out to learn on his or her own at home, are all available.

SUMMARY

1. Differentiation is necessary for intellectually gifted children because of three of their learning characteristics: (1) they often have different interests than nongifted children; (2) they have the ability to learn faster; and (3) they have the ability to learn in greater depth.

2. Class size is one reason why gifted students are *pulled out* from their regular classrooms and served in special programs.

3. The teacher in the regular classroom has a responsibility to have an open attitude about adjusting the pace and depth of work for the gifted children in her class.

4. The major technique for providing appropriate curriculum for intellectually gifted students in the regular classroom is "compacting," "telescoping," or "compressing" the required material. This involves pretesting.

5. Giving a gifted student more work instead of different work often results in having the gifted student try to hide her giftedness.

6. Other means of differentiation are to differentiate by content novelty, by content sophistication. This is usually called *enrichment*.

7. There are at least 15 types of options that could be called acceleration options.

8. Administrators should be aware that the schedule and the Carnegie unit often operate against an optimal education for gifted students.

9. Certain practices by the regular classroom teacher such as compacting, questioning, conducting discussions, and skilled lecturing can contribute to an optimal education for gifted students.

10. There are quite a few out-of-school options for gifted students. These include home schooling, special Saturday and summer programs, special contests and competitions, internships and mentorships, private tutors, and international experiences.

11. Independent studies, correspondence courses, and online interactive courses for credit are all available in cyberspace.

11 Social-Emotional Guidance and Counseling Needs of the Talented

FOCUSING QUESTIONS

1. What would you do if a student with whom you had rapport in one setting defied you in public in another setting?
2. What are the essential aspects of asynchronous development and what are the merits of this definition as a counseling understanding of high-IQ students?
3. What aspects of what research has shown about the psychosocial development of academically talented students merit special counseling and guidance intervention? Why?
4. Discuss two of of the counseling issues that resonate with you. Tell a story.
5. Discuss two of the guidance issues that resonate with you. Tell a story.
6. What are the salient differences between students with high IQs and students with very high IQs?
7. Discuss the counseling issue of self-concept as it relates to gifted youth.
8. Compare and contrast self-concepts of mathematically and verbally precocious youth.
9. What is resiliency and what does it have to do with the manifestation of talent potential?
10. Does underachievement exist? Why or why not?
11. What are the special duties of counselors in guiding talented students?
12. Discuss gender differences in achievement, course selection, and test taking.
13. Discuss the counseling needs of gifted girls.
14. Discuss the counseling needs of gifted boys.
15. Discuss the counseling needs of gay, lesbian, and bisexual students.
16. Do you think the causes of the gender differences are environmentally or genetically induced?
17. Fill out the individual plan (short-term) for a student you know.

Figure 11.1 Overview of Chapter 11

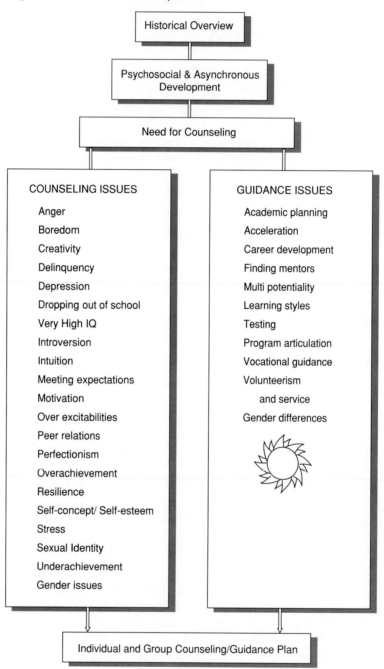

The graduate students studying the education of the talented were discussing problems that had arisen on their jobs as teachers of the talented. Mary Brickman said, "I had an incident happen today that has me really upset. Toby, this sixth grader I am working with, and I really got into it. He had never seen me as a classroom teacher before, only as his resource teacher, pulling him out from study hall to work with him on advanced reading and creative writing. Well, I was scheduled to teach a six-week cycle of reading to the regular class that he's in. He was acting up and talking and drumming his fingers against the table and I asked him quietly to stop disturbing the other students. He just kept on doing it. I asked him again. He kept on. I finally said to him that I would like him to leave. He got up and flounced out, to the study hall. Then when I came to get him for his enrichment lesson in the study hall, he was there with his head in the desk.

"I went over to him and told him to come with me. Now usually he's looking at the door and just rises when I get there. When we got to the library, he just sat there with his arms crossed, and a defiant look on his face. I said, 'Toby, we have to talk about what happened.' I used all my teacher wiles, trying to get him to talk. I patted him on the wrist and he shook my hand off. Finally, I thought, I'm not going to take this anymore, and I pulled out my calendar and said, 'Well, I guess you should go back to study hall. I'll come and get you next Tuesday at this time.'

"But I feel horrible. I went to his folder in the office and got his mother's phone number and I'm going to call her and talk to her about this. What do you guys think?"

"His head in the desk? He actually had his head in his desk?" Ellen Bates said.

"Yes," Mary replied. She went on. "The first week of school, his teacher came up to me and said she couldn't take any more of this. If it's not drumming his fingers, it's banging his head on the desk or on the wall. She said he does no work."

"How are his test scores?" the professor said.

"He's got an IQ of 165 on a Woodcock-Johnson. He's got achievement test scores in the 95th percentile in everything. He's a very good creative writer. Right now in our enrichment period he and another little guy—he's in sixth grade but he has been accelerated a year—are reading fantasy novels and science fiction and writing their own. I have no trouble with Jason, the young one. Only with Toby. And this is the first time."

"165? On an individual test?" the professor said. "He's a highly academically talented boy."

"Yes. Well you wouldn't know it from his grades. Something interesting about his family came up, though. When I was reading his file, I read his mother's request for his kindergarten placement. She said that she wanted him to be in the morning kindergarten because he was so involved in his own projects in the afternoon. That's a little unusual for a kindergartner, isn't it?"

"He thinks you betrayed him when you reprimanded him," another classmate said.

"I know. He's never seen me teach a class before. It's always been one on one," Mary said. "But his behavior was inappropriate and he was disturbing the other kids."

"His subject matter teachers say he does no work?" the professor said.

"None. Zip. He hasn't handed in one homework assignment, and when he's called on, he makes sarcastic remarks. Today, before I asked him to leave, he was saying things in the discussion—we were discussing what makes an eminent writer—and one of the kids said that Stephen King was eminent. He said, 'Stephen King? Come on. Who can stand that simplistic stuff?'"

"He has no tolerance for the other kids," someone observed.

"Well, he's been permitted to underachieve since kindergarten, I'll bet," Karen Brock said. "Has he ever done a project or handed in work?"

"Have you seen any of his work?" the professor said.

"Now that you mention it, no," Mary said. He's just writing and writing on his fantasy story, but when I stand over his shoulder, he puts his arm up and blocks the screen."

"Don't you have a backup of his story?" Carol Warner said.

"No. He takes the disk with him when he leaves and stores it in his locker."

"Then how do you know he's even writing a fantasy story?" said Karen.

"Well, he discusses, he shares, he laughs and is funny when the three of us are together," Mary said. "But now he's shut me out, too. He's shut the whole school out and he trusted me and I reprimanded him and he's shut me out, too."

"Talk to him right away tomorrow morning," Carol said. "Before you see him for the reading class. Get the story."

"Call his mother and ask her what she thinks," Sherry Parke said. "Is he in an intact home? What are his parents like?"

"I think they're kind of odd, too," Mary said. "At least that's what I've picked up from the teachers. His father works in computers, and his mother used to teach. She's a librarian now. Someone said their house is full of books and newspapers, just a mess."

"Do you know?" the professor said. "Rimm makes a good point when she says that no change happens in a student's achievement without three parties—the school, the parents, and the child himself. You've got to see what's up with the family. With that IQ and those achievement test scores in the 90s, he's underachieving. He can get those scores without even trying."

"That banging behavior sounds like Attention Deficit Disorder to me," Ellen said. "Maybe he needs Ritalin. I know a boy who was doing that and they put him on Ritalin and it just cleared right up. He was able to concentrate and do his work."

"But he's so far above. What about accelerating him to eighth grade?" the professor said. "Test him and find him a level of challenge."

"I don't know. I'll keep you tuned in," Mary said.

The next week the class questioned Mary again. She said that the next day, he'd behaved just as if nothing had happened. She had requested permission to do a case study on him for her graduate class, and Toby seemed pleased. "Now you'll find out how psycho I am," he told Mary.

This description of a clash with a very high-IQ boy illustrates some of the difficulties academically talented children and their teachers encounter in the milieu of the school. Such difficulties often call for counseling and guidance interventions.

HISTORICAL TRENDS IN GUIDANCE AND COUNSELING OF THE ACADEMICALLY TALENTED

One of the foremost experts on the guidance and counseling needs of academically talented children is Nicholas Colangelo. In the *Handbook of Gifted Education* that he and Gary Davis edited (1997), he wrote an essay called "Counseling Gifted Students." In this essay, he traced the history of the interest in the counseling needs of academically talented students from the Terman study to the present. Leta Hollingworth (1926, 1942) was credited as being the first to recognize that the academically talented do have emotional and social needs that can be served by counseling.

The 1950s saw such centers as the University of Wisconsin-Madison Guidance Laboratory for Superior Students. The influence of John Curtis Gowan in the 1960s and 1970s was notable. In the late 1970s, Colangelo and Ziffert edited a book called *New Voices in Counseling the Gifted* that heralded that academically talented students did, indeed, have special counseling needs because of their developmental differences. In the 1980s, SENG (Supporting Emotional Needs of the Gifted) was established at Wright State University in Ohio by James Webb. SENG sponsors conferences for parents and educators. In the early 1990s it moved to Kent State University. In 1982, *Guiding the Gifted Child*, the most popular book about the affective needs of gifted children, was published. This was written by James Webb, Elizabeth Meckstroth, and Stephanie Tolan, and it would go on to sell more than 80,000 copies. Galbraith's Free Spirit Press began to feature books for teachers on counseling the gifted, among them *Managing the Social and Emotional Needs of the Gifted: A Teacher's Survival Guide* (Schmitz & Galbraith, 1985). Also in the 1980s, Barbara Kerr established the Guidance Laboratory for Gifted and Talented at the University of Nebraska in Lincoln; in Denver, Linda Silverman established the Gifted Child Development Center; and in Iowa City, Iowa, the Connie Belin & Jacqueline N. Blank International Center for Gifted Education and Talent Development was established at the University of Iowa. By 1993, both James Delisle and Linda Silverman had published substantial books on counseling issues. In addition, Goals 2000 focused on issues having to do with social and emotional development. Colangelo (1997) also applauded the increase in the number of qualitative case studies that has led to in-depth understanding of the counseling and guidance issues pertinent to talented people.

PSYCHOSOCIAL AND ASYNCHRONOUS DEVELOPMENT

Many of these difficulties are caused by the academically talented student's "asynchronous" development. This means that the student is out of sync with his age peers emotionally and intellectually. In fact, what could be called a "counseling" definition of giftedness has been proposed by Morelock (1992) and Silverman (1993). Morelock wrote:

> Giftedness is asynchronous development in which advanced cognitive abilities and heightened intensity combine to create inner experiences and awareness that are qualitatively different from the norm. This asynchrony increases with higher intellectual capacity. The uniqueness of the gifted renders them particularly vulnerable and requires modifications in parenting, teaching and counseling in order for them to develop optimally. (Morelock, p. 14).

As discussed in Chapter 5, Terrasier (1985) said that gifted students experienced "dyssynchrony," uneven development, which has both internal and external aspects, intellectual, language and reasoning, and affective unevenness. The concept of asynchronous development goes beyond Terrasier's concept of dyssynchrony, according to Silverman (1993), in that asynchrony "incorporates the emotional dimension, emphasizing the interrelationship of cognitive complexity and emotional intensity" (p. 2). The emotional repercussions of having a high IQ have long been ignored, or, when recognized, have been thought of as emotional instability. While the physical development of academically talented children is most often similar to those of their age, their cognitive and emotional development often far outstrip their age mates. As a result, these students often experience great stress that can lead to such phenomena as disabling perfectionism, underachievement, acting out behavior, and depression.

Psychosocial Characteristics of Academically Talented Youth

The American Psychological Association published a book in 1985, edited by Frances Horowitz and Marion O'Brien, especially devoted to the development of gifted children. As usual, gifted children were described as those with high IQs. Paul Janos and Nancy Robinson wrote a chapter on the psychosocial development of high IQ (120 to 150) children. Janos and Robinson summarized the research to that date and found these results:

1. In *social cognition*, high-IQ (or intellectually gifted) children generally show more maturity than their age peers, but not as much maturity as their intellectual age mates.
2. In *moral development*, as measured by studies using Kohlbergian dilemmas, high-IQ adolescents seem to be advanced over typical high school and college adolescents.
3. In *play interests*, such as choice of books and aesthetic interests, high-IQ children had interests of older children. They also preferred to play with older children. That older children accepted them shows similar intellectual development.
4. In *personality maturity*, which has implications for whether or not to accelerate a gifted child, high-IQ children seemed to be more mature than age mates. However, Janos and Robinson cautioned that "Better means of assessing both the maturity of individual gifted children and the maturity demands of specific academic settings are essential to prescribing appropriate academic environments." (Janos & Robinson, 1985, p. 156)
5. On *psychosocial adjustment*, researchers have been stymied by the confusion of socioeconomic background factors with intelligence factors, and by the relatively rigid standards for adjustment defined on many personality inventories. For example, a child who plays with older children is called maladjusted on some personality inventories. Nevertheless, there has been a repeated finding that high-IQ youth have average or superior psychosocial adjustment.
6. In *locus of control*, or the internalizing or externalizing of motivation to achieve, talented students, no matter the IQ, generally demonstrated inner drive and determination, especially in areas of talent such as music, mathematics, and any areas that require intense study. This inner locus of control generally describes people who are self-sufficient, independent, autonomous, dominant and individualistic, self-directed, and nonconforming. Nonconformity, though, is tempered in high-IQ youths. Janos and

Robinson said, "they typically do conform to reasoned expectations and engage in cooperative relationships" (p. 165). Creative youths—artists, actors, writers—may demonstrate more nonconformity (Piirto, 1991a, 1992a).

7. In *mental energy, enthusiasm,* and *physical vigor,* studies have confirmed that high-IQ also excel, and these contribute to the wide range of interests found in the gifted. They are both more persistent and more aggressive, and this holds true for both females and males. High aspirations are also an aspect of mental energy. High-IQ, academically talented youths like to think, like to be intellectually challenged, and this is often the cause of their complaints of boredom with the regular watered-down school curriculum. For example, an academically talented fourth grade girl showed her folder from her pullout class to a fourth grade classmate. "Oh, that looks boring," said the classmate. "It's too hard." The academically talented girl, said, "No, it's interesting. It makes me think."

8. In *sociability,* academically talented youths seem to be more introverted than the regular population, as demonstrated by studies using the Myers-Briggs Type Indicator (MBTI). National Merit Scholars were found to favor the "I" dimension more than other students. In fact, while 75 percent of all people prefer the "Extroversion" dimension, more intellectual, creative youths seem to prefer the "I" dimension (Myers & McCaulley, 1985). The *Manual* stated, "The three preferences that appear to contribute most to scholastic success are I, N, and J. The types that possess all three of these 'scholastic preferences,' INTF and INFJ, are quite high" (p. 107).

However, Janos and Robinson cautioned that the developmental research was scattered. The ability to concentrate and to focus on intellectual problems seems apparent in academically talented people, although many high-IQ people do not make life achievements that would be called earthshaking or highly influential. Personality traits that differentiate achievers from nonachievers seem to be "sustained intent and concentrated effort," in all fields and domains of effort. Indeed, high-IQ people who do not achieve would seem to not achieve on the basis of personality characteristics rather than on the basis of high IQ. The reverse is true, also. Average-IQ people who achieve have personality characteristics that encourage intent and effort. (See the Pyramid of Talent Development in Chapter 1.)

Need for Guidance and Counseling of Talented Youth

With these generally positive research findings, what need do academically talented and other talented youth have for guidance and counseling? Won't they make it on their own? The need for guidance is crucial; many academically talented youth, especially females and those in rural or lower socioeconomic situations, do not receive the guidance that they need in terms of career planning, college planning, or definitions of options—mentoring, shadowing, course taking. In the parlance of the guidance and counseling profession, *guidance* has to do with specific options that can be planned, such as taking the PSAT in the junior year, and having a proper schedule for one's abilities. *Counseling* has to do with affective aspects of the students' development, often dealt with in group or individual sessions with counselors trained in process. Counseling often resembles therapy, while guidance resembles advising. This section discusses aspects of counseling.

COUNSELING ISSUES AMONG TALENTED YOUTH

What are foci that counselors of the talented should have? There are several ways to go, but issues among gifted youth, as with the rest of young people, have age-related cycles. For younger academically talented students and others, issues of homework and who does it when, school and playground bullying and competition, peer acceptance and friendship all have importance. The high incidence of introversion among gifted youth may also lead to difficulties with their peers. Janos and Robinson (1985) said that this was an area that was underresearched. Others state that academically talented youth have counseling needs in the areas of self-concept, self-esteem, perfectionism, and underachievement.

Counseling issues that have been particularly applicable to academically talented students are several. Among them are anger, boredom, creativity, delinquency, depression, dropping out of school, gender-related issues, issues that come along with having a very high IQ, introversion, intuition, meeting the expectations of others, motivation, overexcitabilities or intensities, peer relations, perfectionism, overachievement, resilience, self-concept/self-esteem, stress, sexual identity, and underachievement. See Figure 11.2.

Figure 11.2 Counseling Issues for Talented Students

Anger (Goleman, 1997; Vail, 1994)

Genuine boredom (Vail, 1994)

Creativity (Piirto, 1992a/1998; Rimm, 1990a)
- Divergent thinking (Lovecky, 1993; Piirto, 1992a/1998)
- Questioning others' long-held values (Myers & Pace, 1986)

Delinquency (Myers & Pace, 1986)

Depression (Delisle, 1992; Jamison, 1993; Kerr, 1992; Myers & Pace, 1986; Piirto, 1992a/1998; Silverman, 1993; Webb, Meckstroth & Tolan, 1982; Wurtzel, 1994)
- Clinical (Jamison, 1993, 1995; Wurtzel, 1994)
- Existential (Kerr, 1992; Webb, Meckstroth, and Tolan, 1982; Silverman, 1993)
- Suicide (Cross, 1996; Delisle, 1992; Myers & Pace, 1986; Webb, Meckstroth & Tolan, 1983)

Dropping out of school (Myers & Pace, 1986)

Gender related issues
- Gifted girls' unique difficulties (Kerr, 1985, 1991, 1997; Orenstein, 1994; Piirto, 1991b; Pipher, 1994; Silverman, 1993)
- Adolescent females' fear of success (Blackburn & Erickson, 1986; Kerr, 1985, 1991, 1997; Pipher, 1994)

Figure 11.2   *Continued*

- Boys' difficulties (Alvino, 1991; Hébert, 1991, 1996; Kline & Short, 1991)
- Developmental immaturity of young academically talented boys (Blackburn & Erickson, 1986)

Very high IQ (Feldman W. Goldsmith, 1986; Gross, 1993; Hollingworth, 1926; Morelock & Feldman, 1991; Silverman, 1993; Tolan, 1992a, 1992b)

Introversion (Myers & McCaullay, 1985; Piechowski, 1990, 1997a; Piechowski, Colangelo, Grant & Walker, 1983; Silverman, 1993)

Intuition (Myers & McCaullay, 1985; Piirto, 1992a/1998)

Meeting the expectations of others (Delisle, 1992; Miller, 1982/1997; Myers & Pace, 1986; Rimm, 1986; Vail, 1994)

- Parental narcissism (Miller, 1982/1997)
- Parental worship (Feldman & Piirto, 1995; Vail, 1994)

Motivation (Webb, Meckstroth & Tolan, 1982)

- Entelechy (charisma, drive) (Lovecky, 1993)

Overexcitabilities (intensities) (Delisle, 1992; Lovecky, 1993; Piechowski, 1979, 1991, 1992, 1997a, 1997b; Silverman, 1993)

- Perceptiveness
- Sensitivity (Lovecky, in Silverman, 1993; Piechowski, 1979, 1992, 1997)

Peer relations (Delisle, 1992; Kerr, 1992; Myers & Pace, 1986; Webb, Meckstroth & Tolan, 1982; Silverman, 1993)

- Relationships of very high-IQ students (Silverman, 1993)
- Intimate relationships (Kerr, 1992)

Perfectionism (Adderholt-Elliott, 1987, 1991; Blackburn & Erickson, 1986; Delisle, 1992; Kerr, 1991; Silverman, 1993; Webb, Meckstroth & Tolan, 1982)

- Experience of failure, or of not succeeding (Blackburn & Erickson, 1986)

Overachievement (Myers & Pace, 1986)

Resilience (Bland, Sowa, & Callahan, 1994; Block & Kremen,1996; Ford, 1994; Hébert, 1996; Jenkins-Friedman, 1992; Terr, 1992)

Self-concept/Self-esteem (Colangelo, 1997; Delisle, 1992; Jenkins-Friedman, 1992; Rimm, 1995, 1996; Rogers, 1992; Silverman, 1993)

Stress (Kerr, 1991; Webb, Meckstroth & Tolan, 1982)

Sexual identity (Friedrichs, 1997; Lind, 1997; Piirto, 1992a/1998)

Underachievement (Blackburn & Erickson, 1986; Colangelo, 1997; Delisle, 1992; Myers & Pace, 1986; Rimm, 1986, 1990a, 1996; Seeley, in Silverman, 1993;

- As a result of learning disabilities (Bireley, 1993; Seeley, in Silverman, 1993)

Space does not permit a long discussion of the issues listed in Figure 11.2, but following is an overview of how counseling is often helpful.

Anger

Anger in talented students happens the same way it does in everyone: the amygdala is highjacked, as Goleman (1997) says. Vail (1994) described the case of a talented boy who finally snapped, smashing glass:

> Ben's class had thirty-two kids and one teacher—a far cry from the seventeen students, a teacher, and an assistant he had before; and because of a budget cut, there was no music teacher. Music had been Ben's favorite subject at his other school. Because the classes were large, Ben's teachers during those three years kept everyone moving in lock step through the curriculum, making it hard for a shy child to make friends. Thoughtful and imaginative, Ben found no outlet for his intellectual or imaginative energies in school, and the rigidity of the scheduling—mixed with the need for quiet in large groups—meant there were few opportunities for the kind of spontaneous enjoyment which leads to friendship. (p. 96)

Suggestions for counseling the angry student include counseling for recognition of what situation brings the anger out, when the instinct overwhelms the rationality. Anger often occurs during the same kinds of challenges. The student becomes aware of this and uses "emotional intelligence" to bring the anger past the prefrontal cortex so he can deal with it.

Genuine Boredom

Boredom in a class is of three types: (1) boredom because one knows the material; (2) boredom because one doesn't know the material; and (3) boredom because one is not interested in the material being talked about. Little in the literature on counseling suggests what the powerless student can do when subjected to (1) repeated drill and practice in material he/she already knows. Excruciating boredom, when time passes so slowly it is as if a giant were dragging its feet down a long corridor, should be recognized. Alternative activities, testing out of a class, and acceleration to a higher level may be suggested as possibilities. Boredom (2) can be remedied by piercing a hole, shedding some light into the material so that the student can penetrate it and begin to understand (for example, the subject of philosophy or of calculus is often impenetrable at first). Boredom (3) can be helped if the teacher is canny, wise, cunning, funny, and theatrical.

Creativity

That being creative would lead to a need for counseling is sad, but true. The student striding down the halls with the spiked hair, the clothes from the thrift shop, five earrings in one ear, her nose pierced, and clutching her copy of Jack Kerouac to her breast, smelling faintly of incense or patchouli perfume, is making a statement. "I'm different. I'm creative." Her grades are all As in her literature course where her favorite teacher reigns. In math, she barely hands in the homework, coasting to graduation on Cs. She had a poem published in a literary journal sponsored by a major university writing program, but her counselor doesn't know that such a publication is different from the typical poetic publications of high school students, vanity anthologies in which the students have to pay to have their work printed and have to pay to get a copy. She needs to learn how not to be so cutting in her withering verbal barbs; people stay away from her because of her sharp tongue, and while she doesn't mean to be unkind or seem superior, she is taken as such by her teachers as well as peers.

The young rock musician languishing in the third period detention hall in his black leathers and his engineer boots spends many a night in the garage working out some new songs with the band for the gigs they play on weekends. Dyslexic, he has not read one book for the past two years. He is smart, though; he can talk his way out of anything, his teachers say, but this time he went too far. He was late again and cut school yesterday. His parents, themselves musicians, have a house full of interesting friends who crash there when travelling through town. They had backstage passes to the concert and didn't get home until five a.m. He's not old enough to drive, and so he had to stay with them while they partied. He needs flexibility in scheduling and intervention for his dyslexia, books on tape, and counseling about the importance of high school graduation in the long run. (For a more in-depth discussion of the issues surrounding creativity, see *Understanding Those Who Create*, Piirto, 1992a/1998).

Delinquency

While there is little literature about the incidence of delinquency among high-IQ students, that is probably an artifact of the way that giftedness is tested and not of the way that giftedness exists. The gang leader who keeps all the accounts of the drug deals he oversees, is he not bright? The confounding of giftedness with goodness is pervasive, as Margolin (1994) pointed out. But the 10 core attributes of giftedness—communication skills, imagination/creativity, humor, inquiry, insight, interests, memory, motivation, problem solving, and reasoning (Frasier et al., 1994)—exist outside the law as well as within it.

Depression

Depression is of several types. A person may experience bipolar disorder (manic-depressiveness), and this seems to be more common among artists, writers, musicians, and other creative people than among people with talents in the sciences and mathematics. Clinical depression not of the bipolar variety also is common among highly intelligent people. The diagnosis of bipolar or monopolar depression is made by medical people and licensed psychologists and not by school counselors, teachers, or parents. Existential depression is depression when one considers the meaning of life and how one fits into it and what one can do about it. Students may go into depression as they become relativists; that is, when they grow and develop into considering other points of view as having value, and when their own family-based values are in question. The Dabrowski theory of positive disintegration calls this type of depression "multilevel," and the emphasis is on "positive," for one cannot grow without questioning.

Although the tragic popularization of famous suicides of talented students has hit the newspapers, Cross (1996a, 1996b) indicated that suicide seems no more prevalent in the talented population than in other populations. In a case study technique he called "psychological autopsy," he found three themes in suicides in talented adolescents: depression, suicide contagion, and overexcitability. Existential depression may become clinical depression, as Elizabeth Wurtzel, a talented young Harvard graduate who experienced chronic depression, described in her book, *Prozac Nation* (1994):

> Sylvia Plath killed herself in 1963, before there were slackers and before there were even hippies. She killed herself because she was depressed, the same as Ernest Hemingway, Vince Foster, and so many anonymous others. No one shoots himself in the head because he's had a bad fishing season or because the Wall Street Journal's editorial page says mean things about him. Depression strikes down deep. The fact that depression seems to be "in the air" right now can be both the cause and result of a level of societal malaise that so many feel. But once someone is a clinical case, once someone is in a hospital bed or in a stretcher headed for the morgue, his story is absolutely and completely his own. (p. 351)

Dropping Out of School

The incidence of dropping out of school affects academically talented students. A study of Hispanic females in Texas showed that many who had been in programs for the gifted and talented dropped out (Lashaway-Bokina, 1997). A study of students in classes for young unwed mothers in Ohio revealed that 10 percent of them had been in programs for the gifted and talented (Salvo, 1992). A review study of American Indian students (Deyhle & Swisher, 1997) indicated percentages of dropouts who were in gifted and talented programs ranging from 35 percent to 69 percent.

The researchers said that intelligence and achievement tests have long portrayed the American Indian, Hispanic, and African-American student as "a deficit being." The use of such terms as "cultural deprivation" to apply to students from other-than-white ethnic groups, and from cultures other than Anglo, has taken its toll on bright students. Demographic factors that contribute to dropping out are "being two or more years behind grade level, being pregnant, coming from a household where the mother or father was not in the home when the youth was 14 years of age, having relatively little knowledge of the labor market, low classroom grades, negative school attitudes, and delinquent behavior in junior high school" (Deyhle & Swisher, p. 126). Students often felt that they had been "pushed out" of school. Were some of these students talented? Undoubtedly.

Gender-Related Issues

Gender differences should be taken into account by counselors. The adolescent passage is particularly risky for both boys and girls. Pipher (1994), in her devastating collection of case studies of young teenage girls, included many artistically and academically talented students in her warning of the risks of eating disorders, self-mutilation, sexual abuse, date abuse, violence, divorce, drugs and alcohol, problems with mothers, problems with fathers, and the like. One of the problems that is pervasive among girls is what Pipher called "lookism," the desire to look like the models in the magazines and on television, and the resultant discontent with one's own body and its own look. Social isolation, while a problem in adolescence, often strengthens. Pipher said:

> Many strong girls have similar stories. They were socially isolated and lonely in adolescence. Smart girls are often the girls most rejected by peers. Their strength is a threat and they are punished for being different. Girls who are unattractive or who don't worry about their

appearance are scorned. This isolation is often a blessing because it allows girls to develop a strong sense of self. Girls who are isolated emerge from adolescence more independent and self-sufficient than girls who have been accepted by others. (p. 266)

The strategies that have been used by strong girls have been to find "protected space." This space can be created by the student's interests, by books, by families, by their churches, by intentional or unintentional physical or social separation. This can be ameliorated by attendance at special summer institutes where our experience has been overwhelming as far as the student's joy in just being together with others like them.

Talented boys also have issues that counseling could help. Among these are emotionality, bonding, mother-son relationships, father-son relationships, perfectionism, sexuality, the success trap, the images in advertising, competition and ego, and others (Alvino, 1991). Alvino said, "The male ego, augmented by an excessive competition and striving characteristic among the gifted, can become a terrible beast of insatiable hunger" (p. 180). Kline and Short (1991) stated that talented high school boys "decide to shut the door on the emotional insecurity of their junior high experience and put a shield over their vulnerability, suppressing their potential for experiencing feelings and having rewarding relationships" (p. 187). Hébert (1991) summarized six issues with which talented boys must deal: (1) how to manage their images; (2) how to deal with the pressure they put upon themselves; (3) how to meet the expectations of their culture for how a "man" should act; (4) being different from other boys; (5) the need for finding and keeping male friends; (6) gender role conflict. Hébert said, "Many talented young men cherish aspects of their personalities which may be considered non-masculine" (p. 209). This applies to young men in the arts, especially, who are often ridiculed for their interests.

Gender Differences in Socialization

Eccles (1985b; Eccles & Harold, 1992) said that socialization of children is a primary factor in gender differences: (1) cultural milieu; (2) gender role stereotypes; (3) cultural stereotypes of the suitability of the subject matter; (4) the occupational characteristics of the occupations one would go into after having taken that subject matter; (5) the socializer's beliefs and behaviors; (6) the differential aptitudes of the child; and (7) previous achievement-related experiences all contribute to the child's interpretation of the experiences. Peers and values are more important than was previously thought.

Girls are often concerned with social goals more than power and achievement goals (Brown & Gilligan, 1992; Higham & Navarre, 1984; Piirto, 1991b). They are more concerned with social relationships than individual achievement and status. Likewise, they are more interested in people than in things. Gender differences in activity interests, personal interests, and range of interests have surfaced among talented children and youth. Role models are extremely important, especially in the home. For example, who helps with math homework is crucial. Usually it is the father, and this gives the message that men know more than women about math (Navarre, 1979). Who interprets the child's experience? Usually it is the mother. Researchers (Eccles, 1985b; Higham & Navarre, 1984; Kerr, 1985, 1997) also found that the reinforcers for boys and girls are different, and so were the providers of experience; games and toys and special educational experiences were more likely to be provided for boys.

Parents want their daughters to be "happy" and their boys to be achievers in the professions. Mothers are often likely to tell their daughters, "I wasn't any good at mathematics either," and their sons, "Well, you have the math ability; you just didn't work hard enough." When a child hears these messages, the messages have bearing on how difficult courses are perceived. The child's self-concept about ability to do work in hard courses is affected by these messages. The boys think, "Oh, if I work harder, I'll get an A in calculus." The girls think, "I worked so hard in trigonometry and I only got a C. Why should I take calculus and ruin my grade point average?" As a result, the course-taking behavior suffers, and thus the final achievement in such measures as the National Merit Scholarship Program mentioned above.

Female Underachievement

There are also gender differences in underachievement. Colangelo (1990) reported that a large-scale study of underachieving students who had scored above 28 on the ACT and who had grade point averages below 2.0 showed that the majority were white, middle-class or upper middle-class males. Of females who had scored 28 and who had grade point averages that would indicate underachievement, the grade point averages were between 2.0 and 3.0—that is, the females kept their GPAs within respectable limits while the boys seemed to be openly rebellious, didn't hand in papers, didn't do homework, and didn't study for tests while still retaining the information required to score so high on the ACT.

Females underachieve in different ways than males. A 1990 followup study by George and Caroline Vaillant of forty Terman females (mean age 77 years) found that their underachievement came after high school when they married and had children. The most creative and productive had the least numbers of children: of the 30 women who were occupationally the most achieving, only five had become mothers, and the whole group had only seven children. The Vaillants said, "For these women, successful career and childrearing were negatively correlated" (p. 611). Studies like this lead to the conclusion that academically talented girls are lost to underachievement during and after college when their need for intimacy and connection overpowers their need for achievement (Piirto, 1991a, 1992c).

Researchers (Benbow, 1992; Subotnik & Arnold, 1996) have begun to research this perplexing problem. Why do females, who have achieved high grades in high school, and who have entered college as math/science majors (this is particularly the case with these females), drop out of math/science majors, switch to other majors, and sometimes even drop out of the achievement stream (e.g., not go to graduate school, not pursue the Ph.D.)? Some tentative answers were forthcoming in Benbow's 1992 paper. The math/science females were often identified with their fathers: "Perhaps most interesting was that the career choices of these exceptional females often corresponded to their father's career field. That is, these extremely mathematically talented females were following in their father's footsteps" (Benbow, 1992, p. 115). A further conclusion was that mentioned above: that females dropped out as a result of the quality of their junior high school and senior high school academic experiences. Arnold (1993) suggested that the young women do not absorb the tacit knowledge, the practical knowledge that is necessary for building a career; they do not understand or cannot break into the informal networks of connections and acquaintances, of mentors and mentees, that are necessary in building any career.

Still, most students who are targeted in school for special intervention for underachievement are boys, just as most students who are in special education programs are boys. Girls often achieve well enough not to be noticed as underachievers; their underachievement comes in course selection and in getting the gentlewoman's low B instead of the rebellious gentleman's low C. Much insight has been shed on the issue through the essays in *Remarkable Women: Perspectives on Female Talent Development* (Arnold, Noble & Subotnik, 1996).

The Importance of Tacit Knowledge

How does a talented student proceed in a career? Taking the courses is not enough. Tacit knowledge, an aspect of Sternberg's triarchic theory of intelligence (Sternberg, 1985), is necessary. What does one do besides take courses and get good grades, in order to position oneself for success in a career? Tacit knowledge is cognizance of what one must do in order to proceed. This knowledge is often imparted casually, if at all, during a student's life. Sometimes this knowledge is conveyed over what came to be called "the old boys' network," at the golf course, in the private men's club or fraternity, and the talented female might not know what she should do. Arnold (1993) said that while girls and women perceive themselves as good students, they have difficulty in "imagining their career ends." In her study of Illinois valedictorians, Arnold said, "Not only do they have difficulty imagining exactly how career and family will be combined but vocational ends themselves are unclear" (p. 23). Arnold said:

> A major reason many women find it difficult to develop the base of untaught practical knowledge for envisioning, planning, and implementing high level careers is a lack of support, mentorship, and significant interaction with faculty. The most successful women in the valedictorian study were unusual in receiving special opportunities and attention from faculty. Most of the study women did not become close to any faculty person. (p. 25)

Group and individual counseling, and the enlisting of faculty mentors for talented young women, is especially important in late high school and in late college years. One young woman quoted by Arnold said of her high school counselors and teachers, who didn't dissuade her from dropping out of honors mathematics:

> I'm not exactly sure why I dropped out of the honors math program. Part of it was my own fault. But I wished someone had counseled me to really stick it out. I think I would have liked a little more encouragement. For someone to say, "You can do it, Pam." My counselors seemed to accept it as perfectly natural that I would drop out of the math program and not take advanced biology. I think if I'd taken advanced biology in high school I would have realized how interesting I'd find it. (Arnold, p. 26)

Academically Talented Girls and Teen Pregnancy

While many think that academically talented or other talented teenage and young adult girls are virginal and pure, studying hard and achieving, the truth is more mundane. Academically talented young women are just as interested in the opposite sex as are most young women. This leaves them as vulnerable as all young women to the gender issue of teen pregnancy. Sex education is a vital component of any guidance program for academically talented youth. Of course the very title of this section is sexist; that is, isn't an unwanted pregnancy the responsibility of the father as well, whether or not he is gifted and talented?

Very High IQ

Tolan (1992b) noted that parents and theorists/researchers often have conflicting views. Parents of children with high IQs notice more. They notice the pain and the emotion with which the high-IQ child must cope when true intellectual peers are few and understanding is far away. Hollingworth (1926, 1942) noted that students with high IQs have more difficulty in social adjustment than students with less extreme IQs. Tolan called to account theorists who "consciously set out to destroy the concept of the IQ" and thus may have created a situation where the highly academically talented (IQs above 145) no longer exist: "If the definition of this population includes an IQ score, and if IQ scores are no longer valid, does the population disappear?" Tolan asked (p. 14).

She said that these children do, indeed, exist: "There are symptoms." Their extreme precociousness does not smooth out. Parents "see the extremely negative effects of the failure to meet their intense intellectual needs" (p. 14). Tolan said that these children have been called statistically insignificant; that is, their occurrence is too rare for schools and institutions to consider serving them. Tolan said, "Our children are suffering intellectual malnourishment. It is not as obvious as starvation but it is just as real" (p. 18). Gross (1993, 1998) agreed. In her detailed descriptions of the characteristics of high-IQ students in Australia, she asserted that even though they are few in number, they are great in impact on our society.

In Tolan's view, the intellectual malnourishment causes the social and emotional difficulties of many high-IQ students. For example, many have been called hyperactive, needing little sleep. Tolan said that when her own high-IQ son was experiencing an appropriate and challenging education, he would be very tired; the mental activity was necessary for sleep, and if he had not been mentally challenged during the day, he would seek mental challenge all night long, before being able to sleep. "Working the brain is just as, or more tiring than, working the body," she said. (Stephanie Tolan, personal communication, 1992). In trying to provide for academically talented students' needs, counselors should not overlook the intellectual needs of high-IQ students. These students, like handicapped students, didn't ask to be born this way. Morelock and Feldman (1991) said: "It may be, however, that the higher the IQ, the more the benefits are counterbalanced by social adjustment problems imposed by such capacity" (p. 350).

Introversion

Introversion is defined as the tendency to direct one's thoughts and interests inward. On the Myers-Briggs Type Indicator (MBTI), the opposite pole of Introversion is Extroversion, the tendency to direct and to receive strength from the outside world. Only 25 percent of all people are Introverts, but most academically talented students are (Myers & McCaulley, 1985). Silverman (1993) pointed out that the introverts may not be popular during their school years, but that they often "gain prestigious positions at universities and research institutes, they are valued for their knowledge and skills, and they have excellent opportunities to rise to positions of leadership through scholarly efforts and creative contributions to their fields" (p. 25).

Being an introvert in an extroverted world is often painful. Introversion is thought to be genetic, much as the temperaments of being Inhibited/Uninhibited (Kagan, 1995). Sometimes painfully shy, other times willfully arrogant, introverted and talented students may not respond well to counseling. Long pauses may be a feature of counseling sessions. As counselors are often extroverted, this may prove uncomfortable. Myers and McCaulley (1985) said, "Introverts are more likely to look to themselves first for causes of difficulties. They are more intrapunitive than extrapunitive. The counselor may need to focus their attention on the fact that some problems have their source in the environment" (p. 68).The counselor may also want to quote Simonton: "The gregarious who fritter their time away at cocktail parties, social outings, and family get-togethers are less likely to leave enduring impressions on posterity. At death their mouths are silenced forever, while the voices of deceased introverts speak on" (1994, p. 269).

Intuition

Intuition is a way of knowing without using rational processes: "you just know, man," as one of my students said. Intuition involves insight, quick cognition, an ability to penetrate to the truth of a situation. Again, many if not most academically and creatively talented students prefer intuition as a way of seeing the world. Why is having a personality preference of intuition a concern for counseling? Intuitive students may present the problem of not relating to their sensing (S) teachers, as most teachers prefer Sensing (Piirto, Gantz, Ramsay, Steele, Tabacca, and Fraas, 1997a; Piirto, 1998). Most teachers prefer Extroversion, Sensing, Feeling, Judging (ESFJ). Only about eight percent of elementary teachers are NT personality types, the personality types that many academically talented students prefer. As students get into the higher grades and into college, they find more teachers with the same personality preferences, as most N teachers gravitate toward higher education (Keirsey, 1978). Counselors should not be afraid to use metaphor and symbolic discourse with N students, as they respond to such abstractions. As Intuitive students are often quite independent in thinking, helping them to find their own solutions instead of dictating to them works better. Also, Intuitive students often need help in getting organized, as they often underestimate the time it takes to get a task done (an assignment due, a college application in).

Meeting the Expectations of Others

Since academically talented students are often as "good" as they are mythologized to be; that is, they perceive the expectations their teachers and parents have, and they strive conscientiously to meet them, they are often vulnerable to their empathy. Alice Miller's book, *The Drama of the Gifted Child*, about the psychology of the middle-class parent who lives out his/her own dreams and wishes through the child, has hit a worldwide chord so much so that it has been reprinted seven times and in 21 languages since its appearance in 1982. The experience of having been victimized by parental narcissism often calcifies the talented child. Counseling may not be enough; therapy might be necessary.

Many family systems operate on what has been called a dysfunctional level, and these interactions, too, have enhanced talent development. Alice Miller (1990, 1997) theorized that creative adults became creative from family environments of trauma where warmth was present. The trauma may include what Simonton (1984, 1988) called "the orphanhood effect," where a parent may die or be absent. Other traumas that tear apart the traditionally intact family system are divorce, illness, frequent moving, physical, verbal, and sexual abuse, and the like. Talented youths who become scientists, mathematicians, and classical musicians seem to have come from families that were more stable than the families of actors, writers, popular musicians, visual artists, and dancers—people in the arts (Piirto, 1992a, 1992b, 1992c, 1994a, 1992b). Perhaps the long schooling necessary for functioning as an adult scientist, mathematician, or musician is a result of a family striving together to develop the potential of a talented child. The fact that many talented adults came from family situations that were less than ideal illustrates that even the most laissez-faire parenting (or absence thereof) has an impact on talent development.

Two interesting phenomena are operant. One is the "stage mother" or "Little League father" situation, in which the parent is obsessed, even to the point of destructive narcissism, with the development of a child's talent, whether or not the child wants to have his or her talent developed. The other is the "I don't care what you do just so long as you're happy" situation, where busy parents do what is necessary for safety and health, but little beyond that. Both situations can produce talented adults. Judy Garland is an example of the former; her mother was so obsessed with Judy's career as a child actress that she even permitted the use of amphetamines and tranquilizers so that Judy could work longer hours in the studio. An example of the latter is the mother of the actor and comedian Steve Allen, who permitted him to move, alone, from Chicago to the southwest at the age of 16 in order to take a job as a radio announcer. Other parents move with their children to pursue the talent. The mother of the dancer Suzanne Farrell moved Suzanne and her two sisters from Cincinnati to New York City at the offer of an audition with Balanchine, and they lived in one room there while their mother was a private nurse (Farrell, w. Bentley, 1990; Feldman & Piirto, 1995; Vail, 1994).

Talented students may also be torn because of the pressure of certain teachers. Often music, theater, and athletic coaches develop strong relationships with their talented students, and may be in danger of overwhelming them in the desire to develop their talents. Perhaps the coaches and teachers see their young selves in these students. For example, see this phenomenon in the films *Madame Sousatska* and *Mr. Holland's Opus.*

Motivation

Problems of motivation are many. Too much, too little, too outer, too inner are all motivational concerns. Can a student have too much motivation? When health suffers, yes. When relationships with key people in one's life suffer, yes. Too little motivation also needs examining in terms of underachievement. If a student is motivated by external forces only (extrinsic motivation), motivation is said to die when the external forces are removed, though behaviorist theory often advocated using external rewards to motivate students to complete tasks. Internal motivation (intrinsic motivation) is said to be the most useful for achievement; that is, if a student can transfer the external to the internal, he/she is likely to stay on the task. Motivation theory was simplistic once but now it is complicated. We also have to take into account the presence of learned helplessness, where students may not produce without dependence on others, and the presence of internal and external locus of control (see Chapter 12 for a discussion of locus of control in talented minority children in San Diego). Many of the personality attributes in the base of the Pyramid of Talent Development have relationship to motivation: these are discipline, persistence, and the like. One is said to go into a state of "flow" while creating and this state is itself motivating; that is, one wants to come back to it again and again (Csikszentmihalyi, 1991).

Two Greek terms have surfaced in this discussion. Lovecky's (1993) use of the complicated word "entelechy" and Hillman's (1996) use of the word "daimon" also speak to the construct of motivation and the talented. Lovecky contends that the talented individual possesses entelechy; that is, "a vital force urging an individual toward engagement." Hillman offers that the person is motivated by the daimon, which is the tiny acorn of talent born in seed that has the potential to grow into a mighty oak of talent realized. All these should be the focus of some understanding on the parts of those who counsel the talented.

Overexcitabilities: The Dabrowski Theory and Emotional Intensity

A particularly useful theory for understanding how gifted and talented youth cope with what their lives bring along is the Dabrowski theory of emotional development. Dabrowski (1964, 1967, 1972; Dabrowski & Piechowski, 1977), according to his major translator, Michael Piechowski (1975, 1979, 1989, 1991, 1992, 1997a), did not view the intellectually and artistically gifted as maladjusted; rather he saw their intensities in their areas of talent as a higher form of adjustment on a continuum of levels of adjustment. "To varying degrees, these five dimensions give talent its power," said Piechowski (1997a, p. 366).

There are five types of primary intensities, or as they are called in the Dabrowski theory, "overexcitabilities." Piechowski (1991, p. 287) described them this way:

Psychomotor overexcitability—an augmented capacity for being active and energetic, expressed as movement, restlessness, drivenness
Sensual overexcitability—an enhanced differentiation and aliveness of sensual experience
Intellectual overexcitability—avidity for knowledge and the search for truth, expressed as discovery, questioning and love of ideas and theoretical analysis

Imaginational overexcitability—the power of thought creation, expressed through vividness of imagery, richness of association, liking for the unusual, and a facility for dreams, fantasies, and inventions

Emotional overexcitability—the heart, recognized in the great depth and intensity of emotional life expressed through a wide range of feelings, attachments, compassion, heightened sense of resonsibility, and scrupulous self-examination

These intensities, called *overexcitabilities,* provoke both relief and recognition from gifted people and the parents of gifted children who learn about the theory. "I'm not weird, after all" or "I'm not crazy, after all" is a common reaction. Piechowski (1991) said that the "stronger these overexcitabilities are, the less welcome they are among peers and teachers (unless they, too, are gifted)" (p. 287). Children who experience life with such intensity are often made to feel weird, strange, different, and embarrassed. They often learn to squelch their reactions before they are squelched by their peers, their teachers, and even, sometimes, their parents. Their abilities for feeling and for expression thus are quenched, as flames drowned by water or snuffers.

Examples of overexcitabilities present in gifted people often surface when people respond to life. An intellectually gifted teenage boy who wants to be a writer, and who is an avid reader, often reads novels in taking breaks from his homework. When he reads he interacts intensely with the written word, often talking with the characters in the book. Beautiful language gets his mind going. He admires Edgar Allen Poe, and often reads a poem and gets inspired. When he does his homework, which is often boring, he will "zip back and forth" between the books he is reading for pleasure and his homework. When he is writing a story, he will go out to the woods and imagine that he is the character he is writing about (Piirto, 1990b).

Such intense reactions to the world are often uncovered by the use of the Overexcitability Questionnaire (Piechowski & Cunningham, 1985). In one study of adolescents who attended a summer institute, examples of the various types of overexcitability showed through the use of the Overexcitability Questionnaire (OEQs) (Piirto, 1992b). Such questions as "Are you poetically inclined?"; "What kinds of things get your mind going?"; "Do you ever think about your own thinking?"; "Does tasting something mean anything to you?" are examples. A qualitative analysis of 100 questionnaires written in 1989, 1991, and 1995 showed at least five themes in the emotional life of these talented adolescents: hypersensitivity, god, life in other forms, performing, and challenging self and others (Flint et al., 1997). The hypersensitivity was described as "hyperness" by one of the students: "My heartbeat increases, even if I am only intellectually excited. I get very talkative and I gesture a lot."

Of God, one student wrote:

I feel that my most intense pleasure has been brought upon me when I go to a creek with waterfalls and hike around in nature alone or with my closest friend. It gives me a feeling of God and purity and purpose. I love God very much. He has a lot of meaning for me and gives me my most intense pleasure of purity. I even dream of God and heaven. I like to talk deeply with my best friend about God.

A response to and a belief in life in other forms is animistic thinking common to imaginational overexcitability. One student said, "I think everything on the earth is made of energy, and energy is a living thing. Not only nature but thoughts and feelings too." In response to one of the questions about whether or not other things have a life of their own, another student said, "Yes! Yes! Yes! Yes! Yes! I'm always watching out for things. Sometimes I talk to them so they know I care. I know what they're like and how they live."

The love of performing came out in this population, as one of the main themes for two years was musical theater. This is what one student said:

> When I am on stage I feel as if I'm soaring on a cloud with the angels singing beside me. Performing is absolutely my first love. The magic of the theater always seeps into my soul and grasps control of it. When I am acting, I am as happy, or happier, as any person can be.

One young athlete wrote of the joy of competition:

> When the competition is high and I know I can take over the whole scene I use the energy to excel and raise my play up a notch. It is a feeling of freedom and an incredible high. It is a true freedom that unfortunately not everyone can feel. It is to be a winner.

In another theme in this study, the students seemed to thrive on challenge. One student wrote:

> I love to argue. It is almost the only thing that keeps me going in school, challenging my teachers or fellow students. I argue with myself about moral issues, social issues, how I should handle situations, etc. The only problem is that I can often find equally good arguments for both sides. I mentally plan out arguments with other people all the time. Usually the purpose of these arguments is not to prove that I am right or the other person is wrong, but to effectively present another side to think about. I become infuriated easily by people who will not accept anything other than their own ideas or who judge people by whether they have the "right" or the "wrong" answer.

Piechowski's concept of emotional giftedness is similar to what Gardner calls interpersonal and intrapersonal intelligence, but Piechowski noted that Gardner did not delineate the developmental process: "By what developmental process is the mature self realized? What has to take place in a person's development to make gaining advanced self-knowledge and wisdom possible?" (Piechowski, 1997a, p. 370). Few have even called emotional intensity an aspect of giftedness, but such high psychosocial talent is surely among the most valuable of talents. Piechowski (1998) posited the existence of spiritual giftedness, "inner potentials for profound empathy, spiritual awareness, transcendence of emotionally annihilating childhoods, and experience of non-ordinary realities.

Peer Relations

Students who are talented often have difficulty in peer relationships; so do most other students. At a young age, the difficulty may be in finding someone to talk with; students are often amazed at young ages that the other students don't know as much as they. That difficulty may continue through adolescence and into adulthood, but again, it is not known whether this is a function of intelligence or of human nature. Certainly the higher the IQ, the more difficult it is to find intellectual peers as has been already stated. But recent forays into the world of emotional intelligence

(Goleman, 1997) have indicated that the ability to relate to people often takes skills that can be acquired through practice. Contention and difficulty in relationships are not only a function of intelligence or creativity. Several different peer groups may be necessary for such children, just as they are often necessary for adults.

Perfectionism and the Talented

A related counseling issue for both the academically talented student and the student with talent in music, dance, or other domains is their perfectionism. Perfectionism as a psychological difficulty is the presence of a compulsive need to achieve and to be the best in work. By-products of perfectionism can be eating difficulties; paralysis that causes the academically talented student to not even try if not being assured of being rated the best; and timidity. This is called *disabling perfectionism*.

However, a perfectionistic spirit can guide true excellence as well, as the person pays attention to details and to quality in products. The writer will revise his work over and over again, honing and shaping it with a sense of perfectionism until each word and its placement is "perfect." This is a seeking for excellence, *enabling perfectionism*. The short story writer Raymond Carver (1983) said he gleefully awaited each successive draft of his stories from his typist as he revised and revised until the works were as finished as he could make them. Another example is that of the musician who practices the same piece over and over again, paying attention to all the effects, to the dynamics, to the relative weights of eighth and sixteenth notes, in order to prepare a piece for performance. Still another example of enabling perfectionism that leads to excellence in quality is the theater director who rehearses the cast and the play those extra times after the book is put away, shaping and polishing the performance for innuendo of gesture and line.

But perfectionism can also be disabling. A common example of this is the "all but dissertation" (A.B.D.) Ph.D. candidate who spends years on the dissertation, finding more and more references and resources, who is ultimately unable to finish the work, to put it down on paper and complete the degree. The sense of perfectionism that leads to paralysis, to fear, to not even trying because one won't meet one's own standards, is easy to fall into. Academically talented students often set unrealistically high standards for themselves and are unable to forgive themselves if they don't meet those standards. Their self-esteem, while it may seem high, is hooked on accomplishments, the end results, and not on the process of doing the work itself.

This has often been called *external locus of control*, or *extrinsic motivation*, and when perfectionism is disabling, the person is often found to depend on what others say about the work for the pleasure derived from doing the work. How many 4.0 averages, how many gold stars, how many all-As, how many monetary rewards, how many articles in the hometown paper, can the honor student accrue? This becomes the goal and not the by-product of achieving the goal—the finely honed short story, the wonderfully played piece of music, the ensemble theater production that reaches the sublime.

Miriam Adderholt-Elliott has written extensively about perfectionism in her 1987 book, *Perfectionism*. In 1991, in a chapter in *Understanding the Gifted Adolescent*, she wrote that talented adolescents are often at risk for disabling perfectionism because of their strong self-monitoring. She cited seven reasons for perfectionism that may turn out to have negative consequences. These were as follows: (1) birth order (firstborn and only children seem to become more perfectionistic because they learned early to measure their accomplishments against the accomplishments of adults); (2) perfectionistic parents; (3) media influence (watching perfect people on television who solve their problems in less than 30 minutes); (4) pressure from teachers and peers (when perfectionists are brought together, being perfect becomes normal); (5) developmental dysplasia (having disparate mental ages and chronological ages forces undue pressure on children too socially and emotionally young to realize this pressure is unnecessary); (6) "hothousing" or "hurrying" children, in Elkind's terms (1991), which places children at risk for self-doubt and stress; and (7) dysfunctional families (not having control over one's home life leads to an attempt to control one's school and work life).

Adderholt-Elliott also described how perfectionists think. They often experience mood swings; for example, if a child tries out for a play, and her self-esteem is tied to attaining the lead but she "only" gets the second lead, she will feel deflated and disappointed, instead of being happy that she got an important part. One B+ on an all A report card can also produce a black mood, as can one negative work evaluation among many positive ones. Perfectionists often rely on quantity to achieve a feeling of accomplishment. Ten awards is better than one award; Who's Who Among High School Students, National Merit Scholar, President of the Student Council, President of the Band, *and* President of the Sorority is better than being just one of these and doing the job well.

After perfectionists meet a goal, they view the goal as insignificant, Adderholt-Elliott noted. She called this "telescopic thinking" (p. 68). They also remember past failures in explicit detail: a spelling word missed in second grade, or a comment made by a singing teacher in fourth grade. A final way that perfectionists think is that they often put their work ahead of their family, their health, or their friends, and their work becomes paramount. Workaholism is common among perfectionists, and they often measure their worth in the extrinsic rewards the job provides instead of in the intrinsic joys of family life or life among friends.

Because of this valuing of extrinsic reward, Adderholt-Elliott said that perfectionists are often motivated by "all or nothing" thinking (1991, p. 69), which is that they believe that there is either success or there is failure, and there is nothing in between. There is no such thing as a little bit of success or a little bit of failure. A person is either a complete success or a complete failure. This mammoth gap often causes perfectionists to procrastinate. Because they might fail, and there is no such thing as a little bit of failure, perfectionists put off even trying. Then when they do the project at the last minute, they excuse the quality of the project, saying that if they had had more time, they would have done a better job.

Their work is governed by their fear of failure, and so they take the safe road, the road that has led in the past to good grades, to praise, to success. The perfectionist also begins to judge others by her own standards for herself, and people in her circle often feel they are less than adequate because the perfectionist judges them as they judge themselves. A woman told of fearfully changing her children's outfits three or four times before visiting her mother-in-law because her mother-in-law, who had a perfect house, a perfect yard, a perfect husband, and who was perfect herself, scrutinized the babies by how well their shoes were polished and their shirts tucked in, pronouncing the children "cute" if they were unmussed. Likewise, the academically talented child who is a perfectionist may judge friends by his own standards for himself and since he cannot ever meet his own standards, his friends cannot meet his standards either.

What are the consequences of perfectionism, and how can an educator or counselor help the perfectionist whose perfectionism has turned negative? Delisle (1982) warned that perfectionism may be a cause of teenage suicide. When a young academically talented person reaches the point of despair of ever being good enough, of ever reaching his own standards for himself, he may decide to end it all. Another consequence may be eating disorders. These are common in academically talented youth who are interested in fields where their looks matter, such as dance, entertainment, and athletics. In order to attain the ideal, the "perfect" body, the youth may abuse that body by refusing to eat, by bulimic behavior, by using steroids. Obsessive-compulsive behavior disorders may also be caused by perfectionism. Constant hand-washing, house-cleaning, mess-straightening, are examples. Of course, underachievement, which will be discussed in detail later in this chapter, is often caused by perfectionism.

What can the educator or counselor do to help the child who is overly concerned about perfection? Adderholt-Elliott suggested relaxation therapy, reality therapy, group counseling, self-talk, and the use of mental imagery. Rimm (1986) suggested that placing students in situations where they can successfully fail—for example, the second lead in the play, the second chair in the band, the second place in the academic challenge contest—is good for them. When a child sees that people still regard her as successful even though she hasn't won everything, and when she sees this over time, from very early on, the chances of her being constantly so hard on herself will lessen, and she will be able to see that she's better in some things than in others, and that what matters is the process of doing the activity, and not the achievement of being tops in everything.

The counselor's door is always open.

Again, the confusion between perfectionism and excellence should be pointed out; paying attention to the quality of one's work and seeking to produce the best quality is excellence. Letting go of the job, and putting it into the hands of the audience, the judge, the teacher, the critic, is healthy. Paying attention to the quality of one's work and being paralyzed in doing it because it just may not be good enough, and then putting it together at the last minute so that one will have an excuse if the work is judged lacking, is not healthy.

For example, most or all writers have experienced rejection of manuscripts submitted to potential publishers. The perfectionist whose behavior is troubled will not submit himself again and again to the potential rejection letter that will arrive regularly in the mail. This writer will hide his writing, will fill up drawers with unsent, untried manuscripts, and will eventually stop writing. The perfectionist whose behavior is healthy will note which manuscripts receive a few positive comments, will revise or not depending on whether or not she thinks the manuscript needs it, and will continue to attempt to be published, writing all the while. Both are perfectionists, seeking to improve their work, but the unhealthy perfectionist cares so much about extrinsic reward, publication, that the writing stops when the publication is difficult.

Overachievement

The inclusion of this as a counseling issue is just to ask the question: what is overachievement? How can a person achieve more than they can achieve? I think the roots of this as a presented counseling issue in the literature of talent development have to do with the anti-intellectualism of our culture. The attention to mediocrity, to fitting in, to getting by, to not rocking the boat, all feed into the concept of overachievement. The talented student is called an overachiever. That means that he or she should let up a little, should fit in a little, should not have such high standards for herself or himself, should realize that others feel inferior when they see her work and what she has accomplished. If a person can write 10 books and his graduate student friend writes one, who is the overachiever? The high achiever "raises the curve." Of course, concomitant problems follow: ostracism, jealousy, and shunning, becoming a "teacher's pet," and the like. This appears to be a term with a relative meaning; what is overachievement to one peer group may not be to another. And this also seems to be a situation that concerns athletic, minority, and rural poor children more than others.

Resiliency and Its Relationship to Achievement

Resiliency has been studied at the University of Minnesota in Project Competence since the early 1960s by Garmezy and his colleagues (Garmezy & Tellegen, 1984). Those who were resilient were able to communicate their wants and needs; they were able to suppress their impulsivity; their were able to think and reflect about the meaning of their experiences; and they believed they could have some control over their surroundings. Jenkins-Friedman and Tollefson (1992) have constructed a model of resiliency that may explain why some students continue to achieve and some do not. Among disadvantaged children, there continue to be certain children who achieve despite having two strikes against them (e.g. lack of support from home, lack of support in school). These children often have remarkable self-esteem, which is called "resiliency." No matter how far they are down, they seem to have nonintellective characteristics that help them rise to the challenge and to achieve. These are "a mastery orientation, a strong sense of self-efficacy and of optimism, a sense of empowerment, and an attribution orientation characterized by internal, unstable, controllable and intentional explanations for outcomes" (p. 326). These resilient children often have strong maternal influence; their mothers were more optimistic than pessimistic, and the children followed suit. Their mothers also "were both steadily and gainfully employed," even though poor. These resilient children also had belief in themselves that they could prevail, despite the social system or the school environment. Bandura (1986) called this a sense of *self-efficacy*.

Resilient children also attributed their successes to ability rather than luck, and thus they would try again and again, because they knew they had the ability, and they therefore did not attribute failure to succeed to the level they expected to external circumstances such as bad luck. Jenkins-Friedman and Tollefson said that "attribution of an outcome to a stable factor, such as ability, increases expectancy of success after success and decreases expectancy of success after failure, more than does an attribution to effort or luck" (p. 328). Resilient children, in other words, did not show *learned helplessness*, the "poor me" syndrome therapists make people punch pillows about, the dependency fostered by many educational practices. The remarkable triumphs of poor children in such fields as the arts and athletics shows that resiliency is a major factor in the realization of gifted potential when the rest of the world looks away. The counselor and teacher can be major factors in the realization of this potential.

For example, one of my students did a case study of a classical musician/composer. Unlike most classical musicians and composers, this man did not have the support of his family. He had to beg his family for a piano when he was five. His father, who ran a hunting and fishing store, and his mother, a waitress, wanted him to be athletic. He hated athletics. They bought him a beat-up piano and then took it away when he was eight. He had to practice at friends' homes. It was teachers who saw his talent and helped him along. One teacher got him a scholarship to a renowned residential arts academy; another teacher got him a regular touring spot with the American Wind Symphony; another teacher got him an audition with a world-class teacher and that teacher got him a scholarship to a prestigious conservatory where he completed his college degree. He finally disowned his parents, who had broken contact with him because of his homosexuality; his resilience was nurtured by teachers and friends.

A study of childhood trauma by Terr (1990), of the children whose bus was kidnapped in Chowchilla, California, in 1976, showed that repeated exposure to trauma, both real and vicarious, induces a "toughening process" in children (p. 318). Terr believed that traumatic experiences are part of most children's lives, and "most children do not end up traumatized" (p. 318), but carry relatively few postraumatic symptoms into adulthood. However, many artists were traumatized as children, survived, and use their artistic expression as a form of resilience, of auto-therapy. Perhaps the intensity, the presence of overexcitability in imagination, emotion, intellect, or sensation, in the sensitive child magnified the trauma.

The context in which the trauma occurred also encourages resilience. For young children, context, or perspective, is difficult to achieve. Terr said, "Many of us store memories that, if we could uncover them, visualize them, and compare them to what we now know as adults, we could beat. We could lick those horrible memories because of our adult perspective" (p. 336). Resilience also can be encouraged by treatment: trauma "burrows down further and further under the child's defenses and coping strategies," and the child may suppress, displace, overgeneralize, identify with the aggressor, split, or self-anesthetize. "But if the trauma had been effectively treated, the genius probably would have produced a more universal, more versatile kind of art" (Terr, 1990, p. 291). Terr explicated the works of Stephen King, Alfred Hitchcock, and Edgar Allen Poe, who were traumatized children, showing the results of the trauma in their unique accounts of horror.

Resilience in women was discussed by Noble (1996). She credited Kerr (1985) with first pointing out the situation of multipotentiality and the need for support even if one is "gifted." Noble said that women must not only cultivate the personality attributes necessary for resiliency, they must form a community among themselves, and nurture each other as they have always nurtured men.

Resilience in minority youth was discussed by Ford (1996) and Hébert (1996). Ford pointed out that the resilient Black student has "an inner locus of control, a positive sense of self, and feelings of empowerment. They are often bicultural and may "don a facade of racelessness and believe in the American dream" (p. 82). Hébert (1996) noted the positive personalities of resilient youth in his study of three Latino teenagers. He also pointed to the inner locus of control and the intrinsic motivation that seem key. The self-image of these youths permits them to see themselves as winners, and as successes due to their own efforts and their own choices. The presence of a family that encourages and supports, as well as the presence of mentors and other community people who are encouraging, is also important. They are often involved in extracurricular activities and in athletics. In these activities they formed a group of peers who had the same goals and with whom they could bond.

Self-Concept/Self-Esteem

Common counseling issues that are addressed with academically talented students are several: among them is the issue of self-concept. Reva Jenkins-Friedman in 1992 noted that there is confusion about the self-concept of academically talented students. She said that the difficulty comes from how researchers "operationalize" self-concept. Self-concept is defined as "a set of self-expectations and anticipations" (p. 1). The term is often used interchangeably with other terms such as "self-esteem," "efficacy," "instrumentality," and "competence." In fact, psychologists have separated self-concept into several types: people have physical self-concepts, academic self-concepts, social self-concepts.

Academically talented students generally have high academic self-concepts and lower social self-concepts and physical self-concepts (Brounstein, Holahan & Dreyden, 1991). Athletes generally have high physical self-concepts and lower academic self-concepts. Student leaders generally have high social self-concepts and lower academic and physical self-concepts. Janos, Fung, and Robinson (1985) found that academically talented students who had problems in adjustment often had lower social self-concepts. Cornell (1990) found that academically talented students who were unpopular also had lower social self-concepts.

Janos, Fung, and Robinson (1985) noted that while most academically talented youth experience no self-concept difficulties, a minority of academically talented youth do. This is particularly evident in those who have very high IQs, within the third and fourth standard deviation above the mean. These children constantly experience their difference from others, even from other people called academically talented.

Self-Esteem and the Academically Talented

The trendy programs for enhancing self-esteem that are rife in the schools are pervasive reminders of the "me" 1980s and the "feel-good" 1970s, and students who have been identified as academically talented are also subject to concerns about their self-esteem. Critics of such programs argue that true self-esteem comes from accomplishing something difficult, and point out research that shows that students in the United States have the highest self-esteem and low actual achievement, that is, they feel very good about their achievement even though they do not score very well on comparative measures administered across cultures. U.S. students have higher self-esteem than Japan, Taiwan, and China, even though their actual performance is much lower. A 1992 cover story in *Newsweek* (Adler et al., 1992) pointed out that over 10,000 studies of self-esteem have been conducted, using over 200 different tests, despite the fact that, as Jenkins-Friedman pointed out, the definition of self-esteem is unclear. The *Newsweek* writers said, "the actual impact of the self-esteem movement has been an explosion of awards, gold stars and happy-face stickers for the most routine accomplishments of childhood" (p. 49). Academically talented students are just as vulnerable as other students to easy praise that accords false self-esteem for fake accomplishments.

Ego-involvement seems to lower one's self-esteem. For example, Australian high school students whose self-esteem was tied to their task involvement retained higher academic self-esteem than students whose self-esteem was related to their ego-involvement, according to a study conducted by Gross (1998).

Elementary school experiences have great impact on self-esteem (Hamachek, 1990). That is because elementary students' self-esteem is "incomplete and impressionable" (p. 313), and they are vulnerable, with defenses that are not mature. Developmentally, elementary school children are in Erikson's "industry versus inferiority" stage, and students who do not receive recognition and praise are often stymied in making later achievement attempts. Thus elementary school children should not be made to bear untoward criticism and scorn; this is as true for academically talented students as for all students. Academically talented students may gain their self-esteem, though, from all As and many smiley faces, when the work is not challenging enough for them. Then, in the middle grades and in high school, their pictures of themselves are changed and many may succumb to underachievement rather than try hard and receive "only" a B. It is better to hear that one has the ability and if one would only do the work, one could succeed, than to hear that one hasn't succeeded, even though one has worked very hard. Nevertheless, self-esteem is a part of self-concept that is essential.

Stress

Stress occurs when one feels pressure, strain, and tension in one's life. Special situations for the talented have to do with overcommitment, that is, taking on too many activities, courses, and projects. Another reason is trying to please too many people and seeking external praise. Perfectionism causes stress as does meeting the expectations of others, discussed above. Learning how to slow down, to manage stress, to take care of one's body as well as to eat well and to get rest are all ways to cope with stress. Planning and decision making both cause stress and relieve stress. Stress occurs in the interim before the plans and decisions are made, while the student is mulling over the choices in her head. Stress can be "managed," say the experts. The counselor should help in goal setting, in teaching relaxation and meditation, in reducing the number of commitments, in helping students cope with high internal standards and the reality of reaching them. Students should be encouraged to think clearly about what their own preferences are, and be able to separate them from the needs for them that others have.

Sexual Identity

The counseling needs, or even presence, of young gays, lesbians, and bisexuals (GLB) has little attention in the literature on talented youth. However, that there are gay, lesbian, and bisexual talented people cannot be disputed. Gay men were the leaders of the fashion industry until that industry was decimated by AIDS in the late 1980s and early 1990s. The presence of GLB people in intellectual society is the stuff of many biographies and memoirs. My students are assigned to do a biographical study in conjunction with their creativity studies, and gays, lesbians, and bisexual people are often among the ranks of those who have had a biography written about them. A Website (www.users.cybercity.dk/~dko12530/queerher.htm) lists 500 famous gay and lesbian people who have publicly acknowledged their sexual identity. Among them are 24 from across the entire alphabet:

John Ashbery, Pulitzer Prize–winning poet •Joan Baez, singer •Rt. Rev. Otis Charles, retired Episcopal bishop of Utah •Michael Duffy, chair of Massachussets Commission Against Discrimination, appointed by Rep. Gov. William Weld • Melissa Etheridge, rock star •Justin Fashanu, British pro soccer star •David Geffen, billionaire record and film magnate •David Hockney, painter •Janis Ian, singer •Phillip Johnson, architect •Jonathan Ned Katz, historian •Ursula LeGuin, novelist •Rev. Renee McCoy, African-American minister and activist •Martina Navratilova, pro tennis champion •Mary Oliver, Pulitzer Prize–winning poet •Minnie Bruce Pratt, poet and teacher •Ned Rorem, classical composer and writer •John Schlafly, son of anti-gay conservative activist Phyllis Schlafly and lawyer for her organization, the Eagle Forum •Mutsuo Takahashi, Japanese poet •Lily Tomlin, comedian/actress •Annelize van de Stoel, member of Amsterdam City Council •James D. Woods, professor and author (The Corporate Closet) •Ivy Young, head of NGLTF Family Project •Bohdan Zachary, filmmaker.

At the 1997 World Council for the Gifted and Talented Conference, at the 1997 National Association for Gifted Children Conference, and at the 1998 Iowa Wallace Symposium, presentations were given by researchers, GLB educators, and parents of GLB talented students. One of those presenters was Terence Friedrichs, who presented some suggestions for educators in dealing with GLB talented youths. Friedrichs (1997) conducted a study with about 30 gay lesbian and bisexual youths and Table 11.1 shows the issues they most frequently mentioned. A retrospective survey with adult GLB people also affirmed these issues.

Table 11.1 Ways Educators Can Deal Comprehensively with Frequently Stated "Cutting Edge" Needs of Gay, Lesbian, and Bisexual (GLB) Youths

Need	Problem When Need is Addressed	Ways Counselor or Teacher Can Deal with Problem
Sex		
1. To discuss a variety of different sexual behavior patterns	Self-isolation when GLB student gives specific information about self	Answer frequently asked questions by GLB youth nationally, even if they're not asked by particular GLB youth at hand
Peer Relationships		
2. For friends in two or more of these categories: women, gay men, lesbians, bisexuals, non-teens	Continued isolation, even after GLB finds these friends	Find support group explicitly for GLB group, in school or community
3. For GLB student alliances with straight students	Difficulty in GLB and straight students working together for school policy changes	Become actively involved in working for these changes
4. For gay, lesbian, or bisexual role models (teachers or speakers)	Problem in GLB youth relating completely to words and actions of adult speakers or teachers	Speakers can be asked about current trends they support among GLB youth
Parent-Child Relationships		
5. For child's independent search for personal happiness and career choice	Danger of underachievement in GLB youth who seek a "too-independent" course	Schools, churches, social service agencies can be encouraged to offer mentors for GLB youth
6. For parental pointers toward GLB role models in the community	Danger in parents finding "off-the-mark" role models for their GLB youth	Parents seek out a variety of role models through GLB youth centers
7. For independence training		
School Acceptance		
8. For school-provided counseling opportunities for GLB youth	Counseling that doesn't address discrimination or doesn't affirm GLB identity directly	Become actively involved with your own GLB students in affirming their struggle for identity and in redressing discrimination among them
9. To talk and write about troubling issues/feelings in school	GLB youth feelings may not be understood, or may even be betrayed, by teachers or peers	Set, and abide by, rules of confidentiality in class discussions and writings on GLB topics
10. For acceptance of loners	Telltale signs of suicidal ideation or substance abuse may go unnoticed with GLB loners	Follow up on suicide or substance-abuse signs in these students

From T.P. Friedrichs. (November 1997). *The Edge: Social and Emotional Lives of Gifted Gay, Lesbian, and Bisexual Pupils*. Speech at the National Association for Gifted Children Conference, Little Rock, AR.

These students are often highly sensitive and intense. It is important that the counselor or teacher indicate that the student would be safe in talking to or coming to the office. A display of a small Rainbow Coalition flag or books on the shelf indicate the counselor/teacher's awareness that the issue is out there. Students early learn the symbols and signs. The use of nonoffensive language such as "my partner" instead of "boyfriend/girlfriend" or saying the term "Gay/Lesbian/Bisexual"—go ahead, say it—is a beginning. The forming of a gay/straight alliance and letting the students do the networking is another suggestion. "Make your office and classroom a safe place," said Friedrichs.

Lind (1997) had 20 suggestions for helping with the affective needs of lesbian, gay, and bisexual youths (Chandler, 1995; Mallon, 1994; Reynolds & Koski, 1995). Among them were these:

The students' need

1. To understand the meaning of giftedness AND to understand the nature of homosexuality.
2. To deal with the feelings of "differentness" AND to learn to address social isolation and stigmatization.
3. To have a self-concept separate from their achievements AND to have a self-concept separate from their sexuality.
4. To be in classes with at least five or six other gifted students AND to be in settings with other GLB/gifted GLB youths.
5. To be able to be open about one's talents and gifts AND to be open about one's sexuality—to not have to hide.

Peterson (1998) did a qualitative study that asked 14 GLB college students about their experiences. Ten major themes emerged:

1. They said being gay was a reality to be reckoned with, and not to decide about, and that once they realized they were gay, it was not a fluke. By grade 11, most knew they were gay.
2. They felt a sense of inner isolation in spite of being social—some felt as if they were the only ones; others were treated as outcasts. A comment was, "I felt constantly alone. I separated myself from my peers as a way of coping with the prejudice, name-calling, etc."
3. They had a pervasive sense of differentness. A comment was, "I think to be labeled 'gifted' often means to be labeled as 'different,' which is what being gay essentially is. To be both is a very interesting interaction indeed."
4. They had a lack of role models, a lack of the presence of gays in the curriculum, and a lack of validation. A comment was, "I had no role models. I had to create them in my mind. . . . I had to learn what gay was and then unlearn it, as I realized society and stereotypes didn't fit in with my personal expectations or desires."
5. They felt a sense of danger. One female said, "A group of boys made me their pet project. They almost had me cornered several times," and a male said, "I became an easy target for passive and aggressive acts, all of which were anonymous."
6. Hypersensitivity was a reality, being both gifted and gay. One said, "I was oversensitive to comments by classmates. I felt oppressed at school and was absent frequently."

7. They had many behaviors to deflect, to divert in order to be "OK." One male said, "The difficulty of individuation is seriously sompounded by the suspicion that the person you may be becoming will not be readily accepted by your family, friends, and education."

8. They often became overinvolved in school and communty activities as a result of their inner discovery. One said, "I was top of my class, hyper-involved in extracurriculars. Since then I've suspected much of that was avoiding dealing with orientation and socialization issues. In structured activities, I was safe."

9. They felt angst, depression, and experienced suicidal thoughts. None of them "came out" to their teachers, and only one-third came out to their parents.

10. When they went to college, they felt less depressed as they drew closer to the support groups available there. One respondent said, "If it hadn't have been for college I would not be alive. I was at a critical point. College was my last hope."

Underachievement

There are several writers and researchers who have made important contributions to our knowledge of underachievement. Among these are James Gallagher, Joanne Whitmore, Sylvia Rimm, Susanne Richert, James Delisle, and Patricia Supplee. Underachievement continues to plague educators of the talented as one of the most recalcitrant problems that high-IQ youths continue to have. By now we know that each underachiever is different, and that each case of underachievement must be looked at individually to determine the reason for the underachievement and thus to be better able to reverse the underachievement.

What is underachievement? The quick answer most people would give is that underachievement is not receiving the grades that the IQ would indicate are possible. Another quick definition is that underachievement is receiving high scores on standardized achievement tests but low grades in school. Yet another definition of underachievement blames the causes for the underachievement, for example: underachievement is caused by learning disabilities, or underachievement is caused by the social climate of the school, or underachievement is caused by affective characteristics in the child. The underachievement is not defined, but it is usually *assumed* that the underachiever is receiving lower grades than test scores would indicate are possible, and that this failure to achieve is somehow a refusal to achieve on the part of the student with the high IQ score, or high standardized test score.

Underachievement may come about from environmental and from personal factors. Environmental factors are such things as peer influence, poor teaching, and insufficient schools. Changing the environment often changes the pattern of underachievement. The environment can be changed by teaching the student how to cope, or by moving the student from the environment. Personal factors include neurological difficulties such as learning disabilities or physical difficulties such as hearing impairment. Silverman (1989) found that underachievers often had difficulty in sequencing, while being above average in vocabulary, the ability to reason abstractly, the ability to perceive spatial relations, and the ability to analyze mathematical relations.

Gallagher (1991) also noted that personal reasons for underachievement may be psychological, and that recent policy decisions in many states "have established criteria for eligibility to programs for gifted students that require both high aptitude and high achievement" (p. 223), thus mitigating against the underachiever, who must show high performance in order to be served as academically talented. He said that this requirement "would seem to defeat some of our key objectives—to enhance the performance of those students who possess great talent but little motivation or efficiency" (p. 224). The emerging paradigm in the field of talent development education, as described in Chapter 1, features achievement as being predictive for certain manifestations of talent.

Oh, how underachievement bothers educators of the academically talented! Here is a child with a high IQ who refuses to do the work in the classroom. Here is a child with high achievement test scores who refuses to turn in the projects. The educators beg, cajole, compliment, harangue the child. The parents beg, cajole, compliment, harangue the child. "You have such potential! You should be doing better! You won't get into a good college with grades like these! You could do so well; why won't you produce?" The child is the powerful force in these dynamics, both with the parents and with the school, and that is why Rimm (1986) insisted that there must be a "tri-focal" approach to reversing underachievement, and that is that the *school*, the *parents*, and the *child* must all take responsibility for the reversal or the underachievement will continue. The child is the key figure in this triangle.

It is often assumed that children want to do well in school, and schools and parents are often quick to blame themselves for underachievement. It is often assumed that the evils of the society—racism, classism, prejudice against the handicapped—are to blame for underachievement. It is often assumed that children are feckless victims of "the system." Then why do some children from lower social classes, of various races, with learning disabilities and physical handicaps, achieve despite the "system," and others do not? The quality of "resiliency" discussed above seems operational here.

What are the personality traits of people who underachieve? For underachieving males at least, Terman and Oden found in 1947 that those who didn't meet the potential their IQ scores indicated were (1) unable to persevere; (2) unable to formulate goals; (3) preferred to drift rather than to take action; and (4) had low self-confidence. These problems were chronic: that is, they continued from childhood to adolescence to adulthood (Terman & Oden, 1947). Underachievement, Delisle (1992) reminded us, is often in the eyes of the beholder.

Whitmore's Work on Underachievement

Whitmore's 1980 book, *Giftedness, Conflict, and Underachievement*, was a milestone in that she specifically studied children who, in 1970, were put into a special program that sought to remedy underachieving behavior. This program was called the Cupertino Project, and it focused on second and third graders who had very high IQs but who were underachieving. Individualized instruction was offered and results showed that students' achievement generally improved over the long term. Supplee (1990) commented, however, that while masterly in design, the Cupertino program had drawbacks, including the cost. She said that large districts could perhaps afford special classroom settings for underachievers but underachievers are found everywhere, and special classrooms would be cost prohibitive. She also wondered about the "hothouse" nature of the intervention for underachievers, saying, "We need to be sure that once underachieving children reverse self-destructive patterns, they can make it in the 'real' world of traditional classrooms, a temperate climate that blows both hot and cold, good and bad" (p. 22).

Rimm's Work on Underachievement

Rimm (1986) used a behavioral approach to the reversal of underachievement. She described four different categories of underachievers, the "dependent conformers" and the "dependent nonconformers," the "dominant conformers" and the "dominant nonconformers." These are children who are outside what she called the "circle of achievers."

Underachievers were grouped into dependent children and dominant children, conformers and nonconformers. Dependent children manipulate adults and others in their environment by such plaintive pleas as "Help me"; "Nag me"; "Protect me"; "Feel sorry for me"; "Love me"; and "Shelter me." The difficulty is in determining when these pleas are manipulative and when they are "genuine." Rimm said parents and teachers "must assure yourselves that these children can build self-confidence and competence only through effort and perseverance, and that it is indeed a true kindness to permit these children to experience some stress" (Rimm, 1986, p. 148).

Rimm's Suggestions for Remediation   For each of these groups, there are suggested steps in remediation. Rimm was quick to point out that family patterns often foster or encourage underachievement, for passive-aggressive children often have one passive-aggressive parent and one who is made the bad guy; likewise, with aggressive children, there is often aggression in the family. Patterns in the family can be both positive and negative for achievement. It has been called the "family mythology" (Piirto, 1992a/ 1998). Rimm said that potentially harmful family models were these: "I didn't like school either"; having a home that is disorganized; having passive-aggressive parenting; having parents who are overworked and who come home exhausted, complaining, and failing to provide models that work is satisfying, challenging, and life enhancing.

Rimm's work was criticized for being too negative to parents. In a review of Rimm's *How to Parent So Children Will Learn* (1990), Baum (1990) said that "Rimm does not take into account different parenting styles, values, and good instincts" and she stated that Rimm's rules make many parents feel guilty. However, proponents of clinical interventions utilizing behavioral approaches such as Rimm's would say that drastic measures are often needed in reversing underachievement, which is often entrenched, insidious, and a hallmark of dysfunction in the family or school. "Rimm is tough love," said one therapist. Rimm's advice to parents appears regularly on national television and radio.

Divorce and Underachievement

There are also, these days, children of divorce, and gifted children are not immune from this social phenomenon. The family is in chaos. Karnes and Marquardt, in their consideration of legal issues having to do with gifted children, said, "we were surprised by the number of child custody and child support cases where the giftedness of the child became an issue" (Karnes & Marquardt, 1991a, p. 98). Rimm seemed to feel that achievement can continue throughout the divorce, but Wallerstein and Blakeslee, in their longitudinal study of children of divorce, *Second Chances* (1989), noted that underachievement is almost always a by-product of divorce, even years later. Boys who are between the ages of six and eight when their parents get divorced "have a particularly difficult time adjusting to the changes in their lives." They often are unable to concentrate, and may withdraw or "clobber everyone in sight" (p. 77).

Wallerstein and Blakeslee attributed this to fears of being overwhelmed by female authority just at the age when developing strong identifications with their fathers and other male figures was crucial. The authors followed their subjects for 10 years and concluded sadly that about a third of the children they studied still lacked ambition 10 years after the divorce, and said that they were "drifting through life with no set goals, limited educations, and a sense of helplessness."

That gifted and talented youth are exempt from the tragic consequences for children of their parents' divorces is certainly a false notion. Indeed, if we give the theory of asynchrony, and the theory of emotional intensity such as noticed in overexcitabilities, some credence, study after study has shown that gifted and talented youth may be *more* vulnerable, for their sensitivities are often higher tuned and deeper felt, as their advanced intellects and intensities cope with the splits in their nuclear families. In fact, one immutable fact that was found by the Johns Hopkins SMPY researchers was that high academic achievers most often came from families that were intact (Benbow, 1992).

Richert's Work on Underachievement

Richert (1991) presented a refreshingly different definition of underachievement, pointing out the obvious but often overlooked question: What if the IQ is not a good measure of potential after all? What if the IQ test that puts the child in people's minds into "underachieving status" was inaccurate? Richert noted that "underachievement is most often defined in terms of academic achievement" measured by school-related methods such as grades, standardized test scores, and teacher-made test results. What if these are not good ways of assessing underachievement? What if the tests themselves are the problem?

The child's life as a whole should be assessed. Does the child who gets low grades and who has high test scores have an intense life of achievement at home? Does she read seven books a week? Does he program computers and participate in a wide network of computer friends throughout the area? Does she have sketchbooks and do intensive drawing and artwork? Does he practice his music for seven hours a day? How is this child underachieving? Richert pointed out that "Repeated studies have revealed no correlation, or sometimes even a small negative correlation, between academic achievement (good grades) and adult giftedness in a wide range of fields" (p. 139). Richert, in questioning the definition of underachievement, posed an interesting conundrum: If many high achievers in later life found the schools stifling, boring, and the teachers and rules worse, what is the role of the schools in talent development in the various domains?

Delisle's Work on Underachievement

Delisle (1992) also questioned the definition of underachievement. He stated that underachievement should be differentiated from nonproduction. Saying that the sad history in the attempts to reverse underachievement indicates that perhaps there was nothing there to reverse because "the term itself was (and is) too ill defined" (p. 127), Delisle nevertheless attempted to define. A nonproducer is someone who is "very much in touch with both himself and the world of learning but unwilling to do much of his assigned work" and an underachiever is "a lost soul in the academic miasma called school who desperately wants to do better—and feel better—but is at a loss as to how she might begin to do either" (p. 120).

Supplee's Work on Underachievement

In 1990, Supplee wrote *Reaching the Gifted Underachiever*, and she used Abraham Tannenbaum's conception of giftedness to define underachievement. Tannenbaum (1983), in *Gifted Children*, said that giftedness emerges if all five arms in a "starfish" are present (see Figure 1.4). These are the necessary conditions for giftedness to materialize: (1) general intellectual ability (the *g* factor); (2) specific academic abilities (such as math ability or reading ability); (3) nonintellective factors (such as persistence, self-esteem, or creativity); (4) environmental factors (family, school); and (5) chance (proximity, knowing the right people, etc.).

Supplee said that the underachievers she studied were missing one or more of the "starfish" arms; some had high IQs but didn't have other factors; some had fantastic special abilities but didn't have persistence; some were very poor, a negative environmental factor, although they had all four other factors; some had physical or learning disabilities, which fall into the chance arm. The presence of a program for underachieving gifted children is also a chance factor in the life of an underachieving student.

Components of the UAG Program   Funded by the New Jersey Department of Education, the program Supplee described was called the UAG (for "Underachieving Gifted") Program. Stating that typical remediation using the resource room model doesn't work for academically talented students, Supplee designed a program for students with "emotional, social, environmental, [or physical] blocks" (p. 31), and not for students with ability deficits.

She found that beginning with improving the students' self-esteem and proceeding to the improvement of their attitudes, school behaviors, and academic growth, was successful. There was also a parent component that helped parents to understand the causes of the student's underachievement, as well as to examine their expectations for their child, be positive communicators with their child, and to examine familial patterns and familial dynamics. A support group of parents was formed where they could discuss common concerns.

The affective component was quite successful with the students, and they identified their changed self-esteem as most positive. As their time in the program began, the students received direct instruction in these five kinds of skills: (1) pro-social; (2) school-survival; (3) group self-direction; (4) conflict-resolution; and (5) stress-reduction. Students received immediate positive reinforcement when they applied new behaviors taught them.

After affective components were in place, cognitive components began to be taught. The lecture method was never used, but students did group work and hands-on activities such as computer sessions, games, experiments, and field trips. Students were encouraged to give positive reinforcement to themselves and to their fellows. The time schedule was flexible; the breaks were interesting; there were learning centers. The room was organized so that there were large work surfaces and small group areas. Activities commonly used in Outward Bound and Project Adventure were undertaken. These were activities such as ropes courses and trust walks.

School-survival skills were those that Supplee said are "necessary for success in school but normally are not taught there" (p. 144). Many underachievers are not cued to play the school game. They can't "read" their instructors; they are not sensitive to the environment of the classes or the school; they blunder where they should tap dance. School-survival skills were taught using role playing, among other strategies. Some of the school-survival skills the students learned were the following:

School-Survival Skills Needed by Underachievers

1. How to listen, and look as if they were listening
2. How to ask a teacher or a friend for help
3. How to bring needed materials to class
4. How to follow written and oral instructions
5. How to memorize efficiently
6. How to use an assignment pad well
7. How to study for tests
8. How to complete short-term assignments
9. How to complete long-term assignments
10. How to contribute to a class discussion
11. How to ignore distractions
12. How to ask a question in class
13. How to decide what to do when assigned work is finished
14. How to set medium- and long-range goals
15. How to deal with an accusation
16. How to accept consequences for mistakes in work or behavior
17. How to negotiate with the teacher
18. How to make good decisions
19. How to deal with time pressures and schedules
20. How to set priorities
21. Rewarding themselves for tasks well done
22. Learning to say no when work must come first
23. How to overlearn something to make sure it's mastered

(Supplee, 1990, pp. 145–146)

These skills are necessary for all good students, and underachievers lack some or most of them. For gifted underachievers, the ability is not the question; other factors present difficulty in achievement.

The academic portion of the UAG program was targeted to their weaknesses. Using Vygotsky's theory of the Zone of Proximal Development (ZPD), that instruction should take place at the highest level near to the level where the child should be achieving, the teachers in the program assessed the reading abilities of the students, taught them quite rapidly, and raised the levels of instruction as soon as the students demonstrated their knowledge. Reading skills were taught as necessary for comprehension, and not as entities in themselves. An independent reading program was instituted, and the levels of Bloom's taxonomy and the Socratic questioning method were used. Interactive questions, journal writing, telecommunications, and annotated bibliographies of high-interest children's literature were also employed. Skills in the scope and sequence were compacted.

One strategy in mathematics instruction was to let the understanding of mathematical concepts take precedence over the understanding of mathematical computation.

Supplee found that students then mastered the necessary computational facts in order to complete the mathematical process. Another instructional method was to use the "talk aloud" method. One student was asked to talk out loud as he solved an algebraic word problem so the teacher could see where he got stuck. It turned out he had been devising his own algorithms to solve more basic problems, and he had never gotten enough subtraction problems wrong, even in "pages and pages" or problems. The problem was diagnosed, and manipulatives were used to help him "see" where his algorithm was failing. Another strategy used in math instruction for the underachievers was daily problem solving, in short, 10-minute segments. The students went on to stay in school, to get acceptable grades, and to play the school game with adequate skill.

GUIDANCE ISSUES FOR TALENTED YOUTH

Talented students, like most students, do not tend to seek the help of counselors for personal issues (Colangelo, 1991). They do, though, talk with their counselors about guidance issues such as course selection and career advice. Implicit in these choices is often the fact that talented students, especially students from lower socioeconomic groups, may experience ambivalence about the choices available to them. Here are some common guidance issues that should be addressed: academic planning, acceleration, career development, finding mentors, multipotentiality, learning styles, testing, program articulation, vocational guidance, volunteerism and service, and gender issues underlying all of the above. Figure 11.3 lists these guidance issues and some sources that deal with them.

Academic Planning

Depending on geographical region and size and type of school, the college planning help that talented students receive varies greatly. In college towns, suburban areas, and urban academic high schools, talented students are more likely to receive high-level college planning; that is, they are told that they should try to apply to the best college that will take them, and that the money will probably follow. However, in rural areas, especially in the south and in the midwest, and in comprehensive urban high schools, counseling help may often be limited to colleges that the counselor knows about or is familiar with. The vast difference in levels of college planning for talented students often has to do with how well exposed the counselors themselves have been to a wide spectrum of college options; they may be tempted to counsel students to attend their alma maters or similar schools. One counselor from the midwest who was working in an elite overseas school was asked to leave because he was counseling the high school students to attend midwestern state universities and not the top tier, Ivy League, Level I universities that eastern suburban counselors routinely recommend. The superintendent of the school said that he would never again hire a counselor from the midwest, for the reason that their college planning skills advice was limited by their geographical background.

A talented student from the midwest was admitted to M.I.T. His counselor was instrumental in securing this admission. He was also admitted to the regional state university. His family did not think they had the money to send the young man to

Figure 11.3   Guidance Issues for Talented Youth

Anger (Goleman, 1995; Vail, 1995)

Genuine boredom (Vail, 1994)

Creativity (Piirto, 1992a/1998; Rimm, 1992)
- Divergent thinking (Lovecky, 1993; Piirto, 1992a/1998)
- Questioning others' long-held values (Myers & Pace, 1986)

Academic planning (Berger, 1989; Delisle, 1992; Kerr, 1991; Rimm, 1986; VanTassel-Baska, 1994; Wright & Olszewski-Kubilius, 1995)
- Course selection

Acceleration (Benbow, 1992; Southern & Jones, 1991; Stanley, 1979, 1989)

Career development (Delisle, 1992; Hollinger & Flemming, 1992; Kerr, 1991; Myers & Pace, 1986; Silverman, 1993)
- Too-early career closure (Myers & Pace, 1986)
- Coping with delayed gratification (Myers & Pace, 1986)
- Making long-range plans (Myers & Pace, 1986)

Finding mentors (Arnold & Subotnik, 1995; Riley, 1992)

Multipotentiality (Blackburn & Erickson, 1986; Delisle, 1992; Gagné, Neveu, Simard & St. Pére, 1996; Gross, 1993; Kerr, 1991)

Learning styles (Bireley, 1991; Myers & McCaulley, 1985)

Testing (Lupkowski-Shoplik & Assouline,1993; Olszewski-Kubilius & VanTassel-Baska, 1990; Stanley et al., 1992)

Program articulation

Vocational guidance (Greenan, Wu & Broering, 1995)

Volunteerism and service

Gender differences in all of the above

M.I.T. The counselor contacted the state's M.I.T. alumni association and was told, "If he's admitted, we'll help him find the money." The rule of thumb in counseling talented students is for the counselor to make sure that the student knows that if the admittance is secured the money will most likely follow. The student, however, attended the regional state university because his parents, neither of whom had been to college, feared him leaving the state. They thought that he would remain a part of the family if he attended a nearby school.

The biographies of many rural and midwest achievers are illustrative that this probably would have happened. The opportunity to attend a university such as M.I.T., Berkeley, Michigan, Barnard, Sarah Lawrence, Harvard, Princeton, or Yale often makes profound changes in the life of the talented adolescent. The competitiveness and challenge of these top level schools change their lives.The importance for career development, and graduate school admission, of attending such a school if the student can get in cannot be underestimated, and that is where aware counseling of talented youth in their home junior high and high schools must take place. There *is* an "Eastern Establishment." For example, most presidential candidates in the past have graduated from

Yale Law School. Power and influence reside in the graduates from the elite colleges. Counselors should be aware of this and aid their students in attending the best colleges, no matter what geographical area, to which they can be admitted. Recently, the colleges that admitted 100 or more National Merit Scholars were, in descending order, Harvard and Radcliffe, Rice, University of Texas at Austin, Stanford, Texas A & M, Yale, Princeton, Northwestern, Ohio State, M.I.T., Duke, and Brigham Young.

Course Taking

Most intellectually talented students plan to go to college; however, some of them do not receive the course selection advice that they need to do well on precollege examinations such as the Scholastic Aptitude Test or the American College Test. This planning must start early. *Course taking* is the most direct way that guidance counselors can influence talented students. Unfortunately, many adults report that their counselors influenced them in the wrong direction. For example, many talented women were not encouraged to take four years of mathematics and four years of science; when they got to college they found that they had to "catch up" and many of them never did. Others have found, for example, that black youths who take geometry are the most likely ones to go to college. Making sure that geometry is on the course selection agenda should be a priority for school personnel. Guidance counselors who know these facts will be the major influence on course-taking behavior.

Acceleration

Acceleration has been discussed in chapter 2 and chapter 10. The counselor and teacher should be aware that there have been few studies that show acceleration to be a failed strategy for educating young talented learners (Benbow, 1992; Southern, & Jones, 1991; Stanley, 1979, 1989). The most well researched have been the longitudinal studies of SMPY, the Study of Mathematically Precocious Youth.

Research on Acceleration as a Guidance Option

The SMPY studies have shown that acceleration seems to have benefited these students. They conducted studies to elucidate whether accelerated students receive good grades, and found "students who enter college from two to five years early make good grades, win honors, and graduate on time" (Stanley & Benbow, 1983; Stanley & McGill, 1986). Students who had been in fast-paced math classes early were also likely to continue in math/science later on. In fact, one gender difference they found was that girls who had not had challenging high school experiences, who had not crystallized their ambitions by age 18, were likely to drop out of math/science tracks (Benbow, 1992). This loss has great implications for counselors counseling academically talented females. Lynch (1992) found that students in junior high school are probably able to handle advanced science courses as well, and that exposing younger students to more advanced material, consonant with their advanced abilities, is likely to keep them interested in science.

However, the belief that acceleration will harm the social and emotional development of academically talented youth has also been a strong one. The SMPY researchers conducted several studies to see whether this was the case, and they found that "acceleration benefits students academically while not detracting from social and emotional development" (Benbow, 1992, p. 116; Brody & Benbow, 1987). Southern and Jones (1991) said that while the research evidence is clear that academically gifted students do not suffer by acceleration, "the evidence concerning social and emotional harm" is less clear-cut. Because social and emotional maturity, adjustment, and development and even the definitions of these are not clear, it is more difficult to assess the potential impact of acceleration on the social and emotional development of academically talented children.

A rule of thumb is to consider each case individually, with a group of people involved in any decisions, including the student himself. Parents of academically talented youth have often used the strategy of accelerating their students by moving to a new school where they will be perceived freshly, and the peer reactions to skipping grades will not be so noticeable.

Career Development

Most states now have detailed career development planning programs. Students should be plugged into them as a matter of course along the way. From kindergarten through grade 12, certain steps are necessary. For talented youth, the issues are that the student will focus too early on a certain career and not develop in a general education, a "Renaissance" way. This is especially a danger for performers (Allen, 1992). For students who will be entering long courses of study such as those leading to a doctor's degree, there is the issue of coping with delayed gratification and the concomitant need to pay off school loans for a long period of time. It is not at all uncommon for school loans to remain a burden until a talented person is in her forties. The issue of whether going into such debt is worth it is a personal decision. The necessity to make long-range plans is key to this issue as well.

Decisions made in high school are important but not irrevocable. The presence of "late bloomers" in the ranks of the talented is underresearched. In the literature on talented adults, most thinkers give a time line that is somewhat rigid. The lives of those who would go into science, mathematics, and technology are said to be so circumscribed that one cannot make a world-class contribution if one does not get a Ph.D. in one's early twenties (Simonton, 1994). Women and rebels need not apply. So few people make world-class contributions that the phenomenon may not be really worth talking about, even in talent development education circles. Students should be made aware of their potential whether or not they are on the time line needed for world-class contributions. Re-entry into a career path after years of child care, or after bumming around the world and having adventures, is possible. Making significant contributions to the chosen field is also possible, even after the age of forty, fifty, or sixty. Changing careers and trying something new is also possible.

Finding Mentors

The literature on mentoring is vast. Mentor programs are a vital part of the guidance scene in most high schools. Such programs as Tech Prep are part of the vocational and career planning in most states. In the field of talent development education, mentoring is a structured or unstructured relationship between an expert and a novice, where the expert teaches the novice the ins and outs of the domain. The mentor chooses the talented novice and the novice must usually meet three conditions: (1) be available, in proximity to the mentor; (2) be willing to absorb the values of the mentor; and (3) be attractive to the mentor (Arnold & Subotnik,1995). Usually the novice resembles the mentor in ethnicity, family background, and gender: "The more individuals diverge from the traditional traits, values, and backgrounds of professional elites, the less likely their talents will be expressed in ways that elicit the interpersonal network of mentoring" (p. 120).

The mentor provides the novice with judgment and evaluation according to the professional standards of the field: "mentors model what students can become by showing the lifestyles, modes of thinking, professional practices, costs, and advantages associated with high-level achievement in a particular domain" (p. 120). The mentor takes a risk to his/her reputation in sponsoring the novice for membership in the ranks of the domain, and so the novice is chosen carefully (Piirto, 1992a/1998). The mentor communicates the tacit knowledge of the domain, the "unwritten, informal insider information about appropriate, adaptive, professional and career management behavior in a specific talent domain" (p. 120).

There are three stages in the mentoring relationship: (1) initial stages, in which the mentor encourages the novice to step into the river, to feel and experience the delights of the cool water, to smell the fresh air of the domain; (2) technical virtuosity, in which the novice moves beyond the romance and begins the hard work of acquiring automaticity in the domain through intense self-discipline and practice —in this stage, the mentor models the end state for the novice; and (3) mastery, where the novice becomes an expert, a peer of the mentor—in this stage, the mentor is in emotional danger, for the novice may surpass the mentor and move beyond his/her teachings and modeling. If the mentor doesn't hold the novice with an open hand, the novice will not become a respected member of the profession, but a clone of his/her mentor. The difficulty with this process, say Arnold and Subotnik (1995), is that minorities and women may not be found attractive by the mentor, and so the process won't begin.

Multipotentiality

The guidance needs of talented students include the fact that many indicate a potential for achievement in more than one field or domain. This often causes confusion and stress. "What do I like?" "What am I good at?" It is not uncommon for high school and college students to vacillate, change majors, send for more brochures and pamphlets, all in a search for the one, the true, career. However, some research has shown that multipotentiality might not exist to the extent that it has been touted as existing (Gagné et al., 1996). They experienced difficulty when they tried to find people who were in the top 15 percent of two or more distinct domains of talents (as differentiated from aptitudes; see the Gagné model in Chapter 1), for example, "high academic achievement coupled with athletic excellence or with artistic excellence" (p. 6). "Some achievements, while clearly above average, did not appear exceptional enough to attain the threshold of inclusion" (p. 8). Gagné et al. concluded that the concept of multipotentiality, or *polyvalence*, as they called it, presents the same difficulties as most of the concepts in the field of the education of the gifted and talented: identifying polyvalent individuals—people with the potential to excel at the highest levels in more than one talent—poses problems similar to the screening of intellectually gifted and academically talented individuals. It is easy to find the most extreme cases, those who definitely are, or possess the trait, but it is very difficult to find those on the margins, who may or may not.

The issue of multipotentiality as a guidance issue may thus be overblown, except in the few cases where a person is definitely extremely talented in several areas. Perhaps the person with multipotentialities has many interests, but in what lies the extreme talent? In this, it must be the heart, or the *daimon*, that wins; which itch *must* be scratched for well-being and peace of mind? The counselor can aid in guiding the student toward realization of that passion. Another possibility for such students is to plan on having more than one career during a long lifetime.

Differences Between Highly Talented and Moderately Talented

The ongoing studies of highly mathematically and verbally talented youth also have application. In Benbow's 1992 review of SMPY research, comparing highly academically talented youth with moderately academically talented youth, the researchers found that indeed, there is no threshhold such as implied by Renzulli (1977) and Getzels and Jackson (1962). The students who were in the top 25 percent of the top one percent achieved at a "much higher academic level" than those in the bottom 25 percent of the top one percent. That is, those who were moderately academically talented, or who did not score in the highest ranges of the SAT but who were still identified as academically talented, did not have as much potential for academic achievement as those who scored at the highest ranges. The students who had parents who had not attended college and female students were most at risk for not achieving their high mathematical potential, and these are the students to whom counselors should pay special attention. Counselors should note that family factors could be compensated for by the quality of course work in high school. Benbow said, "Achievers had experienced more challenging instruction" (p. 113).

Learning Styles of Talented Youth

The view that students who are high academic achievers have specific personality types or learning styles has been explored by several researchers, among them Marlene Bireley (1991). She listed commonly used learning style instruments and suggested that counselors use one of them "as the basic for counseling the gifted adolescent" (p. 180):

1. The Learning Style Inventory (Dunn, Dunn & Price, 1979)
2. The Learning Style Profile (Keefe & Monk, 1986)
3. The Learning Style Inventory (Renzulli & Smith, 1978a) in the Scales for Rating Behavioral Characteristics of Superior Students (SRBCSS)
4. The Learning Style Inventory (Kolb, 1976)
5. The Gregorc Style Delineator (Gregorc, 1982)
6. The Herrmann Brain Dominance Instrument (Herrmann, 1981)
7. The Learning Prefence Inventory (Silver & Hanson, 1978)
8. The Murphy-Meisgeier Type Indicator for Children (Meisgeier & Murphy, 1987)
9. The Myers-Briggs Type Indicator (Briggs & Myers, 1977)

The most widely researched instrument among these is the Myers-Briggs Type Indicator (MBTI). The *Manual* (Myers & McCaulley, 1985) listed several hundred studies of various groups using the MBTI. The predominant type preference for academically talented students was NF (intuition, feeling). Bireley said that with the pragmatism and concrete disposition of the basic curriculum, and given that almost half of elementary and secondary teachers prefer Sensing, it is not surprising that teachers complain that high-IQ students often "resist completing basic skills assignments" (p. 195).

What is the most commonly found MBTI type for educators? Betkouski and Hoffman (1981) studied 1,389 public school teachers ranging from Canada to California. Their study found that the MBTI type ESFJ seemed to represent the majority of these educators: E = 51 percent to 57 percent; S = 53 percent to 75 percent; F = 55 percent to 66 percent; and J = 63 percent. In the general population, E = 75–80 percent; S = 60 percent; F = 65 percent of females and 35 percent of males; and J = 60 percent. Thus it can be seen that the teachers are close to the general population in preference. About two-thirds of elementary and high school teachers prefer J, with about half of elementary teachers and 40 percent of high school teachers preferring SJ. N teachers are more prevalent in high school, with about half preferring N, while about one-third of elementary school teachers prefer N. Only about one-third of elementary teachers and high school teachers prefer P. Thus the high preference for P in talented students outnumbers those of their teachers and of the society at large. It is notable that most Rhodes Scholars, chosen for their scholar-athlete qualities, prefer P.

A recent study indicated that while teachers of the gifted and talented also prefer Judging, they do so not in the great proportions that regular classroom teachers do (Piirto, 1998a). Of the Sensing-Intuition Preference dyad, the teachers of the talented preferred N. The N types, when coupled with the F, show genuine concern about all aspects of the welfare of their students' social as well as intellectual development. These teachers also prefer to interact on an individual basis and often will individualize instruction as needed. The presence of more N preference among teachers choosing to teach the gifted and talented might be an indication that they have gravitated towards teaching students who have similar preferences to theirs.

The MBTI was administered to 226 tenth and eleventh graders who qualified as gifted and talented. Sixty teachers of the talented were also administered the MBTI. Talented teens preferred ENFP. Gender differences were calculated as well among artistic youth and academically talented youth. Male artistic youth preferred F and academic females preferred T. Teachers of the talented preferred ENFJ (see Table 11.2).

Within the various realms of the education profession, the types seem to gravitate to certain areas based on their combination type. While NFs are about one-third of the teachers, few teachers prefer SP or NT. NTs usually prefer to teach in college; only about 8 percent of K–12 teachers are NTs. Those who prefer NT are often gaining the experience to get into graduate programs in order to become college professors. ENFP student teachers are often very popular among the students, but few of them seem to continue in the teaching professing. Keirsey (1978) said, "SJ teachers . . . are not only the types most likely to choose teaching (56 percent of all teachers), but they are also the types who are most likely to stay in teaching as a lifelong career" (p. 6). The SJ-type teacher may be especially intimidating to a sensitive artistic male, for 97 percent of the artistic males in this study preferred P, and this confirms earlier studies; in the creative males described in Myers and McCaulley

Table 11.2   MBTI Percentages for Talented Teenagers and Teachers of the Talented

	Artistic Teens	Academic Teens	Total Talented Teens	G/T Teachers
	N = 99 M = 33 F = 66	N = 127 M = 36 F = 91	N = 226 M = 69 F = 157	N = 60 M = 0 F = 60
Introversion (I)	N = 55 (56%) 21M = 64% 34F = 52%	N = 65 (51%) 26M = 72% 39F = 43%	N = 110 (49%) 47M = 68% 73F = 46%	N = 25 (42%)
Extroversion	N = 44 (44%) 12M (36%) 32F (48%)	N = 43 (34%) 10M (28%) 52F (57%)	N = 116 (51%) 22M (32%) 84F (54%)	N = 34 (57%)
Sensing	N = 10 (10%) 1M (3%) 9F (13%)	N = 40 (31%) 12M (33%) 28F (30%)	N = 50 (22%) 13M (19%) 37F (24%)	N = 23 (55%)
Intuition (N)	N = 89 (90%) 32M (97%) 57F (87%)	N = 67 (53%) 24M = (67%) 63F (69%)	N = 176 (78%) 56M (81%) 120F (76%)	N = 37 (62%)
Feeling	N = 66 (67%) 23M (70%) 43F (65%)	N = 62 (48%) 12M (33%) 50F (53%)	N = 128 (57%) 35M (50%) 93F (60%)	N = 35 (60%)
Thinking	N = 29 (29%) 10M (30%)	N = 67 (53%) 24M (47%)	N = 96 (43%) 34M (50%)	N = 24 (40%)
Judging	N = 17 (17%) 2M (6%) 15F (22%)	N = 67 (53%) 16M (44%) 43F (48%)	N = 80 (35%) 18M (26%) 62F (40%)	N = 37 (62%)
Perceiving	N = 82 (83%) 31M (94%) 51F (77%)	N = 63 (50%) 20M (56%) 48F (53%)	N = 145 (64%) 51M (73%) 94F (60%)	N = 23 (38%)

(1985), 97 percent of the 112 creative men preferred N. Teachers of the talented as well as regular classroom teachers need to be aware of this finding.

If most educators tend to prefer Sensing, how will they meet the needs of the N-preferring artistically and academically talented students exist in their classrooms? Most talented students are in the regular classroom most of the time during their elementary school years. The answer lies in teachers having a full understanding of the attributes of the N and S types. Briefly, the S type relies on their senses for understanding and learning. They perceive reality as pieces funneled through their senses. If they cannot use their senses, learning will be minimized. On the other hand, the N type is quite the opposite. They rely on their hunches or inner sense. They perceive reality as a world of opportunity and possibilities. The big picture is clear to them and they create ways to be an integral part of it. As teachers understand these differences between the insight-driven N students and their own preference for the concrete S activity, they can then begin to plan and implement the mode of instruction that will produce the highest results for each type's learning preference. Teaching and project-based assignments are preferences for Ns. They do not often like a fill-in-the-blanks, only-one-right-answer style of teaching.

The NPs may have a particularly difficult time being understood and challenged by their SJ teachers in the elementary and high school, but as they grow older, more N teachers will appear (however, these will most likely be NJs, although P-preferring professors seem to gravitate towards the arts), and in fact, studies of college professors have shown that most of them prefer N (for example, see Cooper & Miller, 1991). It could be said without much irony that those with the preference for P are poetic visionaries, and their visions are often undervalued in a prosaic work and school environment.

McCaulley (1976) states that each of the type combinations seems to have its greatest opportunity of success and satisfaction in fields that more closely match the characteristics of that type. According to Jones and Sherman (1979), NPs require the most counseling. They often seem more nonconformist to rules and regulations, and are willing to lock horns with authority. These students can be procrastinators but are usually good at making the system work for them.

Studies of performing and practicing creators showed they are more often intuitive (N) than sensing (S) (Myers & McCaulley, 1985). In fact, in a study of 85 creative and academically talented adolescents, 68 percent were found to prefer the N dimension on the Myers-Briggs Type Indicator (Piirto et al., 1997a), while in the general population only 25 percent prefer N (Myers & McCaullay, 1985). This high proportion of "N" preferers among creative people—including scientists, mathematicians, artists, and writers—seems a prime characteristic. Geiger and Martin (1992) also used the Myers-Briggs with high scorers on the SAT and found that the most frequent MBTI types were INTP (Introversion, Intuition, Thinking, and Perceiving), ENFP (Extroversion, Intuition, Feeling, and Perceiving), and INFP (Introversion, Intuition, Feeling, and Perceiving).

Myers-Briggs Types and Learning Preferences

Some research has been done on which types prefer which teaching/learning environments. Eggins, in 1979, studied junior high students using three models of teaching: (1) the inductive approach, or Bruner's model; (2) the didactic approach, or Ausubel's model using advance organizers; and (3) the concrete to abstract model, or Gagné's model. Students with high intelligence and the intuitive preference liked the Bruner model. High intelligence judging (J) preference students did also. Further matching of type preference with learning preference has shown that not surprisingly, extroverts like to learn in groups, while introverts "not only did not see experiential training as helpful, but were seen by peers as not participating" (p. 131). This might explain the resistance of many academically talented youth to cooperative learning. Probably those with preference for introversion (I) wouldn't like the cooperative learning situation.

Intuitive types (N) like self-paced learning and situations that let them learn on their own. They like essay questions and often feel academically superior to other students at the same time as they have high expectations of themselves that they will achieve high grades. Faculty members find that intuitive types often make the most insightful remarks in class. Thinking types (T) like classes that are laid out for them, classes that have clear objectives and goals, classes with structure. They also like teachers to lecture and to demonstrate. Feeling types (F) have more preference for group activities in classes, and they often report that their social lives interfere with their studies. Judging types (J) work efficiently on their own and can manage their time well. They hand assignments in on time, and they are willing to take courses in improving their study skills or their SAT scores. Like thinking types (T), judging types like orderly classes with clear objectives, and don't mind working in workbooks or listening to lectures.

Perceptive types (P) often report that they procrastinate and they start too late on their work. They like experiential learning, and they are often able to cut through and identify the real issues in problems. In summary, while bright students with high intuition (N), feeling (F), and perception (P) were receptive to teaching/learning situations that used an inductive approach, high achieving students of the J and T preference prefer to learn the traditional way, and might possibly have to be coaxed to participate in such things as "human relations" activities and the like. Like students with S preferences (Sensing), J and T preferences like courses that are laid out clearly, where expectations are made clear, with teacher lectures, workbooks, laboratory exercises, and point systems set out with no surprises. The Myers-Briggs Type Indicator, if one subscribes to the Jungian theory of personality preferences, is a widely used, well-validated instrument with many applications for understanding academically talented high school and college students.

However, recent literature has disclaimed the importance of learning styles as pigeonholing certain groups for less rigorous education. Well-meaning research showed that American Indians prefer to learn by observation: "The American Indian and Inuit children were most successful at processing visual information and had the most difficulty performing well on tasks saturated with verbal content" (Dehyle & Swisher, 1997, p. 140). When such information is used to stereotype students, the cultural deficit model—that certain cultures are deficient—"has been used to stereotype students into specific group styles and to ignore both individual and tribal differences" (p. 151).

Likewise, Howard Gardner (1995b) evinced a worry about the use of his multiple intelligence theory (MI) in schools. He published an article on the "myths" that are being propounded about the multiple intelligences. One of the myths was that multiple intelligences were learning styles. An intelligence is a construct, not a domain, discipline, or learning style. MI theory is empirical and compatible with general intelligence theory. Evidence for this is that a person cannot learn mathematics at the higher levels through a strength in bodily-kinesthetic intelligence. Ultimately each intelligence has its own codified symbol system and a person who is learning a domain based on that intelligence must learn and be able to solve problems within that code.

Testing

Most schools administer standardized achievement tests at all levels. Guidance counselors at all grade levels should "get their hands dirty" with these tests, and mine them for the information that they contain. Much can be gleaned from just looking at the cumulative records of students. One school I consulted with had its tests piled in unopened boxes in the counseling office. The stickers with the test scores were put on the students' folders by the secretaries; the counselors had no clue as to who were their talented students or who were their high achievers. This is an extreme case, but many standardized achievement tests contain useful diagnostic information, especially about skills.

Talent Searches and Out-of-Level Testing

The Talent Searches conducted by the Center for Talented Youth (CTY), and regional talent search organizations [e.g. Northwestern University's Midwest Talent Search; Duke University's Talent Identification Program (TIP)] rely on out-of-level testing. At the higher levels standardized tests are inaccurate; the numbers of items in any category of skill is necessarily small so that the test can be comprehensive. If a child gets all the items right, the school has no idea what the child's actual achievement level is. The tests give a projection of level, in a grade equivalent, but these are just projections, and projections at the upper levels are also inaccurate because of sampling and number of items in the skills. If a child in the third grade receives a grade equivalent of 12.9 (twelfth grade, ninth month) on the standardized achievement test, this does not mean that the child could go to the senior high school class and sit there and achieve with the twelfth graders. It means the child got all the items right on the third grade test.

Higher level tests should be administered to students who score in the top ranges, so that their achievement levels can be clearly assessed and accurate placement can be made (Lupkowski-Shoplik & Assouline,1993; Olszewski-Kubilius & VanTassel-Baska, 1990; Stanley et al., 1992). Schools that do out-of-level testing are quite rare, at least in my experience. That is why opportunities for such children through the Talent Search are important. Usually it is the coordinator of programs for the talented who makes counselors aware of talent search programs, and some coordinators have met with resistance.

The identification of such talent potential when the students are in junior high school is extremely important, so their course selections can be made with care. Students who attend special accelerated summer programs often complete a year of mathematics in an intensive three weeks. A related problem comes when the school system will not give the child credit for the summer work, operating on the assumption that a Carnegie unit takes so much time over so many months and to do the work in a shorter amount of time is not possible. Julian Stanley, who founded the SMPY (Study of Mathematically Precocious Youth) program at Johns Hopkins, said this about the tyranny of the Carnegie unit: "The age-in-grade lockstep is somewhat like the practice of the innkeeper Procrustes in Greek mythology, who tied travelers to an iron bed and amputated or stretched their limbs until they fitted it" (Stanley, 1989, p. 194).

Proficiency Testing

Currently the schools are in a tizzy about proficiency testing. Whole curricula are being modified, teaching styles and methods are being changed, so that the schools can score within acceptable levels on proficiency tests. Some of the tests are high stakes; in some states students cannot graduate from high school without passing a statewide examination for proficiency. In Michigan in 1996, several academically talented students who were National Merit Finalists and who had been accepted to Ivy League universities refused to take the state-mandated exit examination, saying that they already had reached the goals they had set out to reach, and whether or not they graduated from their particular high schools was moot. The state relented.

Proficiency tests have not been studied to any extent for how they relate to the most administered standardized achievement tests such as the California, the Iowa, and the Metropolitan. If studies have been done, they have been done comparing the tests at the lower ends and not at the high ends. What does "proficiency" mean for academically talented students and for those who help them with their education? Will the standards in the schools be lowered to the mean, the norm, of however "proficient" is defined, and will no one worry about how one can teach those who are above proficient?

Program Articulation

Another guidance issue that goes along with course taking is the fact that program articulation must take place from school to school within a school system. Planned program articulation guarantees that repetition does not occur, and that the whole system is operating together, not school by school, or even class by class. High schools often balk at giving junior high school students Carnegie unit credit for courses taken while they are in junior high school. Talented mathematics students are often the victims of this bureaucratic inflexibility, for the development of mathematical talent requires course taking in a sequential manner. The school bureaucracy relies on a schedule and if an anomaly, a talented student, comes along who needs a flexible schedule so he can go to the high school and take mathematics and get Carnegie unit credit for that mathematics and then come back to the middle school to take his social studies and English classes, the schedulers (often counselors) may not like it.

Vocational Guidance

The guidance counselor should have a battery of vocational interest tests that can be used with all students. Talented students especially need vocational counseling because they are often told, "you can do anything that you want to." If a person can do anything she wants to, the burden is heavy, for what does she really want to do? Often, students know only about certain professional choices—doctor, lawyer, scientist, engineer—but do not know about others—linguist, diplomat, historian, professor. Here are some suggestions to improve vocational selection for talented students:

1. Mentoring programs that start early and allow a student to shadow people in certain professions the student may be interested in.

2. A battery of vocational interest inventories available to students early. Many states have computerized career education programs that can be tapped into from the counseling office. The Self-Directed Search and other like instruments can be used fruitfully. The counselor should not wait for student initiation of the process, but should make sure that all talented students take advantage of already present career planning opportunities early.

3. An articulated career education plan beginning in the elementary grades and proceeding through middle school and high school. This should include role models, mentors, career awareness, field trips, internships, and special summer or extracurricular opportunities.

Many people show snobbery about vocational programs. This is mistaken. The need for highly trained technical people keeps growing. Even President Clinton, in a town meeting in November 1997, said "there are thousands of technical jobs going begging today." These jobs are often high paying, and along with them goes a certain job security, often along union lines. But even if there isn't job security such as in old-time union days, the technically trained hospitality, health, business, industry, agriculture, retail, and family and consumer sciences graduate will soon find another job as their knowledge is desperately needed. On the other hand, the sadness of the recent Ph.D. graduate desperately seeking employment in the sciences or in literature is reflected in the hundreds of resumes that pile up in college offices when even a low-level academic position is offered. Something has gone wrong with our value system about what work is admirable and what is not.

Volunteerism and Service

A requirement for high school graduation in many districts has become the mandatory volunteerism and service requirement (an oxymoron to be sure). The results of such programs have been shown to be mixed, but generally of the positive variety. Students who tutor, who visit people in hospitals, who coordinate programs in the community, almost invariably state that the experience was worth it. One academically talented high school girl in a case study done by one of my students credited her career in medicine to her candy-stripe volunteerism while she was in high school. Again, the altruistic nature of many of the students is satisfied when they learn to give and not just to take. Middle school students have also volunteered in their communities as part of the curriculum for their studies (Gosfield, 1993).

GENDER DIFFERENCE CONCERNS
FOR GUIDANCE INTERVENTION

Guidance counselors and educators of the talented should be aware that there are strong gender differences among talented youth. Some of the most profound gender differences have shown up in achievement, in testing, in underachievement, in course taking, and in parents' attitudes and school personnel's behaviors towards their girls.

Even though girls get better grades in high school and college, boys receive better scores on the SAT and are therefore more likely to become National Merit Semifinalists. A group called the National Center for Fair & Open Testing said that the National Merit group indicated that boys take harder courses, especially in mathematics and science, which gives them an edge. For now, suffice it to say that it is true that females are often guided into taking fewer and less rigorous high school courses, and that the more rigorous the junior high school and high school courses for academically talented youths, the more they will achieve in college and perhaps after college.

Gender Differences in Testing

Counselors and educators of the talented should also be aware, in helping students to plan for courses and for tests, that there are great gender differences in test results. In 1992, Julian Stanley and his colleagues reported that of 84 commonly administered achievement tests, 83 showed statistical differences favoring males. This has implications for college and graduate school admissions. These tests included the Differential Aptitude Test, the American College Test, Advanced Placement Tests in all fields, the Graduate Records Examinations, and the Scholastic Aptitude Test. The results of these tests cannot be attributed to test bias or gender bias in test items, according to both Stanley and Benbow. Stanley noted that most test makers throw out items that show gender differences, and that studies that have been showing that gender differences are declining are thus misleading. Benbow noted that "there may be many more exceptionally talented males than females in mathematics," basing her conclusion on data from more than a million subjects tested over 20 years, and concluding, "the gender difference in mathematical talent is not an artifact of test item bias" (Benbow, 1992, pp. 99–100).

THE INDIVIDUAL AND GROUP EDUCATIONAL GUIDANCE PLAN (IEP)

By now it is obvious that the counseling and guidance component in a talented youth's life is as important as is the curricular component, for who but the adult professional guidance person, the adult expert in the education of the talented, can guide the choices the talented youth makes? For this it is necessary to have a regularly updated plan on file. This plan should be jointly made by the school and the student, with active participation and input from the parents and the various instructors of the student. The plan should have components that include specific information about the student's talent areas, assessment instruments or observational instruments that have been administered, or predictive behaviors that have been observed. There should be a short-term component and a long-term component. This plan should follow the student from school to school, level to level, and should be periodically consulted and modified. The specialist in talent education should be aware of this plan, as should all the teachers the student has, especially the teachers in the talent area(s). The plan should be administered by guidance personnel or specialists in talent education. Figure 11.4 shows an outline of such a plan.

A final word: Anti-intellectual feelings are common in a supposedly egalitarian society. While many people think that talented youths will "make it on their own," and while still other people resent these youth and blatantly discriminate against them, seeing them as privileged and lucky and therefore not deserving of special treatment, the facts are obvious. These are children, too. They were born into this world the way they were. They didn't ask to be born with talent potential, with academic potential, with the ability to think quickly, to remember, to formulate abstractions, to question, to love learning. They have social and emotional needs based on the way they are, just as do all other children. They need adult advocates who will guide them, counsel them, and look out for them, just as do all other children.

Figure 11.4   Guidance and Counseling Plan for Talent Development

Name _____ F ___ M ___ Date of Birth _____ Date _____

School _____ District _____ City, State _____

Person administering this plan _____ Title _____

Talent area(s): ____ Mathematics ____ Verbal ____ Science ____ Social Science

____ Foreign Language ____ Visual Arts ____ Vocal Music ____ Instrumental music ____ Drama

____ Dance ____ Athletics ____ Socioemotional ____ Mechanical ____ Technological

____ Invention ____ Leadership ____ Business ____ Other

I. Means of assessment of talent area(s) (Attach protocols)
(Do not use composite scores; use individual content area scores.)

_____ 1. Standardized group ability test. Which? _____ Talent area(s): _____

_____ 2. Standardized individual ability test. Which? _____ Talent area(s): _____

_____ 3. Standardized group achievement test. Which? _____ Talent area(s): _____

_____ 4. Standardized individual achievement test. Which? _____ Talent area(s): _____

_____ 5. Proficiency test. Which? _____ Talent area(s): _____

_____ 6. Behavioral checklist. Which? _____ Describe behaviors checked. (Attach protocol.)

_____ 7. Personality inventory. Which? _____ Comment. (Attach protocol.)

_____ 8. PREDICTIVE BEHAVIORS. ____ OBSERVED BY FAMILY ____ SELF-REFERRED

        ____ OBSERVED BY TEACHERS ____ OBSERVED BY PEERS ____ COMMUNITY

   What behaviors indicate talent in this student?

        ____ Projects ____ Portfolio ____ Extracurricular interests and achievements

        ____ Out-of-school interests ____ Contests ____ Grades ____ Other

   Describe the behaviors indicated.

  9. Student personal and vocational interest inventory administered? ____ Yes ____ No (Attach)
 10. List student interests.

11. Student curriculum modified to accommodate talent area? ____ Yes ____ No (Attach)
12. Student's parents consulted about student's talent? ____ Yes ____ No

   Attach memo of parent conference. Date held: _____

For person in charge of plan:
Attachments: Item 1 ___ 2 ___ 3 ___ 4 ___ 5 ___ 6 ___ 7 ___ 8 ___ 9 ___ 10 ___ 11 ___

Figure 11.4 *Continued*

II. Short-Term (One-Year) Talent Development Plan

A. Interventions in classroom: ＿＿ Placement in special class ＿＿ Honors class
＿＿ Placement in special school ＿＿ Advanced placement ＿＿ Resource teacher
＿＿ Cluster group ＿＿ Pullout program ＿＿ Curriculum compacting ＿＿ Acceleration
＿＿ Enrichment ＿＿ Other
Describe modifications:

B. Interventions outside of class: ＿＿ Individual counseling ＿＿ Group counseling
＿＿ Individual assessment ＿＿ Group assessment ＿＿ Mentor(s) found
＿＿ Individual lessons ＿＿ Group lessons ＿＿ Special club(s) ＿＿ Extracurricular participation
＿＿ Scholarships ＿＿ Summer programs ＿＿ Saturday programs ＿＿ Contests
＿＿ Competitions ＿＿ Projects in area(s) of talent(s) ＿＿ Community involvement
＿＿ Library involvement ＿＿ College planning ＿＿ Other
Describe the items checked:

C. Guidance: ＿＿ Group guidance ＿＿ Individual guidance ＿＿ Mentoring
＿＿ Shadowing ＿＿ Testing ＿＿ Talent and interest guidance ＿＿ Ongoing career information
＿＿ Gender-specific guidance ＿＿ Special projects/programs ＿＿ Peer guidance
＿＿ Parent guidance ＿＿ Scholarship information ＿＿ Other
Describe:

(continued on next page)

Figure 11.4 *Continued*

D. Counseling: _____ Social-emotional; needs group counseling

_____ Social-emotional; needs individual counseling _____ Referral to therapist

_____ Gender-specific counseling _____ Sex/substance abuse counseling

_____ Counseling dealing with asynchrony _____ Peer counseling _____ Family counseling

_____ Cross-age counseling _____ Other

Describe:

III. Long-Term (Two- to Five-Year) Talent Development Plan

A. Interventions in classroom: _____ Placement in special class _____ Honors class

_____ Placement in special school _____ Advanced placement _____ Resource teacher

_____ Cluster group _____ Pullout program _____ Curriculum compacting _____ Acceleration

_____ Enrichment _____ Other

Describe modifications:

B. Interventions outside of class: _____ Individual counseling _____ Group counseling

_____ Individual assessment _____ Group assessment _____ Mentor(s) found

_____ Individual lessons _____ Group lessons _____ Special club(s) _____ Extracurricular participation

_____ Scholarships _____ Summer programs _____ Saturday programs _____ Contests

_____ Competitions _____ Projects in area(s) of talent(s) _____ Community involvement

_____ Library involvement _____ College planning _____ Other

Describe the items checked:

Figure 11.4 *Continued*

C. Guidance: _____ Group guidance _____ Individual guidance _____ Mentoring _____ Shadowing
_____ Testing _____ Talent and interest guidance _____ Ongoing career information
_____ Gender-specific guidance _____ Special projects/programs _____ Peer guidance
_____ Parent guidance _____ Scholarship information _____ Other
Describe:

D. Counseling: _____ Social-emotional; needs group counseling
_____ Social-emotional; needs individual counseling _____ Referral to therapist
_____ Gender-specific counseling _____ Sex/substance abuse counseling
_____ Counseling dealing with asynchrony _____ Peer counseling _____ Family counseling
_____ Cross-age counseling _____ Other
Describe:

Date: _____

Initials:_____

Scheduled update of plan:

CASE EXAMPLE: JUDITH RESNIK

Dr. Judith Resnik (1949–1986) was the second American woman in space, but her accomplishments do not stop there. Resnik was the first Jew to enter space. She received her bachelor's degree in electrical engineering in 1970 from Carnegie-Mellon University. She then went to work for RCA Corporation, where she worked in their missile and surface radar division as well as their service division. She left in 1974 to become a staff scientist in the neurophysiology laboratory at the National Institutes of Health.

She continued her schooling at the University of Maryland, where she received her Ph.D. in electrical engineering in 1977. She went to work as a product developer for Xerox Corporation. When she heard that NASA was going to admit women into the space program, she was determined to become an astronaut. She did everything she could to be in the best physical shape, and learned as much as she could about NASA and space. She joined NASA's space program in 1978.

She and Sally Ride, the first U.S. woman in space, worked together on the design and development of the remote manipulator system. She also worked as a commentator for ABC to explain what was happening on board for the fourth shuttle mission. Tragically, Dr. Resnik was one of the seven astronauts killed in the explosion of the *Challenger* (Shuttle Mission 51L) on January 28, 1986. In her honor, the Society of Women Engineers has named one of their awards for her. It is given to a woman who has helped make advancements in space.

Resnik attended Firestone High School in Akron, Ohio, graduating in 1966. Resnik "maintained top-notch grades, sought further Jewish education, and made her own beginning forays into male-female relationships, all the while enduring parents who were constantly at war," according to biographers Bernstein and Blue (1990, p. 17). She took the most advanced courses in science and mathematics and a photograph of the mathematics club shows her as the only female member. She graduated as valedictorian of her class. One of her mathematics teachers said of her, "She wouldn't stand out in a hill of beans, except for her attitude of excellence." He even saved her advanced placement mathematics test to use as a model of neatness and logical thinking for students.

Judith displayed an attitude of risk taking by dating Len Nahmi, a boy of Arab/Irish heritage, sneaking out of her room at night to meet him, as her parents didn't approve. Her parents divorced while she was in high school, and she lived with her mother, who hated her boyfriend. Her mother Sarah "demanded unceasing perfection from her daughter" (Bernstein & Blue, 1990, p. 18). Judith sued to have her father be given custody of her, and she won. But, she and Len had already broken up under her mother's pressure. Years later, they were reunited, after Judith's divorce from a "suitable" Jewish boy. Len had become a pilot for Canadian Airlines, and he encouraged her in her efforts to become a licensed pilot.

Judith now had the unwavering support of the two men closest to her—her father and her former boyfriend. When her divorce became final, she sent a postcard to Len with two words on it: "I'm single." She also contacted Senator John Glenn of Ohio, the first American astronaut to orbit the earth, asking his help in entering the space program. Len gave her the practical advice that she should share with the National Aeronautics and Space Administration (NASA) whatever good things happened to her while her application was in process:

> If she got a promotion at the National Institutes of Health, she should tell them. When her doctoral degree came through, she should tell them. An academic honor? Tell them that too, Len advised. And don't tell them in a letter. Tell them in a telegram. Make them sit up and take notice. (p. 34)

Dr. Judith Resnik (back right) with the crew of a 1984 space shuttle mission.

Judith began getting into physical condition. She passed the rigorous NASA physical and was one of 200 female candidates. In January 1978, she became one of four women accepted as an astronaut candidate.

Resnik demonstrated the personality and academic qualities referred to throughout this book. She took risks, she demonstrated persistence and resilience, even in the face of personal problems such as her parents' oppositional marriage and their divorce during her vulnerable high school years. She survived her own divorce and went on to become an American heroine.

SUMMARY

1. The guidance and counseling needs of the academically talented have been historically underemphasized.
2. A key internal description of having a high IQ is "asynchronicity."

3. Research into the psychosocial and affective development of high-IQ students indicates generally positive adjustment for moderately high-IQ students, and less positive adjustment for very high-IQ students.
4. Academically talented and other talented youth need specially informed counselors and specialists to help them with their talent development.
5. Among counseling issues for talented youth are issues of anger, boredom, creativity, delinquency, depression, dropping out of school, gender-related issues, issues that come along with having a very high IQ, introversion, intuition, meeting the expectations of others, motivation, overexcitabilities or intensities, peer relations, perfectionism, overachievement, resilience, self-concept/self-esteem, stress, sexual identity, and underachievement.
6. Common guidance issues that should be addressed include academic planning, acceleration, career development, finding mentors, multipotentiality, learning styles, testing, program articulation, vocational guidance, volunteerism and service, and the gender issues underlying all of the above.
7. An individual educational guidance plan (IEP) is necessary for all talented students.
8. *Challenger* astronaut Judith Resnik displayed persistence, resilience, and academic talent in pursuing her goal to be in the space program.

12 CHILDREN OF THE AMERICAN DREAM: POPULATIONS OF TALENTED CHILDREN WHO NEED SPECIAL ATTENTION

FOCUSING QUESTIONS

1. Why have many methods of identifying talented children from special populations failed?
2. What do you think are the most promising methods of identification of talented children from special populations?
3. Discuss the case study approach, its advantages and disadvantages.
4. Discuss the quota approach, its advantages and disadvantages.
5. Why are rural children considered a special population when many of the most talented adults have come from rural backgrounds?
6. Read a biography of an adult from a special population. What factors led to this person's success?
7. Discuss the challenge of finding and serving African-American males.
8. Discuss the challenge of finding and serving African-American females.
9. Discuss the challenge of finding and serving Hispanic (Latino) children.
10. Discuss the challenge of finding and serving American Indian children.
11. Discuss the challenge of finding and serving Asian and Pacific Island children.
12. Interview a learning-disabled talented person. What factors did you uncover in your interview?
13. Interview a physically disabled talented person or an educator of the physically disabled. What did you learn?
14. Do a database search on the consequences of abuse or divorce for the talented. Summarize the results.
15. What personality characteristics and talents of Charlayne Hunter-Gault have led to her position of leadership?

Figure 12.1 Overview of Chapter 12

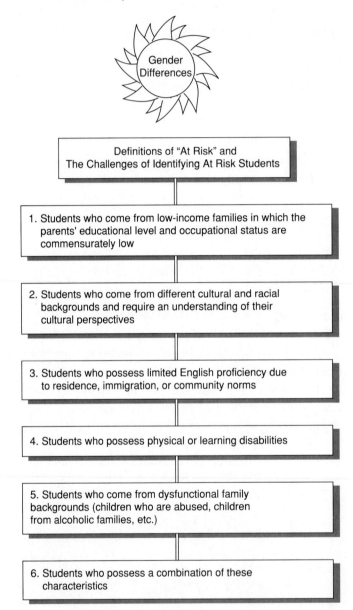

Gender
Differences

Definitions of "At Risk" and
The Challenges of Identifying At Risk Students

1. Students who come from low-income families in which the
   parents' educational level and occupational status are
   commensurately low

2. Students who come from different cultural and racial
   backgrounds and require an understanding of their
   cultural perspectives

3. Students who possess limited English proficiency due
   to residence, immigration, or community norms

4. Students who possess physical or learning disabilities

5. Students who come from dysfunctional family
   backgrounds (children who are abused, children
   from alcoholic families, etc.)

6. Students who possess a combination of these
   characteristics

Lamar is an African-American male in junior high school. He attends an inner-city school and the smallest class he is in has 33 students. He is good at math and gets teased about it by his friends, so he consciously makes mistakes. He is in a special advanced class in math, and during his free periods he goes to the computer lab that his math teacher also runs. She is encouraging him to apply to one of the academic high schools in the city, but his friends want him to stay in the neighborhood. His mother is single and has never been married. He doesn't know who his father is. Chances are he will go on to high school but that he will not finish.

He is a child of the American Dream, one of the many whose childhoods are marred with family trauma, with poverty, with needs for safety, shelter, and care. He is a talented student who has special and difficult challenges in reaching his potential. The American Dream promises immigrants that they will come to a nation whose streets are paved with gold. The American Dream promises everyone that they will have an equal opportunity to raise themselves up by their bootstraps if only they work hard enough. The American Dream promises everyone that people will be considered by the "content of their character and not by the color of their skin," as Martin Luther King, Jr. said in his famous "I Have A Dream" speech in 1965. In reaching the American Dream, Lamar will need more help from the community, the school, and the family than may be offered to him at present. He may be called, by some, "at risk."

DEFINITIONS OF "AT RISK" AND THE CHALLENGE OF IDENTIFICATION

The term "at risk" has undergone some criticism in recent years, and some people have suggested substituting the term "at promise" (Swadener & Lubeck, 1995). The reasons for the criticism of the term "at risk" are that the term "uses a medical language of pathology to label persons based on their race, first language, class, family structure, geographic location, and gender as 'at risk for failure'" (p. 2). The term implies a deficit in the cultural experiences of these children. Swadener and Lubeck said, "The generalized use of the 'at-risk' label is highly problematic and implicitly racist, classist, sexist, and ableist." Formerly, the implication that such children were culturally deficient has become "a 1990s version of the cultural deficit model which locates problems or 'pathologies' in individuals, families, and communities rather than in institutional structures that create and maintain inequality" (Swadener & Lubeck, 1995, p. 3).

Who are these students formerly called "at risk"? A federal study by VanTassel-Baska, Patton, and Prillaman in 1991 defined and made recommendations for students such as Lamar. They suggested the phrase *culturally diverse* to describe these students. The following factors define culturally diverse children who may have special constraints in realizing their talent potentials:

1. Students who come from low-income families in which the parents' educational level and occupational status are also commensurately low

2. Students who come from cultural and racial backgrounds different from the mainstream who require an understanding of their cultural perspectives to find and serve them appropriately
3. Students who possess limited English proficiency due to residence, immigration, or community norms
4. Students who possess physical or learning disabilities that mask their potential
5. Students who come from dysfunctional family backgrounds (children who are abused, children from alcoholic families, etc.)
6. Students who possess a combination of these characteristics
(VanTassel-Baska, Patton, & Prillaman, p. 47)

For example, a middle- or upper-socioeconomic level African-American student is as likely to meet gifted education test score standards as is a middle- or upper-socioeconomic level white student. Therefore, a student's minority status does not necessarily place him or her at risk.

In a survey of state coordinators for the talented, VanTassel-Baska and her colleagues found that very few states include in their definitions of giftedness and talent students who meet these criteria for being at risk. In fact, they found the opposite. Most states pay lip service to the 1972 Marland definition of giftedness and talent that lists six categories—superior cognitive, specific academic, creative, visual and performing arts, leadership, and psychomotor—of varieties of talent, but in reality the students who are served are for the most part those who score high on norm-referenced tests that uncover superior cognitive or specific academic types of talents. VanTassel-Baska, Patton, and Prillaman said, "The limited movement by the states in that direction [of broadening the definition of talent] is surprising" (p. 12). Citing the work of Feldman (Feldman & Goldsmith, 1986), Gardner (1983), Renzulli (1978), and Sternberg (1985), the researchers said that "state standards for administering programs and services have not kept pace with this work" (p. 14). Only one state had developed program standards for serving culturally diverse students with special constraints in realizing their talent potentials. Most states had the same program standards for all students. Passow and Rudnitski (1995) in a more recent study found the same.

The Challenge of Identification

Mary Frasier (1991) said that over the years various solutions have been tried and found wanting. Among these were nominations besides teacher nominations, using special checklists, modifying traditional procedures, using quotas, early childhood and summer interventions, using weighted matrices, teaching to the tests, and the like. "None of these solutions has solved the problem" (p. 236).

Citing the statistics that while minority students make up 30 percent of the population, only 20 percent of students identified as gifted and talented were minorities, and while 30 percent of the population is from low-income families, only 4 percent of those identified as gifted and talented were from low-income families, VanTassel-Baska and her colleagues (1991) pointed out that there is a clear need for gifted and talented policymakers to focus on special populations of talented students.

The conservative use of norm-referenced standardized achievement and ability tests has operated against the inclusion of at-risk students. Therefore, other means of identification are clearly called for. These include the following:

1. Use of a mixture of objective and subjective assessment tools
2. Use of multiple-criteria assessment measures and flexible program cutoff points on assessment measures
3. Use of nontraditional tests and other measures that tap diverse talent areas
4. Use of assessment data as a tool for planning curriculum (p. 47)

These and other researchers (Shore et al., 1991; Shore & Delcourt, 1996) have also made the point that special populations of talented students have different characteristics than talented students who can be easily identified with standardized tests, so the programming as well must be differentiated, just as the identification procedures must be differentiated.

The 1995 study by Frasier et al. showed ten core attributes of giftedness across socioeconomic, ethnic, and racial groups. A qualitative content analysis was used to analyze literature about giftedness to determine characteristics of gifted children in general (*n*=262) and characteristics of gifted children from specific cultural groups (*n*=95), including African-Americans, American Indians, and Hispanics. The 10 attributes were communication skills, imagination/creativity, humor, inquiry, insight, interests, memory, motivation, problem solving, and reasoning. The personality attributes on the bottom of the Pyramid of Talent Development (Figure 1.6) also apply across ethnicities and socioeconomic groups.

Identification

As noted in all the literature about culturally diverse students, the identification procedure must not merely contain an IQ score or any one score; rather, a multitude of methods must be used. Researchers and thinkers are now beginning to realize that test scores and checklists themselves can even be harmful to students, because they are scored in the aggregate, the total, the accumulation. A talented child may have only one of the characteristics, and thus not be selected. The talented child comes from a family with goals, a milieu, a history, a background. For example, it is far more likely for a child to be identified as talented if there are books in the home and the child is read to regularly. This is as true for bilingual talented children as it is for monolingual talented children (Jackson & Lu, 1992). Several promising alternative assessment methods are further discussed here: (1) the Frasier method (1992); (2) the Renzulli revolving door method (1977, 1986); (3) the "quota" method (Mitchell, 1988b); (4) the case study method (Borland & Wright, 1992a, 1992b); and (5) the use of portfolios.

The Frasier Method

Mary Frasier (1992) has designed the Frasier Talent Assessment Profile (F-TAP) system in order to "collect, display, and interpret data from test and non-test sources" (p. 239). This system, or data collection information such as this, is recommended when identifying talented culturally diverse students. The strength of this assessment system is that any one score is an indicator of potential giftedness. The child does not have to have all scores placed on a matrix, which will fail to pull out his or her talents if they lie within one area. The top 50 percent of children are in the screening pool, and there are three different points of entry or departure from the screening pool (see also Frasier, Garcia & Passow, 1995). In 1992, Frasier said that applying the following principles that focus on gifted behaviors and not on test scores has increased ethnic/minority identification in school districts:

1. Focus on the diversity within school populations. The talented are not a homogeneous group, nor do they express their talents in the same way.
2. Adopt a goal of inclusion, not exclusion.
3. Data should be gathered from multiple sources; a single criterion of giftedness should be avoided.
4. Both objective and subjective data should be collected.
5. Involve educators and noneducators who represent various areas of expertise and who know the child who is being observed.
6. Implement an identification program as early as possible, plan it as a series of steps, and find a way to make it continuous.
7. Give special attention to the different ways in which children from different cultures manifest behavioral indicators of giftedness.
8. Decision making should be delayed until all pertinent information on a student has been reviewed.
9. Data collected during the identification process should be used to help make program and instructional decisions. (Frasier, 1992, pp. 46–47)

Renzulli's "Revolving Door" Method

This method is quite popular throughout the country, and for good reason. It identifies a certain percentage of students by placing them into a "talent pool" of about 25 percent of the students. These selected students revolve in and out of special programming. The students are identified by the use of matrices, test scores, and checlists that are given to teachers and parents, and by self-nomination. Type I, or general enrichment activities, are given to the whole population, and then those who are identified receive special Type II activities, which include creative or critical thinking activities (see Figure 9.10 on p. 397). The students then work with special teachers of the talented to complete Type III activities, which are independent investigations, before they revolve out to rest for awhile, and other students can have an opportunity to do Type III activities. This model was adopted by New York City in the 1980s (Renzulli, 1977; Renzulli & Reis, 1989).

Modified Quota System

Mitchell (1988b) said that any program for the talented should have several slots for students who may not be identified or may be underserved. He also described the HUNCHES program in Los Angeles, in which anyone who had a "hunch" that a child was talented was urged to nominate that child. This was step 1 in his recommended program. In step 2, the school district gathers all test information on the students, and puts into a pool all students who have scores at the 75th percentile and above. Step 3 is the completion of a behavioral checklist.

The tendency of educators to emphasize "amount" and "total" should be viewed cautiously. For example, a child who draws constantly may have few of the characteristics listed previously, but may benefit greatly from special programming in art. That is why the case study approach should also be considered by those seeking to identify students with special talent.

Using Case Studies to Identify

The case study, or focusing on the individual child rather than on test scores on group tests, is emerging as the most promising way to identify talented students. Rhodes (1992) noted that when one focuses on the individual, and concentrates on the individual, one can notice predictive behaviors.

Project Synergy, a Javits-funded program in New York City, has used the case study, intense observation over a long period of time, to identify potentially talented young minority students. Borland and Wright (1992b) described a six-year-old kindergarten child named Jenny, whose mother was a pregnant crack addict and whose father was an absent alcoholic. Jenny attended a school that had for supplies one crayon for each child and ranked 617 out of 619 elementary schools in New York City in pupil achievement. Yet Jenny was identified as being potentially talented:

> The daily challenges that Jenny faces seem insurmountable. Yet, she is a survivor. Her inquisitive nature, her tenacious spirit, and the support and encouragement of her kindergarten teacher have enabled her to learn in spite of circumstances that would crush many adults.
>
> Jenny has an intuitive faculty with numbers. Although she has received virtually no formal instruction in the subject, she has somehow learned enough arithmetic to score at the 83rd percentile for children of her age on a test of early mathematical ability. Jenny is also quite adept verbally. She is teaching herself to read, and she writes imaginative stories using inventive spellings. By any reasonable metric, especially in light of her circumstances, Jenny is a talented child. (p. 124)

Project Synergy placed young children like Jenny into a mentor program in which the mentors were achieving adolescents of their ethnic group. Jenny was placed with Narissa, an eighth grader who commutes from a rough neighborhood in Brooklyn to Manhattan to attend a special academy for achieving minority children. Narissa is from a single-parent family also, but the researchers found that her mother emphasizes academic achievement more than Jenny's mother. The pairing of children such as this is a promising practice just now being described in the literature.

Using Portfolios to Identify

A Javits-funded project in Cleveland, Ohio, sought to identify young, talented children of all ethnicities, but primarily poor or African-American talented children. Shaklee and Hansford (1992) described promising practices in assessment. Portfolio assessment was used after extensive staff development. Kent State University's Early Assessment for Exceptional Potential project (Shaklee et al., 1989) included observations of the students during sample lessons, the writing of anecdotal records on the students each week, surveys of parents and the community, and sample products. In 1997 Shaklee reported that the number of young students identified through the portfolio assessment has risen: "portfolio assessment appears to be a viable alternative for the identification of young children from historically underrepresented populations" (p. 6).

VanTassel-Baska, Patton, and Prillaman (1991) posited that there are three philosophical reasons that may have been mitigating against service to at-risk talented learners. The first is that most policymakers believe that equal treatment is fair treatment. The belief that programs for the talented must train future leaders who are knowledgeable and comfortable with the mainstream cultural norms and mores and the concomitant belief that talented learners are advanced learners and that differentiating curriculum for nontypical talented learners insults them and demeans them underlie this philosophical reason.

A second philosophical reason is that affirmative action provides equity, and special populations of talented learners should be placed into programs in numbers proportional to their occurrence in the local population. When this happens, there are often no supports or interventions designed to keep these students in the programs, which are not modified for their needs.

Portfolio assessment is one method that shows promise in identifying talented students.

A third philosophical reason is that individual students have individual needs and individual programs should be designed for them. Therefore, membership in an ethnic group or a group that is, say, abused, should not be a criterion for programming. As a result of any or all of these philosophies about educating talented learners, the special populations of talented students have been falling through the cracks in such numbers that there are basements full of needy children who are bright, talented, and who have high potential that is not being realized. Let us discuss a few of these groups as defined.

RURAL STUDENTS

A student telephoned to arrange her practicum experience. She teaches in a small rural school where most students are below the poverty level and from an Appalachian background. As we arranged for her to be observed during her internship doing a Future Problem Solving program at the school, she commented, "I've come to believe that rural students may be the most challenged of all, because they are away from cultural opportunities and because the community is so protective and conservative." She planned to ask a local egg company for a few dollars for the entry fees for the competition, which is conducted through the mail; thus transportation to an urban site would not be necessary.

Rural students, if they are from poor families, and even, perhaps, if they are from middle-socioeconomic level families, depending on the degree of ruralness, experience special difficulties in realizing their talents. Rural schools are often underfunded. Rural families are often adamant that their children conform to social, religious, and community values, because everyone is looking, everyone knows everyone else, and students who are different stand out. Sex-role stereotypes are especially strong, and what is gender-appropriate is made known to students. Many talented girls in rural areas are pressured to marry young and to forgo further education at the expense of older brothers. If one thinks in global terms, two-thirds of the world's illiterates are females, most of these from rural areas in underdeveloped countries.

Rural schools have certain characteristics that may preclude providing sufficiently challenging academic programs for talented youth. Pendarvis, Howley, and Howley (1990) listed these:

1. Rural schools in some areas may not have sufficient space to house special programs for talented students.
2. Small rural schools may not have sufficient numbers of talented students to justify the implementation of special programs for these students.
3. The distances between rural schools within one district may be so great that the cost and time of transportation to centralized gifted programs may be prohibitive.
4. Parents of rural talented children may oppose programs that require their children to ride buses to gifted programs located at schools other than the local one.
5. Rural high schools may have very few elective options (for example, science courses, foreign language courses, and music courses).
6. Rural high schools may be unable to provide advanced-level courses in required subjects such as English and mathematics. (p. 319)

Just because a student is in a rural district does not mean that the student is in danger of not having his/her talents developed. However, being rural and poor does increase the chances that the student will not fulfill his or her potential giftedness. Howley (1997), in a survey of 758 rural academically talented high school students, noted that very rural gifted students were significantly less satisfied with their communities than gifted students living in more urbanized West Virginia communities.

Many interventions with rural students have been tried and found successful. Among the most successful has been the use of technological advances to educate students who are in rural, isolated districts. Telecourses in advanced subject matters have proven to be very effective in providing bright rural students with course work that will enable them to enter college with the same course background as students in more accessible areas. Satellites and satellite dishes, laser disks and advanced cable equipment, and computers with modems and telephone connections into the Internet have all been shown to be effective in helping students in rural areas.

There are fewer trained counselors, fewer specialists in music and the arts, fewer curriculum specialists in rural areas. Rural districts, which are often extremely competitive with each other as far as athletics and agricultural clubs, should put their differences aside and pool their resources, share personnel and finances, and bus students to special programs, offer courses for college credit, and offer advanced high school courses. The necessity for talented rural youth to have the opportunity to be together with others of like mind is paramount, and when they have such chances, the odds of their talents being overlooked and de-emphasized diminish in proportion to their coming out of isolation.

STUDENTS FROM LOW-INCOME FAMILIES

Repeated studies have shown that poor children, whether rural, urban, or suburban, score lower on standardized tests. A 1987 study by VanTassel-Baska pointed out that economic disadvantage is a clear cause of lower scores on the SAT given in the Midwest Talent Search to students in the seventh grade. About 14 percent of the students who took the SAT (they had to score above the 95th percentile on their school's group achievement test) were economically disadvantaged; that is, their family income was below $20,000 per year. The study showed that economically disadvantaged junior high school students scored significantly lower on the SAT than students from middle- and upper-income homes.

These students would not be able to afford the regional programs offered during the summer by the Talent Search program, and the presence of these students in such numbers should prompt foundations, districts, and corporations to offer help and should prompt state departments of education to formulate policy with reference to these students and their talents. Scholarship programs, counseling for both parents and students, and peer tutoring should also be part of the interventions for these economically disadvantaged youth.

Urban Students

A special program for economically disadvantaged urban students was begun in Boston during the 1980s. Called the Urban Scholars Program, it is a joint effort of the University of Massachusetts at Boston and several urban high schools (Varley, in press). The program provides middle school and high school students identified as gifted and talented with the academic and personal supports necessary for going on to college, and the students who have completed the program have entered some of the most competitive private and public universities in the country.

The director of the program, Joan Becker, was quoted in Varley's study as saying: "the biggest challenge is not in finding black students, but in finding white students. The problem you have with white students is, oftentimes they come from families where, for them to come into a program like this means being in a 'minority' program" (Varley, p. 9). The Urban Scholars Program was funded in 1990 by a Javits grant, and they were able to maintain their intense intervention with gifted and talented urban youth.

Another study of gifted and talented urban youth was done by Lynch (1993). This study, like Varley's, was also part of the Office of Educational Research and Improvement funded case studies. Lynch studied Alika, a gifted and talented student at Walbrook High School in Baltimore, one of the high schools in the Coalition for Essential Schools, which has formed nine principles of essential education. The main influence of the programs founded by the Coalition for Essential Schools for the gifted and talented has been to diminish both honors and Advanced Placement courses in favor of heterogeneous grouping. Alika, a tenth grade girl, was observed for the case study. She is verbally talented. Lynch (1993) observed:

> Alika is never seen in school without a novel, which she pulls out and reads during "down times" in and between her classes. She estimates that she manages to spend about an hour and a half per day doing pleasure-reading at school

Lynch concluded her study with several observations about the fate of gifted and talented learners when there is no ability grouping permitted. She said that such egalitarian treatment "hardly seems fair to the best and the brightest who must be the shining examples, motivators, and teachers of the less able; *unless* they too are helped by their teachers to establish appropriate goals for themselves" (p. 33). She thought that economically disadvantaged gifted and talented students "are accommodating to a curriculum designed for students who are struggling" (p. 34).

ENGLISH-SPEAKING STUDENTS FROM VARIOUS RACIAL BACKGROUNDS

African-Americans

Fenwick (1996) concluded rather cynically that "a pathological image of the African American has infiltrated U.S. education. With desegregation and the arrival of African American children in white America's schools has come the application of psychological and educational labels that create and constrain the educational experiences of the

African American child." Fenwick contended that "these labels have not evolved in an ideological vacuum. They reflect the nature of schools as sites of unequal distribution of economic and cultural capital and they hide the profound interrelations of people, marking the black student as deviant and inferior." Students come to believe that they are destined to underachieve. Fenwick said, "Labels and categories of deviance such as 'at risk' leave educators with the impression that in order for the African American student to succeed, he or she must be exposed to various and repeated treatments." School personnel come to believe that the black student arrives in school "with a natural resistance to learning." Thus, the schools label, certify, and credential students with negative images from an early age. Fenwick called for challenges to the "existing control systems" that schools carry out.

African-Americans are not included in programs for the talented in numbers proportional to their numbers in the population. Researchers (Ford, 1993, 1996; Ford & Harris, 1992; Harris & Ford, 1991) pointed out that only about 63, or less than 2 percent of more than 4,000 articles written about talented students since 1924, were about minority talented students. Alexinia Baldwin, a long-time advocate for African-American talented youth (1977, 1984, 1985, 1987) has, over and over again, pointed out that use of a single measure such as an IQ score to identify talented youngsters leads to the underidentification of African-American talented youngsters. Other researchers have pointed out that in Florida, for example, 22 percent of the students are African-American, but only 4 percent of the students enrolled in gifted classes are African-American (Serwatka, Deering & Stoddard, 1989). Similar ratios occur in other states.

In fact, Jonathan Kozol, in 1991's *Savage Inequalities*, showed that many African-Americans are receiving generally abysmal educations in abysmal schools. His description of the economic disparity in the New York City area is an example:

> The slotting of black children into lower tracks, according to the Public Education Association of New York, is a familiar practice in the city: "Classes for the emotionally handicapped, neurologically impaired, learning disabled and educable mentally retarded are disproportionately black. . . . Classes for the speech, language, and hearing impaired are disproportionately Hispanic." Citywide, the association adds, fewer than 10 percent of children slotted in these special tracks will graduate from school. Nationwide, black children are three times as likely as white children to be placed in classes for the mentally retarded but only half as likely to be placed in classes for the talented: a well-known statistic that should long since have aroused a sense of utter shame in our society. Most shameful is the fact that no such outrage can be stirred in New York City. (p. 119)

Kozol went on to cite per-pupil expenditures in Westchester County, the area just north of New York City, saying that Bronxville spends over $10,000 per pupil while nearby Mount Vernon, mostly African-American, spends $6,400. In New York City the per-pupil expenditure is $5,590, about half that of the Long Island suburb of Jericho, which spends more than $11,000 per pupil. There are no school dropouts in Jericho, and about half of New York City students drop out. Kozol persuasively argued that per-pupil expenditure can mitigate against family and cultural variables that contribute to students' special status:

If the New York City schools were funded, for example, at the level of the highest spending suburbs of Long Island, a fourth grade class of 36 children such as those I visited in District 10 would have had $200,000 more invested in their education during 1987. Although a portion of this extra money would have gone into administrative costs, the remainder would have been enough to hire two extraordinary teachers at enticing salaries of $50,000 each, divide the class into two classes of some 18 children each, provide them with computers, carpets, air conditioning, new texts and reference books and learning games—indeed with everything available today in the most affluent school districts—and also pay the cost of extra counseling to help those children cope with the dilemmas that they face at home. (p. 124)

These inequalities are not unique to the New York City area. Every urban area in the country is ringed by affluent suburbs that tell the tale of "savage inequality." The quality of the school rises with the per-pupil expenditure. Rutter, in 1983, noted that if the family and socioeconomic status variables are held constant, the quality of the school can make as much as one standard deviation's difference in students' achievement measures.

The politics of race and class operate against talented students from groups that are culturally different. One of the most pervasive explanations for the differences in achievement has been called the *cultural deficit*, the *culture of poverty*, or the *cultural underclass* model. In a special issue of *The Journal of Negro Education* focusing on black males, Solorzano (1992) published a study of educational aspirations of African-American and white youth. The cultural deficit model has blamed individuals and families for the lack of educational attainment rather than blaming the schools or the institutions themselves.

A large sample size of 1,500 African-American females, 1,400 African-American males, 8,000 white males and 8,000 white females was used. Solorzano found that African-American females and males believed their mothers had higher educational and career aspirations for them than did the white females and males. The parents' actual aspirations for their children rose as their socioeconomic status rose. Solorzano (1992) proposed a new way of thinking about the underachievement of African-American youth. This disparity between "high educational aspiration-low educational attainment" should raise the question of what these "unfulfilled dreams" (p. 39) mean to both the individuals and to the society. He suggested that the issues be refocused and that the school context be looked at and redefined.

Among the school problems to be analyzed are the "effect of segregated, overcrowded, and underfinanced schools; school staffing, curriculum, and tracking patterns; and teacher expectations and interaction patterns on the educational achievement and attainment of Black students" (Solorzano, 1992, p. 40). Solorzano charged that schools "reproduce minority social inequality" and called for a new model emphasizing the "cultural continuities rather than the cultural deficit approach" (p. 41). His study suggested that the barriers to the achievement of poor black students were social rather than familial or individual. A similar study by Pollard, Farrell, and Sandoval (1986) showed that there was hardly any relationship between aspirations of minority students and the resulting school performance.

What has been called the *American achievement ethic* has not been able to be translated into practice by many African-Americans, especially males, and including the talented. Another 1992 study (Ford, 1992, 1993; Ford & Harris, 1992) showed why. They tried to identify social, psychological, and cultural factors that mitigate against young African-American talented and nontalented children's achievement during their preadolescent years. The American achievement ideology contends that one can attain anything one wants through hard work and dedication, regardless of the ethnic or racial group from which one comes. In addition, a student who believes that hard work pays off can succeed in both life and in school. What Ford and Harris called a "paradox of underachievement" (p. 48) plays itself out with talented African-American youth. On the one hand, as shown earlier by Solorzano's study, African-American youth and their parents have high aspirations. On the other hand, they do less well in school than children who are white or Asian.

The reasons are social, psychological, and cultural, said Ford and Harris in the same special issue of *The Journal of Negro Education.* An "anti-achievement ethic" (p. 48) arises among African-American youth, even talented youth, and especially African-American males: "Some gifted African-American students may sabotage their chances of succeeding outside the African-American community merely to show that they still view themselves as members of the African-American community" (p. 48). Ford and Harris called this a "poverty of spirit." One of the reasons for this feeling is the fact that even African-Americans who do buy into the American achievement ethic and who finish school are not "fairly and equally rewarded" for their efforts by jobs at the end of the pipeline.

Low self-esteem, external locus of control, low achievement motivation, perceived isolation if they achieve, and a fear that they may be perceived to be different from their peers all operate against talented African-American youth. Ford and Harris (1992) said, "gifted students who are forced to choose between psychosocial needs and achievement tend to sacrifice their 'gift'" (p. 49). To be accused of "acting white" was difficult for many talented African-Americans, and thus they chose to excel in athletics or to become the class clown, instead of excelling in academics. Those talented students who showed the most support of the American achievement ethic were those who did best in school: They were "less likely to underachieve and less likely to hold pessimistic beliefs about schooling" (Ford & Harris, 1992, p. 50).

The study (Ford, 1992, 1993; Ford & Harris, 1992) was of 148 identified talented African-American fifth and sixth graders. The comparison group was of similar age in similar schools. The researchers found that students not identified as gifted were more likely to be pessimistic about the efficacy of the American achievement ideology than students identified as gifted. There were no gender differences in this finding. "Thus, academic program (gifted versus nongifted) rather than gender appeared to play a more important role in African-American students' support for the achievement ideology" (Ford & Harris, p. 57). Males not identified as gifted reported lower levels of effort than the gifted students identified as gifted students of both genders and the females not identified as gifted. The students confessed that they were not working at their optimal level in school. The fact that the academic program—participating in the gifted program versus not participating in the gifted program—was the differential, rather than gender or social class, led the authors to speculate about "the ramifications of ability grouping and tracking on the self-esteem and achievement orientation of African American youth" (p. 60).

Perhaps the talented youth had more confidence in their ability and thus were seeing rewards for their adherence to the achievement ideology, Ford and Harris said. Because African-Americans, especially males, do not seem to place much confidence in the educational system or in the achievement ideology, they are at serious risk. Since being placed in a gifted program seemed to be helpful in having students retain their belief in the value of hard work and achievement, the implications for educators of the talented are obvious: Identify and place potentially talented students young, and follow up their progress. Such placement seems to operate to change their beliefs about their possibilities for achievement. Early placement is crucial. For the students who would not be identified as talented, Ford and Harris suggested that a serious look be taken at tracking and ability grouping as predictors of school underachievement.

While the U.S. Office of Education definition of talent stresses more than specific academic ability or superior cognitive ability, in practice, two types of talent—academic or intellectual talent—are the ones that most states and most school districts honor. Harris and Ford (1991) said that there are six shortcomings of the traditional identification process as it applies to minority group members. These shortcomings have led to an underrepresentation (30 to 70 percent) of minority group members in gifted education programs and to an overrepresentation (40 to 50 percent) in special education programs:

1. The process is negatively influenced by the attitudes and expectations of educators who do not believe giftedness exists in culturally different (nonwhite) populations.
2. Sterile IQ-based definitions hinder the process.
3. Identification instruments are misused. (Since environment has been shown to play a role in the manifestation of intelligence, overreliance on intelligence tests and one-dimensional instruments is unwarranted.)
4. A gap exists between research and practice.
5. Inadequate theories are used to account for giftedness among racial minorities. This forces African-American children to manifest giftedness in ways identical to its manifestation in white children.
6. Agreement is lacking on a universal or even acceptable definition of giftedness. (pp. 5–6)

Like many educators before them (for example, Baldwin, 1977; Bernal, 1981; Frasier, 1987; Gallagher & Courtright, 1986; Meeker, & Meeker, 1985; Renzulli, 1986; Richert, Alvino & McDonnel, 1982; Torrance, 1977), Harris and Ford (1991) called for a pluralistic, multimodal assessment procedure for identifying giftedness in African-American youth.

Especially important are checklists that would uncover such characteristics as the ability to concentrate for long periods of time, the ability to speak or to do mathematics well, expressiveness, and dedication. Calling for a "culture-based definition" of giftedness, Harris and Ford pointed out that most contemporary theories of giftedness and creativity emphasize that giftedness arises within a specific culture and what that culture values at the time the person is living. Harris and Ford (1991) also said that the U.S. Office of Education definition of giftedness must reestablish the psychomotor portion of the definition, since many African-American youths manifest their giftedness in their athletic prowess.

However, emphasizing athletics in programs eligible for federal gifted and talented funding may have consequences as well. A controversy has arisen about the numbers of scholarships awarded to African-American athletes by NCAA Division I colleges compared to the numbers of academic scholarships awarded to African-American students. Lederman (1992a, 1992b) reported that one of five full-time African-American male students in college was on an athletic scholarship, compared with one out of 43 white male athletes. Lederman said that critics of these practices pointed out that colleges may be discouraging academically talented African-American youth by awarding so many scholarships to African-American athletes: "Such disparities . . . foster the stereotype that blacks are better suited to physical activities than to intellectual pursuits, and discourage young blacks who are not athletes by suggesting that it's easier to get to college if you play ball" (p. 1). Special admissions procedures for African-American athletes often do not apply to other African-American youth, who have worked hard in high school and who have tried to fulfill the American achievement ideology.

African-American athletes do complete college at a higher rate than do other African-American students, and so proponents of the practices say that giving scholarships to African-American athletes helps them to rise above circumstances of poverty. Arthur Ashe, the tennis player, advocated more difficult academic standards for African-American students and said that the emphasis on athletics sends the wrong message to African-American high school students who are academic achievers, resulting in African-American families pushing their children to be athletes, often at the expense of academic achievement and study time. The fact remained that in 1992, only 6 percent of all college students were African-American, but 22 percent of scholarship athletes were African-American, including 42 percent of football players and 60 percent of basketball players. Overall, however, students who have participated in intercollegiate athletics graduate in larger numbers than students who do not. This is true for all ethnic groups (Lederman, 1992b).

Another study by Olszewski-Kubilius and Scott (1992) compared talented minority middle-class and lower-socioeconomic status students' college aspirations. The study showed that even though the students were equal in test scores, grades, and intention to go to college, the lower-socioeconomic minority students "feel somewhat less prepared to go to college and less confident about being admitted" (p. 146), although their records showed them to be as promising as the others. This lack of confidence could be reflective of the fact that their parents often had no experience with college, college admissions procedures, or college costs, and were not receiving the proper counseling as to these details. The authors recommended that counselors be especially sensitive to these students' needs for mentors, for exposure to college campuses, and for involving the parents early in long-range planning for career and college. However, Olszewski-Kubilius and Laubscher (1996) found that while college counseling for talented economically disadvantaged high school students revealed the same dreams and goals as that for students whose parents had higher incomes, a follow-up study showed the economically disadvantaged high school students were more likely to enter state universities and to experience difficulty in realizing their dreams during college.

Harris and Ford (1991) called for a comprehensive shift in policy toward African-American youth, beginning in their homes and schools. They called for (1) staff development for teachers in the characteristics of children from different cultures; (2) the involvement of parents, beginning in early childhood; (3) the involvement of the community; (4) a re-emphasis on the quality of public eduction; (5) the adoption of a pluralistic philosophy; (6) multimodal assessment procedures; and (7) a curriculum that recognizes "noncognitive, nonacademic skills (e.g., creativity and psychomotor abilities)" (pp. 13–14).

Critics of the latter would say that noncognitive, nonacademic skills are precisely what minority students should not be emphasizing, because this could be construed as another way to enhance racist treatment in schools, permitting majority culture students to be thought of as excelling in cognitive academic skills, while minority culture students would be emphasizing the other skills. What are the reasons for underrepresentation of African-Americans in gifted education classes? A study by Serwatka, Deering, and Stoddard (1989) of talented students in Florida said that such underrepresentation has been blamed on lower verbal skills in standard English among African-American students, and the fact that tests seem to have standard English test content. Others assert that since business is conducted in standard English, all students should learn to express themselves thus.

A study by Wells and Serna (1996) showed that de facto segregation occurs in integrated schools where white students are clustered in programs for the gifted and talented and African-American and Hispanic students are clustered in regular and remedial programs. Attempts by school officials to change this de facto segregation have often incited parents of the white students, who threaten to pull their students out of the public schools and start private schools if their children are to be educated with students of color. The classes where white students are clustered are often fast-paced honors classes, and academically talented black students are relegated to slower-paced regular classes.

Some say that teachers discriminate against their African-American students, and that this is only one in the constellation of school problems that African-American students face. The more African-American teachers a school district has, the more equitably African-American students are identified and placed, the researchers in Florida found. They also found that the more African-American students in educable mentally retarded (EMR) classes, the fewer African-American students in classes for the academically talented. This discounted the accusation that the tests were solely at fault, because the districts that had the most children in EMR classes also had the fewest students in classes for the academically talented. The researchers postulated that use of test data was done in a "less discriminatory manner" in some districts than in others. In addition to emphasizing the importance of having significant numbers of African-American teachers, there is also a need to analyze the way test data are used (Serwatka, Deerin & Stoddard, 1989, p. 530). They also advised studying districts that are successful in balanced placement of students in both EMR and in classes for the academically talented.

Other researchers such as Mary Frasier (1991) have looked at minority (especially African-American) achievers and have found, not surprisingly, that family encouragement is crucial. Racism is a factor in African-American and Hispanic underachievement. Families of academically achieving youth have made their children aware of this, but have also encouraged their children to "cross over" to a certain extent. Fordham and Ogbu (1986) pointed out that academic achievement means that the student must behave like people in the dominant culture, and that this poses some risks for youths among their peers. Fordham (1988) found in a long-term ethnographic study of students in a high school that the academic achievers were teased for "acting white." Ford and Harris (1992) found that academically achieving African-American adolescents preserved their cultural and social awareness but also assumed majority culture achievement standards.

Diane Pollard (1989) did a study of students who were, as she called it, in the "urban underclass" and who had achieved. She said these children were resilient, able to cope under adverse conditions, and that this resiliency was encouraged by certain factors within the achievers' milieu. Pollard said that this resilient behavior needs strong teacher support. Teachers should have high expectations for their students, should help them develop their problem-solving abilities, and should reward them for efforts to achieve. Teachers should also help provide these students with strong self-concepts about their potential to achieve. Understanding and working with the parents of black students is a key component. Ford (1996) offered these suggestions:

Suggestions for Working with Black Parents and Families

1. Remember that parents have the ultimate authority over their children for decisions. Work with rather than against parents to meet students' needs . . .
2. Be receptive to the diversity of family structures. Seek substantive and active parent and family involvement.
3. Recognize that not all parents have the natural ability to parent . . .
4. Establish a good rapport; try to put family members at ease using kindness, friendliness, humor, and informality (if appropriate). Communicate with parents when feedback is positive (opposed to constant negative feedback). If working with underachieving students, contact parents even when progress is small or slow.
5. Use clear language and avoid jargon.
6. Be genuine and sincere. A genuine interest in Black families and their children will increase their trust and self-disclosure about feelings, fears, and concerns.
7. Try to empathize and avoid sympathy. Try to put yourself, to the extent possible, in the place of the family members.
8. Understand and be aware of all means of communication, particularly your own verbal and nonverbal messages; seek consistency between the two.
9. Gather as much information on the child's family as possible before talking with them, educational status, occupation, etc., to better understand the family's circumstances . . . Do not use this information to stereotype or categorize rather to set a tentative framework for understanding.
10. Be familiar with minority child development principles; be aware of the numerous factors affecting minority children's behaviors and achievement.
11. Identify community leaders and how they can work with families on behalf of Black children.
12. Identify resources to help families meet students' needs (e.g., mentors, educational organizations, journals and publications).
13. Avoid being judgmental; try not to show surprise or disapproval of what parents say . . . Make compromises with families that result in win-win situations for children.

14. Be proactive and optimistic—operate from the assumption that Black parents have their children's best interest at heart.
15. Remember that the ultimate goal of family involvement is to enhance the academic and socio-emotional well-being of students. (p. 172)

Suggestions for Identifying African-American Students

Donna Ford (1994b), in a special study for the National Research Center for the Gifted and Talented, published a monograph that listed 10 suggestions for identifying gifted African-American students:

1. A culture of assessment rather than a culture of testing promises to capture the strengths of gifted African American students.
2. There is no "one size fits all" intelligence or achievement test. Multidimensional identification and assessment practices offer the greatest promise for recruiting African American students into gifted programs.
3. Identification instruments must be valid, reliable, and culturally sensitive. If any of these variables are low or missing, the instrument should not be adopted for use with African American and other minority students.
4. To increase the representation of African American students in gifted programs, educators must adopt contemporary definitions and theories of giftedness.
5. Comprehensive services must be provided if the recruitment and retention of African American students in gifted education is to be successful.
6. Teachers who are trained in both gifted education and multicultural education increase their effectiveness in identifying and serving gifted African American students.
7. To prevent underachievement, gifted students must be identified and served early.
8. Qualitative definitions of underachievement offer more promise than quantitative definitions in describing poor achievement among gifted African American students.
9. The representation of African American students in gifted programs must be examined relative to both recruitment and retention issues.
10. Family involvement is critical to the recruitment and retention of African American students in gifted education. Parents and extended family members must be involved early, consistently, and substantively in the recruitment and retention process.

Factors Necessary for Successful Intervention
Family Factors

As the example of Project Synergy showed, parents have a crucial role in encouraging achievement among poor urban and rural students. Johnson (1992) summarized studies of factors outside of school that encourage achievement among junior and senior high school African-Americans. Besides the quality of the school, which is crucial, the home context is also crucial. She said that families who are able to motivate their children to achieve have "strong parental educational values and expectations, academically related activities, optimism, and sense of control" (p. 116).

Personality or Attitudinal Factors

Among other factors necessary for achievement were certain personality factors formed by the interaction of the child with the family, but optimism was critical. Johnson (1992) noted that "those characteristics most involved in motivating achievement behavior among African-American youth—self-concept, locus of control, and self-perceived ability—are quite similar to those found to affect achievement among teens of other racial and ethnic groups" (p. 116).

Locus of control was found to be a major factor in differentiating between those who were successful achievers and those who were underachievers. One of the most well-done Javits grants was a school-university collaboration in San Diego (Johnson, 1994a, 1994b; McLaughlin & Saccuzzo, 1994; Saccuzzo, Johnson & Guertin, 1994 a, 1994b). McLaughlin and Saccuzzo studied gender and ethnic differences in locus of control. The study was of 805 students in grades 5 through 7 who had been referred to psychologists for testing for possible academic talents. Students were given the Nowicki Strickland Internal External Locus of Control Scale for Children (NSLOCS), evaluated for risk factors in six areas (environmental, language, economic, culture, social/emotional, and health), and given the WISC-R. The students who scored high on the WISC-R had more internal locus of control. Ethnic differences in locus of control were also apparent; Caucasian children had more internal locus of control than Filipino, Latino, and African-American students. Students with two or more of the six risk factors had more external locus of control than children with none or one risk factor. Risk factors and ethnic background were related; that is, the more risk factors, the greater the inner locus of control in high-IQ non-Caucasians. Females of all ethnicities had greater inner locus of control. The researchers suggested that a cultural emphasis on independence, self-reliance, and individuation would produce a greater reliance on inner strength. They suggested that locus of control "might be used to produce equity in selecting diverse children for gifted programs" (p. 125). The personality implications of this interesting study need further investigation.

Community Factors

The community in which the child lives has also been studied, and communities that support achievement were those in which the minority children interacted with white children in interracial "friendship networks." Living in integrated neighborhoods was also a factor in teaching children about cultural values that encourage academic achievement. Ogbu (1978) wrote a powerful indictment of what he called a "caste" system in our society, in which minorities, or those who hold a subordinate position with relationship to the power structure of the society, perceive that they have a job ceiling. Those who were "castelike minorities" were those who were involuntarily brought into the society via slavery or colonialism. The perception that hard work and equal educational achievement would still not present a member of a castelike minority with top jobs and top status operates against members of that minority group believing in the value of educational achievement. Moore (1987) found that African-American children who scored highest on the Wechsler Intelligence Scale for Children (WISC-R) and on achievement tests had groups of friends that included whites and lived in neighborhoods that were racially integrated. The elimination of district barriers as manifested in integrated schools and neighborhoods is the main community force that encourages black youths to achieve (Johnson, 1992).

Gender Factors

African-American males and females achieve differently, according to some researchers. Garibaldi (1992) studied the New Orleans school system and found that in the late 1980s, when 43 percent of the public school system was made up of African-American males, these same males received 65 percent of the suspensions, 80 percent of the expulsions, and made up 45 percent of the dropouts. African-American females made up 44 percent of the school population, and were not promoted 34 percent of the time, were expelled 30 percent of the time, and made up 41percent of those who dropped out. Recognizing that not only athletic achievement among African-American males should be emphasized, Garibaldi listed 10 suggestions to positively affect these black males:

1. Teach them how to resist peer pressure and teach them manners, values, and morals both at school and at home.
2. Encourage them to participate in extracurricular activities that are related to academics.
3. Give them tangible recognition, such as letter jackets, for academic achievement.
4. Bring role models, such as African-American male college students, to interact with them at an early age.
5. Encourage volunteers from the community and from the church to serve as mentors.
6. Make teachers aware of the strong risk these males are undergoing, so they can encourage them in academic pursuits from the earliest entry into school.
7. Hire more African-American male teachers in the elementary schools.
8. Encourage parental involvement in the school.
9. Encourage businesses where the parents are employed to provide incentives to the children of employees if they stay in school and do well.
10. Modify the curriculum so that family values and responsibilities are encouraged in African-American males. (pp. 9–10)

African-American females are also considered to be in danger for underachievement, because they are socialized in the early years to be friendly and compliant rather than to achieve academically. However, Ford and Harris (1992) pointed out that there were few gender differences among gifted males and females in their achievement motivation and optimism about achievement. African-American females do attend college in higher numbers than do African-American males (Yeaty & Bennett, 1990). Bronzaft (1991) studied 229 Hispanic, African-American, and white students, and found similarities in their career-family aspirations. Eighty-five percent of them said they wanted to "have it all—marriage, family, career," but the researchers pointed out that this gap in educational attainment between African-American women and African-American men will lead to serious shortages of "marriage eligible" educated African-American men.

A study by Yong (1992) of attitudes toward mathematics among African-American middle school gifted students showed little gender difference in attitudes. Contrary to other studies of young white students, Yong said, "African-American female students perceived that they had good intellectual capacity, did not exhibit fear of success toward mathematics, and were more apt to learn the subject" (p. 138). Yong postulated that this may be due to the fact that the African-American females in the study were "highly androgynous, possessing high degrees of both masculinity and femininity in their perceptions of non-traditional areas of study" (p. 129).

Magnet Schools

Magnet schools, which flourished under orders for desegregation, now attract funding of upwards of $300 million from the U.S. Office of Education Magnet Schools Assistance

Program (Hendrie, 1998). However, they are under fire for their admissions policies now that judges are regularly taking back twenty- and thirty-year-old orders for desegregation. White parents have sued in many states, saying that quotas for minority students were unfair, as less qualified students might be admitted under quota systems. Administrators in such schools as the prestigious Boston Latin School, City Honors School in Buffalo, and Johnston Middle School in Houston are among those struggling to put into place race-neutral admissions policies. The use of lotteries (sometimes in several levels, as in Broward County, Florida) seems to be increasing and the use of IQ and other standardized tests seems to be decreasing. Federal judges throughout the nation have been issuing contradictory rulings, and desegregation experts say that sooner or later the U.S. Supreme Court will have to decide about race-based assignment and admissions to magnet schools.

Promising Programming Practices

Besides enrichment and self-esteem programming for potentially talented minority youth, there seems to be a real need for reinforcement and direct teaching of skills. No matter how many diverse programs provide creative thinking and critical thinking skills, these skills should not be taught in a vacuum. Ultimately, what the student knows about the subject matter is what counts, especially when the outcome measure is admission to college. Sometime or another, the minority, or majority, gifted student will have to learn subject matter. Ultimately one of the factors on which the student will be judged will be scores on standardized tests such as the SAT or the ACT, the GRE or the specialized test for entering his/her profession. Olszewski-Kubilius and Scott (1992) pointed out that the school reform movement that seeks to target all instruction for all students toward the disadvantaged rather than toward the gifted, produces "a group of students who are at high risk for not developing their academic potential" (p. 142). Levin (1992) and his colleagues at Stanford University have also noted that what they call "accelerated schools" should and do use the model of focusing on the potential and not on the disadvantage, which has produced amazing results in turning schools around.

The Center for Talented Youth (CTY) at Johns Hopkins University has for years been offering special programs in subject matter to junior high school and younger high school students who score high on the SAT-Math and SAT-Verbal. Their goal is not to teach the children to have more creative and critical thinking skills, but to teach them subject matter. The fact that fewer ethnic minority students have qualified for these programs than were probably out there prompted the Center for Talented Youth to start a "Skills Reinforcement Program." Lynch and Mills (1990) said, "Affirmative action plans or the alteration of admission criteria for rigorous academic programs, however well-intended, sidestep the fundamental issue: Some children are not as well-prepared as others for demanding academic coursework" (p. 365). This is the fundamental problem, and no amount of sidestepping will solve it. Skills reinforcement, though, seems to work.

The Center for Talented Youth (CTY) took 45 sixth grade students in Pasadena, California, who had scored in the 80th to 90th percentile on the California Achievement Test and offered them academic intervention for 110 hours. The students had special Saturday classes in the spring and in the fall, and they had a summer program. (One is reminded of the popular film, *Stand and Deliver*, in which Jaime Escalante also required that his students, in order to be fully prepared for the Advanced Placement BC-Calculus Examination, attend on weekends and during the summer.)

At the end of this experimental program, CTY found that the students made significant gains in mathematics. Reading scores did not improve significantly, indicating that reading improvement takes a longer time than 110 hours in a spring, a summer, and a fall. Lynch and Mills (1990) noted that "minority students who can demonstrate their abilities by strong performances on standardized tests are sought by many excellent schools and colleges" (p. 375). The instruction was diagnostic-prescriptive in form. The students' weaknesses were diagnosed and remediated. Mathematics skills proved more amenable to such intervention, and the authors suggested that "verbal development may simply require more instructional time and 'homework' time to produce greater advances in proficiency" (p. 376).

The program sought to help the students in test-taking confidence as well, and the students developed a more mature and scholarly attitude toward work. Several of the students received scholarships and admission to special schools as a result of the intervention described here. Critics of such a program may say that it took them out of their communities and made them act more like the dominant culture, more "white," than they should have. Whether the goal is to have students achieve in ways that allow them to function in the dominant culture, or to have students feel good about their own culture and function there, is a key issue when talking about giftedness in black students. It has long been noted that leaders of minority ethnicity, when they reach prominence, often send their children to private or special schools. Jesse Jackson and Marion Wright Edelman are examples. These minority leaders obviously decided, along with members of the majority culture, such as President Bill Clinton, that private schooling was more suitable for their children than public schools.

American Indians

American Indians who are talented may not be served by special programs for the talented to the degree that talent exists. The reasons for this are variously called discrimination or a lack of cultural understanding about differences in American Indian children. Three distinctive schooling environments for AI/AN (American Indian/Alaskan Native) students were examined in a report to the National Bureau of Educational Statistics: the 149 schools operated by the Bureau of Indian Affairs (BIA schools) or by Indian tribes under contract to the BIA (tribal schools), the 1,260 public schools with 25 percent or greater AIAN enrollment (high-AIAN), and the 78,625 public schools with less than 25 percent AIAN enrollment (low-AIAN). BIA/tribal schools serve AIAN students almost exclusively; most are small elementary schools. BIA/tribal schools were more likely than public schools to offer Chapter 1, remedial math, and bilingual education programs, and were less likely than public schools to offer academic enrichment programs for gifted and talented students (Christenson, 1996). In 1997, the Bureau of Indian Affairs (BIA) served over 49,000 K–12 students in 187 schools on 63 reservations in 23 states; 105 of these schools were tribally operated. The BIA also funded 24 tribally controlled colleges and operated two postsecondary institutions. Herring (1996) asserted that the inconsistencies in the identification and assessment of American Indian and Alaska Native gifted and talented youths are neither appropriate nor effective.

Callahan and McIntire (1994) published a monograph called *Identifying Outstanding Talent in American Indian and Alaska Native Students.* They recommended balancing the ideal and the practical; deciding on a concept of talent; recognizing the issues of a particular school; identifying traits that may influence manifestations of talent; recognizing behaviors that distinguish some Native American students from the general population; looking for manifestations of talent potential, alternative behaviors, situations, and interpretations; selecting and constructing appropriate assessment tools; and using the collected student data to make decisions.

Researchers such as Davidson (1992), Meeker (1992), Daniels (1988), Tonemah (1980, 1987; Tonemah & Benally, 1984), and George (1983) have asserted that American Indians process information differently and so using conventional tests to identify them is an exercise in futility.

Davidson (1992) compared 57 American Indians with 60 white students, ages 7 through 12, in a district in Montana. She administered the Kaufman Assessment Battery for Children (K-ABC), and found significant differences in mental processing between the two groups in simultaneous processing and sequential processing. American Indian children were higher in simultaneous processing and white students were higher in sequential processing. Simultaneous processing is more holistic. This study confirmed another study by Krywaniuk and Das (1976) in Canada, in which the American Indian students were found to be better in simultaneous processing than sequential processing.

However, other studies have shown that such conclusions are premature: Davidson (1992) said, "Though research findings . . . provide some support for the theorized view that American Indians tend toward simultaneous or holistic processing strengths, such findings are not consistent, nor are they conclusive" (p. 111). Since about half of the American Indians and three quarters of the whites had no discrepancies between simultaneous and sequential processing, Davidson said it would be overly simplistic to conclude that there are processing differences between the groups. Children should be dealt with as individuals and not as members of a group about whom certain conclusions have been made. Davidson found the Kaufman Assessment Battery for Children "relatively culture-fair" and stated that it "can be appropriately used in assessing the ability of both American Indian and White students of average to superior intelligence" (p. 113).

Other comparisons, using the Wechsler, showed that spatial ability seemed to be higher in the American Indian children, as well. Studies using the Wechsler Intelligence Scale for Children (WISC-R) showed that the greatest strengths of the American Indian children were in Picture Completion, Block Design, and Object Assembly (Connelly, 1983; McShane & Plas, 1982; Teeter, Moore & Peterson, 1982).

Meeker (1992) detailed several studies that have been done, utilizing the Structure of Intellect Learning Abilities Test (SOI-LA) in identifying the strengths of American Indian students. The studies overwhelmingly showed that the American Indian children were strong in visual-spatial, figural abilities, and not in semantic abilities. Most school learning emphasizes semantic and symbolic studies. In studies (Meeker, 1992) that used the SOI-LA test with Navajo, Shoshone, Comanche, Nez Perce, and various tribes of Indians in Canada, "remarkably similar" (p. 11) patterns of abilities were found. The strong abilities were figural-spatial, visual memory for details, auditory memory, and symbolic. The undeveloped, weaker abilities, were convergent production, vocabulary, verbal relations, verbal systems, and classification.

Maker (1997), in the DISCOVER Javits grant, found that "higher percentages of Navajo children (27) are rated 'definitely superior' than Mexican American children (15) on the Pablo activity" (p. 7). Tonemah and Benally (1984) said that while testing may be useful in assessing American Indian talent, a multifactored approach utilizing both qualitative and quantitative data is absolutely necessary. They also cautioned that there are many tribes and that tribes do differ.

Florey et al. (1986) developed an inservice training model to help teachers in identifying American Indian talented youth, noting that there may be several cultural differences such as differences in values and thinking styles, astuteness in judging environmental circumstances, and the ability to think of new ways to do things (creativity) and to take acceptable leadership roles.

George (1983) also cautioned that there is a great diversity among tribes and communities among the American Indian populations, and thus it is difficult to generalize about specific talents generic to American Indian children. However, she said, "Limiting the definition of giftedness to the academic area only seems particularly inappropriate to Native American students, whose experiential background is so rich in areas other than school academics" (p. 222).

Identification should be based on the particular community's history and culture, which is not Western European, but which also differs within the various tribal cultures. American Indians have characteristics that are common to other repressed and minority cultures within the dominant, Western European influenced culture. Identification procedures should take into account the psychological effect of being in a minority, as well as the effects of economic disadvantage and segregation onto reservations. George also pointed out that being identified as talented might go against a cultural belief that people should not be singled out for special treatment. "Who do you think you are? Who does he think he is?" are put-down statements reserved for people who are told they have the potential to achieve great things.

Individual tribal cultures should be consulted as to the efficacy of identification and nomination for special programming, and also the tribe's cultural values should be considered. The question should be asked: What is the goal of special identification and programming for talented American Indian children? and the answers considered when developing programs to identify and assist students in this population.

Using Multiple Intelligence Theory for Assessment

In the early 1990s, a Javits grant called Project STEP-UP directed by Dorothy Sisk of Lamar University in Texas funded studies by C. June Maker at the University of Arizona. Utilizing Gardner's multiple intelligence theory (MI), Maker (1992) formulated a definition of giftedness that emphasized the ability to solve problems. She said:

> The key element in giftedness or high competence is the ability to solve the most complex problems in the most efficient, effective, or economical ways, and gifted, or highly competent individuals are capable of solving simple problems in the most efficient, effective, or economical ways. (p. 13)

Maker, Rogers, Nielson, and Bauerle (1996) formulated a process for finding superior problem-solving ability, and they piloted their process in several elementary schools on Navajo reservations. The process utilized spatial, logical-mathematical, linguistic, interpersonal and intrapersonal problem solving. Students were given problems in each of these areas (for example, tangrams, storytelling, writing, math worksheets, and making figures from cardboard shapes). The children were observed doing these activities, and students who were perceived to be outstanding were discussed by the group of observers. Independent ratings by second or third observers of products were conducted of all products and separate lists of those thought to be outstanding were created. The process has been able to identify American Indian gifted children.

In 1997, a study by DeLeon and Argus-Calvo described a program for identifying talented artists in the American Indian and Hispanic communities in a rural area in New Mexico. Although in the majority in the two program schools, Hispanic and American Indian students were the minority in gifted and talented programs. A multidimensional approach to identification was developed that included the following: nomination by teacher, parent, or self; participation in an art show; teacher assessment on a checklist and a rating scale; assessment by a community artist; portfolio assessment; and student evaluation on two formal tests. Interviews with members of the identification committee indicate that the most effective selection method was the cross-referencing of the community artist's recommendations with those of teachers and students and results of the art show.

Daniels (1988) cited several examples of curricular differentiation useful in special programs for academically talented Indian youth. A science program in South Dakota that included trips to the Badlands and to the Black Hills was developed by Catmull, Hancock, Huckins, and Runyon (1977). A social studies program called Project Necessity was developed by the Bureau of Indian Affairs in 1970 for use with high school Indian youth. It utilized role playing and narratives, with books about Indian culture and interaction about substance abuse. In Washington, Little Soldier (1982) used stories and handicrafts to teach historic contributions of Indians. The growth of predominantly Indian community colleges and colleges near reservations has been a trend of the 1980s. All of these programs seek to instill pride and self-esteem in Indian youth.

STUDENTS WITH LIMITED ENGLISH PROFICIENCY (LEP)

Many of the generalizations made about some African-American talented youth also apply to some Hispanic talented youth. For example, about half of the children in need of bilingual education services are Hispanic and half are of Asian background. For many American Indian youth, English is also their second language, thus they are also LEP. However, more Asians are in programs for the gifted and talented, and more Hispanics are in programs for the mentally retarded, and emotionally disturbed. This discrepancy has been pondered by educators and there have arisen no clear-cut answers as to why recent immigrants who are Asians achieve in traditional academic ways while recent immigrants who are Hispanics experience difficulties in school. Some researchers have posited that time spent doing homework is crucial. Asian students seem to spend the most time doing homework, and time spent doing homework has been shown to be related to academic achievement.

Hispanics (Latinos)

Hispanics and other students whose mother tongue is a language other than English have often been called *language minority* children. The difficulties of identifying these talented children are similar to the difficulties of identifying other talented children of cultural differences, as noted in the preceding section:

1. Commonly used standardized tests may be inadequate, or if adequate, the cutoff scores may be too high, not taking into account the fact that the youngster is often operating in two languages, a very sophisticated procedure not uncovered by commonly used tests.
2. Poverty-related issues may obfuscate the predictive behaviors (as in the case of Jose, in Chapter 3).
3. The mainstream American achievement ideology is not operant, and the children underachieve.
4. Teacher expectations are not consonant with the abilities of the children and teachers do not understand the needs of language minority children.
5. There may be differences in learning styles in language minority children.

Valencia (1985) noted that gifted and talented language minority children are often noticeably articulate in their native language but may not be able to articulate as well in English, and thus may be passed over. They also may be shy, inhibited, or reluctant to express themselves in English, which may result in their language abilities being hidden. Their parents may also not know about programs for the talented, and their culture may impede them from aggressively advocating for the children, even though they recognize the children's extraordinary abilities. Recent immigrants from many cultures feel intimidated by school structures, and some are just grateful to have a free public school to attend. They may then feel it is impolite to point out to the school that their child has special abilities. This can result in underidentification of language minority students who have quite high abilities.

If the student acquires English rapidly and with accuracy; if the child begins to show leadership capabilities that are recognized by the other students; if the youngster begins to understand quickly the new culture's mores and habits; and if the child shows talent in the arts, in music, in mathematics, or in athletics, where knowledge of the dominant language may not be the necessary criterion for excellence, this quickness and talent should be noted and the school should consider the possibility that the child is probably talented. Barkan and Bernal (1991) pointed out that programs for bilingual gifted children should focus on their strengths, and not on their deficits. While instruction in both languages should take place, instruction in English should not be focused on drill, but instead should help them think in English, "so that the child is so focused on what is to be learned that the medium assumes a background role" (p. 146).

Kloosterman (1997) pointed out that bilingualism is similar to giftedness in that it is a complex phenomenon that involves inner cultural dimensions: "Both bilingualism and talent development are multidimensional phenomena involving cognitive, affective, cultural, environmental, and situational factors" (p. 4). Studies of bilingualism show that acquiring and developing competency in two languages requires cognitive abilities that are complex. The lack of appreciation of such complexity in transfer and in simultaneous processing should be focused on. This is a strength and not a weakness (Castellano, 1995).

Identification of Hispanics by standardized testing has not proven successful. The definitive study about the use of the WISC-R compared with the Standard

Raven Progressive Matrices (RPM) was done in 1994 in the San Diego Javits grant (Saccuzzo, Johnson & Guertin, 1994a, 1994b). Testing thousands of children, many of them Hispanic, they found that neither test is suitable for identifying giftedness in Hispanic children. The DISCOVER assessment in the New Mexico Javits grant (Maker et al., 1996) was more successful. Based on Multiple Intelligence assessment, the DISCOVER assessment protocol placed students in programs for the talented and gifted in percentages that "closely parallel the ethnic makeup of the school community" (Maker, 1997, p. 7). Nielson (1992) found that in demographics, identified gifted students had linguistic, economic, and educational backgrounds like other children in their schools, while traditional assessment identified students from English-speaking families with high incomes and high levels of education.

Gender issues are important in considering giftedness in the context of Hispanic culture. Hispanic females of high ability seemed just as likely to drop out of school as other Hispanic students (Lashaway-Bokina, 1997). Latino culture often values the *macho* ethic, and dominance by males. Chicana writer Gloria Anzaldúa said in an interview with Donna Perry:

> For me, personally, the silencing . . . came from my family and my culture, where you were supposed to be seen but not heard. This was especially true for the girl children. You were not supposed to talk back to your elders. You were not suposed to have an opinion that deviated from the tribe's. Because my culture is very family and extended family-oriented, the individual is not that central. It's the family . . . I was also sensitive to the fact that males could talk at any time but not girls . . . A lot of . . . stories in the Chicano/Mexican culture are used to control the children, to keep them from venturing out, especially the girls. (Perry, 1993, p. 27)

In Tucson, a case study method has been used in kindergarten, utilizing a group screening test such as the Raven's Colored Matrices Test (Raven, 1990), a teacher checklist, a parent questionnaire, an abbreviated form of the Wechsler Intelligence Scale for Children-III (WISC-III), a rating of self-esteem, and samples of student work. The number of bilingual children who were accepted into the gifted program substantially increased from 17 to 31 percent (Barkan & Bernal, 1991).

In 1997, Goertz, Rodriguez, and Bernal published a study about Mexican-American secondary gifted students' perceptions about the counseling they had received. The students did not perceive their counselors as being willing or able to help them with personal problems, but saw them as helpful only for career and college concerns. This would seem to parallel the way that most students seem to view their high school counselors.

Pacific Islanders and Asians: Emerging Minorities

Asian groups are as diverse as Hispanic groups. Forty-six percent of recent immigrants to the United States and Canada are from the Asian and Pacific Island groups. It is not uncommon for urban schools that serve immigrant populations to have 50 or 60 different languages represented among the students, and often many of these student immigrants are from Asian and Pacific Island cultures. Asian and Pacific Island immigrants put a great value on education as a means of rising in society and of making good, with about three-quarters of the immigrants having a high school education or beyond (Woliver & Woliver, 1991). College education has been traditionally valued: Woliver and

Woliver said, "Education, for some Asians, even in precolonial times, served as a major vehicle into government, administration, and bureaucracy . . . Education and scholarship were keys to economic advancement" (p. 250).

Therefore, many Asian immigrants are not in trouble educationally; however, their children often feel a lack of fit, a strangeness, a difference between themselves and the majority culture. These children also may not see their parents for long periods of time because parents often work three or four jobs in order to climb the economic ladder. The talented young Asian child may face looking different and feeling different without as much parent support as he or she would like. The friction between traditional values of Asian and Hawaiian people, such as regard for elders and older siblings, the constraint to refrain from calling attention to oneself and one's needs, "indirect rather than direct communication," and "a desire to act as part of a group, rather than an individual" (Woliver & Woliver, 1991, p. 251), conflict with what the young, academically talented Asian child sees among non-Asian peers. Such traditional traits may cause shy, polite, quiet young Asians not to be identified as academically talented. This "incongruence between home and school values" may cause stress and problem behavior.

The presence of racism in society also affects Asian and Pacific Island youths. Some Japanese-American youths still carry family scars of World War II relocation policies. Woliver and Woliver (1991) said:

> While less overt, racism now takes other forms. Recently, a large California university was revealed to have weighted the entrance criteria to discriminate against Asians because the school felt it had too many Asians. Rumors of quotas for Asians among prestigious eastern schools are often heard. The message to Asian youngsters seems to go something like this: "We want you to succeed, but not to excel past the white majority." (p. 256)

Asian youths also face stereotypes. They are perceived to be better at mathematics than at verbal areas, they are not perceived to be athletic, but to be exclusively academic. These stereotypes affect the self-esteem of Asian youth.

Plucker (1996) noted that Asian-American issues have been notably underrepresented in the literature on giftedness and talents. Language issues are, of course, present: "Many gifted Asian-Americans face a 'double-edged sword': they may be excluded from gifted and enrichment programs due to their lack of English fluency but excluded from ESL programs because they are rapidly learning English" (p. 329). Counseling issues are paramount. These include conflicts in cultural values between a student's parents and his/her peers, career issues such as the valuing of mathematics and business-oriented careers over careers in the arts, and reticence in discussing or dealing with personal problems. Students have great pressure to succeed academically, but only in certain areas. A graduate student from Taiwan, given the assignment of looking for predictive behaviors in talented Taiwanese dancers, visual artists, actors, and writers, said she had never thought of these people as gifted (Yu Schu Lin, personal communication, 1995). The best-selling book in Taiwan ever was Goleman's 1997 *Emotional Intelligence*.

Kitano (1997) studied 15 Asian-American women. Their parents' experience of discrimination led them to an extreme focus on academic achievement for their daughters. The women found that other factors besides hard work operate in attaining success. Differences between national groups and social classes showed that one cannot generalize for Asians.

Immigrants

The fact that some immigrant groups achieve better in schools than other immigrant groups has been studied by Duran and Weffer (1992). Several variables are operant in successful, high achievement by immigrants: (1) socioeconomic class (the lower the socioeconomic class, the poorer the achievement, by and large); (2) family educational values (if families expect children to go to college, and if children expect themselves to go to college, achievement is higher); (3) course taking—a strong program in mathematics and science leads to higher achievement; and (4) personality factors such as resilience and persistence. Intervention strategies should include a strong assessment and programming for science in the junior high school, especially reading skills in science.

STUDENTS WITH PHYSICAL OR LEARNING DISABILITIES

Learning-Disabled Talented Youth

Recently, many studies have emphasized that a student can be both learning disabled and talented. Gunderson, Maesch, and Rees (1987) pointed out that learning-disabled and other disabled talented youth are often overlooked because of identification procedures. They may be scoring in average ranges, and school officials may not notice the discrepancy scores that are necessary for being identified as learning disabled. A learning-disabled talented child, like other learning-disabled children, has a discrepancy between Performance and Verbal scores on a WISC. The discrepancy is not noticed by the teacher and thus the student is not referred for evaluation. Group screenings do not necessarily point out learning disabilities.

Another group of students that may be missed are those who are already in learning disability classes. The focus of the intervention for them is on the disability and not on the gift. For example, a child may be verbally facile in speech but may be unable to spell. The spelling is what is called a disability, perhaps a dyslexia, and the speaking ability is ignored or dismissed. Boodoo, Bradley, Frontera, Pitts, and Wright (1989) conducted a survey of procedures in Texas that were used to identify children who are both learning-disabled and talented. They recommended that teachers receive information about the existence of talented, learning-disabled children, especially about the fact that they may display great achievement in only one area and be weak in others.

Besides being aware that these children do exist, and that they may be masked because they are achieving at average levels even though they have high potential, educators should provide appropriate educational experiences, teaching to the gift as well as teaching them to compensate for the disability or handicap (Reis, Neu & McGuire, 1995). Baum (1988) described an enrichment program for talented/learning-disabled students. Noting that these youngsters often shine outside of the school setting in their hobbies and special interests, she and her colleagues created a program for outside of school that was formulated for talented students who were learning disabled. Utilizing Renzulli's enrichment triad model (Renzulli, 1977), the students experienced general exploratory activities and special critical and creative thinking activities before undertaking their Type III activities, individual creative projects in such areas as history, war gaming, and ecology. Students gained in self-esteem as they completed their projects, leading to "an unexpected result," dramatically improved academic achievement (Baum, 1988, p. 229).

Baum provides the following guidelines for programming for learning-disabled youths:

1. Focused attention should be given to the development of a gift or talent in its own right.
2. Talented learning-disabled students require a supportive environment that values and appreciates individual abilities.
3. Students should be given strategies to compensate for their learning problems as well as direct instruction in basic skills.
4. Talented learning-disabled students must become aware of their strengths and weaknesses and be helped to cope with the wide discrepancy between them (1988, p. 230)

Major classroom modifications that teachers of learning-disabled talented children can make include (1) using a variety of teaching approaches—oral, visual, kinesthetic; (2) permitting students to present information in various ways and in various formats (on tape, orally, by demonstration as well as in writing); (3) using alternatives such as puzzles, oral quizzes, math manipulatives, tangrams; (4) placing the child where the child can always be seen; (5) being flexible about deadlines; and (6) using contracts (Whitmore & Maker, 1985).

One caveat should be observed: the learning disability will always be there, and the child must learn to compensate for it. The struggle will always be there; the frustration will always be there. Compensatory skills such as learning to touch type, learning word processing, using calculators and recorders, and learning organization skills should be taught to the learning-disabled talented child. Behavior modification techniques often used in special education may also be tried. Successful talented learning-disabled adults should be sought out as mentors. The world is full of them and most regions have learning-disabled programs for college students at a nearby college. The role model that a successful learning-disabled college student can provide is invaluable to a young, struggling, frustrated learning-disabled talented child.

Physically Disabled Talented Children

Physically disabled talented children are children capable of high performance who also possess some handicapping condition such as hearing, visual, emotional, or orthopedic challenges. Helen Keller, who was blind, deaf, and mute; Franklin Roosevelt, who was a victim of polio; and musicians Stevie Wonder and Ray Charles, who are blind, come to mind. These people are certainly talented and were able to make great contributions to the world in spite of their physical challenges. The National Clearinghouse on Handicapped and Gifted Children estimated in 1985 that there were 300,000 school age children who were talented and disabled. St. Jean (1996) noted that assessing the cognitive abilities of such children can be done using instruments like the Columbia Maturity Test, Detroit Test of Learning Aptitude-2, and the Stanford-Binet. Modifications during the testing situation are usually made. Again, since the disability is highly visible, its presence often masks the talent. Removing the mask is the challenge to the staff members identifying the disabled talented child. The National Clearinghouse Digest on the gifted and talented disabled pointed out:

People with obvious disabilities, such as blindness or deafness, can be readily identified, as can those with obvious mental or creative gifts and talents. But identifying the true ability of a deaf child who has inadequate communication skills or of a physically disabled person who cannot hold a pencil properly presents a unique problem and a challenge. Talent and ability may be present but blocked.

Identification of such children should, like the identification of other special children, include multiple methods. Biographical information, case study information, behavioral checklists, observational information about play and school, and parent and peer information should be part of the identification process.

Brian: Visually Handicapped and Talented

Brian was diagnosed at the age of 4 with a rare brain disease. He began to lose his sight, and by the age of 5 was almost completely blind. He was attending a preschool program in Manhattan. The teachers in the program noticed that Brian had an unusual command of oral language, a superior memory, and was a one-time learner. They recommended to his parents that he be tested for a special school for talented children.

Brian was admitted to the school with an IQ of 140. The school had never served visually handicapped students before, and the administrators had to make arrangements with the New York City Board of Education for specialists in the education of the visually impaired. The school was not affiliated with the Board of Education, but Brian had a right to receive special help under Public Law 94-142. Two specialists were assigned to do work with Brian. One oriented him to the large urban school building. One came in and worked with his teachers to plan his lessons, and to translate them into Braille, sat in on some of his classes, and tutored him when needed. Brian entered the school in the first grade.

The special characteristics of intellectually talented children, their ability to quickly master much material, presented a special challenge to the Braille specialist, who had to spend a lot of extra time translating classroom material into Braille because of the volume of reading material the sighted students in his classes were covering. Brian was expected to cover the same material as his classmates, with the assistance of the Braille specialist. By Brian's second and third grade year, a full-time person was needed just for this purpose, because the challenge of keeping Brian up with the class kept increasing. The school had to pay for half of the services of the Braille translator, because the Board of Education only provided half-time services.

Special teachers noted special challenges in educating Brian. The physical education teacher created special equipment and special lessons while the other children were doing activities that required sight. These activities involved a safe physical risk for Brian, such as balancing on his stomach on a wheeled skateboard and pushing himself along in the gymnasium, or walking on a slightly raised balance beam. The clay art teacher had to devise special tools for Brian because he shaved his clay sculpture by touch. The science specialist created a special workstation for Brian and provided him with a peer tutor who would pour and plug in a safe manner. The whole school learned as a result of educating a disabled talented child.

Identifying Talented Students with Disabilities

Three constraints are present in the talent search: (1) students often have difficulty in expressing themselves so that their talents may be recognized; (2) the classroom itself has an impact on the students and their expressiveness; and (3) inclusion into the regular classroom may be incomplete or done inadequately (Cramond, 1995; Reis, Neu & McGuire, 1995; St. Jean, 1996; Willard-Holt, 1994). Using observational checklists that "cross over" between the characteristics of giftedness and the characteristics of the disabled may help. St. Jean (1996) said, "Recognizing and nurturing talents in children who are unable to speak is extremely difficult. These children cannot explain their thinking processes, respond to or ask questions, or display leadership abilities in conventional ways. They must rely on others or on mechanical devices to interpret for them" (p. 1).

In recent years AD/HD (Attention Deficit/Hyperactivity Disorder) children have increased in numbers. These are children who are unable to pay attention, who must move, and who demonstrate symptoms that are disruptive in quiet classes. The usual therapy is drug therapy, specifically the administration of the drug Ritalin. Often these children are creative and their creativity may be misdiagnosed as Attention Deficit Disorder (Cramond, 1995). Ritalin and other drugs prescribed for AD/HD carry side effects, most notably liver damage. Gifted and talented children with AD/HD may be misdiagnosed as well. Often the gifted and talented child who seems unable to pay attention, does pay attention—to things that interest him (these are most often boys). But the trouble is, nothing in school interests him, so he may be bored and restive. At home, though, he can sit for hours in front of the computer, still and silent, watching the screen. This child is not AD/HD.

Moon, Zentall, Grskovic, and Hall (1997) did a study of the families of three students who exhibited both academic talent and AD/HD and three who were academically talented. All were boys. The families of students who were "twice exceptional" seemed to be more in conflict, more clamorous, and more disorganized. They shared fewer family times than did the families of the other students. The researchers concluded that "intelligence does not moderate family stress in families with a gifted child who also has AD/HD" (p. 198). The parents experience ambiguity and ambivalence at the dual presence of high intellectuality and behavioral difficulty. These families were also more stressed than families whose children had AD/HD but were not academically talented. The families resembled the families of those who raise creative and underachieving children. Are there differences between these families? No one knows, though the families of children who later made creative achievements often have at least one parent who is in a creative field and the family values creative expression (Piirto, 1992a/1998).

As for all children, these students should be in classes that permit individualization, classes where advanced work is possible, and where the atmosphere is such that it values achievement. Science experiments, activities that emphasize the tactile, and field experiences are helpful for students with physical disabilities in order to help them meet situations they might otherwise not encounter. The students with disabilities also need a chance to be in regular classrooms and in classrooms for the gifted and talented (Bireley, 1993).

In addition, there are various measures to enhance the identification of students with specific learning disabilities other than those that are physical. A substantial amount has been published about various traits or characteristics that hamper the identification of high ability students with learning disabilities. Practitioners interested in this population have also identified positive characteristics that can aid educators and parents in recognizing the talents of these students (Baum, 1988; Reis, Neu & McGuire, 1995). Professional development in recognizing talents in the physically and learning disabled is an investment that must be made by the school staff developers.

STUDENTS FROM TROUBLED FAMILY SITUATIONS

The consideration of talented students from troubled, or in the medical terminology, dysfunctional, family backgrounds has been long in coming, but is an appropriate reaction to the growing awareness in the last 20 years that the children of the world are often cruelly abused by the adults in their lives. Talented children are no exception. In fact, Alice Miller, a European psychoanalyst, sounded the cry about the abuse of talented children by their middle-class parents in 1982 (7th edition 1997) in her book, *The Drama of the Gifted Child.* She theorized that parental narcissism— the wish of parents to see their ideal selves reflected in their talented children— caused the talented children themselves to grow up without knowing their true selves, their emotional selves. Miller's work predated that of those who now call for people to seek their inner child in order to become whole adults. This psychic abuse is difficult for school people to recognize and deal with, because it happens at home, and the "good child" and the "great parents" are enacting their own ritualistic dramas far away from the halls of academe. Miller (1997) said that the adults in such a child's life should be enlightened, helpful witnesses. She said:

> The adult who has grown up without helping witnesses in his childhood needs the support of enlightened witnesses, people who have understood and recognized the consequences of child abuse. In an informed society, adolescents can learn to verbalize their truth and to discover themselves in their own story. They will not need to avenge themselves violently for their wounds, or to poison their systems with drugs, if they have the luck to talk to others about their early experiences, and succeed in grasping the naked truth of their own tragedy. (Miller Website: www.amiller.com)

A recent spate of memoirs by creative people has pointed out the presence of extreme abuse in the lives of those who later became successful and admired. Their resiliency, Miller would say, is because they also had a warm presence in their childhoods. Rock musicians such as Elvis Presley have come from poverty; talk show hosts such as Oprah Winfrey tell about sexual abuse by relatives; rich superstars such as Maya Angelou suffered many childhood traumas (Angelou, 1970). I have studied writers for my research (Piirto, in preparation). The current rage for nonfiction memoirs has yielded a memoir on incest from novelist Kathryn Harrison (Harrison, 1997). Her father left the family when she was very young, and her mother left her with her grandparents soon after. Harrison's father reappeared when she was in college at Stanford University (indicating her academic talent), and she had a sexual affair with him for several years. In a television interview, she stated that she wanted to be loved by her mother and by her father, and their abandonment of her at such a young age led her to be so vulnerable as to succumb to her father's sexual advances in young adulthood [Interview on "20/20" (ABC Television), March 14, 1997].

Poet Mary Karr was raped by a neighborhood boy when she was eight. In her memoir, *The Liar's Club*, (1996) she reminisced (confessed) about her early life in Texas and Colorado. Her mother, a sensitive, beautiful, and unstable visual artist, had been married seven times. Her father, a laborer for an oil company, was a rough and ready sort who liked to drink with his friends, ride in pickup trucks, and howl at the moon. The rape in Texas was followed by another by a babysitter in Colorado:

> Later, when he's all done, he backs way off and gets gentle again. The flat of his hand rubs my back while I'm vomiting down the front of my gown. I am grateful for the warm rubbing of his hand, like whatever I did he's forgiven me for. I vomit again till my stomach seizes up on its own hurt, and he's patting on me bent over there. He's saying I'm okay. I did good, though it's clear down in the core of me that I'm no way okay. (pp. 20 ff.)

Karr didn't find out about her mother's many marriages until she was an adult and discovered a jewel box with wedding rings in it. Her mother had had two children who were kidnapped by her second husband and his mother. Karr's mother finally found the children, and kept marrying so she'd have a place and a family to which to bring them, but by the time she married Karr's father, the children were too old to want to come. "Those were my mother's demons, then, two small children, whom she longed for and felt ashamed for having lost." Her mother turned to drink. Her father had his own struggles with the bottle. Karr became a poet. Whether this was cause and effect is not known, for many people have experienced such shocks and have not become poets.

Novelist Amy Tan's parents were immigrants from China. Her father, trained as an engineer, had refused financial help to attend M.I.T. in order to become a minister in the Baptist church. Her mother had been in an arranged marriage in China, and had three children whom she left when she came to the United States with Tan's father. Tan didn't meet her half-sisters until the late 1980s and her mother kept their existence a secret for many years. Her grandmother, after being widowed, was raped and became a concubine. She later committed suicide from shame "after she had a son and his second wife claimed that son as her own" (Pearlman & Henderson, 1992, p. 23). Tan said she suffers from depression.

Novelist Carolyn See said in an interview, "My dad was a hard-luck boy; his mother killed herself; his father drank himself into an early death." Her parents were divorced when she was 11 and her father became a pornographer. See's grandmother's suicide was allegedly because of the sexual demands of See's grandfather. See herself earned money in the 1960s by testifying in defense of pornographers in court cases (Pearlman & Henderson, 1992, p. 167).

It is not known whether writers have more unconventional families than other people in the arts, though other researchers have noted that musicians and visual artists also seem to have their share of family trouble (Piirto, 1992a/1998). Creators in artistic domains seem to follow suit. Perhaps their creativeness spawns from their need to understand what happened in their childhoods through metaphor and making.

But there is a phenomenon that school people can and should recognize, and that is the dramatic social change in the family. With almost half of all couples getting divorced, almost half of the children any teacher teaches are experiencing the trauma of divorce. As Wallerstein and Blakeslee (1989) found, in their longitudinal study of children of divorce, no one escapes unscathed—including talented children. Whatever the custody arrangement, the children will experience periods of underachievement and pain. These children, at this time—and perhaps for a long time—should be watched carefully for signs of depression and underachievement. Many schools have divorce groups, in which children can share their experiences with others in the same situation. Making sure that both parents are informed about the child's progress (depending on the court) and making sure that the term "broken home" is not used are two ways the school and the teacher can be sensitive to the trauma these children are suffering.

Sensitivity to the economic and personal circumstances that single parents experience should also be practiced. Few studies exist about the effects of single parenthood on talented youth, but Gelbrich and Hare's study (1989) showed that, like most children, talented children also suffer from a lag in achievement when they are in single parent homes. The researchers studied the families of 382 students who attended a summer enrichment program and found, "Giftedness does not appear to shield children from the adverse effects on school achievement associated with single parenthood" (p. 116). This phenomenon has been little researched in the field of the education of the talented. Rogers and Nielson (1993) surveyed all the literature on marital status of parents of gifted children and found little information. They said that possible underinclusion of children of divorce is probably taking place.

STUDENTS POSSESSING A COMBINATION OF CHARACTERISTICS

Many children are in double jeopardy because they fall into more than one category. A child may be of a minority group and may be physically disabled. A child may be poor and may be learning disabled. A child may have family trauma—an alcoholic or ill parent—and may be from a group that doesn't speak English as its first language. All these situations compound the danger that the child's talent will not be discovered, that the child's troubles will mask his or her abilities, that the school will be forced to focus on the troubles and pain and ignore the development of talent.

Such students are called "twice exceptional." Benge and Montgomery (1996) did three-year case studies of three male junior high school students who had high academic ability and also emotional difficulties. Using the Dabrowski Theory of Positive Disintegration, the researchers analyzed the life themes of the students. They noted that the students had an acute awareness of how they were manipulated and of how they could manipulate others. The brain power of these students does not permit the institution to "put one over" on them; they are able to see beneath and within with laserlike precision and clarity. This often does not make them willing participants in what they, like Holden Caulfield, see as phony manipulation of their educational and emotional interests.

A 1996 brochure published by Phi Delta Kappa, the organization for school administrators, indicated some strategies for helping students with difficult situations (Dixon, 1996). Teaching strategies suggested were: (1) to step out of the traditional mold; (2) to rethink the classroom; (3) to restructure tests; (4) to be flexible; (5) to provide independent learning time and assistance; (6) to use more manipulatives; (7) to create hands-on classrooms that allow much more movement; and (8) to allow gifted students to take charge of their learning. Parent strategies included (1) reading aloud; (2) reading together; (3) providing access to information; (4) nurturing intense interests; (5) ensuring children do regular homework; (6) ensuring that children participate in school activities; and (7) ensuring gifted and nongifted siblings assume equal roles in family routines.

To summarize, these and other populations of talented children who need special attention are the greatest challenge in the field of talent development education. We now know how to find them and how to serve them; the *will* to do so must be present. The educational institution must work with the social institution, with the family, the church, and the community in providing facilities, expertise, personnel, individual planning, and safety, so that these precious children with talent can be found, nurtured, and educated to reach their potential.

CASE EXAMPLE: Charlayne Hunter-Gault, Civil Rights Heroine

> On January 9, 1961, I walked onto the campus at the University of Georgia to begin registering for classes. Ordinarily, there would not have been anything unusual about such a routine exercise, except in this instance, the officials at the university had been fighting for two and a half years to keep me out. I was not socially, intellectually, or morally undesirable. I was Black. And no Black student had ever been admitted to the University of Georgia in its 176-year history.
>
> —Charlayne Hunter-Gault, 1992, *In My Place*, p. 3

Charlayne Hunter-Gault was born on February 27, 1942, in Due West, South Carolina. Her father was away as a chaplain in the military, and her mother gave birth to her alone at home. Her childhood was typical of the daily experience of African-Americans in the segregated South: What was it like to be forbidden to vote? To be allowed to drink only from a water fountain that was labeled "Colored"? To have your teeth pulled by a white dentist who was too lazy to give you proper treatment? To know that if your young daughter attracted the attention of a white man, there was almost nothing you could do to protect her? These were the realities of the world into which Charlayne Hunter was born, and they helped shape the path she was to take.

Charlayne Hunter lived in Covington, Georgia, and attended the ramshackle "Negro" school there. The family then moved to Atlanta, where she attended a black elementary school and a black high school. Her father was stationed in Alaska for two years, where she attended an integregated high school, but she and her mother returned to Atlanta where she graduated from Turner High School as a member of the National Honor Society, the homecoming queen, and as editor of the school newspaper, third in her graduating class. A fellow student at Turner, Hamilton Earl Holmes, was on the football team and also in the National Honor Society and valedictorian of the senior class. A group of businessmen, professionals, and social activists named the Atlanta Committee for Cooperative Action (ACCA) approached the two honors students with a plan to "crack the lily-white system of higher education" in Georgia (Hunter-Gault, 1992, p. 125). After a dry run at Georgia State University in Atlanta, they set their sights on "the university." The University of Georgia was located in Athens, "seventy-five miles away, on the other side of some of the most backward, racist little towns in Georgia" (p. 127).

Their applications were greeted by headlines on July 11, 1959: "2 NEGROES TRY DOORS AT ATHENS." The registrar said that the university's dorms were full. Charlayne Hunter enrolled in Wayne State University in Detroit and Hamilton Holmes attended Morehouse College in Atlanta for their freshman year. In Atlanta, on March 9, 1960, several thousand students of the Atlanta University Center colleges marched through the streets. They began to sit in to challenge Jim Crow laws. "For us, the summer of '60 was like no other" (p. 145).

While their lawyers were taking their application to the University of Georgia through the courts, as the university gave excuse after excuse why they could not be admitted, except for the excuse of race, the two young honors students participated in the sit-ins and marches. They returned to college in the fall, Hunter to Wayne State and Holmes to Morehouse. In the autumn of 1960, Dr. Martin Luther King, Jr. was put into jail along with protesting students in Atlanta. Dr. King served four months in jail at hard labor. President Kennedy called Mrs. King, pregnant and frightened that her husband would be killed, telling her to call him if she needed anything. The next day Dr. King was released.

In December 1960, Charlayne was summoned back to Georgia, to Athens, for a trial that had been ordered on their motion to be admitted to the University of Georgia. The university argued that her quarter system credits would not transfer to the semester system at the university. The judge delayed his decision until January 6, 1961, after Charlayne had returned to Wayne State University. Thirty-six hours later she arrived at the University of Georgia. The opposition to their enrolling was so great that the university president was opposed and Governor Ernest Vandiver had vowed that "not one, no not one" Negro would attend classes with whites.

The students erupted into riots and Hamilton Holmes and Charlayne Hunter were expelled from the university for their own safety. Bricks flew through windows and fires raged in the streets. Fraternities flew Confederate flags at half mast. The state patrol refused to come, and the city police ended the riots with tear gas. Hamilton and Charlayne drove back to Atlanta in the middle of the night. Judge Bootle ordered the university to readmit them immediately. They returned and spent a year in almost complete silence. They went home every weekend. They had to fight other battles—eating in the cafeteria, swimming in the university pool. Charlayne Hunter graduated with a major in journalism, and Hamilton Holmes graduated with a major in pre-med, in 1963. Hunter-Gault wrote, "Only Hamp and I could really appreciate the special sweetness of this final moment of our unique history together" (p. 212). He went on to be a surgeon, who died at a young age, in the early 1990s, and she went on to international renown as a journalist.

Reporters follow Charlayne Hunter as she walks to class at the University of Georgia.

Charlayne Hunter-Gault began her career in journalism in 1963 as a reporter for *The New Yorker* magazine. In 1967, she joined the investigative news team at WRC-TV, Washington, DC, where she also anchored the local evening news. In 1968, Charlayne joined *The New York Times* as a metropolitan reporter specializing in coverage of the urban black community. Her work was honored with numerous awards during her 10 years with *The Times*, including the National Urban Coalition Award for Distinguished Urban Reporting.

Charlayne Hunter-Gault joined the then "MacNeil/Lehrer Report" in 1977. Her assignments included substitute anchoring and field reporting from various parts of the world. During her association with the broadcast, she was recognized with numerous awards, including two Emmy Awards as well as a Peabody Award for excellence in broadcast journalism for her work on "Apartheid's People," a NewsHour series about life in South Africa. Here is a sampling of Charlayne Hunter-Gault's memorable NewsHour segments: November 19, 1996: Newsmaker with President Jimmy Carter, on his book *Living Faith*; December 16, 1996: Newsmaker interview with Kofi Annan, U.N. Secretary General; October 6, 1994: Newsmaker interview with South African president, Nelson Mandela; December 24, 1996, "Troubled Heart of Africa," a three-part series on the historic roots of the multiple crises in Rwanda, Zaire, and Burundi; October 3 & 4, 1985, "Apartheid's People": a special series on the plight of South Africans.

In addition, she received the 1986 Journalist of the Year Award from the National Association of Black Journalists, the 1990 Sidney Hillman Award, the Good Housekeeping Broadcast Personality of the Year Award, the American Women in Radio and Television Award, and two awards from the Corporation for Public Broadcasting for excellence in local programming. She has honorary degrees from over two dozen institutions. Twenty-five years later she returned to be the commencement speaker at the University of Georgia. In 1997 she left PBS to become the South African correspondent for National Public Radio. She has been married twice and has two children. Her son, Chuma, was a student at the Hunter College Elementary School when I was principal there, and I had the privilege of meeting Charlayne Hunter-Gault on numerous occasions, as she was an active parent in the school.

Charlayne Hunter-Gault is the author of *In My Place*, a personal memoir of her role in the civil rights movement. Vintage Books has an extensive teacher's guide for educators to use in focusing on the U.S. civil rights movement. This is available on the World Wide Web at www.randomhouse.com/acmart or from Random House Academic Marketing, 201 East 50th Street, New York, NY 10022.

SUMMARY

1. The challenge of serving at-risk talented students is the greatest challenge in the field of talent development and education. The six categories of at-risk talented students are as follows:
   a. Students who come from low-income families in which the parents' educational level and occupational status are also commensurately low
   b. Students who come from different cultural and racial backgrounds and require an understanding of their cultural perspectives to find and serve them appropriately
   c. Students who possess limited English proficiency due to residence or immigration or community norms
   d. Students who possess physical or learning disabilities that mask their potential
   e. Students who come from dysfunctional family backgrounds (children who are abused, children from alcoholic families, etc.)
   f. Students who possess a combination of these characteristics
2. Family, community, and personality factors are essential components of the education equation of rescue from "at risk" to "at promise."
3. Charlayne Hunter-Gault represents a child of the American Dream who changed the history of education in the United States.

A COMPARISON OF STANDARDIZED TESTS

Name	Description	Subtests	Theoretical Base or Construct	Reviewers' Comments
Stanford-Binet Intelligence Scale: L-M (1960)	Individual IQ test. Must be administered by a psychologist. Time: 1 hr. +	1. Visual-motor skills 2. Spatial relations 3. General knowledge 4. Picture vocabulary 5. Recall 6. Classification 7. Verbal fluency 8. Abstract reasoning 9. Expressive vocabulary 10. Arithmetical reasoning 11. General knowledge	Spearman, Terman *g*-factor theory	1. The highest-IQ students (182 to 193) lost 46 IQ points on the WISC-III, "making them indistinguishable from moderately gifted children" (Silverman & Kearney, 1992). 2. Primarily a verbal test (Cronbach, 1985).
Stanford-Binet IV (SB$_4$) (1985)	Individual IQ test that superceded the Stanford-Binet L-M. Must be administered by a psychologist. Time: 1 hr. +	1. **Verbal Reasoning (V)** 　Vocabulary 　Comprehension 　Absurdities 　Verbal relations 2. **Quantitative Reasoning (Q)** 　Quantitative 　Number series 　Equation building 3. **ABSTRACT/VISUAL REASONING (A)** 　Pattern analysis 　Copying 　Matrices 　Paper folding and cutting 4. **SHORT-TERM MEMORY (M)** 　Bead memory 　Memory for sentences 　Memory for Digits 　Memory for Objects	Uses a Composite score similar to an IQ that represents a person's overall test performance. Has incorporated the Cattell-Horn G-f and G-c theory of intelligence (Cattell, 1971; Robinson, 1992)	1. Standardized on 5,000 people ages 2 to 23 in 47 states. A stratified random sample based on 1980 census data. "Undersampling of lower strata" (Cronbach, 1985). 2. Students taking the Stanford-Binet Intelligence Scale: L-M scored five points lower taking the new version (Kitano & DeLeon, 1988). 3. "Psychologically interesting and the materials are appealing" (Salvia & Ysseldyke, 1991). 4. Mean of 100, SD of 16, SEMs reported for each area score and composites. 5. "Appears to measure most English-speaking persons well" (Cronbach, 1985).

Name	Description	Subtests	Theoretical Base or Construct	Reviewers' Comments
Wechsler Intelligence Scale for Children-Revised (1974) and III (1991) WISC-R WISC-III	Individual IQ. Must be administered by a psychologist. Time: 1 hr. +	**Verbal subtests** 1. Information 2. Comprehension 3. Similarities 4. Arithmetic 5. Vocabulary 6. Digit span —immediate recall of orally presented numbers 7. Sentences —repeating sentences verbatim Yields verbal IQ **Performance subtests** 8. Picture completion 9. Picture arrangement 10. Block design 11. Object assembly 12. Coding 13. Mazes 14. Geometric design Yields performance IQ **Full-scale IQ is obtained**	1. "Multi-determined and multifaceted, split between verbal and performance scores" (Detterman, 1985) 2. "Wechsler's verbal performance split, despite its popularity, is actually the least theoretically distinct of all" (Robinson, 1992).	1. Children who took the Vocabulary, Picture arrangement, Arithmetic, and Block design and who had a sum of scores above 52 would qualify as academically talented if given the rest of the test (Linn & Lopatin, 1990). 2. The "WISC-III scores are at least five points lower than the WISC-R for children in the gifted range" (Silverman & Kearney, 1992, p. 34). 3. Does not take into account new metacognitive research; tasks essentially the same for all ages, therefore not developmentally appropriate; omits characteristics and attributes of the intelligent person (Witt & Gresham, 1985). 4. WISC-R "predicts academic achievement equally well for blacks and whites," though there are "differences in the average levels of performance . . . between Whites and Blacks, Whites and Hispanics, and Whites and Native Americans" (Witt & Gresham, 1985) 5. "The WISC-R is an anachronistic albatross which hangs gamely around the necks of applied psychologists" (Witt & Gresham, 1985)
Wechsler Intelligence Scale for Children, Split Half Short Form, 2nd Ed.	Individual ability test designed to measure intelligence of children ages 6 to 16. The short form procedure gives all of the diagnostic information provided by the WISC-R, cutting administration time by almost half.	1. General comprehension 2. Arithmetic 3. Similarities 4. Vocabulary 5. Picture completion 6. Picture arrangement 7. Block design 8. Object assembly 9. Mazes		1. Provides new norms for gifted referral in addition to the original norms commonly used for special education.

Name	Description	Subtests	Theoretical Base or Construct	Reviewers' Comments
Slosson Intelligence Test (SIT) Age range 2 weeks to 27 years Slosson Educational Publishers	Individual IQ screening test used by teachers, counselors, and social workers. Time: 15 min.	Quantitative Verbal	No specific theoretical rationale; based on Stanford-Binet and Gessell Development Schedules	1. Normed on 1,109 people in New England, the sample is "meager, narrow, and not representative of the U.S.": not adequate in size or scope (Oakland, 1985b). 2. "Examiners should exercise caution in estimating the IQs of mentally retarded and gifted children" (Oakland, 1985b; Reynolds, 1985). 3. The test "remains a psychometrically poor measure of general intelligence," and to use it for screening brings up ethical considerations with regards to fair testing standards (Reynolds, 1985). 4. "Those who use the SIT to assess children are advised to use the Stanford-Binet, as it provides a more in-depth and qualitative evaluation than the SIT" (Salvia & Ysseldyke, 1991).
Raven Progressive Matrices. There are three forms: Standard Progressive Matrices (SPM), Colored Progressive Matrices (CPM), and Advanced Progressive Matrices (APM) Age Range: 12–64 The Psychological Corporation	A nonverbal test designed for use as an aid in assessing mental ability. Said to be culture fair. Set I covers all intellectual processes covered by the Standard Progressive Matrices Sets. Set II provides a means of assessing all the analytical and integral operations involved in the higher thought processes and differentiates between people of superior intellectual ability. Time: Approx. 40 minutes Number of items: 48	Requires the examinee to solve problems presented in abstract figures and designs.		1. Scores are said to correlate well with comprehensive intelligence tests. This form is designed for use with persons having above-average intellectual ability. Norms are estimated for a British population at ages $11^{1}/_{2}$, 14, 20, 30, and 40. 2. "The particular appeal of the APM is the minimal verbal content needed to understand the instructions and its high correlation with formal IQ measures such as the WAIS and Otis-Lennon" (Baska, 1986). 3. The RPM "may uncover students with intellectual capability who would otherwise go unrecognized, but this must still be well documented" for it is not known exactly what the test measures (Baska, 1986).

Name	Description	Subtests	Theoretical Base or Construct	Reviewers' Comments
Raven Progressive *(continued)*				4. Recommended for use with culturally different, disadvantaged, and limited English proficiency students. It may be suitable for use with learning disabled/gifted students, but should not be used for minority students unless local norms are collected (Mills, Ablard & Brody, 1993). 5. Out-of-level comparisons should be made, with older students as the comparison group, when assessing high ability students. The SPM can be used for younger students for general screening, but the APM should be used for students over age 10 and for high scoring students. Use the RPM and its various forms "cautiously" (Mills, Ablard & Brody, 1993).
Woodcock-Johnson Psycho-Educational Battery Age Range: 2-70 DLM Teaching Resources, P.O. Box 4000, One DLM Park, Allen, TX 75002	Individually administered battery is comprised of 27 subtests (over 877 items), divided according to three major areas of assessment: cognitive ability/scholastic aptitude, scholastic achievement, and interest level. Time: Approx. 2 hrs. Number of Items: 28	1. Memory for names 2. Memory for sentences 3. Visual matching 4. Incomplete words 5. Visual closure 6. Picture vocabulary 7. Analysis-synthesis 1. Visual-auditory learning 2. Memory for words 3. Cross out 4. Sound blending 5. Picture recognition 6. Oral vocabulary 7. Concept formation 8. Delayed recall—memory for names 9. Delayed recall—visual-auditory learning 10. Numbers reversed 11. Sound patterns 12. Spatial relations 13. Listening comprehension 14. Verbal analogies	The diagnostic test battery is based on the Cattell-Horn theory of fluid (Gf) and crystallized (Gc) intelligence (see Chapter 1).	1. Administration of the test should be "only by persons properly prepared by training and/or self-study" (Kaufman, 1985). 2. The Woodcock-Johnson was renormed in the late 1980s, and the ceilings were raised, so that it could be safely used with potentially talented students. 3. "A technically excellent instrument with exceptional reliability and concurrent validity. Predictive validity evidence, though meager, shows impressive results" (Kaufman, 1985). 4. "A significant entry" into the arena of individually administered tests, and it was "commendable" in that its norming was done on the same sample; its subtests represented breakthroughs: "What makes these subtests [Analysis-synthesis, Concept formation, and Visual-auditory learning] especially attractive is that they break with the tradition of Binet and Wechsler style intelligence test items" (Cummings, 1985).

Name	Description	Subtests	Theoretical Base or Construct	Reviewers' Comments
Woodcock-Johnson *(continued)*		**Woodcock-Johnson Tests of Achievement** Standard Achievement Battery 1. Letter-word identification 2. Passage comprehension 3. Calculation 4. Applied problems 5. Dictation 6. Writing samples 7. Science 8. Social studies 9. Humanities Supplemental Achievement battery 1. Word attack 2. Reading vocabulary 3. Quantitative concepts 4. Proofing 5. Writing fluency		
The Kaufman Assessment Battery for Children (K–ABC)	Diagnostic Systems	Sequential Processing Scale 1. Hand movements 2. Number recall 3. Word order Simultaneous Processing Scale 4. Magic window 5. Face recognition 6. Gestalt closure 7. Triangles 8. Matrix analogies 9. Spatial memory 10. Photo series Achievement Scale 11. Expressive vocabulary 12. Faces and places 13. Arithmetic 14. Riddles 15. Reading /decoding 16. Reading /understanding Nonverbal Scale Age 4: Face recognition, Hand movements, Triangles Age 5: Hand Movements, Triangles, Matrix Analogies, Spatial Memory Age 6: Hand Movements, Triangles, Matrix Analogies, Spatial Memory, Photo Series	Information-processing theory of intelligence	1. The KABC was found to be valuable in finding racially and ethnically different children (Kaufman & Harrison, 1986; Woods & Achey, 1980). 2. Woods and Achey found that students who scored above the 86th percentile on the KABC Mental Processing Composite also scored high enough to qualify for the program for academically talented students when they were administered the WISC-R. 3. "Assembled a better standardization sample than the SB$_4$" (Cronbach, 1985).

Name	Description	Subtests	Theoretical Base or Construct	Reviewers' Comments
Kaufman Test of Educational Achievement (K-TEA) Age Range: 5–18 American Guidance Service	Individually administered achievement screening and diagnostic test Time: Brief, 30 min. Comprehensive, 1 hr.	1. Reading comprehension 2. Reading decoding 3. Reading composite 4. Mathematics applications 5. Math computation 6. Math composite 7. Spelling Battery composite	Domains based on textbook content, skills required at grade level, etc.	1. Normed on 2,500 students in a stratified random sample including special education students. 2. Ceilings may not be high enough.
The System of Multicultural Pluralistic Assessment (SOMPA) (1979)	Battery designed to bypass cultural variables and provide a nondiscriminatory system for assessing language minority and socioeconomically disadvantaged children.			1. Use with extreme caution, especially outside California. "At best, SOMPA should be considered experimental" (Salvia & Ysseldyke, 1991).
The Otis-Lennon School Ability Test The Psychological Corporation	Group ability test designed to go along with the Metropolitan Achievement Test. Time: Primary I, II, K–3, 75–85 mins. Elementary, Intermediate, Advanced, Gr 4–12, 1 hr.	Subtests in Quantitative, Verbal, and Nonverbal	Spearman's theory as modified by Guilford and Vernon hierarchical theories of intelligence. Assesses verbal-educational factor.	1. The test yields an SAI—a deviation IQ—instead of an IQ. Dyer (1985) called this differentiation "arbitrary semantics," and asked, "is the SAI measuring intelligent behavior or is it measuring school achievement?" Standard deviation is 16; SEM is 4. 2. Normed on 130,000 pupils. Stratified random sample. 74% White, 20% Black, 4% Hispanic, 2% other. SES accounted for. 3. Adequately reliable in internal consistency, test-retest, and equivalence, but the validity of the content assumptions by which the test was constructed needed to be addressed (Dyer, 1985). 4. Correlation with WISC-R full IQ is .85, with Stanford-Binet is .58, with Metropolitan Achievement Test—.78 to .89. 5. Seems to measure verbal abilities to a greater degree than other abilities (Oakland, 1985).

Name	Description	Subtests	Theoretical Base or Construct	Reviewers' Comments
The Otis-Lennon School Ability Test *(continued)*				6. If a district includes everyone scoring above 115 (one standard deviation above the mean), the test is 90–95% efficient in screening for the high-IQ type of talent (Pegnato & Birch, 1959).
School and College Ability Tests, III	Group ability tests that go along with the Sequential Tests of Educational Progress (STEP)	Subtests in Quantitative, Verbal, and Nonverbal		1. Ahmann (1985) questioned why even to give the test, since it seems to be so highly correlated with the STEP achievement test. 2. The scores from this test are also highly correlated with scores in the Scholastic Aptitude Test. 3. A "polished scholastic aptitude test" suitably normed and validated (Ahmann, 1985).
Cognitive Abilities Test (CogAT) Primary batteries (Gr. K–3); Multilevel (Gr. 3–12) Riverside Publishing Co. Chicago, IL	Group ability test designed to be used with the Iowa Test of Basic Skills	Subtests in 1. **Quantitative** (quantitative relations, number series, and equation building) 2. **Verbal** (vocabulary, sentence completion, verbal classification, verbal analogies) 3. **Nonverbal** (figure analogies, figure classification, and figure synthesis)		1. Carefully normed on a large sample of more than 160,000 students. 2. Well-normed, valid, and reliable, with slightly improved statistical changes from previous versions. (Anastasi, 1989; Fuchs, 1989). 3. Derived score is called Standard Age Score (SAS) with a mean of 100 and SD of 16.
California Achievement Test (CAT)	Group achievement test	Subtests in 1. Reading 2. Mathematics 3. Science 4. Social Science 5. Study Skills		1. "One of the best standardized achievement batteries available" (Wardrop, 1989).
Iowa Test of Basic Skills (ITBS)	Group achievement test			1. State of the art in multilevel comprehensive test batteries" (Willson, 1989).
Metropolitan Achievement Test (MAT)	Group achievement test	Contains both a Diagnostic and a Survey battery		1. Quite useful for testing basic skills in the elementary school, but less useful for testing higher-level skills in the high school (Nitko, 1989).

Name	Description	Subtests	Theoretical Base or Construct	Reviewers' Comments
Comprehensive Test of Basic Skills (CTBS)	Group achievement test			
Stanford Achievement Test (SAT)	Group achievement test			
American College Test (ACT)	Group achievement test			1. Useful in out-of-level testing for junior high school students bound for special academic and summer programs.
Educational Records Bureau (ERB)	Group achievement test			
Wide-Range Achievement Test-Revised (WRAT-R) Ages 5–74	Individual or group achievement test	1. Reading 2. Spelling 3. Arithmetic		1. Standardized on 5,600 stratified by age but no demographic characteristics. Clark (1989) criticized the norming sample, saying that it was "not representative" (p. 901). 2. Harrison (1989) said that the WRAT does not meet the standards of the testing profession, and "there is no supporting evidence that the WRAT-R can be used for placement of children into special education and remedial programs or for prescribing instruction" (p. 905). 3. Not suitable for screening— "may result in a great disservice to students." This test has been widely used because it is quick. Practitioners in talent development education should be cautious. 4. Mean of 100, SD of 15, no SEMs provided. 5. Reliability not established. Items unchanged from 1965 version. 6. Measures codes but not comprehension. A child with comprehension problems could obtain high scores and not be identified as a child with special academic needs.

B GIFTED/TALENTED DATA GATHERING QUESTIONNAIRE

Gifted/Talented Data Gathering Questionnaire
(Adapted from *Educating Able Learners: Programs and Promising Practices* by June Cox, Neil Daniel,
and Bruce O. Boston, Copyright © 1985. Used by permission of University of Texas Press.)

General Information

Name of School _____ Enrollment: K–6 _____

Location of School _____ 7–12 _____

Name of Person Completing Questionnaire _____

Person's Title _____ Telephone _____

Address of School _____

A. Does the school have a board-approved policy or statement of philosophy for educating gifted, talented, able learners?
   _____ yes _____ no   If yes, please attach.

B. Does the school district have a board-approved plan for educating gifted, talented, able learners?
   _____ yes _____ no

   1. If yes, is the plan for _____ 1 year _____ 3 years _____ 5–10 years

   2. Plan is: _____ comprehensive, K–12 _____ partial plan
      If partial plan, please indicate grade levels and talent areas addressed:

C. Does the school district have a systematic plan for identifying gifted/talented/able learners?
   _____ yes _____ no _____ in process of developing

   1. If yes, check areas included:
      _____ general academic

_____ specific academic
_____ creative and productive thinking
_____ fine and performing arts
_____ leadership
_____ other (please specify) _____

   2. Does the plan address special populations? If yes, please check all that apply:

_____ disadvantaged   _____ handicapped
_____ minority   _____ underachieving
_____ other (please specify)

D. Does the district _____ have _____ does not have an advisory/planning committee for the education of able learners?

   1. If yes, the district's advisory/planning committee for able learners includes:
_____ teachers   _____ administrators
_____ parents   _____ school board members
_____ others (please specify)

   2. The district's advisory/planning committee meets:
_____ monthly   _____ bimonthly
_____ other (please specify)

E. Does the district have a budget line item for the gifted/talented program?
_____ yes   indicate amount _____
_____ no

F. Does the district have one or more staff members who coordinate programming for able learners?
_____ yes   _____ no

   1. If yes, give title, grade levels of responsibility, and percent of time spent in coordination of gifted/talented program.

_____

_____

G. Procedures for evaluating programming for able learners are established:

_____ at the elementary level
_____ at the middle school level
_____ at the high school level
_____ not established at any level

Information on Program Components

1. Enrichment in Regular Classrooms. Experiences provided in regular classrooms that are additional and/or supplemental to the established curriculum and/or texts and that are purposefully planned with the needs, interests, and capabilities of particular students in mind.

Indicate percent of classrooms:	K	1–2	3–4	5–6	7–8	9–12
Content is modified for able learners to provide greater depth and variety						
Process is modified for able learners to encourage more complex levels of thought and feeling						
Able learners are given assistance in developing more sophisticated and varied products						
Students are encouraged to pursue areas of interest or talent						

Models/Methods Used:	Indicate grade levels	Percent of classrooms at grade
Bloom's taxonomy		
Enrichment triad		
Future Problem Solving		
Philosophy for Children		
Junior Great Books		
Talents Unlimited		
Creative Problem Solving		
Other creativity training		

Critical thinking training _____

Other _____

_____

_____

2. **Appropriate Pacing.** The content and pacing of curriculum and instruction are matched to students' abilities and needs. Students move ahead on the basis of mastery. Differentiation in pacing and/or depth is needed.

    Please indicate:
    Seldom or never (N)
    Occasionally (O)
    Frequently (F)
    Almost always (A)

	K	1–2	3–4	5–6	7–8	9–12

Students are allowed to move ahead as required skills are mastered:

    Reading

    English

    Math

    Science

    Social Studies

    Art

    Music

    Other

Differentiation in pacing and/or depth is provided:

    Reading

    English

Math	
Science	
Social Studies	
Art	
Music	
Other	

On what basis does a student move from one level to another within the classroom? Check all that apply:

_____ standardized tests   _____ teacher-made tests

_____ pretests, then compacting   _____ mastery of learning objectives

_____ end-of-level tests   _____ common learning objectives

_____ other (please specify)

3. Ongoing Assessment. Students' abilities and needs are continually assessed through both formal and informal means designed to discover and nurture talent. The results are used as the basis for appropriate programming decisions.

Please indicate:
Seldom or never (N)
Occasionally (O)
Frequently (F)
Almost always (A)

	K	1–2	3–4	5–6	7–8	9–12
Assessment is an ongoing process.						
Teachers are encouraged to note behaviors that may be helpful in recognizing and guiding able learners.						
Multiple measures are used to discover talent and assess needs. (Checklist below.)						

Special attention is
given to discovering talent
among special populations:

     minority   _____

     physically disabled   _____

     learning disabled   _____

     economically
     disadvantaged   _____

     underachieving   _____

     female   _____

Out-of-level testing is
done to provide more accurate
information on students who
reach "ceiling" level on
standardized tests.   _____
Students who qualify take
the SAT or ACT in junior
high school for special
talent search summer
programs.   _____

Check assessment measures used:

_____ standardized tests	_____ teacher-made tests
_____ creativity tests	_____ group achievement tests
_____ individual IQ tests	_____ group aptitude tests
_____ individual achievement tests	_____ peer nomination
_____ portfolios	_____ grades
_____ interest inventories	_____ learning style inventories
_____ personality assessments	_____ product assessments
_____ parent checklists	_____ matrices
_____ other	_____ self nomination

4. Guidance and Counseling. Planned activities, sessions, policies that assist gifted and talented students in planning their academic career in-school and after high school, and that also address specific social-emotional needs of gifted/talented students.
    Please indicate:
    Seldom or never (N)
    Occasionally (O)
    Frequently (F)
    Almost always (A)

	K	1–2	3–4	5–6	7–8	9–12
Students are taught to value their abilities and to use their individual strengths.						
Planned guidance activities in preparation for high school, college, and career choices are provided.						
Specialized guidance and counseling is provided for the highly (high-IQ) gifted.						
Specialized guidance and counseling is provided for visual and performing arts gifted students.						
Planned guidance seminars are provided for parents of all gifted students.						
Information on out-of-school and summer opportunities is provided to gifted students.						

5. Within-Class Cluster Grouping. Any classroom with a group of identified gifted/talented students purposefully organized to provide planned differentiated instruction most of the time.

	Percent of classrooms with within-class groups	Average number of identified gifted/talented students
Kindergarten		
First grade		
Second grade		
Third grade		

Fourth grade   _____

Fifth grade   _____

Sixth grade   _____

Do teachers of cluster classrooms receive special training?   _____ yes   _____ no
If yes, please describe:

6. Across-Class Departmental Ability Grouping. Grouping for high-ability students in special subject matter (e.g., math or reading) in combination with other classes at grade level.

Grade levels	Subject(s)

7. Special Enrichment Classes During School Day. Group organized from one or more classrooms and meets on a regular basis to provide experiences beyond the established curriculum.

	K	1–2	3–4	5–6	7–8	9–12
Approximate number of classes per year						
Approximate number of students per class						
Average number of students per class						
Total percent of students involved throughout year						

8. Interest Groups. Any group organized from one or more classrooms on the basis of interest in a topic; usually short term in duration.

	K	1–2	3–4	5–6	7–8	9–12
Approximate number of groups per year						
Approximate number of hours per group						
Total percent of students involved throughout the year						

9. Resource Room. Students are released from their regular classroom on a scheduled basis to work with a teacher specializing in education of the gifted in a resource room setting.

Number of resource rooms in operation: _____

Grade levels served: _____

Percent of students served at grade levels designated: _____

Average number of hours per week a student spends in the resource room: _____

Focus of resource room instruction: _____

_____

_____

10. Convocations and Workshops. Special short-term sessions where students focus on one area of study.

<table>
<tr><td align="center">Name of convocation
or workshop</td><td align="center">percent of students
involved in grades designated</td></tr>
</table>

11. Competitions. Organized opportunities for students to enter competitions or contests in a variety of subject areas.

	Grade levels	Percent of students per designated grade
Equations or other academic games		
Future Problem Solving		
Odyssey of the Mind		
Quiz Bowl		
Spelling Bee		
Science Olympiad		
Math Olympiad		
Social Science Olympiad		
Language Arts Olympiad		
Geography Bee		
History Day		
Power of the Pen		
Other writing competitions (name)		
Invention Convention		
Math competitions (name)		
Science competitions (name)		
Foreign language competitions (name)		
Music contests (name)		
Drama contests (name)		
Visual arts contests (name)		

12. Acceleration. Administrative practice designed to allow students to progress through the school grades at a rate faster than the average; e.g., early school entrance, content area acceleration, etc. Please check beneath yes or no and indicate the percent of students permitted to be accelerated.

A.   yes   no   percent

1. Early entrance

2. Grade skipping

3. Continuous progress

4. Self-paced instruction

5. Subject-matter
   acceleration

6. Combined classes

7. Curriculum compacting

8. Telescoping curriculum

9. Mentorships

10. Extracurricular programs

11. Concurrent enrollment

12. Advanced placement

13. Credit by examination

14. Correspondence courses

15. Early entrance into junior
    high, high school, college

16. Long-range planning
    and follow-up support is
    provided for students
    who are accelerated

B. Are there written guidelines or policy statements regarding any of the accelerated options? If yes, please attach.

_____ at the building level
_____ at the district level

	K	1–2	3–4	5–6	7–8	9–12

How many students were
involved last year?

Did students receive monetary compensation or credit for internship? _____ yes _____ no

16. Mentorships. A program that pairs individual students with someone who has advanced skills and experiences in a particular discipline and who can serve as a guide, advisor, counselor, and role model.

	K	1–2	3–4	5–6	7–8	9–12

How many students were
involved in a mentorship
during the last school year?

Which staff personnel or volunteer personnel are responsible for setting up mentorships?

_____

_____

_____

_____

17. Independent Study. Individually contracted in-depth study of a topic.

	K	1–2	3–4	5–6	7–8	9–12

What percent of students
completed an independent
study last year?

Do students receive a grade for independent study? _____ yes _____ no

Can students receive course credit for independent study? _____ yes _____ no

18. Correspondence Courses. Courses taken by correspondence through a college, university, or other accrediting institution.

	Number of students last year	Grade level(s)	Fees paid?	Credit given?
English				

Foreign language   _____

Math   _____

Science   _____

Social studies   _____

Other (describe)   _____

19. Concurrent or Dual Enrollment. Usually refers to high school students taking some college courses before they graduate from high school, but may also refer to students at any level who are allowed to take some classes at the next school level, e.g., elementary/junior high or junior high/high school.

Are students allowed to enroll in courses at two levels? _____ yes _____ no

If yes, please describe. _____

_____

_____

_____

20. International Baccalaureate. A rigorous, comprehensive program that enhances and extends the quality of the eleventh and twelfth grade course offerings. The internationally recognized IB curriculum provides students with a comprehensive background in English, foreign language, the social sciences, physical and life sciences, mathematics, and the arts. The IB diploma is accepted at many foreign universities and at American colleges, where full first-year credit is often granted.

Does the district offer IB course leading to the IB diploma?
_____ yes _____ no

If yes, please complete the following:

IB course offered (please list)	Percent of students enrolled

21. Special Schools. Special schools for high-ability students are located in some areas. These schools have a special preprofessional or technical focus (e.g., performing arts, visual arts, mathematics, science, mechanics).

Do any of your students attend special schools?

_____ yes   _____ no
_____ all day   _____ part of the day

If yes, please complete the following:

Name of school	Grade (s)	Percent of students

22. Summer Enrichment Programs. Enrichment classes or courses offered during the summer months.

Does the district provide a summer enrichment program for able learners?

_____ yes   _____ no

If yes, please complete the following:

Topic	Grade level(s)	Number of students last year

Do students pay a fee? _____ yes   _____ no

23. Saturday Enrichment Programs. Enrichment classes taught at a central site on Saturdays, geared for able learners.

Does the district provide Saturday enrichment programs for able students?

_____ yes   _____ no

If yes, please complete the following:

Topic(s)	Grade level(s)	Number of students last year

Do students pay a fee? _____ yes _____ no

24. Fast-Paced or Telescoped Courses. An arrangement that allows a student to complete two or more courses in a discipline in an abbreviated time span.

Does your district offer fast-paced courses? _____ yes _____ no

If yes, how many students were enrolled last year?
_____ Mathematics   _____ Foreign language
_____ Science   _____ Social studies
_____ Other (please describe)

When are the fast-paced courses offered?
_____ during the regular school day
_____ before or after the regular school day
_____ on Saturday
_____ during the summer

25. Other. If your school district has a provision or program for gifted/talented students that is not listed above, please describe.

_____

_____

_____

_____

REFERENCES

Note: References indicated with a bullet are new to this edition.

Ackerman, D. (1990). *A natural history of the senses.* New York: Random House.

Adderholt-Elliott, M. (1987). *Perfectionism: What's bad about being too good?* Minneapolis: Free Spirit.

Adderholt-Elliott, M. (1991). Perfectionism and the gifted adolescent. In J. Genshaft & M. Bireley (Eds.), *Understanding the gifted adolescent* (pp. 65–75). New York: Teachers College Press.

Adler, J., et al. (1992, February 17). Hey, I'm terrific. *Newsweek*, pp. 51–56.

•Adler, M. (1952). *The great ideas: A syntopticon* of Great Books of the Western World. Chicago: The Encyclopedia Britannica.

Adler, M. (1984). *The Paideia Program: An educational syllabus.* New York: Collier.

•*Affluenza.* (1997, October). [Television broadcast]. Public Broadcasting System.

African American Male Task Force. (1990). *Educating African American males: A dream deferred.* Milwaukee: Milwaukee Public Schools.

Ahmann, J. S. (1985). Review of School and College Ability Tests, Series III. In J. Kramer (Ed.), *The Ninth Mental Measurements Yearbook* (pp. 1315–1318). Lincoln, NE: University of Nebraska Press.

Albert, R. S. (1975). Toward a behavioral definition of genius. *American Psychologist, 30,* 140–151.

•Alexander, J. (1997). Long-term effects of an early intervention program for gifted and talented students. In T. Cross (Ed.), *Research briefs* (pp. 158–173). Washington, DC: National Association for Gifted Children Service Publications.

Allen, J. S. (1992). Educating performers. *The American Scholar, 61*(2), 197–209.

Alter, J. (1984). Creativity profile of university and conservatory dance students. *Journal of Personality Assessment, 48,* 153–158.

•Alvino, J. (1991). An investigation into the needs of gifted boys. *Roeper Review, 13*(4), 174–180.

Alvino, J., McDonnel, R. & Richert, E. (1981). National survey of identification practices in gifted and talented education. *Exceptional Children, 48*(2), 124–132.

Amabile, T. M. (1983). *The social psychology of creativity.* New York: Springer-Verlag.

Amabile, T. M. (1989). *Growing up creative.* New York: Crown.

•Ambrose, D., Allen, J., & Huntley, S. (1994). Mentorship of the highly creative. *Roeper Review, 17*(2), 131–133.

American Association of University Women Educational Foundation. (1992). *How schools shortchange girls: The AAUW report.* New York: Marlowe & Company.

American college testing program. Iowa City, IA: Author.

Ames, B. (1988). *Self-study in music for middle states evaluation.* Unpublished manuscript.

Anastasi, A. (1989). A review of the Cognitive Abilities Test, Form 4. In J. C. Conoley & J. J. Kramer (Eds.), *The Tenth Mental Measurements Yearbook* (pp. 192–193). Lincoln, NE: University of Nebraska Press.

•Anderson, M. B., Denson, E. L., Brewer, B. W., & Van Raalte, J. L. (1994). Disorders of personality and mood in athletes: Recognition and referral. *Applied Sport Psychology, 6,* 168–184.

• Angelou, M. (1970). *I know why the caged bird sings.* New York: Random House.

• Anshel, M. H., & Porter, A. (1996). Self-regulatory characteristics for competitive swimmers as a function of skill level and gender. *Journal of Sport Behavior, 19*(2), 91–110.

• Apple, M. (Ed.). (1995–1996). *Review of research in education.* (Vol. 21). Washington, DC: American Educational Research Association.

• Archambault, F. X., Westberg, K. L., Brown, S. W., Hallmark, B. W., Emmons, C. L., & Zhang, W. (1993). *Regular classroom practices with gifted students: Results of a national survey of classroom teachers.* Storrs, CT: The University of Connecticut. National Research Center on the Gifted and Talented, Research Monograph 93101.

Argulewicz, E. N. (1985). Review of scales for rating the behavioral characteristics of superior students. In [Buros Institute of Mental Measurements]. *The Ninth Mental Measurements Yearbook* (Vol. II, pp. 1311–1312). Lincoln, NE: University of Nebraska Press.

• Armenta, C. (1997). Understanding our passion for the gifted. In T. Cross (Ed.), *Research briefs* (pp. 100–111). Washington, DC: National Association for Gifted Children Service Publications.

• Armstrong, D. (1989). Appropriate programs for the gifted: An analysis of gifted elementary students' perceptions. *Journal for the Education of the Gifted, 12*(4), 277–292.

• Armstrong, D. (1997). Gifted students: Preferred practices: A follow-up study. *The Journal Portfolio of the Illinois Association for Gifted Children, 13,* 27–32.

• Armstrong, D. (1994, November). Preparing teachers to successfully implement outcomes. Paper presented at the National Association for Gifted Children Convention, Salt Lake City, UT.

• Armstrong, D. (1995, November). Validation of innovative collaborative techniques with gifted students. Paper presented at the National Association for Gifted Children Convention, Tampa, FL.

Arnold, K. D. (1993). The Illinois Valedictorian Project: Academically talented women in the 1980s. In D. T. Schuster & K. D. Hulbert (Eds.), *Women's lives through time: Educated American women of the twentieth century.* New York: Jossey Bass.

• Arnold, K. D., & Subotnik, R. F. (1995). Mentoring the gifted: A differentiated model. *Educational Horizons, 73,* 3, 118–23.

• Arnold, K. D., Noble, K. D., & Subotnik, R. F. (Eds.). (1996). *Remarkable women: Perspectives on female talent development.* Cresskill, NJ: Hampton Press.

Arter, J. (1990). *Using portfolios in instruction and assessment: State of the art summary.* Northwest Educational Research Laboratory 503-275-9562.

Assouline, S. G., & Lupowski, A. E. (1992). Extending the Talent Search Model: The potential of the SSAT-Q for identifying mathematically talented students. In N. Colangelo, S. G. Assouline & D. L. Ambroson (Eds.), *Talent development* (pp. 223–232). Unionville, NY: Trillium Press.

Astin, H. S. (1985). The meaning of work in women's lives: A sociopsychological model of career choice and work behavior. *The Counseling Psychologist, 12*(4), 117–126.

Bachtold, L. M., & Werner, E. E. (1970/1984). Creative psychologists: Gifted women. *American Psychologist, 25,* 234–243.

Baer, J. (1991). Generality of creativity across performance domains. *Creativity Research Journal, 4*(1) 23–39.

• Baer, J. (1993/1994). Why you shouldn't trust creativity tests. *Educational Leadership, 51*(4), 80–83.

• Baer, J. (1994). Performance assessments of creativity: Do they have long-term stability? *Roeper Review, 17*(1), 7–11.

Bagley, M., & Hess, K. (1983). *200 ways of using imagery in the classroom.* New York: Trillium Press.

Baird, L. L. (1972a). Review of Remote Associates Test. In O. K. Buros (Ed.), *The Seventh Mental Measurements Yearbook* (Vol. I, pp. 827–829). Highland Park, NJ: Gryphon Press.

Baird, L. L. (1972b). Review of Torrance Tests of Creative Thinking. In O.K. Buros (Ed.), *The Seventh Mental Measurements Yearbook* (Vol. I, pp. 836–838). Highland Park, NJ: Gryphon Press.

Baird, L. L. (1985). Do grades and tests predict adult accomplishment? *Research in Higher Education, 23*(1), 3–85.

• Baker, E. L., & Schachter, J. (1996). Expert benchmarks for student academic performance: The case for gifted children. *Gifted Child Quarterly, 40*(2), 61–69.

Baldwin, A. Y. (1977). Tests do underpredict: A case study. *Phi Delta Kappan, 58,* 620–621.

Baldwin, A. Y. (1984). *The Baldwin Identification Matrix 1 for the identification of the gifted and talented: A handbook for its use.* New York: Trillium Press.

Baldwin, A. Y. (1985). Programs for the gifted and talented: Issues concerning minority populations. In F. D. Horowitz & M. O'Brien (Eds.), *The gifted and talented: Developmental perspectives* (pp. 223–247). Washington, DC: American Psychological Association.

Baldwin, A. Y. (1987). I'm Black but look at me, I am also gifted. *The Gifted Child Quarterly, 31*(4), 180–185.

Baldwin, A. Y., & Wooster, J. (1977). *Baldwin identification matrix inservice kit for the identification of gifted and talented students.* Buffalo: D.O.K.

•Balzer, C. (1991). *The effect of ability grouping of gifted elementary students, combined with instruction modified for level and rate of learning on student achievement: A review of the literature.* ERIC Document Reproduction Service ED 345392.

Bamberger, J. (1986). Cognitive issues in the development of musically gifted children. In R. Sternberg & J. Davidson (Eds.), *Conceptions of giftedness* (pp. 388–415). New York: Cambridge.

Bandura, A. (1986). *Social foundations of thought and action: A social cognitive theory.* Englewood Cliffs, NJ: Prentice Hall.

Bandura, A. (1989). Self-regulation of motivation and action through internal standards and goal systems. In L. A. Pervin (Ed.), *Goal concepts in personality and social psychology.* Hillsdale, NJ: Erlbaum and Associates, Inc.

Barkan, J. H., & Bernal, E. M. (1991). Gifted education for bilingual and limited English proficient students. *Gifted Child Quarterly, 35,* 144–147.

Barron, F. (1968). *Creativity and personal freedom.* New York: Van Nostrand.

Barron, F. (1972). *Artists in the making.* San Francisco: Seminar Press.

•Barron, F. (1995). *No rootless flower: An ecology of creativity.* Cresskill, NJ: Hampton Press.

Baska, L. K. (1986). The use of the Raven Advanced Progressive Matrices for junior high school gifted programs. *Roeper Review, 8*(2), 181–184.

Bass, B. M. (1985). *Leadership and performance beyond expectations.* New York: Free Press.

Bass, B. M., & Barrett, G. V. (1981). *People, work, and organizations: An introduction to industrial and organizational psychology.* Boston: Allyn & Bacon.

•Basu, S. (1996). Pioneering Hindu women in India: Overcoming barriers and claiming their places in today's society. In K. Arnold, K. D. Noble, & R. F. Subotnik (Eds.), *Remarkable women: Perspectives on female talent development* (pp. 81–92). Cresskill, NJ: Hampton Press.

Bates, B. (1987). *The way of the actor.* Boston: Shambhala.

•Bateson, M. C. (1989). *Composing a life.* New York: Plume Books.

Baum, S. (1988). An enrichment program for gifted learning disabled students. *Gifted Child Quarterly, 32,* 226–230.

Baum, S. (1990). Review of *How to parent so children will learn. Gifted Child Quarterly, 34*(4), 169–170.

Beckwith, A. H. (1988, April). Tapping their potential. *Teaching K–8,* 58–60.

•Belenky, M. F., Clinch, B. M., Goldberger, M. R., & Tarule, J. M. (1986). *Women's ways of knowing: The development of self, voice, and mind.* New York: Basic Books.

•Bell, C. S., & Chase, S. E. (1996). The gendered character of women superintendents' professional relationships. In K. D. Arnold, K. D. Noble & R. F. Subotnik (Eds.), *Remarkable women: Perspectives on female talent development* (pp. 117–132). Cresskill, NJ: Hampton Press.

Bell, Q. (1976). *Virginia Woolf: A biography.* New York: Harcourt Brace Jovanovich.

Benbow, C. P. (1992). Mathematical talent: Its nature and consequences. In N. Colangelo, S. G. Assouline & D. L. Ambroson (Eds.), *Talent development: Proceedings from the 1991 Henry B. and Jocelyn Wallace National Research Symposium on Talent Development* (pp. 95–123). Unionville, NY: Trillium Press.

•Benbow, C. P., & Lubinski, D. (1995). Optimal development of talent: Respond educationally to individual differences in personality. *Educational Forum, 59*(4), 381–392.

•Benbow, C. P., & Lubinski, D. (1997). Intellectually talented children: How can we best meet their needs? In N. Colangelo & G. A. Davis (Eds.), *Handbook of gifted education* (2d ed., pp. 155–169). Boston: Allyn & Bacon.

Benbow, C. P., & Minor, L. L. (1990). Cognitive profiles of verbally and mathematically precocious students: Implications for the identification of the gifted. *Gifted Child Quarterly, 34,* 21–26.

Benbow, C. P., & Wollins, L. (submitted). Gender differences in mathematical precocity: A function of test item bias?

•Benge, B., & Montgomery, D. (1996). Understanding the emotional development of twice exceptional rural students. ERIC ED 394784.

Bentley, J. E. (1937). *Superior children.* New York: W.W. Norton & Co.

•Berger, S. (1989). *College planning for gifted students.* Reston, VA: The Council for Exceptional Children.

Bernal, E. M. (1981). *Special problems and procedures for identifying minority gifted students.* San Antonio,

TX: Creative Educational Enterprises. ERIC Document Reproduction Service ED 103653.

Bernal, E. M. (1982). Identifying minority gifted students: Special problems and procedures. In *Identifying and educating the disadvantaged gifted/talented. Selected proceedings from the fifth national conference on disadvantaged gifted/talented.* Los Angeles: The National/State Leadership Training Institute on the Gifted and Talented.

•Bernstein, J. E., & Blue, R., w. Gerber, A. J. (1990). *Judith Resnik: Challenger astronaut.* New York: Dutton Lodestar.

Berryman, J. (1950). *Stephen Crane.* New York: William Sloan Associates.

Bessemer, S. P., & Treffinger, D. J. (1981). Analysis of creative products: Review and synthesis. *Journal of Creative Behavior, 15*, 159–179.

•Betkouski, M., & Hoffman, L. (1981). A summary of Myers-Briggs Type Indicator research application in education. *Research in Psychological Type, 3,* 3–41.

Betts, G. (1988). The autonomous learner model. In J. S. Renzulli & S. Reis (Eds.), *Systems and models for developing programs for the gifted and talented* (pp. 134–156). Mansfield Center, CT: Creative Learning Press.

Bireley, M. K. (1991). Learning styles: One way to help gifted adolescents understand and choose lifestyles. In M. K. Bireley & J. Genshaft (Eds.), *Understanding the gifted adolescent: Educational, developmental, and multicultural issues* (pp. 189–200). New York: Teachers College Press.

•Bireley, M. K. (1993). *Crossover children: A sourcebook for helping the learning disabled/gifted child.* Beavercreek, OH: Greyden Press.

Birnbaum, J. A. (1975). Life patterns and self-esteem in gifted family-oriented and career-committed women. In M. Mednick, S. Tangri, & L. W. Hoffman (Eds.), *Women and achievement: Social and motivational analysis* (pp. 396–419). New York: Hemisphere-Halstead.

•Bishop, B. (1995, January 25). Teen wins national science honor. Eugene, OR: *The Register Guard* (p. 1A).

Blackburn, A. C., & Erickson, D. B. (1986). Predictable crises of the gifted student. *Journal of Counseling and Development, 64,* 552–555.

Blackshear, P. B. (1979). A comparison of peer nomination and teacher nomination in the identification of the academically gifted black, primary level student. *Dissertation Abstracts International,* 2525A [University Microfilms No. 79-25739].

Blake, R. R., & Mouton, J. S. (1964). *The managerial grid III.* Houston: Gulf Publishing.

•Bland, L. C., Sowa, C. J., & Callahan, C. M. (1994). An overview of resilience in gifted children. *Roeper Review, 17*(2), 77–79.

•Block, A. A. (1997). *I'm only bleeding: Education as the practice of violence against children.* New York: Peter Lang.

Block, J., & Kremen, A. M. (1996). IQ and ego resiliency. *Journal of Personality and Social Psychology, 70*(2), 346–361.

Bloom, B. S. (1980). *All our children learning.* New York: McGraw-Hill.

Bloom, B. S. (Ed.). (1985). *Developing talent in young people.* New York: Ballantine.

Bloom, B. S., Englehart, M., Furst, E., Hill, W., & Krathwohl, D. (1956). *Taxonomy of educational objectives: The classification of educational goals. Handbook I, cognitive domain.* New York: Longmans Green.

•Bloom, H. (1994). *The western canon: The books and school of the ages.* New York: Harcourt, Brace, and Company.

Blumberg, S. A., & Panos, L. G. (1990). *Edward Teller: Giant of the golden age of physics.* New York: Macmillan.

•Bly, R. (1990). *Iron John: A book about men.* New York: Addison-Wesley.

Boodoo, G. M., Bradley, C., Frontera, R., Pitts, J., & Wright, L. (1989). A survey of procedures used for identifying gifted learning disabled children. *Gifted Child Quarterly, 33,* 110–114.

•Bookspan, M., & Yodkey, R. (1981). *Andre Previn: A biography.* New York: Doubleday.

Booth, J. (1985). The administrator's role in the education of gifted and talented children. *ERIC Digest.* Reston, VA.: ERIC Clearinghouse on Handicapped and Gifted Children.

Borkowski, J. G., & Peck, V. A. (1986). Causes and consequences of metamemory in gifted children. In R. J. Sternberg & J. E. Davidson (Eds.), *Conceptions of giftedness* (pp. 182-200). New York: Cambridge University Press.

Borland, J. H. (1986a). A note on the existence of certain divergent-production abilities. *Journal for the Education of the Gifted, 9,* 239–251.

Borland, J. H. (1986b). IQ tests: Throwing out the bathwater, saving the baby. *Roeper Review, 8*(3), 163–167.

Borland, J. H. (1989). *Planning and implementing programs for the gifted.* New York: Teachers College Press.

•Borland, J. H. (1996). Gifted education and the threat of irrelevance. *Journal for the Education of the Gifted, 29*(2), 129–147.

•Borland, J. H. (1997, March). *Curriculum development.* Speech at the National Curriculum Conference at the College of William and Mary, Williamsburg, VA.

Borland, J. H., & Wright, L. (1992a) Identifying young, potentially gifted, economically disadvantaged students. Submitted for publication.

Borland, J. H., & Wright, L. (1992b). A special friend: Adolescent mentors for young, economically disadvantaged, potentially gifted students. *Roeper Review, 14,* 124–129.

Bouchard, T. J., Lykken, D. T., McGue, M., Segal, N. L., & Tellegen, A. (1990). Sources of human psychological differences: The Minnesota Study of Twins Reared Apart. *Science, 250*(4978), 223–228.

Bouchard, T. J., Lykken, D. T., McGue, M., Segal, N., et al. (1991). Sources of human psychological differences: The Minnesota Study of Twins Reared Apart: Response. *Science, 252*(5003), 191–192.

Bowie, E. L. (1979). The utility of Piagetian tasks for the assessment of arithmetic reasoning ability in intellectually gifted first and second grade students. *Dissertation Abstracts International, 40, 723A* [University Microfilms No. 79-15542].

•Boyce, L. N., VanTassel-Baska, J., Burrus, J. D., Sher, B. T., & Johnson, D. T. (1997). A problem-based curriculum: Parallel learning opportunities for students and teachers. *Journal for the Education of the Gifted, 20*(4), 363–379.

Boyd, J. (1992). *Musicians in tune.* New York: Simon & Schuster.

Brande, D. (1992). *Becoming a writer.* Los Angeles: Tarcher.

Brandwein, P. (1955). *The gifted student as future scientist.* New York: Harcourt, Brace & World.

Brauer, R. (1988). *Favorite books of Hunter College Elementary School students.* Unpublished handout to parents and staff.

Brauer, R., Dolgins, J., & Marvuglio-Schwake, C. (1988). *Self-study for language arts for middle states evaluation.* Unpublished manuscript, Hunter College Elementary School, New York.

•Breard, N. (1996). *Exploring a different way to identify gifted African American students.* Unpublished doctoral dissertation, University of Georgia, Athens, GA.

Brescia, D. A. (1988). Building a new gifted program is like building a new house. *Roeper Review, 11*(2), 64–66.

Briggs, K. C., & Myers, I. B. (1977). *Myers-Briggs Type Indicator.* Palo Alto, CA: Consulting Psychologists Press.

Brody, L. E. (1989, November). *Characteristics of extremely mathematically talented females.* Paper presented at the Thirty-sixth National Association for Gifted Children Conference, Cincinnati, OH.

Brody, L. E., & Benbow, C. P. (1986). Social and emotional adjustment of adolescents extremely talented in verbal or mathematical reasoning. *Journal of Youth and Adolescence, 15,* 1–18.

Brody, L. E., & Benbow, C. P. (1987). Accelerative strategies: How effective are they for the gifted? *Gifted Child Quarterly, 31,* 105–110.

Bronzaft, A. L. (1991). Career, marriage, and family aspirations of young black college women. *Journal of Negro Education, 60,* 110–118.

Brook, P. (1969). The act of possession. In T. Cole & H. Chinoy (Eds.). (1970/1989). *Actors on acting* (pp. 223–229). New York: Crown.

Brookhiser, R. (1993, May). Intense: Reflections on a personality type. *The Atlantic,* pp. 20–24.

Brophy, B., & Goode, E. E. (1988, December 12). Amazing families. *U.S. News & World Report,* pp. 78–87.

Brounstein, P., Holahan, W., & Dreyden, J. (1991). Chance in self-concept and attributional styles among academically gifted adolescents. *Journal of Applied Social Psychology, 21*(3), 198–218.

Brown, L., & Gilligan, C. (1992). *Meeting at the crossroads: Women's psychology and girls' development.* Cambridge, MA: Harvard University Press.

Bruner, J. (1960). *The process of education.* Cambridge, MA: Harvard University Press.

Bruner, J. (1983). *In search of mind: Essays in autobiography.* New York: Harper & Row.

Burkes, B. S., Jenson, D. W., & Terman, L. (1930). The promise of youth: Follow-up studies of a thousand gifted children. In L. Terman (Ed.), *Genetic studies of genius, II.* Stanford, CA: Stanford University Press.

Burns, J. M., Collins, M. D., & Paulsell, J. C. (1991). A comparison of intellectually superior preschool accelerated readers and nonreaders: Four years later. *Gifted Child Quarterly, 35*(3), 118–127.

Cage, J. (1973). Silence: Lectures and writings. Middletown, CT: Wesleyan University Press.

Callahan, C. M. (1991). The assessment of creativity. In N. Colangelo & G. A. Davis (Eds.), *Handbook of gifted education* (pp. 219–235). Needham Heights, MA: Allyn & Bacon.

•Callahan, C. M. (1996). A critical self-study of gifted education: Healthy practice, necessary evil, or sedition? *Journal for the Education of the Gifted, 19*(2), 148–163.

•Callahan, C. M., & McIntire, J. (1994). *Identifying outstanding talent in American Indian and Alaska native students.* The National Research Center on the Gifted and Talented Research Monograph. Charlottesville, VA: University of Virginia.

Callahan, C. M., Cornell, D. G., & Loyd, B. H. (1992). The academic development and personal adjustment of high ability young women in an early college entrance program. In N. Colangelo, S. G. Assouline & D. L. Ambroson (Eds.), *Talent development: Proceedings from the 1991 Henry B. and Jocelyn Wallace National Research Symposium on Talent Development* (pp. 248–260). Unionville, NY: Trillium Press.

Callahan, C. M., Tomlinson, C. A., & Pizzat, P. M. (Eds.). (1993). *Contexts for promise: Noteworthy practices and innovations in the identification of gifted students.* Charlottesville, VA: National Research Center on the Gifted and Talented, University of Virginia.

•Callahan, C. M., Adams, C. M., Bland, L. C., Moon, T. R., Moore, S. R., Perie, M., & McIntire, J. A. (1996). Factors influencing recruitment, enrollment, and retention of young women in special secondary schools of mathematics, science, and technology. In K. Arnold, K. D. Noble & R. F. Subotnik (Eds.), *Remarkable women: Perspectives on female talent development* (pp. 243–260). Cresskill, NJ: Hampton Press.

Cameron, J. (1992). *The artist's way: A spiritual path to higher creativity.* Los Angeles: Tarcher/Perigee.

Campbell, D. T. (1960). Blind variation and selective retention in creative thought as in other knowledge processes. *Psychological Review, 67,* 380–400.

•Campbell, J. (1996). Early identification of mathematics talent has long-term positive consequences for career contributions. *International Journal of Educational Research, 26*(6), 497–522.

Carr, M., & Borkowski, J. G. (1987). Metamemory in gifted children. *Gifted Child Quarterly, 31,* 40–44.

•Carroll, H. A. (1940). *Mental hygiene: The dynamics of adjustment.* Englewood Cliffs, NJ: Prentice Hall.

Carroll, J., & Howieson, N. (1991). Recognizing creative thinking talent in the classroom. *Roeper Review, 14*(2), 68–71).

•Carver, R. (1983). Fires. In S. Berg (Ed.), *In praise of what persists* (pp. 33–44). New York: Harper & Row.

•Castellano, J. (1995). Revisiting gifted education opportunities for linguistically and culturally diverse students. *National Association for Bilingual Education News, 18*(6), 27–28.

•Castillo, L. (1994). *The effect of analogy on young children's metaphor comprehension.* Unpublished doctoral dissertation, City University of New York Graduate Center.

Catmull, J., Hancock, J., Huckins, R., & Runyon, J. (1977). Alternative programming for the gifted. Tallahassee: Florida State Department of Education. ERIC Document Reproduction Service ED 141967 .

Cattell, R. B. (1971). *Abilities: Their structure, growth, and action.* Boston: Houghton Mifflin Co.

Cattell, R. B., & Cattell, M. C. (1969). *Handbook for the High School Personality Questionnaire (HSPQ).* Champaign, IL: Institute for Personality and Ability Testing.

Cattell, R. B., Cattell, M. D., & Johns, E. F. (1984). *Manual and norms for the High School Personality Questionnaire.* Champaign, IL: Institute for Personality and Ability Testing.

•Chan, L. K. S. (1996). Motivational orientations and metacognitive abilities of intellectually gifted students. *Gifted Child Quarterly, 40*(4), 184–193.

•Chandler, K. (1995). *Passages of pride: Lesbian and gay youth come of age.* New York: Times Press.

Cheever, S. (1984). *Home before dark.* Boston: Houghton Mifflin.

•Christenson, B. (1996). *What academic programs are offered most frequently in schools serving American Indian and Alaska Native Students?* Issue Brief. ERIC Document ED395751

•Christopher. (1997). *Released from the past.* [Recording on compact disc.] Berea, OH: Shirtless Records.

Cipriani, A., & Divi, N. (1988). *Self-study of foreign languages for Middle States Evaluation.* Unpublished manuscript. Hunter College Elementary School, New York.

•Clark, B. (1979). *Growing up gifted* (1st ed). Columbus: Macmillan.

Clark, B. (1992). *Growing up gifted* (4th ed). Columbus: Macmillan.

Clark, E. (1989). Review of the Wide Range Achievement Test-Revised. In J. C. Conoley & J. J. Kramer (Eds)., *The Tenth Mental Measurements Yearbook* (pp. 901–903). Lincoln, NE: University of Nebraska Press.

Clark, G. (1989). *Drawing abilities test.* Bloomington, IA: Arts Publishing Co.

Clark, G., & Zimmerman, E. (1983, November). Identifying artistically talented students. *School Arts,* pp. 23–31.

Clark, G., & Zimmerman, E. (1984). *Educating artistically talented students.* Syracuse, NY: Syracuse University Press.

Clark, G., & Zimmerman, E. (1986). A framework for educating artistically talented students based on Feldman's and Clark and Zimmerman's models. *Studies in Art Education, 27*(3), 115–122.

Clark, G., & Zimmerman, E. (1987). Tending the special spark: Accelerated and enriched curricula for highly talented art students. *Roeper Review, 105*(1), 10–16.

Clark, R. (1971). *Einstein: The life and times.* New York: World.

• *Code of fair testing practice in education.* (1968). Washington, DC: Joint Committee on Testing Practices, American Psychological Association.

Cohen, E. G., & Lotan, R. A. (1995). Producing equal-status interaction in the heterogeneous classroom. *American Educational Research Journal, 32*(1), 99–120.

Cohen, L. (1988). To get ahead, get a theory. *Roeper Review, 11,* 2.

Colangelo, N. (1990, April). *Underachieving and achieving gifted students: A national comparison based on ACT scores.* Invited address at the Annual Meeting of the American Educational Research Association, Boston.

Colangelo, N. (1991). Counseling gifted students. In N. Colangelo & G. Davis (Eds.), *Handbook of gifted education* (pp. 273–284). Needham Heights, MA: Allyn & Bacon.

• Colangelo, N. (1997). Counseling gifted students. In N. Colangelo & G. A. Davis (Eds.), *Handbook of gifted education* (2d ed., pp. 253–265). Needham Heights, MA: Allyn & Bacon.

Colangelo, N., & Davis, G. (Eds.). (1991). *Handbook of gifted education.* Needham Heights, MA: Allyn & Bacon.

• Colangelo, N., & Davis, G. a. (Eds.). (1997). *Handbook of gifted education* (2d ed.). Needham Heights, MA: Allyn & Bacon.

Colangelo, N., & Kerr, B. A. (1990). Extreme academic talent: Profiles of perfect scorers. *Journal of Educational Psychology, 82,* 404–409.

Colangelo, N., & Ziffert, R. T. (1979). *New voices in counseling the gifted.* Dubuque: Kendall/Hunt.

Colangelo, N., Assouline, S. G., & Ambroson, D. L. (Eds.). (1991). *Talent development: Proceedings of the Henry B. and Jocelyn Wallace National Research Symposium on Talent Development.* Iowa City, IA: The University of Iowa.

• Colangelo, N., Assouline, S. G., & D. L. Ambroson (Eds.) (1992). *Talent development: Proceedings of the Henry B. and Jocelyn Wallace National Research Symposium on Talent Development* (University of Iowa). Trumansburg, NY: Trillium Press.

• Colangelo, N., Assouline, S. G., & D. L. Ambroson (Eds.) (1994). *Talent development, II: Proceedings of the Henry B. and Jocelyn Wallace National Research Symposium on Talent Development* (University of Iowa). Scottsdale, AZ: Gifted Psychology Press.

Colangelo, N., Kerr, B. A., Husman, R., Hallowell, & Gaeth, J. (1991). The development of a scale to identify mechanical inventiveness. In N. Colangelo, S. G. Assouline & D. L. Ambroson (Eds.), *Talent development: Proceedings of the Henry B. and Jocelyn Wallace National Research Symposium on Talent Development* (pp. 223–232). Iowa City, IA: The University of Iowa.

• Cole, P. (1993). Learner-generated questions and comments: Tools for improving instruction. ERIC Document 62160.

• Coleman, L. J. (1994). Being a teacher: Emotions and optimal experience while teaching gifted children. *Gifted Child Quarterly, 38,* 146–152.

Coleman, M. R., & Gallagher, J. J. (1992). *Report on state policies related to the identification of gifted students.* University of North Carolina at Chapel Hill, Gifted Education Policy Studies Program. U.S. Office of Educational Research and Improvement grant number R206A00596.

Coles, R. (1991). *The spiritual life of children.* New York: Houghton Mifflin.

Connelly, J. B. (1983). Recategorized WISC-R score patterns of older and younger referred Tlingit Indian children. *Psychology in the Schools, 20,* 271–275.

Connolly, A., Nachtman, W., & Pritchett, E. (1976). *Manual for the KeyMath Diagnostic Arithmetic Test.* Circle Pines, MN: American Guidance Service.

• Conoley, J. C., & Impard, J. C. (Eds.). (1995). *The Twelfth Mental Measurements Yearbook.* Lincoln, NE: The Buros Institute of Mental Measurements.

•Cooper, S., & Miller, J. (1991). MBTI learning style-teaching style discongruencies. *Educational and Psychological Measurement, 51*(3), 699–706.

Cornell, D. G. (1990). High ability students who are unpopular with their peers. *Gifted Child Quarterly, 34*(4), 155–160.

Corner, S. M., & Hagman, J. D. (Eds.) (1987). *Transfer of learning* (pp. 81–120). New York: Academic Press.

Corno, L., & Kanfer, R. 1993. The role of volition in learning and performance. In L. Darling-Hammond (Ed.), *Review of research in education, 19* (pp. 301–342). Washington, DC: American Educational Research Association.

Costa, A. (Ed.). (1985). *Developing minds: A resource book for teaching thinking.* Alexandria, VA: Association for Supervision and Curriculum Development.

Cox, C. (1926). The early mental traits of three hundred geniuses. In L. M. Terman (Ed.), *Genetic studies of genius* (Vol. 2). Stanford, CA: Stanford University Press.

Cox, J., Daniel, N. & Boston, B. O. (1985). *Educating able learners: Programs and promising practices.* Austin: University of Texas Press.

Crabbe, A. B. (1990). *Creating more creative people.* Aberdeen, NC: Think.

Crabbe, A. B. (1991, March/April). Preparing today's students to solve tomorrow's problems. *Gifted Children Today*, 2–5.

Crabbe, A. B. (1992). Creating creative curriculum focus: Science. Aberdeen, NC: Think.

Crabbe, A. B., & Betts, G. (1990). *Creating more creative people II.* Greely, Co: Autonomous Learner Press.

Cramond, B. (1993). Predictive validity of the Torrance Tests of Creative Thinking. In R. F. Subotnik & K. D. Arnold (Eds.), *Beyond Terman: Longitudinal studies in contemporary gifted education.* Norwood, NJ: Ablex.

•Cramond, B. (1994). We can trust creativity tests. *Educational Leadership*, 52(1), 70.

•Cramond, B. (1995). The coincidence of attention deficit hyperactivity disorder and creativity. National Research Center on the Gifted and Talented Research-based Decision-making Paper No. 9508. Storrs, CT: University of Connecticut.

Crockenberg, S. B. (1972). Creativity tests: A boon or boondoggle for education? *Review of Educational Research, 42,* 27–45.

Cronbach, L. J. (1960). *Essentials of psychological testing* (2d ed.). New York: Harper and Row.

•Cronbach, L. J. (1985). Review of Stanford Binet Intelligence Scale, Fourth Edition. In J. Kramer (Ed.), *The Ninth Mental Measurements Yearbook* (pp. 773–775). Lincoln, NE: University of Nebraska Press.

Cross, J. W. (1903). *George Eliot's life as related in her letters and journals.* New York & London: Abbey.

•Cross, T. (1996a, January/February). Examining claims about gifted children and suicide. *Gifted Child Today Magazine, 19*(1), 46–48.

•Cross, T. (1996b, May/June). Psychological autopsy provides insight into gifted adolescent suicide. *Gifted Child Today Magazine, 19*(3), 22–23, 50.

Csikszentmihalyi, M. (1991). Commentary. *Human Development, 34,* 32-34.

•Csikszentmihalyi, M. (1995). *Creativity.* New York: HarperCollins.

•Csikszentmihalyi, M., Rathunde, K., & Whalen, S. (1993). *Talented teenagers: The roots of success and failure.* New York: Cambridge University Press.

CTB/McGraw-Hill. (1985). *California Achievement Test.* Monterey, CA: Author.

CTB/McGraw-Hill. (1991). *Comprehensive Tests of Basic Skills, Fourth Edition.* Monterey, CA: Author.

•Cummings, C., & Piirto, J. (1997). The education of young talented children in the context of school reform. In J. Smutny (Ed.), *The young gifted child: Potential and promise, an anthology.* (pp. 380–389). Cresskill, NJ: Hampton Press.

Cummings, J. A. (1985). Review of Woodcock-Johnson Psycho-Educational Battery. In J. Kramer (Ed.), Ninth Mental Measurements Yearbook (pp. 1759–1762). Lincoln, NE: University of Nebraska Press.

Curie, E. (1937). *Madame Curie: A biography.* Trans. V. Sheean. New York: Literary Guild of America.

Dabrowski, K. (1964). *Positive disintegration.* Boston: Little, Brown.

Dabrowski, K. (1967). Personality-shaping through positive disintegration. Boston: Little, Brown.

Dabrowski, K. (1972). *Psychoneurosis is not an illness.* London: Gryf.

Dabrowski, K., & Piechowski, M. M. (1977). *Theory of levels of emotional development* (2 vols.). Oceanside, NY: Dabor.

Damarin, F. (1985). Review of Creativity Packet. In J. Kramer (Ed.), *The Ninth Mental Measurements Yearbook,* Vol. I, (pp. 410–411). Lincoln, NE: University of Nebraska Press.

Daniels, R. R. (1988). American Indians: Gifted, talented, creative, or forgotten? *Roeper Review, 10*(4), 241–244.

• Dark, V. J., & Benbow, C. P. (1994). Type of stimulus mediates the relationship between working-memory performance and type of precocity. *Intelligence, 19*(3), 337–57.

Darwin, C. (1845/1906). *Journal of researches into the geology and natural history of the various countries visited during the voyage of the* H.M.S. *Beagle round the world.* London: J. M. Dent & Sons, Ltd.

Darwin, C. (1859). *On the origin of species.* London: Murray.

Das, J. P. (1984). Simultaneous and successive processes and K-ABC. *Journal of Special Education, 18*(3), 229–237.

Davidson, J. E. (1986). The role of insight in giftedness. In R. J. Sternberg & J. E. Davidson (Eds.), *Conceptions of giftedness* (pp. 201–222). Cambridge: Cambridge University Press.

Davidson, J. E. (1992). Insights about giftedness: The role of problem solving abilities. In N. Colangelo, S. G. Assouline & D. L. Ambroson (Eds.), *Talent development: Proceedings from 1991 Henry and Jocelyn Wallace National Research Symposium on Talent Development* (pp. 125–142). Unionville, NY: Trillium Press.

Davidson, K. L. (1992). A comparison of Native American and white students' cognitive strengths as measured by the Kaufman Assessment Battery for Children. *Roeper Review, 14*(3), 111–114.

Davis, G. A. (1981). *Creativity is forever.* Cross Plains, WI: Badger Press.

Davis, G. A. (1989). Testing for creative potential. *Contemporary Educational Psychology, 14,* 257–274.

• Davis, G.A. (1997). Identifying creative students and measuring creativity. In N. Colangelo & G. A. Davis (Eds.), *Handbook of gifted education* (2nd ed., pp. 269–281). Needham Heights, MA: Allyn & Bacon.

Davis, G. A. & Rimm, S. B. (1982). Group inventory for finding interests (GIFFI) I and II: Instruments for identifying creative potential in the junior and senior high school. *Journal of Creative Behavior, 16,* 50–57.

Davis, G. A., & Rimm, S. B. (1989). *Education of the gifted and talented* (2nd ed.). Englewood Cliffs, NJ: Prentice Hall.

• Davis, G. A., & Rimm, S. B. (1997). *Education of the gifted and talented.* (4th Ed.). Needham Heights, MA: Allyn & Bacon.

DeAvilla, E. (1976). *Cartoon Conservation Scale.* Linquametrics Group.

deBono, E. (1970). *Lateral thinking.* New York: Harper Colophon.

deBono, E. (1978). *CoRT thinking lesson series.* Blanford Forum, Corset, UK: Direct Education Services.

DeHaan, R. F., & Havighurst, R. J. (1957). *Educating gifted children.* Chicago: University of Chicago Press.

• Delcourt, M. A. B., Loyd, B. H., Cornell, D. G., & Goldberg, M. D. (1994). *Evaluation of the effects of programming arrangements on student learning outcomes.* The National Research Center on the Gifted and Talented, Research Monograph 94108. Charlottesville, VA: The University of Virginia.

• DeLeon, J., & Argus-Calvo, B. (1997). Model program for identifying culturally and linguistically diverse rural gifted and talented students. ERIC Document ED 406125.

Delisle, D., & Delisle, J. R. (1992). Classroom strategies for meeting multiple needs: A five-step model. In *Challenges of gifted education* (pp. 89–96). Columbus, OH: Ohio Department of Education.

Delisle, J. R. (1982). Striking out: Suicide and the gifted adolescent. *Gifted Child Today, 24,* 16–19.

• Delisle, J. R. (1992). *Guiding the social and emotional needs of the gifted.* New York: Longman.

• Delisle, J.R. (1995, November/December). Au contraire. *Gifted Child Today,* 10–11.

• Delisle, J. R. (1996, November/December). Multiple intelligences: Simple, convenient, wrong. *Gifted Child Today,* 12–13.

Delisle, J. R., & Govender, S. P. (1988). Educators of gifted and talented students: Common bonds, unique perspectives. *Roeper Review, 11*(2), 72–76.

DeSalvo, L. (1989). Virginia Woolf: *The impact of childhood sexual abuse on her life and work.* Boston: Beacon Press.

Detterman, D. (1985). Review of Wechsler Intelligence Scale for Children. In J. Kramer (Ed.), *The Ninth Mental Measurements Yearbook* (pp. 1715–1716). Lincoln, NE: University of Nebraska Press.

• Detterman, D. (1993). *Evaluate yourself.* Storrs, CT: The National Research Center on the Gifted and Talented.

• Deyhle, D., & Swisher, K. (1997). Research in American Indian and Alaska Native Education: From assimilation to self-determination. In M. Apple (Ed.), *Review of Educational Research, 22* (pp. 113–194). Washington, DC: American Educational Research Association.

Digest: Education of the gifted and talented handicapped. (1985). Reston, Va: National Clearinghouse for the Council for Exceptional Children-The Association for the Gifted.

Dillon, J. (1979). Alternatives to questioning. *High School Journal, 62*, 217–222.

•Dixon, C. (1996). *Gifted and at risk.* Phi Delta Kappa Fastback 398. Bloomington, IN: Phi Delta Kappa Educational Foundation.

Dobbs, S. (1989). Some second thoughts on the application of left brain/right brain research. *Roeper Review, 12*(2), 119–121.

Dos Passos, J. (1966). *The best times.* New York: New American Library.

Dover, A., & Shore, B. M. (1991). Giftedness and flexibility on a mathematical set-breaking task. *Gifted Child Quarterly, 35*(2), 99–105.

Drevdahl, J. E., & Cattell, R. B. (1958). Personality and creativity in artists and writers. *Journal of Clinical Psychology, 4*, 107–111.

Duke, P. & Turan, K. (1987). *Call me Anna.* New York: Banton.

Dunn, R., Dunn, K., & Price, G. (1979). *Learning Style Inventory.* Lawrence, KS: Price Systems.

Duran, B. J. & Weffer, R. E. (1992). Immigrants' aspirations, high school process, and academic outcomes. *American Educational Research Journal, 29*(1), 163–181.

Durden, W.G. (1985). Editorial: Talent and creativity require information. *Academic Talent, 1*(2), 7–9.

Durden, W.G., & Tangherlini A.E. (1993). Smart kids: *How academic talents are developed and nurtured in America.* Kirkland, WA: Hogrefe & Huber Publishers.

Dyer, C. O. (1985). Review of Otis-Lennon School Ability Test. In J. Kramer (Ed.), *The Ninth Mental Measurements Yearbook* (pp. 1107–1111). Lincoln, NE: University of Nebraska Press.

Eberle, B. (1982). *Visual thinking.* Buffalo: D.O.K.

Eby, J. W., & Smutny, J. F. (1990). *A thoughtful overview of gifted education.* White Plains, NY: Longman.

Eccles, J. (1985a). Model of students' mathematics enrollment decisions. *Educational Studies in Mathematics, 16*, 311–314.

Eccles, J. (1985b). Why doesn't Jane run? Sex differences in educational and occupational patterns. In F. D. Horowitz & M. O'Brien (Eds.), *The gifted and talented: Developmental perspectives* (pp. 251–300). Washington, DC: American Psychological Association.

Eccles, J., & Harold, R. D. (1992). Gender differences in educational and occupational patterns among the gifted. In N. Colangelo, S. G. Assouline & D. L. Ambroson (Eds.), *Talent development: Proceedings from the Henry B. and Jocelyn Wallace National Research Symposium on Talent Development* (pp. 2–32). Iowa City, IA: The University of Iowa.

Education Products Information Institute (EPIE). (1979). *Grant progress report NIE-G-790083.* Mimeographed. Stonybrook, NY EPIE.

Educational Records Bureau Comprehensive Testing Program. Princeton, NJ: Educational Testing Service.

Edwards, A. (1975). *Judy Garland.* New York: Simon and Schuster.

Edwards, B. (1979). *Drawing on the right side of the brain.* Los Angeles: Tarcher.

Edwards, F. & Kleine, P. (1986). Counseling to multimodal profiles of gifted youth. *Journal of Counseling Psychology, 10*, 134–147.

•Egan, K. (1992). *Imagination in teaching and learning: The middle school years.* Chicago: University of Chicago Press.

Eggins, J. A. (1979). *The interaction between structure in learning materials and the personality type of learners.* Unpublished doctoral dissertation, Indiana University.

Eisner, E. W. (1979). *The educational imagination* (1st ed.) . New York: Macmillan.

Eisner, E. W. (1985). *The educational imagination* (2d ed.). New York: Macmillan.

•Eisner, E. (1994). *The educational imagination* (4th ed.). New York: Prentice Hall.

•*Elementary and Secondary Education Act.* (1988, April 28). Public Law 100-297. Title IV, Part B—Gifted and Talented Children.

Flkind, D. (1981). *The hurried child: Growing up too fast too soon.* Reading, MA: Addison-Wesley.

Elmore, R., & Zenus, V. (1991). Cooperative learning and middle school gifted. In R. Swassing & A. Robinson (Eds.), *Research briefs of the National Association for Gifted Children.* Washington, DC.

Etheredge, L. S. (1978). Personality effects on American foreign policy, 1898–1968: A test of interpersonal generalization theory. *American Political Science Review, 78*, 434–451.

Eysenck, H. J. (1985). The nature and measurement of intelligence. In J. Freeman (Ed.), *The psychology of gifted children* (pp. 115–140). London: John Wiley.

•Eysenck, M. (1990). Creativity. In Eysenck, M. K. (Ed.), *The Blackwell dictionary of cognitive psychology* (pp. 86–87). London: Blackwell Ltd.

Fairbairn, D. M. (1986, September). The art of questioning your students. *Clearinghouse*, 19–22.

•Fairhurst, A. M., & Fairhurst, L. L. (1995). *Effective teaching: Effective learning.* Palo Alto, CA: Davies-Black.

Falk, G. (1987). Gifted children's perception of divorce. *Journal for the Education of the Gifted, 11*(1), 29–43.

Farmer, H. S. (1985). Model of career and achievement motivation for women and men. *Journal of Counseling Psychology, 32*, 363–390.

Farrel, S. W., Bentley, T. (1990). *Holding on to the air.* New York: Summit.

•Farrell, W. (1986). *Why men are the way they are.* New York: McGraw-Hill.

•Feiring, C., Louis, B., Ukeje, I., & Lewis, M. (1997). Early identification of gifted minority kindergarten students in Newark, NJ. *Gifted Child Quarterly, 41*(3), 76–82.

Feldhusen, J. F. (1986). A conception of giftedness. In R. Sternberg & J. Davidson (Eds.), *Conceptions of giftedness* (pp. 112–127). New York: Cambridge University Press.

Feldhusen, J. F. (1992a). From the editor: Talent identification and development in education. *Gifted Child Quarterly, 36*, 123.

Feldhusen, J. F. (1992b). *Talent identification and development in education (TIDE).* Sarasota: Center for Creative Learning.

Feldhusen, J. F. (1992c). *Talent identification and development as an alternative to gifted education.* Symposium at National Association for Gifted Children Conference. Los Angeles, CA.

•Feldhusen, J. F. (1995). *Talent development: The new direction in gifted education.* Roeper Review, *18*, 92.

Feldhusen, J. F., & Baska, L. K. (1985). Identification and assessment of the gifted and talented. In J. F. Feldhusen (Ed.), *Excellence in educating the gifted* (pp. 87–88). Denver, CO: Love.

Feldhusen, J. F., & Clinkenbeard, P. (1986). Creativity instructional materials: A review of research. *Journal of Creative Behavior, 20*, 176–188.

Feldhusen, J. F., & Moon, S. (1992). Grouping gifted students: Issues and concerns. *Gifted Child Quarterly, 36*, 63–67.

Feldhusen, J. F., Asher, J. W., & Hoover, S. M. (1984). Problems in the identification of giftedness, talent, or ability. *Gifted Child Quarterly, 28*(4), 149–151.

Feldhusen, J. F., Baska, L. K., & Womble, S. R. (1981). Using standard scores to synthesize data in identifying the gifted. *Journal for the Education of the Gifted, 4*, 177–185.

Feldhusen, J. F., Hoover, S. M., & Sayler, M. F. (1990). *Identifying and educating gifted students at the secondary level.* Monroe, NY: Trillium Press.

•Feldman, D. H. (1971). Map understanding as a possible crystallizer of cognitive structures. *American Educational Research Journal, 8*, 485–501.

Feldman, D. H. (1974). Universal to unique: A developmental approach to creativity and education. In S. Rosner & L. Abt (Eds.), *Essays in creativity.* Croton-on-Hudson, NY: North River Press.

Feldman, D. H. (1982). A developmental framework for research with gifted children. In D. Feldman (Ed.), *New directions for child development* (pp. 31–46). San Francisco: Jossey-Bass.

Feldman, D. H., w. Goldsmith, L. (1986). *Nature's gambit.* New York: Basic.

Feldman, D. H. (1988). Dreams, insights, and transformations. In R.J. Sternberg (Ed.), *The nature of creativity: Contemporary psychological perspectives* (pp. 271–297). New York: Cambridge University Press.

Feldman, D. H. (1991, Fall). Has there been a paradigm shift in gifted education: Some thoughts on a changing national scene. *Educating Able Learners*, 14–19.

Feldman, D. H. (1992). Has there been a paradigm shift in gifted education? In N. Colangelo, S. G. Assouline & D. L. Ambroson (Eds.), *Talent development: Proceedings from 1991 Henry b. and Jocelyn Wallace National Research Symposium on Talent Development* (pp. 89–94). Unionville, NY: Trillium Press.

•Feldman, D. H. (1994). *Beyond universals in cognitive development* (2d ed.). Norwood, NJ: Ablex.

•Feldman, D. H. (1997). *Developmental theory and the expression of talent.* Paper presented at the 12th World Conference of the World Council for Gifted and Talented Children. Seattle, WA. August 1, 1997.

•Feldman, D. H., & Piirto, J. (1995.) Parenting talented children. In M. Bornstein (Ed.), *Handbook of parenting* (pp. 285–304). NJ: Lawrence Erlbaum.

•Feldman, D. H., Csikszentmihalyi, M., & Gardner, H. (1994). *Changing the world: A framework for the study of creativity.* Westport, CT: Praeger.

Feldman, R. D. (1982). *Whatever happened to the Quiz Kids?* Chicago: Chicago Review Press.

•Fenwick, L. T. (1996). *School reform: Challenging the race orthodoxy.* ERIC Document ED405407.

•Fetterman, D. M. (1993). *Evaluate yourself.* The National Research Center on the Gifted and Talented; Research-based Decision Making Series. Storrs, CT: University of Connecticut.

Feuerstein, R. (1979). *The dynamic assessment of retarded performers.* Baltimore: University Park Press.

Fiedler, F. E. (1967). *A theory of leadership effectiveness.* New York: McGraw-Hill.

Fincher, J. (1976). *Human intelligence.* New York: Putnam.

• Finley, C.L. (1995). Review of the Metropolitan Achievement Test, 7th edition. In J. C. Conoley & J. C. Impara. (Eds.), *The Twelfth Mental Measurements Yearbook.* Lincoln, NE: The Buros Institute of Mental Measurements.

Fitz-Gibbon, C. (1975). The identification of mentally gifted "disadvantaged" students at the eighth grade level. *Journal of Negro Education, 43*(1), 53–66.

Fitzgibbon, C. (1965). *The life of Dylan Thomas.* Boston: Little, Brown.

Flanagan, J. C., Dailey, J. T., Shaycoft, M. F., Gorham, W. A., Orr, D. B., & Goldberg, I. (1962). *Design for a study of American youth.* Boston: Houghton Mifflin.

Flavell, J. H. (1977). *Cognitive development.* Englewood Cliffs, NJ: Prentice Hall.

• Flavell, J. H. (1979). Metacognition and cognitive monitoring: A new area of cognitive-developmental inquiry. *American Psychologist, 34,* 906–911.

Fleming, E., & Hollinger, C. (1994). Project CHOICE: A longitudinal study of the career development of gifted and talented young women. In R. F. Subotnik & K. D. Arnold (Eds.), *Beyond Terman: Contemporary longitudinal studies of giftedness and talent* (pp. 316–348). Norwood, NJ: Ablex.

Fliegler, L. A. (1961). *Curriculum planning for the gifted.* Englewood Cliffs, NJ: Prentice-Hall.

• Flint, L., Schottke, N., Willmore, S., & Piirto, J. (1997). *Intensities in talented teenagers: Themes from the Dabrowski Overexcitability Questionnaire (OEQ).* Master's paper for the Inquiry Seminar in Talent Development Education, July, 1997. Ashland University, Ashland, OH.

Florey, J. E., et al. (1986). *Identification of gifted children among the American Indian population: An inservice model.* ERIC Reproduction Document Service ED 273399.

Fogler, K., & Gottling, C. (1985). *Hunter College Elementary School Mathematics Curriculum.* Unpublished manuscript. NY: Hunter College Elementary School.

Ford, D. Y. (1992). Determinants of underachievement as perceived by gifted, above-average, and average black students. *Roeper Review, 13,* 130–135.

Ford, D. Y. (1993). Black students' achievement orientation as a function of perceived family achievement orientation and demographic variables. *Journal of Negro Education, 62*(1), 47–66.

• Ford, D. Y. (1994a). Nurturing resilience in gifted Black youth. *Roeper Review, 17*(2), 80–85.

• Ford, D. Y. (1994b). *The recruitment and retention of African-American students in gifted education programs: Implications and recommendations.* The National Research Center on the Gifted and Talented Research Monograph 9405. Charlottesville, VA: University of Virginia.

• Ford, D. Y. (1996). *Reversing underachievement among gifted black students: Promising practices and programs.* New York: Teachers College Press.

Ford, D. Y., & Harris, J. J. (1992). The American achievement ideology and achievement differentials among preadolescent gifted and nongifted African American males and females. *Journal of Negro Education, 61*(1), 45–64.

• Ford, D. Y., Harris, J. J., & Winborne, D. G. (1990). The coloring of IQ testing: A new name for an old phenomenon. *The Urban League Review Policy Research Journal, 13*(1/2), 99–111.

• Fordham, S. (1988). Racelessness as a factor in black students' school success: Pragmatic strategy or Pyrrhic victory? *Harvard Educational Review, 58*(1), 54–84.

Fordham, S. & Ogbu, J. U. (1986). Black students' school success: Coping with the 'burden' of 'acting white.' *The Urban Review; 18*(3), 176–206.

Forrest, D. W. (1974). *Francis Galton: The life and work of a Victorian genius.* New York: Taplinger.

Forster, M. (1988). *Elizabeth Barrett Browning: A biography.* New York: Doubleday.

Frady, M. (1992, February 10). Profiles (Jesse Jackson—Part II). *The New Yorker,* pp. 41–75.

Frasier, M. M. (1987). The identification of gifted Black students: Developing new perspectives. *Journal for the Education of the Gifted, 10*(3), 155–180.

Frasier, M. (1990, April). *The equitable identification of gifted and talented children.* Paper presented at the Annual Meeting of the American Educational Research Association, Boston, MA.

Frasier, M. (1991). Disadvantaged and culturally diverse gifted students. *Journal for the Education of the Gifted, 14,* 234–245.

Frasier, M. (1992). Ethnic/minority children: Reflections and directions. In *Challenges in gifted education* (pp. 41–48). Columbus, OH: Ohio Department of Education.

•Frasier, M., Garcia, J., & Passow, A. H. (1995). *A review of assessment issues in gifted education and their implications for identifying gifted minority students.* The National Research Center on the Gifted and Talented Research Monograph 95204. Storrs, CT: University of Connecticut.

Frasier, M., Hunsaker, S., Lee, J., Mitchell, S., Cramond, B., Krisel, S., Garcia, J., Martin, D., Frank, E., & Finley, S. (1995). *Core attributes of giftedness: A foundation for recognizing the gifted potential of minority and economically disadvantaged students.* National Research Center on the Gifted and Talented. Storrs, CT: University of Connecticut.

Freehill, M. (1961). *Gifted children: Their psychology and education.* New York: Macmillan.

Freeman, D., Holder, S., & Varlese, R. (1988). *Self-study for pre-primary for middle state evaluation.* Unpublished manuscript. New York: Hunter College Elementary School.

Freeman, J. (Ed.). (1986). *The psychology of gifted children: Perspectives on development and education.* New York: Wiley.

•Freire, P. (Ed.). (1997). *Mentoring the mentor: A critical dialogue with Paolo Freire.* New York: Peter Lang.

•Friedrichs, T.P. (1997, November). *The edge: Social and emotional lives of gifted gay, lesbian, and bisexual pupils.* Paper presented at the National Association for Gifted Children Conference, Little Rock, AR.

From risk to renewal: Charting a course for reform. (Feb. 10, 1993). *Education Week*/special report.

Fuchs, D. (1989). A review of the Cognitive Abilities Test, Form 4. In J. C. Conoley & J. J. Kramer (Eds.), *The Tenth Mental Measurements Yearbook* (pp. 193–197). Lincoln, NE: University of Nebraska Press.

Fuller, B. (1981). *Critical path.* New York: St. Martin's Press.

Gagné, F. (1985). Giftedness and talent: Reexamining a reexamination of the definition. *Gifted Child Quarterly, 29,* 103–112.

Gagné, F. (1990). Toward a differentiated model of giftedness and talent. In N. Colangelo & G. Davis (Eds.), *Handbook of gifted education* (pp. 65–81). Needham Heights, MA: Allyn & Bacon.

Gagné, F. (1992, November). *Talent identification and development as an alternative to gifted education.* Symposium at the National Association for Gifted Children Conference, Los Angeles, CA.

Gagné, F. (1993). Constructs and models pertaining to exceptional human abilities. In K. A. Heller, F. J.

Mönks, and A. H. Passow (Eds.), *International handbook of research and development of giftedness and talent* (pp. 69–87). Oxford: Pergamon Press.

Gagné, F. (1995). Hidden meaning of the "talent development" concept. *The Educational Forum, 59*(4), 350–362.

Gagné, F. (1996, Fall). A thoughtful look at the concept of talent development. *Tempo: The Journal of the Texas Association for Gifted and Talented,* pp. 5–10.

Gagné, F., Bégin, J., & Talbot, L. (1993). How well do peers agree among themselves when nominating the gifted or talented? *Gifted Child Quarterly, 37*(1), 39–45.

•Gagné, F., Neveu, F., Simard, L., & St. Père, F. (1996). How a search for multitalented individuals challenged the concept itself. *Gifted and Talented International, 11*(1), 5–11.

Gallagher, J. J. (1985). *Teaching the gifted child.* (3rd ed.) Boston: Allyn & Bacon.

Gallagher, J. J. (1991). Personal patterns of underachievement. *Journal for the Education of the Gifted, 14,* 221–233.

•Gallagher, J. J. (1996). A critique of critiques of gifted education. *Journal for the Education of the Gifted, 19*(2), 234–239.

Gallagher, J. J., & Courtwright, R. D. (1986). The educational definition of giftedness and its policy implication. In R. J. Sternberg & J. E. Davidson (Eds.), *Conceptions of giftedness* (pp. 93–111). Cambridge: Cambridge University Press.

Gallagher, J. J., & Lucito, L. (1960). Intellectual patterns of gifted compared with average and retarded. *Peabody Journal of Education, 38,* 131–136.

•Gallagher, S.A. (1997). Problem-based learning: Where did it come from, what does it do, and where is it going? *Journal for the Education of the Gifted, 20*(4), 332–362.

Galton, F. (1869). *Hereditary genius: An inquiry into its law and consequences.* London: Macmillan and Co.

Gardner, E. F., Rudman, H. C., Karlsen, B., & Merwin, J. C. (1982). *Stanford Achievement Test* (7th ed.). San Antonio: The Psychological Corporation.

Gardner, H. (1982). *Art, mind, and brain.* New York: Basic Books.

Gardner, H. (1983). *Frames of mind.* New York: Basic Books.

Gardner, H. (1985). *The mind's new science.* New York: Basic Books.

Gardner, H. (1988). Creative lives and creative works: A synthetic scientific approach. In R. Sternberg (Ed.), *The nature of creativity* (pp. 298–321). New York: Cambridge University Press.

Gardner, H. (1989, December). Learning Chinese style. *Psychology Today*, 54–56.

Gardner, H. (1991). *The unschooled mind.* New York: Basic Books.

•Gardner, H. (1993a). *Creating minds: An anatomy of creativity seen through the lives of Freud, Einstein, Picasso, Stravinsky, Eliot, Graham, and Gandhi.* New York: Basic Books.

•Gardner, H. (1993b). *Multiple intelligences: The theory in practice.* New York: Basic Books.

Gardner, H., with the collaboration of Laskin, E. (1995). *Leading minds: An anatomy of leadership.* New York: Basic Books. Basic Books Paperback with a new introduction, 1996.

Gardner, H. (1995a, April). *Assessment of projects.* Speech for Ohio Association for Gifted Children meeting, Columbus, OH.

•Gardner, H. (1995b, November). Reflections on Multiple Intelligences: Myths and messages. *Phi Delta Kappan, 77*, 3, 200–203, 206–209.

Gardner, H. (1997). *Extraordinary minds: Portraits of exceptional individuals and an examination of our extraordinariness.* New York: Basic Books.

•Gardner, H., & Boix-Mansilla, V. (1994, February). Teaching for understanding—within and across disciplines. *Educational Leadership, 51*(5) 14–18.

Gardner, J. (1982). *On becoming a novelist.* New York: Colophon/Harper & Row.

Garibaldi, A. M. (1992). Educating and motivating African American males to succeed. *Journal of Negro Education, 61*, 4–11.

Garmezy, G., & Tellegen, A. (1984). Studies of stress-resistant children: Methods, variables, and preliminary findings. In F. J. Morrison, C. Lord & D. P. Keating (Eds.), *Applied developmental psychology* (pp. 241–283). Orlando: Academic Press.

Gawain, S. (1979). *Creative visualization.* New York: Bantam.

Geary, D. C., & Brown, S. C. (1991). Cognitive addition: Strategy choice and speed-of-processing differences in gifted, normal, and mathematically disabled children. *Developmental Psychology, 27*(1), 398–408.

Geften, L. (1989). Editorial. *Roeper Review, 12*(3), 72.

Geiger, R., & Martin, R. P. (1992). Personality differences of academically gifted students with different cognitive strengths. In N. Colangelo, S. G. Assouline & D. L. Ambroson (Eds.), *Talent development: Proceedings from the 1991 Henry B. and Jocelyn Wallace National Research Symposium on Talent Development* (pp. 376–389). Unionville, NY: Trillium Press.

Gelbrich, J. A., & Hare, E. K. (1989). The effects of single parenthood on school achievement in a gifted population. *Gifted Child Quarterly, 33*, 115–117.

George, K. R. (1983). Native American Indian: Perception of gifted characteristics. In B. M. Shore, F. Gagné, S. Larivee, H. Tali & R. E. Tremblay (Eds.), *Face to face with giftedness* (pp. 220–249). Montreal: McGill University.

George, K. R. (1987). *A guide to understanding gifted American Indian students.* Las Cruces, NM: ERIC Clearinghouse on Rural Education and Small Schools. ED 284715.

Getzels, J. (1987). Creativity, intelligence, and problem finding: Retrospect and prospect. In S. Isaksen (Ed.), *Frontiers of creativity research* (pp. 88–102). Buffalo: Bearly Ltd.

Getzels, J., & Csikszentmihalyi, M. (1976). *The creative vision: A longitudinal study of problem finding in art.* New York: Wiley.

Getzels, J., & Jackson, P. (1962). *Creativity and intelligence: Explorations with gifted students.* New York: Wiley.

Ghiselin, B. (1952). *The creative process.* New York: Mentor.

•Gillespie, C. (1991) Questions about student-generated questions. *Journal of Reading, 34*(4), 250–257.

Ginzberg, E. (1966). *Life styles of educated women.* New York: Columbia University Press.

•Giroux, H. A. (1997). *Pedagogy and the politics of hope: Theory, culture and schooling.* New York: Westview Press.

•Glascoe, F. P. (1996). Can the BRIGANCE Screens detect children who are gifted and academically talented? *Roeper Review, 19*(1), 20–26.

Glass, P. (1987). *Music by Philip Glass.* New York: Harper & Row.

Glover, J. S., Ronning, R. R., & Reynolds, C. R. (1989). *Handbook of creativity.* New York: Plenum.

•Goertz, J., Rodriguez, A. M., & Bernal, E. (1997). Mexican-American secondary gifted students' perceptions of counselors. In T. Cross (Ed.), *Research briefs* (pp. 90–99). Washington, DC: National Association for Gifted Children Service Publications.

Goertzel, V., & Goertzel, M. G. (1962). *Cradles of eminence.* Boston: Little, Brown.

Goertzel, V., Goertzel, M. G., & Goertzel, T. (1978). *Three hundred eminent personalities: A psychosocial analysis of the famous.* San Francisco: Jossey-Bass.

•Goldberg, N. (1986). *Writing down the bones.* New York: Quality Paperbacks.

•Goleman, D. (1995). *Emotional intelligence.* New York: Bantam Books.

Good, T. L., & Brophy, J. E. (1990). *Educational psychology: A realistic approach.* New York: Longman.

Goodenough, F. L. (1926). *Measurement of intelligence by drawings.* Yonkers-on-Hudson, NY: World Book Company.

•Goodlad, J. I. (1984). *A place called school: Prospects for the future.* New York: McGraw-Hill Book Co.

Gordon, E. E. (1965). *Music aptitude profile.* Boston: Houghton Mifflin.

Gordon, E. E. (1970–1971). *Iowa tests of musical literacy.* Iowa City, IA: Bureau of Educational Research and Service, University of Iowa.

Gordon, W. (1961). *Synectics: The development of creative capacity.* New York: Harper & Row.

•Gosfield, M. (1993). Developing leadership during the middle school years. In J. Drum (Ed.), Special issue on middle school gifted. *Communicator 23*(2). Journal of the California Association for the Gifted. ERIC Document ED 365037.

Gottfredson, L.S. (1981). Circumscription and compromise: A developmental theory of occupational aspirations. *Journal of Counseling Psychology, 28*(6), 545–579.

Gough, H. G. (1952). *Adjective checklist.* Palo Alto, CA: Consulting Psychologists Press.

Gough, H. G. (1979). A creative personality scale for the Adjective Checklist. *Journal of Personality and Social Psychology, 37,* 1398–1405.

Gough, H. G., & Heilbrun, A. B. (1983). *The adjective checklist.* Palo Alto, CA: Consulting Psychologists Press.

Gould, S. J. (1981). *The mismeasure of man.* New York: Norton.

Gourley, T. J. (1981). Adapting the varsity sports model for nonpsychomotor gifted students. *Gifted Child Quarterly, 25,* 164–166.

Graffman, G. (1981). *I really should be practicing: Reflections on the pleasures and perils of playing the piano in public.* New York: Avon.

Gray, W. A. (1982). Mentor-assisted enrichment projects for the gifted and talented. *Educational Leadership, 40*(2), 16–21.

Gray, W. A. (1983). *Challenging the gifted and talented through mentor-assisted enrichment projects.* Bloomington, IN: Phi Delta Kappa Educational Foundation.

Green, D. (1992). School-related predictive behaviors in mathematics. Unpublished document.

Green, J. (1961). *Diary: 1928–1957.* New York: Carroll & Graf.

Green, K. C. (1989). A profile of undergraduates in the sciences. *American Scientist, 77,* 475–480.

•Greenan, J. P., Wu, M., & Broering, K. (1995). Talented students in career, vocational, and technical education programs. *The Educational Forum, 59*(4), 409–422.

Gregorc, A. (1982). *Gregorc Style Delineator: A self-assessment instrument for adults.* Columbia, CT: Author.

•Griffin, D. R., Cobb, J. B., Ford, M. B., Gunter, P. A. Y., & Ochs, P. (1993). *Founders of constructive postmodern philosophy: Peirce, James, Bergson, Whitehead, and Hartshorne.* Albany: State University of New York Press.

Griffin, J. (1992). Catching the dream for gifted children of color. *Gifted Child Quarterly, 36,* 126–130.

•Gross, M. (1993). *Exceptionally gifted children.* London: Routledge.

•Gross, M. (1998, May). *Ability grouping, self-esteem, and the gifted.* Keynote presentation at the Fourth Biennial Henry B. and Jocelyn Wallace National Research Symposium on Talent Development. Iowa City, IA: University of Iowa.

Grover, E. (1990). *Talented characters in juvenile literature.* Unpublished manuscript.

Gruber, H. (1982). *Darwin on man* (2d ed.). Chicago: University of Chicago Press.

Gruber, H., & Davis, S. (1988). Inching our way up Mount Olympus: the evolving-systems approach to creative thinking. In R. J. Sternberg (Ed.), *The nature of creativity: Contemporary psychological perspectives* (pp. 243–270). New York: Cambridge University Press.

Gruen, J. (1988). *People who dance.* Princeton, NJ: Princeton Book Co.

•Grumet, M., & Pinar, W. (1996). The curriculum: What are the basics and are we teaching them? In J. L. Kincheloe & S. R. Steinberg (Eds.), *Thirteen questions: Reframing education's conversions* (pp. 13–31). New York: Peter Lang.

Grun, B. (1992). *The timetables of history.* New York: Simon and Schuster.

•Gubbins, E.J. (1992, Fall). NRC/GT destination: So near and so far. *NRC G/T Newsletter,* pp. 1–2.

Guilford, J. P. (1950). Creativity. *American Psychologist, 5,* 444–454.

Guilford, J. P. (1967). *The nature of human intelligence.* New York: McGraw Hill.

Guilford, J. P. (1970). Traits of creativity. In P. E. Vernon (Ed.), *Creativity* (pp. 167–178). Harmondsworth: Penguin.

Guilford, J. P. (1977). *Way beyond the IQ: Guide to improving intelligence and creativity*. Buffalo: Creative Education Foundation.

Guilford, J. P. (1987). Creativity research: Past, present and future. In S. Isaksen (Ed.), *Frontiers of creativity research* (pp. 33–66). Buffalo: Bearly.

Gulbenkian Report (1978). *The arts in schools*. London: Calouste Gulbenkian Foundation.

Gunderson, C. W., Maesch, C., & Rees, J. W. (1987). The gifted/learning disabled student. *Gifted Child Quarterly, 31*, 158–160.

Gustin, W. C. (1985). The development of exceptional research mathematicians. In B. Bloom (Ed.), *Developing talent in young people* (pp. 270–331). New York: Ballantine.

Halperin, J. (1986). *The life of Jane Austen*. Baltimore: Johns Hopkins.

Halpin, G., & Halpin, G. (1973). The effect of motivation on creative thinking abilities. *Journal of Creative Behavior, 7*, 51–53.

Halstead, J. W. (1988). *Guiding gifted readers*. Columbus, OH: Ohio Psychology Publishers.

Hamachek, D. (1990). *Psychology in teaching, learning, and growth* (4th ed.), Needham Heights, MA: Allyn & Bacon.

•Hannah, C. L., & Shore, B. M. (1995). Metacognition and high intellectual ability: Insights from the study of learning-disabled gifted students. *Gifted Child Quarterly, 39*(2), 95–109.

•Hanninen, G.E. (1994). *Blending gifted education and school reform*. ERIC Document ED 371520. ERIC Digest E525.

Harkins, J. D., & Macrosson, W. D. K. (1990). Creativity training: An assessment of a novel approach. *Journal of Business and Psychology, 5*(1), 143–148.

Harmon, L. W. (1985). What's new? A response to Astin. *The Counseling Psychologist, 12*(4), 127–128.

•Harnadek, A. (1978). *Mind benders*. Pacific Grove, CA: Midwest Publications.

•Harnadek, A. (1980). *Critical thinking, Books 1 and 2*. Pacific Grove, CA: Midwest Publications.

Harrington-Lueker, D. (1991, November). Empty promises. *The Executive Educator*, 18–25.

Harris, C. R. (1990). The Hollingworth longitudinal study: Follow-up, findings, and implications. *Roeper Review, 12*(3), 216–221.

Harris, J. J., & Ford, D. Y. (1991). Identifying and nurturing the promise of gifted black American children. *Journal of Negro Education, 60*(1), 3–18.

•Harrison, K. (1997). *The kiss*. New York: Random House.

Harrison, P. L. (1989). Review of the Wide Range Achievement Test-Revised. In J. C. Conoley & J. J. Kramer (Eds.), *The Tenth Mental Measurements Yearbook* (pp. 903–905). Lincoln, NE: University of Nebraska Press.

Hartounian, J. (1993, Winter). Identification of the musically talented student: The assessment of musical potential and musical performance. *NRCG/T Newsletter*, pp. 12–13.

Hatch, T. C., & Gardner, H. (1986). From testing intelligence to assessing competencies: A pluralistic view of intellect. *Roeper Review, 8*(3), 147–150.

Hausman, C. (1987). Philosophical perspectives on the study of creativity. In S. Isaksen (Ed.), *Frontiers of creativity research* (pp. 380–389). Buffalo: Bearly Ltd.

H'Doubler, M. (1968). *Dance: A creative art experience*. Madison, WI: The University of Wisconsin Press.

Heausler, N., & Thompson, B. (1988). Structure of the Torrance Tests of Creative Thinking. *Educational and Psychological Measurement, 48*, 463–468.

•Hébert, T. (1991). Meeting the affective needs of bright boys through bibliotherapy. *Roeper Review, 13*(4), 201–212.

•Hébert, T. (1996). Portraits of resilience: The urban life experience of gifted Latino young men. *Roeper Review, 19*(2), pp. 82–90.

•Heller, K. A., Mönks, F. J., & Passow, A. H. (Eds.). (1993). *International handbook of research and development of giftedness and talent*. Oxford: Pergamon Press.

Hendrie, C. (1998, June 10). New Magnet school policies sidestep an old issue: Race. Education Week, pp. 10–12.

Helson, R. (1983). Creative mathematicians. In R. Albert (Ed.), *Genius and eminence: The social psychology of creativity and exceptional achievement* (p. 211–30). London: Pergamon Press.

•Hennessey, B. A. (1997). Teaching for creative development: A social psychological approach. In N. Colangelo & G. A. Davis (Eds.), *Handbook of gifted education* (2d ed., pp. 282–291). Needham Heights, MA: Allyn & Bacon.

Hennessey, B., & Amabile, T. (1988). Storytelling as a means of assessing creativity. *Journal of Creative Behavior, 22*, 235–247.

•Hernandez, A. (1995, July). *HARG study*. Paper presented at Ashland University, Ashland, OH.

•Herring, R. (1996). The unrecognized gifted: A more humanistic perspective for indigenous students. *Journal of Humanistic Education and Development, 35*(1), 4–11.

Herrmann, N. (1981). *Herrmann Brain Dominance Instrument.* Lake Lure, NC: Applied Creative Services.

•Herrnstein, R., & Murray, C. (1994). *The Bell Curve: Intelligence and class structure in American life.* New York: The Free Press.

Hieronymous, A. N., Hoover, H. D., & Lindquist, E. F. (1986). *Iowa Tests of Basic Skills.* Chicago: Riverside.

Higham, S. Lynch, & Navarre, J. Piirto (1984). Gifted adolescent females require differential treatment. *Journal for the Education of the Gifted, 8,* 43–49.

•Hillman, J. (1996). *The soul's code: In search of character and calling.* New York: Random House.

Hinkley, L. (1945). *The Brontës: Charlotte and Emily.* New York: Hastings House.

Hirsch, E. D. (1987). *Cultural literacy: What every American needs to know.* New York: Houghton Mifflin.

Hirsch, E. D. (1990). *A first dictionary of cultural literacy.* New York: Houghton Mifflin.

Hirsch, E. D. (Ed.). (1992). *What your first grader needs to know.* New York: Doubleday.

•Hirsch, E.D. (1993, October). Esprit de core. *Core Knowledge Foundation Newsletter,* p. 1.

•Hirsch, E.D. (1996). *The schools we need.* New York: Doubleday.

Hirsch, E. D., Kett, J. F., & Trefil, J. (1988). *Dictionary of cultural literacy.* New York: Houghton Mifflin.

Hocevar, D. (1980). Intelligence, divergent thinking, and creativity. *Intelligence, 4,* 25–40.

Hoehn, L., & Bireley, M. K. (1988). Mental processing preferences of gifted children. *Illinois Council for the Gifted Journal, 7,* 28–31.

Hoffman, E. (1992). *Visions of innocence: Spiritual and inspirational experiences of childhood.* Boston: Shambhala.

Hoge, R. (1988). Issues in the definition and measurement of the giftedness construct. *Educational Researcher, 43,* 12–16.

Holland, J. L. (1961). Creative and academic performance among talented adolescents. *Journal of Educational Psychology, 52*(2), 136–147.

Hollander, L. (1987). Music, the creative process, and the path of enlightenment. *Roeper Review, 10*(1), 28–32.

•Hollinger, C. (1996). An examination of the lives of gifted black young women. In K. Arnold, K. D. Noble & R. F. Subotnik (Eds.), *Remarkable women: Perspectives on female talent development* (pp. 383–398). Cresskill, NJ: Hampton Press.

•Hollinger, C. L., & Fleming, E. S. (1992). A longitudinal examination of life choices of gifted and talented young women. *Gifted Child Quarterly, 36,* 207–212.

Hollingworth, L. S. (1926). *Gifted children: Their nature and nurture.* New York: Macmillan.

Hollingworth, L. S. (1942). *Children above 180 IQ Stanford Binet: Origin and development.* New York: World Book.

•Hooks, b. (1994). *Teaching to transgress: Education as the practice of freedom.* New York: Routledge.

Horn, J. (1986). Intellectual ability concepts. In R. J. Sternberg (Ed.), *Advances in the psychology of human intelligence 3* (pp. 35–77). Hillsdale, NJ: Lawrence Erlbaum.

•Horowitz, F. D., & O'Brien, M. (Eds). *The gifted and talented: Developmental perspectives* (pp. 149–196). Washington, DC: American Psychological Association.

•Howard, D. D. (1997). A naturalistic study of the psychological development of highly gifted young girls. In T. Cross (Ed.), *Research briefs* (pp. 74–89). Washington, DC: National Association for Gifted Children Service Publications.

Howard, J. (1984). *Margaret Mead: A life.* New York: Ballantine.

Howell, H., & Bressler, J. (1988). Research on teaching styles of teachers of the gifted. *Roeper Review, 10,* 144–146.

Howley, A., Howley, C., & Pendarvis, E. (1986). *Teaching gifted children.* Boston: Allyn & Bacon, Inc.

Howley, C. (1992). Early school entry is essential for many gifted children. *The ERIC Review, 2*(1), 19–20.

Howley, C. (1997). *Rural scholars or bright rednecks? Aspirations for a sense of place among rural youth in Appalachia.* ERIC Document ED 404063.

•Howley, C., Howley, A., & Pendaravis, E. (1995). *Out of our minds: Anti-intellectualism and talent development for American schooling.* New York: Teachers College Press.

Humphreys, L. (1986). Concepualization of intellectual giftedness. In F. D. Horowitz & M. O'Brien (Eds.), *The gifted and talented: Developmental perspectives* (pp. 331–360). Washington: American Psychological Association.

•Hunter-Gault, C. (1992). *In my place.* New York: Farrar Straus Giroux.

Hurwitz, A. (1983). *The gifted and talented in art: A guide to program planning.* Worcester, MA: Davis.

International Association for the Evaluation of Educational Achievement (IEA). (1988). *Science achievement in seventeen countries: A preliminary report.* Oxford: Pergamon Press.

Isaksen, S. G., & Treffinger, D. J. (1985). *Creative problem solving: The basic course.* Buffalo: Bearly Limited.

Jackson, N. E. (1988). Precocious reading ability: What does it mean? *Gifted Child Quarterly, 32,* 200–204.

Jackson, N. E. (1991, June). Are early readers gifted? *The National Research Center on the Gifted and Talented Newsletter,* p. 12.

Jackson, N. E. (1992). Understanding giftedness in young children: Lessons from the study of precocious reading. In N. Colangelo, S. G. Assouline & D. L. Ambroson (Eds.), *Talent development: Proceedings from the 1991 Henry B. and Jocelyn Wallace National Research Symposium on Talent Development* (pp. 163–179). Unionville, NY: Trillium Press.

Jackson, N. E., & Lu, W. (1992). Bilingual precocious readers of English. *Roeper Review, 14,* 120–123.

Jacobs, H. H., & Borland, J. A. (1986). The interdisciplinary concept model: Theory and practice. *Gifted Child Quarterly, 30*(4), 159–163.

•Jamison, K. (1993). *Touched with fire: Manic depressive illness and the artistic temperament.* New York: The Free Press.

•Jamison, K. (1995). *An unquiet mind: A memoir of moods and madness.* New York: Vintage Books.

Janos, P. M., & Robinson, N. M. (1985). Psychosocial development in intellectually gifted children. In F. D. Horowitz & M. O'Brien (Eds.), *The gifted and talented: Developmental perspectives* (pp. 149–196). Washington, DC: American Psychological Association.

Janos, P. M., Fung, H. C., & Robinson, N. M. (1985). Self-concept, self-esteem, and peer relations among gifted children who feel "different." *Gifted Child Quarterly, 29,* 78–82.

Jarrell, R. H., & Borland, J. A. (1990). The research base for Renzulli's three-ring conception of giftedness. *Journal for the Education of the Gifted, 13*(4), 288–308.

Jarvie, I. E. (1981). The rationality of creativity. In D. Dutton & M. Kraus (Eds.), *The concept of creativity in science and art* (pp. 109–128). The Hague: Martinus Mijhoff.

Jastak, S., & Wilkinson, G. (1984). *Wide Range Achievement Test-Revised.* Wilmington, DE: Jastak Assessment Systems.

Jenkins-Friedman, R. (1992). Zorba's conundrum: Evaluative aspects of self-concept in talented individuals. *Quest, 3*(1), 1–7.

Jenkins-Friedman, R., & Tollefson, N. (1992). Resiliency in cognition and motivation: Its applicability to giftedness. In N. Colangelo, S. G. Assouline & D. L. Ambroson (Eds.), *Talent development: Proceedings from the 1991 Henry B. and Jocelyn Wallace National Research Symposium on Talent Development* (pp. 325–333). Unionville, NY: Trillium Press.

John-Steiner, V. (1985). *Notebooks of the mind: Explorations of thinking.* New York: Harper & Row.

•Johnsen, S. K., & Ryser, G. R. (1996). The validity of portfolios in predicting performance in a gifted program. *Journal for the Education of the Gifted, 20*(3), 253–267.

Johnson, D. W., & Johnson, R. T. (1987). *Learning together and alone: Cooperative, competitive, and individualistic learning* (2d ed.). Englewood Cliffs, NJ: Prentice Hall.

Johnson, D. W., Johnson, R. T., & Holubec, E. J. (1986). *Circles of learning: Cooperation in the classroom* (1st ed.) Edina, MN: Interaction Book Company.

Johnson, D. W., Johnson, R. T., & Holubec, E. (1990). *Circles of learning: Cooperation in the classroom* (3rd ed.). Edina, MN: Interaction Book Company.

Johnson, D. W., Maruyama, G., Johnson, R., Nelson, D., & Skon, L. (1981). Effects of cooperative, competitive, and goal structures on achievement: A meta-analysis. *Psychological Bulletin, 89*(1), 47–62.

•Johnson, N. E. (1994a). *Understanding gifted underachievers in an ethnically diverse population.* ERIC ED 368101.

•Johnson, N. E. (1994b). *Evaluation of risk factors in selecting children for gifted programs. Part 1: Gifted children at risk: Evidence of an association between low test scores and risk factors. Part 2: Intelligence, aptitude, and achievement in gifted children with and without language risk.* ERIC ED 368098.

Johnson, S. T. (1992). Extra-school factors in achievement, attainment, and aspiration among junior and senior high school-age African American youth. *Journal of Negro Education, 61,* 99–118.

Johnson, S. T., Starnes, W. T., Gregory, D., & Blaylock, A. (1985). Program of Assessment, Diagnosis, and Instruction (PADI): Identification and nurturing potentially gifted and talented minority students. *Journal of Negro Education, 54,* 416–430.

•Jones, J. H., & Sherman, R. G. (1979). Clinical uses of the Myers-Briggs Type Indicator. *Research in Psychological Type, 2,* 32–45.

Jordan, J. B., & Grossi, J. A. (1980). *An administrator's handbook on designing programs for the gifted and talented.* Reston, VA: CEC-TAG.

Jung, C. G. (1965). *Memories, dreams, reflections.* New York: Vintage.

Kabanoff, B., & Bottger, P. (1991). Effectiveness of creativity training and its relationship to selected personality factors. *Journal of Organizational Behavior, 12*(3), 218–235.

•Kagan, J. (1995). *Galen's prophecy: Temperament in human nature.* New York: Basic Books.

Kagan, S. (1989/1990). The structural approach to cooperative learning. *Educational Leadership, 47*(4), 12–15.

Kaltsounis, B., & Honeywell, L. (1980). Instruments useful for studying creative behavior and creative talent. Part IV. Non-commercially available instruments. *Journal of Creative Behavior, 5,* 117–126.

Kamin, L. J. (1981). Separated identical twins. In H. J. Eysenck & L. Kamin (Eds.), *The intelligence controversy* (pp. 106–113). New York: Wiley.

Kanevsky, L. (1991, October). *Metacognitive activities.* Paper presented at Regional CEC-TAG meeting, Columbus, OH.

Kant, I. (1976). The critique of judgment. Trans. J. C. Meredith. In A. Rothenberg & C. Hausman (Eds.), *The creativity question* (pp. 37–41). Durham, NC: Duke University Press.

Karnes, F. A. (1991). Leadership and gifted adolescents. In M. Bireley and J. Genshaft (Eds.), *Understanding the gifted adolescent* (pp. 122–138). New York: Teachers College Press.

Karnes, F. A., & Marquardt, R. G. (1989). *Legal issues and the gifted: Implications for education.* Monograph for the Indiana Department of Education. ERIC Document ED 323 687.

Karnes, F. A., & Marquardt, R. G. (1991a). *Gifted children and legal issues in education: Parents' stories of hope.* Dayton, OH: Ohio Psychology Press.

Karnes, F. A., & Marquardt, R. G. (1991b). *Gifted children and the law: Mediation, due process, and court cases.* Dayton, OH: Ohio Psychology Press.

Karnes, F. A., Chauvin, J. C., & Trant, T. J. (1985). Comparison of personality profiles for intellectually gifted students and students outstanding in the fine and performing arts attending self-contained secondary schools. *Psychology in the Schools, 22,* 122–126.

Karnes, M., & Johnson, P. L. (1987). Bringing out Head Start talents: Findings from the field. *Gifted Child Quarterly, 31*(4), 174–179.

•Karr, M. (1996). *The liar's club: A memoir.* New York: Penguin Books.

•Kastberg, S.M., & Miller, D.G. (1996). Of blue collars and ivory towers: Women from blue-collar backgrounds in higher education. In K. Arnold, K. D. Noble & R. F. Subotnik (Eds.), *Remarkable women: Perspectives on female talent development* (pp. 49–67). Cresskill, NJ: Hampton Press.

Kaufman, A. S. (1985). Review of the Woodcock-Johnson Psychoeducational Battery. In J. Kramer (Ed.), *The Ninth Mental Measurements Yearbook* (pp. 1761–1764). Lincoln, NE: University of Nebraska Press.

Kaufman, A. S., & Harrison, P. (1986). Intelligence tests and gifted assessment: What are the positives? *Roeper Review, 8*(3), 154–159.

Kaufman, A. S., & Kaufman, F. A. (1983). *Kaufman Assessment Battery for Children.* Circle Pines, MN: American Guidance Services.

Kaufmann, F. A., Harrel, G., Milam, C. P., Woolverton, N., & Miller, J. (1986). The nature, role, and influence of mentors in the lives of gifted adults. *Journal of Counseling and Development, 64,* 576–578.

Kearns, D. T., & Doyle, D. F. (1989). *Winning the brain race.* San Francisco: ICS Press.

Keating, D. P. (1983). The creative potential of mathematically precocious boys. In R. Albert (Ed.), *Genius and eminence: The social psychology of creativity and exceptional achievement* (pp. 128–137). London: Pergamon.

Keefe, J. W., & Monk, J. S. (1986). *Learning style profile.* Reston, VA: National Association of Secondary School Principals.

•Keen, S. (1991). *Fire in the belly: On being a man.* New York: Bantam Books.

•Keirsey, D. (1978). *Please understand me: An essay on temperament styles.* DelMar, CA: Promethean Books.

Keller, E. F. (1983). *A feeling for the organism: The life and work of Barbara McClintock.* New York: W.H.

•Kemnitz, T. M., Martin, E. G., Hegeman, K. T., & Hickey, J. G. (1982). *Management systems for gifted and special educational programs.* New York: Trillium Press.

Kemp, A. E. (1982). Personality traits of successful music teachers. *Psychology of Music,* 72–73.

Kennedy, J. (1992, October). Outcome based education (OBE) and the high ability student. *North Carolina Association for the Gifted and Talented Newsletter*, pp. 16–17.

Kerr, B. A. (1985). *Smart girls, gifted women*. Columbus, OH: Ohio Psychology Press.

•Kerr, B.A. (1991). *A handbook for counseling the gifted and talented*. Washington, DC: American Association for Counseling and Development.

Kerr, B. A. (1992). A twenty-year follow-up of gifted women. In N. Colangelo, S. G. Assouline & D. L. Ambroson (Eds.), *Talent development: Proceedings from the 1991 Henry B. and Jocelyn Wallace National Research Symposium on Talent Development* (pp. 240–247). Unionville, NY: Trillium Press.

•Kerr, B. A. (1997). *Smart girls : A new psychology of girls, women, and giftedness*. Scottsdale, AZ: Gifted Psychology Press.

Khatena, J., & Torrance, E. P. (1973). *Norms-technical manual: Thinking creatively with sounds and words*. Lexington, MA: Personnel Press/Ginn.

•Kincheloe, J. L., & Steinberg, S. R. (Eds.). (1996a). *Thirteen questions: Reframing education's conversation*. New York: Peter Lang.

•Kincheloe, J. L., & Steinberg, S. R. (1996b). Who said it can't happen here? In J. L. Kincheloe, S. R. Steinberg & A. D. Gresson (Eds.), *Measured lies*: The Bell Curve *examined* (pp. 3-47). New York: St. Martin's Press.

•Kincheloe, J. L., Steinberg, S. R., & Gresson, A. D. (Eds.). (1996). *Measured lies*: The Bell Curve *examined*. New York: St. Martin's Press.

King, J. M. (1992). *The art of mathematics*. New York: Plenum.

Kirkland, G., & Lawrence, G. (1986). *Dancing on my grave: An autobiography*. New York: Doubleday.

Kirschenbaum, R. J. (1990a, July/August). An interview with C. June Maker. *Gifted Children Today*, pp. 45-50.

Kirschenbaum, R. J. (1990b, November/December). An interview with Howard Gardner. *Gifted Children Today*, 26–32.

Kirst, M. W. (1982). How to improve schools without spending more money. *Phi Delta Kappan, 64*(7), 465–470.

•Kitano, M.K. (1997). Gifted Asian American women. *Journal for the Education of the Gifted, 21*(1), 3–39.

Kitano, M. K., & DeLeon, J. (1988). Use of the Stanford-Binet Fourth Edition in identifying young gifted children. *Roeper Review, 10*, 156–159.

Kitano, M. K., & Kirby, D. F. (1986). *Gifted education: A comprehensive view*. Boston: Little, Brown.

•Kline, B. E., & Short, E. B. (1991). Changes in emotional resilience: Gifted adolescent boys. *Roeper Review, 13*(4), 184–187.

•Kloosterman, V. I. (1997, Spring). Building a bridge: A combined effort between gifted and bilingual education. *The Newsletter of the National Research Center on the Gifted and Talented*, pp. 3–5.

Kogan, J. (1987). *Nothing but the best: The struggle for perfection at the Juilliard School*. New York: Random House.

Kolb, D. A. (1976). *Learning style inventory*. Boston: McBer.

Kolloff, P. B. (1989). A comparison of self-contained and pullout models. In R. Swassing (Ed.), *Research briefs*. Washington, DC: National Association for Gifted Children.

Kough, J. (1960). *Practical programs for the gifted*. Chicago: Science Research Associates.

Kough, J., & DeHaan, R. F. (1957). *Helping students with special needs*. Chicago: Science Research Associates.

Kozol, J. (1991). *Savage inequalities*. New York: Crown.

•Kozol, J. (1995). *Amazing grace: The lives of children and the conscience of a nation*. New York: Crown Publishers.

Kruteskii, V. (1976). *The psychology of mathematical abilities in schoolchildren*. I. Wirszup & J. Kilpatrick, (Eds.), J. Teller (Trans.). Chicago: University of Chicago Press. (Original work published 1968).

Krywaniuk, L. W., & Das, J. P. (1976). Cognitive strategies in native children: Analysis and intervention. *The Alberta Journal of Educational Research, 22*(4), 271–280.

Kubat, J., & Ghnassia, B. (1988). *Self-study for health and physical education for Middle States Evaluation*. Unpublished manuscript. New York: Hunter College Elementary School.

Kuhn, T. (1952/1970). *The structure of scientific revolution*. Chicago: University of Chicago Press.

•Kuhn, T. (1959). The essential tension. In C. W. Taylor (Ed.), *Research conference on the identification of creative science talent* (pp. 123–145). Salt Lake City: University of Utah Press.

Kuhn, T. (1977). *The essential tension: Selected studies in scientific tradition and change*. Chicago: University of Chicago Press.

Kulik, J. A. (1985, August). *Effects of inter-class ability grouping on achievement and self-esteem*. Paper presented at the 93rd annual convention of the American Psychological Association, Los Angeles.

Kulik, J. A. (1992a). Ability grouping and gifted students. In N. Colangelo, S. G. Assouline & D. L. Ambroson (Eds.), *Talent development: Proceedings from the 1991 Henry B. and Jocelyn Wallace National Research Symposium on Talent Development* (pp. 261–266). Unionville, NY: Trillium Press.

Kulik, J. A. (1992b). An analysis of the research on ability grouping: Historical and contemporary perspectives. Research-based Decision Making Series. The National Research Center on the Gifted and Talented. Storrs, CT: University of Connecticut.

Kulik, J. A., & Kulik, C.-L. C. (1982). Effects of ability grouping on secondary school students: A meta-analysis of evaluation findings. *American Educational Research Journal, 19,* 415–428.

Kulik, J. A., & Kulik, C.-L. C. (1984a). Effects of accelerated instruction on students. *Review of Educational Research, 54,* 409–425.

Kulik, J. A., & Kulik, C.-L. C. (1984b). Synthesis of research of effects of accelerated instruction. *Educational Leadership, 42,* 84–89.

Kulik, J. A., & Kulik, C.-L. C. (1987). Effects of ability grouping on student achievement. *Equity and Excellence, 23,* 22–30.

Kulik, J. A., & Kulik, C.-L. C. (1990). Ability grouping and gifted students. In N. Colangelo & G. A. Davis (Eds.), *Handbook of gifted education* (pp. 178–196). Boston: Allyn & Bacon.

Kulik, J. A. & Kulik, C.-L. C. (1991). Ability grouping and gifted students. In N. Colangelo & G. A. Davis (Eds.), *Handbook of gifted education* (pp. 178–196). Needham Heights, MA: Allyn & Bacon.

Kurcinka, M. S. (1991). *Raising your spirited child: A guide for parents whose child is more intense, sensitive, perceptive, persistent, energetic.* New York: Harper Perennial.

Kurtz, B. E., & Weinert, F. E. (1989). Metamemory, memory performance, and causal attributions in gifted and average children. *Journal of Experimental Child Psychology, 48,* 45–61.

Langer, S. K. (1953). *Feeling and form.* New York: Charles Scribner's Sons.

Langley, P., & Jones, R. (1988). A computational model of scientific insight. In R. J. Sternberg (Ed.), *The nature of creativity: Contemporary psychological perspectives* (pp. 177-201). New York: Cambridge University Press.

LaRose, B. (1978). A quota system for gifted minority children: A viable solution. *Gifted Child Quarterly, 22,* 394–403.

•Lashaway-Bokina, N. (1997, Spring). Gifted, but gone: High ability, Mexican-American, female dropouts. *The National Center on the Gifted and Talented Newsletter,* p. 12.

Lawton, M. (1992, February 5). Gifted elementary students languishing in regular classrooms, studies suggest. *Education Week,* p. 4.

Lederman, D. (1992a, June 12). Blacks make up large proportion of scholarship athletes, yet their overall enrollment lags at Division I colleges. *Chronicle of Higher Education,* pp. A 1, 30–34.

Lederman, D. (1992b, July 8). Black athletes graduate at a higher rate than other blacks, NCAA reports. *Chronicle of Higher Education,* pp. A 31–32.

Leiter, R. G. (1980). *Leiter International Performance Scale.* Chicago: Stoelting Co.

Levin, H. (1992, April). *Toward an evaluation model for accelerated schools.* Paper presented at the Annual Meeting of the American Educational Research Association, San Francisco, CA.

Lewin, K., & Lippitt, R. (1938). An experimental approach to the study of autocracy and democracy: A preliminary note. *Sociometry, I,* 292–300.

Lewis, M., & Louis, B. (1990). Young gifted children. In N. Colangelo and G. A. Davis (Eds.), *Handbook of gifted education* (pp. 365–381). Needham Heights, MA: Allyn & Bacon.

•Lewis, M., & Macedo, D. (1996). Power and education: Who decides the forms schools have taken, and who should decide? In J. L. Kincheloe & S. R. Steinberg (Eds.), *Thirteen questions: Reframing education's conversations* (pp. 33–42). New York: Peter Lang.

Lewis, M., & Michalson, L. (1985). The gifted infant. In J. Freeman (Ed.), *The psychology of gifted children* (pp. 35–57). Chichester: John Wiley.

Lewontin, R., Rose, S., & Kamin, L. (1984). *Not in our genes.* New York: Pantheon Books.

•Lind, S. (1997, November). *Affective needs of gifted, lesbian, gay, and bisexual youth.* Speech presented at National Association for Gifted Children Conference, Little Rock, AR, November 7, 1997.

Linn, M., & Lopatin, E. (1990). A simultaneous screening/assessment procedure for identifying the gifted student. *Psychology in the Schools, 27*(4), 303–309.

•Lipman, M. (1974). *Harry Stottlemeier's discovery.* Upper Montclair, NJ: IAPC.

•Lipman, M. (1976). *Lisa.* Upper Montclair, NJ: IAPC.

•Lipman, M. (1978). *Suki.* Upper Montclair, NJ: IAPC.

•Lipman, M. (1980). *Mark,* Upper Montclair, NJ: IAPC.

•Lipman, M. (1981). *Pixie.* Upper Montclair, NJ: IAPC.

•Lipman, M. (1984). *Kio and Gus.* Upper Montclair, NJ: IAPC.

Lipman, M. (1985). Thinking skills fostered by Philosophy for Children. In J. W. Segal, S. F. Chipman & R. Glaser (Ed.), *Thinking and learning skills* (Vol. 1, pp. 83–108). Hillsdale, NJ: Lawrence Erlbaum.

•Lipman, M. (1988) "Critical thinking: What can it be?" *Educational Leadership, 44,* pp. 38–41.

•Lipman, M. (1990). *Elfie.* Upper Montclair: NJ: IAPC.

•Lipman, M. (1991). *Thinking in education.* Cambridge: CUP.

Lissitz, R., & Wilhoft, J. (1985). A methodological study of the Torrance Tests of Creativity. *Journal of Educational Measurement, 22,* 1–11.

Little, C. W. (1992). The Wellington Schools identification matrix. Unpublished document.

Little Soldier, I. (1982). Now is the time to dispel the myths about Indians. *Learning, 11*(4), 44–45.

Lohman, D. (1992). Encouraging the development of fluid abilities in gifted students. In N. Colangelo, S. G. Assouline & D. L. Ambroson (Eds.), *Talent development: Proceedings from 1991 Henry and Jocelyn Wallace National Research Symposium on Talent Development* (pp. 143–162). Unionville, NY: Trillium Press.

Louis, B., & Lewis, M. (1992). Parental beliefs about giftedness in young children and their relationship to actual ability level. *Gifted Child Quarterly, 36*(1), 27–31.

Lovecky, D. V. (1986). Can you hear the flowers singing? Issues for gifted adults. *Journal of Counseling and Development, 64,* 572–575.

•Lovecky, D. V. (1993). The quest for meaning: Counseling issues with gifted children and adolescents. In L. K. Silverman (Ed.), *Counseling the gifted and talented* (pp. 29–50). Denver, CO: Love Publishing.

Lozanov, G. (1978). *Suggestology and outlines of suggestopedia (psychic studies).* New York: Gordon & Breach.

•Luke, A. (1995-1996). Text and discourse in education: An introduction to critical discourse analysis. Review of Research in Education (Vol. 21, pp. 3–48). Washington, DC: American Educational Research Association.

Lupkowski, A. E., & Assouline, S. G. (1992). *Jane and Johnny love math: Recognizing and encouraging mathematical talent in elementary students: A guidebook for educators and parents.* ERIC Document ED 381365.

Lupkowski-Shoplik, A. E., & Assouline, S. G. (1993). Identifying mathematically talented elementary students: Using the lower level of the SSAT. *Gifted Child Quarterly, 37*(3) 118–23.

Lupkowski-Shoplik, A.E., & Assouline, S. G. (1994). Evidence of extreme mathematical precocity: Case studies of talented youths. *Roeper Review, 16*(3) 144–51.

Lynch, S. (1992). Fast-paced high school science for the academically talented: A six-year perspective. *Gifted Child Quarterly, 36*(3) 147–154.

Lynch, S. (1993, April). *The gifted and talented at Walbrook High: A Coalition of Essential Schools Case Study.* Paper presented at American Educational Research Association annual meeting, Atlanta, GA.

•Lynch, S. (1996). Four remarkable Polish women: Antecedents to success. In K. Arnold, K. D. Noble & R. F. Subotnik (Eds.), *Remarkable women: Perspectives on female talent development* (pp. 93–116). Cresskill, NJ: Hampton Press.

Lynch, S., & Mills, C. J. (1990). The Skills Reinforcement Project (SRP): An academic program for high potential minority youth. *Journal for the Education of the Gifted, 13,* 364–379.

Maccoby, E. E., & Jacklin, C. N. (1974). *The psychology of sex differences.* Stanford, CA: Stanford University Press.

•Macedo, D. (1996). Power and education: Who decides the forms schools have taken, and who should decide? In J. L. Kincheloe and S. R. Steinberg (Eds.), *Thirteen questions: Reframing educators' conversations* (2nd ed., pp. 43–59). New York: Peter Lang.

•MacKinnon, D. (1975). IPAR's contribution to the conceptualization and study of creativity. In I. A. Taylor & J. W. Getzels (Eds.), *Perspectives in creativity* (pp. 60–89). Chicago: Aldine Publishing Co.

MacKinnon, D. (1978). *In search of human effectiveness.* Buffalo: Bearly Ltd.

•Maker, C. J. (1982a). *Curriculum development for the gifted.* Rockville, MD: Aspen.

Maker, C. J. (1982b). *Teaching models for the education of the gifted.* Rockville, MD: Aspen.

Maker, C. J. (1992). Intelligence and creativity in multiple intelligences: Identification and development. *Educating Able Learners, 17*(4), 12–19.

•Maker, C. J. (1997). DISCOVER problem solving assessment. *Quest, 8*(1), 3, 4, 7.

•Maker, C. J., & Nielson, A. B. (1996a). *Teaching models in the education of the gifted* (2d ed.). Austin, TX: Pro-Ed.

• Maker, C. J., & Nielson, A. B., (1996b). *Curriculum development and teaching strategies for gifted learners* (2d ed.). Austin, TX: Pro-Ed.

Maker, C. J., Rogers, J. A., Nielson, A. B., & Bauerle, P. R. (1996). Multiple intelligences, problem solving, and diversity in the general classroom. *Journal for the Education of the Gifted, 19*(4), 437–460.

• Mallon, G. P. (1994). Counseling strategies with gay and lesbian youth. In T. DeCrescenzo (Ed.), *Helping gay and lesbian youth: New policies, new programs, new practice.* New York: Harrington Park Press.

• Margolin, L. M. (1994). *Goodness personified: The emergence of gifted children.* Hawthorne, NY: Aldine de Gryuter.

Marland, S. (1971). *Education of the gifted and talented: Report to the Congress of the United States by the U.S. Commissioner of Education.* Washington, DC: U.S. Government Printing Office.

Marsh, H. W., & Young, A. S. (1997). Coursework selection: Relations to academic self-concept and achievement. *American Educational Research Journal, 34*(4), 663–720.

Martorano, S. C. (1977). A developmental analysis of performance on Piaget's formal operations tasks. *Developmental Psychology, 13*, 666–672.

Maslow, A. (1968). *Toward a psychology of being* (2d ed.). New York: Van Nostrand Reinhold.

Mason, R., Fogler, K., Yost, C., Stearns, P., & Gottling, C. (1988). *Self-study for mathematics for Middle States Evaluation.* Unpublished manuscript. New York: Hunter College Elementary School.

Mason, R., Halkitis, P., Cruz, B., & Arafat, L. (1988). *Self-study for science for Middle States Evaluation.* Unpublished manuscript. New York: Hunter College Elementary School.

Mayr, E. (1982). *The growth of biological thought.* Cambridge, MA: Belknap Press.

McCandliss, B., & Watson, A. (1988). *Problemoids: Math challenge.* Unionville, NY: Trillium Press.

McCarthy, K., & Navarre, J. Piirto. (1985, March). *A validated procedure for the identification of young gifted children.* Paper presented at American Association of School Administrators Conference, Dallas, TX.

McCarthy, K., Rosenfield, S., & Navarre, J. Piirto. (1984, August). *A validated procedure for the identification of young gifted children.* Paper presented at the American Psychological Association meeting, Toronto, Canada.

• McCaulley, M. H. (1976). *The Myers-Briggs Type Indicator and the teaching-learning process.* Paper presented at the meeting of the American Educational Research Association, Chicago.

McClelland, D. C. (1961). *The achieving society.* New York: The Free Press.

McDonald, R. A. F. (1915). *Adjustment of school organization to various population groups.* New York: Teachers College Press.

McDonnell, D., & LeCapitaine, J. (1985). *The effects of group creativity training on teachers' empathy and interactions with students.* ERIC ED 294858.

McGregor, D. (1960). *The human side of enterprise.* New York: McGraw-Hill.

McKenzie, J. A. (1986). The influence of identification practices, race, and SES on the identification of gifted students. *Gifted Child Quarterly, 30*(2), 93–95.

• McLaughlin, S. C., & Saccuzzo, D. P. (1994). *Ethnic and gender differences in locus of control in at risk and nongifted children.* ERIC Document ED 368100.

McShane, D. A., & Plas, J. M. (1982). Wechsler scale performance patterns of American Indian children. *Psychology in the Schools, 19*, 8–17.

Meeker, M. (1969). *The structure of intellect.* Columbus, OH: Charles Merrill.

Meeker, M. (1973). *Divergent production sourcebook.* Vida, OR: SOI Institute.

Meeker, M. (1992). *How the SOI-LA tests and SOI-curriculum identify, develop, and maintain giftedness in disadvantaged learners.* Vida, OR: SOI Systems.

Meeker, M., & Maxwell, J. (1976). *Sourcebooks for SOI.* Vida, OR: SOI Institute.

Meeker, M., & Meeker, R. (1976). *The structure of Intellect Learning Abilities Test.* Vida, OR: M & M Enterprises.

Meeker, M., & Meeker, R. (1985). *SOI-Learning Abilities Test: Screening form for atypical gifted.* Vida, OR: M & M Enterprises.

Meeker, M., & Meeker, R. (1992). *Learning modules for SOI.* Vida, OR: SOI Institute.

Meier, N. C. (1939). Factors in artistic aptitude: Final summary of a ten year study of special ability. *Psychological Monographs, 51* (pp. 140–158). Princeton, NJ: The Psychological Review Company.

Meininger, L.K. (1991, May). *(Toward) a theory of intellectual giftedness in kindergarten age children.* Paper presented at the Henry B. and Jocelyn Wallace National Research Symposium on Talent Development. Iowa City, IA: University of Iowa.

Meisgeier, C., & Murphy, E. (1987). *The Murphy-Meisgeier Type Indicator for Children.* Palo Alto, CA: Consulting Psychologists Press.

Mercer, J. (1979). *System of Multicultural Pluralistic Assessment Technical manual.* Cleveland: The Psychological Corporation.

Mercer, J., & Lewis, J. (1978). Using the System of Multicultural Pluralistic Assessment (SOMPA) to identify the gifted minority child. In A. Baldwin, G. Gear & L. Lucito (Eds.), *Educational planning for the gifted* (pp. 7–14). Reston, VA: Council for Exceptional Children.

Miklus, S. (1989, April). Forum. *Omni,* p. 16.

Milgram, R. M., & Hong, E. (1993). Creative thinking and creative performance in adolescents as predictors of creative attainment in adults: A follow-up study after 18 years. *Roeper Review, 15*(3), 135–140.

•Milgram, R. M., Hong, E., Shavit, Y. W., & Peled, R. W. (1997). Out-of-school activities in gifted adolescents as a predictor of vocational choice and work accomplishment in young adults. *The Journal for Secondary Gifted Education, 8*(3), 111-120.

Miller, A. (1982). *The drama of the gifted child.* New York: Doubleday.

Miller, A. (1990). *The untouched key.* New York: Doubleday.

•Miller, A. (1997). *The drama of the gifted child: The search for the true self* (7th ed.). New York: Basic Books.

Mills, C., Ablard, K. E., & Brody, L. E. (1993). The Raven's Progressive Matrices: Its usefulness for identifying gifted/talented students. *Roeper Review, 15*(3), 185–186.

Mills, C., & Durden, W. (1992). Cooperative learning and ability grouping: An issue of choice. *Gifted Child Quarterly, 36*(1), 11–16.

Mills, J. R., & Jackson, N. E. (1990). Predictive significance of early giftedness: The case of precocious reading. *Journal of Educational Psychology, 82*(3), 410–419.

Mitchell, B. (1988a). The latest national assessment of gifted education. *Roeper Review, 10*(4), 239–240.

Mitchell, B. (1988b). A strategy for the identification of the culturally different gifted/talented child. *Roeper Review, 10,* 163–165.

Model for the identification of creative-thinking ability. (1992). Columbus, OH: Ohio Department of Education Research and Demonstration Series in Gifted Education.

Moi, T. (1985). *Sexual/textual politics: Feminist literary theory.* New York: Routledge.

Moloney, D. P., Bouchard, T. J., & Segal, N. L. (1991). A genetic and environmental analysis of the vocational interests of monozygotic and dizygotic twins reared apart. *Journal of Vocational Behavior, 39*(1), 76–109.

Moon, S. M., & Feldhusen, J. F. (1991). PACE: A follow-up study. *Research briefs of the National Association for Gifted Children.* Washington, DC: NAGC.

Moon, S. M., Feldhusen, J. F., & Kelly, K. W. (1991, January/February). Identification procedures: Bridging theory and practice. *Gifted Children Today,* 30–36.

Moon, S. M., Zentall, S., Grskovic, J., & Hall, A. (1997). Families of boys with intellectual giftedness and AD/HD. In T. Cross (Ed.), *Research briefs* (pp. 185–203). Washington, DC: National Association for Gifted Children Service Publications.

Moore, E. G. J. (1987). Ethnic social milieu and Black children's intelligence test achievement. *Journal of Negro Education, 56,* 44–52.

Moore, L. (1981). *Does this mean my kid's a genius?* New York: McGraw-Hill.

Morelock, M. J. (1992, January). Giftedness: The view from within. *Understanding Our Gifted, 4*(3), 1, 11–15.

•Morelock, M. J. (1996). On the nature of giftedness and talent: Imposing order on chaos. *Roeper Review, 19,* 4–12.

Morelock, M. J., & Feldman, D. H. (1991). Extreme precocity. In N. Colangelo & G. Davis (Eds.), *Handbook of gifted education* (pp. 347–364). Needham Heights, MA: Allyn & Bacon.

•Morocco, C. C., Riley, M. K., Gordon, S. M., & Howard, C. L. (1996). The elusive individual in teachers' planning. In G. G. Brannigan (Ed.), *The enlightened educator* (pp. 154–176). New York: McGraw-Hill.

Morrison, M., & Dungan, R. (1992). *Model for the identification of creative thinking ability: A multifactored approach.* Ohio Department of Education: Gifted Education Research and Demonstration Project.

Morse, D., & Khatena, J. (1989). The relationship of creativity and life accomplishments. *Journal of Creative Behavior, 23,* 23–30.

Moyers, B. (1990). An interview with Evelyn Fox Keller. In A. Tucher (Ed.), *Bill Moyers: A world of ideas, II* (pp. 73–81). New York: Doubleday.

Munsinger, H. (1975). The adopted child's IQ: A critical review. *Psychological Bulletin, 82,* 623–659.

•Murphy, E. (1995, October). *Training workshop on the Murphy-Meisgeier.* Columbus, OH: Consulting Psychologists.

Myers, I. B. (1962). *Manual: The Myers-Briggs Type Indicator.* Princeton, NJ: Educational Testing Service.

Myers, I. B., & McCaulley, M. H. (1985). *Manual: A guide to the development and use of the Myers-Briggs Type Indicator.* Palo Alto, CA: Consulting Psychologists Press.

Myers, R. S., & Pace, T. M. (1986). Counseling gifted and talented students: Historical perspectives and contemporary issues. *Journal of Counseling and Development, 64,* 548–551.

Myers, S. A. (1983). The Wilson-Barber Inventory of Childhood Memories and Imaginings: Children's form and norms for 1337 children and adolescents. *Journal of Mental Imagery, 7*(3), 83–94.

•Napier, L. A. (1996). Nine native women: Pursuing the obstacles and aspiring to positions of leadership. In K. Arnold, K. D. Noble & R. F. Subotnik (Eds.), *Remarkable women: Perspectives on female talent development* (pp. 133–148). Cresskill, NJ: Hampton Press.

Nash, D., & Treffinger, D. (1986). *The mentor.* East Aurora, NY: D.O.K. Publishers.

Naslund, R. A., Thorpe, L. P., & LeFever, D. W. (1978). *SRA Achievement Series.* Chicago: Science Research Associates.

National Commission on Excellence in Education. (1983). *A nation at risk.* Washington, DC: Government Printing Office, ERIC ED 226006.

National excellence: A case for developing America's talent. (1993). Washington, DC: U.S. Department of Education. Office of Educational Research and Improvement.

National Merit Program biased against girls, testing group says. (May 13, 1992). *Education Week,* p. 2.

Navarre, J. Piirto (1978, November). *A study of creativity in poets.* Paper presented at National Association for Gifted Children Conference, Houston, Texas.

Navarre, J. Piirto (1979). Is what is good for the goose, good for the gander? Should gifted girls receive differential treatment? *Roeper Review, 2*(3), 21–25.

Neisser, V. (1979). The concept of intelligence. *Intelligence, 3,* 217–227.

Nevo, D. (1983). The conceptualization of educational evaluation: An analytical review of the literature. *Review of Educational Research, 53,* 117–128.

Nielson, A. (1992). Grouping gifted young children: A qualitative study of three classrooms of gifted children. In N. Colangelo, S. G. Assouline & D. L. Ambroson (Eds.), *Talent development: Proceedings from the 1991 Henry B. and Jocelyn Wallace National Research Symposium on Talent Development* (pp. 410–414). Unionville, NY: Trillium Press.

Niemark, E. D. (1975). Intellectual development during adolescence. In F. D. Horowitz (Ed.), *Review of child development research* (Vol. 4). Chicago: University of Chicago Press.

Nitko, A. J. (1989). Review of the Metropolitan Achievement Test, Sixth Edition. In J. C. Conoley & J. J. Kramer (Eds.), *The Tenth Mental Measurements Yearbook* (pp. 510–515). Lincoln, NE: University of Nebraska Press.

•Noble, K. D. (1996). Resilience, resistance, and responsibility: Resolving the dilemma of the gifted woman. In K. Arnold, R. F. Subotnik, & K. D. Noble (Eds.), *Remarkable women: Perspectives on female talent development* (pp. 413-415). Cresskill, NJ: Hampton Press.

•Noble, K. D., Subotnik, R. F., & Arnold, K. D. (1996). A new model for adult female talent development: A synthesis of perspectives from remarkable women. In K. Arnold, K. D. Noble, and R. F. Subotnik (Eds.), *Remarkable women: Perspectives on female talent development* (pp. 427–440). Cresskill, NJ: Hampton Press.

Noller, R. B., Parnes, S. J., & Biondi, A. M. (1976). *Creative actionbook.* New York: Scribners.

Nowell, E. (1960). *Thomas Wolfe: A biography.* New York: Doubleday & Co.

Oakes, J. (1985). *Keeping track.* New Haven, CT: Yale University Press.

Oakland, T. (1985a). Review of Otis-Lennon School Ability Test. In J. Kramer (Ed.), *The Ninth Mental Measurements Yearbook* (pp. 1111–1112). Lincoln, NE: University of Nebraska Press.

Oakland, T. (1985b). Review of Slosson Intelligence Test. In J. Kramer (Ed.), *The Ninth Mental Measurements Yearbook* (pp. 1401–1402). Lincoln, NE: University of Nebraska Press.

Oates, J. C. (1988). *(Woman) Writer.* New York: E.P. Dutton.

O'Brien, G. (1991). Reliability and validity of four subscales of a Scale For Rating Behavioral Characteristics of Superior Students as self reporting tools. *Psychological Reports, 68*(1) 285–286.

O'Connell-Ross, P. (1997). Federal policy on gifted and talented education. In N. Colangelo & G. Davis (Eds.), *Handbook of gifted education* (2d ed., pp. 553–559). Boston: Allyn & Bacon.

•Office of Indian Education Programs, Bureau of Indian Affairs: 1997 Fingertip Facts. ERIC ED 408124.

Ogbu, J. U. (1978). *Minority education and caste: The American system in cross-cultural perspective.* New York: Academic Press.

• *Ohio Gifted Course of Study*. (1989). Columbus: Ohio Department of Education.

Okuda, S. M., Runco, M. A., & Berger, D. A. Creativity and the finding and solving of real-world problems. *Journal of Psychoeducational Assessment, 9*, 45–53.

Olenchak, R. (1989). Teachers of the gifted: Backgrounds behind their success. In R. Swassing (Ed.), *Research briefs*. Washington, DC: National Association for Gifted Children.

Olson, L. (1992, August 5). 11 design teams are tapped to pursue their visions of 'break the mold' schools. *Education Week*, pp. 1, 47–52.

• Olszewski-Kubilius, P. M., & Laubscher, L. (1996). The impact of a college counseling program on economically disadvantaged gifted students and their subsequent college adjustment. *Roeper Review, 18*(3), 202–208.

Olszewski-Kubilius, P. M., & Scott, J. M. (1992). An investigation of the college and career counseling needs of economically disadvantaged minority gifted students. *Roeper Review, 10*, 163–165.

Olszewski-Kubilius, P. M., & VanTassel-Baska, J. (Eds.). (1990). *Patterns of influence*. New York: Teachers College Press.

• Orenstein, P. (1994). *Schoolgirls: Young women, self-esteem, and the confidence gap*. New York: Doubleday.

Osborn, A. (1963). *Applied imagination* (3rd ed.). New York: Charles Scribners.

Ostrander, S. (1979). *Superlearning*. New York: Delacourte.

Otis, A. S., & Lennon, R. T. (1989). *Otis-Lennon School Ability Test*. San Antonio, TX: The Psychological Corporation.

Oxford English Dictionary, 3rd Edition. (1981). Cambridge: Oxford University Press.

• Pagano, J., & Miller, J. (1996). Women and education: In what ways does gender affect the educational process? In J. L. Kincheloe & S. R. Steinberg (Eds.), *Thirteen questions: Reframing education's conversations* (pp. 139–156). New York: Peter Lang.

Parke, B. (1989). *Gifted students in regular classrooms*. Boston: Allyn & Bacon.

Parloff, M. B., Datta, L., Kleman, M., & Handlon, J. H. (1968). Personality characteristics which differentiate creative male adolescents and adults. *Journal of Personality, 36*(4), 528–552.

Parnes, S. (1967). *Creative behavior guidebook*. New York: Scribners.

Parnes, S. (1987). The Creativity Studies Project. In S. Isaksen (Ed.), *Frontiers of creativity research: Beyond the basics* (pp. 156–188). Buffalo: Bearly Ltd.

Parnes, S. J., Noller, E. B., & Biondi, A. M. (1977). *Guide to creative action*. New York: Scribners.

• Passow, H. A., & Rudnitski, R. A. (1995). *State policies regarding education of the gifted as reflected in legislation and regulation*. National Research Center on the Gifted and Talented Research Monograph. Storrs, CT: The University of Connecticut.

Pastore, N. (1949). *The nature-nurture controversy*. New York: Columbia University, Kings Crown Press.

Peak, L., et al. (1996). *Pursuing excellence: A study of U.S. eighth-grade mathematics and science teaching, learning, curriculum, and achievement in international context. Initial Findings from the Third International Mathematics and Science Study*. U.S. Department of Education, Office of Research and Improvement.

• Pearlman, M. & Henderson, K. U. (19900. *A voice of one's own: Conversations with America's writing women*. New York: Houghton Mifflin.

Pegnato, C., & Birch, J. (1959). Locating gifted children in junior high school. *Exceptional Children, 25*(7), 300–304.

Pendarvis, E. D., & Howley, A. (1996). Playing fair: The possibilities of gifted education. *Journal for the Education of the Gifted, 18*, 2, 215–233.

Pendarvis, E., Howley, A., & Howley, C. (1990). *The abilities of gifted children*. Englewood Cliffs, NJ: Prentice Hall.

Perkins, D. N. (1981). *The mind's best work*. Boston: Harvard University Press.

Perkins, D. N. (1988). The possibility of invention. In R. Sternberg (Ed.), *The nature of creativity* (pp. 362–386). New York: Cambridge.

Perkins, D. N. (1991, October). Educating for insight. *Educational Leadership, 49*(2), 4–8.

Perkins, D. N. (1993, Fall). Teaching for understanding. *American Educator: The Professional Journal of the American Federation of Teachers, 17*(3), 8, 28–35.

Perleth, C., Sierwald, W., & Heller, K. (1993). Selected results of the Munich Longitudinal Study of Giftedness: The Multidimensional/Typological giftedess model. *Roeper Review, 15*(3), 149–155.

Perrone, V. (1991). On standardized testing. *Childhood Education, 67*(3), 132–142.

• Perry, D. (Ed.). (1993). *Backtalk: Women writers speak out*. New Brunswick, NJ: Rutgers University Press.

• Peterson, J. S. (1998, May). *Gifted, gay, and at risk: A study of the adolescent experience*. Paper presented at the Fourth Biennial Henry B. and Jocelyn

Wallace National Research Symposium on Talent Development. Iowa City, IA: University of Iowa.

•Peterson, J. S., & Margolin, R. (1997). Naming gifted children: An example of unintended "reproduction." *Journal for the Education of the Gifted, 21*(1), 82–101.

Phenix, P. (1964). *Realms of meaning.* New York: McGraw-Hill.

Piaget, J. (1947/1960). *Psychology of intelligence* (2d ed.). Paterson, NJ: Littlefield, Adams & Company.

Piechowski, M. M. (1975). A theoretical and empirical approach to the study of development. *Genetic Psychology Monographs, 92,* 231–297.

Piechowski, M. M. (1979). Developmental potential. In N. Colangelo & R. Zaffer (Eds.), *New voices in counseling the gifted* (pp. 25–57). Dubuque: Kendall-Hunt.

Piechowski, M. M. (1989). Developmental potential and the growth of self. In J. VanTassel-Baska & P. Olszewski-Kubilius (Eds.): *Patterns of influence: The home, the self, and the school* (pp. 87–101). New York: Teachers College Press.

•Piechowski, M. M. (1990). Inner growth and transformation in the life of Eleanor Roosevelt. *Advanced Development, 2,* 35–53.

Piechowski, M. M. (1991). Emotional development and emotional giftedness. In N. Colangelo & G. Davis (Eds.), *Handbook of gifted education* (pp. 285–306). Needham Heights, MA: Allyn & Bacon.

Piechowski, M. M. (1992). Giftedness for all seasons: Inner peace in a time of war. In N. Colangelo, S. G. Assouline & D. L. Ambroson (Eds.), *Talent development: Proceedings from the 1991 Henry B. and Jocelyn Wallace National Research Symposium on Talent Development* (pp. 180–203). Unionville, NY: Trillium Press.

Piechowski, M. M. (1997a). Emotional giftedness: The measure of intrapersonal intelligence. In N. Colangelo & G. Davis (Eds.), *Handbook of gifted education* (2d ed., pp. 366–381). Needham Heights, MA: Allyn & Bacon.

Piechowski, M. M. (1997b). *Emotional giftedness: An expanded view.* Paper presented at the 19th World Conference of the World Council for Gifted and Talented Children, Seattle, WA, July 29, 1997.

•Piechowski, M. M. (1998, May). *Spiritual giftedness and the transpersonal dimension of experience.* Paper presented at the Fourth Biennial Henry B. and Jocelyn Wallace National Research Symposium on Talent Development. Iowa City, IA: University of Iowa.

Piechowski, M. M., & Cunningham, K. (1985). Patterns of overexcitability in a group of artists. *Journal of Creative Behavior, 19*(3), 153–174.

Piechowski, M. M., Colangelo, N., Grant, B. A., & Walker, L. (1983, November). *Developmental potential of gifted adolescents.* Paper presented at the National Association for Gifted Children annual convention, Philadelphia.

Piers, E. V., & Harris, D. (1984). *Piers-Harris Children's Self Concept Scale, Revised.* Los Angeles: Western Psychological Corporation.

Piirto, J. (1987). *The existence of writing prodigy.* Paper presented at the National Association for Gifted Children Conference, New Orleans.

Piirto, J. (1988). *Syllabus summary.* Unpublished manuscript. New York: Hunter College Elementary School.

Piirto, J. (1989a). Does writing prodigy exist? *Creativity Research Journal, 2,* 134–135.

Piirto, J. (1989b, May/June). Linguistic prodigy: Does it exist? *Gifted Children Monthly,* 1–2.

Piirto, J. (1989c, July/August). What do you do in a primary gifted program? *Gifted Children Today,* 33–34.

Piirto, J. (1989d, November/December). What did Robert Kennedy die of? Cultural literacy for gifted students. *Gifted Children Today,* 51–53.

Piirto, J. (1990a, January). Profiles of creative adolescents. *Understanding Our Gifted, 1,* 10–12.

Piirto, J. (1990b, April). *Creative adolescents at a Governor's Institute.* Paper presented at the Ohio Association for Gifted Children Conference, Columbus, OH.

Piirto, J. (1990c). Early IQ or high achievement? Predicting high school success. *Research briefs.* Washington, DC: National Association for Gifted Children.

Piirto, J. (1991a). Encouraging creativity in adolescents. In J. Genshaft & M. Bireley (Eds.), *Understanding gifted adolescents* (pp. 104–122). New York: Teachers College Press.

Piirto, J. (1991b). Why are there so few? (Creative women: mathematicians, visual artists, musicians). *Roeper Review, 13*(3), 142–147.

Piirto, J. (1992a/1998). *Understanding those who create.* Dayton, OH: Ohio Psychology Press.

Piirto, J. (1992b). The existence of writing prodigy: Children with extraordinary writing talent. In N. Colangelo, S. G. Assouline & D. L. Ambroson (Eds.), *Talent devÚelopment: Proceedings from the 1991 Henry B. and Jocelyn Wallace National Research Symposium on Talent Development* (pp. 387–389). Iowa City, IA: University of Iowa.

Piirto, J. (1992c, November). *The lives of creative women.* Paper presented at the National Association for Gifted Children Conference, Los Angeles, CA.

Piirto, J. (1993, April). *Case study: A midwestern suburban gifted program.* Paper presented at the American Educational Research Association annual conference, Atlanta, GA.

Piirto, J. (1994a). *Talented children and adults: Their development and education.* New York: Macmillan.

Piirto, J. (1994b). A few thoughts about actors. *Spotlight: Newsletter of the Visual and Performing Arts Division of the National Association for Gifted Children, 4*(1), 2–5.

Piirto, J. (1995a). Deeper and broader: The pyramid of talent development in the context of the giftedness construct. In M. W. Katzko & F. J. Mönks (Eds.), *Nurturing talent: Individual needs and social ability* (pp. 10–20). Proceedings of the Fourth Conference of the European Council for High Ability. The Netherlands: Van Gorcum, Assen.

Piirto, J. (1995b). Deeper and broader: The pyramid of talent development in the context of the giftedness construct. *Educational Forum, 59*(4), 363–371.

Piirto, J. (1995c). *A location in the Upper Peninsula: Poems, stories, essays.* New Brighton, MN: Sampo Publishing.

Piirto, J. (1995d). *Themes in the lives of female creative writers at midlife.* Invited paper presented at the 1995 Henry B. and Jocelyn Wallace National Research Symposim on Talent Development, Iowa City, IA.

Piirto, J. (1996). Why does a writer write? Because. *Advanced Development, 7,* 39–59.

Piirto, J. (1997). *Between the memory and the experience* (2d ed.). Ashland, OH: Sisu Press.

•Piirto, J. (1998a). *Feeling boys and thinking girls: Talented adolescents and their teachers.* A paper presented at the Center for the Application of Personality Type Conference, Orlando, FL, March 8, 1998.

•Piirto, J. (1998b). Review of Slattery, P., Curriculum development in the postmodern era (1995). *Gifted Child Quarterly, 42*(2), 130–133.

•Piirto, J. (1998c, May). *Twelve issues: Implications of postmodern curriculum theory for the education of the talented.* Paper presented at the Fourth Biennial Henry B. and Jocelyn Wallace National Research Symposium on Talent Development. Iowa City, IA: University of Iowa.

•Piirto, J. (in press). Themes in the lives of successful contemporary U.S. women creative writers at midlife. *Roeper Review,* special issue on creativity.

•Piirto, J. (in preparation). *My teeming brain: Creativity and creative writers.* Cresskill, NJ: Hampton Press.

Piirto, J. (Submitted). An ethnographic of a suburban pullout gifted program. Washington, DC: U.S. Department of Education, U.S. Office of Research and Improvement.

•Piirto, J., & Fraas, J. (1995). Androgyny in the personalities of talented teenagers. *Journal of Secondary Gifted Education,* (2), 93–102.

•Piirto, J., Cassone, G., & Wilkes, P. (1998). Talent development in the middle school. In C. Walley and W. G. Gerrick (Eds.), *Affirming middle grades education* (pp. 247–262). Needham Heights, MA: Allyn & Bacon.

•Piirto, J., Gantz, B., Ramsay, L., Steele, K., Tabacca, G., & Fraas, J. (1997). Quantitative analysis of The Myers-Briggs Type Indicator (MBTI) from Ohio Summer Institutes at Ashland University. In J. Piirto (Ed.), *Five studies on talented adolescents.* An Inquiry Seminar at Ashland University, Summer 1997.

•Piirto, J., Hohman, L., Nickle, M., & Ryan, R. (1997). A quantitative analysis of the High School Personality Questionaire (HSPQ) from Ohio Summer Institutes at Ashland University. In J. Piirto (Ed.), *Five studies on talented adolescents.* An Inquiry Seminar at Ashland University, Summer 1997.

•Pinar, W., Reynolds, W., Slattery, P., & Taubman, P. (1995). *Understanding curriculum.* New York: Peter Lang.

•Pipher, M. (1994). *Reviving Ophelia: Saving the selves of adolescent girls.* New York: Putnam.

Plato. The ion. In *Great books of the western world* (Vol. 7). (1952) Chicago, IL: Encypedia Britannica.

Plato. The republic. Trans. P. Shorey. (1930-1935). In R. Ulich (1954) (Ed.), *Three thousand years of educational wisdom* (pp. 53, 61). Loeb Classical Library. Cambridge, MA: Harvard University Press.

Plimpton, G. (Ed.). (1988). *Writers at work* (8th series). New York: Penguin.

Plomin, R. (1986). *Development, genetics, and psychology.* Hillsdale, NJ: Lawrence Erlbaum.

Plomin, R. (1989). Environment and genes: Determinants of behavior. *American Psychologist, 23,* 1–4.

•Plomin, R. (1997). Genetics and intelligence. In N. Colangelo & G. Davis (Eds.), *Handbook of Gifted Education* (2d ed., pp. 67–74). Boston: Allyn & Bacon.

•Plucker, J. A. (1996). Gifted Asian-American students: Identification, curricular, and counseling concerns. *Journal for the Education of the Gifted. 19* (3), 315–343.

Polette, N. (1980). *Exploring books with gifted children.* Littleton, CO: Libraries Unlimited, Inc.

Pollard, D. S. (1989). Against the odds: A profile of academic achievers from the urban underclass. *Journal of Negro Education, 58,* 297–308.

Pollard, D. S., Farrell, W. G., and Sandoval, P. (1986, April). *Ethnicity, gender, and relationships between academic performance, perceived performance, and aspirations for college.* Paper presented at Annual Meeting of the American Educational Research Association, San Francisco, CA. [Referred to in Pollard, 1989].

Porath, M. (1991, November). Stage and structure in the development of children with various types of giftedness. *The National Research Center on the Gifted and Talented Newsletter,* p. 12.

Porter, R. B. (1964). A comparative investigation of the personality of sixth grade gifted children and a norm group of children. *Journal of Educational Research, 58,* 132–134.

Prescott, G. A., Balow, I. H., Hogan, T. R., & Farr, R. C. (1984). *Metropolitan Achievement Tests 6: Survey Battery.* San Antonio, TX: The Psychological Corporation.

Project necessity—Secondary program. (1970). Washington, DC: Bureau of Indian Affairs. ERIC Document Reproduction Service ED 049856.

•The Psychological Corporation. *Metropolitan Achievement Tests* (7th ed.)

Pugh, S. L., Hicks, J. W., Davis, M., Venstra, T. (1992). *Bridging: A teacher's guide to metaphorical thinking.* ERIC Clearinghouse on Reading and Communication Skills, Bloomington, IN. ERIC Document Reproduction Service ED 341985.

Pupin, M. (1922/1960). *From immigrant to inventor.* New York: The Scribner Library.

Purkey, W. W. & Novak, J. (1983). *Inviting school success.* Belmont, CA: Wadsworth Publishing Co.

•*Pursuing excellence: A study of U.S. eighth-grade mathematics and science teaching, learning, curriculum, and achievement in international context.* (1996). Washington, DC: U.S. Government Bookstore Superintendent of Documents, U.S. Government Printing Office. [Internet: www.access.gpo.gov/su_docs].

•*Pursuing Excellence: A study of U.S. fourth-grade mathematics and science achievement in international nontext.* (1997). Washington, DC: U.S. Government Bookstore Superintendent of Documents, U.S. Government Printing Office. [Internet: www.access.gpo.gov/su_docs].

•*Pursuing Excellence: A study of U.S. twelfth-grade mathematics and science achievement in international nontext.* (1998). Washington, DC: U.S. Government Bookstore Superintendent of Documents,

U.S. Government Printing Office. [Internet: www.access.gpo.gov/su_docs].

•Pyryt, M.C. (1996). IQ: Easy to bash, hard to replace. *Roeper Review, 18*(2), 255–257.

Radford, J. (1990). *Child prodigies and exceptional early achievers.* New York: Macmillan.

Ramos-Ford, V., & Gardner, H. (1990). Giftedness from a multiple intelligence perspective. In N. Colangelo & G. Davis (Eds.), *Handbook of gifted education* (pp. 55–64). Needham Heights, MA: Allyn & Bacon.

•Ramos-Ford, V., & Gardner, H. (1997). Giftedness from a multiple intelligence perspective. In N. Colangelo & G. Davis (Eds.), *Handbook of gifted education* (2d ed., pp. 54–66). Needham Heights, MA: Allyn & Bacon.

Raven, J. C. (1980). *Standard Progressive Matrices.* New York: Psychological Corporation.

Raven, J. (1990). *Raven manual research supplement, 3: American and international norms—neuropsychological uses.* Oxford: Oxford Psychologists Press.

Ravitch, D. (1985). *The schools we deserve: Reflections on the educational crises of our times.* New York: Basic Books.

Ravitch, D. (Ed.). (1990). *An American reader.* New York: HarperCollins.

Ravitch, D., & Finn, C. (1987). *What do our 17-year-olds know?* New York: Harper and Row.

Rees, M. E., & Goldman, M. (1961). Some relationships between creativity and personality. *The Journal of General Psychology, 65,* 145–161.

Reich, C. (1971). *The greening of America.* New York: Random House.

Reis, S. M. (1989, May). *Curriculum compacting.* Keynote address at Michigan Association for Gifted and Talented Educators Conference. Flint, MI.

•Reis, S. M. (1996). Older women's reflections on eminence: Obstacles and opportunities. In K. Arnold, K. D. Noble & R. F. Subotnik (Eds.), *Remarkable women: Perspectives on female talent development* (pp. 149–170). Cresskill, NJ: Hampton Press.

Reis, S. M., & Burns, D. (1991). Developing a thinking skills component in the gifted education program. *Roeper Review, 14*(2), 72–79.

Reis, S. M., & Renzulli, J. S. (1988). The role and responsibilities of the gifted program coordinator. *Roeper Review, 11*(2), 66–71.

Reis, S. M., & Renzulli, J. S. (1991). The assessment of creative products in programs for gifted and talented students. *Gifted Child Quarterly, 35*(3), 128–134.

•Reis, S. M., Burns, D. E., & Renzulli, J. S. (1992). *Curriculum compacting: The complete guide to modifying the regular curriculum for high ability students.* Mansfield, CT: Creative Learning Press, Inc.

•Reis, S. M., Neu, T. W., & McGuire, J. (1995). *Talents in two places: Case studies of high ability students with learning disabilities who have achieved.* The National Research Center on the Gifted and Talented Research Monograph 95114. Storrs, CT: University of Connecticut.

•Reis, S. M., Westberg, K. L., Kulikowich, J., Caillard, F., Hébert, T., Plucker, J., Purcell, J. H., Rogers, J. B., & Smist, J. M. (1993). *Why not let high ability students start school in January? The curriculum compacting study.* The National Research Center on the Gifted and Talented Research Monograph 93105. Storrs, CT: The University of Connecticut.

•Renzulli, J. S. (1975). *A guidebook for evaluating programs for the gifted and talented.* Wethersfield, CT: Creative Learning Press.

Renzulli, J. S. (1977). *The enrichment triad model: A guide for developing defensible programs for the gifted and talented.* Wethersfield, CT: Creative Learning Press.

Renzulli, J. S. (1978). What makes giftedness? Re-examining a definition. *Phi Delta Kappan, 60,* 180–181, 261.

Renzulli, J. S. (1986). The three-ring conception of giftedness: A developmental model for creative productivity. In R. J. Sternberg & J. E. Davidson (Eds.), *Conceptions of giftedness* (pp. 53–92). Cambridge: Cambridge University Press.

Renzulli, J. S. (1988). A decade of dialogue on the Three-Ring Conception of giftedness. *Roeper Review, 11*(1), 18–15.

Renzulli, J. S. (1992a). *Talent identification and development as an alternative to gifted education.* Symposium at National Association for Gifted Children Conference, Los Angeles, CA.

Renzulli, J. S. (1992b). A general theory for the development of creative productivity through the pursuit of ideal acts of learning. *Gifted Child Quarterly, 36*(4), 170–182.

•Renzulli, J. S. (1995). *Building a bridge between gifted education and total school improvement.* National Research Center on the Gifted and Talented Talent Development Research-based Decision Making Series 9502. Storrs, CT: The University of Connecticut.

Renzulli, J. S., & Reis, S. M. (1985). *The schoolwide enrichment model.* Mansfield Center, CT: Creative Learning Press.

Renzulli, J. S., & Reis, S. M. (1989). The enrichment triad/revolving door model: A schoolwide plan for the development of creative productivity. In J. Renzulli & S. Reis (Eds.), *Systems and models in gifted education* (pp. 217–275). Mansfield Center, CT: Creative Learning Press.

Renzulli, J. S., & Westberg, K. (1991). The reform movement and the quiet crisis in gifted education. *Gifted Child Quarterly, 35*(1), 26–35.

Renzulli, J. S., & Smith, L. H. (1978a). *Learning Styles Inventory: A measure of student preferences for instructional techniques.* Mansfield Center, CT: Creative Learning Press.

Renzulli, J. S., & Smith, L. H. (1978b). *The compactor.* Mansfield Center, CT: Creative Learning Press.

Renzulli, J. S., & Westberg, K. (1990, November). *The 1990 revision of the Scales for Rating the Behavioral Characteristics of Superior Students.* Mansfield Center, CT: Creative Learning Press.

•Reynolds, A. I., & Koski, M. H. (1995). Lesbian, gay, and bisexual teens and the school counselor: Building alliances. In G. Links (Ed.), *The gay teen: Educational practice and theory for lesbian, gay, and bisexual adolescents* (pp. 85–94). New York: Routledge.

•Reynolds, F. C. (1997). *Reifying creativity during the adolescent passage.* Paper presented at Ashland University Ohio Summer Institute. July 13, 1997.

Reynolds, W. M. (1985). Review of Slosson Intelligence Test. In J. J. Kramer (Ed.), *The Ninth Mental Measurements Yearbook* (pp. 1403–1404). Lincoln, NE: University of Nebraska Press.

Rhodes, L. (1992). Focusing attention on the individual in the identification of gifted black students. *Roeper Review, 14,* 108–110.

Richardson, T. M., & Benbow, C. P. (1990). Long-term effects of acceleration on the social and emotional adjustment of mathematically precocious youth. *Journal of Educational Psychology, 82,* 464–470.

Richert, E. S. (1989, November). *Organizing a gifted program.* Paper delivered at the National Association for Gifted Children Conference, Cincinnati, OH.

•Richert, S. (1990a). *Gifted program assessment and planning checklist.* Speech given at the Ohio Association for Gifted Children Annual Meeting, Columbus, OH.

Richert, E. S. (1990b). Rampant problems and promising practices in identification. In N. Colangelo & G. Davis (Eds.), *A handbook of gifted education* (pp. 81–96). Needham Heights, MA: Allyn & Bacon.

Richert, E. S. (1991). Patterns of underachievement among gifted students. In J. Genshaft & M. Bireley (Eds.), *Understanding the gifted adolescent* (pp. 139–162). New York: Teachers College Press.

Richert, E. S., Alvino, J., & McDonnel, R. (1982). *The national report on identification: Assessment and recommendations for comprehensive identification of gifted and talented youth.* Sewell, NJ: Educational Information and Resource Center, for U.S. Department of Education.

Rico, G. (1983). *Writing the natural way.* Los Angeles: Tarcher.

Riley, J. (1992). Mentorship: The essential guide for schools and business. Dayton, OH: Ohio Psychology Press.

•Riley, T. L., & Karnes, F. A. (1996, January/February). Tracking interests: Curriculum interests of elementary intellectually gifted students. *Gifted Child Today,* 36–37.

Rimm, S. B. (1986). *The underachievement syndrome.* Apple Valley, WI: Apple Valley Press.

Rimm, S. B. (1990a). *How to parent so children will learn.* Watertown, WI: Apple Publishing.

Rimm, S. B. (1990b, November). *Identifying creativity: The characteristics approach.* Paper presented at National Association for Gifted Children Conference, Little Rock, AR.

•Rimm, S. B. (1995). *Why bright kids get poor grades: And what you can do about it.* New York: Crown Publishers.

•Rimm, S. B. (1996). *Dr. Sylvia Rimm's smart parenting: How to raise a happy, achieving child.* New York: Crown Publishers.

•Rimm, S. B., & Davis, G. A. (1976). GIFT: An instrument for the identification of creativity. *Journal of Creative Behavior, 10,* 178–182.

Rivers, L. S., Meininger, L. K., & Batten, J. (1991, November). *Kindergarten screening and program placement: Possible relationships.* A paper presented at the National Association for Gifted Children Convention, Kansas City, MO.

Robinson, A. (1990). Cooperation or exploitation? The argument against cooperative learning for talented students. *Journal for the Education of the Gifted, 12,* 46–61.

Robinson, A. (1992). *Cooperative learning and the academically talented student.* Storrs, CT: National Research Center on the Gifted and Talented.

Robinson, N. M. (1987). The early development of precocity. *Gifted Child Quarterly, 31*(4), 161–164.

Robinson, N. M. (1992). Which Stanford-Binet for the brightest? Stanford-Binet IV, of course! Time marches on. *Roeper Review, 15*(1), 32–33.

Robinson, N. M., & Chamrad, D. L. (1986). Appropriate uses of intelligence tests with gifted children. *Roeper Review, 8*(3), 160–163.

Robinson, R. (1989). *Georgia O'Keeffe: A life.* New York: Harper & Row.

Rodriguez-Mylinski, S. (1989). *Jose: A culturally different talented child.* Unpublished manuscript.

Roe, A. (1953). *The making of a scientist.* New York: Dodd Mead.

Roe, A. (1973). Psychological approaches to creativity in the sciences. In M. Coles & H. Hughes (Eds.), *Essays on creativity in the sciences* (pp. 231–237). New York: New York University Press.

Roe, A. (1975). Painters and painting. In C. Taylor & J. Getzels (Eds.), *Perspectives in creativity* (pp. 157–172). Chicago: Aldine.

Roedell, W., Jackson, N., & Robinson, H. (1980). *Gifted young children.* New York: Teachers College Press.

Roets, L. (1986). *Roets Rating Scale for Leadership.* Des Moines, IA: Leadership Publishers.

•Rogers, J. A., & Nielson, A. (1993). Gifted children and divorce: A study of the literature on the incidence of divorce in families with gifted children. *Journal for the Education of the Gifted, 16*(3), 251–267.

Rogers, K. B. (1991). *The relationship of grouping practices to the education of the gifted and talented learner.* Storrs, CT: National Research Center on the Gifted and Talented.

Rogers, K. B. (1992). Self-concept and giftedness. *Quest, 3*(1), 6, 9–10.

Rogers, K. B., Cussler, B., & Anderson, L. (1991, November). *Cooperative versus individualistic learning in English: Which works?* Paper presented at 38th Convention of the National Association for Gifted Children, Kansas City, MO.

Rose, L. H., & Lin, H. (1984). A meta-analysis of long-term creativity training programs. *Journal of Creative Behavior, 18*(1), 11–22.

Rosen, C. L. (1985). Review of Creativity Packet. In [Buros Institute of Mental Measurements] *The Ninth Mental Measurements Yearbook* (Vol. I, pp. 411–412). Lincoln, NE: University of Nebraska Press.

Rosenfield, S. (1987). *Retesting of Hunter College Elementary School students.* Unpublished report.

Rosenthal, A., DeMers, S. T., Stilwell, W., Graybeal, S., & Zins, J. (1983). Comparison of interrater reliability on the Torrance Tests of Creative Thinking for gifted and nongifted students. *Psychology in the Schools, 20,* 35–40.

Rothenberg, A. (1971). The process of Janusian thinking in creativity. *Archives of General Psychiatry,* (Vol. 24, pp. 195–205). In A. Rothenberg & C. Hausman (Eds.). (1976). *The creativity question* (pp. 311– 327). Durham, NC: Duke University Press.

Rothman, R. (1992, November 4). Performance-based assessment gains prominent place on research docket. *Education Week, 1,* 22-24.

Rousseau, J. (1773). *Selections from Emilius; or, a treatise of education,* translated from the French of J. J. Rousseau, citizen of Geneva. In R. Ulich (Ed.). (1954). *Three thousand years of educational wisdom* (p. 353). Cambridge, MA: Harvard University Press.

Roy, A. (1991). A look at the Johnson and Johnson research base for cooperative learning. In R. Swassing & A. Robinson (Eds.), *Research briefs of the National Association for Gifted Children.* Washington, DC: National Association for Gifted Children.

•Rubin, L. (1983). Artistry in teaching. *Educational Leadership, 40,* 44–49.

Rubin, L. (1996). *The transcendent child.* New York: Harper Perennial.

Runco, M. (1986). Maximal performance on divergent thinking tests by gifted, talented, and nongifted children. *Psychology in the Schools, 23,* 308–315.

Runco, M. (1987). The generality of creative performance in gifted and nongifted children. *Gifted Child Quarterly, 31,* 121–125.

Runco, M. (1991). *Divergent production.* New York: Ablex.

•Runco, M. (1992). *Creativity as an educational objective for disadvantaged students.* The National Research Center on the Gifted and Talented Research-based Decision Making Series. Storrs, CT: University of Connecticut.

Runco, M. (1993). Divergent thinking, creativity, and giftedness. *Gifted Child Quarterly, 37*(1), 16–22.

Runco, M., & Albert, R. (1986). The threshold theory regarding creativity and intelligence: An empirical test with gifted and nongifted children. *The Creative Child and Adult Quarterly, 11,* 212–218.

Russell, B. (1967). *The autobiography of Bertrand Russell,* 1872–1914. Boston: Little, Brown.

Rust, J. O. (1985). Review of Scales for Rating the Behavioral Characteristics of Superior Students. In [Buros Institute of Mental Measurements] *The Ninth Mental Measurements Yearbook* (Vol. II, p. 1312–1313). Lincoln, NE: University of Nebraska Press.

Rutter, M. (1983). School effects on pupil progress. Research findings and policy implications. *Child Development, 54,* 1–29.

•Saccuzzo, D. P., Johnson, N., & Guertin, T. L. (1994a). *Identifying underrepresented disadvantaged gifted and talented children: A multifaceted approach* (Vol. 2). ERIC Document ED 368095.

•Saccuzzo, D. P., Johnson, N., & T. L. Guertin. (1994b). Identifying underrepresented disadvantaged gifted and talented children: A multifaceted approach (Vol. 2). ERIC Document ED368095.

•Sadker, M., & Sadker, D. (1994). *Failing at fairness.* New York: Scribners.

•St. Jean, D. (1996, Spring). Valuing, identifying, cultivating, and rewarding talents of students from special populations. *National Research Center on the Gifted and Talented Newsletter,* pp. 1, 3.

Salvia, J., & Ysseldyke, J. E. (1991). *Assessment* (5th ed.). Boston: Houghton Mifflin.

Salvo, S. (1992). *A grant proposal for services for gifted girls.* Unpublished master's practicum. Ashland University, Ashland, OH.

Samples, B. (1976). *The metaphoric mind.* Reading, MA: Addison-Wesley.

•Sandel, A., McCallister, C., & Nash, W. R. (1993). Child search and screening activities for preschool gifted children. *Roeper Review, 16*(2), 98–101.

•Sapon-Shevin, M. (1994). *Playing favorites: Gifted education and the disruption of community.* Albany, NY: State University of New York Press.

Saul, J. R. (1995). *The unconscious civilization.* Concord, ON, Canada: Anansi.

Sawyer, R. (1988). In defense of academic rigor. *Journal for the Education of the Gifted, 11*(2), 5–21.

•Scarborough, E., & Furumoto, L. (1987). *Untold lives: The first generation of American women psychologists.* New York: Columbia University Press.

Schack, G. (1991). Differential effects of a problem-solving curriculum. In R. A. Swassing & A. Robinson (Eds.), *Research briefs.* Washington, DC: National Association for Gifted Children Publications.

Schafer, E. W. P. (1982). Neural adaptability: A biological determinant of behavioural intelligence. *International Journal of Neurosciences, 17,* 183–191.

Schickel, R. (1986). *Intimate strangers: The culture of celebrity.* New York: Fromm.

•Schiever, S. W., & Maker, C. J. (1997). Enrichment and acceleration: An overview and new directions. In N. Colangelo & G. A. Davis (Eds.), *Handbook of gifted education* (2d ed., pp. 113–125). Needham Heights, MA: Allyn & Bacon.

•Schmidt, W. (1998, February 24). *Are there surprises in the TIMSS twelfth grade results?* [Press release]. East Lansing, MI: Michigan State University TIMSS Center.

Schmitz, C., & Galbraith, J. (1985). *Managing the social and emotional needs of the gifted: A teacher's survival guide.* Minneapolis: Free Spirit Press.

Schorer, M. (1961). *Sinclair Lewis.* New York: Random House.

•Schuler, P. A. (1997, Winter). Cluster grouping coast to coast. *The National Center for the Gifted and Talented Newsletter.* Storrs, CT: University of Connecticut.

Schuster, D. T. (1986/1987). *The interdependent mental stance: A study of gifted women at midlife* (Doctoral dissertation, The Claremont Graduate School, 1986). *Dissertation Abstracts International, 48,* 88A.

Schuster, D. T. (1990). Fulfillment of potential, life satisfaction, and competence: Comparing four cohorts of gifted women at midlife. *Journal of Educational Psychology, 82*(3), 471–478.

•Schwanenflugel, P. J., Stevens, T. P. M., & Carr, M. (1997). Metacognitive knowledge of gifted children and nonidentified children in early elementary school. *Gifted Child Quarterly, 41*(2), 24–35.

Scott, M. S., Perou, R., Urbano, R., Hogan, A., & Gold, S. (1992). The identification of giftedness: A comparison of white, Hispanic, and black families. *Gifted Child Quarterly, 36,* 121–139.

Scriven, M. (1967). The methodology of evaluation. In R. E. Stake (Ed.), *AERA monograph series on curriculum evaluation* (No. 1). Chicago: Rand McNally.

Seashore, C., Lewis, D., & Saetveit, J. (1960). *Seashore measures of musical talents.* New York: Psychological Corporation.

Serwatka, T. S., Deering, S., Stoddard, A. (1989). Correlates of the underrepresentation of black students in classes for gifted students. *Journal of Negro Education, 58,* 520–530.

Shaklee, B. D. (1991, June). Early assessment for exceptional potential and cooperative alliance in gifted education. *NRC/GT Newletter,* p. 13.

•Shaklee, B. D. (1997). Early assessment portfolios, *Quest, 8*(1), 2, 4, 7.

Shaklee, B. D., & Hansford, S. (1992). Identification of underserved populations: Focus on preschool and primary children. In *Challenges in gifted education* (pp. 35–50). Columbus, OH: Ohio Department of Education.

Shaklee, B. D., Whitmore, J., Barton, L., Barbour, N., Ambrose, R., & Viechnicki, K. (1989). *Early assessment for exceptional potential for young and/or economically disadvantaged students.* Washington, DC: Office of Educational Research and Improvement, U.S. Department of Education. Grant No. R206A00160.

•Shallcross, D. J. (1985). *Teaching creative behavior: How to evolve creativity in children of all ages.* Buffalo: Bearly Ltd.

Sharan, S., & Sharan, Y. (1976). *Small group teaching.* Englewood Cliffs, NJ: Educational Technology Publications.

Sheets, M. (1966). *The phenomenology of dance.* Madison, WI: University of Wisconsin Press.

•Shepherd, L. J. (1993). *Lifting the veil: The feminine face of science.* Boston: Shambhala.

Sherman, R., & Rosenthal, A. (1988). *Self-study in visual arts for Middle States Evaluation.* New York: Hunter College Elementary School. Unpublished manuscript.

Sherman, R., Gottling, C., Ames, B., & Rosenthal, A. (1988). *Self-study for Middle States Evaluation.* New York: Hunter College Elementary School. Unpublished manuscript.

Sherwood, J., & Nataupsky, M. (1968). Predicting the conclusions of Negro-white intelligence research from biographical characteristics of the investigator. *Journal of Personality and Social Psychology, 8*(1), Part I, 53–58.

•Shore, B. M., & Delcourt, A. B. (1996). Effective curricular and program practices in gifted education and the interface with general education. *Journal for the Education of the Gifted 20*(2), 138–154.

Shore, B. M., Cornell, D. G., Robinson, A., & Ward, V. (1991). *Recommended practices in gifted education: A critical analysis.* New York: Teachers College Press.

Siegler, R. S., & Richards, D. D. (1982). The development of intelligence. In R. J. Sternberg (Ed.), *Handbook of human intelligence* (pp. 897–971). Cambridge: Cambridge University Press.

Silver, H. F. & Hanson, J. R. (1978). *Learning Preference Inventory.* Moorestown, NJ: Institute for Cognitive and Behavior Studies.

Silverman, L. K. (1986). The IQ controversy: Conceptions and misconceptions. *Roeper Review, 8*(3), 136–140.

Silverman, L. K. (1989a, November). *Lost: One IQ point per year for the gifted.* Paper delivered at National Association for Gifted Children Conference, Cincinnati, OH.

Silverman, L. K. (1989b). Invisible gifts, invisible handicaps. *Roeper Review, 12,* 37–42.

Silverman, L. K. (Ed.). (1993). *Counseling the gifted and talented.* Denver, CO: Love.

•Silverman, L. K. (1994). The moral sensitivity of gifted children and the evolution of society. *Roeper Review, 17*(2), 110–115.

Silverman, L. K., & Kearney, K. (1992). The case for the Stanford-Binet L-M as a supplemental test. *Roeper Review, 15*(1), 34–37.

Simonton, D. K. (1975). Age and literary creativity: A cross-cultural and transhistorical survey. *Journal of Cross-cultural Psychology, 6,* 259–277.

Simonton, D. K. (1984). *Genius, creativity, and leadership: Historiometric inquiries.* Cambridge, MA: Harvard University Press.

Simonton, D. K. (1986). Biographical typicality, eminence and achievement styles. *Journal of Creative Behavior, 20*(1), 17–18.

Simonton, D. K. (1988). *Scientific genius.* New York: Harvard University Press.

Simonton, D. K. (1992). The child parents the adult: On getting genius from giftedness. In N. Colangelo, S. G. Assouline & D. L. Ambroson (Eds.)., *Talent development: Proceedings from 1991 Henry B. and Jocelyn Wallace National Research Symposium on Talent Development* (pp. 278–297). Unionville, NY: Trillium Press.

•Simonton, D. K. (1994). *Greatness: Who makes history and why.* New York: The Guilford Press.

Simpson, E. (1982). *Poets in their youth.* New York: Random House.

Singal, M. (1991, November). The other crisis in education. *The Atlantic,* pp. 34–36, 71.

•Sizer, T. R. (1984). *Horace's compromise—The dilemma of the American high school.* Boston: Houghton Mifflin.

Slattery, P. (1995a). A postmodern vision of time and learning: A response to the National Education Commision Report *Prisoners of Time. Harvard Educational Review, 65*(4), 612–633.

Slattery, P. (1995b). *Curriculum development in the postmodern era.* New York: Garland.

Slavin, R. (1987). Ability grouping and student achievement in elementary schools: A best evidence synthesis. *Review of Educational Research, 57,* 293–336.

Slavin, R. (1991). Synthesis of research on cooperative learning. *Educational Leadership, 47*(4), 3.

Sloan, K. D., & Sosniak, L. A. (1985). The development of accomplished sculptors. In B. Bloom

(Ed.), *Developing talent in young people.* New York: Ballantine.

Slosson, R. L. (1971). *Slosson Intelligence Test.* East Aurora, NY: Slosson Educational Publications.

•Smutny, J. (Ed.) (1997) *The young gifted child: Potential and promise, an anthology.* Creskill, NJ: Hampton Press.

Smutny, J., & Blockson, R. (1990). *Education of the gifted: Programs and perspectives.* Bloomington, IN: Phi Delta Kappa Educational Foundation.

Smutny, J., Veenker, K., & Veenker, S. (1989). *Your gifted child: How to recognize and develop the special talents in your child from birth to age seven.* New York: Ballantine.

•Solars, M. (1995). *City schools follow-up study of 1995 seniors.* A Research Practicum Report for Master's of Education Degree. Ashland University, Ashland, OH.

Solorzano, D. G. (1992). An exploratory analysis of the effects of race, class, and gender on student and parent mobility aspirations. *Journal of Negro Education, 61*(1), 30–41.

Sosniak, L. A. (1985a). Learning to be a concert pianist. In B. Bloom (Ed.), *Developing talent in young people* (pp. 348–408). New York: Ballantine.

Southern, W. T., & Jones, E. (1991). *The academic acceleration of gifted children.* New York: Teachers College Press.

Speare, E. G. (1983). *The sign of the beaver.* New York: Dell.

Spicker, H. H., Southern, W. T., & Davis, B. I. (1987). The rural gifted child. *Gifted Child Quarterly, 31,* 155–157.

Spoto, D. (1985). *The kindness of strangers: The life of Tennessee Williams.* Boston: Little, Brown.

Stankon, L., & Chen, K. (1988). Can we boost fluid and crystallized intelligence? A structural modelling approach. *Australian Journal of Psychology, 40*(4), 363–376.

Stanley, J. C. (1979). The case for extreme educational acceleration of intellectually brilliant youths, In J. Gowan, J. Khatena & E. P. Torrance (Eds.), *Educating the ablest: A book of readings* (2d ed.). Itasca, IL: F. E. Peacock Publishers.

Stanley, J. C. (1989). Guiding gifted students in their academic planning. In J. VanTassel-Baska & P. Olszewski-Kubilius (Eds.), *Patterns of influence on gifted learners* (pp. 192–200). New York: Teachers College Press.

Stanley, J. C., & Benbow, D. P. (1983). Extremely young college graduates: Evidence of their success. *College and University, 58,* 361–371.

Stanley, J. C., & McGill, A. M. (1986). More about "Young entrants to college: How did they fare?" *Gifted Child Quarterly, 30,* 70–73.

Stanley, J. C., Benbow, C. P., Brody, L. E., Dauber, S., & Lupkowski, A. E. (1992). Gender differences on eighty-six nationally standardized achievement and aptitude tests. In N. Colangelo, S. G. Assouline & D. L. Ambroson (Eds.), *Talent development: Proceedings from the 1991 Henry B. and Jocelyn Wallace National Research Symposium on Talent Development* (pp. 42–65). Unionville, NY: Trillium Press.

•Starko, A. J. (1995). *Creativity in the classroom.* White Plains, NY: Longman Publishers.

Stein, M. (1987). Creativity assessment. In S. Isaksen (Ed.). *Frontiers of creativity research: Beyond the basics* (pp. 45–87). Buffalo: Bearly Ltd.

Sternberg, R. J. (1982a). Natural, unnatural, and supernatural concepts. *Cognitive Psychology, 14,* 451–458.

Sternberg, R. J. (Ed.) (1982b). *Advances in the psychology of human intelligence.* Hillsdale, NJ: Lawrence Erlbaum.

Sternberg, R. J. (1985). *Beyond IQ: A triarchic theory of human intelligence.* New York: Cambridge University Press.

Sternberg, R. J. (1988a). *The triarchic mind: A new theory of human intelligence.* New York: Viking.

Sternberg, R. J. (1988b). A three-facet model of creativity. In R. J. Sternberg (Ed.), *The nature of creativity: Contemporary psychological perspectives* (pp. 125–147). New York: Cambridge University Press.

Sternberg, R. J. (1991). Giftedness according to the triarchic theory of human intelligence. In N. Colangelo & G. A. Davis (Eds.), *Handbook of gifted education.* Needham Heights, MA: Allyn & Bacon.

•Sternberg, R. J. (1997). Giftedness and successful intelligence. In T. Cross (Ed.), *Research briefs* (pp. 1–14). Washington, DC: National Association for the Gifted Service Publications.

Sternberg, R. J., & Davidson, J. E. (1985). Cognitive development in the gifted and talented. In F. J. Horowitz & M. O'Brien (Eds.). *The gifted and talented: A developmental perspective* (pp. 37–74). Washington, DC: American Psychological Association.

Sternberg, R. J., & Davidson, J. (Eds.) (1995). *The nature of insight.* Cambridge, MA: The MIT Press.

Sternberg, R. J., & Lubart, T. I. (1991). An investment theory of creativity and its development. *Human Development, 34,* 1–31.

Sternberg, R. J., & Lubart, T. I. (1992). Creative giftedness. In N. Colangelo, S. G. Assouline, D. L. Ambroson (Eds.), *Talent development: Proceedings from the 1991 Henry B. and Jocelyn Wallace National Research Symposium on Talent Development* (pp. 66–88). Unionville, NY: Trillium Press.

Sternberg, R. J. & Lubart, T. I. (1993). Creative giftedness: A multivariate investment approach. *Gifted Child Quarterly, 37*(1), 7–15.

•Sternberg, R. J., Zhang, L. (1995). What do we mean by giftedness? A pentagonal implicit theory. *Gifted Child Quarterly, 29*(2), 88–94.

Subotnik, R. F., & Arnold, K. D. (1993). Longitudinal studies of giftedness: Investigating the fulfillment of promise. In K. S. Heller, F. J. Mönks & A. H. Passow (Eds.), *International handbook for research on giftedness and talent.* London: Pergamon Press.

Subotnik, R. F., & Arnold, K. D. (Eds.). (1994). *Beyond Terman: Longitudinal studies of giftedness and talent.* Norwood, NJ: Ablex.

•Subotnik, R. F., & Arnold, K. D. (1996). Success and sacrifice: The costs of talent fulfillment for women in science. In K. Arnold, K. D. Noble & R. F. Subotnik (Eds.), *Remarkable women: Perspectives on female talent development* (pp. 263–280). Cresskill, NJ: Hampton Press.

Subotnik, R. F., & Steiner, C. (1994). Adult manifestations of adolescent talent in science: A longitudinal study of 1983 Westinghouse Science Talent Search winners. In R. F. Subotnik & K. D. Arnold (Eds.), *Beyond Terman: Contemporary longitudinal studies of giftedness and talent* (pp. 52–76). Norwood, NJ: Ablex.

Subotnik, R. F., Karp, D. E., & Morgan, E. R. (1989). High IQ children at midlife: An investigation into the generalizability of Terman's *Genetic Studies of Genius. Roeper Review, 11*(3), 139–145.

•Subotnik, R. F., Kassan, L., Summers, E., & Wasser, A. (1993). *Genius revisited: High IQ children grown up.* Norwood, NJ: Ablex.

•Sulloway, F. (1996). *Born to rebel: Birth order, family dynamics, and creative lives.* New York: Pantheon Books.

•Supovitz, J. A., & Brennan, R.T. (1997). Mirror, mirror on the wall, which is the fairest test of all? An examination of the equitability of portfolio assessment relative to standardized tests. *Harvard Educational Review, 67*(3), 472–502.

Supplee, P. (1990). *Reaching the gifted under-achiever: Program strategy and design.* New York: Teachers College Press.

Suzuki, S. (1983). *Nurtured by love: The classic approach to talent education.* Smithtown, NY: Exposition Press.

•Swadener, B. B., & Lubeck, S. (1995). *Children and families "at promise."* Albany, NY: State University of New York.

Swassing, R., & Fichter, G. (1992). Residential, regional, and specialized schools. *Challenges of gifted education* (pp. 97–102). Columbus, OH: Ohio Department of Education.

Swiatek, M. A., & Benbow, C. P. (1991). A ten-year longitudinal follow-up of participants in a fast-paced mathematics course. *Journal for Research in Mathematics Education, 22,* 138–150.

Tannenbaum, A. (1983). *Gifted children: Psychological and educational perspectives.* New York: Macmillan.

Tannenbaum, A. (1986). The enrichment matrix model. In J. Renzulli (Ed.), *Systems and models for developing programs for the gifted and talented* (pp. 391–429). Mansfield Center, CT: Creative Learning Press.

•Tannenbaum, A. (1997). The meaning and making of giftedness. In N. Colangelo & G. A. Davis (Eds.), *Handbook of gifted education* (2d ed., pp. 27–42). Boston, MA: Allyn & Bacon.

Tardif, T. Z., & Sternberg, R. J. (1988). What do we know about creativity? In R. J. Sternberg (Ed.), *The nature of creativity: Contemporary psychological perspectives.* New York: Cambridge University Press.

Taylor, B. M., & Frye, B. J. (1988). Pretesting: Minimum time spent on skill work for intermediate readers. *The Reading Teacher, 42*(2), 100–103.

Taylor, C. W. (Ed.). (1955, 1957, 1959). *Research conference on the identification of creative scientific talent.* Salt Lake City: University of Utah Press.

Taylor, C. W. (1965). Who are the exceptionally creative? In J. J. Gallagher (Ed.), *Teaching gifted students: A book of readings* (pp. 51–64). Boston: Allyn & Bacon.

Taylor, C. W. (1969). The highest talent potentials of man. *Gifted Child Quarterly, 13,* 9–20.

Taylor, C. W., & Ellison, R. L. (1975). Moving toward working models in creativity. In I. A. Taylor & J. W. Getzels (Eds.), *Perspectives in creativity* (pp. 191–223). Chicago, IL: Aldine Publishing.

Teeter, A., Moore, C. L., & Peterson, J. D. (1982). Wechsler scale performance patterns of American Indian children. *Psychology in the Schools, 19,* 8–17.

Terman, L. M., et al. (1925, 1926, 1930, 1947, 1959). *Genetic studies of genius.* Stanford, CA: Stanford University Press.

Terman, L. M. (1925). *Mental and physical traits of a thousand gifted children, I.* Stanford, CA: Stanford University Press.

Terman, L. M. (1930). *The promise of youth, follow-up studies of a thousand gifted children: Genetic studies of genius, III.* Stanford, CA: Stanford University Press.

Terman, L. M. (1965). Are scientists different? In J.J. Gallagher (Ed.), *Teaching gifted students: A book of readings* (pp. 43–50). Boston: Allyn & Bacon.

Terman, L. M., & Merrill, M. (1916). *Stanford-Binet Intelligence Scale.* Boston: Houghton Mifflin.

Terman, L. M., & Merrill, M. (1937). *Stanford-Binet Intelligence Scale.* Boston: Houghton Mifflin.

Terman, L. M., & Merrill, M. (1973). *Stanford-Binet Intelligence Scale.* Chicago: Riverside.

Terman, L. M., & Oden, M. H. (1947). *The gifted child grows up, twenty-five years follow up of a superior group: Genetic studies of genius, IV.* Stanford, CA: Stanford University Press.

Terman, L. M., & Oden, M. H. (1959). *The gifted group at mid-life, thirty-five years follow-up of the superior child: Genetic studies of genius* (Vol. 3). Stanford, CA: Stanford University Press.

Terr, L. (1990). *Too scared to cry.* New York: Basic.

Terrasier, J. C. (1985). Dyssynchrony: Uneven development. In J. Freeman (Ed.), *The psychology of gifted children* (pp. 265–274). Chichester: John Wiley.

Terry, W. (1971). *Dance in America.* New York: Harper & Row.

•Terry, W. (1997, January 7). How he found himself—again and again. *Parade Magazine.*

Thomas, B. (1973). *Marlon: Portrait of the rebel as an artist.* New York: Random House.

Thorndike, R. L., & Hagen, E. (1986). *Cognitive Abilities Test.* Chicago: Riverside.

Thorndike, R. L., Hagen, E., & Sattler, J. (1985). *Stanford-Binet Intelligence Scale.* Chicago: Riverside.

Thorndike, R. L., Hagen, E., & Sattler, J. (1986). *Technical manual, The Stanford-Binet Intelligence Scale: Fourth Edition.* Chicago: Riverside.

Thurstone, L. L. (1960). *The nature of intelligence.* Paterson, NJ: Littlefield, Adams & Co.

Thurstone, L. L. (1958). *SRA primary mental abilities.* Chicago: Science Research Associates.

Tittle, C. K. (1983). Studies of the effects of career interest inventories: Expanding outcome criteria to include women's experiences. *Journal of Vocational Behavior, 22,* 148–158.

Tolan, S. S. (1992a). Special problems of highly gifted children. *Understanding Our Gifted, 4*(3), 3, 5.

Tolan, S. S. (1992b). Parents vs. theorists: Dealing with the exceptionally gifted. *Roeper Review, 15*(1), 14–18.

•Tolan, S. S. (1994). Discovering the ex-gifted child. *Roeper Review, 17,* 2, 134–137.

•Tomlinson, C. A. (1994). Gifted learners: *The boomerang kids* of middle school? *Roeper Review, 16*(3), 177–182.

Tomlinson, C. A. (1995a). Deciding to differentiate instruction in middle school: One school's journey. *Gifted Child Quarterly, 39*(2), 77–87.

•Tomlinson, C. A. (1995b). *Differentiating instruction for advanced learners in the mixed-ability middle school classroom.* ED 389141. ERIC Digest E536.

•Tomlinson, C. A., Callahan, C. M., & Lelli, K. M. (1997). Challenging expectations: Case studies of high potential, culturally diverse young children. *Gifted Child Quarterly, 41*(2), 5–18.

•Tomlinson, C. A., Coleman, M. R., Allan, S., Udall, A., and Landrum, M. (1996). Interface between gifted education and general education: Toward communication, cooperation, and collaboration. *Gifted Child Quarterly, 40*(3), 165–171.

Tomlinson-Keasey, C. (1990). Developing our intellectual resources for the 21st century: Educating the gifted. *Journal of Educational Psychology, 82*(3), 399–403.

Tomlinson-Keasey, C., & Little, T. D. (1990). Predicting educational attainment, occupational achievement, intellectual skill, and personal adjustment among gifted men and women. *Journal of Educational Psychology, 82*(1), 442–455.

Tonemah, S. A. (1980, January). *Indian education in the 1980s.* ERIC Document Reproduction Service ED 194478.

Tonemah, S. A. (1987). Assessing American Indian gifted and talented student abilities. *Journal for the Education of the Gifted, 10,* 181–194.

Tonemah, S. A., & Benally, E. R. (1984). *Trends in American Indian education: A synthesis and bibliography of selected ERIC resources.* Las Cruces, NM: Center for Rural Education and Small Schools. ERIC Document Reproduction Service ED 247042.

Torrance, E. P. (1962). *Guiding creative talent.* Englewood Cliffs, NJ: Prentice Hall.

Torrance, E. P. (1966). *Torrance Tests of Creative Thinking: Norms and technical manual.* Princeton, NJ: Personal Press.

Torrance, E. P. (1969). Creative positives of disadvantaged children and youth. *Gifted Child Quarterly, 13*(2), 71–81.

Torrance, E. P. (1974). *Torrance Tests of Creative Thinking: Norms-technical manual.* Princeton, NJ: Personal Press.

Torrance, E. P. (1977). *Discovery and nurturance of giftedness in the culturally different.* Reston, VA: Council for Exceptional Children.

Torrance, E. P. (1979). *The search for satori and creativity.* Buffalo, NY: Bearly Ltd.

Torrance, E. P. (1987a). *Teaching for creativity.* In S. Isaksen (Ed.), *Frontiers of creativity research: Beyond the basics* (pp. 190–215). Buffalo: Bearly Ltd.

Torrance, E. P. (1987b). Recent trends in teaching children and adults. In S. Isaksen (Ed.), *Frontiers of creativity research: Beyond the basics* (pp. 205–215). Buffalo: Bearly Ltd.

Torrance, E. P. (1990). *The Torrance Tests of Creative Thinking: Norms-technical manual, Figural (Streamlined) Forms A & B.* Bensenville, IL: Scholastic Testing Service.

Torrance, E. P., & Goff, K. (1989). A quiet revolution. *Journal of Creative Behavior, 23,* 219–223.

Torrance, E. P., & Myers, R. E. (1970). *Creative learning and teaching.* New York: Dodd and Mead.

•Torrance, E. P., & Safter, H. T. (1983). *Incubation teaching: Getting beyond the aha!* New York: Ginn.

Torrance, E. P., & Safter, H. T. (1989). The long range predictive validity of the Just Suppose Test. *Journal of Creative Behavior, 23,* 219–223.

Torrance, E. P., Bruch, C., & Torrance, J. P. (1978). Interscholastic futuristic problem solving. *Journal of Creative Behavior, 10,* 117–125.

Toth, S. A. (1984). *Ivy days: Making my way out east.* Boston: Little, Brown.

Trager, J. (1992). *The people's chronology.* New York: Holt, Rinehart & Winston.

Treffinger, D. J. (1986). Research on creativity. *Gifted Child Quarterly, 30*(1), 15-19.

Treffinger, D. J. (1987). Research on creativity assessment. In S. Isaksen (Ed.), *Frontiers of creativity research: Beyond the basics* (pp. 103–119). Buffalo: Bearly Ltd.

Treffinger, D. J. (1991). Future goals and directions. In N. Colangelo and G. Davis (Eds.), *Handbook of* gifted education (pp. 441–447). Boston: Allyn & Bacon.

Treffinger, D. J., & Isaksen, S. (1992). *Creative problem solving: An introduction.* Sarasota: Center for Creative Learning.

Twins. (Dec. 6, 1981). Episode of *Nova.* [Television broadcast]. Coproduced by Canadian Broadcast Company and WGBH-Boston.

•Tucker, B., & Hafenstein, N.L. (1997). Psychological intensities in young gifted children. *Gifted Child Quarterly, 41*(3), 66–75.

Tyler, R. (1949). *Basic principles of curriculum and instruction.* Chicago: University of Chicago Press.

Tyler-Wood, T. L., & Carri, L. (1991). Identification of gifted children: The argument of various measures of cognitive ability. *Roeper Review, 14*(2), 63–65.

•U.S. Department of Education Office of Educational Research and Improvement. (1994). *Javits Gifted and Talented Students Education Program Grants Projects Abstracts 1992–1993.*

Useem, E. L. (1992). Getting on the fast track in mathematics: School organizational influences on math track assignment. *American Journal of Education, 100*(3), 325–353.

•Vail, P. (1994). *Emotion: The on/off switch for learning.* Rosemont, NJ: Modern Learning Press.

Vaillant, G., & Vaillant, C. (1990). Determinants and consequences of creativity in a cohort of gifted women. *Psychology of Women Quarterly, 14,* 607–616.

Valencia, A. A. (1985). Curriculum perspectives for gifted limited-English-proficient students. *The Journal for the National Association for Bilingual Education, 10*(1), 65–77.

VanTassel-Baska, J. (1987). The ineffectiveness of the pull-out model in gifted education: A minority perspective. *Journal for the Education of the Gifted, 10*(4), 255–264.

VanTassel-Baska, J. (Ed.). (1988). *Comprehensive curriculum for gifted learners.* Needham Heights, MA: Allyn & Bacon.

VanTassel-Baska, J. (1989). Characteristics of the developmental path of eminent and gifted adults. In J. VanTassel-Baska and P. Olszewski-Kubilius (Eds.), *Patterns of influence on gifted learners* (pp. 140–156). New York: Teachers College Press.

VanTassel-Baska, J. (1992, November). *Educational reform: Issues, concerns and implications for gifted education.* Paper delivered at National Association for Gifted Children Conference. Los Angeles, CA.

VanTassel-Baska, J. (1994a). *Comprehensive curriculum for gifted learners* (2d ed.). Needham Heights, MA: Allyn & Bacon.

•VanTassel-Baska, J. (1994b). *Planning and implementing curriculum for the gifted.* Denver, CO: Love.

VanTassel-Baska, J. (1997). *Keynote speech at National Curriculum Conference.* College of William and Mary, March, 1997.

•VanTassel-Baska, J., & Avery, L. (1997). Perspectives on evaluation: Local considerations. In T. Cross (Ed.), *Research briefs* (pp. 118–128). Washington, DC: National Association for Gifted Children Service Publications.

VanTassel-Baska, J., & Willis, G. (1987). A three-year study of the effects of low income on SAT scores among the academically able. *Gifted Child Quarterly, 31,* 169–173.

VanTassel-Baska, J., Patton, J. M., & Prillaman, D. (1991). *Gifted youth at risk: A report of a national study.* Reston, VA: Council for Exceptional Children.

•Vars, G. F., & Rakow, S. R. (1993). Making connections: Integrative curriculum and the gifted student. *Roeper Review, 16*(1), 48–53.

Varley, P. (in press). *Nurturing talents in the inner city: The Urban Scholars middle school program.* U.S. Office of Education: Office of Educational Research and Improvement.

Vaughn, V. L., Feldhusen, J. F., & Asher, J. W. (1991). Meta-analyses and review of research on pull-out programs in gifted education. *Gifted Child Quarterly, 35*(2), 92–98.

Vernon, P. A. (1971). *The structure of human abilities.* London: Methuem.

Vernon, P. A. (Ed.). (1987). *Speed of information-processing and intelligence.* Norwood, NJ: Ablex.

Viadero, D. (1992, November 25). Standards groups ponder value of setting ability levels. *Education Week.*

Vidal, G. (1992, September/October). Lincoln: Screening history. *The American Poetry Review, 21*(5), 21–29.

von Oech, R. (1983). *A whack on the side of the head.* New York: Warner.

Vygotsky, L. S. (1962). *Thought and language.* Trans. E. Hanfmann & G. Vakar. Cambridge, MA: Massachusetts Institute of Technology Press.

Wakefield, D. (1988). *Returning: A spiritual journey.* New York: Doubleday.

Walker, B. (1989, November). *The effects of gifted women's perceptions on their personal and professional lives*. Keynote address at National Association for Gifted Children Conference, Cincinnati, OH.

Walker, S., & Simonson, R. (Eds.) (1988). *The Gray-wolf annual five multi-cultural literacy*. St. Paul, MN: Graywolf.

Wallach, M., & Kogan, N. (1965). *Modes of thinking in young children: A study of the creativity-intelligence distinction*. New York: Holt, Rinehart, & Winston, Inc.

Wallerstein, J. S., & Blakeslee, S. (1989). *Second chances: Men, women and children a decade after divorce*. New York: Ticknor & Fields.

Ward, V. (1961/1980). *Differential education for the gifted*. Ventura, CA: Ventura County Superintendent of Schools.

Wardrop, J. L. (1989). Review of the California Achievement Test, Forms E and F. In J. C. Conoley & J. J. Kramer (Eds.), *The Tenth Mental Measurements Yearbook* (pp. 128–133). Lincoln, NE: University of Nebraska Press.

•Webb, J., Meckstroth, E., & Tolan, S. (1982). *Guiding the gifted child*. Scottsdale, AZ: Gifted Psychology Press.

Wechsler, D. (1974). *Manual for the Wechsler Intelligence Scale for Children-Revised*. Cleveland: The Psychological Corporation.

Wechsler, D. (1981). *Manual for the Wechsler Intelligence Scale for Children-Revised*. Cleveland: The Psychological Corporation.

Weinberg, R. (1989). Intelligence and IQ: Landmark issues and great debates. *American Psychologist, 44*(2), 98–104.

Weiner, J. (1990). *The next one hundred years: Shaping the fate of our living earth*. New York: Bantam.

Weisner, T. S. & Garnier, H. (1992). Nonconventional family life-styles and school achievement: A 12-year longitudinal study. *American Educational Research Journal, 29*(3), 605–632.

Wells, A. S., & Serna, I. (1996). The politics of culture: Understanding local political resistance in detracking in racially mixed schools. *Harvard Educational Review, 66*(1), 93–118.

•Werner, E. E., & Bachtold, L. M. (1969). Personality factors of gifted boys and girls in middle childhood and adolescence. *Psychology in the Schools 6*(2), 177–182.

Wertsch, J. V. (1988). L. S. Vygotsky"s "new" theory of mind. *The American Scholar, 57*(1), 81–90.

•West, J. I. (1996). In God's country: Rural gifted women. In K. Arnold, K. D. Noble & R. F. Subotnik

(Eds.), *Remarkable women: Perspectives on female talent development* (pp. 69–80). Cresskill, NJ: Hampton Press.

•Westberg, K. L., & Archambault, F. X. (1997). A multi-site case study of successful classroom practices for high ability students. *Gifted Child Quarterly, 41*(1), 42–51.

•Westberg, K. L., Archambault, F. X., Dobyns, S. M., & Salvin, T. J. (1993). *An observational study of instructional and curricular practices used with gifted and talented students in regular classrooms*. The National Research Center on the Gifted and Talented Research Monograph 93103. Storrs, CT: University of Connecticut.

Wheeler, D. L. (1992, July 29). Championing the philosophy and beauty of mathematics. *The Chronicle of Higher Education*, p. A6–7.

White, B. (1985). Competence and giftedness. In J. Freeman (Ed.), *The psychology of gifted children* (pp. 59–73). Chichester: John Wiley.

Whitmore, J. (1980). *Giftedness, conflict, and underachievement*. Boston: Allyn & Bacon.

•Whitmore, J., & Maker, D. J. (1985). *Intellectual giftedness in disabled persons*. Rockville, MD: Aspen.

•Widman, N. (1997). *A follow-up study of the academically talented students*. Research Practicum Report for Master's of Education. Ashland University, Ashland, OH.

•Wiggins, G. (1992). *The case for authentic assessment*. ERIC Digest ED 328611.

•Wiggins, G. (1996). Anchoring assessment with exemplars: Why students and teachers need models. *Gifted Child Quarterly, 40*(2), 66–70.

•Wildenhaus, K. J. (1996). The talented female athlete: Issues in the development of competitive excellence. In K. Arnold, K. D. Noble & R. F. Subotnik (Eds.), *Remarkable women: Perspectives on female talent development* (pp. 335–350). Cresskill, NJ: Hampton Press.

•Willard-Holt, C. (1994). *Recognizing talent: Cross-case study of two high potential students with cerebral palsy*. The National research Center on the Gifted andTalented Research Monograph CRS94307. Storrs, CT: University of Connecticut.

Williams, F. (1970). *Classroom ideas for encouraging thinking and feeling*. Buffalo: D.O.K.

•Williams, F. (1972). *A total creativity kit*. Englewood Cliffs, NJ: Educational Technology Publications.

Willson, V. L. (1989). Review of the Iowa Test of Basic Skills, Forms G and H. In J. C. Conoley & J. J. Kramer (Eds.), *The Tenth Mental Measurements*

Yearbook (pp. 393–400). Lincoln, NE: University of Nebraska Press.

•Winebrenner, S. (1992). *Gifted kids in the regular classroom.* Minneapolis: Free Spirit.

Winebrenner, S., & Devlin, B. (1991). *Cluster grouping fact sheet.* Lombard, IL: Phantom Press.

•Winner, E. (1996). *Gifted children: Myths and realities.* New York: Basic Books.

Witt, J. C. & Gresham, F. M. (1985). Review of Wechsler Intelligence Scale for Children. In J. Kramer (Ed.), *Ninth Mental Measurements Yearbook* (pp. 1716–1719). Lincoln, NE: University of Nebraska Press.

•Wittig, A. F., & Shurr, K. T. (1994). Psychological characteristics of women volleyball players: Relationships with injuries, rehabilitation, and team success. *Personality and Social Psychology Bulletin, 20*(3), 322–330.

Witty, P. A. (Ed.). (1951). *The gifted child.* Boston: D.C. Heath & Co.

Wolf, D., Bixby, J., Glenn II, J., & Gardner, H. (1991). To use their minds well: Investigating new forms of student assessment. In G. Grant (Ed.), *Review of Research in Education, 17*, 31–74. Washington: American Educational Research Association.

Woliver, R., & Woliver, G. M. (1991). Gifted adolescents in the emerging minorities: Asians and Pacific Islanders. In M. Bireley and J. Genshaft (Eds.), *Understanding the gifted adolescent* (pp. 248–258). New York: Teachers College Press.

Woodcock, R. W., & Johnson, M. B. (1989). Woodcock-Johnson Psycho-Educational Battery-Revised. Allen, TX: DLM.

Woods, S. B., & Achey, V. H. (1990). Successful identification of gifted racial/ethnic group students without changing classification requirements. *Roeper Review, 13*(1), 21–32.

•Wright, A. L., & Olszewski-Kubilius, P. (1995). *Helping gifted children and their families prepare for college: A handbook designed to assist economically disadvantaged and first-generation college attendees.* National Research Center for the Gifted and Talented. ERIC Document ED 379848. Storrs, CT: University of Connecticut.

•Wurtzel, E. (1994). *Prozak nation: Young and depressed in America.* New York: Houghton Mifflin.

Yeatey, C. C., & Bennett, C. T. (1990). Race, schooling, and class in American society. *Journal of Negro Education, 59*, 3–18.

Yong, F. L. (1992). Mathematics and science attitudes of African-American middle grade students identified as gifted: Gender and grade differences. *Roeper Review, 14*, 136–140.

Yost, C. (1988). *Self-study for computer studies for Middle States Evaluation.* Unpublished manuscript. New York: Hunter College Elementary School.

Zakrajsek, D. B., Johnson, R. I., & Walker, D. B. (1984). Comparison of learning styles between physical education and dance majors. *Perceptual and Motor Skills, 58*, 583–588.

Zarnegar, Z., Hocevar, D., & Michael, W. (1988). Components of original thinking in gifted children. *Educational and Psychological Measurement, 48*, 5–16.

Zigler, E., & Seitz, V. (1982). Social policy and intelligence. In R. J. Sternberg (Ed.), *Handbook of human intelligence* (pp. 586–641). Cambridge: Cambridge University Press.

Zimmerman, B. J. (1989). A social cognitive view of self-regulated learning. *Journal of Educational Psychology, 81*, 329–339.

Zimmerman, B. J., Bandura, A., & Martinez-Pons, M. (1992). Self-motivation for academic attainment: The role of self-efficacy beliefs and personal goal setting. *American Educational Research Journal, 29*(3), 663–676.

Zuckerman, H. (1977). *The scientific elite.* New York: Free Press.

Name Index

Rimm, S. B., 64, 69, 172, 227, 466, 470, 471, 486, 494–496, 501
Rivers, L., 197, 202
Robinson, A., 53, 66, 67, 80, 107, 108, 115, 259, 527
Robinson, H., 199, 243
Robinson, N., 12, 197, 199, 203, 468–470, 489, 490
Rockefeller, J. D., 240
Rodgriguez, M., 550
Rodriguez-Mylinski, S., 130
Roe, A., 232
Roedell, W., 199, 243
Roets, L., 306
Rogers, J. B., 71, 208, 547, 558
Rogers, K., 53, 66, 67, 471
Rorem, N., 491
Rose, S., 13
Rosen, C. L., 172
Rosenfield, S., 198, 199
Rosenthal, A., 169
Rothman, R., 376
Rousseau, H., 388
Roy, A., 53
Rubin, L., 77, 353
Rudnitski, R., 55, 327, 526
Runco, M., 144, 147, 151, 153, 156, 168, 169
Runyon, J., 548
Russell, B., 239, 320, 330
Rust, J., 172
Rutter, M., 535
Ryan, M., 43
Ryan, R., 277
Ryser, G. R., 179

Sabin, F., 390
Saccuzzo, D. P., 116, 116, 542
Sadker, D., 413
Sadker, M., 413
St. Jean, D., 98, 553, 555
St. Père, F., 501, 504
Safter, T., 156, 168, 442
Salvia, J., 116
Salvin, T., 71
Salvo, S., 474
Samples, R., 156
Sandoval, P., 535
Santi, B., 390
Sapon-Shevin, M., 36, 53, 72
Saul, J. R., 404, 412
Sawyer, R., 367, 384, 385
Say, A., 218
Sayler, M. F., 282, 291, 294
Sayre, A. P., 218
Schack, G., 396

Schacter, J., 61
Schickel, R., 251
Schlafly, J., 491
Schmidt, W., 374
Schottke, N., 408, 482
Schuler, P., 63
Schurr, K. T., 303
Schuster, D. T., 344, 345
Schwanenflutel, P. J., 22
Schwartz, A., 218
Scott, J. M., 538, 544
Scott, M., 228, 229
See, C., 557
Segal, N. L., 14, 115
Seitz, V., 115
Serna, I., 410, 539
Serwatka, T. S., 534, 539
Shaklee, B., 191, 207, 529
Shallcross, D., 156
Shankar, R., 250
Shavit, Y. W., 127
Shelby, A., 218
Shepherd, L. J., 347
Sher, L., 442
Sherman, R., 509
Sherwood, J., 13
Shiever, S., 208
Shoenherr, J., 218
Shore, B. M., 22, 67, 80, 107, 108, 115, 197, 259, 401, 527
Short, E., 470, 475
Shurr, K. T., 303
Sierwald, W., 129
Silver, H. F., 505
Silverman, E., 218
Silverman, L. K., 31, 33, 108, 123, 197, 200, 349, 467, 470, 471, 479, 494
Simard, L., 501, 504
Simon, T., 9
Simonson, R., 392
Simonton, D. K., 32, 142, 151, 196, 232, 234, 237, 244, 276, 281, 322–324, 328, 329, 335, 347, 404, 457, 479, 480, 503
Simpson, E., 294
Singal, M., 367
Sisk, D., 547
Sizer, T., 74, 362
Slattery, P., 364, 398, 402, 404
Slavin, R., 53, 61–63
Sloan, K. D., 304
Slobodkina, E., 218
Smist, J. M., 71
Smith, L., 102, 227, 253, 305, 427, 461, 505
Smutny, J., 72, 190, 209, 227
Socrates, 15, 33, 436

Solars, M., 82
Solorzano, D., 535
Sosniak, L., 237, 249, 250, 283, 292, 298, 304, 328, 329
Southern, W. T., 64, 431, 432, 501–503
Sowa, C., 471
Speare, E., 423
Spearman, C., 9, 11
Spoto, D., 244
Stanley, D., 390
Stanley, J., 64, 501, 502, 511, 513
Starko, A., 158
Stearns, P., 216
Steele, K., 277, 479, 508
Stein, M., 165
Steinberg, S., 10, 114, 405
Steiner, C., 287
Stepien, B., 443
Stern, W., 9, 127
Sternberg, R. J., 4, 18, 21, 22, 31, 36, 95, 99, 100, 115, 126, 151, 152, 165, 227, 228, 279, 361, 363, 395, 477, 526
Stevens, T. P. M., 22
Stewart, R., 250
Stieglitz, A., 303
Stilwell, W., 169
Stoddard, A., 534, 539
Strauss, L., 43
Streep, M., 253
Strindberg, A., 340
Subotnik, R. F., 99, 198, 237, 274, 287, 324, 325, 328, 345, 346, 476, 501, 504
Suess, Dr., 218
Sulloway, F., 281
Summers, E., 99, 324, 346
Supovitz, J., 177
Supovitz, T., 376
Supplee, P., 494, 495, 498–500
Suzuki, S., 247
Swadener, B., 525
Swiatek, M. A., 291
Swisher, K., 474, 510
Szilard, L., 236

Taba, H., 387
Tabacca, G., 277, 479, 509
Takahashi, M., 491
Talmey, M., 235
Tan, A., 557
Tangherilni, A., 376
Tannenbaum, A., 4, 18, 25, 31, 50, 52, 58, 95, 99, 108, 227, 233, 236, 276, 364, 365, 384, 387, 498
Tatum, A., 163
Taubman, P. M., 364, 398, 402

SUBJECT INDEX